P9-BJA-570

# MANAGING ORGANIZATIONAL BEHAVIOR

JOHN WILEY & SONS, INC.

FOURTH EDITION

# MANAGING ORGANIZATIONAL BEHAVIOR


**JOHN R. SCHERMERHORN, JR.**
Ohio University

**JAMES G. HUNT**
Texas Tech University

**RICHARD N. OSBORN**
Wayne State University



NEW YORK CHICHESTER BRISBANE TORONTO SINGAPORE

*Acquisitions Editor* Cheryl Mehalik
*Developmental Editor* Barbara Heaney
*Production Manager* Katharine Rubin
*Cover/Text/Illustration Designer* Karin Gerdes Kincheloe
*Production Supervisor* Sandra Russell
*Manufacturing Manager* Lorraine Fumoso
*Copy Editors* Gilda Stahl/Marjorie Shustak
*Cover Illustration* Steve Jenkins

Recognizing the importance of preserving what has been written, it is a policy of John Wiley & Sons, Inc. to have books of enduring value published in the United States printed on acid-free paper, and we exert our best efforts to that end.



***Library of Congress Cataloging in Publication Data:***

Schermerhorn, John R.
Managing organizational behavior / John R. Schermerhorn, Jr., James G. Hunt, Richard N. Osborn. -- 4th ed.
Includes bibliographical references and indexes.
ISBN 0-471-52199-X (cloth)
1. Organizational behavior. 2. Management. I. Hunt, James G., 1932- . II. Osborn, Richard. III. Title.
HD58.7.S34 1991
658--dc20 90-24652
CIP

**Printed and bound by Von Hoffmann Press, Inc.**

10 9 8 7 6 5 4

# PREFACE

Circles, inverted triangles, ellipses, squares, and rectangles—such symbols represent *the shape of things to come in tomorrow's organizations.* The traditional "pyramid" concept is giving way to new organizational forms that emphasize employee involvement, work teams and lateral relations, and flexibility in day-to-day management practices. These trends and other related themes are reported daily in the media—from the pages of *The Wall Street Journal, Fortune, Business Week,* and other business periodicals, to your local newspapers and television stations. They are also ever-present in the conversations and "networks" through which progressive managers share approaches and discuss problems with one another.

We are part of the dawning of a new era of management in which the old ways and standards just don't seem to be good enough anymore. Importantly, we live in a society that now expects productivity and quality-of-work-life to go hand-in-hand; in which ethics and social responsibility are of paramount importance; where the workforce is increasingly diverse; and where the realities of a global economy are evident everywhere.

In line with these challenges, the fourth edition of *Managing Organizational Behavior* has been reorganized, updated, and redesigned. With our first opportunity to revise the book for the 1990s, we have retained the "OB" core of past editions while enhancing the managerial tone of each chapter and the book overall. "High performance" and "managerial application" are key themes in chapter introductions, concept discussions, the many real-life examples, and end-of-chapter materials.

An all-new book design with full color format and open page layouts in the style of the professional literature that well-informed executives must read is used to facilitate understanding. Among other pedagogical features, a "Visions" commentary introduces each chapter's subject matter by illustrating a progressive management approach or philosophy. Photo essays in each chapter also highlight all-important ethics, inter-

national, and skills perspectives as found in the current activities of well-known organizations and their managers.

As in the past, this edition of *Managing Organizational Behavior* tries to make the field of OB accessible to the reader without sacrificing content or application. Through three successful editions, thousands of students and instructors around the world have communicated their satisfaction with our efforts. We believe this book can once again meet the needs of instructors who want to give their students an introduction to organizational behavior with a strong managerial emphasis. Thus, we are pleased to offer you the fourth edition of *Managing Organizational Behavior.*

## *ACKNOWLEDGMENTS*

*Managing Organizational Behavior,* fourth edition, benefits from insights provided by a dedicated group of management educators who carefully read and critiqued draft chapters of this edition. We are pleased to express our appreciation for the contributions of those who reviewed the manuscript for this new edition:

Chi Anyansi-Archibong, North Carolina A & T State University
Terry Armstrong, University of West Florida
Leanne Atwater, State University of New York-Binghamton
Gene E. Burton, California State University-Fresno
Deborah Crown, University of Colorado, Boulder
Dennis Duchon, University of Texas at San Antonio
Daniel Ganster, University of Nebraska
Eugene Gomolka, University of Dayton
Barbara Goodman, Wayne State University
Bengt Gustafsson, Gustavus Adolphus College
Nell Hartley, Robert Morris College
Neil J. Humphreys, Louisiana Tech University
Eugene Hunt, Virginia Commonwealth University
Paul N. Keaton, University of Wisconsin-Lacrosse
Charles Milton, University of South Carolina
Sandra Morgan, University of Hartford
Ralph F. Mullin, Central Missouri State University
Dennis Pappas, Columbus State University
Edward B. Parks, Marymount University
Charles L. Roegiers, University of South Dakota
Michael Rush, University of Tennessee, Knoxville
Richard J. Sebastian, St. Cloud State University
Allen N. Shub, Northeastern Illinois University
Dayle Smith, Georgetown University
Paul L. Starkey, Delta State University
W. Fran Waller, Central Missouri State University
Fred A. Ware, Jr., Valdosta State College
Harry Waters, Jr., California State University-Hayward
Wayne Wormley, Drexel University

as well as those reviewers from previous editions:

Robert Barbato, Rochester Institute of Technology
Bonnie Betters-Reed, Boston College
Gerald Biberman, University of Scranton
Dale Blount, Southern Illinois University at Edwardsville

Joseph F. Byrnes, Bentley College
Paul Collins, Purdue University
Delf Dodge, Corporate Strategic Planning, General Motors Corporation
Dalmar Fisher, Boston College
Cynthia V. Fukami, University of Denver
Joe Garcia, Western Washington University
Frederick Greene, Manhattan College
William Hart, University of Mississippi
David Hunt, Miami University
Harriet Kandelman, University of Portland
Donald Latham, University of Mississippi
Kathy Lippert, University of Cincinnati
David Luther, University of Mississippi
James McFillen, Bowling Green State University
Herff L. Moore, University of Central Arkansas
Paula Morrow, Iowa State University
Richard Mowday, University of Oregon
Linda Neider, University of Miami
Robert F. Pearse, Rochester Institute of Technology
Lawrence Peters, Texas Christian University
Joseph Porac, University of Illinois
Steven Ross, University of Pugeot Sound
Anson Seers, University of Alabama
Walter W. Smock, Rutgers University
Sharon Tucker, Washington University
Joyce Vincelette, University of South Florida
David Vollrath, New York University
Andrea F. Warfield, Ferris State University
Joseph W. Weiss, Bentley College
Barry L. Wisdom, Southwest Missouri State University
Raymond Zammuto, University of Colorado

Efforts to deepen the international coverage of *Managing Organizational Behavior,* fourth edition, led to special contributions from our Canadian colleagues—R. Julian Cattaneo and Andrew J. Templer, both of the University of Windsor. Their initial draft of Chapter 3 allowed for a timely cross-cultural introduction to organizational behavior issues important to our global economy. Among the subject-matter specialists contributing to this edition, we thank Rick Milter of Ohio University for his fine work with the end-of-chapter exercises.

As always, the support staff at John Wiley & Sons was most helpful in the various stages of developing and producing this edition. Our editor, Cheryl Mehalik, continued her push for quality and currency—in all aspects of the book's content and design, and also with the supplements. Karin Gerdes Kincheloe was the creative force behind the new design, while Barbara Heaney's special efforts resulted in the many photo essays which enhance this edition. We thank Katharine Rubin and Sandra Russell in Production, Gilda Stahl and Marjorie Shustak in Copyediting, and Marinita Timban for her research and administrative assistance.

*John Schermerhorn*
*Jerry Hunt*
*Dick Osborn*

# ABOUT THE BOOK

*Managing Organizational Behavior,* fourth edition, brings to its readers the content core of prior editions, along with many revisions, updates, and enhancements that reflect the management challenges and opportunities of the 1990s. Readers who are familiar with our book will find that it still progresses in an orderly sequence of major parts. This edition begins with a managerially-oriented introduction, proceeds through the basic building blocks of organizational behavior (individuals, groups, organizations, and processes), and concludes with selected managerial issues in our dynamic work environment. In each part, readers will find a solid introduction to the basic theories and concepts of organizational behavior, along with many examples and guidelines dealing with their practical application in management. Briefly, the following highlights indicate what there is about the content of *Managing Organizational Behavior,* fourth edition, that can make it a useful resource for instructors and students alike.

## Part One

Two thoroughly revised opening chapters provide a managerial framework for studying OB, while a third all-new chapter allows for special attention to the international dimensions. Topics include *cultural and workforce diversity* and other *key forces in the contemporary environment,* issues of *managerial ethics and social responsibility,* the *nature of managerial work, productivity and quality of work life,* and the complexities of *managing in a global economy.*

## Part Two

Four revised and updated chapters begin with basic issues of *individual performance, individual differences,* and *values, attitudes, and needs.* Coverage includes *key motivation theories, goal-setting and MBO, social learning, positive reinforcement, merit pay and reward systems, alternative work arrangements, practical approaches to job design,* and *job enrichment,* while remaining sensitive to individual diversity and an increasingly global workforce.

## Part Three

Two revised chapters streamline our treatment of group and intergroup dynamics, while highlighting *group-based organization and management approaches.* Readers learn a *diagnostic model of work groups,* explore *new directions in work group designs,* and examine management applications including *self-managing work teams* and *quality circles, managerial aspects of group dynamics, team-building strategies,* and *cooperation and competition in intergroup dynamics.*

## Part Four

Along with two chapters covering the fundamentals of organizational structures and design, this part includes an all-new chapter on *organizational cultures. New-form organizations* are identified in the context of *basic structural alternatives,* an emphasis on *innovation and adaptation in organizational design,* and an examination of the increasing importance placed on *core values and strong cultures* in high-performing organizations.

## Part Five

A comprehensive four-chapter treatment of the processes of organizational behavior addresses the full range of interpersonal dynamics critical to managerial success. An all-new chapter segment on *negotiation in organizations* is combined with revised coverage of *decision making,* with special attention to *intuition, judgmental heuristics,* and *participation.* Our treatments of *communication* and *interpersonal conflict* are updated; *empowerment* is a major theme in *power and politics;* while *leadership* is addressed with expanded attention to *transformational leadership* and related considerations.

## Part Six

This book concludes with special attention to the challenges of change in a dynamic environment, and to related stress-management and career-management implications. Topics include the *manager's role as change agent,* the available *change strategies* and *approaches to resistance to change,* and the various *organization development interventions. Personal wellness* and *stress management* are highlighted, as are basic issues of *career planning and development, dual-career challenges,* and the complexities of *family and work responsibilities.*

## Supplementary Modules

Offered at the end of the book, these short but focused modules provide special attention to *historical roots of OB, the scientific method, research designs,* and *performance appraisal methods.*

# CONTENTS

PHOTO ESSAYS



## CHAPTER 6 ■ LEARNING, REINFORCEMENT, AND EXTRINSIC REWARDS 159

PHOTO ESSAYS

PHOTO ESSAYS

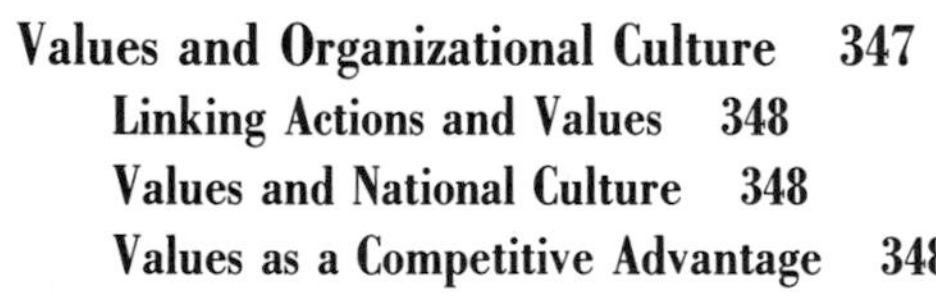

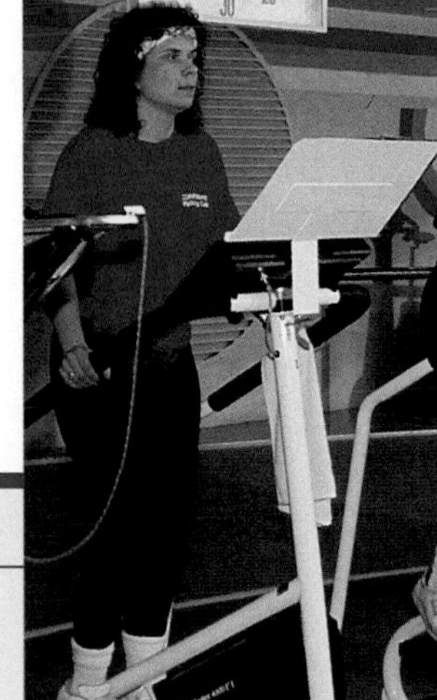

# MANAGING ORGANIZATIONAL BEHAVIOR

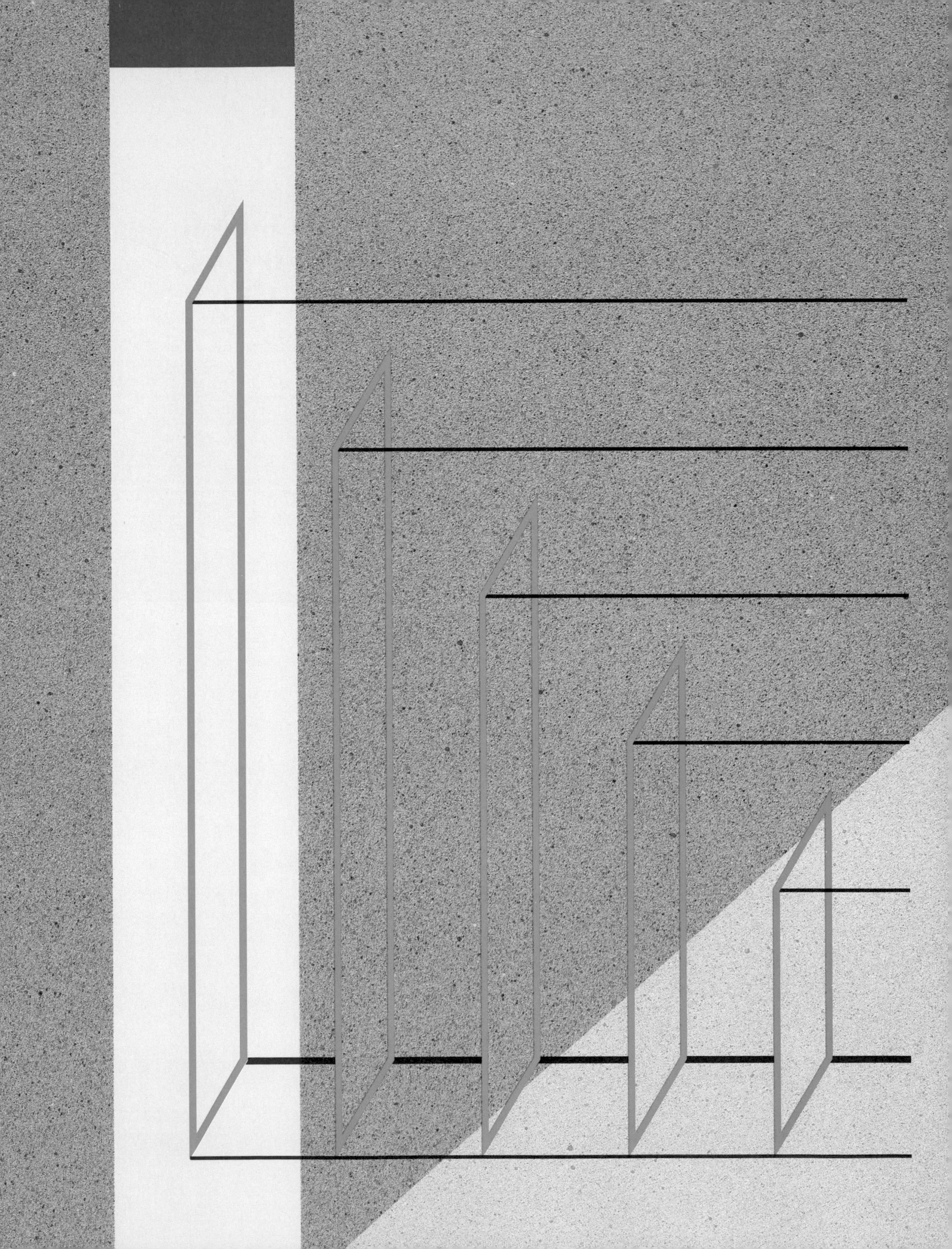

# PART ONE

# INTRODUCTION

This study outline of major topics is meant to organize your reading now; it is repeated in the Summary to structure your review.

## STUDY OUTLINE

### ■ Foundations of Organizational Behavior (OB)

Historical Foundations of OB   Scientific Foundations of OB
The Organization of This Book

### ■ Learning about Organizational Behavior

Experiential Learning   Life-long Learning

### ■ The Nature of Organizations

Why Do Organizations Exist?   Ingredients of Organizations
Organizations as Open Systems   Synergy in Organizations

### ■ Managers in Organizations

What Is an Effective Manager?   Four Functions of Management
The Manager's Challenge

# CHAPTER 1

# ORGANIZATIONAL BEHAVIOR AND THE MANAGER

## The Manager's Changing Environment

Focus on Productivity   The Global Economy   Organizational Transitions
Information Technologies   New Ways of Organizing
Changing Demographics and Work Force Diversity   Human Rights in the Workplace

## Managerial Ethics and Quality of Work Life

Ethical Managerial Behavior   Corporate Social Responsibility
Work and the Quality of Life

## PHOTO ESSAYS

Skills Perspective   HYATT HOTELS

International Perspective   McDONALD'S

Ethical Perspective   THE BODY SHOP

# VISIONS 1

Vision is a popular word these days in management circles. Todays' complex and ever-changing environment demands that managers of the 1990s have "vision" and the capacity to exercise "visionary leadership." Sam Walton, founder of Wal-Mart stores had a vision built upon a great respect for people and their potential to contribute to the well-being of the enterprise. This visionary approach to people has had remarkable results. Wal-Mart is highly regarded in American industry for high-quality management and its stellar profit-as-a-percent-of-sales performance.

At Wal-Mart people work as *associates* and not employees, they are given *responsible* jobs, and they *participate* in making workplace decisions. When David Glass, Walton's successor as CEO says, "At Wal-Mart, our philosophy is that the best ideas come from the people on the firing line," he means it. Department managers in the company's retail stores run their operations as if they were individual businesses. "Instead of having one entrepreneur who founded the business," Glass says, "we have got 250,000 entrepreneurs out there running their parts of the business." People are a competitive advantage for Wal-Mart. Or, as Glass puts it, "We have no superstars . . . We have average people operating in an environment that encourages everyone to perform way above average."

Managers

This book is about people at work in organizations. It is also about ***managers,*** those persons in an organization who are responsible for the work performance of one or more others. Being a manager is a special type of challenge. People—as well demonstrated in the case of Wal-Mart—are key resources of organizations, and managers must ensure that these human resources are well utilized. Simply put, a manager's job is to get things done through people.

Organizational behavior

***Organizational behavior***, or ***"OB"*** for short, is the study of individuals and groups in organizations. It is a body of knowledge that has special implications for the effective management of people as the human resources in any work setting. Learning about OB will help develop your "vision" about people at work and ensure your capacity to exercise "visionary leadership" when serving in any managerial job.

# FOUNDATIONS OF ORGANIZATIONAL BEHAVIOR

*Good managers* are opportunity seekers and problem solvers. They continually analyze work situations to identify opportunities to be examined or problems to be solved. They develop possible responses to these situations and make decisions to choose and implement appropriate actions. They also follow through to make sure that any actions taken achieve the desired results.

Good managers know what to look for in work situations and how to understand what they find. This, for example, is a process for which physicians are carefully trained. During a physical exam, the doctor systematically asks questions and is quick to note where one condition (such as a recurrent facial sore) may be symptomatic of a problem that requires further medical attention (treatment for a small skin cancer). Instead of such things as sores and headaches, the manager's action indicators are more likely to deal with the attitudes and behaviors of people at work, as well as events occurring in the work unit, organization as a whole, and even in the external environment. Successful managers are able to recognize the significance of these indicators (for example, a decline in work group morale) and take constructive action to improve things as a result of this insight (such as engaging the work group in a "team-building" activity).

Every manager's day is filled with human resource problems to be solved and opportunities to be explored. Although these problems and opportunities will vary in magnitude and immediacy, they all have the potential to affect the performance of organizations and the satisfaction of their members. The field of organizational behavior (let's call it "OB" from now on) offers a knowledge foundation that managers can use to analyze work situations and better understand their consequences for people and organizations.[1] As you proceed with the study of OB, remember:

- OB provides managers with a way of systematically thinking about the behavior of people at work.
- OB provides managers with a vocabulary of terms and concepts that allow work experiences to be clearly analyzed, shared, and discussed.
- OB provides managers with techniques for dealing with the problems and opportunities that commonly occur in work settings.

## Historical Foundations of Organizational Behavior

The field of organizational behavior first emerged as a scientific discipline during the late 1940s. An historical sketch of the various "roots" of OB is provided in *Supplementary Module A* at the end of this book. Here, we should note that OB has developed as a body of knowledge that draws on a variety of scholarly vantage points to build its concepts, theories, and understandings about human behavior in organizations. OB has strong ties to the behavioral sciences—psychology, sociology, and anthropology—as well as to allied social sciences such as economics and political science. Out of this historical background and interdisciplinary character, however, OB has emerged with the following special characteristics.

- *OB Has a contingency orientation.* Rather than assume that there is "one best" or a universal approach to management, OB researchers recognize that behavior in organizations may vary systematically depending upon the nature of the circumstances and people involved. Through a **contingency approach,** they seek to identify how situations can be understood and managed in ways that respond appropriately to their unique characteristics.
- *OB Has an applied focus.* OB is an applied scientific discipline that seeks answers to practical questions. An important criterion of OB research is relevancy. The body of knowledge made available as the field of OB is ultimately designed to help people achieve high performance and experience satisfaction through their work in organizations.
- *OB Rests on scientific foundations.* Researchers in the field of OB use scientific methods to develop and test empirically generalizations about behavior in organizations. Common sense explanations and "armchair speculations" are not routinely accepted; they require scientific justification.

## Scientific Foundations of Organizational Behavior

The scientific foundations of OB, with an emphasis on research methods and designs, are described in *Supplementary Module B* at the end of this book. In addition, it is important to recognize that the value of *scientific thinking* applies not just to OB researchers and scholars, but also to the managers who try to apply the results of their efforts in actual practice. Consider the following short case.

> Joan Brady, a representative of Better Management, Inc., was telling Don Black, the director of personnel for Osdo Corporation, about a new management training package her firm was offering. It was based, she said, on lengthy interviews with five outstanding company presidents. The interviews were analyzed to create a set of assessment materials that could be used to determine the strengths and weaknesses of managers. Better Management, Inc., was prepared to conduct the assessments for Osdo and then offer a training program. The assessment procedure first identifies the personal traits of a firm's managers, and then compares them with a trait profile of successful managers developed from the interviews.
>
> Don noticed that the traits were neatly listed and carefully defined. He was also impressed that each of his managers could be profiled against this list to identify their strengths and weaknesses. He worried, though, whether or not Better Management's assessment and training package really had all the answers.

Good managers will be selective and careful in accepting advice and/or responding to sales overtures such as the one depicted in this case. A proper response to Don's concerns would begin by examining the source of the data used by Better Management. It makes common sense that successful executives are in a position to identify the traits of a good manager. However, this source of data is anecdotal; that is, the executives are simply reminiscing and using recollections to identify the desirable managerial traits. Don Brady and other informed managers should insist on a more *systematic and controlled process of data collection.* This is the first basic characteristic of scientific thinking.

Second, scientific thinking is concerned with *systematically testing proposed explanations* and examining relationships among variables. This includes considering more than one possible explanation for a given question or event. It also includes trying to locate the most feasible explanation and rule out the less feasible alternatives. In our example, none of these things was done. The only explanation given for managerial success was selected personal traits. Other possibilities such as special knowledge, economic conditions, nature of the organization, and so on were completely neglected.

Finally, scientific thinking is *unwilling to accept metaphysical explanations.* These are arguments that cannot be subjected to scientific proof. "It is God's will" is one example of metaphysical reasoning. In the case, attributing someone's managerial success to his or her "gutsiness" is also a basically metaphysical argument.

As a manager, you will be better able to consume the advice and recommendations of others if you develop your scientific thinking. The same argument holds true as you consume the theories, concepts, and advice of organizational researchers. Fortunately, the field of OB is founded on insights developed by scholars who apply scientific methods to study human behavior in organizations.

## The Organization of This Book

OB is an academic discipline that can be used by managers to improve the performance of organizations and the satisfactions of their members. You should find that the many topics presented in this book offer a meaningful study of organizational behavior and its managerial implications. Specifically, our goal is to help you become a successful and respected manager of individuals and groups in organizations.

Figure 1.1 describes the way this book is organized. There are six major parts, with each addressing concepts and theories related to an important OB topic. *Part 1 emphasizes contemporary issues in organizational behavior and management.* The present chapter introduces the foundations of OB with an emphasis on environmental trends and ethical considerations. Chapter 2 gives more specific attention to issues of managerial behavior and performance. Chapter 3 examines the international dimensions of organizational behavior and management.

*Part 2 is dedicated to managing individuals in organizations.* Chapter 4 reviews individual differences in respect to abilities, values, attitudes,

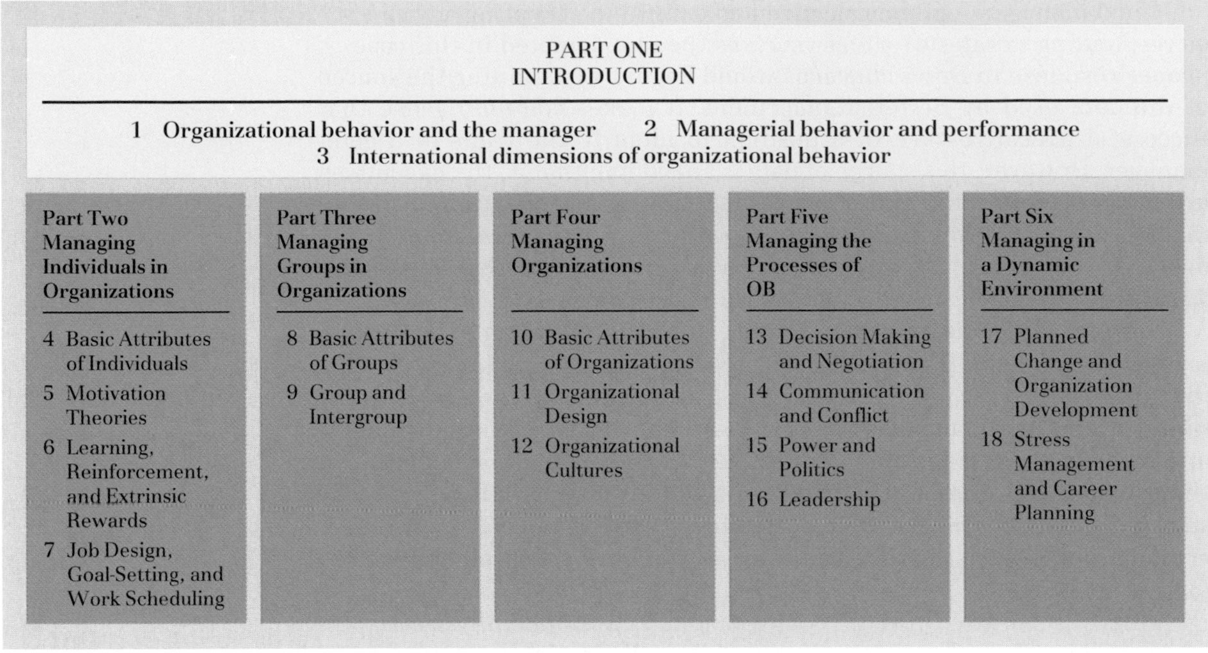


*FIGURE 1.1 Major topics in the study of organizational behavior.*

and perceptions and personalities. Chapter 5 introduces various theories of motivation. Chapters 6 and 7 discuss how these theories can be used to manage rewards and design jobs to encourage high levels of individual work performance and job satisfaction.

*Part 3 is dedicated to managing groups in organizations.* Chapter 8 explains a framework for better understanding groups as human resources of organizations. Chapters 9 and 10 examine group and intergroup dynamics and there is an emphasis on current trends in work group design and team management.

*Part 4 is dedicated to managing organizations.* The three chapters in this part focus on understanding the entire organization as a complex social system. Chapter 11 presents basic structural attributes of organizations. Chapter 12 reviews alternatives in organizational design and the influences of environment, technology, and size. Chapter 13 is devoted to the concept of organizational "culture" and the creation of high performance systems.

*Part 5 reviews the interpersonal processes of OB.* The four chapters in this part explore the following processes through which good managers translate a knowledge of individuals, groups, and organizations into effective action: Chapter 14—decision making and negotiation, Chapter 15—communication and conflict, Chapter 16—power and politics, and Chapter 17—leadership.

*Part 6 deals with the dynamic environment of management.* The focus of both chapters here is on personal managerial applications in an ever-changing environment. Chapter 18 examines the challenges of managing planned change and organization development. Chapter 19 reviews managerial stress and a number of issues relevant to personal career planning and development.

Finally, three supplemental modules at the end of the book offer additional opportunities to extend your study of OB in selected directions. These modules provide additional background on the history of OB *(Module A)*, the scientific foundations of OB *(Module B)*, and performance appraisal *(Module C)*.

# LEARNING ABOUT ORGANIZATIONAL BEHAVIOR

**Learning**

***Learning*** is a change in behavior that occurs as a result of experience. Your learning about OB only begins with the pages of this book and your formal education. It can and should continue in the future as you benefit from actual work experiences.

## Experiential Learning

Experiential learning is a means of initially learning and then continuing to learn about OB.[2] The learning sequence involves an initial experience and subsequent reflection. Theory-building follows to explain what took place, and the theory is tested through experimentation at the next opportunity.

This book is a formal opportunity for you to learn more about OB. It is also written to capitalize on the values of experiential learning. Your other course activities will complement the book to help you to take full

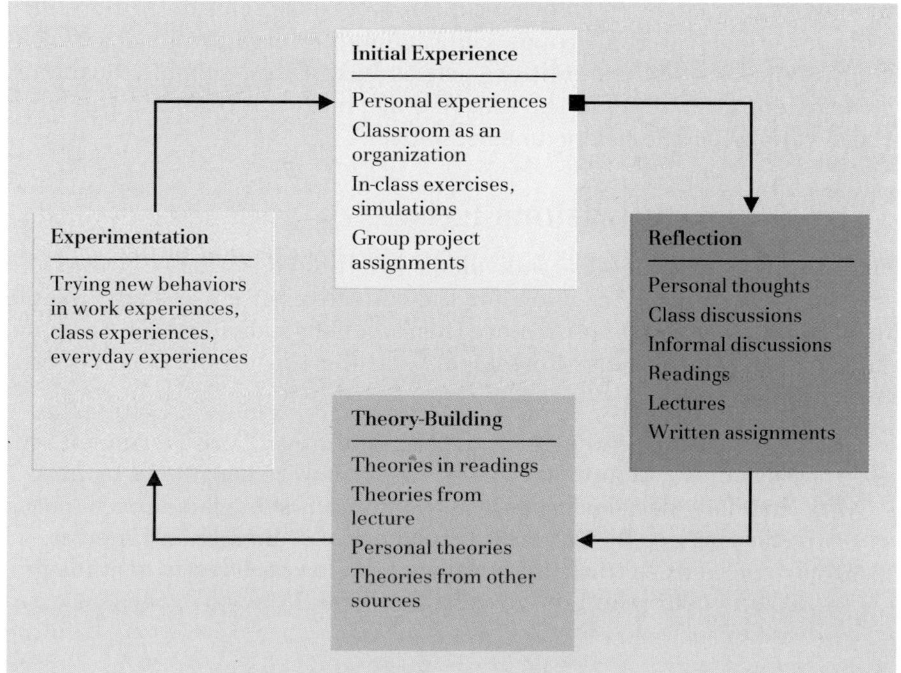


*FIGURE 1.2 Experiential learning in the typical OB course.*

advantage of the experiential learning cycle in Figure 1.2. Along with your instructor we can offer special cases and exercises to provide you with initial experience. We can even stimulate your reflection and theory-building by presenting theories and discussing their practical implications. Sooner or later, however, you must become an active participant in the learning process. Only you can do the active experimentation required to complete the learning cycle.

## Life-long Learning

**Life-long learning**

***Life-long learning,*** continuous learning from the full variety of one's actual work and life experiences, is both a personal responsibility and a prerequisite to your long-term career success. Day-to-day work experiences, conversations with colleagues and friends, counsel and advice from mentors, "success models," training seminars and workshops, professional reading and videotapes, and the information available in the popular press and radio/television media, all provide frequent opportunities for day-to-day learning about OB. All it takes to derive full advantage from life-long learning is your commitment to pursue actively such opportunities and incorporate the results into your thinking and behavior. Managerial success in today's complex and dynamic environment demands this commitment to continuous learning and personal development.

# THE NATURE OF ORGANIZATIONS

**Organization**

The study of OB must begin with the nature of organizations themselves. Formally defined, an organization is a collection of people working together in a division of labor to achieve a common purpose. This definition fits a wide variety of fraternal groups, clubs, voluntary organizations, and religious bodies, as well as entities such as businesses, schools, hospitals, government agencies, and the like. We are most interested in the work organizations people belong to as employees.

## Why Do Organizations Exist?

Organizations exist because individuals are limited in their physical and mental capabilities. They allow for the collective efforts of many people to be combined to accomplish more than what any individual can do alone. This logic may be as old as time itself. Consider this example as reported in the Bible.[3]

> Some time after leading his people out of Egypt, Moses camped at the base of the Mountain of God. His days were consumed by making the many decisions required to maintain the tribe. Moses took care that his people had proper food and clothing. He listened to their concerns, settled their disputes, and responded to all those who came before him inquiring about God.

> Moses was fortunate to be joined in this camp by his father-in-law, Jethro. After observing Moses' daily routine, the wise counsel Jethro commented, "thou wilt surely wear away, both thou and this people that is with thee; for this thing is too heavy for thee; thou are not able to perform it thyself alone."
>
> Jethro went on to give Moses the following advice. He counseled Moses to select other persons to assist him in these many managerial chores. He further suggested that these people be given the responsibility to rule over groups of thousands, hundreds, fifties, and tens. Finally, he encouraged Moses to let them judge the small matters for the people under their control and to only bring the large matters to him.

Jethro, in effect, gave Moses a way to organize his people. Moses' "organization" was created when certain people were appointed as "managers" to whom others reported at various levels of responsibility. Similar forms of organization emerge in many different circumstances. In all cases, the goal is to best utilize everyone's talents *and* achieve outcomes that are beyond individual capabilities alone.

## Ingredients of Organizations

Organizations begin with people. Beyond that, however, they involve a purpose, division of labor, and hierarchy of authority.

### *Purpose*

**Purpose of an organization**

The purpose of an organization is to produce a good or service. Nonprofit organizations, for example, produce services with public benefits, such as health care, education, judicial processing, and highway maintenance. Businesses produce consumer goods and services such as automobiles, appliances, gourmet dining, and accommodations.

The following are the stated purposes found in annual reports of four familiar businesses. Note that each defines a domain or intended arena of operations for each organization in the broader society.

> *CBS, Inc.* To serve as a broad-based entertainment and communications company.
>
> *Apple Computer, Inc.* To bring technology to individuals through computers.
>
> *Chesebrough-Pond's.* To serve as a diversified worldwide manufacturer and marketer of branded consumer products for the health and well-being of the entire family.
>
> *Wal-Mart.* To offer quality name brand merchandise at an everyday low price.

### *Division of Labor*

The essence of any organization is human effort. The process of breaking the work to be done into tasks that can be performed by individuals or

**Division of labor**

groups is called the ***division of labor.*** It is through the division of labor that organizations mobilize the work of many people to achieve a common purpose.

Consider the example of McDonald's, where the division of labor is quite clear in any of the company's restaurants. What do you see upon entry? There are certain people waiting on customers, others cooking hamburgers, others cooking french fries, and still others cleaning up. By dividing up the labor and training employees to perform highly specialized tasks, the company strives for excellence in task accomplishment and high operating efficiency.

### *Hierarchy of Authority*

**Authority**

***Authority*** is the right to act and to command other persons. Managers have authority over their subordinates. When organizations divide labor into small components, something must be done to coordinate the efforts to ensure that work results accomplish the organization's purpose. A ***hierarchy of authority,*** wherein work positions are arranged in order of increasing authority, facilitates this coordination. Persons of higher authority are able to make decisions that result in the proper coordination and direction of work activities at lower levels.

**Hierarchy of authority**

The hierarchy of authority is well defined in a McDonald's restaurant. Supervisors wear different color uniforms and have special name tags. It is also quite clear that they make the big decisions when problems or special situations arise.

## Organizations as Open Systems

Organizations are complex social systems that ultimately depend upon the activities and collective efforts of many people to achieve performance results. But even though people are the human resources of organizations, organizations are more than people. They also include the machinery, equipment, raw materials, facilities, and money that allow people to produce some good or service. These are the physical or material resources of organizations.

**Open systems**

As ***open systems,*** organizations transform human and physical resources received as inputs from their environments into goods and services that are then returned to the environment for consumption. The goods or services are created by work activities that transform resource inputs into product outputs. All this is made possible by the direct interaction of the organization with its environment.

Take, for example, the way your McDonald's functions in terms of Figure 1.3. The figure views this organization as an open system. People, the human resource inputs, work with various physical resource inputs to create and deliver fast food for customers. Each local McDonald's obtains needed human and physical resource inputs from its external environment. These resources are then combined in a transformation process that results in food items being prepared and sold as product outputs. In this business example, furthermore, the price paid by customers for their

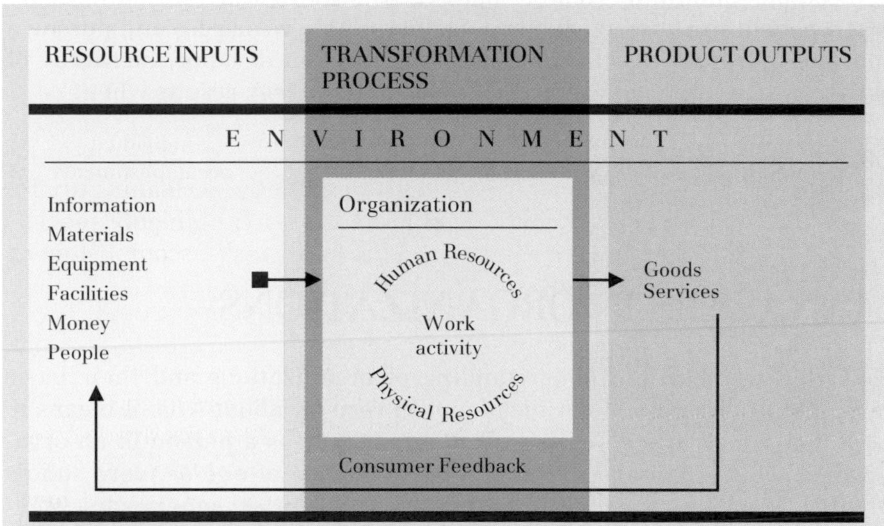


*FIGURE 1.3 The organization as an open system: Turning resource inputs into product outputs.*

food becomes an important monetary input to the organization. The company's ability to sell today is a significant influence on its ability to be in business again tomorrow.

A major contribution of the open systems perspective is increased managerial awareness that organizational survival depends on satisfying environmental demands. The input–output interdependency between a system and its environment is an important influence on organizations and the people who work within them. Like all organizations, McDonald's is an open system that must successfully interact with its environment to survive and prosper in the long run. Probably the best recent examples of external challenges to the firm are concerns expressed about the environmental impact of its food packaging and about the nutritional value of the food itself. In both cases, the company has responded, in part at least, with extensive public information campaigns.

## Synergy in Organizations

**Means–end chains**

A well-defined organization includes ***means-end chains*** that clearly link the work efforts of individuals and groups to a common purpose. Think of this purpose as an end sought by the chief executive officer (CEO). In the division of labor, those managers directly reporting to the chief executive each have a set of performance goals. These are the means for accomplishing the end represented by the CEO's view of the organization's purpose. Such a division of labor should flow clearly throughout an organization so that performance goals at any one level of responsibility become the means for accomplishing ends at the next higher level.

**Synergy**

There is something more, however, to the organization as a collection of means–end chains. ***Synergy*** is the creation of a whole that is greater than the sum of its parts. You might think of it as the potential to make 2

+ 2 equal something greater than 4. Synergy in organizations occurs when people work well together to use available resources and pursue a common purpose. It is facilitated by the division of labor, hierarchy of authority and effective managerial behavior. Synergy results when:

Organizational accomplishments $\xrightarrow[\text{than}]{\text{are more}}$ group accomplishments $\xrightarrow[\text{than}]{\text{are more}}$ individual accomplishments

# MANAGERS IN ORGANIZATIONS

Now that we share an understanding of organizations and their basic ingredients, it is possible to speak more precisely about what it means to be a manager. Earlier, we identified a ***manager*** as a person in an organization who is responsible for the performance of one or more subordinates. Managers are identified by various job titles: supervisors, principals, administrators, general managers, presidents, and group leaders are a few examples.

**Manager**

## What Is an Effective Manager?

**Work unit**

A ***work unit*** is a task-oriented group in an organization that includes the manager and his or her immediate subordinates. Examples include departments in a retail store, divisions of a corporation, branches of a bank, and wards in a hospital. Even the college classroom can be considered a work unit, with the instructor as its manager.

**Task performance**

**Human resource maintenance**

A manager's immediate concerns about a work unit are two-fold. First, the manager is concerned with ***task performance,*** the quality and quantity of work produced or services performed. Second, the manager is concerned with ***human resource maintenance,*** the attraction and continuation of a viable work force. This last notion focuses a manager's attention on individual job satisfaction, job involvement, commitment, absenteeism, and turnover, as well as performance. Without proper maintenance of the people who do the work, no work unit or organization will be able to perform at consistently high levels over time. One potential sign of improper human resource maintenance is "job burnout," a term commonly used to describe the feelings of mental exhaustion sometimes experienced by people facing too many demands and pressures in their work.

**Effective manager**

This book treats task performance and human resource maintenance as key results sought by any manager. Indeed, an ***effective manager*** is defined as someone whose work unit achieves high levels of *both* task accomplishment *and* human resource maintenance.

## Four Functions of Management

A basic foundation for managerial effectiveness is found in the four functions of management shown in Figure 1.4. Considered action responsibilities of all managers, these functions are:

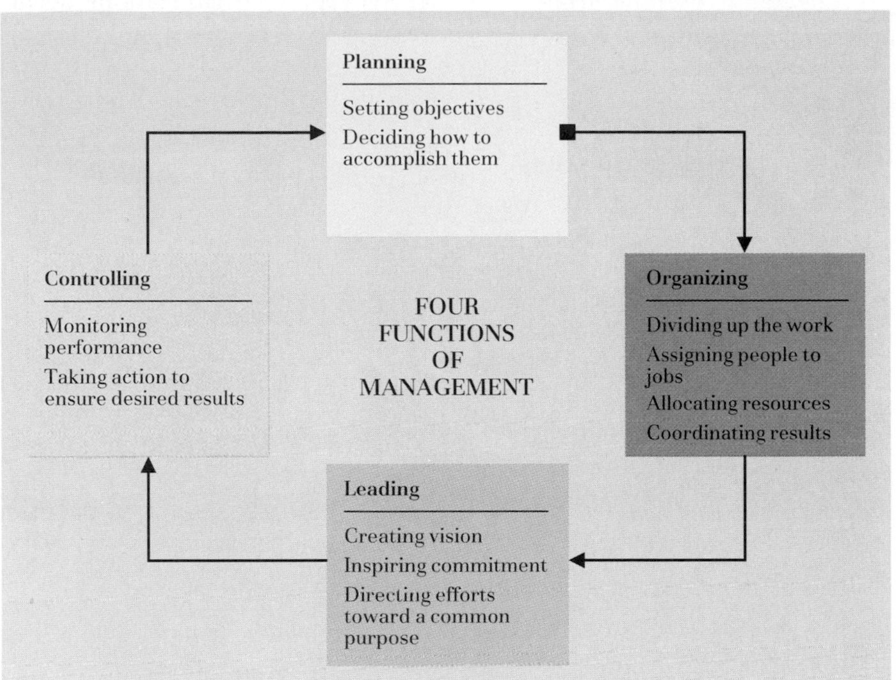


*FIGURE 1.4 Planning, organizing, leading, and controlling—four functions of management.*

1. **Planning** the process of setting performance objectives and identifying the actions needed to accomplish them. **Planning**
2. **Organizing** the process of dividing up the work to be done and then coordinating results to achieve a desired purpose. **Organizing**
3. **Leading** the process of directing the work efforts of other people to successfully accomplish their assigned tasks. **Leading**
4. **Controlling** the process of monitoring performance, comparing actual results to objectives, and taking corrective action as necessary. **Controlling**

The four functions of management are part of the historical foundations of OB described in *Supplementary Module A* at the end of the book. The functions apply in all occupational settings and they offer a useful framework for managerial action. To take just one example, consider this case from a small but growing fast-food chain hoping to compete successfully with McDonald's.

> *In respect to planning,* the president of the chain senses the need for a new product line in order to stay competitive with the industry leaders. After talking things over with the company's top management team, a decision is made to have a new breakfast item ready for field testing within six months.
>
> *In respect to organizing,* the president convenes a special task force to create the new product. People with various skills are selected and assigned to the task force. A budget, clerical support, facilities, and equipment are also made available. Someone is appointed to "head" the task force and is assigned under the direct supervision of the president.

## SKILLS PERSPECTIVE

# HYATT HOTELS

Courtesy of Hyatt Hotels Corporation.

**When a company the size of Hyatt Hotels Corporation shuts down its corporate headquarters for a day, you know something must be happening. But who would have guessed that the president and other corporate employees went to spend the day carrying bags, bussing tables, and making beds in the firm's hotels? This first annual "Hyatt In Touch Day" was intended to get people at the top back in touch with customers and the tasks of workers who directly serve them. Darryl Hartley-Leonard, Hyatt's president, carried bags at the Hyatt Regency Chicago. "It's reality testing," he says of the skills involved at this level. "Those luggage carts are awfully tough to get through the doors." That may seem to be a small point to most people, but to Hartley-Leonard, it means getting new luggage carts. That way, the workers can concentrate on giving service to the hotel's clients—not on maneuvering carts.**

*In respect to leading,* at the first task force meeting, the president states the performance objective, answers questions, and explains why the new product is so important to the firm. The task force head is introduced as someone within whom the president has complete confidence. Before leaving, the president encourages everyone to be enthusiastic and work hard to accomplish the objective.

*In respect to controlling,* the president holds frequent conversations with the task force head to stay informed on efforts to create the new product. Sometimes the president attends task force meetings to ask and answer questions with the group as a whole. When it appears the timetable is slipping, additional personnel are assigned and the budget increased slightly. At last, all task force members are present when the new breakfast item is offered for the first time in one of the company's restaurants.

## The Manager's Challenge

Most managers are simultaneously subordinates and superiors. Think about this statement and what it can mean. As subordinates, managers are held accountable by their superiors (or "bosses") for the task performance and human resource maintenance of their work units. This creates what we refer to as the *manager's challenge:* At the same time that they are held accountable by their superiors for work unit results, managers are dependent upon the efforts of their subordinates to make these results possible.

The last sentence says a great deal. Assume that you are a shift supervisor at a McDonald's restaurant. Look at the diagram in Figure 1.5. This diagram depicts your manager's challenge. At the same time that you are held accountable by the franchise manager for the restaurant's performance during your shift, you depend upon the contributions of 15 subordinate employees to make this performance possible. In effect, and like all managers, you are being held accountable for work that is in large part produced by someone else! This reality is most evident on those days when the shift fails to meet its quality goals. When this happens, the franchise manager does not ask the employees what went wrong; he or she goes directly to you and asks the questions. You cannot say, in return, "but my subordinates are the ones who did not do the work." It is the manager's job to ensure that work unit performance and human resource maintenance are successfully accomplished.

# THE MANAGER'S CHANGING ENVIRONMENT

A knowledge of organizational behavior, defined earlier as the study of individuals and groups in organizations, can help you master the man-

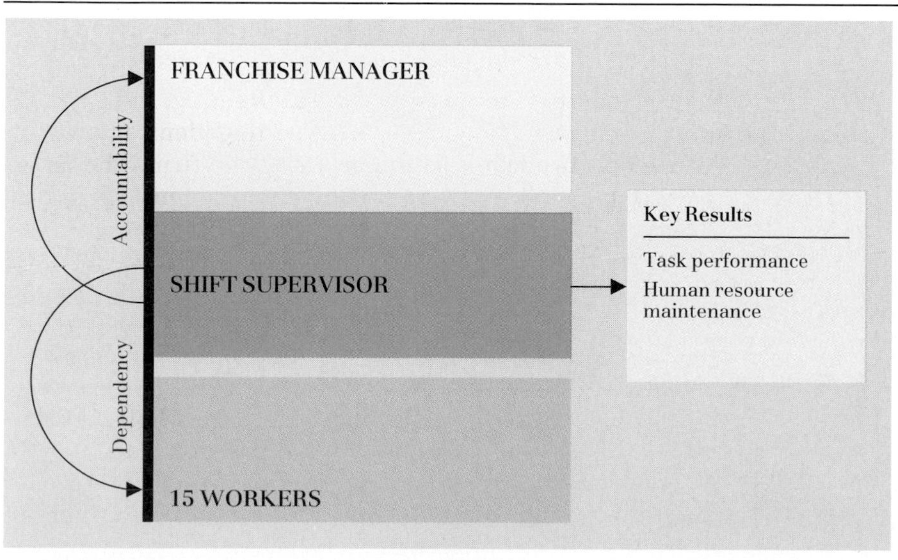


*FIGURE 1.5 The manager's challenge: Case of the production shift supervisor at a McDonald's restaurant.*

ager's challenge as depicted in the last figure. Yet, this challenge must always be addressed in the context of today's dynamic environment. Managers of the 1990s and beyond must be able to perform under the pressures of rapid and even unprecedented change. *Future shock*—the discomfort that comes about in times of continual and uncertain change—is a characteristic of the modern workplace. Managers must be willing and able to anticipate and deal with changing environmental circumstances and help others do the same. As you prepare for such responsibilities, it is helpful to consider several trends representative of what faces managers of tomorrow.[4]

## Focus on Productivity

**Productivity**

***Productivity*** is defined as a summary measure of the quantity *and* quality of work performance with resource utilization considered. As a criterion of work accomplishment in and by organizations, productivity has maintained its place in the vocabulary of management as the watchword of the 1990s. It is sure to be an anchor point for management long into the future.

A major part of a manager's job is to establish and maintain the conditions needed to ensure workplace productivity. Figure 1.6 illustrates the blend of both *performance effectiveness*—a measure of goal attainment—and *performance efficiency*—a measure of resource utilization, that high productivity requires. In complex and challenging times, it is no longer acceptable for managers to simply get a job done (that is, to be effective

*FIGURE 1.6 High productivity = performance effectiveness + performance efficiency.*

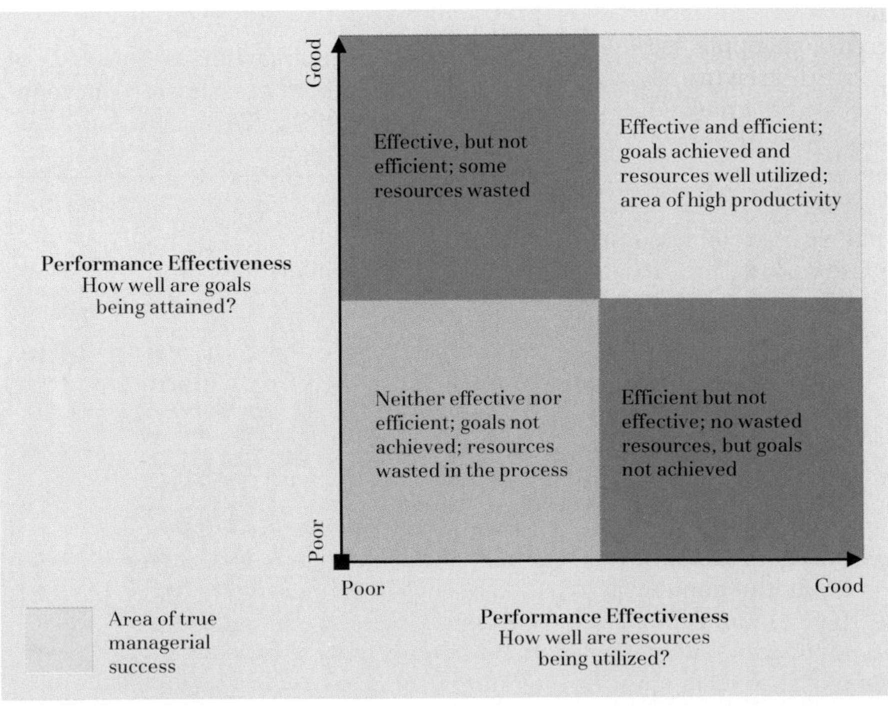

in accomplishing goals). The goals must be achieved efficiently in the use of both human and material resources as well. The study of OB offers many insights in both respects.

High productivity, in turn, requires the efforts of what are now being referred to as ***value-added managers***—managers whose efforts clearly improve "bottom-line performance" for the organization as a whole. It also requires the creation of a total performance system in which individuals and groups in an organization truly work well together. For example,

**Value-added managers**

> ***Inland Fisher Guide*** It used to take seven weeks to manufacture one of 15 styles of steering wheels Inland Fisher Guide produces for the automobile industry. Parts were made in batches and stored until needed, and unfinished wheels were stored between production steps. Now, a single model is made in a work shift by groups of workers doing multiple tasks. There is 50 percent less scrap, 85 percent less reworking, 20 percent less labor cost per unit, 99 percent less lead time, and 25 percent less floor space used under the new methods.

## The Global Economy

No one can doubt that we live at a time in which the many nations and cultures of the world are increasingly interdependent. The *global economy* is real, and it continues to emerge in shape and power. Developments such as the 1992 agreement for an increased integration of Europe, continued business and commercial growth in the Pacific Rim, and dramatic changes in the political economies of Eastern Europe and the Soviet Union are but a few recent examples.

Today's managers are being urged to respond to this dynamic environment by "thinking global" and becoming more competitive in pursuing commercial opportunities around the world. More and more senior executives are arriving at their positions with the benefit of "overseas experience" and knowledge gained from working abroad. More and more junior executives are being asked and encouraged to take such assignments. More and more businesses are integrating themselves through "joint ventures" and "strategic alliances" to become major players in the global economy. And, more and more domestic workers are finding themselves working for "foreign" employers in their local communities. For example,

> ***British Petroleum*** About half of British Petroleum's assets are in the United States, and it pumps more crude oil from U.S. territory than any oil company. The green and yellow "BP" logo appears over some 8000 U.S. service stations and 22,000 world-wide. The company is also looking for another major acquisition to expand its base in America.

In this complex global economy, there is also a growing recognition that managers around the world can learn a lot from one another. Spurred, in part, by the popularization of "Japanese management" approaches in the 1980s, management scholars now recognize that good management and good ideas about management are not confined to one country or region of the world alone. We all have things to share and learn with one

**INTERNATIONAL PERSPECTIVE**

## McDONALD'S

Courtesy of McDonald's Corporation.

**They're calling it "McWorld"—a McDonald's Corporation in which earnings growth is increasingly tied to continued success in international markets. From Moscow to the Caribbean island of Aruba, from the fashionable streets of Budapest to busy Hong Kong, McDonald's is there to offer the same food, quick service, and clean surroundings that U.S. customers are familiar with. As the firm continues to expand abroad, it is exporting its business and management skills as well. Management of the new Moscow restaurant, for example, is not only concerned with training the restaurant workers. Long before the restaurant opened, McDonald's carefully evaluated the local supply of potatoes and beef and worked with local producers to make sure the highest standards were met, even going so far as to introduce a new variety of potatoes to local Soviet farmers. The restaurant—a joint venture between McDonald's–Canada and the Soviet Union—continues to be backed up by a food production and distribution center that monitors quality and food processing and coordinates production with Soviet farmers. The internationalization of McDonald's is a classic example of business trends in a global society.**

another. Chapter 3 of this book is devoted to international dimensions of organizational behavior. You will also find international perspectives and themes emphasized throughout the text.

## Organizational Transitions

Over the last two decades the global economy has not only materialized, it has also demonstrated a tremendous power that for many of us was very new in its demands on organizations and their members—the reality of economic decline as opposed to growth. The emphasis on "downsizing," "restructuring," and "demassing"—all which became business buzzwords in the late 1980s—is sure to be with us for some time. And even though we do not offer the prospects of organizational retrenchment and decline as undeniable facts of a future manager's life, we can and do support the view that tomorrow's managers must be prepared to succeed in both the peaks and valleys of changing economic times. Among the special challenges in managing decline are the increased stress and conflict within and between organizations and their subunits that accompany decline. Significant, too, are the associated demands for increased adaptation and change, including the need for work-force adjustments and alternative organizational structures.

No longer can the scholar or manager be content to view the management of growth as a predominant concern. Learning to live with, cope with, and manage in situations of decline are now equally significant sources of challenge and concern. Perhaps a situation of decline may even test the manager to the ultimate as a sponsor of "productivity" in the broadest use of the term. For example,

> ***Navistar International Corporation*** Forces of economic decline and mismanagement led Navistar International to the brink of bankruptcy. A successful transition into a streamlined company, now increasingly known as a world-class competitor and innovator, was accomplished when new management downsized the firm, changed the company culture in a positive way, and created a new structure and strategies to compete in the global economy.

## Developments in Information Technologies

Another undeniable aspect of our dynamic work environment is the continued emergence of information and computer technology as a dominant force in our lives. We live at a time when *expert systems* are increasingly using techniques of artificial intelligence to facilitate complex diagnosis and decision making for businesses; we live in a time when organizations are creating new top management jobs for a position called "chief information officer"; and, we live in a time when managerial work stations are being constructed around personal computers linked together in local and wide area networks to serve a variety of functions. Indeed, the modern "computer-literate" worker and manager must—at a minimum—be able to use a "PC" and take advantage of popular word-processing, database, spreadsheet, graphics, and networking programs.

Yet most of the technological revolution probably lies before us. As the pace of change in information and computer technology quickens, the results will be revolutionary indeed—for workers, for managers, and for organizations. What it presently means, at a minimum, is that machines are now able to do many routine chores more cheaply and accurately than people; that more information for planning and control is now available at all levels of operations; and that both people and organization structures must now adjust to new ways of doing things. For example,

> ***Next, Inc.*** Steve Jobs—one of Apple Computers' co-founders—has used technology to create a highly advanced manufacturing system at

Next, Inc. Computer circuit boards move on an assembly line where robots place tiny components, lasers make the electrical connections, and 1700 tiny dabs of solder are applied. Only after 20 minutes, when the board reaches the end of the line, does a person appear to check the work. Not much checking is needed, since Next, Inc. circuit boards have a defect rate one-tenth the industry standard.

## New Ways of Organizing

One outgrowth of changes in the contemporary environment has been the emergence of new ways of organizing the workplace—and we're talking about more than the introduction of new technologies. For example,

***Corning Glass, Inc.*** The company's Blacksburg, Virginia plant was renovated; 7,500 applicants were screened for 100 new jobs. There are no timeclocks in the plant and no supervisors; there are just eight managers. Employees spend one-fifth of their time in training and earn pay increases for mastering new skills. The emphasis is on teamwork, job rotation, and self-management. Everyone belongs to a team whose six or so workers set their own goals, make schedules, and assign work. All this is a stark contrast to the plant's former assembly-line organization where each worker toiled alone at one, and only one, job.

More and more organizations are turning to new ways of bringing people and technology together to create the "high-performance" systems discussed earlier in this chapter. Like Corning, they are experimenting with revised production and service operations that emphasize teamwork and group-based tasks, performance-based incentives and reward systems, intense training and development of employees, continuous learning and improvement for the organization as a whole, reduced external supervision and increased individual responsibilities, fewer levels of management, fewer numbers of staff personnel, and greater emphasis on organizational adaptation, innovation, and performance.

Any manager must be informed about such developments, and be willing and able to fully participate in the new-form workplaces they represent. It may be that the 1990s will become known as the decade that fundamentally changed the way people work.

## Changing Demographics and Work Force Diversity

A most significant trend involves developments in population demographics and work force diversity. Changes in population demographics are affecting the job mix and career opportunities in the 1990s and will continue to do so. Whereas reports like *Workplace 2000* note that jobs are growing more complex and demand workers with higher levels of skills, these reports express great concern over the current availability of skilled workers and the quality of education being offered to create future ones. This is a most important issue—both in the United States and elsewhere.[5] For example, *The Economist* refers to a world-wide "population time bomb" in which a shortage of skilled young workers is projected even as the number of jobs continues to grow. For example,

> *Shering-Plough Corp.* Management is worried about a shortage of scientists and engineers at this New Jersey medical-products firm. Recruiting strategies are under review, and the company is going to be more aggressive in its efforts to find job candidates on college campuses.

For the 1990s it is expected that:

- America's work force will grow more slowly, the number of people aged 16–24 will fall, and those over 35 will rise.
- The countries of the European Community—notably Ireland, Britain, France, and West Germany, will have fewer younger workers.
- Japan will experience a slight growth in population but will see a steady decline in workers under the age of 25.

Forecasts of where the jobs will be in the 1990s indicate that many will be available, but they will mostly be found in the service sectors of the economy—including *business services* (e.g., management consulting, public relations, advertising, and lobbying), *professional services* (e.g., law, accounting, and engineering) *specialized services* (e.g., maintenance and repair of computers, copiers, and communications equipment), and *financial services* (e.g., banking, insurance, and brokerage). As *big* business has been losing jobs, job creation includes *small*- and *medium-sized* businesses that stress entrepreneurship and innovation.

The manager of tomorrow will work and perform in settings where personal creativity and small organizational size are the norms. This person will also need to be skilled at managing ***work force diversity,*** that is a work force consisting of a broad mix of workers from different racial and ethnic backgrounds, of different ages and genders, and of different domestic and national cultures. In the United States alone, the proportion of native white men in the new work force is decreasing while that of women grows, the proportion of both non-white men and women is growing, and the proportion of immigrant men and women is also growing. Indeed, nearly two-thirds of the new entrants to the 1990s work force will be women and another 20 percent will be non-white or immigrant men.

**Work force diversity**

Work force diversity brings with it new demands for managerial sensitivity and understanding, as well as for responsive employment practices. More and more employers are training managers to better handle the new diversity—a subject discussed in the *Skills Perspective* and at many points throughout this book. Many employers are setting up special programs to help workers, often from "dual-career" or "single-parent" households, who require assistance in such areas as child-care and elder-care as they try to balance work and family responsibilities. As employers search for employees in scarce labor markets to fill "high skill" jobs, some are getting involved in education to help insure the future availability of qualified job candidates. For example,

***Eastman Kodak*** President Kay Whitmore says that Eastman Kodak is actively helping restructure the Rochester, N.Y. schools where the firm has major corporate operations. Although it helps the community, Kodak's initiative serves its own needs as well. "If we can't expand the pool of qualified people," Whitmore says, "we won't get the people we need."

## Human Rights in the Workplace

All of the prior changes and trends create pressures for new ways of managerial thinking and for new relationships between managers and the persons who report to them. *Human rights* and *social justice* are increasingly revered in the workplace, as they are in the world at large. All managers, accordingly, must be willing to deal with:

- *Pressures for self-determination.* People seek greater freedom to determine *how* to do their jobs and *when* to do them. Pressures for increased worker participation in the forms of job enrichment, autonomous work groups, flexible working hours, and compressed workweeks will grow.
- *Pressures for employee rights.* People expect their rights to be respected on the job as well as outside of work. These include the rights of individual privacy, due process, free speech, free consent, freedom of conscience, and freedom from sexual harassment.
- *Pressures for job security.* People expect their security to be protected. This includes their physical well-being in terms of occupational safety and health matters, and their economic livelihood in terms of guaranteed protection against layoffs and provisions for cost-of-living wage increases.
- *Pressures for equal employment opportunity.* People expect and increasingly demand the right to employment without discrimination on the basis of age, sex, ethnic background, or handicap. Among these demands will remain a concern for furthering the modest but dramatic gains made in recent years by women and other minorities in the workplace. "Progress" will be applauded but it will not be accepted as a substitute for true equality of opportunity.
- *Pressures for equity of earnings.* People expect to be compensated for the "comparable worth" of their work contributions. What began as a concern for earnings differentials between women and men doing the same jobs has been extended to cross-occupational comparisons. Questions such as why a nurse receives less pay than a carpenter and why a maintenance worker is paid more than a secretary are asked with increasing frequency. They will require answers other than the fact that certain occupations (such as nursing) have traditionally been dominated by women, whereas others (such as carpentry) have been dominated by men.

Good managers will understand and respond to these and related social pressures. Although progress is not always as fast as one would like, there are an increasing number of organizations whose managers are trying to respond in positive ways. For example,

*U.S. West, Inc.* A Study of its management ranks showed that although one out of 21 white males reached middle-management or higher at U.S. West, Inc., only one out of 138 white women did so. Even worse, only one of every 289 non-white women did so. Now the firm has a special leadership development program for "women of color" which is designed to increase their odds of success in advancing up the management ladder.

# MANAGERIAL ETHICS AND QUALITY OF WORK LIFE

The word "ethics" is often in the news these days. Formally defined, ***ethical behavior*** is that which is morally accepted as "good" and "right" as opposed to "bad" or "wrong" in a particular setting. *Is it ethical,* for example, to pay a bribe to obtain a business contract in a foreign country? *Is it ethical* to allow your company to dispose of hazardous waste in an unsafe fashion? *Is it ethical* to withold information that might discourage a job candidate from joining your organization? *Is it ethical* to ask someone to take a job you know will not be good for their career progress? *Is it ethical* to do personal business on company time?

**Ethical behavior**

Our list of examples could go on and on. Regardless of your initial inclinations in response to these questions, the major point of it all is to remind you that the public-at-large is demanding that government officials, managers, workers in general, and the organizations they represent all act in accordance with high ethical and moral standards.

## Ethical Managerial Behavior

***Managerial ethics*** are standards and principles that guide the actions and decisions of managers and determine if they are "good" or "bad" in a moral sense. Ethical managerial behavior, accordingly, is that which conforms not only to the dictates of law, but also to a broader moral code common to society as a whole. An ***ethical dilemma*** is a situation in which a person must decide whether or not to do something that, although benefiting oneself or the organization or both, may be considered unethical.

**Managerial ethics**

**Ethical dilemma**

Ethical dilemmas are common in the workplace. Research, in fact, suggests that managers encounter such dilemmas in their working relationships with superiors, subordinates, customers, competitors, suppliers, and regulators. Common issues underlying the dilemmas involve honesty in communications and contracts, gifts and entertainment, kickbacks, pricing practices, and employee terminations.[6]

Whereas some organizations have published *codes of conduct* to help guide behavior in such circumstances, in all organizations the ultimate test is the strength of an individual manager's personal ethical framework. Because of this, more and more organizations are offering ethics training programs to help managers clarify their ethical frameworks and practice self-discipline when making decisions in difficult circumstances. What follows is a useful seven-step checklist for dealing with an ethical dilemma:[7]

1. Recognize and clarify the dilemma.
2. Get all possible facts.
3. List your options—all of them.
4. Test each option by asking: "Is it legal? Is it right? Is it beneficial?"
5. Make your decision.
6. Double check your decision by asking: "How would I feel if my family found out about this? How would I feel if my decision was printed in the local newspaper?"
7. Take action.

There is one more point that must be considered on this subject of ethical managerial behavior. Each of us can too easily use rationalizations to help justify actual or potential misconduct. The best way to prevent these rationalizations from leading us astray is to recognize them for what they are. Common rationalizations used to justify *un*ethical behavior include:[8]

- Pretending the behavior is not really unethical or illegal.
- Excusing the behavior by saying it's really in the organization's or your best interest.
- Assuming the behavior is okay because no one else would ever be expected to find out about it.
- Expecting your superiors to support and protect you if anything should go wrong.

## Corporate Social Responsibility

Some absolutely notorious cases of organizational wrongdoing have been in the public eye. It wasn't too long ago, for example,

> ***Beech-nut*** Two senior executives were sentenced to jail for their roles in covering up the fact that Beech-nut was selling adulterated apple juice for infants. The juice was labeled "100% fruit juice," but turned out to be a blend of chemical ingredients.

**Whistleblower**

A ***whistleblower*** is someone who exposes organizational wrongdoings in order to preserve ethical standards and protect against wasteful, harmful, or illegal acts. The fact that it was a whistleblower who brought the Beech-nut case to public attention is generally well known. What is not so well known is that whistleblowers are often subject to retaliatory action by disgruntled employers. To cite just three examples—Agnew Connolly was fired after pushing her employer to report two toxic chemical accidents; Dave Jones was fired after reporting his company was using unqualified suppliers in a nuclear power plant construction project; two IRS officials were harassed and demoted after implicating their superior in a pattern of work misconduct and corruption.[9]

**Corporate social responsibility**

***Corporate social responsibility*** is the obligation of organizations to behave in ethical and moral ways as institutions of the broader society. The whistleblowers we have just been discussing have all been persons who exposed *ir*responsible corporate behavior to outside scrutiny. Today's

ETHICAL PERSPECTIVE

## THE BODY SHOP

Courtesy of The Body Shop.

**Anita Roddick turned a $6,500 investment into one of Great Britain's most noteworthy new enterprises. Since 1976, her storefront-cosmetics firm has grown into a 37-country network of franchises expected to be a $1 billion enterprise by 1995. The firm is known for its innovative "natural" cosmetics and a commitment to the environment. Roddick's social activism is reflected in the spirit of her business, which promotes environmental consciousness by supporting such causes as Greenpeace, Save the Whales, and the Stop the Burning (of the rain forest) Campaign. Internally, the firm has an Environmental Projects department to monitor compliance with its principles, which include using only biodegradable products and refillable containers.**

organizations and their managers face increased accountability for their decisions. We expect socially responsible organizations to deliver safe and quality products and/or services to customers and clients; we expect socially responsible organizations to avoid harming the environment; we expect socially responsible organizations to provide working conditions that support employee health, safety, and personal needs; we expect socially responsible organizations to contribute positively to the general well-being of their host communities. And the list can go on.

What this concept of corporate social responsibility suggests, in turn, is that managers—the people who make the decisions that guide the behavior of organizations—must ensure that their ethical frameworks extend to the organization as a whole. Managers must be the role models for other organizational members and take the lead in committing the organization to act in ways that are consistent with both the quest for high productivity and the objective of corporate social responsibility.

## Work and the Quality of Life

Quality of work life

One way for organizations to show socially responsible behavior is to provide their members—employees—with high-quality work environments. ***Quality of work life,*** or *QWL*, for short, is a term that has gained deserved prominence in OB as an indicator of the overall quality of human experiences in the workplace. It expresses a special way of thinking about people, their work, and the organizations in which careers are fulfilled. It establishes a clear objective that high productivity can and should be achieved along with satisfaction of the human resources—the people who do the required work.

Quality of work life activities represent special applications of the many OB concepts and theories to be introduced in this book. In particular, managerial commitments to QWL entail a willingness to pursue:[10]

- *Participative problem solving.* Getting people at all levels of responsibility involved in decision making, such as is found in quality circles and employee group meetings.
- *Work restructuring.* Rearranging the jobs people do and the work systems and structures surrounding them, such as is found in job enrichment and autonomous work groups.
- *Innovative reward systems.* Creating new ways of making rewards available for contributed work performance, such as is found in the Scanlon Plan and skills-based pay.
- *Improved work environments.* Making the work setting more pleasant and responsive to individual needs, such as in alternative work schedules and better physical conditions.

Furthermore, managers should remember that what happens to people at work can affect how they feel and what they do outside work, and vice versa. Someone who is having a "bad day" on the job, for example, may be responding to worries about family responsibilities or other pressures in their nonwork life. The central importance of work in the total life experience also varies from one person to the next—and, this centrality may change over the course of a career. Work may mean quite different things to the young single adult, to the mid-career adult with a working spouse and school-age children involved in a variety of sports and activities, and to the late-career adult making retirement plans. Indeed, what satisfies different people and even the same individual at different life and career stages will vary significantly.

Thus, the field of OB recognizes that every employee of a work organization lives two overlapping lives, a work life and a nonwork life. The environment created by managers for people at work may have consequences that extend beyond the time an individual spends in the work setting. Managers should be fully aware that the quality of any individual's life, even their own, can be heavily influenced by the quality of life at work. Poor management can decrease the quality of overall life, not just the quality of work life. Hopefully, good management can increase both.

# SUMMARY

■ **Foundations of Organizational Behavior** include research insights developed from strong scientific foundations, a contingency orientation, and an applied focus. Together with historical roots in the applied behavioral sciences, the foundations introduce an academic discipline devoted to helping organizations and their members perform. "OB" is formally defined as the study of individuals and groups in organizations. The understandings of OB are useful to all managers who must make good decisions in complex and dynamic environments.

■ **Learning about Organizational Behavior** is a life-long process. Good managers are able to understand, predict and influence human behavior in organizations. Studying and thinking about the many insights made available in the field of OB will help you establish these important capabilities. Only a true willingness to apply these insights and learn from your experiences will allow you to sustain and continually improve them throughout your career.

■ **The Nature of Organizations** of all types and sizes rests with their shared existence as collections of people working together in a division of labor to achieve a purpose. As open systems, organizations interact with their environments as they transform human and physical resource inputs into product or service outputs.

■ **Managers in Organizations** are persons to whom one or more others report—that is, they serve at the head of work units staffed by one or more subordinates. Key results sought by managers are task performance and human resource maintenance at the individual, group and organizational levels. All managers share the common challenge of being held accountable by a higher authority for work which they are dependent upon their subordinates to produce.

■ **The Manager's Changing Environment** includes many important trends. Significant issues facing managers of the 1990s include: a focus on productivity, the global economy, organizational transitions, information and computer technologies, changing population demographics and job mix, new ways of organizing, and concerns for human rights in the workplace.

■ **Managerial Ethics and Quality of Work Life** are topics of utmost importance to managers and the persons they ultimately serve—members of broader society. Ethical managerial behavior involves making decisions based on moral concepts of what is "right" and "wrong" from the societal perspective. Managers must develop strong ethical frameworks to help them

**resolve the ethical dilemmas common to the workplace and assist in the development of corporate social responsibility—the obligation of organizations as a whole to act in ethical ways. A quality work life is increasingly recognized as a component of corporate social responsibility and the discipline of OB offers many insights to help managers contribute positively to the achievement of this objective.**

## KEY TERMS

Authority
Contingency Approach
Controlling
Corporate Social Responsibility
Division of Labor
Effective Manager
Ethical Behavior
Ethical Dilemma
Hierarchy of Authority
Human Resource Maintenance
Leading
Learning
Life-Long Learning
Manager
Managerial Ethics
Means-End Chain
Open Systems
Organization
Organizational Behavior
Organizational Purpose
Organizing
Planning
Productivity
Quality of Work Life
Synergy
Task Performance
Value-Added Manager
Whistleblower
Work Force Diversity
Work Unit

## REVIEW QUESTIONS

1. Explain what it means to say that OB is an academic discipline with a "contingency orientation," "applied focus," and "scientific foundation."
2. Define the term "organization" and describe how an organization with which you are familiar operates as an "open system."
3. Describe the "manager's challenge" that might be faced by someone in this organization. Explain how the four functions of management—planning, organizing, leading, and controlling—can assist them in mastering this challenge.
4. What is an "effective" manager, and why would an effective manager be concerned with the achievement of "synergy?"
5. What is "productivity" and how does this concept relate to the terms "performance efficiency" and "performance effectiveness?"
6. Choose three environmental trends and developments you believe are especially important in today's world. Explain their significance to managers of the 1990s.
7. Describe an "ethical dilemma" that might be faced by a manager in his or her dealings with subordinates. Explain how you feel this dilemma could be handled in an ethical fashion.

8. Is it a manager's responsibility to (a) be a "whistleblower" when organizational wrongdoings are detected, (b) be concerned about the quality of *non-work* life experienced by persons under his or her supervision? Explain your answers to both questions.

## AN OB LIBRARY

Peter F. Drucker, *The New Realities* (New York: Harper Collins, 1989).

John Naisbitt and Patricia Aburdene, *Megatrends 2000: Ten New Directions for the 1990s* (New York: William Morrow, 1990).

Gary N. Powell, *Women and Men in Management* (Newbury Park, Calif.: Sage, 1988).

Barbara Ley Toffler, *Tough Choices: Managers Talk Ethics* (New York: John Wiley & Sons, 1986).

*Workforce 2000: Work and Workers for the 21st Century* (Indianapolis: The Hudson Institute: 1987).

# EXERCISE

## PART A "MY BEST MANAGER"

### *Objectives*

1. To help you reflect seriously on the attributes of a good manager.
2. To allow you to share your views with others and compare their thoughts with yours.
3. To provide an opportunity for you to get to know other participants in the course and learn about their work experiences.

### *Time*

30 to 40 minutes

### *Procedure*

1. Make a list of the attributes that describe the *best* manager you have ever worked for. If you have trouble identifying with an actual manager, make a list of attributes you would like the manager in your next job to have.
2. Form a group of four to five persons and share your lists.
3. Create one list that combines all the unique attributes of the "best" managers represented in your group. Make sure that you have all attributes listed, but list each only once. Place a check mark next to those that were reported by two or more members. Have one of your members prepared to present the list in general class discussion.

4. After all groups have finished Step 3, spokespersons should report to the whole class. The instructor will make a running list of the "best" manager attributes as viewed by the class.
5. Feel free to ask questions and discuss the results.

## PART B "MY BEST JOB"

### *Objectives*

1. To have you state and examine a set of professional goals.
2. To help you identify unrealistic or superficial work goals.
3. To allow you to compare your goals with those of others.

### *Time*

45 to 70 minutes

### *Procedure*

1. Make a list of the top five things you expect from your first (or next) full-time job.
2. Exchange lists with a nearby partner. Assign probabilities (or odds) to each goal on your partner's list to indicate how likely you feel it is that the goal can be accomplished. (Note: Your instructor may ask that everyone use the same probabilities format.)
3. Discuss your evaluations with your partner. Try to delete superficial goals or modify them to become more substantial. Try to restate any unrealistic goals to make them more realistic. Help your partner do the same.
4. Form a group of four to six persons. Within the group have everyone share what they now consider to be the most "realistic" goals on their lists. Have a spokesperson prepared to share a sample of these items with the entire class.
5. Discuss what group members have individually learned from the exercise. Await further class discussion led by your instructor.

# CASE

## PRODUCTIVITY IMPROVEMENT AT A BRITISH PLANT

The setting is Halewood, England. The factory is a Ford Motor Company plant. Up until recently, the factory displayed classic British industrial ills. Labor strife permeated the plant, with turmoil so common that the local newspaper used to call daily to check on possible troubles. Once, when the unusual occurred and nothing bad did happen, the headline read: "Smooth Night Shift at Ford."

Now cooperation has replaced conflict on the shop floor at the Halewood facility, located just outside of Liverpool. Along with other segments of British industry, it has been transformed. Productivity is up dramatically as production has increased and labor costs have fallen. One worker says: "If you had told me (10 years ago) that I would be producing more cars with fewer workers, I would have told you to go see a psychiatrist."

Ford's European operations are a major contributor to its profits, and the British operations are important to Ford. Its confidence is reflected in a decision to invest $950 million more in the facility. The turning point occurred five years ago after word leaked out that the head of Ford Europe considered inefficient plants, like the old Halewood, to be an "endangered species." In other words, they may have had to be shut down.

The cities of Halewood and Liverpool could ill afford to lose the plant and its contributions to the region's economy. The local labor unions called for meetings with management to discuss matters. The operations manager seized the opportunity to explain the "competition" Ford faced and what it would take to survive and prosper in the current and highly competitive European marketplace. He met with everyone—all 8000 workers—in groups ranging from 40 to 200 people to explain things. He sent some 2000 over time to visit Ford's Saarlouis, Germany plant where productivity was high. He asked them upon returning to consider what they could do to help turn around the Halewood operation.

Joint work committees consisting of union and management personnel were formed. A new atmosphere of discussion and problem-solving gradually emerged to replace the old "class warfare" in the plant. Although the union still bargains hard in behalf of workers on wages and such matters, it is highly involved in constructive dialog with management. Everyone wants to keep the facility competitive—and keep the jobs in town. Most feel that the changes at Halewood are permanent. Says one union representative: "It's gone on for a few years, and both sides trust each other much more now."

## *Questions*

1. Identify what you would consider to be the more "progressive" management responses made in this case that helped turn around the Halewood plant. Why do you think these specific responses worked—that is, what appeal did they have to the union workers in the facility?
2. What does "productivity" mean when applied at the Halewood facility? Why is productivity an important concern for both the management and union groups? Is there something about productivity that leads to a natural antagonism between management and unions? Please explain.
3. Discuss how the following issues apply in the setting of this case: (a) managerial ethics, (b) corporate social responsibility, (c) quality of work life. What lessons does this case offer, if any, that may be of use to managers concerned about similar issues in other places?

This study outline of major topics is meant to organize your reading now; it is repeated in the Summary to structure your review.

## STUDY OUTLINE

### ■ Work and the Psychological Contract

What Is a Psychological Contract? The Inducements–Contributions Balance

### ■ The Nature of Managerial Work

Managerial Roles and Activities Managerial Networks
Managerial Skills and Competencies

### ■ Perception and Managerial Behavior

What is Perception? Factors Influencing Perceptions
Common Perceptual Distortions

### ■ Perception, Attribution and Performance

Attribution Error and the Self-Serving Bias
Managing the Perception and Attribution Processes

CHAPTER 2

# MANAGERIAL BEHAVIOR AND PERFORMANCE



## PHOTO ESSAYS

# VISIONS 2

**Herman Miller Corporation, a Michigan-based office furniture manufacturer, is often cited for its innovative management, high productivity, and humane work environment. The person behind the firm is chairperson and retired CEO Max DePree whose vision includes a relationship with employees based more on mutual respect and shared commitments to values, goals, and ideas, than on legal and contractual considerations.**

**At Herman Miller, there are no managers or supervisors—just work-team leaders. There is a "vice president for people." Management training focuses on the company's two goals: (1) to make money, and (2) to be a great place to work. The company culture encourages diversity in the pursuit of innovation; it encourages participation and communication; and it encourages employee ownership. What's the bottom line of all this? As one employee puts it, "People just sincerely and genuinely enjoy working for a company with this kind of philosophy."**

Work

***Work*** is an activity that produces value for other people. It is something people do in exchange for things, like money and retirement security, that they cannot directly provide for themselves. But work is also a transaction that can and should result in mutually beneficial relationships between individuals and organizations. These relationships are evident at Herman Miller, Inc., and they are important foundations for the company's success as exemplified by Max DePree's management visions.

Managerial work

All managers, from the CEO level of Max DePree to the head of a production-floor work team, must be concerned about the people who work for and with them. After all, ***managerial work***—as introduced in Chapter 1—involves influencing the activities of other people so that organizational performance objectives are well served *and* so that the people themselves experience personal satisfaction from their work. But as you also learned in Chapter 1, the manager's world of the 1990s is complicated by times of unprecedented societal change. Global competition, new technologies, shifting demographics, and changing values are just a few of the significant trends. Today's managers face an unrelenting push for high performance in ever-more demanding conditions and with an increasingly diverse work force. The pressures are only likely to increase even further tomorrow.

This chapter continues your introduction to OB with a more specific focus on managerial behavior and human performance in the workplace.

Before you begin, consider these quotations as reminders of the very challenging nature of managerial work.[1]

> My day always ends when I'm tired, not when I am done. A manager's work is never done: There is always more to be done, more than should be done, always more that can be done.—Andrew Grove, president of Intel Corporation and author of *High Output Management.*

> No matter what kind of managerial job, managers always carry the nagging suspicion that they might be able to contribute just a little bit more. Hence they assume an unrelenting pace in their work.—Henry Mintzberg, management scholar and author of *The Nature of Managerial Work.*

# WORK AND THE PSYCHOLOGICAL CONTRACT

You are probably familiar with the work "contract" as it pertains to relations between labor unions and organizations employing their members. Such a contract is written and formal. Contract negotiations may cover such items as pay, work hours, vacations, and seniority rights, among others. There is another, less formal, contract that underlies what we have been referring to as the "relationship" between every employee and his or her work organization. We call this contract the *psychological contract.*

## What Is a Psychological Contract?

**Psychological contract**

A ***psychological contract*** is the set of expectations held by the individual and specifying what the individual and the organization expect to give to and receive from one another in the course of their working relationship. This contract represents the expected exchange of values that causes the individual to work for the organization and causes the organization to employ that person. During the time when the individual is being recruited by the organization, this exchange is an anticipated one. Later, during actual employment, expectations are either confirmed or not. Needless to say, part of the manager's job is to ensure that both the individual and the organization continue to receive a fair exchange of values under the psychological contract.

## The Inducements–Contributions Balance

**Contributions**

Figure 2.1 depicts an exchange of values between the individual and the organization as expressed in this concept of the psychological contract. To begin, the individual offers ***contributions*** or work inputs of value to the organization. These contributions—things like effort, skills, loyalty, creativity, and others—make each person a true human resource to the organization. In fact, one important measure of any organization's success is its ability to attract and maintain a high-quality work force.

*FIGURE 2.1 Inducements–contributions balance and the psychological contract.*

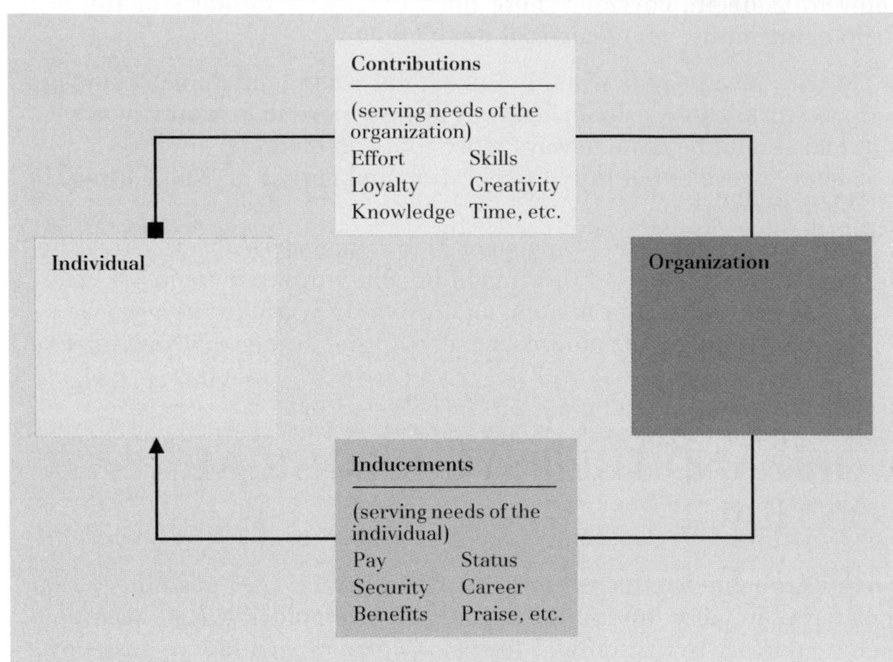


**Inducements**

Those things that the organization gives to individuals in return for their contributions are called ***inducements.*** The term means exactly what it implies. To induce participation, the organization offers the individual things of value—including pay, benefits, status, and job security, among others. As with the organization, these inducements are of value to the individual as ways of satisfying one or more important needs.

**Inducements–contributions balance**

When the exchange of values in the psychological contract is felt to be fair, a state of ***inducements–contributions balance*** exists. In this ideal condition, the individual can be expected to feel good about his or her work and have a positive relationship with the organization. When the exchange of values is perceived to be *un*fair, however, people may develop bad attitudes, lose their desire to work hard, and/or even quit to take "better" jobs elsewhere.

It is important for managers to help create and maintain healthy and balanced psychological contracts among people at work. The introductory example of Herman Miller, Inc., suggests the positive things that can happen when this is accomplished. However, some of the pressures in the present-day economic and business environment can make the management of psychological contracts difficult. Think about the sense of betrayed loyalty experienced by people who lose their jobs, or see others lose theirs, when an organization is "downsized" or "restructured" in order to increase productivity. For example, *Sibson & Company's* Craig Schneier, managing principal of this consulting firm, says: "There's no question that a psychological contract develops." But in times when layoffs even in the managerial ranks are common, he is concerned about employees who are counting on being retained until retirement in return for the loyalty they show to their employers. Schneier comments: "The first major cut in people is a very visible breach of that contract."

# THE NATURE OF MANAGERIAL WORK

Henry Mintzberg's classic book, *The Nature of Managerial Work,* reports an in-depth examination of the daily activities of corporate chief executives. One insightful excerpt from his observations regarding an executive's workday follows.[2]

> There was no break in the pace of activity during office hours. The mail (average of 36 pieces per day), telephone calls (average of 10–15 per day), and meetings (average of eight) accounted for almost every minute from the moment these executives entered their offices in the morning until they departed in the evenings. A true break seldom occurred. Coffee was taken during meetings, and lunchtime was almost always devoted to formal or informal meetings. When free time appeared, ever-present subordinates quickly usurped it. If these managers wished to have a change of pace, they had two means at their disposal—the observational tour and the light discussions that generally preceded scheduled meetings. But these were not regularly scheduled breaks, and they were seldom totally unrelated to the issue at hand: managing the organization . . .
>
> Why do managers adopt this pace and workload? One major reason is the inherently open-ended nature of the job. The manager is responsible for the success of the organization. There are really no tangible mileposts where one can stop and say, "Now my job is finished." The engineer finishes the design of a casting on a certain day; the lawyer wins or loses a case at some moment in time. The manager must always keep going, never sure when he or she has succeeded, never sure when the whole organization may come down because of some miscalculation. As a result, the manager is a person with a perpetual preoccupation. The manager can never be free to forget the job, and never has the pleasure of knowing, even temporarily, that there is nothing else to do.

Clearly, a manager's job in any organization will be busy and demanding. The results of continuing research on managerial work can be summarized as follows.[3]

- *Managers work long hours.* A workweek of at least 50 hours is typical, and up to 90 hours is not unheard of. The length of the workweek tends to increase as one advances to higher managerial levels. Heads of organizations often work the longest hours.
- *Managers are busy.* Their work is intense and involves doing many different things each workday. The busy day of a manager includes up to 200 separate incidents or episodes in an eight-hour period at supervisory levels and at least 20 to 30 for chief executives.
- *Managers are often interrupted.* Their work is fragmented and variable. Interruptions are frequent and many tasks are completed quickly.

- *Managers work mostly with other people.* They spend little time working alone. Time spent with others includes working with bosses, peers, subordinates, subordinates of their subordinates, as well as outsiders such as customers, suppliers, and the like.
- *Managers are communicators.* Much of their work is face-to-face verbal communications during formal and informal meetings. They spend a lot of time getting, giving, and processing information. Higher-level managers spend more time in scheduled meetings than do lower-level managers.

## Managerial Roles and Activities

From his research, Mintzberg identifies three major categories of roles that managers must be prepared to enact—*interpersonal roles, informational roles,* and *decisional roles.* Each of these roles derives from the manager's position of formal authority in the organization and involves a number of distinct action responsibilities. Table 2.1 identifies ten major roles falling into the three categories.

The importance of a better understanding of the specific task activ-

*TABLE 2.1*
MINTZBERG'S TEN ACTION ROLES OF MANAGERS

| *Interpersonal Roles* | |
|---|---|
| Figurehead | To attend ceremonies and represent the organization/ work unit to external constituencies. |
| Leader | To motivate subordinates and integrate their needs with those of the organization/work unit. |
| Liaison | To develop and maintain contacts with outsiders to gain benefits for the organization/work unit. |
| *Informational Roles* | |
| Monitor | To seek and receive information of relevance to the organization/work unit. |
| Disseminator | To transmit to insiders information relevant to the organization/work unit. |
| Spokesperson | To transmit to outsiders information relevant to the organization/work unit. |
| *Decisional Roles* | |
| Entrepreneur | To seek problems and opportunities and to take action in respect to them. |
| Disturbance handler | To resolve conflicts among persons within the organization/work unit or with outsiders. |
| Resource allocator | To make choices allocating resources to various uses within the organization/work unit. |
| Negotiator | To conduct formal negotiations with third parties such as union officials or government regulators. |

*Source:* Abridged and adapted from p. 46 in *The Nature of Managerial Work* by Henry Mintzberg (New York: Harper & Row, 1973). Copyright © 1973 by Henry Mintzberg. Reprinted by permission of Harper & Row Publishers, Inc.

ities performed by managers was underscored in Professor Fred Luthans' presidential speech to the Academy of Management on the occasion of its 50th anniversary. He began with this question—"What do we really know about managers and managing?" In response, he reported a study of over 300 managers working at all levels in a variety of organizations. The study identified four major sets of activities that were emphasized by *effective* managers.[4]

1. *Routine communication*—processing paperwork and exchanging information with others.
2. *Human resource management*—motivating, reinforcing, disciplining, punishing, staffing, and developing.
3. *Traditional management*—planning, decision making, and controlling.
4. *Networking*—interacting with outsiders, as well as socializing, and politicking.

Figure 2.2 summarizes research showing that somewhat different tasks are emphasized by managers working at different levels of organizational responsibility.[5] First-level managers (such as department heads or supervisors) tend to emphasize one-on-one activities with subordinates. They are very concerned about managing individual performance and instructing subordinates. The concerns of middle-level managers (persons to whom other managers report) deal more with group and inter-group issues. Here, attention shifts toward planning and allocating resources, coordinating interdependent groups, and managing group performance. Among top-level managers (executives), we see "an eye to the outside." These senior managers are concerned with monitoring the organization's environment to keep informed on important trends and developments.

**Top-Level Managers**

Monitoring the environment
Representing one's staff

**Middle-Managers**

Planning and allocating resources
Coordinating interdependent groups
Managing group performance
Representing one's staff

**First-Level Managers**

Managing individual performance
Instructing and coaching subordinates
Representing one's staff

*FIGURE 2.2 Task priorities of managers at different levels of responsibility.* (*Source:* Based on Allen I. Kraut, Patricia R. Pedigo, D. Douglas McKenna, and Marvin D. Dunnette, "The Role of the Manager: What's Really Important in Different Management Jobs," *Academy of Management Executive,* Vol. III (No. 4), 1989, pp. 286–293.)

Looking again at the figure, you will see that all levels of management in this study reported equal concern for representing one's staff—something the researchers identify as an "ambassadorial" task. This is comparable to Mintzberg's spokesperson role and what Luthans calls "networking." As it turns out, this latter concept is increasingly singled out for its importance to managerial work. All managers must establish and maintain good working relationships with a multitude of other people in order to get their work done. The ability to do so is indispensable to managerial success.

## Managerial Networks

Managers enact roles and fulfill their action responsibilities through relationships with other persons inside and outside of the organization. The nature of these *interpersonal networks* is illustrated by this description in John Kotter's book *The General Managers.*[6]

> B.J. Sparksman had a good working relationship with his four bosses and a close mentor–protege relationship with one of them. He had cordial-to-good relations with his peers, some of whom were

*FIGURE 2.3 Vertical and lateral relationships in a manager's interpersonal networks.*

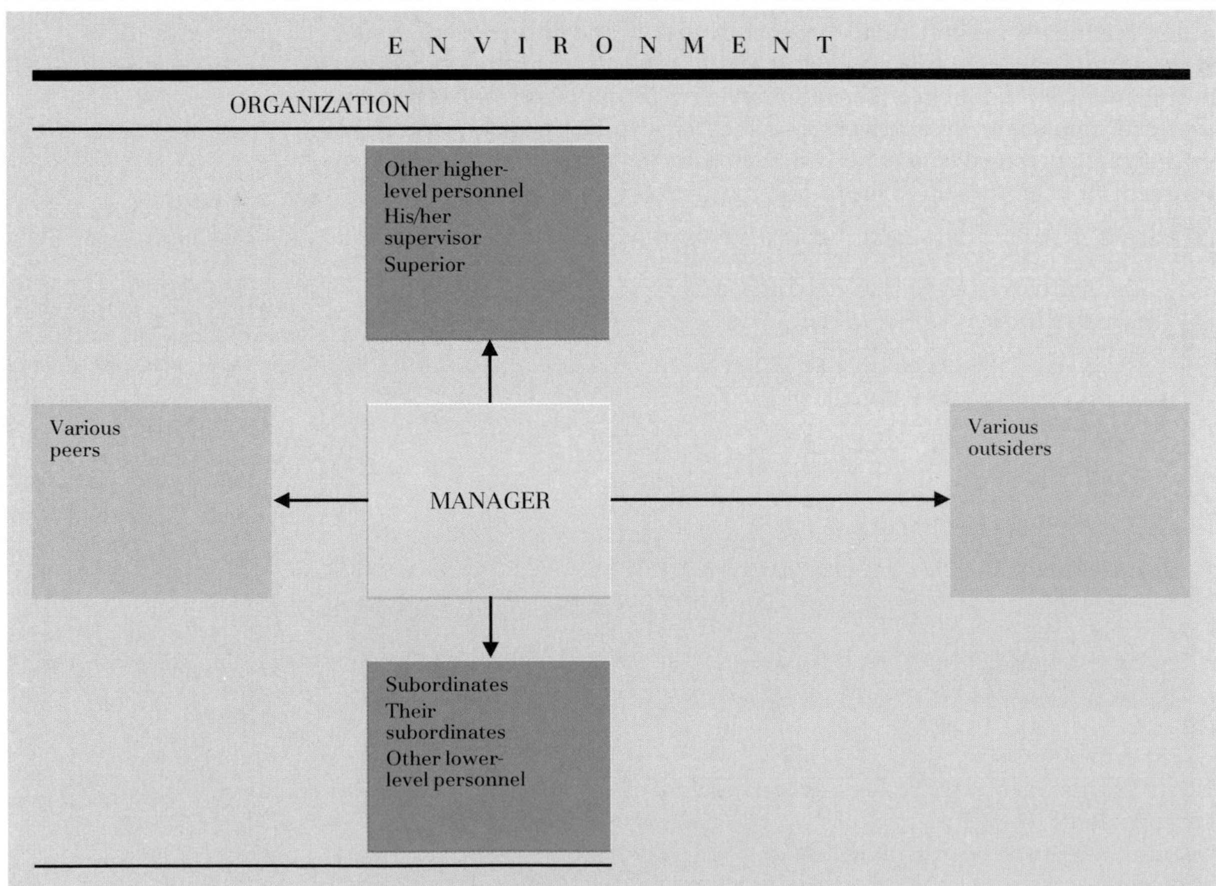

> friends and all of whom were aware of his track record . . . He also had a good working relationship with many of the subordinates of his peers (hundreds of people) based mostly on his reputation. B.J. had a close and strong working relationship with all but one of his main direct reports because they respected him, because he was the boss, and the fact that he tried to treat them fairly and with respect. Outside the firm, B.J. maintained fairly strong relationships with dozens of top people in firms that were important clients for his organization . . . He also had relationships with dozens of other important people in the local community.

What this example shows is a manager who uses a complex set of interpersonal *networks,* many falling outside the formal chain of command, to help get the job done. Inside the organization Sparksman's networks included both vertical relationships with a variety of superiors and subordinates, and lateral relationships with peers. They also included relationships with many outsiders such as customers and suppliers. Figure 2.3 portrays in full detail the potential complexity of the interpersonal networks maintained by managers.

The ability to develop, maintain, and work well within networks is increasingly recognized as an important aspect of managerial work. Effective general managers, for example, have been observed to "allocate significant time and effort when they first take their jobs to developing a network of cooperative relationships among those people they feel are needed to satisfy their emerging agendas." Later on—"their attention shifts toward using the networks to both implement and help in updating the agendas."[7]

## Managerial Skills and Competencies

When executives of today talk about what it will take to become a corporate leader in the year 2000, they see increased emphasis on:[8]

- Visionary and strategic thinking.
- Effective communications.
- Human resource management.
- Ethical behavior.
- International outlook.

Interestingly enough, American executives and their counterparts around the globe differ a bit regarding the last two items on the list. The Americans place *more* emphasis on ethical behavior on the part of tomorrow's executive; but, although they considered international outlook to be increasingly important, it was considered even more important by executives from other countries.

This brief look toward the future relates to an important question: What "skills" are required to achieve managerial success in a dynamic environment? A ***skill*** is an ability to translate knowledge into action that results in desired performance. It is a *competency* that allows someone to achieve superior performance in one or more aspects of their work.

**Skill**

Table 2.2 lists selected skills and personal characteristics identified by the AACSB (American Assembly of Collegiate Schools of Business) as important foundations of managerial success. This table can be used as a quick "checklist" to assess your skills and identify possible areas for further personal development. In addition, the *Skills Perspectives* found in each chapter of this book can serve a similar purpose.

**Technical skill**

Robert Katz offers a useful way to view the skills development challenge.[9] He divides the *essential managerial skills* into three categories—technical, human, and conceptual. A ***technical skill*** is an ability to apply specialized knowledge or expertise to perform a job. This involves being highly proficient at using select methods, processes, and procedures to accomplish tasks. Good examples are the work of accountants, engineers, and attorneys whose technical skills are acquired through formal education. Most jobs have some technical skill components. Some require

*TABLE 2.2*
**SELECTED SKILLS AND PERSONAL CHARACTERISTICS CONSIDERED IMPORTANT FOR MANAGERS**

*Analytic thinking.* The ability to identify fundamental ideas, concepts, themes or issues that help integrate, interpret, and/or explain patterns in a set of information or data.

*Behavioral flexibility.* The ability to modify personal behavior to reach a goal; to adapt personal behavior to respond to changes in a situation or in the environment.

*Decision making.* The ability to use logic and information to choose among alternative courses of action; to form judgments and make commitments in complex situations.

*Leadership.* The ability to stimulate and guide individuals or groups toward goal and/or task accomplishment.

*Oral communication and presentation.* The ability to effectively express ideas to others in individual or group situations.

*Personal impact.* The ability to create a good early impression; to command attention and respect; to show confidence through verbal and nonverbal presentations.

*Planning and organizing.* The ability to establish a course of action to accomplish specific goals; to properly assign personnel and allocate supporting resources.

*Resistance to stress.* The ability to maintain work performance even while experiencing significant personal stress.

*Self-objectivity.* The ability to realistically assess personal strengths and weaknesses; to gain insight into personal motives, skills, and abilities as applied to a job.

*Tolerance for uncertainty.* The ability to maintain work performance under uncertain or unstructured conditions.

*Written communication.* The ability to clearly express ideas in writing and in appropriate grammatical form.

*Source:* Developed from the *Outcome Measurement Project of the Accreditation Research Committee, Phase II: An Interim Report* (St. Louis: American Assembly of Collegiate Schools of Business, 1984), pp. 15–18.

SKILLS PERSPECTIVE

## HALLMARK

Courtesy of Hallmark Cards, Incorporated.

**"Creativity" sets the tone at Hallmark Cards—America's famous cardmaker. From the level of Irvine Hockaday, president and CEO, to the people who design the cards and write the verses, brainstorming sessions are used to maintain creativity among the people behind the motto: "Hallmark: When you care enough to send the very best." Interpersonal and group skills are essential to the success of these work sessions, and the firm's employees know it. But then again, they also know that creativity counts . . . and that sometimes it takes a little help from someone else to achieve and maintain the creative edge.**

preparatory education, whereas others allow skills to be learned through appropriate work training and on-the-job experience.

***Human skill*** is the ability to work well in cooperation with other persons. It emerges as a spirit of trust, enthusiasm, and genuine involvement in interpersonal relationships. A person with good human skills will have a high degree of self-awareness and a capacity to understand or empathize with the feelings of others. This skill is clearly essential to the manager's "networking" responsibilities as just described.

**Human skill**

All good managers ultimately have the ability to view the organization or situation as a whole and solve problems to the benefit of everyone concerned. This ability to analyze and diagnose complex situations is a ***conceptual skill.*** It draws heavily on one's mental capacities to identify problems and opportunities, gather and interpret relevant information, and make good problem-solving decisions that serve the organization's purpose.

**Conceptual skill**

The relative importance of these essential skills varies across levels of management. Technical skills are more important at lower management levels where supervisors are dealing with concrete problems. Broader, more ambiguous, and longer-term decisions dominate the manager's concerns at higher levels, where conceptual skills gain in importance. Human skills are consistent in importance across all managerial levels.

# PERCEPTION AND MANAGERIAL BEHAVIOR

When it comes to using skills and competencies effectively, a good manager is able to understand situations and such things as task objectives and individual needs *as other people view them.* At a minimum, this understanding is an important foundation for creating inducements–contributions balances, and healthy psychological contracts. Unfortunately, gaps often exist between the way a work situation is "perceived" by managers and by the people they supervise.

## What Is Perception?

**Perception**

***Perception*** is the process through which people select, receive, organize, and interpret information from their environment. Through perception,

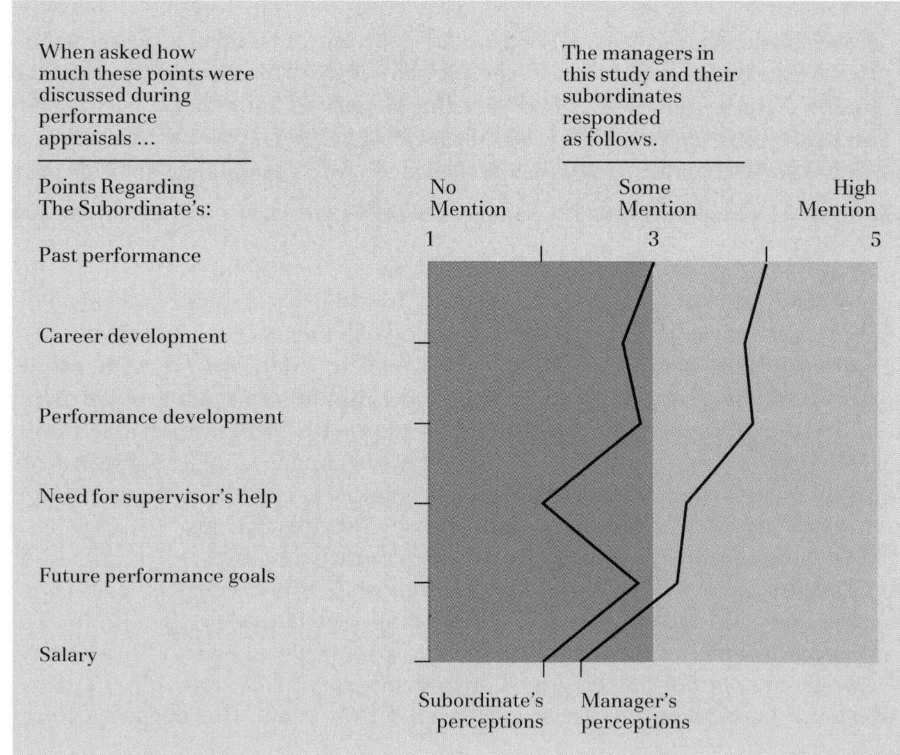


*FIGURE 2.4 Contrasting perceptions between managers and their subordinates: The case of the performance appraisal interview.*
(*Source:* Data reported in Edward E. Lawler III, Allan M. Mohrman, Jr., and Susan M. Resnick, "Performance Appraisal Revisited," *Organizational Dynamics,* Vol. 13 (Summer 1984), pp. 20–35.)

people process information inputs into decisions and actions. It is a way of forming impressions about yourself, other people, and daily life experiences. It is also a screen or filter through which information passes before having an effect on people. The quality or accuracy of a person's perceptions, therefore, has a major impact on the quality of any decisions made or actions taken in a given situation.

People respond to situations in terms of their perceptions. And the fact that the "perceived" meaning of the same work situation often varies from one person to the next is an important dynamic for all managers to understand. Consider Figure 2.4, which contrasts the viewpoints of managers and their subordinates over what transpires during performance appraisal interviews. Rather substantial differences exist in the two sets of perceptions—and the consequences can be significant. In this case, managers who perceive they already give adequate attention to past performance, career development, and supervisory help are unlikely to increase emphasis on them in future performance appraisal interviews. Their subordinates, by contrast, are likely to experience continued frustration, since they perceive these subjects as not being given sufficient attention.

## Factors Influencing Perceptions

A number of factors contribute to perceptual differences among people at work. As shown in Figure 2.5, these include:

1. *Characteristics of the Perceiver:* A person's needs, past experience, habits, personality, values, and attitudes may all influence the perception process. Someone with a strong need for ego satisfaction, for example, may select from a situation and emphasize signals that either tend to satisfy or deny the desire for self esteem. By the same token, negative attitudes toward unions may cause a manager to look for antagonisms even during routine visits by local union officials to the organization. These and other personal factors will impact what a person gives attention to in a situation and how these cues are interpreted as a basis for decision making and action responses.
2. *Characteristics of the Perceived:* The physical attributes, appearance, and behavior of other persons in the situation also influence how that situation is perceived. We tend to notice the physical attributes of a person in terms of age, sex, height, and weight, for example. A young person attempting to exert authority in a situation may be viewed quite differently from an older person doing exactly the same thing. Personal attire and appearance are also relevant factors. Characteristics of the perceived can and do influence how one person perceives another and the situation in which they are involved.
3. *Characteristics of the Situation:* The physical, social, and organizational settings of the situation or event in question can also influence perceptions. Hearing a subordinate call his or her boss by a first name may be perceived quite differently when observed in an office hallway as opposed to an evening social reception. By the same token, a conversation with the "boss" may be perceived differently when

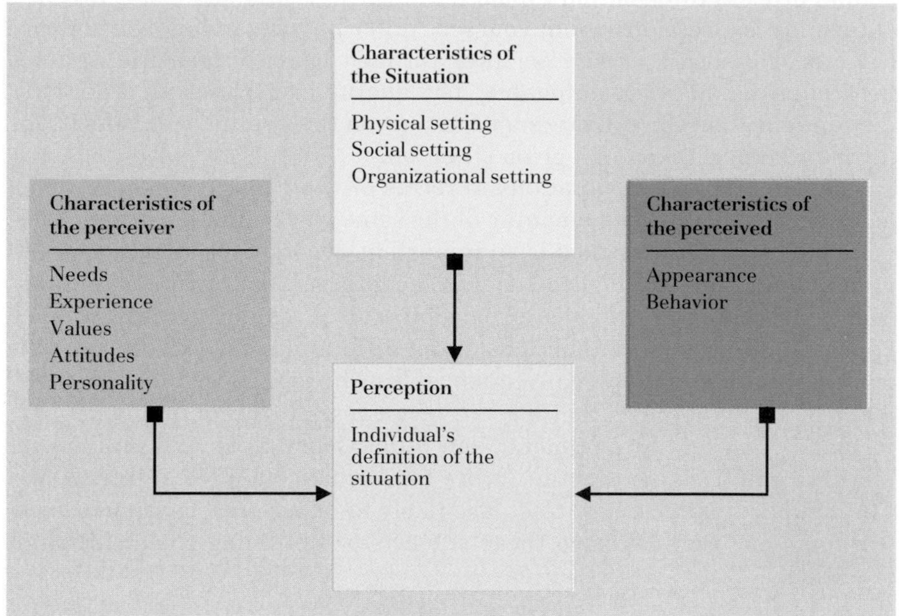


*FIGURE 2.5 Multiple influences on the perception process: Why different people may perceive the same situation differently.*

taking place in a casual reception area than when held in the boss's office with the door closed. Such background characteristics of the situation context are additional factors that can affect how a situation is perceived by the different persons involved.

## Common Perceptual Distortions

Perception influences a manager's view of people and events, and it influences the manager's responses to them. Other people, in turn, draw their impressions of the manager from *their* perceptions of how the manager behaves in these same daily situations. It is thereby essential for managers to understand the common perceptual distortions and recognize their potential impact on workplace affairs. These are stereotypes, halo effects, selective perception, projection, and expectancy.

### *Stereotypes*

**Stereotype**

A ***stereotype*** occurs when an individual is assigned to a group or category (for example, youth), and then the attributes commonly associated with the group or category are assigned to the person in question (e.g., "young people dislike authority"). Stereotypes obscure individual differences. They can prevent managers from getting to know people as individuals and from accurately assessing their needs, preferences, and abilities.

A person's race and ethnicity are often the source of negative stereotypes, as are one's gender and age. All such stereotypes are unfortunate at a time when fair treatment in the workplace and equal employment opportunities are cherished human rights. Many progressive employers are making strides in eliminating these biases. For example,

***Xerox Corporation*** This company is noted for putting minorities into fast-track management jobs. The firm supports minority caucuses and national networks offering advice and support to female, black, and other minority employees. A company spokesperson says, "We believe we will have an edge on people who are trying to catch up to the work force of the '90s."

Yet even though progress is in evidence, a ***glass ceiling effect*** still exists as a hidden barrier limiting the advancement of minorities in some occupations and employment settings.[10] Inappropriate stereotypes based on race, gender, and age all contribute to the "ceiling," which operates in subtle ways. How, for example, do you explain the fact that women managers under the age of 35 earn only about three-quarters of what their male counterparts earn in similar jobs? Why is the proportion of American women in senior management positions very small? Why is the representation of blacks in managerial and executive ranks minuscule in proportion to their share of the U.S. population? And why are older workers sometimes denied opportunities by managers who assume they are hesitant to change and unable or unwilling to learn new tasks? Progressive managers and employers are shedding such stereotypes and recognizing that an increasingly diverse work force can be a truly competitive advantage.

**Glass ceiling effect**

## *Halo Effects*

A ***halo effect*** occurs when one attribute of a person or situation is used to develop an overall impression of the individual or situation. Halo effects are common in our everyday lives. When meeting a new person, for example, one trait such as a pleasant smile can lead to a positive first impression of an overall "warm" and "honest" person. The result of a halo effect, however, is the same as with a stereotype; individual differences are obscured.

**Halo effect**

Halo effects are very significant in the performance appraisal process since they can influence a manager's evaluations of subordinates' work performance. People with good attendance records, for example, tend to be viewed as intelligent and responsible; those with poor attendance records are considered poor performers. Such conclusions may or may not be true. It is the manager's job to get true impressions rather than allow halo effects to result in biased and erroneous evaluations.

## *Selective Perception*

***Selective perception*** is the tendency to single out those aspects of a situation or person that are consistent with one's beliefs, values, and needs. This perceptual distortion is identified in a classic research study involving executives in a manufacturing company.[11] When asked to identify the key problem in a comprehensive business policy case, each one selected problems consistent with their functional area work assignments. Most marketing executives viewed the key problem area as sales; production people tended to see it as a problem of production and organization. These differing viewpoints would certainly affect how the executives would

**Selective perception**

approach the problem; they may also have created difficulties once these persons tried to work together to improve things.

Managers should test whether or not situations and individuals are being selectively perceived. The easiest way to do this is to gather additional opinions from other people. When these opinions are contradictory, an effort should be made to check the original impression. This tendency toward selectivity in perception is one that a manager must be able to control in terms of his or her own behavior as well as recognize in the behavior of others.

## *Projection*

**Projection**

***Projection*** is the assignment of personal attributes to other individuals. A classic projection error is the manager who assumes that the needs of subordinates are the same as his or her own. Suppose, for example, that you enjoy responsibility and achievement in your work. Suppose, too, that you are the newly appointed manager of a group whose jobs seem dull and routine. You might move quickly to expand these jobs to help the workers achieve increased satisfaction from more challenging tasks. Why? Because you want them to experience things that you personally value in work.

This may not be a good decision. By projecting your needs on subordinates, individual differences are lost. Rather than designing the subordinates' jobs to fit their needs best, you have designed their jobs to fit yours. The problem is that they may be quite satisfied and productive doing jobs that, to you, seem dull and routine. Projection can be controlled through a high degree of self-awareness and by *empathy,* the ability to view a situation as others see it.

## *Expectancy*

**Expectancy**

Another perceptual distortion is ***expectancy***. This is the tendency to create or find in another situation or individual that which you expected to find in the first place. Expectancy is sometimes referred to as the "pygmalion effect."[12] Pygmalion was a mythical Greek sculptor who created a statue of his ideal mate and then made her come to life. His expectations came true! Through expectancy, you may also create in the work situation that which you expect to find.

Expectancy can have both positive and negative results for the manager. Suppose a manager assumes that his or her subordinates basically prefer to satisfy most of their needs outside the work setting and want only minimal involvement with their jobs. This manager is likely to provide simple, highly structured jobs designed to require little involvement. Can you predict the response of the subordinates to this situation? Their most likely response is to show the lack of commitment that the manager assumed in the first place. Thus, the manager's initial expectations are confirmed as a *self-fulfilling prophecy*.

Research on the positive side of expectancy may further stimulate your thinking. Psychologists, for example, have found that rats introduced

Courtesy of Scandinavian Airline System.

## INTERNATIONAL PERSPECTIVE

### SAS

Good management isn't just found at home. In today's global community we are learning more and more from what successful managers in other countries do. One model of progressive management is Jan Carlzon, president and CEO of Swedish Scandinavian Airline System. With an emphasis on innovation and commitment to customers, Carlzon has helped forge a dynamic and growing firm known for excellence in the travel industry. In a global marketplace, SAS has formed an alliance with traditional rivals Finnair and Swissair to provide better service throughout Europe and the world. Its hubs have expanded from within Europe to other destinations such as Newark, Toronto, Bangkok, and Tokyo. To attract more customers, SAS has expanded its services, offering more flights, punctual arrivals and departures, booking services, and hotel and travel connections. When it comes to understanding the needs of customers, Carlzon says the key words are: Trust, Simplicity, and Care. Putting these words into action is the cornerstone of SAS's strategy for the 1990s.

to their handlers as "maze bright" run mazes more quickly than do rats introduced to their handlers as being "dumb"; students identified to their teachers as "intellectual bloomers" do better on achievement tests than do counterparts who lack such a positive introduction; job trainees pointed out to their supervisors as having "special potential" have higher job performance than do trainees not so identified.

The expectancy effects in these cases argue strongly for managers to adopt positive and optimistic approaches to people at work. Positive self-fulfilling prophecies may occur as managers:

- Create a warmer interpersonal climate between themselves and subordinates.
- Give more performance feedback to subordinates.
- Spend more time helping subordinates to learn job skills.
- Give subordinates more opportunities to ask questions.

# PERCEPTION, ATTRIBUTION, AND PERFORMANCE

**Attribution**
**Attribution theory**

An ***attribution*** is an attempted explanation of why something happened the way it did. ***Attribution theory*** is the study of how people attempt to (1) understand the causes of a certain event, (2) assess responsibility for outcomes of the event, and (3) evaluate the personal qualities of people involved in the event.

## Attribution Error and the Self-Serving Bias

**Attribution error**

**Self-serving bias**

Look at the data in Table 2.3. Obtained from a group of health care managers, they are consistent with predictions of attribution theory.[13] When supervisors were asked to identify or *attribute* causes of poor performance by subordinates, they more often chose internal deficiencies of the individual—ability and effort—than external deficiencies in the situation—support. This shows a possible ***attribution error,*** or the tendency to *under*estimate the influence of situational factors and *over*estimate the influence of personal factors in evaluating someone else's behavior. When asked to identify causes of their own poor performance, however, the supervisors overwhelmingly chose lack of support—an external or situational deficiency. This shows a ***self-serving bias,*** an attributional tendency to deny personal responsibility for performance problems but accept it for performance success.

The managerial implications of attribution theory and data such as these trace back to the fact that perceptions influence behavior. A manager who feels subordinates are *not* performing well and perceives the reason to be lack of effort is likely to respond with attempts to "motivate" them to work harder. The possibility of changing situational factors to remove job constraints and provide better organizational support may be largely ignored. This oversight could sacrifice major performance gains. It is also an interesting oversight since, when it comes to evaluating their own behavior, the supervisors in this study indicated that *their* performance would benefit from having better support. This implies that *their* abilities or willingness to work hard were not at all felt to be at issue. "Why," you can and should ask, "if the supervisors only needed more

*TABLE 2.3*
HEALTH CARE MANAGERS' ATTRIBUTIONS OF CAUSES FOR POOR PERFORMANCE

| Cause of Poor Performance by Their Subordinates | Most Frequent Attribution | Cause of Poor Performance by Themselves |
|---|---|---|
| 7 | Lack of *ability* | 1 |
| 12 | Lack of *effort* | 1 |
| 5 | Lack of *support* | 23 |

*Source:* Data reported in John R. Schermerhorn, Jr., "Team Development for High Performance Management," *Training & Development Journal,* Vol. 40 (November 1986), pp. 38–41.

support to improve their work performance, couldn't the same be said for their subordinates?"

### Managing the Perception and Attribution Processes

Successful managers recognize that perceptual differences are likely to exist among people in any given situation, and they are aware of the common perceptual distortions. They understand the attribution process and individual tendencies toward a self-serving bias when explaining performance situations. They are also informed about ***impression management,***[14] the systematic attempt to behave in ways that create and maintain desired impressions of oneself in the eyes of others. Impressions, especially first impressions, can count in how other people evaluate and respond to us. They can be managed through such things as choice of manners, dress, appearance, and use of verbal and nonverbal communications. As a result, good managers try to make decisions and take action with a true understanding of the work situation as it is viewed by all persons concerned. A manager who is skilled in the perception process will:

**Impression management**

1. Have a high level of self-awareness.
2. Seek information from various sources to confirm or disconfirm personal impressions of a decision situation.
3. Be empathetic—that is, be able to see a situation as it is perceived by other people.
4. Avoid common perceptual distortions that bias our views of people and situations.
5. Avoid inappropriate attributions.
6. Influence the perceptions of other people.

## JOB SATISFACTION

Formally defined, ***job satisfaction*** is the degree to which individuals feel positively or negatively about their jobs. It is an emotional response to one's tasks, as well as the physical and social conditions of the workplace. In concept, job satisfaction also indicates the degree to which the expectations in someone's psychological contract are fulfilled. Job satisfaction is likely to be higher for persons who perceive an inducements–contributions balance in their relationship with the employing organization.

**Job satisfaction**

Two closely related concepts are "job commitment" and "job involvement." ***Organizational commitment*** refers to the degree to which a person strongly identifies with and feels a part of the organization. ***Job involvement*** refers to the willingness of a person to work hard and apply effort beyond normal job expectations. An individual who has high organizational commitment is considered very loyal; an individual who is highly involved in a job is considered a good corporate or organizational citizen.

**Organizational commitment**

**Job involvement**

## Measuring Job Satisfaction

Job satisfaction is identified in Chapter 4 as among the important *attitudes* that can and do influence human behavior in the workplace. Thus, OB researchers are interested in accurately measuring job satisfaction and understanding its consequences for people at work. On a daily basis, managers must be able to infer the job satisfaction of others by careful observation and interpretation of what they say and do while going about their jobs. At times it is also useful to examine more formally the levels of job satisfaction among groups of workers. This is usually done through formal interviews or questionnaire surveys.

Among the many available job satisfaction questionnaires, two popular ones are the Minnesota Satisfaction Questionnaire (MSQ) and the Job Descriptive Index (JDI).[15] Both address things that good managers should be concerned about for the people reporting to them. For example, the MSQ measures satisfaction with working conditions, chances for advancement, freedom to use one's own judgment, praise for doing a good job, and feelings of accomplishment, among others. The JDI also measures five facets of job satisfaction that nicely summarize the kinds of things that can influence whether or not people develop positive feelings about their work. These are:

1. *The work itself*—responsibility, interest, and growth.
2. *Quality of supervision*—technical help and social support.
3. *Relationships with co-workers*—social harmony and respect.
4. *Promotion opportunities*—chances for further advancement.
5. *Pay*—adequacy of pay and perceived equity vis-à-vis others.

## Job Satisfaction Trends and Issues

Job satisfaction in the labor force is a topic of continuing social interest. Over the years, a number of studies and opinion polls have addressed the issue in the United States.[16] Even though there is always concern that most workers are unhappy with their jobs, the empirical evidence generally indicates that most American workers are moderately satisfied with their jobs. At worst, job satisfaction has declined slightly on the average since the early 1960s. Furthermore, a person's level of job satisfaction seems relatively consistent, even when jobs and occupations are changed. Someone who is unhappy in one work setting is likely to feel the same in another, and vice-versa.[17] Within the labor force, however, general patterns of satisfaction seem to vary among different groups of workers. For example,[18]

- *White-collar workers appear more satisfied than blue-collar workers*—with blue-collar workers sensing lack of opportunity, respect, and financial rewards.
- *Men appear more satisfied than women*—with women remaining troubled by sexual harassment, salary inequities, and the "glass ceiling" of limited advancement.

ETHICAL PERSPECTIVE

## CELESTIAL SEASONINGS

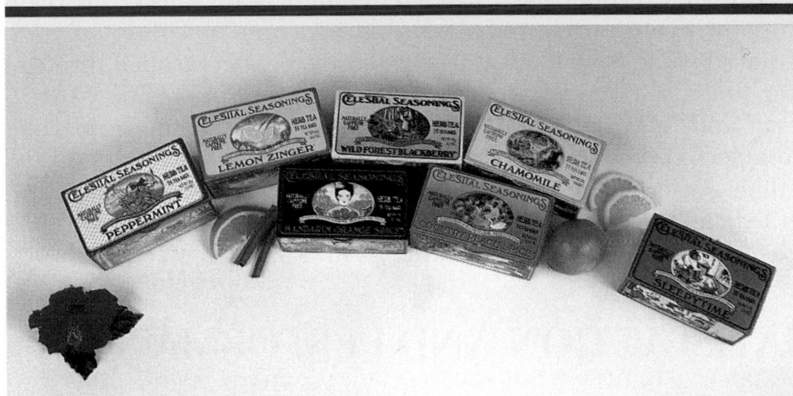


Courtesy of Celestial Seasonings, Inc.

**Celestial Seasonings, Inc. is a successful marketer of herbal teas as flavorful, healthy beverages. It all began in 1969 when 19-year-old Mo Siegel made tea from herbs gathered in the Colorado forests. What began as a cottage industry is today a 200+ employee company rated by the U.S. Council of Economic Priorities as one of America's most socially responsible firms. You will find among Celestial's corporate "beliefs" this significant statement: "We believe in the dignity of the individual, and we are totally committed to the fair, honest, kind, and professional treatment of all individuals and organizations with whom we work."**

- *Older workers appear more satisfied than younger workers*—with younger workers with high expectations concerned about lack of authority, and jobs which lack the status and challenge they desire.

These and related job satisfaction issues continue to attract research interest and public scrutiny. Of special recent concern are reports that managers, professionals, and hourly workers all show decreased satisfaction with the respect and consideration given to them by their employers.[19] At issue here is "loyalty"—both loyalty of the employer to the employee and loyalty of the employee to the employer. For example,

- We live at a time when firms in many industries are pursuing acquisitions, mergers, and staff cutbacks in the quest for increased productivity—employee security and loyalty may be suffering as a result.
- As the workforce grows more "professional" in nature, these employees may identify more with their professions and external reference groups than with their employers—thus reducing loyalty.
- Values may be shifting toward greater emphasis on the importance of family, leisure, and other aspects of one's nonwork life—loyalty to the employer may be losing ground in competition with loyalty to personal affairs.

Finally, job satisfaction trends and developments must be viewed in respect to how the nature of work itself is changing in many settings. *Technology* is a most important factor here and managers must be alert to the impact of new technology—such as computers—on workers.[20] Take the machinist who once prepared all the settings on a machine tool and did the required work. Now the settings are likely to be controlled through a computer that also operates the machine. This machinist is now more of a "helper" and "observer," and less of a "doer." Or, think of the airline reservation clerks whose work is done via a computer that also closely monitors their performance. After suffering a nervous breakdown brought on in part by job pressures, one clerk said: "Management is acting as if I am supposed to have a digital clock in my head. I'm not a machine."

# JOB SATISFACTION AND PERFORMANCE

It is helpful to view job satisfaction in the context of two decisions people make about their work. First is the decision to belong, that is to initially join and then stay a member of an organization. Second is the decision to perform, that is to work hard in pursuit of high levels of task performance while there.

## Job Satisfaction and the Decision to Belong

**Absenteeism**

Job satisfaction influences ***absenteeism,*** or the failure of people to attend work. Satisfied workers are more regular in attendance and less likely to be absent for unexplained reasons than dissatisfied ones. Job satisfaction can also affect ***turnover,*** or decisions by workers to terminate their employment. Satisfied workers are less likely to quit; dissatisfied ones are more likely to leave when they can.

**Turnover**

Both absenteeism and turnover are of major concern to managers. When people fail to show up for work or quit, valuable human resources are wasted. The costs of turnover are especially high. They include the expenses of recruiting, selecting, and training replacements, as well as productivity losses caused by any operational disruptions and low morale that may occur.

Still, a manager must be careful when dealing with these issues. Neither absenteeism nor turnover should be viewed as entirely negative phenomena. For people who are "burned out" or highly stressed in their work, a day or more of *functional absenteeism* might be beneficial—for both the individuals and the organization. Likewise, *functional turnover* can be an opportunity to bring replacements with creative ideas and new energy into the work unit. It may also reduce conflict by removing a dissatisfied employee from the work setting and/or increase morale by providing position vacancies into which others may advance.[21]

One way to successfully manage absenteeism and turnover is to create a work environment that fulfills the expectations of everyone's psychological contract. Indeed, absenteeism and turnover sometimes develop because unrealistic expectations are created during the recruiting process. In contrast to traditional recruiting, which tries only to "sell" job candidates on the organization, realistic recruitment is the preferred approach. This method utilizes ***realistic job previews*** which give prospective employees as much pertinent information—both good and bad—about the job as

**Realistic job previews**

possible, and without distortion.[22] They communicate organizational realities and help keep the job candidate's expectations as reasonable as possible. In today's day and age, this recruiting approach not only makes sense from a staffing perspective—it is also the only *ethical* thing to do.

## Job Satisfaction and the Decision to Perform

Somewhere near a Ford Motor Company plant in Dearborn, Michigan, a tavern once displayed this sign.

> I SPEND FORTY HOURS A WEEK HERE—AM I SUPPOSED TO WORK TOO?

The sign communicates a simple but potent message. It is one thing for people to come to work everyday; it is quite another thing for them to work hard and achieve *high performance* while they are there.

**Performance**

***Performance*** is formally defined as the quantity and quality of task accomplishments—individual, group, or organizational. Your study of OB will emphasize the foundations of high-performance outcomes at all three levels, and *Supplementary Module C* at the end of the book offers special insights on the performance appraisal process. For now, our focus is on the question: "What is the relationship between job satisfaction and performance?" The debate on this question, sometimes called "the job-satisfaction–performance controversy," involves three alternative points of view.[23]

1. Satisfaction causes performance (S→P).
2. Performance causes satisfaction (P→S).
3. Rewards cause both performance and satisfaction (R→P, S).

### *Argument: Satisfaction Causes Performance*

If job satisfaction causes high levels of performance, the message to managers would be quite simple. In order to increase someone's work performance, make them happy.

Research indicates that there is no simple and direct link between individual job satisfaction at one point in time and work performance at a later point in time. This conclusion is well respected among OB scholars, even though some continue to suggest that the S→P relationship may exist to various degrees depending upon the exact situation. These alternative views continue to be debated and justify our use of the qualifiers "simple" and "direct" in summarizing the research evidence.

Managers should recognize that job satisfaction alone is probably not a consistent predictor of individual work performance. It may well be, however, an important component of a larger set of variables that together can predict performance—and it may predict performance for certain persons. Finally, regardless of whether or not job satisfaction causes work performance, it is certainly a part of the quality of work life. Job satisfaction, accordingly, deserves a manager's attention on this point alone.

## *Argument: Performance Causes Satisfaction*

If high levels of performance cause job satisfaction, the message to managers is quite different. Rather than focusing first on someone's job satisfaction, attention should be given to helping them experience high performance accomplishments. From this outcome, job satisfaction would be expected to follow.

Research indicates an empirical relationship between individual performance measured at one point in time and later job satisfaction. A basic model of this relationship, based on the work of Edward E. Lawler and Lyman Porter, is presented in Figure 2.6.[24] In the figure, performance accomplishment leads to rewards that, in turn, lead to satisfaction. Rewards in this model are *intervening variables,* that is they "link" performance with later satisfaction. In addition a *moderator variable*—perceived equity of rewards—further affects the relationship. The moderator indicates that performance will lead to satisfaction only *if* rewards are perceived as equitable. If an individual feels his or her performance is unfairly rewarded, the performance-causes-satisfaction effect will not hold.

This viewpoint is important to managers not because it resolves the satisfaction–performance controversy, but because it highlights the importance of rewards in the management process. Rewards are subject to managerial control. Rewards are also important to the ongoing health of an individual's psychological contract with the organization.

## *Argument: Rewards Cause Both Satisfaction and Performance*

This final argument in the satisfaction–performance controversy is the most compelling. It suggests that a proper allocation of rewards can positively influence *both* performance and satisfaction.

The key word in the last sentence is "proper." Research indicates that people receiving high rewards report higher job satisfaction. But research

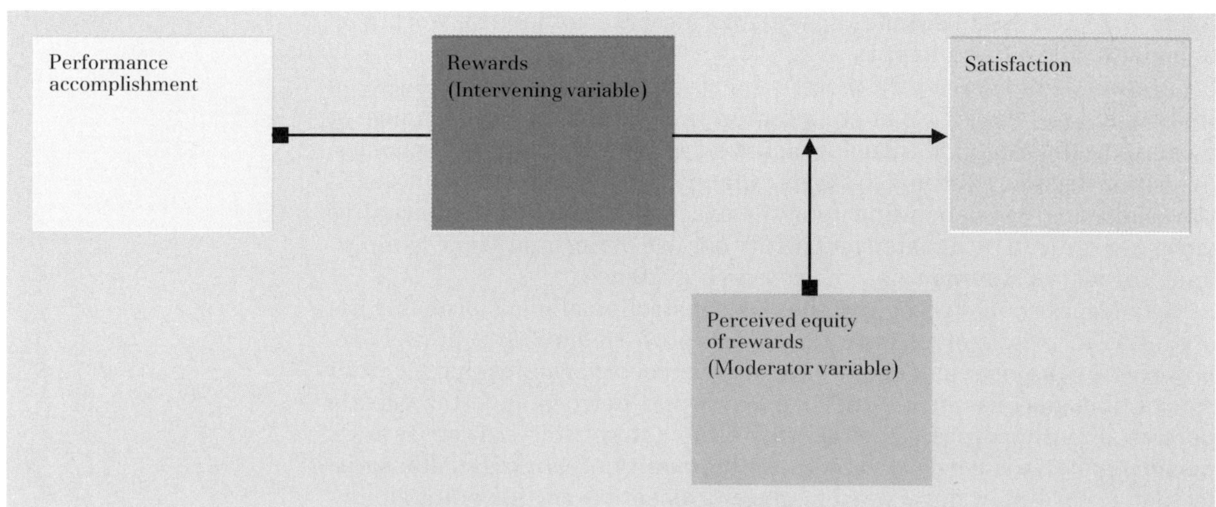


*FIGURE 2.6 Simplified version of the Porter-Lawler model of the performance–satisfaction relationship.*

also indicates that giving people ***performance-contingent rewards*** influence their work performance. This means that the size and value of the reward varies in proportion to the level of one's performance accomplishment. Large rewards are given for high performance; small or no rewards are given for low performance. And while giving a low performer only small rewards may lead to initial dissatisfaction, the expectation is that individual efforts will be made to improve performance to obtain greater rewards in the future.

**Performance-contingent rewards**

Managers should consider satisfaction and performance as two separate but interrelated work results that are affected by the allocation of rewards. Whereas job satisfaction alone is not a good predictor of work performance, well-managed rewards can have a positive influence on both satisfaction and performance. In particular, you will find that the concept of performance-contingent rewards is very important in the study of organizational behavior.

# SUMMARY

**■ Work and the Psychological Contract are OB concepts dealing with the basic relationship between individuals and organizations. Work is an activity that produces value for other people. The psychological contract is the individual's expectations of what she or he and the organization expect to give and receive from one another as a mutual exchange of values. A "healthy" psychological contract involves a perceived balance between the contributions someone makes to the organization and the various inducements they receive in return. Much of OB deals with issues which can help managers create healthy psychological contracts for people at work.**

**■ The Nature of Managerial Work is characterized by long hours, intense activity and frequent interruptions. Effective managers—those who achieve both high levels of task performance and human resource maintenance—fulfill a variety of interpersonal, informational, and decisional roles. They also pursue action agendas through a variety of complex interpersonal networks involving higher level superiors, peers and outsiders, as well as subordinates. Among the essential managerial skills—Human skills are uniformly important at all levels of management; technical skills are more important at lower levels of management; conceptual skills increase in importance at higher levels of management.**

**■ Perception and Managerial Behavior are interrelated as managers take action based on their interpretations of work situations. Since perceptions vary from one individual to the next, managers and others often develop different views of the same work situation. Perceptions are influenced by a variety of factors including the social and physical aspects of the situation, as well as personal factors like individual needs and values. The**

**common perceptual distortions of stereotypes, halo effects, projection, selective perceptions, and expectancy, can all affect managerial judgment and behavior.**

■ **Perception, Attribution and Performance** **are also interrelated in the management process. Attribution is the human tendency to try to understand or explain the causes of events. Attribution error is the tendency to underestimate the importance of situational factors and overestimate the importance of personal factors when evaluating someone else's performance. A self-serving bias often occurs as people blame external factors for their performance failures and accept personal credit for performance successes.**

■ **Job Satisfaction** **is usually measured in respect to a worker's feelings about various facets of the job, including the work itself, pay, promotion, co-workers, and supervision. Studies tend to show that most workers are neither highly satisfied nor highly dissatisfied with their jobs. However, there are some observed differences among occupational groups—younger vs. older workers, male vs. female workers, and white-collar vs. blue-collar workers. Recent trends also indicate a decline in workers' feelings of loyalty and trust for their employers.**

■ **Job Satisfaction and Performance** **are both work outcomes of great interest to OB researchers and managers alike. Job satisfaction is related to employee turnover and absenteeism, and is a key managerial concern in its own right. But, the relationship of job satisfaction to performance is controversial. Current thinking in OB rejects the notion that satisfaction causes performance. It focuses instead on how well-managed rewards can influence both satisfaction and performance. A key concept in this respect is *performance-contingent rewards*—giving rewards that vary according to the level of someone's performance accomplishments.**

## ▶ KEY TERMS

Absenteeism
Attribution
Attribution Error
Attribution Theory
Conceptual Skill
Contributions
Expectancy
Halo Effect
Human Skill
Glass Ceiling Effect
Impression Management
Inducements
Inducements–Contributions Balance
Job Involvement
Job Satisfaction
Managerial Work
Organizational Commitment
Perception
Performance
Performance-Contingent Reward
Projection
Psychological Contract
Realistic Job Previews
Selective Perception
Self-Serving Bias
Skill
Stereotype
Technical Skill
Turnover
Work

## REVIEW QUESTIONS

1. Explain the managerial significance of the "psychological contract" and "inducements–contributions balance." What can a manager do to establish and maintain healthy psychological contracts among the members of a work unit?
2. List Mintzberg's 10 managerial roles. Give examples of each as they might apply to (a) a department head or first-level supervisor, and (b) the president of a large organization.
3. How do the tasks and activities emphasized by managers vary across managerial levels? How do the essential managerial skills as described by Katz vary across management levels?
4. What is "perception"? List five common perceptual distortions and give an example of how each may work *against* a manager's best interests.
5. What is an "attribution"? Why is attribution theory important to the study of organizational behavior and management?
6. What are the major facets of job satisfaction measured by the Job Descriptive Index? What can a manager do to make a subordinate feel better about each of these facets?
7. Why is a subordinate's "job satisfaction" important to a manager? What do we know about job satisfaction and what the textbook calls (a) the decision to belong, and (b) the decision to perform?
8. Explain the concept of "performance-contingent rewards." Give an example that explains how well-managed rewards can positively influence someone's satisfaction and performance.

## AN OB LIBRARY

Richard E. Boyatzis, *The Competent Manager* (New York: John Wiley & Sons, 1982).

David L. Bradford and Allan R. Cohen, *Managing for Excellence* (New York: John Wiley & Sons, 1984).

John P. Kotter, *The General Managers* (New York: The Free Press, 1982).

Fred Luthans, Richard M. Hodgetts, and Stuart A. Rosenkrantz, *Real Managers* (New York: Harper Collins, 1988).

Marvin A. Weisbrod, *Productive Workplaces: Organizing and Managing for Dignity, Meaning, and Community* (San Francisco: Jossey-Bass, 1987).

# EXERCISE

## PERSONAL MANAGERIAL SKILLS

### *Objectives*

1. To create an awareness of necessary managerial skills.
2. To help you gain experience in self-analysis.

### *Total Time*

20 to 30 minutes

### *Procedure*

1. Look over the skills listed below and ask your instructor to clarify those you do not understand.
2. Complete each category by checking either the "Strong" or "Needs Development" category in relation to your own level with each skill.
3. After completing each category, briefly describe a situation in which each of the listed skills has been utilized.

### *Instrument*

| | *Strong* | *Needs Development* | *Situation* |
|---|---|---|---|
| Communication | ________ | ________ | ________ |
| Conflict Management | ________ | ________ | ________ |
| Delegation | ________ | ________ | ________ |
| Ethical Behavior | ________ | ________ | ________ |
| Listening | ________ | ________ | ________ |
| Motivation | ________ | ________ | ________ |
| Negotiation | ________ | ________ | ________ |
| Performance Appraisal and Feedback | ________ | ________ | ________ |
| Planning and Goal Setting | ________ | ________ | ________ |
| Power and Influence | ________ | ________ | ________ |
| Presentation and Persuasion | ________ | ________ | ________ |
| Problem Solving and Decision Making | ________ | ________ | ________ |
| Stress Management | ________ | ________ | ________ |
| Team Building | ________ | ________ | ________ |
| Time Management | ________ | ________ | ________ |

CASE

# ASIAN AND AMERICAN CEOS: ARE THEY DIFFERENT?

"Japanese and American management are 95 percent the same, and differ in all important respects." Or so says T. Fujisawa, the cofounder of Honda. What do you think of this statement? Could it be that these significant differences exist between American managers and those of Japan and other nations of the economically important Asia-Pacific Rim? And if they do exist, is it possible that alternative approaches to managerial behavior and performance are preferable to the American or more generally "western" ones?

In a recent study of Asian and American CEOs, management scholar Robert H. Doktor of the University of Hawaii reports the following comparison of a typical work day by an American and Japanese CEO. In the situation, each faces the same problem: dealing with an oil leak that has just been discovered at the firm's Indonesian refinery. Here's the way each CEO's work day developed.

## *The American CEO's Day*

6:30 AM
Mr. Mann, president of Eastern Oil, begins his day with a cup of coffee.

7:15
To beat traffic he leaves early for work.

7:15–7:45
Along the way he uses his minicassette recorder to dictate instructions to his secretary and employees.

7:45–8:00
Mr. Mann's mobile phone rings as he pulls into Eastern Oil. His refinery production manager tells of an oil leak at the Indonesia plant. The manager wants instructions on what to do next. The president says he will call him back with a plan of action.

8:00
Mr. Mann has his secretary call in all necessary personnel for an 8:30 meeting and his assistant gathers all related files.

8:20–8:30
He asks the legal department about legal problems that could result from the spill.

8:30–8:50
He briefs subordinates on what is known so far about the spill.

9:00–9:15
The legal staff submits reports on what can and should be done.

9:17–10:00
Mr. Mann meets with plant and design engineers and discusses suggestions on how to contain the oil spill.

10:03
The VP of marketing and communications says the press is calling for a story. She wants to know what the angle should be.

10:10–10:25
The Indonesia plant manager calls back, asking for the plan of attack.

10:31–10:47
The plant engineers at the headquarters decide to shut down the plant until the leak is contained.

10:55–11:15
The accounting department is asked how much the plant shutdown will cost. The comptroller says he will have the figures in an hour.

11:30
The Indonesia plant manager calls back, saying that only the affected area of the plant has been shut down, so production will continue at 60 percent capacity.

11:45 AM–12:15 PM
Mr. Mann holds another meeting with the chief assistants to get an update on the situation.

12:15–12:30
He has a hurried lunch while talking on the phone to the legal department about insurance clauses.

12:30
At this point Mr. Mann already has had many times as many meetings as his Japanese counterpart in half the time. The remainder of his day is a mirror image of his morning.

9:45 PM
Mr. Mann finishes his day, having had a grand total of 18 meetings, 20 phone calls, 2 vending-machine meals, and a late night at the office.

### *The Japanese CEO's Day*

8:00 AM
Mr. Nakamura, president of Congee Oil, begins his day with a limousine ride from home.

9:00
Mr. Nakamura arrives. He proceeds to have tea and read the newspaper.

10:00 AM–12:00 noon
He meets with subordinates to discuss why the planned effort in the South China Sea isn't working. (Earlier the CEO was made aware of the problem and informed his subordinates indirectly of his solution. The subordinates then met together and developed a consensus of opinion on the solution.) At the same time, the subordinates, already aware that there has been an oil leak at an Indonesian plant, do not mention the leak to the CEO. Rather, their staff makes a considerable effort to develop an appropriate response plan to the leak problem.

12:15–12:30
The subordinates and staff inform Mr. Nakamura of the oil leak and the plan of action already in place to address the problem. Mr. Nakamura acknowledges the information and compliments the staff on their quick action.

12:30–2:30
He meets with an MITI (Ministry of International Trade and Industry) representative for lunch to discuss long-term production goals.

3:00–5:00
He meets with two department heads to discuss the 25-year plan for the Yokohama refinery.

5:30 PM–1:00 AM
He has cocktails with a supplier, followed by dinner and evening entertainment at a private restaurant club in the Ginza.

### *Questions*

1. Use the frameworks of managerial work and behavior presented in this chapter to make a list of differences in the "approaches" of Mr. Mann and Mr. Nakamura to this managerial situation. Make your list as extensive as possible.
2. What are the most significant differences between Mann's and Nakamura's approaches? Why do you consider these "significant" differences? Is one approach preferable to the other? Why or why not?
3. Assume that Eastern Oil and Congee Oil suddenly merged. What would you anticipate to be the most important problems Mr. Mann and Mr. Nakamura would face if they were asked to work together as a top executive team of the new company? Is it likely that each would be able to accommodate the other's style, perform well, and experience personal satisfaction in their work? Please explain and defend your answer.

The following study outline is meant to organize your reading now; it is repeated in the Summary to structure your review.

## STUDY OUTLINE

### ■ Management and the International Imperative

Implications of a Global Economy   Emphasis on International Business
Changing Employment Patterns

### ■ People at Work: International Perspectives

Multinational Employers   Multi-Cultural Work Forces
Expatriate Managers and Workers

### ■ What Is Culture?

Popular Dimensions of Culture   Values and National Cultures

### ■ Dealing with Cultural Diversity

Understanding Our Own Culture   Developing Cross-Cultural Sensitivity

CHAPTER 3

# INTERNATIONAL DIMENSIONS OF ORGANIZATIONAL BEHAVIOR

## Comparative Management and Organizational Practices

Communication in an International Arena   Employee Motivation Across Cultures
Leadership and Supervision Across Cultures
Organizational Structures for International Operations

## A "Global" View on Learning About Organizational Behavior

Management Lessons from Abroad   A Special Look at Japanese Management

## PHOTO ESSAYS

Skills Perspective   PEPSICO

International Perspective   TOYS 'Я' US

Ethical Perspective   CORNING

# VISIONS 3

**The "competitive advantage of *nations*?" Yes. In his new book of that title, Harvard's Michael Porter examines the factors that make nations as well as their industries truly competitive in the global marketplace. In a four-year study of ten countries, Porter focuses on their successes and failures in international commerce. What he finds is that sustainable economic advantage is only possible with the right combination of industries, support institutions, people . . . and competition. Yes. Competition at home, the more the better, tends to create the foundations for industries to achieve their potential internationally.**

**Porter believes the United States is slipping. But his vision is of a U.S. that regains its competitive advantage. To do so, he points out, America must take stock of its existing advantages and then upgrade them to the next level of competition. Two big assets are America's technology and its human resources. Of course, success in this national-level business strategy will take lots of commitment—especially from government and industry leaders. But it can be accomplished.**

---

Global manager

With all the emphasis these days on international business and the global economy, *Fortune* reports that there is a search on for a new breed of manager—"the global manager."[1] Depicted as a scarce commodity, the ***global manager*** is defined as someone who knows how to do business across borders. Often multi-lingual, this manager really "thinks" with a world view and is able to map strategy accordingly. If this is you, or soon will be you, get ready. Corporate recruiters are scrambling to find people with these types of skills and interests. If you're still in college, the new global thrusts of business and management curricula should be to your advantage—especially with a good dose of liberal arts, language study, and foreign travel. If you're an experienced executive looking for personal growth along these lines, more and more international assignments are opening up. Then, too, there are special management development programs available. For example,

> ***The University of Michigan*** Executives from various nations come together to study worldwide management at the University of Michigan. In a five-week long course they learn from experienced educators from the United States and abroad, engage in a variety of cross-cultural team exercises and projects, and even go together on special "fact-finding" visits to selected countries. All this is

designed to increase participants' awareness of the complications and challenges of global management.

This chapter is designed to raise your level of awareness regarding the international dimensions of organizational behavior. Throughout the book, discussion, examples, and photo essays on the "International Perspective" serve as a continual reminder of the need to think cross-culturally and globally. Here, we introduce key themes to assist you in fully integrating your study of OB with an international outlook—something any global manager can't be without.

# MANAGEMENT AND THE INTERNATIONAL IMPERATIVE

The 1990s began with exciting news, and this last decade of the twentieth century promises to be a tumultuous and challenging one—especially in respect to the world's community of nations and global economy. We have seen the arrival of democracy and change in the former "Eastern Bloc" nations; we are witnessing political upheaval and socio-economic change of great magnitude in the Soviet Union; we have been disappointed with the events of June 4, 1989, when China's student-led "democracy movement" was so violently suppressed; and we see signs of progress in apartheid-troubled South Africa. Yet everyday personal opportunities are increasingly international as well. The world is ever-smaller and within the daily reach of even those with modest resources. While the supersonic Concorde takes elite business travelers from New York to London or Paris in just over three hours, we can board planes in Detroit, Chicago, Dallas, and Los Angeles, and step off in the business centers of Asia within 24 hours. There are, simply put, absolutely incredible opportunities for a person to see and become involved in all of the splendor and variety of today's world.

Given all this—and more—we believe it is *imperative* for you to admit, and embrace, the international aspects of today's work environment. It must be recognized, at a minimum, that:

- We all live in an increasingly global economy.
- International work opportunities are becoming part of more and more careers.
- Even so-called "domestic" organizations feel the impact of international competition at home.
- More and more people are now working at-home for foreign employers.

## Implications of a Global Economy

The "new awakening" and increasing recognition of the global economy is helped by international communications. In our "global village," news is received across the world sometimes even before it reaches the next town. This is particularly evident with such global news channels as CNN, which reaches more than 90 countries, including the offices of the heads of state of the United States, the Soviet Union, Canada, Britain, Cuba, and many others. While the international news brings the world at large into our homes and thoughts daily, the transnational movement of products, trends, values, and innovations continues to raise and change lifestyles at a rapid pace. The movement of people from one country to another is having profound implications in many nations and for their work forces. At the same time that valuable skills and investment potential enter these economies, cultural diversity among the populations and work forces increases as well. Today, perhaps more than ever before, the major cities of the western world are culturally heterogeneous.

The "world" is also coming center stage in respect to business and commerce. A recent listing by *The Wall Street Journal* showed that of the world's 100 largest public companies, 65 have their headquarters outside the United States. This globalization is even more evident in the banking arena, where just 12 headquarters of the world's 100 largest banks are in America. The implication of these figures is that companies that wish to compete successfully in world markets need to recognize this global economy and develop international links.[2]

Perhaps the most powerful reason for the growing recognition of the global economy is the growth of international trade groupings and pacts. Everyone is talking about 1992, the year of European economic integration. The evident strength of the European Common Market was one of the incentives for the development of the Canada–USA Free Trade Agreement. It may also be contributing to the current inclusion of Mexico in a North American trading group. It is clear that domestic self-sufficiency is no longer enough for many businesses. In a study of U.S. industrial competitiveness, for example, the Congressional Office of Technology Assessment reported that "where a global market exists, firms operating on a worldwide basis may have advantages over those that restrict themselves to a domestic market, even one as large as that of the United States."[3] Even so, there is growing dominance of overseas companies in fields such as automobiles, computers, and electronic goods; it is also becoming true in the service and even in the agricultural and resource sectors. According to RCA's Robert Frederick, chairperson of the National Foreign Trade Council, 80 percent of U.S. industry now faces international competition. He points out that no longer is the United States the only big kid on the block. For example,

> ***Motorola*** When it lost a contract to a Japanese company in France, Motorola was told by one of the French executives: "We may just have more in common with the Japanese than we do with the Americans. We both attach great importance to form and style." The company is now quite successful internationally with more than one-half of their cellular telephone systems' revenues coming from outside the United States.

## Emphasis on International Business

Perhaps you are still wondering whether the international management imperative is really important to you individually. Sooner or later, your career choices will almost certainly be influenced by the international dimension. Three important possibilities are:

1. You may work overseas in the foreign operation of a domestic firm.
2. You may work overseas as an expatriate employee of a foreign firm.
3. You may work as a domestic employee of a foreign firm operating in your country.

In an era in which foreign ownership of domestic commercial assets is increasing through mergers and acquisitions, you should also remember that many of the fastest growing economies are outside of the United States. This is all too clear in the hardships faced by the domestic industries as they find themselves challenged by highly competitive companies from abroad.

While the international dimension in business and management is pervasive, it cannot be treated lightly . . . and it cannot be assumed that success in international dealings is easily achieved. The costs of doing business internationally are high and there are many barriers to be overcome. Success depends on the ability to perform well—with trans-national responsibility. And this competence is a function of cultural sensitivity as well as technical skills. Failure overseas rarely results from professional incompetence. But even high-achievers with proven skills at home too often find that their skills, style, and attitudes just don't work well overseas. Of concern to North Americans, especially, is that these mistakes seem to be less frequently made by our overseas competitors. Perhaps it is because they prepare better for assignments here, or perhaps it is because they are simply building on a base of much greater cross-cultural and international experience to begin with.

## Changing Employment Patterns

When you travel—for leisure or for business—you expect to encounter international differences. What may not be so obvious, though, is that the most powerful impact of the international dimension may be right at home in so-called "domestic organizations." Perhaps the most immediate impact is felt through foreign ownership. Because of the dependence of its economy on the United States, Canada has been aware of this impact for years. But now ***foreign direct investment*** is becoming more evident in the United States. In one year alone, foreigners bought nearly 400 U.S. businesses worth $600 billion. Foreigners now own all or parts of such American symbols as Howard Johnson's, Baskin-Robbins, Saks Fifth Avenue, Alka-Seltzer, and Rockefeller Center. Less immediate to the eye is the key role played by international suppliers in the operations of many industries. The U.S. automobile industry imports Japanese, Mexican, and Brazilian engines; uses German instruments and British electronics; and employs Italian designers.

**Foreign direct investment**

Another more visible and important impact of the international imperative is in the international character of the work force that domestic organizations employ. As reports such as *Workforce 2000* point out, the domestic work force is—and will continue to be—"multi-cultural."[4] More than ever before, domestic employers draw their workers from "nontraditional" labor sources and from ethnic backgrounds representing all corners of the globe. Managers, in turn, must respond by being sensitive and comfortable in dealing with such ***work force diversity***.

**Work force diversity**

# PEOPLE AT WORK: INTERNATIONAL PERSPECTIVES

**International management**

**International organizational behavior**

***International management*** is a term used to describe management that involves the conduct of business or other operations in foreign countries. ***International organizational behavior*** involves the study of individuals and groups in organizations in this international setting.[5] International management and OB scholars study to learn how the principles and concepts of the disciplines apply across cultural and national boundaries. Practicing managers benefit from these efforts when they are able to selectively transfer practices and work successfully in alternative settings.

## Multinational Employers

**Multinational corporation**

**Multinational organization**

There are many different ways of setting up international business such as direct import and export, portfolio investment, contract and other foreign manufacturing, foreign licensing, and turn-key projects.[6] Of particular interest is the ***multinational corporation,*** or "MNC"—a business firm with extensive international operations in more than one foreign country. MNCs are more than companies that just do "business abroad." They are *global concerns* whose missions and strategies are truly transnational in scope. These large multinational businesses are complemented by other ***multinational organizations*** **(MNOs)** whose non-profit missions and operations also span the globe. Good examples are the International Red Cross, the United Nations, and the World Bank.

Multinational corporations, in particular, play an extremely important role in international management. Most employees who are employed in more than one location around the world work for an MNC, and many of the premier businesses in the world are found in any listing of MNCs. Table 3.1 shows the largest 25 industrial enterprises in the world. Only nine of them are still based in the United States, whereas the other 15 are based in eight different countries overseas. It is difficult to exaggerate the impact of the MNCs. Most of the largest ones have revenues in excess of $23 billion dollars, and the largest 200 multinationals in the world have affiliates in 20 or more countries.

MNCs are relatively complex organizations in which a diverse network of wholly or partially owned production and marketing affiliates located in some very different countries have to be effectively coordinated. This raises many management problems and is a rich field of study for the OB scholar. Alvin Toffler has an apt description: "The transnational corporation . . . may do research in one country, manufacture components in another, assemble them in a third, sell the manufactured goods in a fourth, deposit its surplus finds in a fifth, and so on. It may have operating affiliates in dozens of countries. The size, importance, and political power of this new player in the global game has skyrocketed."[7]

***Maquiladoras***

MNCs, and prospective MNCs, are also sometimes controversial in their impact on host countries. Perhaps nowhere is this more noticeable than in the case of the U.S./Mexican border, where ***maquiladoras*** or foreign-owned plants are springing up on the Mexican side of the border. In towns like Nuevo Laredo and Nogales, employment is up as workers typically assemble parts sent from across the border and ship them back when finished. Labor is cheap for the foreign operators, and Mexico benefits from reduced unemployment and more foreign exchange earnings. But on the "downside" of the *maquiladoras* are complaints that:[8]

- Population explosions in the border towns stress housing and public services.
- Inequities exist in the way Mexican workers are treated—wages, working conditions, production quotas—in comparison to their U.S. counterparts.
- Women are given job preference over men in many instances.
- Some companies are highly suspect in terms of toxic pollution and poor environmental protection from the Mexican operations.

*TABLE 3.1*
**WORLD'S TOP 25 INDUSTRIAL CORPORATIONS**

| *Rank* | *Company* | *Nationality* | *Industry* |
|---|---|---|---|
| 1 | General Motors | USA | Motor Vehicles |
| 2 | Ford Motor | USA | Motor Vehicles |
| 3 | Exxon | USA | Petroleum Refining |
| 4 | Royal Dutch/Shell Group | British/Dutch | Petroleum Refining |
| 5 | International Business Machines | USA | Computers |
| 6 | Toyota Motor | Japanese | Motor Vehicles |
| 7 | General Electric | USA | Electronics |
| 8 | Mobil | USA | Petroleum Refining |
| 9 | British Petroleum | British | Petroleum Refining |
| 10 | IRI | Italian | Metals |
| 11 | Daimler-Benz | German | Motor Vehicles |
| 12 | Hitachi | Japanese | Electronics |
| 13 | Chrysler | USA | Motor Vehicles |
| 14 | Siemens | German | Electronics |
| 15 | Fiat | Italian | Motor Vehicles |
| 16 | Matsushita Electric Industrial | Japanese | Electronics |
| 17 | Volkswagen | German | Motor Vehicles |
| 18 | Texaco | USA | Petroleum Refining |
| 19 | E.I. Du Pont de Nemours | USA | Chemicals |
| 20 | Unilever | British/Dutch | Food |
| 21 | Nissan Motor | Japanese | Motor Vehicles |
| 22 | Philips' Gloeilampenfabrieken | Dutch | Electronics |
| 23 | Nestlé | Swiss | Food |
| 24 | Samsung | Korean | Electronics |
| 25 | Renault | French | Motor Vehicles |

*Source:* Excerpted and adapted from "The New Shape of Global Business," *Fortune* (31 July, 1989), pp. 280–323.

**SKILLS PERSPECTIVE**

## PEPSICO

Reproduced with permission, © PepsiCo, Inc. 1990.

**When Mexico suffered a severe economic crisis in the 1980s, Sabritas, S.A.—PepsiCo's Foods International company there—succeeded in increasing value for its snack food lines. The Sabritas management team knew their market well enough to respond quickly and innovatively when the government restricted advertising and consumer product promotion. They created an educational program, *juego limpio* ("play cleanly") designed to encourage Mexican citizens to protect their environment. The program kept the Sabritas name in the public eye. It also reinforced the firm's role as a responsible corporate citizen.**

## Multi-Cultural Work Forces

One of the most important issues to be examined later in the chapter is how to manage the multi-cultural work force. There is no easy answer. Research has shown that styles of leadership, motivation, decision making, planning, organizing, staffing, and controlling vary among different countries. This is an obvious problem for an MNC in a project abroad. For example, it would be expected that there would be problems in managing a construction project in Saudi Arabia with very different work forces employed side by side, or that it would take a great deal of patience—as many are finding—to successfully conclude a joint venture within the USSR.

**Domestic multi-culturalism**

Managing across cultures, however, is also a key problem at home. This is a result of what Nancy Adler, an international OB scholar and consultant, terms ***domestic multi-culturalism***—cultural diversity within a given national population.[9] What has happened over the past 20 years in Los Angeles is but one case in point. This city, with the second largest

Mexican population after Mexico City, is a popular home to many immigrant groups. Los Angeles no longer has a majority population, but must constantly adjust to the shifting rhythms of ethnic diversity from its Samoan, Thai, Salvadorean, Armenian, and many other subcultures. Some 20 percent of the city's school children, in fact, speak one of a 100+ languages more fluently than English.

## Expatriate Managers and Workers

**Expatriates**

Individuals who work as ***expatriates***—that is, who take employment and live in a foreign country—often face problems when entering a foreign culture to work. They also can face problems when re-entering their domestic culture after the assignment abroad. All this is complicated by the cost of an overseas assignment to the employer. It is estimated, for example, that an executive earning $100,000 per year in the United States would cost her company $300,000 in the first year—compensation and benefits, transfer and other costs—if transferred to Great Britain.[10]

Figure 3.1 shows the typical cycle of an expatriate work assignment. It begins with the potential of *initial assignment shock* after someone is informed of the foreign posting. The nature of the recruitment, selection, and orientation provided during this stage can have an important influence on the assignment's eventual success. Ideally, the employee along with his or her spouse and family are allowed free choice on whether or not to accept the opportunity. Ideally too, proper pre-departure support and counseling (including an exploratory visit) are made available to prepare "realistic expectations" for what is to come.

As a foreign assignment begins, the expatriate faces the challenge of adjusting to the new country.[11] There are three phases of adjustment stretching over several months. First is the *tourist stage,* where the expatriate enjoys discovering the new culture. Second is the *disillusionment stage,* where the expatriate's mood descends as the difficulties with the new culture become more evident. This typically includes an inability to converse intelligently in the local language, difficulty in obtaining certain supplies and brands of personal preference, and so on. Third, the expatriate's mood hits bottom in the ***culture shock stage***—when a point of frustration and confusion results from the continuing challenge of living in a foreign environment. If the culture shock is handled successfully, the expatriate begins to feel better, to function more effectively, and to lead a reasonably normal life. If not, the expatriate's work performance will continue to deteriorate and she or he will eventually return home having not really enjoyed the time or performed well abroad. The employer can minimize this possibility by:

**Culture shock**

- Carefully recruiting and selecting employees who have the appropriate skills and motivation to go abroad.
- Providing adequate training and orientation in preparation for life in the foreign culture.
- Actively supporting employees while on assignment abroad, particularly during the first few months.

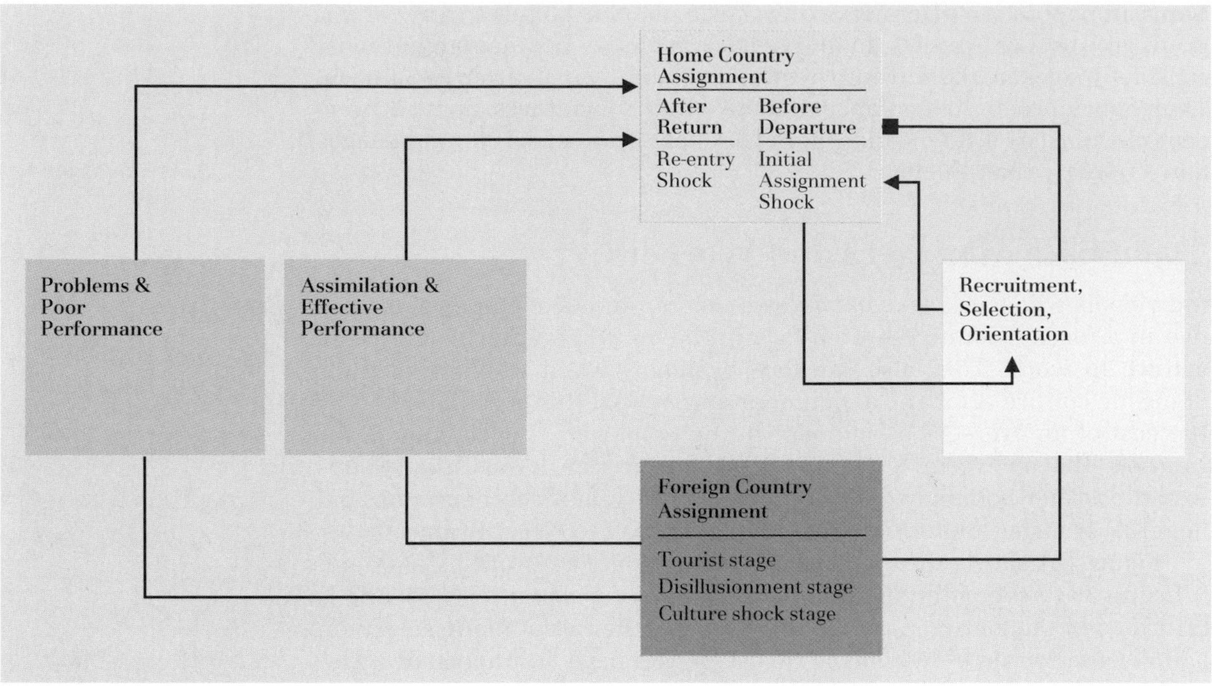


*FIGURE 3.1 Stages in the expatriate international career cycle: Adjustment problems in the home and foreign countries.*
*Source:* Developed from Nancy J. Adler, *International Dimensions of Organizational Behavior* (Boston: Kent, 1986), p. 192.

- Paying careful attention to needs of the employees' spouses and families, since many failures are due to their inability to adapt to the new country.

At the end of the assignment, perhaps after three or four years, the expatriate returns home. Surprisingly, this re-entry process can be even more stressful than the adaptation to the foreign culture![12] There are two major reasons for this problem. One is that after several years abroad, the expatriate and his or her family have changed, and the home country has changed as well. So rather than just falling back in, it takes time to get used to living at "home" again. The second problem is that in too many instances little thought is given to assigning the returned expatriate a job that matches his or her current skills and abilities. While abroad, furthermore, the expatriate has often developed the ability to function with a great degree of independence—something that may or may not be permissible at home. This issue is an important concern for serious international employers. For example,

> ***General Electric Company*** Even a successful tour abroad has been found by GE to be accompanied by some re-entry problems. A. Lawrence Buckley, a personnel manager at the company, says: "Sometimes the re-entry process isn't as smooth as you'd like it to be . . . it's still a problem for us, and for U.S. industry in general." He adds that GE is making progress in this area.

Two strategies can help minimize *re-entry shock*. One is to plan for re-entry as carefully as for the initial assignment. This includes providing for adequate contact back to the home country during the foreign assignment, as well as actually supporting the move both before departure and upon arrival. The second is for the company to recognize the skills and abilities gained during the foreign assignment, and to assign the returned expatriates to jobs commensurate with their abilities. This implies carrying out career planning on a global scale.

# WHAT IS CULTURE

We have used the word *culture* several times already in this book—both in connection with the concept of *organizational culture* (to be covered in Chapter 12) and in connection with broad differences among people around the world. It is now time to clarify the concept in its international dimension. Specialists tend to agree that ***culture*** is the learned, shared way of doing things of a particular society—how its members eat, dress, greet one another, teach their offspring, and so on. It is this constellation of factors that makes, for example, the culture of America distinguishable from that of Spain.

**Culture**

We are not born with a culture; we are born into a society that teaches us its culture. Also, culture consists of many interrelated facets. If a culture is modified in one place, everything else is affected. Finally, culture is shared by people and it defines the "boundaries" of different groups of people.

For our purposes it is convenient to think of two aspects of culture. First, are the *popular dimensions* or more observable aspects of expressed culture. We will examine them in terms of language, time and space etiquettes, and religion. Second, are the *subjective dimensions* or aspects of culture that represent internalized influences on the way people think and behave. We will examine them in terms of value differences among national cultures.

## Popular Dimensions of Culture

The popular dimensions of culture are the things that are most apparent to the traveler. They include language, time orientation, use of space, and religion, among other possibilities.

### *Language*

Perhaps the most conspicuous aspect of culture and certainly the one the traveler notices first is language. Languages reflect their culture, and the vocabulary of any language will reveal the history of its society and the things that are or were important to it. Arabic, for example, has over 6000 different words for the camel, its parts, and related equipment. As you might expect, English is very poor in its ability to describe camels. The structure of the language one uses can also influence the manner in which one understands one's environment.[13]

There are over 3000 languages in the world. Some are spoken by only a handful of people, whereas others, like English, Spanish, and Chinese, are spoken by millions of people. Some countries, like France, have an official language whereas others, like the United States, do not. In some countries, like Canada, Switzerland, India, and the Soviet Union, there is more than one official language.

The fact that many people apparently speak the same language should be taken with caution. For example, there are differences between versions of English. An American can be quite puzzled by the English "lorry" (truck) or the Canadian "hydro" (electric power). Even within American English, differences abound. Grocery shoppers in the Midwest might include "pop" in their "sacks," whereas their East Coast counterparts would have "soda" in their "bags." As we shall see in Chapter 12, even organizations develop their own languages, or jargons, which become important mainstays of the organizational culture.

## Time Orientation

Attitudes toward time vary in different cultures. Many cultures hold what could be called a *traditional* concept of time, where time is a circle, therefore suggesting repetition and another chance to pass this way—for example, if today is lost, that is no problem, because it will return tomorrow. The focus is on the present with little concern for the future. The modern view of time is quite different. Time is perceived as a straight line, rather than a circle. The past is gone; the present is here briefly; and the future is almost upon us. Rather than measuring time with recurring natural events, time is measured with the precise movement of a clock. Rather than "flowing" with time, people measure it, save it, and waste it. Long-range goals become important and planning is a way of managing the future. In many societies both views of time coexist uneasily. Mexicans, for example, may specify *hora americana* (American time) if they want to emphasize the importance of being punctual.

Another way of looking at time is presented by anthropologist Edward T. Hall, who distinguishes between cultures that are monochronic (do one thing at a time) and polychronic (do more than one thing at a time).[14] Monochronic cultures distinguish clearly between different activities, such as work and rest: polychronic cultures do not. For example, a North American or Northern European manager will allot half an hour to deal with a visitor and will give this visitor his or her undivided attention during this time. When the visitor leaves, this manager will proceed to the next task or receive the next visitor. This is monochronic behavior. A cabinet minister in a Mediterranean country, on the other hand, may have a large reception area outside his or her office. People wait in this area—and transact business in public with government officials who move around the room conferring with one person, then another, then perhaps back to the first, and so on.

## Use of Space

The ways in which humans use space can also vary among cultures. Personal space is the "bubble" that surrounds us.[15] We feel uncomfortable when others invade or "close in" on our personal space. But then again, if people are too far away communication becomes difficult. The size of the personal-space bubble varies from one culture to another. Arabs and

South Americans, for example, are comfortable at closer distances than North Americans. When a Saudi moves close enough to feel comfortable, an American executive may back away. Cross-cultural misunderstandings result from such natural tendencies.

In some cultures, space is organized in a way to permit many activities to be carried out simultaneously. Spanish and Italian towns are organized around central squares (*plazas* or *piazzas*), whereas American towns are structured linearly along Main Street. Cultural influences are also seen in how we organize the workspace. North Americans prefer individual offices, whereas the Japanese prefer an open floor plan. The most important office in an American company will typically be the biggest and probably be located in a corner of the top floor. The French are more likely to put supervisors in the middle of their subordinates—where they can presumably exercise control more easily.

### *Religion*

Religion is also a major element of culture and can be one of its more visible manifestations. The influence of religion often prescribes rituals, holy days, and foods that can be eaten. Codes of ethics and moral behavior often have their roots in religious beliefs. And the influence of religion on economic matters can be significant.[16] In the Middle East, for example, one finds "Islamic" banks that operate on principles prescribed in the *Koran.*

## Values and National Cultures

Cultures can vary in their values and attitudes foundations. Values/attitudes toward such matters as achievement and work, wealth and material gain, risk and change, may all influence how people view employment and organizations. The popular work of Geert Hofstede, a Dutch scholar and consultant, offers one approach to value differences across national cultures.[17] He studied 116,000 employees of a U.S.–based MNC operating in more than 40 countries. As a result of his analysis, Hofstede identified four dimensions of national culture illustrated in Table 3.2 and defined as:

1. *Power distance* The degree to which a society accepts a hierarchical or unequal distribution of power in organizations.
2. *Uncertainty avoidance* The degree to which a society perceives unequal and ambiguous situations as threatening and as things to be avoided.
3. *Individualism–collectivism* The degree to which a society focuses on individuals or groups as resources for work and social problem solving.
4. *Masculinity–femininity* The degree to which a society emphasizes so-called "masculine" traits such as assertiveness, independence, and insensitivity to feelings as dominant values.

Research on Hofstede's framework of national cultures is popular in the comparative management and organizational behavior literatures. More recently Hofstede has worked with Michael Bond, a cross-cultural psy-

*TABLE 3.2*
**EXAMPLES OF HOFSTEDE'S FOUR DIMENSIONS OF NATIONAL CULTURE**

| *Power–Distance Dimension* | |
|---|---|
| *Small Power Distance* | *Large Power Distance* |
| Superiors consider subordinates to be "people like me" | Superiors consider subordinates to be a different kind of people |
| Superiors are accessible | Superiors are inaccessible |
| All should have equal rights | Power holders are entitled to privileges |
| ***Uncertainty–Avoidance Dimension*** | |
| *Weak Uncertainty Avoidance* | *Strong Uncertainty Avoidance* |
| Time is free | Time is money |
| There is more willingness to take risks in life | There is great concern with security in life |
| There should be as few rules as possible | There is a need for written rules and regulations |
| ***Individualism–Collectivism Dimension*** | |
| *Collectivist* | *Individualist* |
| "We" consciousness holds sway | "I" consciousness holds sway |
| Identity is based in the social system | Identity is based in the individual |
| Belief is placed in group decisions | Belief is placed in individual decisions |
| ***Masculinity Dimension*** | |
| *Feminine* | *Masculine* |
| Sex roles in society are more fluid | Sex roles in society are clearly differentiated |
| Interdependence is the ideal | Independence is the ideal |
| Small and slow are beautiful | Big and fast are beautiful |

*Source:* Adapted by permission of the author from Geert Hofstede, "Motivation, Leadership, and Organization: Do American Theories Apply Abroad?" *Organizational Dynamics,* Vol. 9 (Summer 1980), pp. 46–49.

chologist whose Chinese Values Survey was developed in Chinese to examine national values from an alternative to the western point of view.[18] In comparing this research to Hofstede's, they identified a fifth value dimension called "Confucian Dynamism." Values on this scale include persistence, ordering relationships, thrift, sense of shame, personal steadiness, reciprocity, protecting "face," and respect for tradition. Interestingly, the "Anglo" countries in Figure 3.2 score quite low on this dimension, whereas the Asian "Dragons"—Hong Kong, Singapore, Japan, South Korea, Taiwan—score quite high. Hofstede and Bond argue that this cultural value may, in part at least, account for the surge of recent economic successes by these Asian nations.

Continuing research on Hofstede's framework examines the way countries can be grouped into clusters sharing generally similar cultures.

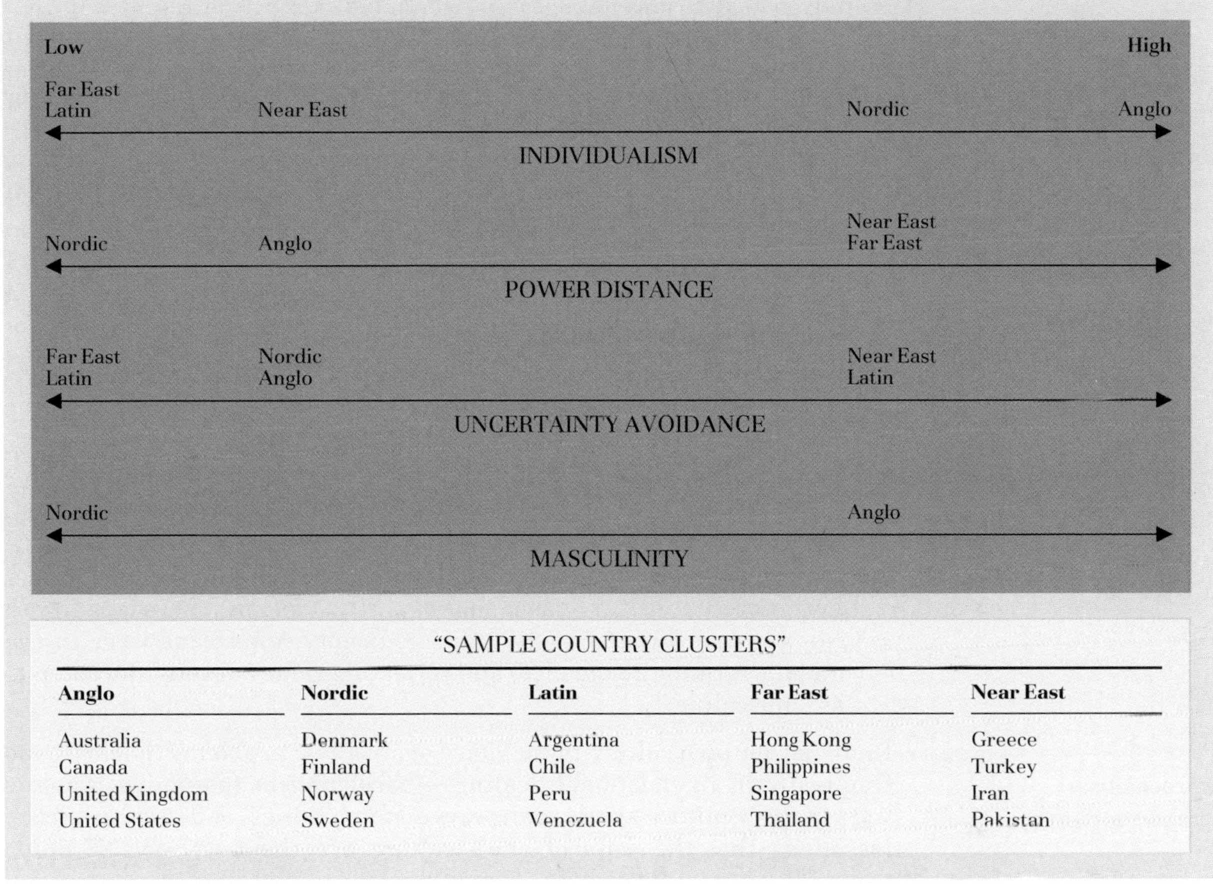


"SAMPLE COUNTRY CLUSTERS"

| Anglo | Nordic | Latin | Far East | Near East |
|---|---|---|---|---|
| Australia | Denmark | Argentina | Hong Kong | Greece |
| Canada | Finland | Chile | Philippines | Turkey |
| United Kingdom | Norway | Peru | Singapore | Iran |
| United States | Sweden | Venezuela | Thailand | Pakistan |

*FIGURE 3.2 Sample "country clusters" on Hofstede's four dimensions of national cultures.* (*Source:* Developed from Betty Jane Punnett, *Experiencing International Management* (Boston: PWS-Kent, 1989), p. 19.)

One grouping is shown in Figure 3.2. Scholars are interested in such cluster maps as they try to determine how management practices can and do transfer across cultures.

# DEALING WITH CULTURAL DIVERSITY

It is not necessary to travel or work abroad to experience different cultures. As we mentioned earlier, there are many places across the United States—from Los Angeles to Marysville, Ohio to Miami—where multicultural work forces are becoming the norm rather than the exception. As the number of foreign-owned firms operating domestically is increasing, the potential for problems in the interactions between the local and the expatriate employees grows. For example,

> ***Kotobuki Electronics Industries*** A Japanese executive at this Panasonic subsidiary in Vancouver, Washington was surprised to learn of these criticisms by American employees: Japanese managers don't trust the American workers and appear secretive; American managers have little decision-making authority; Japanese managers criticize but never praise.

## Understanding Our Own Culture

The starting point for being able to better deal with cultural diversity is to understand our own culture. Frankly, we are usually unaware of our own culture until we come into contact with a very different one. Hofstede's framework can be helpful here. Take, for example, the question: "What is American culture like?" In Hofstede's work, Americans compared with nationals of other countries in this way:

- *Power Distance* Americans ranked 15 out of 40 countries, reflecting a moderate tolerance of unequal power distribution; Singapore and Hong Kong ranked much higher.
- *Uncertainty Avoidance* Americans ranked 9 out of 40, which reflects considerable tolerance for ambiguity; Greek managers showed the least tolerance and Singaporeans the most.
- *Individualism–Collectivism* Americans were the most individualistic, (ranked 40 out of 40) whereas Colombian and Venezuelan managers were the least individualistic.
- *Masculinity–femininity* The country with the most "masculine" values (assertiveness, independence, insensitivity to feelings) was Japan, with Norway and Sweden at the other extreme. Americans were in the middle, ranking 28 out of 40 and reflecting values usually stereotyped as "masculine."

**Parochialism**
**Ethnocentrism**

Knowing our own culture helps guard against two problems that arise too frequently in international dealings—***parochialism*** (assuming that the ways of one's culture are the *only* ways of doing things) and ***ethnocentrism*** (assuming that the ways of one's culture are the *best* ways of doing things).[19] An apt illustration of parochialism is found in radio and TV sports announcements. The U.S. networks informed their listeners that the Detroit Pistons had won the 1990 "world championship" of basketball. Considering that at the same time, teams from 24 different countries were competing in Italy for the World Cup of soccer—the final to be beamed live to 1.1 *billion* viewers in 148 countries—the claim to "world" status for the champion of a league composed entirely of U.S. teams does seem a little stretched.

## Developing Cross-Cultural Sensitivity

To become more aware of our own cultural conditioning, we must be able to see ourselves as others see us—that is, to understand how we may be viewed through the eyes of foreigners. The learning available from good listening can be very valuable. Consider the following comments, which indicate how the "intricacies" of American culture may appear in the eyes of others.[20]

"Americans seem to be in a perpetual hurry." (India)

"Americans appear to us rather distant." (Kenya)

"[To Americans] work seems to be the one type of motivation." (Colombia)

## INTERNATIONAL PERSPECTIVE

# TOYS 'Я' US

Courtesy of Toys 'R' Us.

**It would be a rare kid in America that didn't know about Toys 'Я' Us. But would you expect the same to hold true for kids in Kuala Lumpur, Malaysia; London, England; and Cologne, Germany? Under the leadership of Charles Lazarus, Toys 'Я' Us is now the world's largest and fastest-growing toy specialty retail chain. With close to 400 U.S. stores, the company first went international by moving to Canada, where it now has over 20 stores. Now the world seems to be its target, with the company committed to what it calls an "intelligent and aggressive expansion throughout the U.S. and around the world." Toys 'Я' Us is a good example of a domestic success whose story is likely to continue now that it has gone international.**

> "[For Americans] even the littlest thing has to be 'why, why, why'?" (Indonesia)
>
> "The American is very explicit; [he or she] wants a 'yes' or 'no'." (Ethiopia)

Another useful approach for improving cultural empathy is *role reversal.* Imagine that you are a foreign person. Imagine the family you come from, the background of your parents, how many brothers and sisters you have, the education you received, the ways in which you reached your present position, and so on.[21] You may have to do some research to truly place yourself in the shoes of this person, but in the process you will be able to perceive the similarities and differences between the foreigner and yourself, and to see the foreigner as a complete person. Try to go one step further: describe yourself and your culture from the viewpoint of this person. You will likely be amazed at the insights you have gained, and how much you have learned about your own culture.

Finally, there are a few practical things that you can do to foster your cross-cultural sensitivity. Probably the best is to learn a foreign language.

It is also important to learn some facts about the outside world. Consider geography—where the different countries are, what their main physical features are, and where their resources and main activities are to be found. Read international history. Read current events. If you can, travel—with your eyes and ears open—both "looking at" and "listening to" the world around you.

# COMPARATIVE MANAGEMENT AND ORGANIZATIONAL PRACTICES

All levels of concern in the study of management and organizational behavior—the individual, the group, and the organization—can be affected by the international dimension. This point should be kept in mind throughout the study of various topics in this book. Here we provide an introductory look at some fundamental issues.

## Communication in an International Environment

Language is an important element in the communication process (the subject of Chapter 14). It is certainly a critical concern when communicating internationally. And although many people in the world are learning English, relatively few English-speakers are learning other languages. This places limits on the international business person who must rely on others being able to speak English. Potential problems include:

- We will only be able to learn what the other party wishes us to learn.
- The others may not speak English as well as they (or we) think.
- Because not all the people can be reached in English, some opportunities may have to be forgone.

When dealing with someone who speaks an unfamiliar language, translation is used. However, translating is difficult and there may be some lack of correspondence between the languages being compared. Idioms and figures vary from one culture to the next and speech may complicate matters further. For example, General Motors' well-known "Body by Fisher" label was translated into Flemish as "Corpse by Fisher." When Ford introduced a low-cost truck, the "Fiera," into some developing countries, it belatedly discovered that the name means "ugly woman" in colloquial Spanish.[22] We also need to be aware that the meanings of body language and gestures also vary across cultures. It is possible to insult people without meaning to. The familiar "go get them"/"jolly good" western "thumbs up" gesture, for example, is vulgar and insulting in Ghana and Iran.

The language of symbols is also variable in international communications. Although some symbols are practically universal (such as the colors for traffic lights), others have different meanings in different cultures. Problems can unexpectedly arise if we are unaware of this . . . as executives at Eastern Airlines once found out. When the firm inaugurated its Hong Kong–U.S. service, the Hong Kong VIPs who boarded the maiden flight were greeted by smiling flight attendants who handed them white carnations. Eastern was totally unaware that in that part of the world white flowers are given only at funerals!

## Employee Motivation Across Cultures

Motivation refers to the reasons why people do what they do and will be discussed in depth in Chapter 5. In the international arena, we run the risk of being parochial or ethnocentric by assuming that all people will be motivated by the same things, and in the same ways, as we are. As you will see, furthermore, the most popular management theories of motivation have been developed in the United States. While these theories may help explain the behavior of Americans, serious questions must be raised as to their generalizability across cultures.[23]

Individual values and attitudes, including attitudes to work, have strong cultural ties. Managers, therefore, must be careful in designing reward systems to ensure that the rewards are truly motivational in the local cultural framework. Consider Hofstede's framework again. While Americans value individual rewards (which reflects their high individualism score), the Japanese (with higher collectivism) prefer group rewards. Members of a culture with high power distance will expect to see people higher in the hierarchy get bigger and better rewards than those lower in the hierarchy.

## Leadership and Supervision Across Cultures

There are also important cross-cultural differences affecting leadership and supervision, the subject of Chapter 16. A recent in-depth study of international airlines found substantial differences in the leadership styles of different airlines. This was true despite the fact that international airline technology, types of jobs and skills required from employees, and basic operations are very similar from one company to another.[24]

Employees in some cultures want their superiors to be experts as well as to be decisive and authoritarian. Latin American employees, for example, may feel uncomfortable with a boss who delegates too much authority to them. In other cultures, such as the Scandinavian, employees want their managers to emphasize a participative, problem-solving approach.

Planning and decision making are important aspects of a leader's activities. We have seen that cultures differ in their attitude toward, and perception of, time—a crucial component of planning. In order to plan effectively, the planner must be able to visualize the future; the planner must believe that the future can be influenced; and the planner must believe that it is desirable to influence the future. The amount of planning done by a manager, the degree and detail of the planning, and the time frame for the planning will all be affected by cultural differences on just such matters.

Decision making, reviewed in Chapter 13, is essential to planning. Like time orientation, it is also affected by cultural differences. As noted previously, employees from cultures with high power distance expect their supervisors to make the decisions and may not expect or wish to be involved in the process. Individualism–collectivism also affects the desire to participate in decision making. Employees from a more collectivist culture are more likely to want decisions to be made using a team approach. In "collectivist" Japan, many companies use the *Ringi* system for making decisions. This is a group decision approach where all affected company members affix their sign of approval to widely circulated written proposals. In more "individualistic" France, decisions tend to be made at the top of companies and passed down the hierarchy for implementation.

Culture may even play a role in determining whether a decision is necessary at all—in other words, whether the situation should be changed or not. North Americans tend to perceive situations as problems to be solved. Others, like Thais and Indonesians, tend to accept situations as they are. Thus a North American is more likely to decide that a problem exists and that something should be done about it.[25]

## Organizational Structures for International Operations

As we will see in Chapters 10 and 11, the structure used by an organization will depend on a variety of factors, including the industry, technology, and environment of the organization. In addition, cultural preferences regarding communication, the role of leaders in decision making, and so on, can affect the structure of the organization in a number of ways. This includes the number of subordinates reporting to a manager, the number of levels in the hierarchy, and the degree of centralization, among other possibilities. Such cross-cultural differences in structures can be a source of management learning. A few years ago, for example, it was recognized that the Japanese auto manufacturers had about half the levels of management compared to the American "Big Three." Since then, Ford, GM, and Chrysler have tried to streamline their operations by eliminating entire levels of management.[25]

There are important structural implications when organizations expand their international operations. Usually a firm enters the international market on a small scale, such as by exporting one of its products—perhaps even through an independent export company. As the international side of the business grows, a manager responsible for export sales is usually appointed. This person reports to the Marketing Vice-President or the Chief Executive Officer (CEO). With further international growth, the firm eventually finds that it must establish subsidiaries in foreign countries. The management of these subsidiaries is quite decentralized at the beginning and the subsidiaries have a lot of autonomy. As the number of foreign subsidiaries grows, a headquarters group is put together to take

Courtesy of Corning Glass Works.

**ETHICAL PERSPECTIVE**

## CORNING

**Corning's philosophy is "Total Quality" equals "Total Ethics," says Van C. Campbell, the firm's vice-chairperson. He goes on to say: "I think that in this day and age, every responsible person in business or elsewhere had better be or become something of an ethicist or an environmentalist." Speaking for a company known for its commitment to quality and ethics, Campbell challenges managers and leaders in all organizations to meet these standards of a "transnational ethical system": Does the intended action do the most good for the greatest number of people? Does the intended action meet standards of justice for the individual? With companies like Corning as role models, high ethical standards in international business and management are getting more and more attention.**

control of all of the firm's international operations. This development—the creation of an *international division*—tends to reduce the autonomy of the subsidiaries. But it also tries to mobilize better headquarters' support and guidance.

As international operations continue to grow, a new structure is needed. It appears that when international sales account for more than a quarter of total sales, or when they are as important to the organization as the sales of one of the domestic product lines, then the international division approach becomes unwieldy. At this point the organization has acquired experience in international operations and top management is ready to perceive it as a *multinational enterprise,* not just a domestic company with some international sales. Strategic decisions can no longer be made separately for the domestic and international operations; they must be shifted to a global orientation. The company must also adopt an appropriate global organization structure. Three typical forms are:

**Global product divisions**

1. ***Global Product Divisions***—separate divisions, as shown in Figure 3.3, with each responsible for a line of products for the entire world.

**Global geographic divisions**

2. ***Global Geographic Divisions***—separate divisions, as shown in Figure 3.3, for different geographical areas.

**Multidimensional global structure**

3. ***Multidimensional Global Structure***—representing a hybrid of the prior two.[26]

*FIGURE 3.3 Organization structures for global operations: The global product division and the global area division structures.*

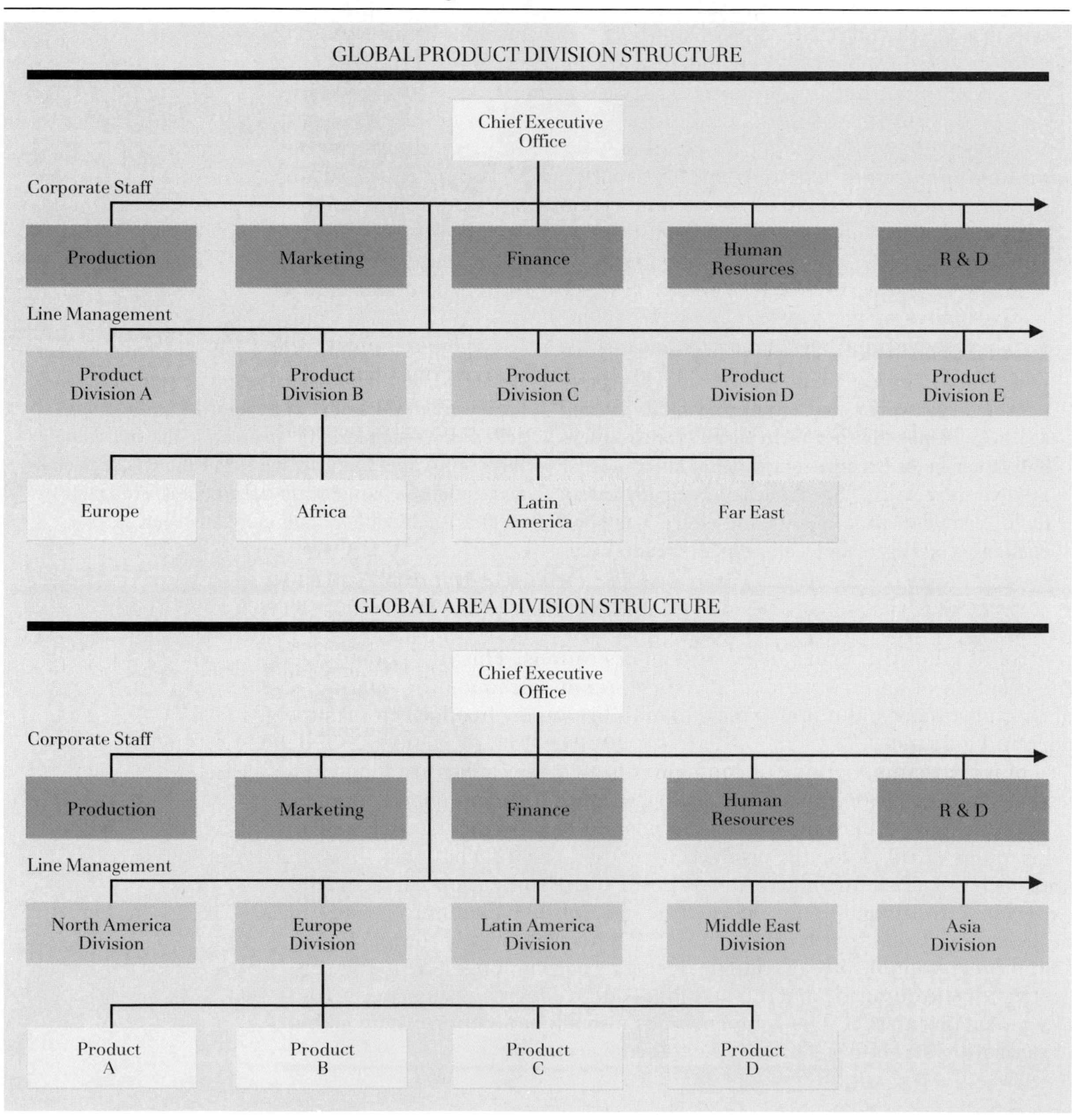

# A "GLOBAL" VIEW ON LEARNING ABOUT ORGANIZATIONAL BEHAVIOR

One thing that should be clear from this chapter—we believe the international dimensions of OB are increasingly important in today's world. We also believe that managers in the various cultures and parts of the world have a lot to learn from one another about what it takes to succeed in a global economy. It is no longer sufficient to accept local practices and beliefs as the most, or only, correct ones. In order to develop the competitive edge introduced by Michael Porter's work in the chapter opening *Visions,* we must test what we are doing against what others are doing. And we must always ask ourselves—"What can we learn from *them*?"

## Management Lessons from Abroad

Throughout this book you will be exposed to examples of progressive management and organizational practices from other countries. Notable among these is our extensive discussion in Chapter 8 of the innovative team-based approach to job design being taken in Sweden's Volvo plants. The eyes of the world are literally on Volvo's Kalmar and Udevalla production facilities to see how the experiments work and learn *if* there is a real alternative to the traditional assembly line.

Business firms are increasingly finding, too, that they can't just "go it alone" anymore and succeed in all aspects of international business. What they are finding is that they need to "team up," cooperate, and generally work with partners from abroad to accomplish certain objectives. ***Joint ventures*** and ***strategic alliances***—where two firms, often from different countries, make joint investments in an operation—are becoming more and more common. Part of the issue in any joint venture is learning—each partner presumably gains, in part, by learning from the other partner. As Toyota has shown in its joint venture with General Motors at the New United Motor Manufacturing Company, Inc. (NUMMI), in California, this can prove important in succeeding in new markets. Not only is NUMMI doing well as a joint venture, the Japanese company used the opportunity to learn more about American workers and markets. It helped when they opened their own U.S. manufacturing facility in Tennessee. Of course, GM should be learning too as examples about NUMMI's use of work teams will show. Many U.S. firms are pursuing joint ventures as key parts of their overall business strategies. For example,

**Joint ventures**
**Strategic alliances**

> ***AT&T Microelectronics*** Vice-President Rock Pennella says, "These days it's just too expensive to go it alone." AT&T has recently joined with the big Japanese chip maker NEC to trade computer-assisted design (CAD) technology for some of NEC's advanced logic chips.

The importance of international learning is further illustrated by trends in U.S. industry where the résumés of top executives increasingly show "hands-on" foreign experience. For example,

> ***Proctor & Gamble*** A major force behind P&G's high priority on international operations is new CEO Edwin Artzt. After largely

revamping their European operations, Artzt took over the international unit. Now this relatively neglected direction is a key part of the firm's business strategy.

*Ford Motor Company* International experience is fast becoming a priority if you expect to make it to top management at Ford. Most of the current senior management staff have extensive overseas experience, often in Europe where Ford's products are highly successful.

## A Special Look at Japanese Management

The runaway popularity of William Ouchi's book *Theory Z: How American Business Can Meet the Japanese Challenge* and Richard Tanner and Anthony Athos's book *The Art of Japanese Management,* speaks of the force with which Japanese management came onto the scene in the 1980s.[27] Along with it came a premature rush on the part of many western managers to find out exactly *how* the Japanese were managing and then to simply *copy* it to improve their own operations. Now that we are beyond this simplistic approach to learning the "lessons" of Japanese management, we've much to gain.

*TABLE 3.3*
**DO "JAPANESE"-STYLE MANAGEMENT PRACTICES PRODUCE COMPANY COMMITMENT AND JOB SATISFACTION IN JAPAN *AND* IN THE UNITED STATES?**

| *"Japanese" Management/ Employment Practice* | *Impact on Work Attitudes* |
|---|---|
| Long-Term Employment and Age/ Seniority Grading | Positive in Both Countries[a] |
| Cohesive Work Groups | Positive in Both Countries |
| Dense Supervision; Close Supervisor–Subordinate Contact | Positive in Japan; Negative in United States |
| "Tall," Finely-Layered Hierarchies | Negative in Both Countries; but Contributes to Management–Labor Consensus in Japan |
| Formal Centralization/De Facto Decentralization of Decision-Making | Positive in Both Countries |
| *Ringi* System | Positive in Japan[b] |
| Quality Circle Participation | Positive in Both Countries |
| Welfare Services | Positive in Both Countries |
| Unions (Enterprise-Specific in Japan; Industry/Occupation-Specific in the United States) | Weak Negative to Null in Japan; Strongly Negative in United States |

[a]In the sense that psychological attachment to the firm is found in both countries to rise with age and seniority.

[b]No comparable measure from the U.S. survey.

*Source:* Copyright © 1989 by the Regents of the University of California. Reprinted from *California Management Review,* Vol XX, Fall 1989, p. 103, by permission of the Regents.)

On Hofstede's scale of national cultures Japan is a collectivist society. This contrasts markedly with the highly individualistic cultures of the United States and other western nations. One would, therefore, expect to find differences in Japanese and western approaches to management and organization. In general, the Japanese approach has been described as involving: lifetime employment practices, slow promotion and career advancement, non-specialized career paths, and consensus-building and slow decision making (the *ringi* system). Although this pattern remains, it must be recognized that changes are emerging among Japan's younger workers which suggest that Japanese management itself may be undergoing, or at least facing, substantial changes as well.[28] These include shifting values among younger workers—with a reduced sense of loyalty toward the employer and greater concern for self-interests; enhanced focus on monetary gain and extrinsic rewards—as opposed to the intrinsic satisfactions of a "job well done;" and, new pressures for equal work opportunities for women—who still experience considerable job discrimination.

The basic practices that are now most typically associated with the "Japanese-style" of management are listed on the left side of Table 3.3. The table also summarizes recent research on the impact of these practices on worker attitudes in Japan and in America, when the practices are used by American employers. As the table suggests, Japanese approaches to management can have a positive impact on work attitudes. The lessons are there, particularly in respect to a number of themes you will find in the following parts of this book: work-group cohesion, consensus decision making, participative groups, "flatter" structures, and company-sponsored employee services.[29]

Thus, the special and popular case of Japan is still a good example of how careful study and analysis of "foreign" management and organizational practices can have important implications at home. As we have matured in our study of Japanese management, we seem to be learning more about what is really taking place in that culture. And as we have done so, we are learning more about what can positively transfer from that culture to ours. This is really the bottom-line of global learning about organizational behavior. We want to be alert to what managers are doing around the world, and we want to carefully examine what they are accomplishing and why. Then, finally, we want to apply this understanding with a strong cultural sensitivity to selectively change and enhance our own practices.

# SUMMARY

■ **Management and the International Imperative are at the forefront of current interest in the global economy. As America and other nations struggle to achieve and maintain a truly competitive edge in international commerce, "global managers" with a strong world view are needed.**

The situation is complicated by great transnational product and labor mobility. Many nations—such as those in Europe—are working more cooperatively together to gain economic strength, and wherever you live the major businesses of the world are "foreign" owned. A career in today's work environment will typically include some contact with international issues and considerations.

■ **People at Work: International Perspectives** is a theme of ever greater significance to most people in most careers. Multinational corporations (MNCs) are major employers and international business is being strategically viewed as the route to continued growth and prosperity for many companies. Expatriate employees who work abroad for extended periods of time face special challenges. These include both adjustment problems in the foreign country and assignment, and re-entry problems upon returning home. Increasingly, too, the domestic work force is culturally diverse, and managers must be willing and able to work with people of different cultural backgrounds in their places of employment.

■ **What Is Culture?** In its popular dimensions, culture represents observable differences in the activities and expressions—such as language, time and space orientation, and religion—of people. In its subjective dimensions, culture represents deeply ingrained influences on the way people from different societies think and behave. National cultures may vary on Hofstede's four dimensions of power distance, individualism–collectivism, uncertainty avoidance, and masculinity–femininity. Research shows how countries of the world may form clusters which differ somewhat on these dimensions.

■ **Dealing with Cultural Diversity** is an important consideration for the global manager and for the manager of a diverse work force. To be effective here, we must begin with an understanding of our own cultures. This involves breaking the pattern of parochialism and ethnocentrism that views one's culture as the only and/or best way of doing things. It requires empathy and an ability to understand things from another person's/culture's point of view. And it often involves becoming fluent in one or more foreign languages, a major asset in expanding one's cross-cultural horizons.

■ **Comparative Management and Organizational Practices** are studied by international scholars in management and OB. Major issues relate to the complexities of communication in an international environment, where language—spoken and non-spoken—is often a source of misunderstandings and unintentional mistakes. Management issues such as "motivation" also vary across cultures, as value differences affect the way rewards are viewed in the workplace. The global product division and global geographic division are two popular organization structures used by firms when the international component in their operations becomes significantly large. Cross-cultural differences in preferences for leadership and supervision can also be noted, as cultures vary on such aspects as Hofstede's power-distance and individualism–collectivism dimensions.

■ **A Global View on Learning About Organizational Behavior** can be an important asset. There are many innovations taking place

**in the world's industries and organizations, and they are often directly relevant to the field of OB. This includes our interest in this book in work teams, enriched job designs, alternative organization structures, and the like. And as interest in Japan continues in business circles, a new and more refined understanding of Japanese management is contributing to our ability to learn from this popular model of industrial success. Research shows common "Japanese" approaches such as long-term employment, cohesive work groups, quality-circle participation, and employee services can have a positive impact on worker attitudes in Japan *and* on American workers in the United States. When transferred selectively and with cultural sensitivity, valuable management lessons can be found in many alternative settings. The future will see more of this "learning" about management and organizational behavior becoming available from cultures other than those of North America and Western Europe.**

## KEY TERMS

Culture
Culture Shock
Domestic Multi-Culturalism
Expatriates
Foreign Direct Investment
Global Geographic Division Structure
Global Manager
Global Product Division Structure
International Management
International Organizational Behavior
Joint Venture
Maquiladoras
Multinational Corporation
Multinational Organization
Strategic Alliance
Work Force Diversity

## REVIEW QUESTIONS

1. Write a one-paragraph essay in which you explain the significance of a "global economy" to (a) the United States or another country of your choice, and (b) yourself and your future career progress.
2. Explain how the concept of *work force diversity* becomes significant to a "domestic" employer as well as to a multinational corporation.
3. According to the discussion in this chapter, what are some of the special challenges you might anticipate if asked to work for a time as an expatriate employee?
4. What is "culture"? Give examples of cultural differences as they may relate to culture in its (a) popular dimensions, and (b) subjective dimensions.
5. Explain the four dimensions of national culture expressed in Hofstede's research framework. Do you think this framework is useful to a global manager? Why or why not?
6. What can you do to become more aware of your culture? In what ways can this help you deal better when working with cultural diversity at home and/or abroad?
7. Choose two of the following areas and give an example to show how

management and organizational practices may vary across cultures: communication, motivation, and leadership.

8. Draw a diagram of a global product division structure and a global geographic division structure. List what you might consider to be the major advantages and disadvantages of each.
9. Use Table 3.3 to explain at least three "Japanese" management practices that you feel could be used by an American manager. Explain and defend your answer.

## AN OB LIBRARY

James A. Austin, *Managing in Developing Countries* (New York: The Free Press, 1990).

Geert Hofstede, *Culture's Consequences* (Newbury Park, CA: Sage, 1984).

Kenichi Ohmae, *Borderless World* (New York: Harper Collins, 1990).

Richard T. Pascale and Anthony G. Athos, *The Art of Japanese Management* (New York: Simon & Schuster, 1981).

Michael E. Porter, *The Competitive Advantage of Nations* (New York: The Free Press, 1990).

# EXERCISE

## CROSS CULTURAL AWARENESS

### *Objectives*

1. To assist you in establishing a better awareness of differences among various cultures.
2. To explore different cultural norms and values.
3. To enhance your awareness of the demands of global competition.

### *Total Time*

60 to 90 minutes

### *Procedure*

1. Form a group of four to five people and choose a specific country to target for this exercise.
2. In your group, develop a profile on the country you have selected. Profiles may include such things as:
   a. What the inhabitants look like.
   b. Climate and geographic characteristics.
   c. Socioeconomic structure.

   d. Expected roles for various persons in this society.
   e. Moral/ethical beliefs and traditions.
   f. Competitive strength/advantages in the global marketplace.
   g. Greatest weaknesses/needs.
3. Your group will present a brief overview of the country's profile to the rest of the class.
4. After the group presentations, your instructor will pair your group with another group. You are to assume the role of manager in a company in your profiled country that has recently experienced a corporate merger with a company represented by your paired group. Managers from both companies are assigned to a special task force to address the merger. Specific issues to be discussed include:
   a. What problems will the new management team have?
   b. What can be done to make it work effectively?
   c. What major cultural issues may be cause for concern?
5. Following your task-force discussion, you will be asked to share your findings with the entire class.

CASE

## AMERICAN WORKERS AND JAPANESE EMPLOYERS

Foreign-owned businesses in the United States are a rapidly growing segment of the economy. Along with the British, the Japanese are major investors. In the automobile industry alone, Mitsubishi, Toyota, Nissan, Honda, Fuji-Isuzu, and Mazda together have seven facilities in the midwestern states and California. Two are joint ventures with American firms; in two others, American firms own significant shares of stock; the others are wholly owned by the Japanese. Projections are that within two years Japanese automakers will be providing American workers with over 110,000 jobs.

A study by the Brookings Institution says that these plants improve U.S. competitiveness, reduce the trade deficit, and improve technology throughout the auto industry. President Bush is on record as saying: "I welcome Japanese investment in this country. Jobs, American jobs, . . . people working that wouldn't have a job necessarily if there wasn't that investment."

The success of these plants depends on a successful blending of Japanese management practices and the ways of American workers. But it isn't all rosy. Look at what has been happening at Mazda's Flat Rock, Michigan, plant. Turnover is up among Mazda's American managers and the blue-collar rank-and-file are growing increasingly resentful. Several top American managers have left and they have been replaced by Japanese who are now in most of the top posts. Labor relations are difficult and union workers have boycotted Mazda's suggestion box—something that is a mainstay of the company's normal operations at home in Japan.

"Culture" seems to be somewhat of a divide at the Flat Rock facility. Even before it opened, Japanese executives were wondering if the American workers could "hustle" like their Japanese counterparts. While the Japanese managers complain about the American's work attendance, the workers complain about the Japanese managers. Says one: "I think they need to listen more. I like to see that an employee's word is being taken."

Although Mazda had an agreement with the UAW that the Flat Rock plant might be organized, it's no secret that Japanese employers aren't high on American unions. The firm took great pains initially to screen job applicants and weed out potential trouble-makers. Elsewhere in the industry, the UAW lost a bitter battle to organize Nissan's Smyrna, Tennessee, plant. Says the plant manager: "In my opinion the work ethic is stronger down here."

### *Questions*

1. Do you agree or disagree with the Brookings report on the benefits of Japanese automobile plants in the United States? Please explain and defend your answer. As you do so, state a personal position on the significance of growing foreign direct investment in the United States.
2. Based on the case and your personal feel for the issues, what is there about the American "culture" that might make it difficult for Japanese managers to deal with American workers? What about the reverse situation—that is, what is there about the Japanese culture that may make it hard for American workers to deal with Japanese managers? Make a list of suggestions you would give Japanese managers to help them work "better" with American workers. Defend your list.
3. Would you consider working here at home for a "foreign" employer? What is there about your personal skills, needs, and career aspirations that causes you to answer this way? Please explain.

# PART TWO

# MANAGING INDIVIDUALS IN ORGANIZATIONS

This study outline of major topics is meant to organize your reading now; it is repeated in the Summary to structure your review.

## STUDY OUTLINE

### ■ Individual Performance Factors

Individual Attributes   Work Effort   Organizational Support
A Manager's Viewpoint on Work Performance

### ■ Demographic Differences Among Individuals

The Special Case of Stereotypes   A Final Note on Demographics

### ■ Competency Differences Among Individuals

### ■ Values and Attitudes

Values   Attitudes

CHAPTER 4

# BASIC ATTRIBUTES OF INDIVIDUALS

## Personality

Personality Theories and Personality Development Locus of Control Authoritarianism/Dogmatism Problem-Solving Style Machiavellianism Type A and Type B Orientation

## Managing Individual Differences

## PHOTO ESSAYS

Skills Perspective L.L. BEAN

International Perspective DU PONT

Ethical Perspective WALGREENS

# VISIONS 4

There's a lot of concern these days for job skills and educational qualifications of the new work force. Michigan Bell recently finds only 2 out of each 15 applicants for clerical jobs can pass reading and math tests. New York Telephone tested 60,000 applicants to find 2100 people qualified for entry-level positions. At the same time that the entry-level qualifications of job applicants are declining, the level of skills required for these jobs is rising. Companies with vision are working hard to get on top of this situation and address the problem head-on.

Aetna Life & Casuality Insurance is one of these. In one innovative program—"Hire and Train"—the firm is training highly motivated but underqualified employees for entry-level jobs. They take classes in basic areas such as writing, math, and word processing; and they take a class called the "world of work" to learn office protocols and acceptable business behavior. Says Badi Foster who heads up the company's training institute: "There is a high price to pay for ignorance. The quality of the workers you have is critical to success . . . We must invest in people."

The visionary companies in the chapter opener have recognized the importance of individual differences in employee attributes and the fit of these differences with job requirements. In other words, they are dealing with some key things a manager must be concerned about when attempting to influence individual performance—the primary emphasis of this chapter. Our discussion begins with what we call, "the individual performance equation" that identifies major influences on work performance. The rest of the chapter then looks in some detail at each of the three components of the equation and gives special attention to several basic attributes of individuals.

## INDIVIDUAL PERFORMANCE FACTORS

The individual performance equation is

$$\text{Performance} = \begin{matrix}\text{individual} \\ \text{attributes}\end{matrix} \times \begin{matrix}\text{work} \\ \text{effort}\end{matrix} \times \begin{matrix}\text{organizational} \\ \text{support}\end{matrix}$$

This equation views performances as the result of the personal attributes of individuals, the work efforts they put forth, and the organizational support that they receive. The multiplication signs indicate that all three factors must be present for high performance to be achieved. This means that each factor should be maximized for each person in a work setting if the desired levels of accomplishment are to be realized. Every manager should understand how these three factors, acting alone and in combination, can affect performance results.

As shown in Figure 4.1, it helps to recognize that[1]

- Individual attributes relate to a *capacity* to perform.
- Work effort relates to a *willingness* to perform.
- Organizational support relates to the *opportunity* to perform.

## Individual Attributes

Three broad categories of attributes create individual differences relevant to our study of OB: demographic characteristics (gender and age, for example), competency characteristics (i.e., aptitude/ability), and psychological characteristics (e.g., values, attitudes, and personality). These characteristics are the major topics of study in this chapter. We examine them in detail after taking a look at the other two components of the performance equation. Of course, the importance of the various attributes depends on the nature of a job and its task requirements. Managerially speaking:

Individual attributes must match task requirements to facilitate job performance

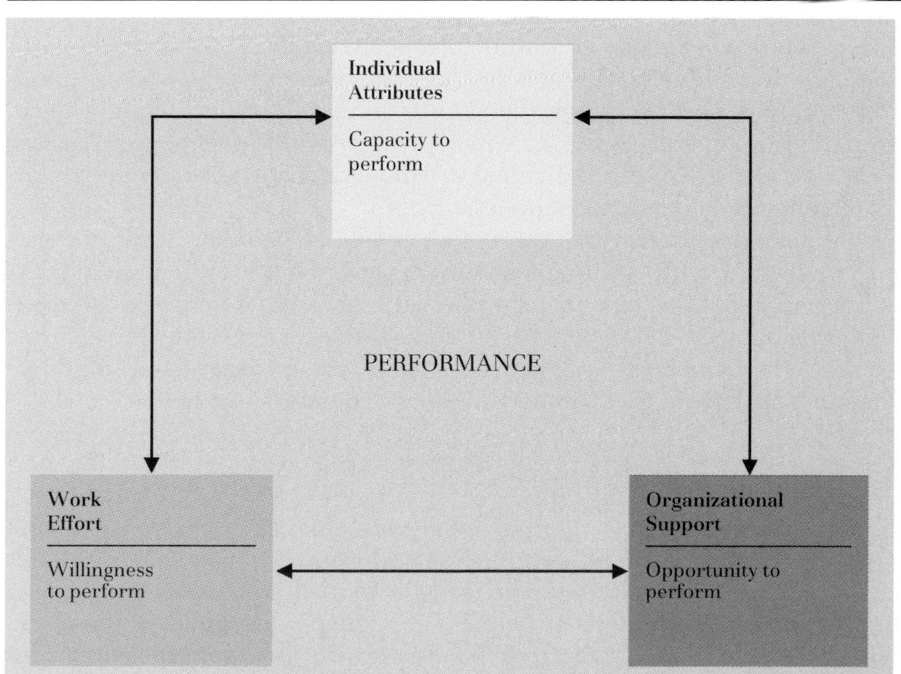


*FIGURE 4.1 Dimensions of individual performance factors.* (Suggested by Melvin Blumberg and Charles D. Pringle, "The Missing Opportunity in Organizational Research: Some Implications for a Theory of Work Motivation," *Academy of Management Review,* Vol. 7 (1982), p. 565.)

## Work Effort

Suppose that a manager has a subordinate whose individual attributes fit the task requirements as closely as possible. Can we predict that the individual will be a high performer? The answer is "no," and the reason is because of the important variable we call work effort.

To achieve high levels of performance, even people with the right individual attributes must have the willingness to perform; that is, they must put forth adequate work effort. Consider the college classroom. In your present course, for example, the chances are that the actual abilities, ages, and social backgrounds of you and your colleagues are quite similar. Does that mean that your instructor can expect the same level of performance from everyone? "Certainly not." The typical end of the course grade distribution supports this position. But why, as you look around the class, does performance vary when the individual characteristics of students are pretty much the same? Part of the answer rests with effort. Some students work harder at their learning tasks than do others.

**Motivation to work**

Instead of using the term "effort," your response to our question may have been different. Perhaps you said, "performance will vary because some students are more motivated than others." ***Motivation to work*** is a term used in OB to describe the forces within an individual that account for the level, direction, and persistence of *effort* expended at work. A highly motivated person works hard. But, notice that this definition links motivation to work effort, not to performance results. The distinction is important. Motivation predicts effort. Effort combines with individual attributes and organizational support to predict performance.

The concept of motivation is a most important addition to our study of individual work performance. Earlier, we described people who had the necessary individual attributes to perform but did not put forth the effort required to achieve high-performance results. They were not motivated to do so. The converse is just as real. Some people are very motivated, that is, they work very hard but still do not achieve high levels of performance. The performance equation suggests this might occur because of a lack of fit between individual attributes and task requirements, or inadequate organizational support, or both.

Managers must develop ways of positively influencing other people's motivations to work. Willingness to exert effort is up to the individual. A manager cannot do someone else's work. This is the essence of the manager's challenge—being held accountable for work that someone else has to do. As a manager therefore, you should be very interested in understanding individual motivation. Chapters 5, 6, and 7 can help.

## Organizational Support[2]

**Situational constraints**

The third component of the individual performance equation is support from the organization. Even the person whose individual characteristics satisfy job requirements and who is highly motivated to exert work effort may not be a good performer because of inadequate support in the workplace. OB researchers refer to such inadequacies as ***situational constraint*** and include among them[3]

- Lack of time.
- Inadequate budgets.
- Inadequate tools, equipment, supplies.
- Unclear instructions, job-related information.
- Unfair levels of expected performance.
- Lack of job-related authority.
- Lack of required services and help from others.
- Inflexibility of procedures.

You have probably experienced how a lack of organizational support can intrude on work performance. Having to rush a job because of a short deadline, not having the best tools, or not receiving clear instructions are common examples. In fact, you might argue that such failures of support are often found in the college classroom. They can include unrealistic due dates for assignments, inability to get library reference material, and not getting a clear statement of what the instructor is looking for in the first place.

All such problems share a common theme. They direct a manager's attention to the question, "How well is the motivated and capable individual supported as he or she seeks to perform assigned tasks?" They challenge all managers to ensure that organizational support for performance exists in their areas of supervisory responsibility. For example,

> ***Quad/Graphics*** A big Wisconsin printing company, Quad/Graphics builds in time for job instruction into every employee's workweek. Each one gets time off from the factory for one-half day of skills training per week. The firm is often cited for its quality management and high performance.

Chapter 7 will examine organizational support in terms of alternate job designs including work arrangements. In Part Three we discuss how the work group can provide or withhold support for individual task performance and similarly influence human resource maintenance. Part Four deals with organizational size, structure, technology, and culture, all of which are additional sources of support. Finally, Part Five includes a treatment of leadership and other interpersonal processes that, when provided by the manager and other key persons in the work setting, become additional and very significant support mechanisms.

## A Manager's Viewpoint on Work Performance

Table 4.1 summarizes the action implications associated with each major variable in the individual performance equation. To ensure the presence of capable people, a manager must do a good job of recruiting, selecting, and training subordinates. Motivating workers to put forth maximum effort is accomplished by creating enthusiasm and through a good allocation of rewards. Proper planning, organizing, leading, and controlling the affairs of the workplace are ways of ensuring necessary support.

*TABLE 4.1*
**MANAGEMENT IMPLICATIONS FOR VARIABLES IN THE INDIVIDUAL PERFORMANCE EQUATION**

| *Variable* | *Key Factors* | *Managerial Implications* |
|---|---|---|
| Individual attributes | Demographic, competency, and psychological characteristics | Increase *capacity* to perform by doing a good job of recruting, selecting, and training employees |
| Work effort | Motivation to work | Increase *willingness* to perform by creating enthusiasm and doing a good job of allocating work-related rewards |
| Organizational support | Resources, tools, organization structure and size, technology and culture, job design, group and interpersonal processes | Increase *opportunity* to perform by doing a good job of planning, organizing, leading, and controlling affairs of the workplace. |

The remainder of this chapter reviews three sets of individual differences—demographic, competency, and psychological characteristics. The discussion can help you better understand the individualities of people at work and also recognize their managerial implications.

# DEMOGRAPHIC DIFFERENCES AMONG INDIVIDUALS

**Demographic characteristics**

***Demographic characteristics*** are background variables that help shape what a person has become. Some are current, such as a person's socioeconomic status; others are historical, such as where and how many places a person lived while growing up, size of family, family socioeconomic status, and the like.

Three such characteristics in the work force are gender, race or ethnicity, and age. As already discussed in Chapter 1, the work force is rapidly becoming more diverse and "managing diversity" is a major concern of employers. Let's recall that by the year 2000[4]:

- Ethnic minorities will be a majority of the American work force.
- Nearly two thirds of new work force entrants will be women, with an additional 20 percent expected to be non-white or immigrant men.
- White native born males will comprise only 15 percent of new entrants between now and the year 2000.

The rapidly changing work force has led many organizations to establish management diversity training programs.

## The Special Case of Stereotypes

In dealing with this diverse work force, managers are having to come to grips with the kinds of stereotyping discussed in Chapter 2 as applied to gender, race, and age.

You should remember that managers (and others) who fall prey to stereotypes lose sight of individual differences among people. The quality of their decisions can suffer as a result. Someone who believes older people aren't creative, for example, may mistakenly decide not to assign a very inventive 60-year-old person to an important task force, or someone who believes handicapped people are not independent may fail to hire a capable person for a job. Rather than accepting such prejudices blindly, stereotypes should be challenged.

For example, consider the evidence on gender-related job performance differences. Simply put, there are fewer differences between males and females that affect job performance than many stereotypes suggest. There are no consistent gender differences in problem-solving ability, analytical skills, competitive drive, motivation, leadership, learning ability, or sociability. In terms of job turnover, the evidence is so mixed that firm conclusions cannot be drawn. Women, however, do have higher absence rates than men—possibly in large measure because of extra family responsibilities.[5]

Closely related to stereotyping are such behaviors as employment discrimination and sexual harassment in the workplace. Although illegal in this country as a part of equal opportunity legislation, such behavior still affects many women.

To avoid stereotyping, even the words we use can make a difference. A study involving children and snow statues demonstrates the importance of "de-sexing" our language and everyday assumptions. One group of children was asked to build snowmen; another group was told to build snow statues. With one exception, the first group built several traditional snowmen. The other group (separated some distance from the first) built snowmen, snow women, snow animals, and a snow spaceship.[6]

## A Final Note on Demographics

Demographic variables are convenient starting points when considering individual differences in everyday life. They are important to consider in the workplace, too, in order to respect and best deal with the needs or concerns of people of different genders, from different ethnic backgrounds, and of different ages. These differences, however, are often too easily linked with inaccurate stereotypes when it comes to an individual's work potential. This must be avoided—demography is not a good indicator in seeking good individual job fits. Matters of competency and/or values, attitudes, and personality are much more relevant considerations.

# COMPETENCY DIFFERENCES AMONG INDIVIDUALS

Competency is the central issue in respect to the aptitudes and abilities of people at work. ***Aptitude*** represents the capability to learn something. ***Ability*** reflects an existing capacity to perform the various tasks needed for a given job.[7] Aptitudes, in fact, are potential abilities. Abilities are

**Aptitude**

**Ability**

skills that an individual already possesses. In Chapter 2 we gave special attention to the skills essential for managerial competency—technical, human, and conceptual.

Competency is also an important consideration when a manager is initially hiring or selecting individuals to do a job. Once people with the appropriate aptitudes or abilities have been selected, then on-the-job and continuing education or training activities can be used to develop or enhance the required job skills. These are important investments in the human resources of an organization or work unit, since competency is a motivational force that can stimulate work effort. Psychologists call this the

**Effectance motive**

***effectance motive*** and relate its impact to the sense of mastery it gives a person over the environment. People who feel competent in their work can be expected to work harder at it. In this sense, competency becomes an internal force that stimulates and encourages people to work hard. Both physical and mental competencies are involved here.

Table 4.2 presents sample mental and physical or motor competencies recognized by industrial/organizational psychologists for their job rele-

***TABLE 4.2***
**SAMPLE MENTAL AND MOTOR COMPETENCIES USED IN THE JOB RECRUITMENT AND SELECTION PROCESSES**

| | *Description* | *Example* |
|---|---|---|
| *Mental Competencies* | | |
| Numerical ability | To be speedy and accurate in arithmetic computations such as adding, subtracting, multiplying, dividing | Making change at a cash register |
| Verbal comprehension | To understand the meanings of words and comprehend readily what is read or heard | Understanding and answering customer inquiries |
| Inductive reasoning | To be able to discover a principle and apply it in solving a problem | Determining what is wrong when a machine fails to function |
| *Motor Competencies* | | |
| Response orientation | To make correct and accurate movements in relation to a stimulus under highly speeded conditions | Flicking a switch to halt a machine when a warning horn sounds |
| Manual dexterity | To make skillful arm and hand movements in handling objects under speeded conditions | Adding parts to items moving rapidly on an assembly line |
| Finger dexterity | To manipulate skillfully small objects with the fingers | Screwing a nut on a small bolt in a tight space |

*Source:* Summarized from a discussion in Marvin D. Dunnette, ed., *Handbook of Industrial and Organizational Psychology* (Chicago: Rand McNally, 1976), pp. 473–520.

Courtesy of L.L. Bean, Inc.

## SKILLS PERSPECTIVE

## L.L. BEAN

**"Satisfaction" is guaranteed at L.L. Bean, Inc. But it takes a lot of work by a lot of dedicated employees to make it happen. At this $600 million outdoor sporting specialty retailer in Freeport, Maine, some 3500+ regular and temporary employees know what it means to be considered the company's critical resource. President Leon Gorman believes that people with ability are the cornerstone of success, and a great emphasis is placed on training in technical communication skills—the foundation of "performance through people." The telephone operators you talk to when placing an order are trained to process orders swiftly and pleasantly; the warehouse worker who pulls your order is trained to fill them accurately. Indeed, in all of Bean's major functions, employee ability through technical skills training is a high priority.**

vance. It is important to remember that this relevancy varies from job to job and it should always be confirmed before becoming a part of the selection process. A manager should always know the exact requirements of jobs to be done and be able to clearly document why particular competencies are essential to master them.

Each of us is acquainted with various tests used to measure mental aptitudes and abilities. Some provide an overall "IQ" score (e.g., the Stanford–Binet IQ test). Others provide measures of more specific competencies required of people entering various educational programs or career fields. Surely you have taken the ACT or SAT college entrance tests. Perhaps you plan to take a test for graduate study in law, medicine, or management. All such tests seek to measure mental aptitude or ability and thereby facilitate the screening and selection of applicants. Of course, there is controversy over the validity of such tests and their trends over time, particularly as they apply to persons from diverse backgrounds. Controversies also continue over such matters as college grades and class rank, which are often used by potential employers as indicators of a person's mental competencies and performance potential. As with the prior discussion concerning demographic diversity, however, the manager's job is to focus on what each individual can do and determine his or her best fit with job requirements.

# VALUES AND ATTITUDES

Psychological characteristics

The third category of individual attributes covers ***psychological characteristics.*** While there is a wide range of these characteristics, they share a common tendency to predispose an individual to behave in predictable ways. These predispositions can have a substantial influence on behavior. Extroverted salespersons, for example, are likely to see things differently from introverts and to be seen differently by others. These differences will influence their behavior and perhaps the sales they are able to generate. Our treatment of psychological differences looks first at values and attitudes, and then at personality.

## Values

Values

The noted psychologist Milton Rokeach defines ***values*** as global beliefs that guide actions and judgments across a variety of situations.[8] The study of values has an important place in OB because values are individual attributes that can affect such things as the attitudes, perceptions, needs, and motivations of people at work.

### *Sources and Types of Values*

Parents, friends, teachers, and external reference groups can all influence individual values. Indeed, a person's values develop as a product of learning and experience in the cultural setting in which he or she lives. As learning and experiences vary from one person to the next, value differences are the inevitable result.

Terminal values
Instrumental values

Rokeach classifies values into two broad categories. ***Terminal values*** reflect a person's beliefs about "ends" to be achieved; ***instrumental values*** reflect beliefs about the "means" for achieving desired ends. Among the values Rokeach places in each category are

| *Terminal Values ("ends")* | *Instrumental Values ("means")* |
|---|---|
| Comfortable life | Ambition |
| Sense of accomplishment | Courage |
| Family security | Honesty |
| Mature love | Helpfulness |
| Self-respect | Independence |
| Wisdom | Imagination |

Another classification of human values was developed in the early 1930s by psychologist Gordon Allport and his associates. They categories values into six major types.[9]

1. *Theoretical.* Interest in the discovery of truth through reasoning and systematic thinking.

INTERNATIONAL PERSPECTIVE

## DU PONT

Courtesy of Du Pont.

In 1990, Du Pont was honored by the President's Committee on Employment of People with Disabilities as National Employer of the Year. The chairperson of the committee stated: "Du Pont has been a driving force in promoting the employment of people with disabilities." This employment policy is true throughout all Du Pont operations, domestic and worldwide. Internally and with other organizations, they share their findings that their disabled employees are equivalent to all other Du Pont employees in terms of job performance, attendance, and safety. Internationally, Du Pont helped develop the Job Accommodation Network as an information resource to people with disabilities in the United States and Canada. A Du Pont representative also served on an international task force advising concerned Lebanese businesspeople on how to employ persons disabled by war. DuPont is committed to employment opportunities for persons with disabilities.

2. *Economic.* Interest in usefulness and practicality, including the accumulation of wealth.
3. *Aesthetic.* Interest in beauty, form, and artistic harmony.
4. *Social.* Interest in people and love as a human relationship.
5. *Political.* Interest in gaining power and influencing other people.
6. *Religious.* Interest in unity and understanding the cosmos as a whole.

A final set of values has been developed in specific respect to people at work.[10]

1. *Achievement.* Getting things done and working hard to accomplish difficult things in life.
2. *Helping and Concern for Others.* Being concerned with other people and helping others.
3. *Honesty.* Telling the truth and doing what you feel is right.
4. *Fairness.* Being impartial and doing what is fair for all concerned.

## *Patterns and Trends in Values*

Values are important to managers and the field of OB because of their potential to influence workplace behavior. They can do this either through their direct impact on employee perceptions, feelings and behavior or through ***value congruence.*** This occurs when individuals express greater positive feelings when they encounter others who exhibit values similar to theirs. When values differ or are incongruent, conflicts over such things as goals and means to achieve them may well result. Consider this short case.[11]

**Value congruence**

> Sal Henderson, the marketing manager, approaches Jim Reynolds, the engineering project leader, and asks when a new computer model will be ready for display. Sal reminds Jim that the new model is needed for a sales convention in two weeks. Jim tells her that the engineers are not satisfied with the computer's speed and don't want to release it for at least six weeks. Jim's people don't want it released until it is perfect. Sal looks for a compromise by asking for a prototype to show, with a promise of increased speed later. But Reynolds will have none of that. "Forget it, engineers don't work that way. We've got to deliver and not just promise—and besides sending a prototype is dishonest."

This very common situation shows a lot of conflict potential between salaried professionals—such as engineers and scientists, who practice their crafts within organizations—and managers. The professional will probably view things from an individual perspective, as did Jim. In contrast, the manager sees things from an organizational or managerial point of view, as did Sal. Clearly, the values in this case are incongruent. Sometimes, such incongruencies trace to differences in the time periods when people grew up and during which their values were set. For example, the so-called "60's generation" (that is, the group attending college in the 1960s), identified with values that may contrast with organizational reality. These include:[12]

- *Defiance of authority.* A willingness to challenge the status quo, to exercise self-control, and to reject imposed structure and authority.
- *Participation in decision making.* A willingness and desire to get involved, exercise individual autonomy, be responsible, and use one's competencies.
- *Service.* A willingness to serve society by advancing the quality of life and to demand personal treatment and a high quality of life inside an organization.
- *Social justice.* A willingness to set aside "careerism" per se and seek the "right" and socially responsible things in one's work, not just the easy ones.

Geert Hofsteade's work, discussed in Chapter 3, adds an international context to our discussion of values. Recall that he showed differences across 40 countries in the emphasis on the four value dimensions of power distance, uncertainty avoidance, individualism–collectivism, and masculinity. For example, U.S. managers tended to show: a moderate tolerance for unequal power distribution; above-average tolerance for uncertainty; the highest of all the countries' scores on individuality; and above-average masculinity. Once again, some problems may be expected when people whose national cultures vary must work together.

A recent study using the achievement, helping, honesty, and fairness values described earlier, reinforces the importance of value congruence. It was found that when such employee values were congruent with those of their leader, there was greater employee satisfaction with the leader.[13] Finally, we must be aware of applied research on values trends over time. Daniel Yankelovich, for example, is known for his informative public opinion polls.[14] Among American workers, he notes trends away from valuing economic incentives, organizational loyalty, and work-related identity and sees trends toward valuing meaningful work, pursuit of leisure, and personal toward valuing meaningful work, pursuit of leisure, and personal identity and self-fulfillment. Yankelovich believes that the modern manager must be able to recognize value differences and trends among people at work. He reports, for example, finding higher productivity among younger workers employer in jobs that match their values and/or who are supervised by managers who share their values.

In concluding this discussion of values, we should reiterate that they are individual attributes but, as we have shown, many of them tend to be shared within cultures. Our examples have covered national culture or societal culture. However, you should be aware that there are also shared values within organizations. The use of values in this context is so important that we devote Chapter 12 to *organizational culture.*

## Attitudes

Attitudes constitute another psychological attribute of individuals While similar to values, they are more specific. Formally defined, an ***attitude*** is a predisposition to respond in a positive or negative way to someone or something in one's environment. When you say, for example, that you "like" or "dislike" someone or something, an attitude is being expressed. One important work-related attitude we previously discussed in Chapter 2 is job satisfaction. This attitude expresses peoples' positive or negative feelings about various aspects of their job and/or work environment.

**Attitude**

### *Components of Attitudes*

It is useful to classify three primary components of an attitude. These are[15]

1. *Cognitive component.* Beliefs and values representing information and observations regarding the object of a person's attention. These are antecedent conditions to the actual attitude itself.
2. *Affective component.* A specific feeling regarding the personal impact of the antecedent conditions. This is the actual attitude in respect to the object of attention.
3. *Behavioral component.* An Intention to behave in a certain way in response to the feelings. This is a result of the attitude; it is a predisposition to act in a specific way.

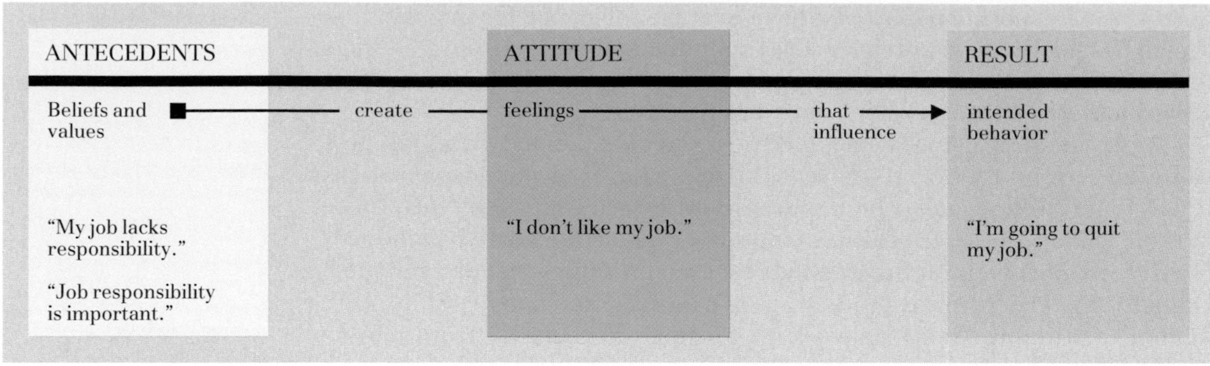


*FIGURE 4.2 A work-related example of the three components of attitudes.*

Figuratively speaking, the components of attitudes systematically relate to one another in the following way:

$$\text{Beliefs and values} \xrightarrow{\text{creates}} \text{attitudes} \xrightarrow[\text{predispose}]{\text{That}} \text{behavior}$$

Thus, another way to view an attitude is as a variable that intervenes between beliefs and values as antecedent conditions, on the one hand, and intended behavior that is a result, on the other. Figure 4.2 presents this logic in the context of a work-related example.

## *Attitudes and Behavior*

Look again at the figure. It is essential to recognize that the link between attitudes and behavior is tentative. An attitude results in *intended* behavior. This intention may or may not be carried out in any given circumstance. Take a person with a favorable attitude toward labor unions. Other things being equal, this attitude would predict such intentions as saying nice things about labor unions and buying union-made products. Practically speaking, however, other factors in a given situation may override the intentions. Hearing a good friend say negative things about unions, for example, may lead to the suppression of the tendency to say something nice about them in the same conversation. The person's favorable attitude in this case, has not changed, but its associated intention to behave was not carried out.

Even though attitudes do not always predict behavior, the link between attitudes and potential or intended behavior is important for managers. Think about your work experiences and/or conversations with other people about their work. It is not uncommon to hear concerns expressed about someone's "bad attitude." These concerns are expressed for a reason, and that reason is usually displeasure with the behavioral consequences with which the poor attitude is associated. In Chapter 2, we noted that unfavorable attitudes in the form of job dissatisfaction can result in costly labor turnover. They may also result in absenteeism, tardiness, low productivity, and even impaired physical or mental health. One of a manager's responsibilities, therefore, is to recognize attitudes and understand both their antecedents and potential implications.

In the international arena, a large-scale study examined people's attitudes toward work goals in seven countries: Belgium, Great Britain, Israel, Japan, the Netherlands, the United States, and West Germany. A range of professional, service, clerical, production, and managerial employees were asked to rank the importance of the following goals: learning new things, good interpersonal relations; upgrading or promotion, convenient work hours; lots of variety; interesting work; good job security; match between abilities/experience and job requirements; good pay; good working conditions; and lots of autonomy. Interesting work turned out to be the most important work goal across the seven countries. For all employee groups, including managerial, it ranked either first or very close to first. Good pay and good interpersonal relations were next in order. The latter, however, was ranked much lower in the United States. Pay also tended to be ranked lower by managers than by other occupational groups in all countries.[16]

Once again, it should be remembered that an attitude is hypothetical construct. One never sees, touches, and/or actually isolates an attitude. What actually happens is that attitudes are *inferred* from things people say and do. Hence, we often "attribute" the reasons for things happening the way they do to the presence of certain attitudes held by the people involved. This is a major foundation of attribution theory as introduced in Chapter 2.

One additional avenue of research on attitudes is interest in cognitive consistency, that is, in the consistency between a person's expressed attitudes and his or her actual behavior. Let us go back to the example in Figure 4.2. The person in this illustration has an unfavorable attitude toward a job. She knows and recognizes this fact. Now assume that her intentions to quit are not fulfilled and she continues to work at the same job day-in and day-out. The result is an inconsistency between the attitude (job dissatisfaction) and the behavior (continuing to work at the job).

**Cognitive dissonance**

Leon Festinger, a noted social psychologist, uses the term **cognitive dissonance** to describe a state of inconsistency between an individual's attitudes and behavior.[17] He predicts that the discomfort experienced by someone experiencing such an inconsistency results in a desire to reduce or eliminate it. This is achieved by changing the underlying attitude, changing future behavior, and/or developing new ways of explaining or rationalizing the inconsistency.

Festinger's cognitive dissonance theory offers yet another perspective on attitudes as special attributes of people at work. Among the work-related implications of the theory are:

1. A recognition that behavior may influence attitudes, as well as that attitudes may influence behavior.
   *Work example:* a person who actually tries a new task and likes it may change a previously held negative attitude toward the task.
2. A recognition that attitudes may develop consistent with a person's initial emotional response to a new person or object.
   *Work example:* a person who has a quick negative reaction to the unshaven appearance of a new co-worker may develop the attitude that the person is untrustworthy.

# PERSONALITY

Personality

A *Fortune* article recently reported that "America's toughest bosses" are: "steely, super-demanding, unrelenting, sometimes abusive, sometimes unreasonable, inpatient, driven, stubborn, and combative."[18] What's at issue here is "personality," an often-heard term when someone is describing someone else's characteristics. ***Personality*** is used here to represent the overall profile or combination of traits that characterize the unique nature of a person.

Just as with values and attitudes, attempts to describe or classify personalities are important to OB because of the expectation that there is a predictable interplay between personality and behavior. A common understanding, for example, is that introverts tend not to be sociable. Sometimes attempts are made to measure personality with questionnaires or special tests. Frequently, personalities is inferred from behavior, such as with the toughest bosses. Either way, personality is an important individual attribute for managers to understand.

## Personality Theories and Personality Development

Four personality theories of interest in OB are:

1. *Psychoanalytic theory* Based on the work of Sigmund Freud and Carl Jung, emphasizing the contribution of the "unconscious" as a component of personality.
2. *Trait theory* Popularized by Gordon Allport and Raymond Cattell, using observable traits such as values, abilities, and temperament to describe personalities.
3. *Humanistic theory* Represented in the work of Abraham Maslow and Carl Rogers, emphasizing the importance of individual growth, improvement, and the self-concept to personality.
4. *Social learning theory* Well described by Albert Bandura, recognizing the importance to personality of learning from other people and person–situation interactions.

In addition to studying these theories of personality, experts also investigate personality development and its implications. One approach is to view an individual's personality as developing in a series of "stages" over time. Freud, for example, viewed the important stages as a progression of one's psycho*sexual* development; Erik Erikson, a child psychologist, viewed them as a progression of psycho*social* development. Two other developmental perspectives with more direct managerial implications follow.

Figure 4.3 shows various stages in the adult life cycle. This age-based view of personality development is described by Daniel Levinson.[19] It includes four key transitions—age-30, mid-life, age-50, and late adult—that may have significant impact on a person's relationship with his or her job, career, and employing organization. As we will further discuss in a section on careers in Chapter 18, people at various adult life stages may have different work needs and thus require quite different managerial responses. The interests of a single person taking his or her first job, for example, may be quite dissimilar to those of a married manager with a family and substantial personal responsibilities.

Another developmental view is offered by Chris Argyris, a management expert who is concerned about possible conflicts between individuals and organizations.[20] He notes that people develop along a continuum of dimensions from immaturity to maturity. A person progresses during life.

| *From Immaturity* | *To Maturity* |
|---|---|
| Passivity | Activity |
| Dependence | Independence |
| Limited behavior | Diverse behavior |
| Shallow interests | Deep interests |
| Short-time perspective | Long-time perspective |
| Subordinate position | Superordinate position |
| Little self-awareness | Much self-awareness |

Argyris believes the nature of the mature adult personality can sometimes be inconsistent with work opportunities. Organizations and their managers may neglect the "adult" sides of people. They may use close

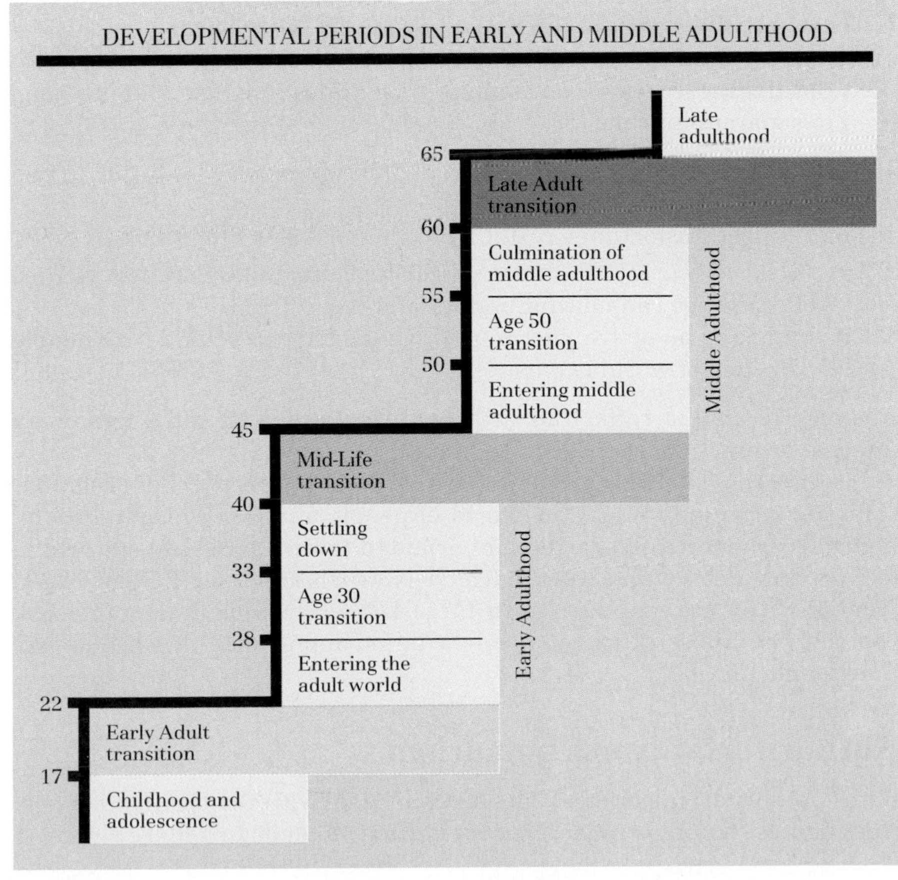


*FIGURE 4.3 Developmental periods in early and middle adulthood.* (*Source:* From *The Seasons of a Man's Life*, by Daniel J. Levinson, et al., copyright © 1978 by Daniel J. Levinson. Reprinted by permission of Alfred A. Knopf, Inc.)

supervision and control more typically needed by "infants" whose personalities are still immature.

Personality theories have had a noticeable impact on the concepts of motivation and learning discussed in the next chapter. In addition, OB research has tended to focus on specific personality traits (or "styles") that are considered important in the workplace. Five traits of special relevance to managers are: locus of control, authoritarianism/dogmatism, problem-solving style, Machiavellianism, and Type A-Type B personality style. As you read on, think about where you and others might fit regarding each of these traits. Think, too, about how that aspect of personality may affect what you and they do in response to things that happen at work.

## Locus of Control

**Locus of control**

***Locus of control*** measures the internal–external orientation of a person, that is, the extent to which a person feels able to affect his or her life.[21] People have general conceptions about whether events are controlled primarily by themselves, which indicates an internal orientation, or by outside forces, characteristic of an external orientation. "Internals," or persons with an internal locus of control, believe they control their own fate or destiny. "Externals," or persons with an external locus of control, believe that much of what happens to them is uncontrolled and determined by outside forces. In terms of attribution theory, we can say that internals attribute causes for events primarily to themselves, whereas externals attribute causes to things outside their control.

Consider these items from a much longer questionnaire that has been used to separate internals from externals.

1. a. Many of the unhappy things in people's lives are partly due to bad luck.
   b. People's misfortunes result from the mistakes them make.
2. a. As far as world affairs are concerned, most of us are the victims of forces we can neither understand nor control.
   b. By taking an active part in political and social affairs, the people can control world events.

Answers 1a and 2a reflect an external orientation; 1b and 2b show an internal orientation.

In general, externals are more extroverted in interpersonal relationships and oriented toward the world of people and things around them. Internals are more introverted and oriented toward their inner world of feelings and ideas. Other ways in which externals and internals have been found to differ are summarized in Table 4.3. As you look at the table, ask yourself how these differences might be of importance in various jobs that people may hold.

## Authoritarianism/Dogmatism

**Authoritarianism**

Both "authoritarianism" and "dogmatism" deal with the rigidity of a person's beliefs. A person high in ***authoritarianism*** tends to adhere rigidly to

*TABLE 4.3*
**SOME WAYS IN WHICH INTERNALS DIFFER FROM EXTERNALS**

| | |
|---|---|
| Information processing | Internals make more attempts to acquire information, are less satisfied with the amount of information they possess, and are better at utilizing information. |
| Job satisfaction | Internals are generally more satisfied, less alienated, less rootless, and there is a stronger job satisfaction/performance relationship for them. |
| Performance | Internals perform better on learning and problem-solving tasks, when performance leads to valued rewards |
| Self-control, risk, and anxiety | Internals exhibit greater self-control, are more cautious, engage in less risky behavior, and are less anxious. |
| Motivation, expectancies and results | Internals display greater work motivation, see a stronger relationship between what they do and what happens to them, expect that working hard leads to good performance, feel more control over their time. |
| Response to others | Internals are more independent, more reliant on their own judgment, and less susceptible to the influence of others; they are more likely to accept information on its merit. |

conventional values, readily obeys recognized authority, is concerned with toughness and power, and opposes the use of subjective feelings. A person high in ***dogmatism*** sees the world as a threatening place, often regards legitimate authority as absolute, and accepts or rejects others according to how much they agree with accepted authority. Superiors possessing these traits tend to be rigid and closed. Dogmatic subordinates tend to want certainty imposed upon them.[22]

**Dogmatism**

## Problem-Solving Style

**Problem-solving style**

Another personality characteristic is ***problem-solving style,*** the way in which a person goes about gathering and evaluating information in solving problems and making decisions. In this process, information gathering and evaluation are separate activities. *Information gathering* involves getting and organizing data for use. Style of information gathering vary from sensation to intuitive. *Sensation-type individuals* prefer routine and order, and emphasize well-defined details in gathering information. They would rather work with known facts than look for possibilities. *Intuitive-type people* prefer the big picture, like solving new problems, dislike routine, and would rather look for possibilities than work with facts.

*Evaluation* involves making judgments about how to deal with information once it has been collected. Styles of information evaluation vary from an emphasis on feeling to an emphasis on thinking. *Feeling-type individuals* are oriented toward conformity and try to accommodate themselves to other people. They try to avoid problems that might result in disagreements. *Thinking-type people* use reason and intellect to deal with problems. They downplay emotional aspects in the problem situation.

When these two dimensions of information gathering and evaluation are combined, the matrix of problem-solving styles shown in Table 4.4 results. The table contains descriptions of four basic problem-solving styles: sensation–feeling (SF), intuitive–feeling (IF), sensation–thinking (ST), and intuitive–thinking (IT), together with various occupational pairings. "Tough" boss Robert Crandall, chairperson of American Airlines would probably be a strong sensation–thinker (ST) with his incessant demand for details. Soichiro Honda, CEO of Honda, has been characterized as an intuitive-thinker type. He built Honda by emphasizing new possibilities and being creative in the marketplace.[23]

Research indicates there is a fit between individuals' styles and the decision strategy they select. For example, "analytics" (sensation–thinkers) preferred analytical strategies, "intuitives" (intuitive–feelers) preferred intuitive strategies, and those with mixed styles preferred mixed decision strategies.[24] Also, there are findings that thinkers tend to have higher motivation than feelers and those emphasizing sensations have higher job satisfaction than intuitives. These findings suggest basic differences between different problem-solving styles and that it may be important to try to fit such styles with a task's information processing and evaluation requirements.[25]

Problem-solving styles are typically measured by the Myers–Briggs Type Indicator. Firms such as Apple, AT&T, and Exxon as well as hospitals, educational institutions, and the U.S. Armed Forces have used the Myers–Briggs for various aspects of management development.[26]

### *TABLE 4.4*
### FOUR PROBLEM-SOLVING STYLES AND THEIR OCCUPATIONAL MATCH-UPS

| | |
|---|---|
| **Sensation–Thinking:** decisive, dependable, applied thinker, sensitive to details | **Sensation–Feeling:** pragmatic, analytical, methodical, and conscientious |
| Accounting<br>Production<br>Computer programming<br>Market research<br>Engineering | Direct supervision<br>Counseling<br>Negotiating<br>Selling<br>Interviewing |
| **Intuitive–Thinking:** creative, progressive, perceptive thinker, with many ideas | **Intuitive–Feeling:** charismatic, participative, people oriented, and helpful |
| Systems design<br>Systems analysis<br>Law<br>Middle/top management<br>Teaching business, economics | Public relations<br>Advertising<br>Personnel<br>Politics<br>Customer services |

*Source:* Developed in part from Don Hellriegel, John W. Slocum, Jr., and Richard W., Woodman, *Organizational Behavior*, 5th ed. (St. Paul, Minn.: West Publishing Co., 1989), Ch. 4.

## Machiavellianism

Niccolo Machiavelli! Why the very name itself evokes visions of a master of "guile," "deceit," and "opportunism" in interpersonal relations. This sixteenth-century author earned his place in history by writing a nobleman's guide to the acquisition and use of power—*The Prince.*[27] From its pages emerges the personality profile of a ***Machiavellian,* someone who views and manipulates others for purely personal gain.**

The subject of Machiavelli's book is manipulation as the basic means of gaining and keeping control of others. Among his admonitions to the prices of his day were

> "It is far better to be feared than loved if you cannot be both"
>
> "Princes should delegate to others the enactment of unpopular measures and keep neither own hands the distribution of favors."

From just these two short examples it is easy to see why Machiavelli's ideas have been so avidly read *and* heavily criticized over the years.

Psychologists have developed a series of instruments (called Mach scales) to measure a person's Machiavellian orientation.[28] A *high-Mach* personality is someone with tendencies to behave in ways consistent with Machiavelli's basic principles.

Additional predispositions of the high-Mach personality are: tendencies to approach situations logically and thoughtfully; capability of lying to achieve personal goals; they are not easily swayed by loyalty, friendships, past promises, or the opinions of others; and they are skilled at influencing others.

Research using the Mach scales has led to a number of predictions regarding the way high and low Machs behave in various situations. A "cool" and "detached" high-Mach personality can be expected to take control and try to exploit loosely structured situations, but will perform in a perfunctory, even detached manner in highly structured situations. Low Machs tend to accept direction imposed by others in loosely structured situations; they work hard to do well in highly structured ones.

## Type A and Type B Orientation

Let's switch gears for the moment and focus a bit more directly on *you.* Take the following quiz, and then read on.[29] Circle the number that best characterizes you on each of the following pairs of characteristics.

| | | | | | | | | | |
|---|---|---|---|---|---|---|---|---|---|
| Casual about appointments | 1 | 2 | 3 | 4 | 5 | 6 | 7 | 8 | Never late |
| Not competitive | 1 | 2 | 3 | 4 | 5 | 6 | 7 | 8 | Very competitive |
| Never feel rushed | 1 | 2 | 3 | 4 | 5 | 6 | 7 | 8 | Always feel rushed |
| Take one thing at a time | 1 | 2 | 3 | 4 | 5 | 6 | 7 | 8 | Try to do many things |
| Do things slowly | 1 | 2 | 3 | 4 | 5 | 6 | 7 | 8 | Do things fast |
| Express my feelings | 1 | 2 | 3 | 4 | 5 | 6 | 7 | 8 | Hold in my feelings |
| Many outside interests | 1 | 2 | 3 | 4 | 5 | 6 | 7 | 8 | Few outside interests |

**Type A orientation**
**Type B orientation**

The point of the quiz is to determine your orientation toward Type A or Type B behavior. This personality dimension has attracted a lot of interest from medical and organizational researchers alike. Those with a ***Type A orientation*** are characterized by impatience, desire for achievement, and perfectionism. Those with ***Type B orientations,*** on the other hand, are characterized as more easy-going and less competitive in relation to daily events.[30] Total your points for the seven items in the quiz. Multiply this total by 3 to arrive at a final score. Use this total to locate your Type A/Type B orientation on the following list.

| *Final Points* | *A/B Orientation* |
|---|---|
| Below 90 | B |
| 90–99 | B+ |
| 100–105 | A− |
| 106–119 | A |
| 120 or more | A+ |

Think about your Type A/Type B orientation and its implications—both in terms of your work and nonwork behaviors and your personal health. This issue will come up again in a career context in Chapter 18. For now, let's admit that Type A's tend to work fast and be impatient, uncomfortable, irritable, and aggressive. Such tendencies indicate "obsessive" behavior, a fairly widespread—but not always helpful—trait among managers. Many are hard-driving, detail-oriented people who have high-performance standards and thrive on routine. But when such work obsessions are carried to the extreme, they may lead to greater concerns for the details than the results, resistance to change, an over control of subordinates, and interpersonal difficulties.

# MANAGING INDIVIDUAL DIFFERENCES

Throughout Chapter 4, we stressed the importance of achieving a good fit between individual attributes and job requirements. An interesting example of how the nature of this fit can vary across cultures is shown in a recent comparison of Soviet and American female top managers.[31] Both sets of executives were similar in that they were highly educated, made their own opportunities, and were totally committed. However, there were differences. The Americans emphasized analytical abilities and specialized functional area knowledge; they also emphasized individualism, competitiveness, and discipline. In contrast, the Soviets emphasized team-oriented and general abilities, and interactions with groups outside their organization.

Differing job demands tied to national cultures and political economies may call for the differing attributes exhibited in these samples of female executives. It will be interesting to see if these differences fade as the Soviets economy becomes more market-driven and its political foundation turns more democratic.

The fit between individual attributes and the job is important at the management level of work responsibility. For example,

Courtesy of Walgreen Co.

ETHICAL PERSPECTIVE

## WALGREENS

**Walgreen Company is a large retail drugstore chain with over 1500 stores located in 28 states and Puerto Rico. Although dedicated to conservative fiscal policy and aggressive growth, the firm also recognizes its responsibility to be a good corporate citizen in the communities in which it operates. Carmen Pineiro, the chief pharmacist at Walgreen's Plaza Rio Hondo store in Bayamon, Puerto Rico, knows this commitment well—and she willingly helps fulfill it. She serves as a mentor and trainer for pharmacy students from the University of Puerto Rico. This helps them learn the practical sides of the pharmacy business. "It's also quite an honor for Walgreens too," says Carmen. "The University selects only the best community pharmacies."**

*General Motors* To be more competitive with foreign imports, GM spent billions of dollars on automation but found that its people didn't have the required abilities to function in these sophisticated plants (i.e., their abilities didn't "fit" the job requirements). GM's chairperson Roger Smith found out to his sorrow that "technology alone can't get the job done."

To achieve the desired fit between the person and job, managers need to pay special attention to individual differences. This can be done through special efforts in communications, training and development programs, and reward systems. Let's look at the management of values as an example. Among the things that can be done to help develop strong and desired values among organization members are:[32]

- *Programs to clarify and communicate values.* In order for values to provide the "rules of the road" for employees, they must be stated, shared, and understood by everyone in an organization. Formal programs to clarify and communicate important values can help accomplish this objective.

- *Proper attention to employee recruitment, selection, and orientation.* The values of prospective employees should be examined and discussed, and the results used in making selection decisions. A person's first encounters with an organization and its members also "say" a lot about key beliefs and values. Every attempt should be made to expose new hires to the "correct" values and expectations, and to teach them "the way we do things here."
- *Appropriate training and development programs.* Any organization should offer a variety of training and development opportunities to establish and maintain the skills of members. Values can and should be emphasized along with other important individual attributes.
- *Progressive reward systems.* Rewards in the form of monetary compensation, employee benefits, and special recognition can reinforce individual values and maintain enthusiasm in support of organizational values. Creative managers can find many ways to reward people for displaying the values that are considered essential to organizational success.

These and other strategies can be used by managers to achieve the best continuing match between job demands and the personal attributes of the individuals who must master them. The specific individual differences covered in this chapter are illustrative rather than exhaustive. We have simply tried to familiarize you with some of the important ones and with the related issues. Remember, high-performance foundations are first established when a manager achieves a good match between the requirements of a job and the individual attributes of any person asked to do it.

## SUMMARY

**Individual Performance Factors** are highlighted in this equation: Performance = individual attributes × work effort × organizational support. Individual attributes consist of the demographic, competency, and psychological characteristics discussed in this chapter. Work effort is reflected in the motivation to work and is treated in detail in the remaining three chapters in Part Two. Organizational support consists of a wide range of organizational support mechanisms such as tools, resources, instructions, and the like, which provide the opportunity for an individual to perform if he or she has the capacity and willingness. These important managerial issues are dealt with throughout the book.

**Demographic Differences Among Individuals** are background variables that help shape what a person has become. Some are current (e.g., socioeconomic status) and some are historical (e.g., where a person lived growing up). Age, gender, and race or ethnicity are particularly subject to stereotypical misconceptions. However, they are important individual attributes to address in managing successfully an increasingly diverse work force. Instead of resorting to stereotypes on such matters as male/female differences, it is always more meaningful to examine individual job competencies.

■ **Competency Differences Among Individuals** consist of aptitude (the capability to learn something) and ability (the existing capacity to do something). Aptitudes are potential abilities. Both physical and mental competencies are used in employee selection and training. Here, the assessments should be valid and job-related.

■ **Values and Attitudes** are a category of psychological characteristics that predispose one to behave in predictable ways. Values are global beliefs that guide actions and judgments across a variety of situations. They are especially important because they can influence such things as attitudes, perceptions, needs, and motivations. Values can also reflect differences among various societal and organizational cultures. Attitudes are similar to values but are more specific. They express predispositions to respond positively or negatively to someone or something in one's environment.

■ **Personality** represents an overall profile or a combination of traits that characterizes the unique nature of a person. Four personality theories widely studied by scholars are: psychoanalytic theory, trait theory; humanistic theory and social learning theory. Five personality traits especially relevant to managers in OB settings are: *locus of control* (the extent to which a person feels able to affect his or her life); *authoritarianism/dogmatism* (the rigidity of a person's beliefs); *problem-solving style* (one's orientation toward information gathering and evaluation in solving problems and making decisions); *Machiavellianism* (the extent to which one feels it appropriate to use manipulative behavior to influence others); and *Type A/Type B orientation* (the degree to which one is characterized as being impatient, pushing hard for achievement, and being perfectionist and highly competitive).

■ **Managing Individual Differences** involves attempting to get a good fit between individual attributes and job requirements. Such a fit involves giving special managerial attention to individual differences in such things as employee communications, recruitment, selection, new employee orientation, training and development programs, and reward systems. The achievement of this fit, in combination with work effort and organizational support aspects, is critical to the managerial implications of the individual performance equation.

## KEY TERMS

Ability
Aptitude
Attitude
Authoritarianism
Cognitive Dissonance
Demographic Characteristics
Dogmatism
Effectance Motive
Instrumental Values
Locus of Control

Machiavellianism
Motivation to Work
Personality
Problem-Solving Style
Psychological Characteristics
Situational Constraints
Terminal Values
Type A Orientation
Type B Orientation
Values
Value Congruence

## REVIEW QUESTIONS

1. Describe the individual performance equation. Use examples to show how each of the three major variables must be present if high performance is to be truly facilitated in the work setting.
2. List some forms of organizational support. Describe how a lack of organizational support might inhibit the otherwise capable and motivated person from doing a good job.
3. State and defend a list of competency characteristics that might be associated with high performance as (a) a market researcher, (b) personnel specialist, and (c), assembly-line worker.
4. Find an example from a newspaper or magazine of age, gender, or other improper discrimination in employment. Analyze and explain why such discrimination occurs and state how it might be eliminated.
5. Do you believe that entrance tests (e.g., SAT, GMAT) are useful and fair as screening devices for selecting applicants to colleges and various professional schools? Why or why not?
6. Make a list of the values and attitudes you expect to be associated with success as a manager. Defend your list.
7. Make a list of the personality characteristics that you expect to be associated with success as a manager. Defend your list.
8. Describe the basic tendencies of a Type A orientation. Discuss the challenges likely to be encountered as the supervisor of someone with strong Type A tendencies.

## AN OB LIBRARY

Albert J. Bernstein and Sydney Craft Rozen, *Dinosaur Brains: Dealing with All Those Impossible People at Work* (New York: John Wiley & Sons, 1989).

Dov Eden, *Pygmalion in Management: Productivity as a Self-Fulfilling Prophesy* (Lexington, MA: Lexington Books, 1990).

Joseph A. Raelin, *Clash of Cultures: Managers and Professionals* (Cambridge, MA: Harvard University Press, 1986).

Peter B. Vaill, *Managing as a Performing Art* (San Francisco: Jossey-Bass, 1989).

John P. Wanous, *Organizational Entry: Recruitment, Selection, and Socialization of Newcomers* (Reading, MA: Addison-Wesley, 1980).

EXERCISE

# ALLIGATOR RIVER STORY

## *Objectives*

1. To help you realize the different perceptions, values, and attitudes that people have on common, everyday happenings.
2. To give you an opportunity to compare your values with those of your classmates.

## *Total Time*

60 to 75 minutes

## *Procedure*

1. Read "The Alligator River Story,"[33] which follows. After reading the story, rank the five characters in the story beginning with the one whom you consider as the most offensive and end with the one whom you consider the least objectionable. That is, the character who seems to be the most reprehensible to you should be entered first in the list following the story, then the second most reprehensible, and so on, with the least reprehensible or objectionable being entered fifth. Of course, you will have your own reasons as to why you rank them in the order that you do. Very briefly note this too.
2. Form groups as assigned by your instructor (at least four persons per group with gender mixed).
3. Each group should:
   a. Elect a spokesperson for the group.
   b. Compare how the group members ranked the characters.
   c. Examine the reasons used by each of the members for their rankings.
   d. Seek consensus on a final group ranking.
4. Following your group discussions, you will be asked to share your outcomes and reasons for agreement or non-agreement. A general class discussion will then be held.

## *The Alligator River Story*

There lived a woman named Abigail who was in love with a man named Gregory. Gregory lived on the shore of a river. Abigail lived on the opposite shore of the same river. The river that separated the two lovers was teeming with dangerous alligators. Abigail wanted to cross the river to be with Gregory. Unfortunately, the bridge had been washed out by a heavy flood the previous week. So she went to ask Sinbad, a riverboat captain, to take her across. He said he would be glad to if she would consent to go to bed with him prior to the voyage. She promptly refused and went to a friend named Ivan to explain her plight. Ivan did not want to get involved at all in the situation. Abigail felt her only alternative was to accept Sinbad's terms. Sinbad fulfilled his promise to Abigail and delivered her into the arms of Gregory.

When Abigail told Gregory about her amorous escapade in order to cross the river, Gregory cast her aside with disdain. Heartsick and rejected, Abigail turned to Slug with her tale of woe. Slug, feeling compassion for Abigail, sought out Gregory and beat him brutally. Abigail was overjoyed at the sight of Gregory getting his due. As the sun set on the horizon, people heard Abigail laughing at Gregory.

| *Rank* | *Name* | *Reasons* |
|---|---|---|
| First | | |
| Second | | |
| Third | | |
| Fourth | | |
| Fifth | | |

CASE

## REVERSE DISCRIMINATION[33]

At a meeting of all management personnel, the legal advisor to the Rampart Insurance Company spoke on the subject of employee discrimination with special emphasis on subjects relating to employees of minority groups and female employees. Essentially the message was that there should be no discriminatory decisions by managers relating to the selection and hiring process, promotion policies, seniority, recognition, vacations, work loads, and so forth.

The managers of the company accepted the advice seriously, and under a climate established and implemented by the president, administered the philosophy vigorously. In some cases, women who had good performance records, equal seniority with men, and other minimal qualifications were promoted to supervisory positions, even though they might be married, have several children, and could not work overtime when needed. In other cases, employees who were classed as members of minority groups were purposely rated high on employee evaluation reports so a basis could be established for justifying a forthcoming promotion.

After about a year had passed, other nonmanagement employees gave signs that they were upset, dissatisfied, and angry about the newly introduced managerial philosophy. When no attention was given to their statements that they were now being discriminated against, and when no action came forth when they requested a hearing with the president, the informal leaders of the group posted a notice on all bulletin boards which read as follows:

All employees who are dissatisfied with present management practices and who desire to meet and discuss the organization of an independent union or discuss the possibility of affiliating with a natural union, please sign below.

### *Questions*

1. Where and how does the individual performance equation apply to this case? Give specific examples of the individual attributes that appear to be of special importance.
2. In view of your response to the prior question, has Rampart's president done a good job on the issue of employee discrimination? Why or why not?
3. What would you do now as president of Rampart Insurance Company? Why?

This study outline of major topics is meant to organize your reading now; it is repeated in the Summary to structure your review.

## STUDY OUTLINE

- Content and Process Theories
- Maslow's Hierarchy of Needs Theory

Aldefer's ERG Theory

- McClelland's Acquired Needs Theory

Three Types of Acquired Needs   The Research

- Herzberg's Two-Factor Theory

Dissatisfiers or Hygiene Factors   Satisfiers or Motivator Factors
Research and Practical Implications

- Questions and Answers on the Content Theories
- Equity Theory

Resolving Felt Inequities   Managing the Equity Dynamic

# CHAPTER 5

# MOTIVATION THEORIES



## PHOTO ESSAYS

# VISIONS 5

**While almost everyone is looking at the business world for tips on executive excellence, nonprofit organizations are doing their jobs too. In fact, there's a lot to be learned from people like Frances Hesselbein. Says management guru Peter F. Drucker: "If I had to put somebody in to take Roger Smith's place at GM, I would pick Frances."**

**Frances Hesselbein is the recently retired head of the Girl Scouts. Her accomplishments in turning around this organization—struggling for its life in 1976 when Frances took over and now counting a robust 2.3 million in membership—are legendary. She managed the Girl Scouts with a clear sense of mission: helping girls reach their highest potential. Of this clear sense of mission, she says, "more than any one thing made the difference." With that mission and her dedication to excellence, Frances and the people she motivated accomplished great things.**

In this chapter we examine a number of current motivation theories. These are an important foundation for the ideas to be developed throughout the rest of this book. Before looking at the separate theories, recall the definition of motivation given in Chapter 4. ***Motivation to work*** refers to the forces within an individual that account for the level, direction, and persistence of effort expended at work.

Motivation to work

## CONTENT AND PROCESS THEORIES

Content

Needs

Motives

It is useful to think of two broad categories of motivation theories. ***Content theories*** emphasize the reasons for motivated behavior and/or what causes it. They explain behavior in terms of specific human ***needs*** or ***motives***—terms we use interchangeably. Content theories help to represent physiological or psychological deficiencies that an individual feels some compulsion to eliminate. Content theories lend insight into people's needs and, thus, help a manager to understand (1) what it is within individuals that energizes and sustains their behavior, and (2) what they will and will not value as work rewards. The theories of Maslow, Alderfer, McClelland, and Herzberg are addressed here as two of the better known representatives of the "content" orientation.

Process theories

Content theories are sometimes criticized as being static and descriptive. The ***process theories*** offer a more dynamic alternative. They strive to provide an understanding of the thought or cognitive processes that take place within the minds of people and that act to influence their behavior. We will discuss two process theories that offer significant managerial implications: the equity theory and the expectancy theory.

The content and process motivation theories complement rather than compete with one another. While the content theories are less directly linked with work efforts than job satisfactions, the process theories tend to be directly concerned with work efforts and their performance implications. Together they address both performance and satisfaction as key work outcomes. Ultimately, we will use expectancy theory to integrate the insights of the content and process theories in a way that is most useful to the practicing manager.[1]

# MASLOW'S HIERARCHY OF NEEDS THEORY

Maslow's hierarchy of needs theory as shown in Figure 5.1, identifies ***higher-order needs***—self-actualization and esteem—and ***lower-order needs***—social, safety and physiological. His formulation suggests a pre-

**Higher-order needs**
**Lower-order needs**

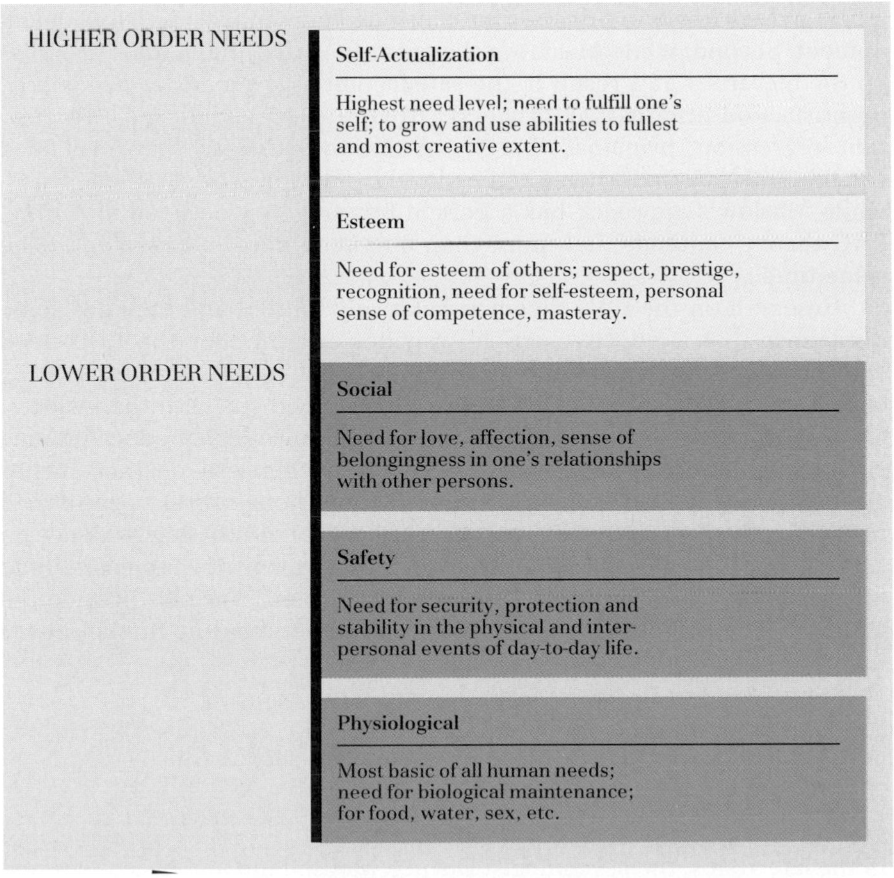

*FIGURE 5.1 Maslow's Hierarchy of Needs.*

| | |
|---|---|
| HIGHER ORDER NEEDS | **Self-Actualization**<br>Highest need level; need to fulfill one's self; to grow and use abilities to fullest and most creative extent. |
| | **Esteem**<br>Need for esteem of others; respect, prestige, recognition, need for self-esteem, personal sense of competence, masteray. |
| LOWER ORDER NEEDS | **Social**<br>Need for love, affection, sense of belongingness in one's relationships with other persons. |
| | **Safety**<br>Need for security, protection and stability in the physical and interpersonal events of day-to-day life. |
| | **Physiological**<br>Most basic of all human needs; need for biological maintenance; for food, water, sex, etc. |

potency of these needs. Some are assumed to be more important (potent) than others and must be satisfied before the other needs can serve as motivators. Thus, according to the figure, the physiological needs must be satisfied before the safety needs are activated and the safety needs must be satisfied before the social needs are activated, and so on.

Research identifies some tendency for higher-order needs to increase in importance over lower-order needs as individuals move up the managerial hierarchy.[2] Other studies report that needs vary according to a person's career stage,[3] organization size,[4] and even geographical location.[5] However, there is no consistent evidence that the satisfaction of a need at one level will decrease its importance and increase the importance of the next higher need.[6] As a result, some theorists have tried to modify Maslow's theory and make it more realistic in terms of daily individual behavior. One of the most promising among these latter efforts is the ERG (existence, relatedness, growth) theory of Clayton Alderfer.

### Alderfer's ERG Theory

**Existence needs**

**Relatedness needs**

**Growth needs**

ERG theory differs from Maslow's theory in three basic respects.[7] First, the theory collapses Maslow's five need categories into three: ***existence needs*** relate to people's desires for physiological and material well-being; ***relatedness needs*** represent desires for satisfying interpersonal relationships; ***growth needs*** are desires for continued personal growth and development. Second, while Maslow's theory argues that individuals progress up the hierarchy as a result of the satisfaction of lower-order needs (i.e., a satisfaction-progression process), ERG theory includes a "frustration–regression" principal whereby an already satisfied lower-level need can become activated when a higher-level need cannot be satisfied. Third, while Maslow's approach has a person focusing on one need at a time, ERG theory contends that more than one need may be activated at the same time.

Research on the ERG theory is relatively limited and includes some disclaimers.[8] A supportive article provides evidence for the ERG need categories and reports additional findings.[9] Among the more interesting of these are: (1) blacks had greater existence need strength than whites, (2) growth needs were greater for those with more highly educated parents, and (3) women had lower strength of existence needs and higher strength of relatedness needs than men. Even though future research is needed to shed additional light on its validity, the supporting evidence on ERG theory is stronger than for Maslow's theory. For now, the combined satisfaction–progression and frustration–regression principles provide the manager with a more flexible approach to understanding human needs than does Maslow's strict hierarchy.

## McCLELLAND'S ACQUIRED NEEDS THEORY

In the late 1940s, the psychologist David I. McClelland and his co-workers began experimenting with the Thematic Apperception Test (TAT for short)

Courtesy of Mary Kay Cosmetics, Inc.

SKILLS PERSPECTIVE

## MARY KAY COSMETICS

**The "pink luxury cars" driven by Mary Kay Cosmetics, Inc., superstars are almost legendary in some parts of the United States. Founder Mary Kay Ash's skill at using recognition and rewards to motivate employees is also becoming legendary in management circles. Founded in 1963 on a $5000 investment, the company now operates in 12 countries and is considered one of the world's largest cosmetics empires. The sales force pursues a program structured with many contests and rewards in addition to regular income. Recognition for outstanding performance ranges from photos in monthly magazines to incentive gifts such as cars, vacation trips, and diamond jewelry. The company's ability to motivate employees adds a strong performance push to a company which was initially founded to help provide women with unlimited opportunity for success.**

as a way of measuring human needs.[10] The TAT asks people to view pictures and write stories about what they see.

## Three Types of Acquired Needs

In one case, McClelland tested three executives using a photograph that shows a man sitting down and looking at family photos arranged on his work desk. One executive wrote of an engineer who was daydreaming about a family outing scheduled for the next day. Another described a designer who had picked up an idea for a new gadget from remarks made by his family. The third saw an engineer who was intently working on a bridge-stress problem that he seemed sure to solve because of his confident look.[11]

McClelland distinguishes three themes that appear in such TAT stories. Each theme corresponds to an underlying need that he feels is important for understanding individual behavior. These needs are:

**Need for achievement**

- ***Need for Achievement (nAch):*** The desire to do something better or more efficiently, to solve problems, or to master complex tasks.

**Need for affiliation**

- ***Need for Affiliation (nAff):*** The desire to establish and maintain friendly and warm relations with other persons.

**Need for power**

- ***Need for Power (nPower):*** The desire to control other persons, to influence their behavior, to be responsible for other people.

McClelland's basic theory is that these three needs are acquired over time and as a result of life experiences. People are motivated by the needs, and each can be associated with individual work preferences. The theory encourages managers to learn how to identify the presence of nAch, nAff, and nPower in themselves and other people and to be able to create work environments that are responsive to the respective need profiles.

Let's go back to the picture of the man sitting at his desk. McClelland scored the stories given by the three executives as follows:

| | |
|---|---|
| Person dreaming about family outing: | nAch = +1 |
| Person pondering new idea for gadget: | nAch = +2 |
| Person working on bridge-stress problem: | nAch = +4 |

## The Research

Research lends considerable insight into nAch and includes some particularly interesting applications in developing nations. For example, McClelland trained business people in Kakinda, India to think, talk, and act like high achievers by having them write stories about achievement and participate in a business game that encouraged achievement. They also met with successful entrepreneurs and learned how to set challenging goals for their own businesses. Over a two-year period following these activities, these people engaged in activities creating twice as many new jobs as those who didn't get training.[12]

There are two especially relevant managerial applications of McClelland's theory. First, it is especially useful in linking each need with a set of work preferences as shown in Table 5.1. Second, if these needs are truly acquired, it may be possible to acquaint people with the need profiles required to be successful in various types of jobs. One interesting direction of McClelland's research, for example, seeks to identify the need profiles typical of successful managers. Working with what he calls the "leadership motive pattern," McClelland has found that the combination of moderate to high need for power and lower need for affiliation enables people to be effective managers at higher levels in organizations. High nPower creates the willingness to have influence or impact on others; lower nAff allows the manager to make difficult decisions without undue worry of being disliked.[13]

The Power need is particularly interesting. A management consultant, Charles M. Kelly, uses the term "destructive achiever" to describe executives high in nPower, but who misuse that power. These people usually have charisma and other characteristics to get promoted to high-level positions but because they misuse their power, they usually don't make it to the top—they tend to get sabotaged by those they stepped on earlier.[14] This example reinforces McClelland's point that nPower is most useful

*TABLE 5.1*
**WORK PREFERENCES OF PERSONS HIGH IN NEED FOR ACHIEVEMENT, AFFILIATION, AND POWER**

| *Individual Need* | *Work Preferences* | *Example* |
|---|---|---|
| High need for achievement | Individual responsibility<br>Challenging but doable goals<br>Feedback on performance | Field sales person with challenging quota and opportunity to earn individual bonus; entrepreneur |
| High need for affiliation | Interpersonal relationships<br>Opportunities to communicate | Customer service representative; member of work unit subject to group wage bonus plan |
| High need for power | Influence over other persons<br>Attention<br>Recognition | Formal position of supervisory responsibility; appointment as head of special task force or committee |

for managers when it is used to accomplish group and organization goals, rather than being used selfishly.

# HERZBERG'S TWO-FACTOR THEORY[15]

Some time ago Frederick Herzberg began his research on motivation by asking workers two straightforward questions:

1. "Tell me about a time when you felt exceptionally good about your job."
2. "Tell me about a time when you felt exceptionally bad about your job."

After analyzing almost 4000 responses to these questions, as shown in Figure 5.2, Herzberg and his associates developed the *two-factor theory*. They noticed that respondents identified different things as sources of work satisfaction—subsequently called satisfiers or motivator factors—than they did as sources of dissatisfaction—subsequently called dissatisfiers or hygiene factors.

## Dissatisfiers or Hygiene Factors

**Hygiene factors**
**Job context**

***Hygiene factors*** are associated with the ***job context,*** which are aspects of a person's work setting. That is, job satisfaction is linked more to where people work than to the nature of the work itself. Among the hygiene factors shown on the left in Figure 5.2, perhaps the most surprising is salary. Herzberg found that low salary makes people dissatisfied but paying them more does not satisfy or motivate them. Improved working conditions (e.g., special offices, air conditioning) act in the same way. The reason for these conclusions is that in the two-factor theory, job satisfac-

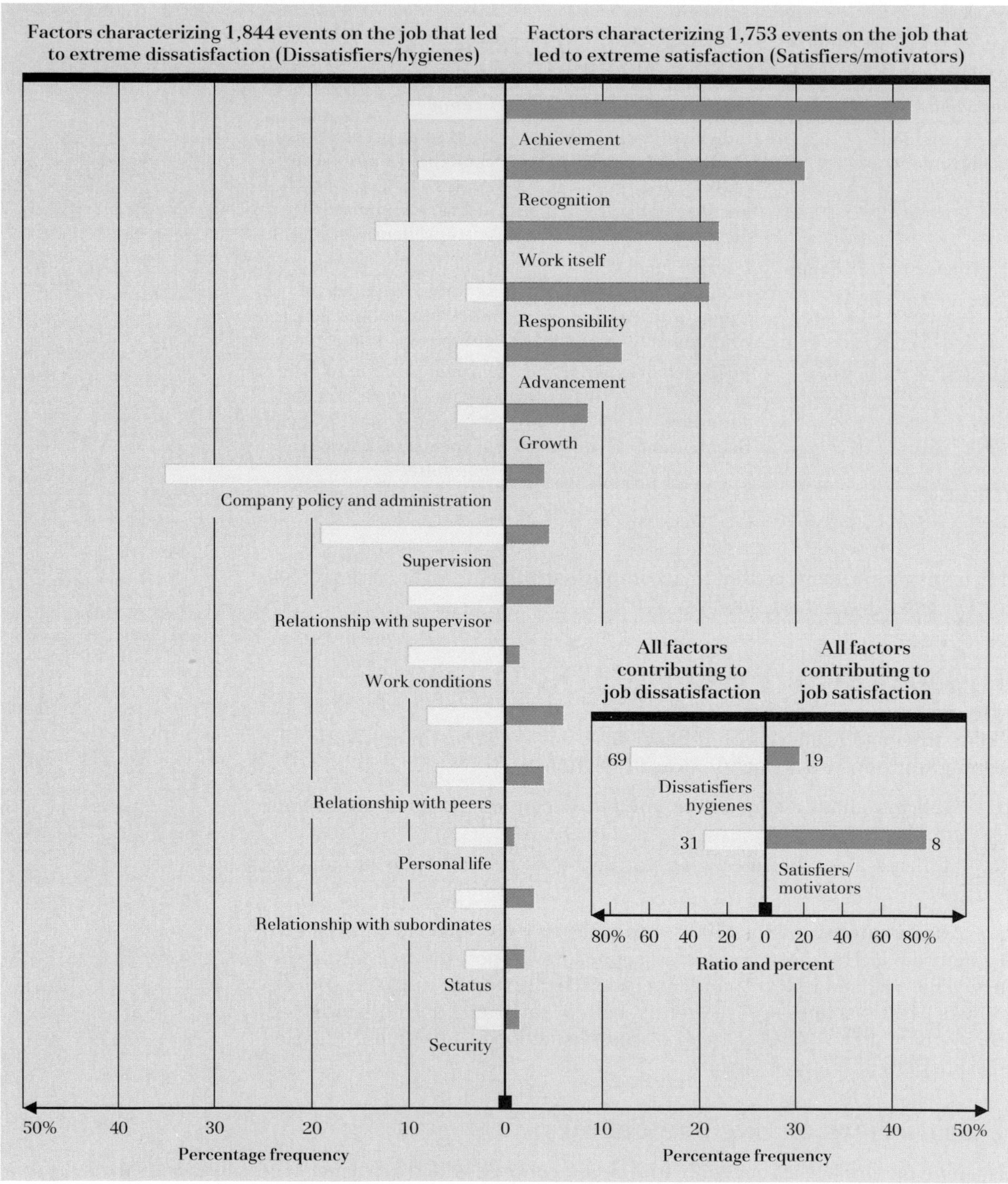


*FIGURE 5.2 Herzberg's Two-factor Theory: Sources of satisfaction and dissatisfaction as reported in 12 investigations.*
(Adapted from Frederick Herzberg, "One More Time: How Do You Motivate Employees?" Harvard Business Review, Vol. 46, January–February, 1968, p. 57. 

*TABLE 5.2*
**SAMPLE HYGIENE FACTORS FOUND IN WORK SETTINGS**

| *Hygiene Factors* | *Examples* |
|---|---|
| Organizational policies, procedures | Attendance rules<br>Vacation schedules<br>Grievance procedures<br>Performance appraisal methods |
| Working conditions | Noise levels<br>Safety<br>Personal comfort<br>Size of work area |
| Interpersonal relationships | Co-worker relations<br>Customer relations<br>Relationship with boss |
| Quality of supervision | Technical competence of boss |
| Base salary | Hourly wage rate or salary |

tion and job dissatisfaction are totally separate dimensions. Table 5.2 shows other examples of a number of hygiene factors in work settings.

## Satisfiers or Motivator Factors

Improving a hygiene factor, such as working conditions, will not make people satisfied with their work. It will only prevent them from being dissatisfied. To improve ***satisfaction*** the manager must use ***motivator factors*** as shown in the right of Figure 5.2. They are related to ***job content***: what people actually do in their work. Adding these satisfiers or motivators to people's jobs is Herzberg's link to performance. These cover such things as sense of achievement, recognition, responsibility, and so on. According to Herzberg, when these opportunities are absent, workers will neither be satisfied nor perform well.

**Motivator factors**
**Job content**

## Research and Practical Implications

OB scholars debate the merits of the two-factor theory.[16] Herzberg's continuing research and that of his followers supports the theory. Some researchers have used different methods and find they are unable to confirm the theory. It is therefore criticized as being method-bound, that is, as being supportable only by applying Herzberg's original methodology. This is a serious criticism, since the scientific approach requires that theories be verifiable when different research methods are used.

With all this debate, you may ask if the two-factor theory is of any value. We think it is because of the discipline it adds to managerial thinking. Many managers allocate considerable time, attention, and other resources to things that Herzberg would consider hygiene factors. Special office fixtures, piped-in music, fancy lounges for breaks, and high-base salaries are examples. The two-factor theory suggests caution in expecting too much performance impact from these investments. Herzberg's theory is perhaps even more useful because it is associated with a specific technique for building satisfiers into job content. This approach is called job enrichment, and we give it special attention in Chapter 7.

## QUESTIONS AND ANSWERS ON THE CONTENT THEORIES

There is a lot of similarity in the content theories as shown in Figure 5.3. Although content theorists disagree somewhat concerning the exact nature of human needs, they do agree that:

$$\text{Individual needs} \xrightarrow{\text{activate}} \text{tensions} \xrightarrow[\text{influence}]{\text{that}} \text{attitudes and behavior}$$

Stated even more precisely, content theorists suggest that the manager's job is to create work environments that respond positively to individual needs. Such things as poor performance, undesirable behaviors, and/or decreased satisfaction can be partially explained in terms of "blocked" needs or those that are not satisfied on the job. Also the motivational value of rewards can be analyzed in terms of "activated" needs to which a given reward either does or does not respond. Ultimately, content theorists argue that managers must:

- ▶ Understand how individuals differ in what they need from their work.
- ▶ Know what can be offered to these individuals in response to their needs.
- ▶ Know how to create work settings that give people the opportunity to satisfy their needs by contributing to the task performance of the work unit and organization.

*FIGURE 5.3 Comparison of content motivation theories.*

| MASLOW | ALDEFER | McCLELLAND | HERZBERG |
|---|---|---|---|
| Need hierarchy | ERG Theory | Acquired needs theory | Two-factor theory |
| Self-actualization<br>Esteem | Growth | Need for achievement<br>Need for power | Motivators satisfiers |
| Social | Relatedness | Need for affiliation | Hygiene dissatisfiers |
| Safety and security<br>Physiological | Existence | | |

Finally, let's look at some questions you still may have about these content theories and their managerial implications.

1. *How many different individual needs are there?* Research has not yet defined the complete list of work-related individual needs. Each of the needs we have discussed has been found to be especially useful by various experts. As a manager, you can use these needs as a starting point for understanding the many different needs that people may bring with them to the work setting.
2. *Can one work outcome satisfy more than one need?* Yes, some work outcomes or rewards can satisfy or block more than one need. Pay is a good example. It is a source of performance feedback for the high need achiever. Pay can also be a source of security as well as a way of satisfying physiological and social needs.
3. *Is there a hierarchy of needs?* Research evidence fails to support the existence of a precise five-step hierarchy of needs as postulated by Maslow. Rather, the evidence seems to suggest that it is more legitimate to picture needs operating in a more flexible hierarchy, such as the one in ERG theory. Also, it appears useful to distinguish between lower-order and higher-order needs in terms of motivational properties.
4. *How important are the various needs?* Research is inconclusive as to the importance of various needs. Individuals probably vary in this regard. Also, they may value needs differently at different times.
5. *What is the manager's responsibility as defined by the content theories?* Although their details vary, each content theory generally suggests that the manager is responsible for creating a work environment within which individual subordinates find opportunities to satisfy their important needs. To the extent that some needs are acquired, the manager's responsibility may also include acquainting subordinates with the value of needs to which the work setting can positively respond.

# EQUITY THEORY

As useful as they are, content theories still emphasize the "what" aspect of motivation and do not provide information on thought processes (the "how" aspect). For these things we must turn to process theories of motivation like the equity theory, which is based on the phenomenon of social comparison. We know it best through the writings of J. Stacy Adams.[17] He argues that when people gauge the fairness of their work outcomes in comparison with others, felt inequity is a motivating state of mind. That is, when people perceive inequity in their work, they will be aroused to remove the discomfort and restore a sense of felt equity to the situation. Inequities exist whenever people feel that the rewards or inducements received for their work inputs or contributions are unequal to the rewards other persons appear to have received for their inputs. For the individual, the equity comparison or thought process that determines such feeling is

$$\frac{\text{Individual rewards}}{\text{Individual inputs}} \underset{\text{with}}{\overset{\text{compared}}{\longleftrightarrow}} \frac{\text{Others' rewards}}{\text{Others' inputs}}$$

INTERNATIONAL PERSPECTIVE

## COLGATE-PALMOLIVE

Courtesy of Colgate-Palmolive Co.

**Colgate Overseas is a major contributor to Colgate-Palmolive's profit growth. In fact, the company believes long-term growth will mainly be achieved through the firm's worldwide marketing and sales network in more than 160 countries. Rallying the talents and energies of over 25,000 employees around the globe is no small challenge for Colgate. An improved compensation system for the international sales force now links commissions with corporate profitability, and new labor agreements call for increased flexibility, greater teamwork, and more employee involvement in decision making.**

## Resolving Felt Inequities

Felt inequity

A ***felt negative inequity*** exists when an individual feels that he or she has received relatively less than others in proportion to work inputs. ***Felt positive inequity*** exists when an individual feels he or she has received relatively more than others. Both felt negative and felt positive inequity are motivating states. When either exists, the individual is predicted to engage in one or more of the following behaviors (shown with examples for perceived negative inequity) to restore a sense of equity.

1. Change work inputs (e.g., reduce performance efforts).
2. Change rewards received (e.g., ask for a raise).
3. Leave the situation (e.g., quit).
4. Change the comparison points (e.g., compare self to a different co-worker).
5. Psychologically distort the comparisons (e.g., rationalize that the inequity is only temporary and will be resolved in the future).

6. Take actions to change the inputs or outputs of the comparison person (e.g., get a co-worker to accept more work).

Equity theory predicts that people who feel under-rewarded or over-rewarded for their work will act to restore a sense of equity. The research of Adams and others, largely accomplished in laboratory settings, lends tentative support to this prediction.[18] People who feel overpaid (felt positive inequity) have been found to increase the quantity or quality of their work, while those who are underpaid (felt negative inequity) do the opposite. The research is most conclusive in respect to felt negative inequity, it appears people are less comfortable when underrewarded than when overrewarded.

## Managing the Equity Dynamic

Figure 5.4 shows that the equity comparison actually intervenes between a manager's allocation of rewards and his or her impact on the work behavior of subordinates. Feelings of inequity are determined solely by the individual's interpretation of the situation. Thus, the assumption that all employees in a work unit will view their annual pay raise as fair is incorrect. It is not how a manager feels about the allocation of rewards that counts; it is how the individuals receiving the rewards feel or perceive them that will determine the motivational outcomes of the equity dynamic.

Managing the equity dynamic thus becomes quite central to the manager who strives to maintain healthy psychological contracts, that is, fairly balanced inducements and contributions, among subordinates. For example,

> ***Toronto Sun Publishing, Corporation*** "Equal pay for equal work" is becoming a reality as the Toronto Sun's employees experience the effects of Ontario's new law on pay equity. A comprehensive review of all jobs was conducted and points assigned to each according to set criteria. Where less-paid but equivalent jobs performed mostly by women were found equivalent to others performed mostly by men, salary adjustments were made.

Rewards that are received with feelings of equity can foster job satisfaction and performance; rewards received with feelings of negative inequity can damage these key work results. The burden lies with the manager to take control of the situation and make sure that any negative consequences of the equity comparison are avoided, or at least minimized, when rewards are allocated. A manager should:

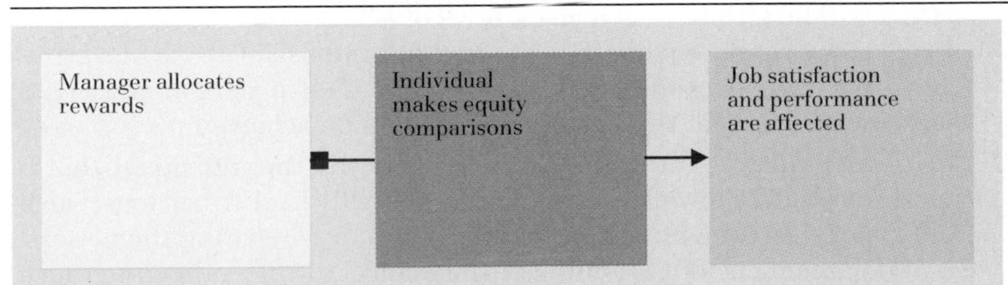


*FIGURE 5.4 The equity comparison as an intervening variable in the rewards, satisfaction, and performance relationship.*

- Recognize that an equity comparison will likely be made by each subordinate whenever especially visible rewards such as pay, promotions, and so on are being allocated.
- Anticipate felt negative inequities. Carefully communicate to each individual your evaluation of the reward, an appraisal of the performance upon which it is based, and the comparison points you consider to be appropriate.

# EXPECTANCY THEORY

In 1964, a book by Victor Vroom covering an expectancy theory of work motivation made an important contribution to the OB literature.[19] The theory seeks to predict or explain the task-related effort expended by a person. The theory's central question—of both theoretical and managerial relevance—is "What determines the willingness of an individual to exert personal effort to work at tasks that contribute to the performance of the work unit and the organization?" To answer this question, Vroom argues that managers must know three things.

1. The person's belief that working hard will enable various levels of task performance to be achieved.
2. The person's belief that various work outcomes or rewards will result from the achievement of the various levels of work performance.
3. The value the individual assigns to these work outcomes.

## The Theory

Expectancy theory argues that work motivation is determined by individual beliefs regarding effort–performance relationships and the desirabilities of various work outcomes that are associated with different performance levels. Simply put, the theory is based on the logic: "People *will do* what they *can do* when they *want to*."[20]

### Key Terms

Figure 5.5 illustrates the managerial foundations of expectancy theory. Individuals are viewed as making conscious decisions to allocate their behavior toward work efforts and serve self-interests. The three key terms in the theory are:

**Expectancy**

1. ***Expectancy:*** The probability assigned by an individual that work effort will be followed by a given level of achieved task performance. Expectancy would equal "0" if it were felt impossible to achieve the given performance level; it would equal "1" if a person were 100 percent certain that the performance could be achieved.

**Instrumentality**

2. ***Instrumentality:*** The probability assigned by the individual that a given level of achieved task performance will lead to various work outcomes. Instrumentality also varies from "1," meaning the reward is 100 percent certain to follow performance, to "0," indicating there is no chance that performance will lead to the reward."[21]

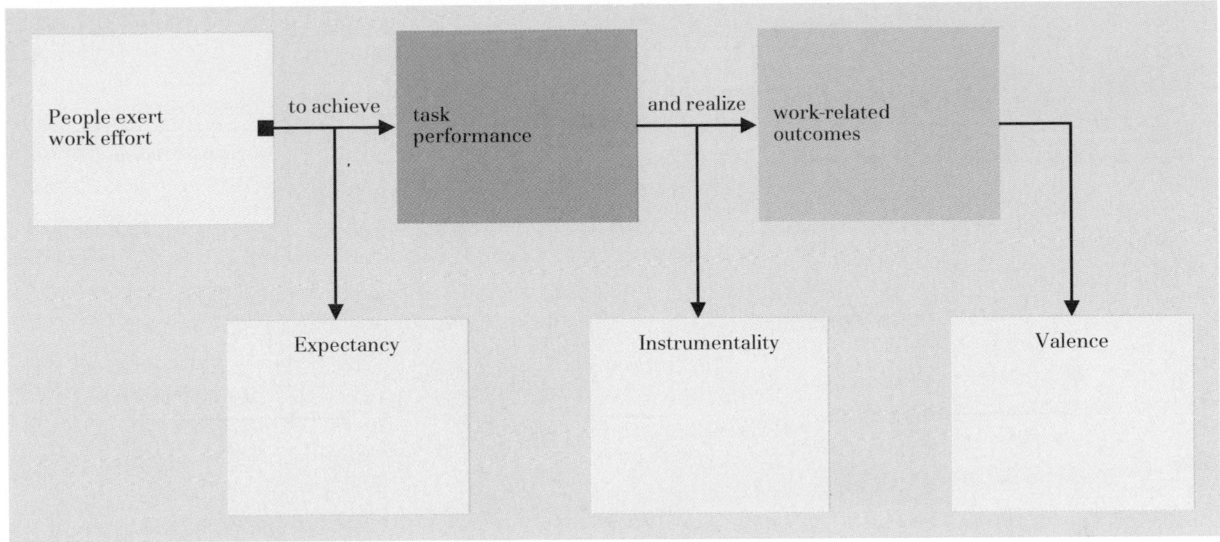


FIGURE 5.5 Expectancy theory terms in a managerial perspective.

**Valence**

3. ***Valence:*** The value attached by the individual to various work outcomes. Valences form a scale from -1 (very undesirable outcome) to +1 (very desirable outcome).

## *Multiplier Effects and Multiple Outcomes*

Vroom posits that motivation ($M$), expectancy ($E$), instrumentality ($I$), and valence ($V$) are related to one another by the equation.

$$M = E \times I \times V$$

The equation states that motivation to work results from expectancy times instrumentality times valence. This multiplicative relationship means that the motivational appeal of a given work path is sharply reduced whenever any one or more of expectancy, instrumentality, or valence approaches the value of zero. Conversely, for a given reward to have a high and positive motivational impact as a work outcome, the expectancy, instrumentality, and valence associated with the reward must all be high and positive.

Suppose that a manager is wondering whether or not the prospect of earning a merit pay raise will be motivational to a subordinate. Expectancy theory predicts that motivation to work hard to earn the merit pay will be *low* if:

1. Expectancy is low—a person feels that he or she cannot achieve the necessary performance level.
2. Instrumentality is low—the person is not confident a high level of task performance will result in a high merit pay raise.
3. Valence is low—the person places little value on a merit pay increase.
4. Any combination of these exists.

The multiplier effect requires managers to act to maximize expectancy, instrumentality, and valence when seeking to create high levels of work

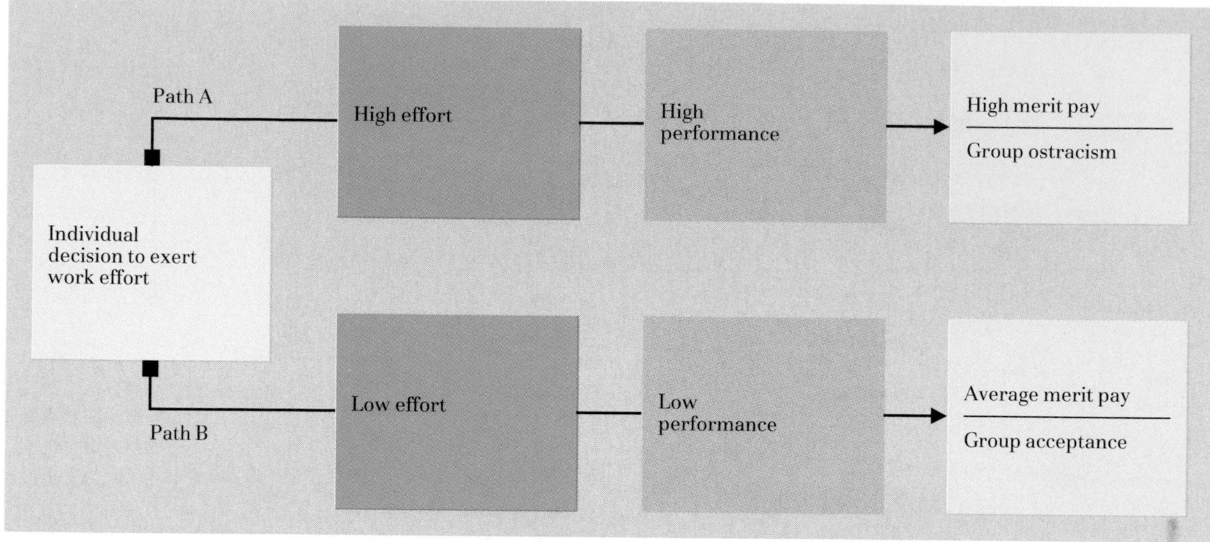


*FIGURE 5.6 An example of individual thought processes as viewed by expectancy theory.*

motivation among subordinates through the allocation of certain work rewards. A "zero" at any location on the right side of the expectancy equation will result in "zero" motivation.

Expectancy theory is able to accommodate multiple work outcomes in predicting motivation. Going back to the earlier case (see Figure 5.6), the outcome of a merit pay increase may not be the only one affecting the individual's decision to work hard. Relationships with co-workers may also be important, and they may be undermined if the individual stands out from the group as a high performer. Even though merit pay is both

*TABLE 5.3*
**MANAGERIAL IMPLICATIONS OF EXPECTANCY THEORY**

| *Expectancy Term* | *The Individual's Question* | *Managerial Implications* |
|---|---|---|
| Expectancy | "Can I achieve the desired level of task performance?" | Select workers with ability<br>Train workers to use ability<br>Support ability with organizational resources<br>Identify performance goals |
| Instrumentality | "What work outcomes will be received as a result of the performance?" | Clarify psychological contracts<br>Communicate performance → reward possibilities<br>Confirm performance → reward possibilities by making actual rewards contingent upon performance |
| Valence | "How highly do I value the work outcomes?" | Identify individual needs or outcomes<br>Adjust available rewards to match these |

Courtesy of Wal-Mart Stores, Inc.

ETHICAL PERSPECTIVE

## WAL-MART

**Sam Walton, Wal-Mart's founder, is considered to be America's richest man. Obviously, "Mr. Sam" knew what he was doing when he established the principles upon which his large and fast-growing retail chain still operates. The core customer strategy is a good one—"everyday low prices." But this strategy wouldn't succeed without Wal-Mart's "team spirit" and the belief that its employees make the difference. Employees, who are called "associates," are treated with great respect. Associates are encouraged to buy company stock, participate in profit-sharing, and qualify for bonuses. In addition, they are regularly asked for suggestions. Says one senior executive: "Most of the good ideas come from the bottom up." Staying in touch with employees isn't just good ethics at Wal-Mart, it's also good business.**

highly valued and considered accessible to the individual, its motivational power can be canceled out by the negative effects of high performance on the individual's social relationships with his or her co-workers. One of the advantages of expectancy theory is its ability to help managers take into account such multiple outcomes when trying to determine the motivational value of various work rewards to individual subordinates.

## Managerial Applications

The managerial implications of Vroom's expectancy theory are summarized in Table 5.3. Basically, expectancy logic argues that a manager must try to understand individual thought processes and then actively intervene in the work situation to influence them. This includes trying to maximize work expectancies, instrumentalities, and valences that support the organization's production purposes. Said differently, a manager should strive to create a work setting so that work contributions serving the organization's needs also will be valued by the individual as paths toward desired personal outcomes or rewards.

Table 5.3 shows that a manager can influence expectancies by selecting individuals with proper abilities, training people to use these abilities, supporting people with abilities by providing the needed resources, and identifying desired task goals. Instrumentality is influenced by clarifying performance → reward relationships in the psychological contract, by communicating revised performance → reward relationships specific to a given situation, and by confirming performance → reward expectations through direct action, that is, by actually rewarding desirable performance once it occurs.

## The Research

There's a lot of research on expectancy theory, and good review articles are available.[22] Although the theory has received substantial support, specific details, such as the operation of the multiplier effect, remain subject to question. Rather than charging that the underlying theory is inadequate, however, researchers indicate that their inability to generate more confirming data may be caused by problems of methodology and measurement. Thus, while awaiting the results of more sophisticated research, experts seem to agree that expectancy theory is a useful source of insight into work motivation.

One of the more popular modifications of Vroom's original version of the theory distinguishes between extrinsic and intrinsic rewards as two separate types of possible work outcomes.[23] ***Extrinsic rewards*** are positively valued work outcomes that are given to the individual by some other person in the work setting. An example is pay. Workers typically do not pay themselves directly; some representative of the organization administers the reward. ***Intrinsic rewards,*** on the other hand, are positively valued work outcomes that are received by the individual directly as a result of task performance. They do not require the participation of another person. A feeling of achievement after accomplishing a particularly challenging task is one example of an intrinsic reward. This distinction is important because each type of reward demands separate attention from a manager seeking to use rewards to increase motivation. We discuss these differences more thoroughly in Chapters 6 and 7.

**Extrinsic rewards**

**Intrinsic rewards**

# AN INTEGRATED MODEL OF MOTIVATION

Each of the theories presented in this chapter has potential usefulness for the manager. Although the equity and expectancy theories have special strengths, current thinking argues forcefully for a combined approach that develops and tests contingency-type models that point out where and when various motivation theories work best.[24] Thus, before leaving this discussion, we should pull the content and process theories together into one integrated model of individual performance and satisfaction.

We will begin with the individual performance equation (see Chapter 4), and then proceed in building-block fashion. The equation directs our attention to individual attributes, work effort, and organizational support as three variables that influence individual performance. Simply put,

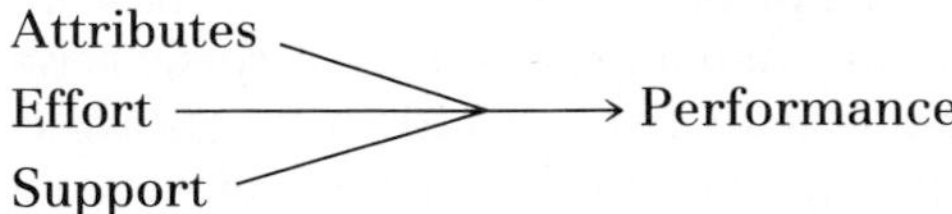


Recall, too, that we went on to say that because the individual alone controls his or her work effort, the manager attempts to influence effort through the concept of motivation. Thus, the foregoing relationships can be modified to

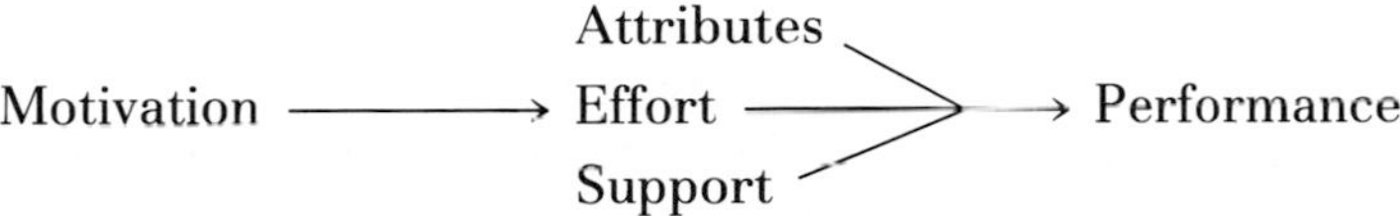


Note further, however, that managers are also interested in promoting high levels of individual satisfaction as a part of their concern for human resource maintenance. Remember, too, that we concluded our Chapter 2 review of the satisfaction–performance controversy by noting that when rewards are allocated on the basis of past performance (i.e., when rewards are performance-contingent) they can cause both future performance and satisfaction. Figuratively speaking,

performance-contingent rewards —influence→ performance *and* satisfaction

Now, we have used the logic of expectancy theory to integrate these latter ideas with insights of the other motivational theories and create the model of individual performance and satisfaction shown in Figure 5.7. In the figure, performance is determined by individual attributes, work effort, and organizational support. Individual motivation directly deter-

*FIGURE 5.7 Predicting individual work performance and satisfaction: an integrated model.*

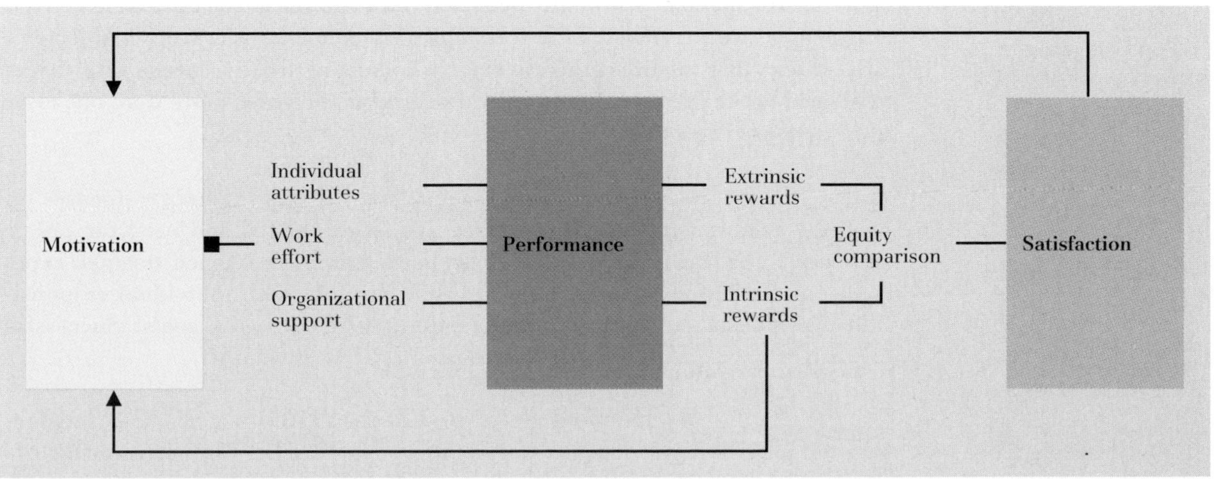

mines work effort, and the key to motivation is the manager's ability to create a work setting that positively responds to individual needs and goals. Whether or not a work setting provides motivation depends on the availability of rewards. When the individual experiences intrinsic rewards for work performance, motivation will be directly and positively affected. Motivation can also occur when job satisfactions result from either extrinsic or intrinsic rewards that are felt to be equitably allocated. When felt negative inequity results, satisfaction will be low and motivation reduced.

Figure 5.7 is an extension of Vroom's original expectancy theory and an expanded model by Porter and Lawler.[25] The figure is based on the foundation of the individual performance equation. It includes a key role for equity theory and recognizes job performance and satisfaction as separate, but potentially interdependent, work results. The content theories enter the model as the manager's guide to understanding individual attributes and identifying the needs that give motivational value to the various work rewards allocated by the manager.[26]

## SUMMARY

**■ Content and Process Theories are useful ways of organizing the study of motivation. Content theories emphasize the reasons for motivated behavior or what causes it. They include the work of Maslow, Alderfer, McClelland, and Herzberg. Process theories are dynamic and emphasize the "how" aspects of motivation. They focus on understanding the thought or cognitive processes that act to influence behavior. The equity and expectancy theories fall in this category.**

**■ Maslow's Hierarchy of Needs Theory arranges human needs into the following five-step hierarchy: physiological, safety, social (the three lower-order needs), esteem, and self-actualization (the two higher-order needs). Satisfaction of any need activates the one at the next higher-level, and people are presumed to move step-by-step up the hierarchy. Alderfer's ERG theory has modified this theory by collapsing the five needs into three: existence, relatedness, and growth. Alderfer also allows for more than one need to be activated at a time.**

**■ McClelland's Acquired Needs Theory focuses on need for achievement (nAch), need for affiliation (nAff), and need for power (nPower). The theory argues that these needs can be developed through experience and training. Persons high in nAch like jobs with individual responsibility, performance feedback, and moderately challenging goals. Successful executives have a high nPower that is greater than their nAff.**

**■ Herzberg's Two-Factor Theory treats job satisfaction and job dissatisfaction as two separate issues. Satisfiers or motivator factors are associated with job content. They include such factors as achievement, responsibility, and recognition. When job content is improved, this is expected**

to increase satisfaction and motivation to perform well. In contrast, dissatisfiers or hygiene factors are associated with the job context. They consist of such factors as working conditions, relations with co-workers, and salary. When job context is improved this does not lead to more satisfaction but is expected to reduce dissatisfaction.

■ **Questions and Answers on the Content Theories** suggest that—there is no definitive list of human needs, one outcome can satisfy multiple needs, and there is no formal "hierarchy" of needs. All managers should, nonetheless, try to create work environments in which people can satisfy important needs.

■ **Equity Theory** is a process theory of motivation. It points out that people compare their rewards (and inputs) with those of others. The individual is then motivated to engage in behavior to correct any perceived inequity. At the extreme, feelings of inequity may lead to reduced performance or job turnover.

■ **Expectancy Theory** is also a process theory of motivation. It argues that work motivation is determined by an individual's beliefs concerning effort–performance relationships (expectancy), work–outcome relationships (instrumentality), and the desirability of various work outcomes (valence). Based on Vroom's classic work, the theory states that Motivation = Expectancy × Instrumentality × Valence. Managers, therefore, must build positive expectancies, demonstrate performance–reward instrumentalities, and use rewards with high positive valences in their motivational strategies.

■ **An Integrated Model of Motivation** builds from the individual performance equation developed in Chapter 4, which relates performance to individual attributes, work effort, and organizational support. The integrated motivational model integrates the content and process theories to show how well-managed rewards can lead to high levels of both individual performance and satisfaction.

## KEY TERMS

Content Theories
Esteem Needs
Existence Needs
Expectancy
Extrinsic Rewards
Felt Inequity
Growth Needs
Higher-Order Needs
Hygienes (Hygiene Factors)
Instrumentality
Intrinsic Rewards
Job Content
Job Context
Lower-Order Needs
Motivation to Work
Motivator (Motivator Factors)
Need
Need for Achievement (nAch)
Need for Affiliation (nAff)
Need for Power (nPower)
Physiological Needs
Process Theories
Relatedness Needs
Safety Needs
Self-Actualization Needs
Social Needs
Valence

## REVIEW QUESTIONS

1. What is the key difference between the approaches taken by the content and process theories concerning their explanations of work motivation?
2. Two OB experts are discussing the topic of work motivation. One says "motivation can never come from the boss," while the other states "if people aren't motivated, managers are to blame." How can each position be defended? How can the two positions be reconciled with one another?
3. Suppose that you are a manager and find yourself with one group of subordinates who apparently seek higher-order need satisfactions at work, and another group that seems concerned only with lower-order needs. What would you do to motivate each group of subordinates? Why?
4. What are the major differences between Maslow and Alderfer in their approaches to human needs in the workplace?
5. If David McClelland is right, and it is possible to stimulate certain needs in people, what is the managerial significance of this finding?
6. Use Herzberg's two-factor theory to identify possible sources of dissatisfaction-satisfaction in a job with which you are familiar.
7. Choose an example of how the equity dynamic has affected your behavior as a student or in a work situation. What guidelines would you suggest to instructors or managers that could help them to minimize the negative consequences potentially associated with this equity dynamic?
8. What is one major modification that you would make to the model of motivation to work presented in Figure 5.6 to increase its usefulness to practicing managers? Please explain.

## AN OB LIBRARY

Peter Drucker, *Management: Tasks, Responsibilities, and Practices* (New York: Harper Collins, 1973).

Andrew Grove, *High Output Management* (New York: Random House, 1985).

Abraham Maslow, *Motivation and Personality,* Second Edition (New York: Harper Collins, 1970).

Douglas McGregor, *The Human Side of Enterprise* (New York: McGraw-Hill, 1960).

Robert E. Quinn, *Beyond Rational Management* (San Francisco: Jossey-Bass, 1988).

EXERCISE

# ESSENTIALS OF MOTIVATION

*Objectives*

1. To stimulate personal analysis of social and academic motivators.
2. To contrast and compare social and academic motivators.
3. To provide insight into a variety of motivators for yourself and other people in groups.

*Total Time*

45 to 70 minutes

*Procedure*

1. Make a list for each category of worker below in response to the question: "What are the five most important 'turn-ons' or things that motivate you in your job?"
   a. Yourself.
   b. A skilled worker.
   c. A white collar manager.
   d. A professional (e.g., physician, attorney).
2. Form a group of five to seven individuals, share your lists, and reach agreement as to the top five motivators for each worker listed above.
3. Discuss as a group whether any conflicts were discovered among the workers, and if so, why?
4. Compare and contrast each worker's motivators. Emphasis should be placed on differences and reasons for differences.
5. Await further class discussion led by your instructor.

CASE

# PERFECT PIZZERIA

Perfect Pizzeria in Southville, in deep southern Illinois, is the second largest franchise of the chain in the United States.[27] The headquarters is located in Phoenix, Arizona. Although the business is prospering, employee and managerial problems exist.

Each operation has one manager, an assistant manager, and from two to five night managers. The managers of each pizzeria work under an area supervisor. There are no systematic criteria for being a manager or becoming a manager trainee. The franchise has no formalized training period for the manager. No college education is required. The managers for whom the case observer worked during a four-year period were relatively young (ages 24 to 27) and only one had completed college. They came from the ranks of night managers or assistant managers, or both. The night managers were chosen for their ability to perform the duties of the regular employees. The assistant managers worked a two-hour shift during the luncheon period five days a week to gain knowledge about bookkeeping and management. Those becoming managers remained at that level unless they expressed interest in investing in the business.

The employees were mostly college students, with a few high school students performing the less challenging jobs. Since Perfect Pizzeria was located in an area with few job opportunities, it had a relatively easy task of filling its employee quotas. All the employees, with the exception of the manager, were employed part time and were paid the minimum wage.

The Perfect Pizzeria system is devised so that food and beverage costs and profits are computed according to a percentage. If the percentage of food unsold or damaged in any way is very low, the manager gets a bonus. If the percentage is high, the manager does not receive a bonus; rather, he or she receives only his or her normal salary.

There are many ways in which the percentage can fluctuate. Since the manager cannot be in the store 24 hours a day, some employees make up for their paychecks by helping themselves to the food. When a friend comes in to order a pizza, extra ingredients are put on the friend's pizza. Occasional nibbles by 18 to 20 employees throughout the day at the meal table also raise the percentage figure. An occasional bucket of sauce may be spilled or a pizza accidentally burned.

In the event of an employee mistake, the expense is supposed to come from the individual. Because of peer pressure, the night manager seldom writes up a bill for the erring employee. Instead, the establishment takes the loss and the error goes unnoticed until the end of the month when the inventory is taken. That's when the manager finds out that the percentage is high and that there will be no bonus.

In the present instance, the manager took retaliatory measures. Previously, each employee was entitled to a free pizza, salad, and all the soft drinks he or she could drink for every 6 hours of work. The manager raised this figure from 6 to 12 hours of work. However, the employees had received these 6-hour benefits for a long time. Therefore, they simply took advantage of the situation whenever the manager or the assistant was not in the building. Although the night manager theoretically had complete control of the operation in the evenings, he did not command the respect that the manager or assistant manager did. This was because he received the same pay as the regular employees, he could not reprimand other employees, and he was basically the same age or sometimes even younger than the other employees.

Thus, apathy grew within the pizzeria. There seemed to be a further separation between the manager and his workers, who started out as a closely knit group. The manager made no attempt to alleviate the problem, because he felt it would iron itself out. Either the employees that were dissatisfied would quit or they would be content to put up with the new regulations. As it turned out, there was a rash of employee dismissals. The manager had no problem in filling the vacancies with new workers, but the loss of key personnel was costly to the business.

With the large turnover, the manager found that he had to spend more time in the building, supervising and sometimes taking the place of inexperienced workers. This was in direct violation of the franchise regulation, which stated that a manager would act as a supervisor and at no time take part in the actual food preparation. Employees were now placed under strict supervision with the manager working alongside them. The operation no longer worked smoothly because of differences between the remaining experienced workers and the manager concerning the way in which a particular function should be performed.

Within a two-month period, the manager was again free to go back to his office and leave his subordinates in charge of the entire operation. During this two-month period, the percentage had returned to the previous low level, and the manager received a bonus each month. The manager felt that his problems had been resolved and that conditions would remain the same, since the new personnel had been properly trained.

It didn't take long for the new employees to become influenced by the other employees. Immediately after the manager had returned to his supervisory role, the percentage began to rise. This time the manager took a bolder step. He cut out any benefits that the employees had—no free pizzas, salads, or drinks. With the job market at an even lower ebb than usual, most employees were forced to stay. The appointment of a new area supervisor made it impossible for the manager to "work behind the counter," since the supervisor was centrally located in Southville.

The manager tried still another approach to alleviate the rising percentage problem and maintain his bonus. He placed a notice on the bulletin board, stating that if the percentage remained at a high level, a lie detector test would be given to all employees. All those found guilty of taking or purposefully wasting food or drinks would be immediately terminated. This did not have the desired effect on the employees, because they knew if they were all subjected to the test, all would be found guilty and the manager would have to dismiss all of them. This would leave him in a worse situation than ever.

Even before the following month's percentage was calculated, the manager knew it would be high. He had evidently received information from one of the night managers about the employees' feelings toward the notice. What he did not expect was that the percentage would reach an all-time high. That is the state of affairs at the present time.

### *Questions*

1. Consider the situation where the manager changed the time period required to receive free food and drink from 6 to 12 hours of work. Try to apply each of the motivational approaches discussed in this chapter to explain what happened. Which of the approaches offers the most appropriate explanation? Why?
2. Repeat Question 1 for the situation where the manager worked beside the employees for a time and then later returned to his office.
3. Repeat Question 1 for the situation as it exists at the end of the case.
4. Establish and justify a motivational program based on one or a combination of motivation theories to deal with the situation as it exists at the end of the case.

This study outline of major topics is meant to organize your reading now; it is repeated in the Summary to structure your review.

## STUDY OUTLINE

### ■ Learning

Classical Conditioning   Operant Conditioning   Cognitive Learning   Social Learning

### ■ Reinforcement

Reinforcement and Rewards   Reinforcement Strategies

### ■ Positive Reinforcement

Examples of Positive Reinforcement   Scheduling Positive Reinforcement
Guidelines for Positive Reinforcement

### ■ Extinction

A Case of Extinction   Extinction and Positive Reinforcement

CHAPTER 6

# LEARNING, REINFORCEMENT, AND EXTRINSIC REWARDS

# VISIONS 6

**Employers are going to great lengths to attract, retain, and motivate highly capable workers. In today's increasingly tight labor markets, the task isn't easy. Au Bon Pain, a popular and fast-growing chain of sandwich shops based on the east coast, seems up to the job. With the help of Len Schlesinger, a business professor on leave from Harvard, the company has turned to its compensation system as one way to lower costs, improve service, and boost productivity.**

**At Au Bon Pain, store managers earn about twice as much as the industry average and can go much higher if their store's sales and profits are up. Even crew workers, the people making the bread and sandwiches, are well paid according to industry standards. But they are expected to put in long hours. The result? The firm has an annual turnover of entry-level workers of only 75 percent; the rest of the industry runs over 200 percent. At Au Bon Pain, a willingness to compensate workers for jobs well done seems to offer high returns. With a vision like this, both the company and its employees reap the benefits.**

In this chapter we address one major question: How can a manager allocate *extrinsic rewards,* including pay, so that desired work behaviors are encouraged and facilitated, rather than discouraged and inhibited? To examine this question we need to be especially familiar with learning, and the management of various forms of reinforcement and rewards. As we saw in Au Bon Pain, it's possible to use extrinsic rewards very effectively. They are an important part of any broad-based motivational strategy.

## LEARNING

Learning

***Learning,*** previously defined in Chapter 1 as a relatively permanent change in behavior resulting from experience, is an important part of rewards management. It is the process through which people acquire the competencies and beliefs that affect their behavior in organizations. An understanding of basic learning principles will deepen your perspectives on the concepts and theories of motivation already studied in Chapter 5. Managers with such an awareness are well positioned to help other persons "learn" the behaviors necessary to achieve maximum positive outcomes from their work.

There are four general approaches to learning—classical conditioning, operant conditioning, cognitive learning, and social learning. Each offers insights of potential value to managers and the field of OB.[1]

## Classical Conditioning

Classical conditioning

***Classical conditioning*** is a form of learning through association. As shown in Figure 6.1, it involves the manipulation of *stimuli* to influence behavior. Classical conditioning associates a previously neutral stimulus, one having no effect on behavior, with another stimulus that does affect behavior. The former thus becomes a *conditioned stimulus* which, upon its occurrence, also draws forth the now *conditioned response*. This process is illustrated in the well-known experiments by Ivan Pavlov, the Russian psychologist, who "taught" dogs to salivate (conditioned response) at the sound of a bell (conditioned stimulus). He did so by ringing the bell when feeding the dogs, something that caused then to salivate. The dogs eventually "learned," through the association of the bell with the presentation of meat, to salivate by the ringing of the bell alone. Involuntary behaviors of humans are also susceptible to classical conditioning. Someone who is verbally reprimanded on several occasions after being "asked to step into the boss's office," for example, may become conditioned to display apprehensiveness and nervous reactions whenever "asked" to come into the office in the future.

## Operant Conditioning

Operant conditioning

***Operant conditioning*** is learning achieved when the *consequences* of behavior lead to changes in the probability of its occurrence. You may think of it as learning through reinforcement. Figure 6.1 clarifies how this operant or behaviorist approach contrasts with classical conditioning. It views behavior as "operating" on its environment to produce conse-

*FIGURE 6.1 Differences between the classical and operant conditioning approaches to learning.*

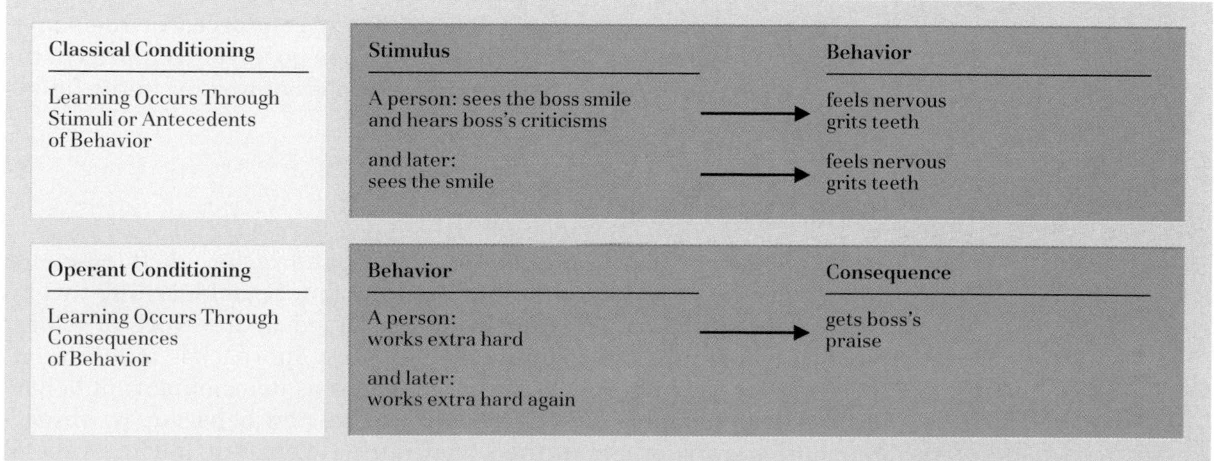

quences that affect its future occurrence. The noted psychologist B. F. Skinner has popularized operant conditioning as a way of controlling behavior by manipulating its consequences.[2] Whereas classical conditioning works only on behaviors that are involuntary in nature, operant conditioning has a broader application to almost any human behavior. Thus, it has rather substantial applications in the workplace. For example,

> ***Nordstrom's*** The customer is always right at Nordstrom's—a Seattle-based department-store chain. The chain pays its employees 20 percent more than competitors and deliberately congratulates and encourages them for good work. If customers complain, employees are instructed to replace anything on demand, no questions asked. Workers have "learned" through the positive consequences of their behavior to continue to do the right things.

## Cognitive Learning

**Cognitive learning**

***Cognitive learning*** is learning achieved by thinking about the perceived relationship between events and individual goals and expectations. The process motivation theories reviewed in Chapter 5 are good examples of how this approach is applied to the work setting. They are concerned with explaining "why" people decide to do things. They do so by examining how people come to view various work activities as perceived opportunities to pursue desired rewards, eliminate felt inequities, and the like. These cognitive explanations of learning differ markedly from the acognitive or behaviorist explanations of operant conditioning. Take the example of a person walking down the street and finding a $10 bill on the pavement.[3] Thereafter, this person is observed to spend more time looking down when walking. The question is, "why?"

*The Cognitive Learning Explanation:* The person does so with the goal of finding more money, something held in high value. The person *reasons* that more money may be lost in the streets, and thus *decides* to look down more frequently when out walking in the future.

*The Operant Conditioning Explanation:* When the initial behavior of "looking down" occurred, it was positively reinforced by the consequences of finding the $10 bill. Having been positively reinforced, the behavior is then repeated when the person is out walking in the future. No cognitive explanation is needed.

## Social Learning

**Social learning**

***Social learning*** is learning achieved through the reciprocal interactions among people, behavior, and their environment. Social learning theory, as introduced in Chapter 4 and well expressed in the work of Albert Bandura, integrates the cognitive and operant approaches to learning.[4] It recognizes the importance of consequences as determinants of behavior. But, it also emphasizes that people acquire new behaviors by observing and imitating others in the social setting. Learning is not a case of environmental determinism (classical and operant views) or of individual determinism (the cognitive view). Rather, it is a blending of both influences.

Social learning theory places special emphasis on three aspects of the learning process—modeling or vicarious learning, symbolism, and self-control. Through ***vicarious learning*** or ***modeling,*** people acquire behaviors by directly observing and imitating others. The "models," such as the manager or a co-worker, demonstrate desirable behaviors, and a person may attempt to acquire these behaviors by modeling them through practice. "Mentors," or senior workers who befriend younger and more inexperienced proteges, can also be very important models. In fact, a shortage of mentors for women in management is sometimes cited as a major constraint to their progression up the corporate ladder.[5]

**Vicarious learning**
**Modeling**

Symbolic behavior can also help people learn. Words and other symbols used by managers and people at work can help communicate values, beliefs, and goals, and thus become guides to behavior. Finally, people can learn to exercise self-control over their behavior. By observing things that happen, thinking about them, and then trying to manage them to better achieve goals, humans are capable of self-regulation and able to influence their own behavior.

# REINFORCEMENT

Reinforcement plays a key role in the learning process. The foundation for this relationship is the "law of effect" as stated by E. L. Thorndike.[6]

> ***Law of Effect:*** Behavior that results in a pleasant outcome is likely to be repeated; behavior that results in an unpleasant outcome is not likely to be repeated.

**Law of effect**

The implications of the law of effect are straightforward. Rewards are outcomes or environmental consequences that are considered by the reinforcement orientation to determine individual behavior. Thus, one way in which to increase your ability to successfully manage rewards is to understand their nature and the principles of reinforcement as they apply to the work setting. Let's consider these.

## Reinforcement and Rewards

You should remember the distinction between extrinsic and intrinsic rewards as clarified in Chapter 5. The relationship between reinforcement and extrinsic rewards is especially important here.

***Extrinsic rewards*** are positively valued work outcomes that are given to the individual by some other person. They are important external reinforcers or environmental consequences that can substantially influence people's work behaviors through the law of effect. Table 6.1 presents a sample of extrinsic rewards that can be allocated by managers to their subordinates. Some of these are *contrived* or *planned* rewards, which have direct costs and budgetary implications—examples are pay increases and cash bonuses. Others are *natural* rewards, having no cost other than the

**Extrinsic rewards**

*TABLE 6.1*
A SAMPLE OF EXTRINSIC REWARDS ALLOCATED BY MANAGERS

| Contrived Rewards: Some direct cost | | Natural Rewards: No direct cost |
|---|---|---|
| refreshments | promotion | smiles |
| piped-in-music | trips | greetings |
| nice offices | company car | compliments |
| profit-sharing | pay increase | special jobs |
| office parties | gifts | recognition |
| cash bonuses | paid insurance | feedback |
| sport tickets | stock options | asking advice |

*Source:* Developed from Fred Luthans and Robert Kreitner, *Organizational Behavior Modification and Beyond* (Glenview, IL.: Scott, Foresman, 1985), p. 126–130.

manager's personal time and efforts—included here are such things as verbal praise and recognition.

## Reinforcement Strategies

**Applied behavior analysis**

***Applied behavior analysis*** is the systematic reinforcement of desirable work behavior and the nonreinforcement or punishment of unwanted work behavior. It includes four basic reinforcement strategies: positive reinforcement, negative reinforcement, or avoidance, punishment, and extinction. Let us look at these in some detail.[7]

**Positive reinforcement**

- ***Positive reinforcement:*** administration of positive consequences that tend to increase the likelihood of repeating the behavior in similar settings—for example, a Texas Instruments manager nods to express approval to a subordinate after she makes a useful comment during a staff meeting.

**Negative reinforcement**

- ***Negative reinforcement*** or ***Avoidance:*** withdrawal of negative consequences that tend to increase the likelihood of repeating the behavior in similar settings—for example, a manager at McDonald's regularly nags a worker about his poor performance and then stops nagging when the worker does not fall behind one day. Your parents ground you for poor grades. When you study hard and make good grades, they remove the grounding.

Note that there are two aspects here: First, the negative consequences, then the withdrawal of these when desirable behavior occurs. The term "negative reinforcement" comes from this withdrawal of the negative consequences. This strategy is also sometimes called "avoidance" because its intent is for the person to avoid the negative consequence by performing the desired behavior—for example, we stop at a red light to avoid a traffic ticket; a worker (who prefers the dayshift) is allowed to return to the dayshift if she performs well on the nightshift.

Both positive and negative reinforcement seek to encourage desirable behavior. The first provides a pleasant consequence; the second provides an unpleasant consequence followed by its withdrawal when the desired behavior occurs.

Courtesy of Hilton Hotels Corporation.

**SKILLS PERSPECTIVE**

## HILTON HOTELS

**"Hilton" is a famous name worldwide in the hospitality industry. And "service" is synonymous with success in this competitive industry. At Hilton, service is not left to chance. In a new "Performance for Excellence Program," the company has carefully examined all aspects of its hotel operations. Rigorous behavior standards have been set, and a multimillion dollar staff training program has been instituted to communicate the standards and build the skills necessary to attain them. This involves everything from viewing videotapes of positive customer contacts to more standard classroom instruction and discussion. Hilton expects this performance-based training to pay off handsomely in the future.**

- *Punishment:* administration of negative consequences that tend to reduce the likelihood of repeating the behavior in similar settings—a Burger King manager docks a worker's pay when she reports late for work one day. (Punishment)
- *Extinction:* withdrawal of the reinforcing consequences for a given behavior—Jack often is late for work and his co-workers cover for him (positive reinforcement). The manager instructs Jack's co-workers to stop such covering. (Extinction)

The manager has deliberately used extinction here to get rid of an undesirable behavior. Note that we need to be careful not to use it inadvertently to eliminate a desired behavior. This sometimes happens when we stop positively reinforcing that behavior. A subordinate shows unusual initiative and we ignore it.

Sometimes negative reinforcement and punishment are confused. A major difference is their effects on behavior. Negative reinforcement *increases* the likelihood of repeating the behavior; punishment *decreases* the likelihood. Negative reinforcement *removes* negative consequences following behavior; punishment *presents* negative consequences following behavior.

The four strategies are illustrated in Figure 6.2 in terms of directing work behavior toward practices desired by management. Notice that both positive and negative reinforcement are used to strengthen desirable behavior when it occurs; both punishment and extinction are applied to undesirable behavior to try to decrease its frequency. These strategies may be used in combination with each other as well as alone. In the discussion that follows we emphasize especially the managerial significance of positive reinforcement, extinction, and punishment.

# POSITIVE REINFORCEMENT

B. F. Skinner and his followers advocate positive reinforcement. To use positive reinforcement well in the work setting, you must first be aware of the wide variety of things that have potential reward value. We showed

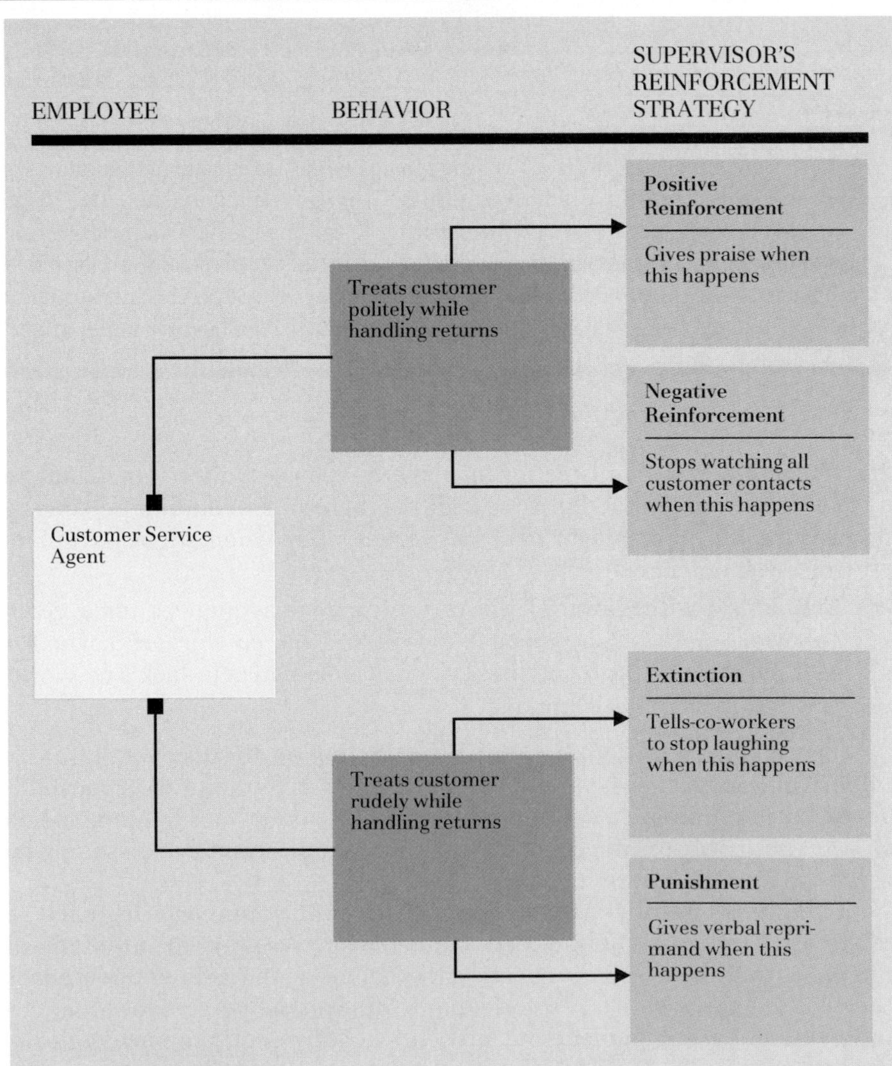


*FIGURE 6.2 An illustration of four reinforcement strategies.*

a number of these in Table 6.1. But in using these for reinforcement purposes, several things must be kept in mind.

To begin, we need to be aware that positive reinforcers and rewards are not necessarily the same. Recognition is both a reward and a positive reinforcer *if* a person's performance later improves. Sometimes, however, apparent rewards turn out not to be positive reinforcers. For example, a supervisor at Boeing may praise a subordinate in front of other group members for finding errors in a report. But the group members may then give the worker the silent treatment who, in turn, may stop looking for errors in the future. In this and other related cases, the supervisor's "reward" does not serve as a positive reinforcer.

In order to have maximum reinforcement value, a reward must also be delivered only if the desired behavior is exhibited. The reward must be *contingent* on the desired behavior. This is the ***law of contingent reinforcement.*** Finally, the reward must be given as soon as possible after the desired behavior. This is the ***law of immediate reinforcement.***[8]

**Law of contingent reinforcement**

**Law of immediate reinforcement**

## Examples of Positive Reinforcement

In Alaska's remote Bering Strait School District, students often missed class because they were out whaling with their parents. Officials decided to use such items as backpacks and T-shirts to try to increase attendance.[9]

At the Bering Mission School, students accumulate points each time they show up for class or after-school study sessions. Each Monday they can cash these in for coffee mugs, pennants, Frisbees, T-shirts, and other items with the school emblem. Prizes are similar but not necessarily identical at other individual schools in the district. Backpacks are especially popular at many schools.

All the cash to support the program is raised by the students themselves, using student council funds. Thus, they are providing the resources for their own rewards.

Has the program worked? "As far as I know, it has been having a substantial impact" on attendance, said Bob Collins, an associate superintendent of attendance for the district. He was contacted by phone some 400 miles northwest of Anchorage.

Let's look at this example in terms of our earlier reminders. First, it does look as if these goodies are both rewards and reinforcers. Behavior has changed in the desired direction. The fact that students are involved in raising the money probably helped them to "buy into" the program.

Second, the rewards appear clearly linked to the desired behavior and are given promptly. So the two reinforcement laws are being utilized. Internationally we see a somewhat similar plan used in a company in Mexico that needed to cut down on tardiness—an especially severe problem among Mexican workers. In the previous year 131 workers accumulated 750 tardies. The firm then gave a bonus if workers punched in on time. The plan was successful in reducing tardiness.[10] Thus, these workers seem to have responded in much the same way as U.S. workers.

The school district and Mexican plant in the previous examples used positive reinforcement well and apparently the district was satisfied that it had increased its attendance. Sometimes if the desired behavior is more

**Shaping**

specific in nature and difficult to achieve, another form of positive reinforcement called shaping will be used. ***Shaping*** is the creation of a new behavior by the positive reinforcement of successive approximations to the desired behavior.

For example, city workers in Bellevue, Washington are awarded "points" with a monetary value on the cost of their health insurance—currently one point must be given up for each dollar of health benefits used—and the value of the points increases as the number of claims filed by all workers decreases. This is a straightforward positive reinforcement strategy.[11]

However, suppose the amount spent on insurance and the number of claims filed still were too high. The city might set a goal that was harder to reach to further contain its costs. Rather than give rewards only for reaching the new goal, the city might continue with current rewards and then increase these in increments until the new goal is reached. Once reached, the new level of rewards would be continued to stabilize the behavior. In this way, behavior could be gradually shaped, rather than changed all at once.

## Scheduling Positive Reinforcement

**Continuous reinforcement**
**Intermittent reinforcement**

Positive reinforcement can be given according to continuous and intermittent schedules. ***Continuous reinforcement*** administers a reward each time a desired behavior occurs. ***Intermittent reinforcement*** rewards behavior only periodically.

These alternatives are important since the two schedules may have significantly different impacts on behavior. In general:

1. Continuous reinforcement draws forth a desired behavior more quickly than intermittent reinforcement; but continuous reinforcement is more costly in the consumption of rewards, and is more easily extinguished when reinforcement is no longer present.
2. Behavior acquired under intermittent reinforcement lasts longer upon the discontinuance of reinforcement than does behavior acquired under continuous reinforcement. In other words, it is more resistant to extinction.

*TABLE 6.2*
FOUR WAYS TO SCHEDULE INTERMITTENT POSITIVE REINFORCEMENT

| Reinforcement Schedule | Example |
|---|---|
| *Fixed interval*—Give reinforcer after specific time passes | Weekly or monthly paychecks |
| *Fixed ratio*—Give reinforcer after specific number of responses | Piece rate pay or sales commissions |
| *Variable interval*—Give reinforcer at random times | Occasional praise by boss on unscheduled "walk arounds" |
| *Variable ratio*—Give reinforcer after a random number of responses | Random quality checks with praise for zero defects |

Courtesy of Citibank.

**INTERNATIONAL PERSPECTIVE**

## CITICORP

**Visit a Citicorp office in Australia or Hong Kong, or anywhere else for that matter, and a high-tech global network will allow you to get the best exchange rates and terms from any of its offices. As part of its global thrust, the firm keeps its trading rooms in New York, London, and Tokyo open 24 hours a day. But it expects Citibankers in each location to work as ad hoc teams and help one another. To encourage such behavior, the bank has started a system of cross-evaluations. An employee in New York who is supposed to work well with an employee in London gets rated by that person, and vice-versa. Financial bonuses are based in part on how well they collaborate with one another.**

Intermittent reinforcement, as shown in Table 6.2, can be given according to fixed or variable schedules. The variable schedules are considered to result in more consistent patterns of desired behaviors than are fixed reinforcement schedules. *Fixed interval schedules* provide rewards at the first appearance of a behavior after a given time has elapsed; *fixed ratio schedules* result in a reward each time a certain number of the behaviors has occurred. A *variable interval schedule* rewards behavior at random times, while a *variable ratio schedule* rewards behavior after a random number of occurrences.

Let's look at an example of some unionized beaver trappers working for a large Pacific Coast lumber company. Their job was to keep the beavers from eating newly planted tree seedlings.[12]

The trappers alternated under two different pay plans. In the first plan, each trapper earned $7 per hour plus $1 for each beaver caught, paid as a continuous reinforcement schedule. The second plan paid $7 per hour plus a 25 percent chance (determined from rolling the dice) of receiving $4 for each beaver (a variable ratio schedule). In the long run, both plans gave an average bonus of $1 per beaver. However, when the trappers were under the variable ratio plan, they were 58 percent more productive than under the continuous reinforcement plan. A recent study of new car dealership mechanics tended also to support on-the-job lotteries as low cost incentive systems. Those of you familiar with Las Vegas operations also have seen intermittent reinforcement in action. Players will stay and keep putting in coins since they don't have any idea when they will hit the jackpot.[13]

All of these examples show the usefulness of using intermittent reinforcement schedules.

### Guidelines for Positive Reinforcement

To ensure that the allocation of extrinsic work rewards has the desired positive reinforcement effects, a manager should[14]

1. Clearly identify the desired behaviors. That is, determine what specific behaviors will result in positive contributions to organizational goal attainment by each person in the work unit.
2. Maintain an inventory of rewards that have the potential to serve as positive reinforcers for these people.
3. Recognize individual differences in the rewards that actually will have positive value for each person.
4. Let each person know exactly what must be done to receive a desirable reward. Set clear targets, and give performance feedbacks.
5. Allocate rewards contingently and immediately upon the appearance of the desired behaviors. Make sure the reward is given only if the desired behavior occurs.
6. Allocate rewards wisely in terms of scheduling the delivery of positive reinforcement.

## EXTINCTION

**Extinction**

Recall that ***extinction*** is the withholding of reinforcement for a behavior that previously has been positively reinforced. This decreases the frequency or weakens the behavior. The behavior is not "unlearned," it simply is not exhibited. Since it no longer is reinforced, it will reappear if reinforced again. Whereas positive reinforcement seeks to establish and maintain desirable work behaviors, the goal of extinction is to weaken and eliminate undesirable ones. How would you apply this new strategy to the following case?

### A Case of Extinction

A manager at Motorola is worried.[15] One of her bright young assistants is developing a problem behavior that could eventually erode his credibility. At the weekly staff meeting, Jason has started acting more like a comedian than an aspiring executive. He interjects "one-liners" and makes "wisecracks" with increasing frequency during discussions. As a result, the meetings are often disrupted. The manager is becoming annoyed and is especially concerned because Jason's behavior has gotten worse during the last month.

If you were the manager, how would you use reinforcement theory to analyze this situation?

The manager decided not to reprimand Jason. Rather, she tried to analyze his behavior in terms of the environmental consequences that it produced for him. She reasoned that his behavior must be receiving some sort of positive reinforcement. At the next two meetings, she closely observed Jason's disruptive behavior and its results. She noticed that two other staff members usually acknowledged Jason's remarks with smiles and by nodding approval. In fact, the manager noticed that Jason immediately looked to these persons each time after making one of his disruptive comments.

In terms of reinforcement theory, the manager has found that Jason is being positively reinforced by these two persons for a behavior that is organizationally undesirable. Given this diagnosis, the manager decided on a strategy of extinction. She went to Jason's two colleagues and asked them to avoid approving his disruptive behavior. They did so. In future meetings the frequency of his "joking" decreased dramatically.

## Extinction and Positive Reinforcement

Extinction can be especially powerful when combined with positive reinforcement. In fact, this is what actually occurred in the previous case. Extinction caused Jason to stop making disruptive comments. However, the manager was still concerned that Jason maintain and even increase his useful contributions. Whenever such a valuable comment was made, therefore, she provided him with immediate acknowledgement and approval. These extrinsic rewards had a positive reinforcing effect on desirable behavior. Thus, the combined strategy of extinction and positive reinforcement is a most useful tool for managers.

# PUNISHMENT

Another reinforcement strategy, besides extinction, that managers use to eliminate undesirable behavior is ***punishment.*** Earlier we said that this involves administration of negative consequences that tend to reduce the likelihood of repeating the behavior in similar settings. To punish an employee, a manager may deny the individual a valued reward such as praise or even merit pay; or the manager may administer an adversive or unpleasant stimulus, such as reprimand or monetary fine. It is just as important to understand punishment as a reinforcement strategy as it is to understand the principles of positive reinforcement.

**Punishment**

One recent study illustrates this by showing that punishment administered for poor performance led to *increased* performance without a significant effect on satisfaction. However, punishment seen by the workers as arbitrary and capricious led to very low satisfaction as well as low performance.[16] Thus, punishment can be done poorly, or it can be done well. Of course, your goal is to know when to use this strategy and when to use it correctly.

## Problems with the Punishment Strategy

Problems such as resentment and sabotage may accompany a manager's use of punishment. It is also wise to remember that:

- *Although a behavior may be suppressed as a result of punishment, it may not be permanently abolished.* An employee, for example, may be reprimanded for taking unauthorized work breaks. The behavior may stop, but only when the manager is visible. As soon as the threat of punishment is removed from the situation, such as when the manager is no longer present, the breaks may occur once again.
- *The person who administers punishment may end up being viewed negatively by others.* A manager who frequently punishes subordinates may find that he or she has an unpleasant effect on the work unit even when not administering punishment. This manager has become so associated with punishment that his or her very presence in the work setting is an unpleasant experience for others.
- *Punishment may be offset by positive reinforcement received from another source.* A worker may be reinforced by peers at the same time that punishment is being received from the manager. Sometimes the positive value of such peer support may be strong enough to cause the individual to put up with the punishment. Thus, the undesirable behavior continues. As many times as a student may be verbally reprimanded by an instructor for being late to class, for example, the "grins" offered by other students may well justify the continuation of the tardiness in the future.

Does all of this mean that you should never punish? No. The important things to remember are to administer punishment selectively, and then do it right. Consider the following case.

## A Case of Punishment

Peter Ramirez is a forklift operator in a large supermarket warehouse.[17] This is the highest paid nonsupervisory job in the firm. It is considered a high-status job, and it took Peter five and a half years to work himself into the position. Unfortunately, he is prone to "show off" by engaging in a variety of unsafe driving habits that violate federal safety codes. Pete's manager "chews him out" regularly as a negative reinforcement, but the unsafe driving continues.

Pete's boss analyzed the situation from a reinforcement perspective. He sought to determine what environmental consequences were associated with Pete's unsafe driving habits. As you may have predicted, he found that the undesirable behavior was typically followed by laughter and special attention from the other warehouse workers. He decided that it would be impossible to enlist their aid to implement a strategy of extinction similar to the one followed by the manager at Motorola.

The next time Pete was observed to drive unsafely, Pete's boss took him off the forklift truck, explained what he was doing wrong and what was desired, and reassigned him to general warehousing duties. When finally allowed back on the forklift, Pete drove more safely.

### Punishment and Positive Reinforcement

Punishment can also be combined with positive reinforcement. Pete, for example, could now be positively reinforced when observed to drive safely. Then he would know exactly what was wrong and the unpleasant consequences associated with it, and what was right and the pleasant consequences associated with it. This combined strategy is advantageous in that it may help a manager to avoid the first problem identified: having an undesirable behavior suppressed for a period of time but not eliminated entirely.

### Guidelines for Administering Punishment

The following five guidelines are useful for managers using punishment as a reinforcement strategy.[18]

1. *Tell the individual what is being done wrong.* Clearly identify the undesirable behavior that is being punished.
2. *Tell the individual what is right.* Identify clearly the desirable alternative to the behavior that is being punished.
3. *Punish in private.* Avoid public embarrassment by punishing someone in front of others.
4. *Punish in accord with the laws of contingent and immediate reinforcement.* Make sure that the punishment is truly contingent upon the undesirable behavior and follows its occurrence as soon as possible.
5. *Make the punishment match the behavior.* Be fair in equating the magnitude of the punishment with the degree to which the behavior is truly undesirable.

## REINFORCEMENT PERSPECTIVES: RESEARCH AND ETHICAL ISSUES

The effective use of reinforcement strategies can assist in the management of human behavior at work. Testimony to this effect is found in their application in formal programs used by many substantial corporations, including General Electric, B. F. Goodrich, Emery Airfreight, and many others. It is also supported by the growing number of consulting firms who specialize in reinforcement techniques. However, we must also recognize that managerial use of these approaches is not without criticism. Some reports on the "success" of specific programs, for example, are single cases analyzed without the benefit of scientific research designs. It is hard to conclude definitively that the observed results were "caused" by reinforcement dynamics. In fact, one critic argues that the improved

ETHICAL PERSPECTIVE

## BEN & JERRY'S

Courtesy of Ben & Jerry's Homemade Inc.

**Wanted: "Visionary Chief Financial Officer" read the ad one day in papers around the country. It went on to state that the potential employer was Ben & Jerry's—"a progressive, socially responsible, slightly left-of-center ice cream manufacturer . . . whose goal is to successfully blend profitability, high quality, and social activism." You wouldn't think this highly regarded, $600 million per year firm would have much trouble filling the job, but they did. The reason? Neither Ben nor Jerry believes anyone in the company should earn more than five times the salary of the lowest paid worker. This sense of "ethics" places a cap on executive salaries—an unusual policy indeed in today's corporate America. No matter. They found a candidate from within. She's expected to do fine in the new job.**

performance may well have occurred only because of the goal-setting involved—that is, because specific performance goals were clarified and workers were individually held accountable for their accomplishment.[19]

Another criticism rests with the potential value dilemmas associated with the use of applied operant conditioning techniques to influence human behavior at work. For example, there is expressed concern that the systematic use of reinforcement strategies[20]

1. Leads to a demeaning and dehumanizing view of people that stunts human growth and development
2. Results in managers abusing the power of their position and their knowledge by exerting external control over individual behavior.

Advocates of the reinforcement approach attack the problem straight on. They agree that behavior modification involves the control of behavior. But they also argue that behavior control is an irrevocable part of every manager's job. "Managers manipulate people all the time," they might say. The real question is, "How are we to ensure that this manipulation is done in a positive and constructive fashion"? William Scott and Philipp Podsakoff, two such advocates, argue that managers can avoid exploitation in applied behavior analysis only by a careful examination of the controlling features of their own behavior and of the short- and long-range results of their practices. These managers need to promote self-control and avoid weakening subordinates by ignoring worker self-interest since leaders are only as effective as the subordinates they lead.[21]

Others have argued that the ethics of social influence processes, such as applied behavior analysis, may be judged by how much they promote freedom of choice. Such choice can be increased by recognizing individuals' preferences in design of the reinforcement contingencies and through designing self-reinforcement systems where people regulate their own behavior. These self-management systems and their ethics have been discussed by Fred Luthans and Robert Kreitner. In other words, managers should be sensitive to possible exploitation by carefully examining their own behavior and practices, by involving subordinates in design of the system, and by encouraging self-reinforcement systems whenever feasible.[22]

We expect continuing research will mainly refine our knowledge of the reinforcement strategies rather than dramatically change existing insights. Their worth in work settings seems clearly established. Future research will probably tell us how, as managers, to better use the various reinforcement strategies. That we should be using them already seems well established. Such use should be tempered with a strong managerial emphasis on employee involvement wherever possible and by explicit efforts to avoid exploitation. In other words, reinforcement should always be pursued from strong ethical foundations.

# MANAGING PAY AS AN EXTRINSIC REWARD

Pay is one of the important extrinsic rewards made available to people through working. It can help organizations attract and retain highly capable workers, and it can help satisfy and motivate these workers to work hard to achieve high performance. But if there is dissatisfaction with it, pay can also lead to strikes, grievances, absenteeism, turnover, and sometimes even poor physical and mental health. Indeed, pay is a very complex reward whose many aspects make it a good example for us to use in this discussion of reinforcement and the management of extrinsic rewards.[23]

## Multiple Meanings of Pay

To begin, a manager must understand why pay is important to people if he or she is to use it effectively as a reward. Various OB theories recognize multiple meanings of pay and the potential of these meanings to vary from one person or situation to the next. When it comes to the relationship between pay and job satisfaction, for example, each of the following theories with which you are already familiar offers a slightly different perspective.

*Under Maslow's hierarchy of needs theory* pay is a unique reward that can satisfy many different needs. It is used directly to satisfy lower-order needs, such as the physiological; and it is of symbolic value in satisfying higher-order needs, such as ego fulfillment.

*Under McClelland's acquired needs theory* pay is important as a source of performance feedback for high-need achievers; it can be attractive to persons with high needs for affiliation when offered as a group bonus; it is valued by the high-need-for-power person as a means of "buying" prestige or control over others.

*Under Herzberg's two-factor theory* pay in the form of base wage or salary can prevent dissatisfaction but cannot lead to motivation. However, merit pay raises given as special rewards for jobs done well can cause increased satisfaction and motivation.

Expectancy and equity theories, as well as the various reinforcement strategies, give additional insight into the multiple meanings of pay and their potential relationships to job performance. These ideas are summarized in Table 6.3, and they each show that pay can serve as a good motivator of work effort . . . *when properly managed.* The highlighted phrase is the real key. For pay to prove successful as a reward that is truly motivational to the recipient, it must be given (1) contingent on the occurrence of specific and desirable work behaviors and (2) equitably. Merit pay and a variety of emerging creative pay practices are applications that deserve special consideration.

## Merit Pay

**Merit pay**

Edward Lawler is a management expert whose work has contributed greatly to our understanding of pay as an extrinsic reward. His research generally concludes that, for pay to serve as a source of work motivation, high levels of job performance must be viewed as the path through which high pay can be achieved.[24] ***Merit pay*** is defined as a compensation system that bases an individual's salary or wage increase on a measure of the person's performance accomplishments during a specified time period. That is, merit pay is an attempt to make pay contingent upon performance. This application is closely related to the performance appraisal foundations discussed in Module C. There, specific ways of appraising performance are treated. Such appraisal is a vital part of making sure that any merit pay plan works well.[25]

***Lincoln Electric*** This well-regarded builder of welding machinery and electric motors in Cleveland, Ohio, uses "pay-for-performance" incentives to inspire workers. Each worker is paid only for what he or she produces, and workers must repair defects on their own time. One says: "The individual's own ability is the only factor limiting them." Turnover in the firm is only 3 percent.

Although research supports the logic and theoretical benefits of merit pay, it also indicates that the implementation of merit pay plans is not as universal or as easy as we might expect. One recent article, in fact, reports that 75 percent of American workers believe that their performances have deteriorated—because there is little link between their pay and their performance. Only 20 percent believe that they are rewarded for

*TABLE 6.3*
**THE MULTIPLE MEANINGS OF PAY AS VIEWED FROM A PERFORMANCE PERSPECTIVE**

| Theory | The Meaning of Pay |
|---|---|
| Equity theory | Pay is an object of social comparison. People are likely to compare their pay and pay increases with those received by others. When felt inequity occurs as a result of such comparisons, work effort may be reduced in the case of negative inequity or increased in the case of positive inequity. |
| Expectancy theory | Pay is only one of many work rewards that may be valued by individuals at work. When valence, instrumentality, and expectancy are high, pay can be a source of motivation. The opportunity to work hard to obtain high pay will, however, be viewed in the context of other effort-outcome expectancies and the equity dynamic. |
| Reinforcement theory | Pay is one of the extrinsic rewards that a manager may use to influence the work behavior of subordinates. Through the techniques of operant conditioning, pay can be used as a positive reinforcer when the laws of contingent and immediate reinforcement are followed. |

extra effort.[26] An effective merit pay system is one approach to dealing with this problem. To work well, a merit pay plan should

- Be based on realistic and accurate measures of individual work performance.
- Create a belief among employees that the way to achieve high pay is to perform at high levels.
- Clearly discriminate between high and low performers in the amount of pay reward received.
- Avoid confusing "merit" aspects of a pay increase with "cost-of-living" adjustments.

## Creative Pay Practices

Merit pay plans are but one way of trying to enhance the positive value of pay as a work reward. Indeed some argue that merit pay plans are not consistent with the demands of today's organizations since they fail to recognize the high degree of task interdependence among employees. Still others contend that the nature of any incentive scheme should be tied to the overall organizational strategy and the nature of the desired behavior. For example, where a firm needs highly skilled individuals in short supply, a pay system emphasizing employee retention, rather than performance, should be emphasized.[27]

With these points in mind, let us look at a variety of creative pay practices that deserve your attention. These "nontraditional" practices tend to be used in firms facing increased competition in order to try to become more competitive by getting more from their workers.[28] They include *skill-based pay, gain-sharing plans, lump-sum pay increases,* and *flexible benefit plans.*

## "Skill-Based" Pay

**Skill-based pay**

***Skill-based pay*** rewards people for acquiring and developing job-relevant skills. Pay systems of this sort pay people for the mix and depth of skills they possess, not for the particular job assignment they hold. In a typical manufacturing plant, for example, a worker may know how to perform several different jobs, each of which requires different skills. He or she would be paid for this "breadth" of capability, even though working primarily in one job assignment. Of course, this person must be willing to use any of the compensated skills in other assignments and at any time in accordance with the company's needs.

Close to 70 percent of such skilled-based pay systems have been only very recently established. Thus, there is very little research on them. But, they do seem to offer flexibility to the organization in making work assignments and do seem to increase productivity. The opportunity to master skills and be rewarded for it can also be a source of motivation and satisfaction for workers. One of the difficulties is that the measurement of skill acquisition can sometimes be difficult and even controversial.[29]

## "Gain-Sharing" Plans

Cash bonuses, or extra pay for performance above standards or expectations, have been common practice in the compensation of managers and executives for a long time. Top managers in some industries earn annual bonuses of 50 percent or more of their base salaries. This is a substantial "bonus," indeed, and it can be highly motivating. Growing in number and significance today are attempts to extend such opportunities to all employees. Popular among them is ***gain-sharing,*** an approach which links pay and performance by giving workers the opportunity to share in productivity gains through enhanced earnings.

**Gain sharing**

The Scanlon Plan is probably the oldest and best known gain-sharing plan. Others you may hear or have heard about are the Lincoln Electric Plan, the Rucker Plan, IMPROSHARE, or more generally, profit-sharing plans. All build from a common premise that workers having an impact on productivity increases and improved operating results should share in the benefits.[30] For example, the basic Scanlon Plan operates as follows:

- A business unit (e.g., plant, division, or department) is defined for purposes of performance measurement.
- Some concrete measure of costs is agreed upon for this business unit, as well as appropriate time periods for performance measurement.
- Employee bonuses are paid to all members of the business unit according to a predetermined formula relating the size of bonuses to realized cost savings.

The intended benefits of gain-sharing plans include increased worker motivation, due to the pay-for-performance incentives, and greater sense of personal responsibility for making performance contributions to the organization. Because they can be highly participative in nature, gain-sharing plans may also encourage cooperation and teamwork in the workplace. Although more remains to be learned about gain-sharing, it is being used by a growing number of large and small organizations. And recent surveys on gain-sharing plans show:

1. Employee reactions were reported as favorable in more than 80 percent of the firms surveyed.[31]
2. Of 170 firms surveyed, 81 percent reported a positive impact of gain-sharing plans on productivity.[32]
3. The effectiveness of these plans is influenced by such characteristics as employee unionization and overall employee-management attitudes.[33]

### "Lump-Sum Pay Increases"

Do you know what an annual pay raise of $1200 is worth when spread over 52 pay checks? It means exactly $23.08 per week! This figure is even further reduced when taxes and other deductions are made. Most of us don't have any choice in such matters. Our "annual" pay increases are distributed in proportionate amounts as part of weekly, biweekly, or monthly paychecks. And, as a result, they may lose considerable motivational impact in the process.

Lump-sum pay increase

An interesting alternative is the ***lump-sum pay increase*** program, which lets people elect to receive an increase in one or more lump-sum payments. The full increase may be taken at the beginning of the year and used for some valued purpose (e.g., a down payment on a car or a sizable deposit in a savings account). Or, a person might elect to take one-half of the raise early and get the rest at the start of the winter holiday season. In either case, the motivational significance of the pay increase is presumably enhanced by allowing the individual to receive it in larger doses and realize the most personal significance out of its expenditure as possible.

Another related, but more controversial development in this area is the lump-sum *payment* as differentiated from the lump-sum *increase.* The lump-sum payment is an attempt by employers to hold labor costs in line and still give workers more money—if corporate earnings allow. It involves giving workers a one-time lump-sum payment, often based upon a gain-sharing formula, instead of a yearly percentage wage or salary increase. In this way a person's base pay remains fixed, while overall monetary compensation varies according to the bonus added to this figure by the annual lump-sum payment. American labor unions, in particular, are somewhat resistant to this approach. However, a survey of 487 firms showed that 66 percent thought these programs had a positive effect on performance. In another survey, employee reactions were found to be favorable in 63 percent of the cases.[34]

### "Flexible Benefit" Plans

The total compensation package of an employee includes not only direct pay but also any fringe benefits that are paid by the organization. These fringe benefits often add an equivalent of 10 to 40 percent to a person's salary. It is argued that organizations need to allow for individual differences when developing such benefit programs. Otherwise the motivational value of this indirect form of pay incentive is lost. One approach is to let individuals choose their total pay package by selecting benefits, up to a certain dollar amount, from a range of options made available by the organization. These ***flexible benefit plans*** allow workers to select benefits according to needs. A single worker, for example, may prefer quite a different combination of insurance and retirement contributions than a married person. The predicted result is increased motivational benefit from pay as an extrinsic work reward.

**Flexible benefit plans**

*The Bank Mart* Employees use a "spending credit" at this savings bank in Bridgeport, Connecticut, to tell the personnel department what benefits they want each year. Within the limits of their credit, which includes employer contributions, they have flexibility in choosing among health, life, and liability insurance coverages and other benefits. The bank feels it helps contain costs and the employees feel it gives them better individual packages of benefits.

Flexible benefit plans are popular with employers and with many employees. The plans offer flexibility to both parties in the employment relationship, but they can also contain some disadvantages. Some plans shift costs to the employee by raising the required co-payments and deductibles on such things as medical and dental coverage. Also, federal income tax complications continue to influence the amount of flexibility that can be allowed in the plans. Nevertheless, they do offer some additional opportunities to tie more closely this form of monetary compensation to worker needs.[35]

# SUMMARY

■ **Learning is a relatively permanent change in behavior resulting from experience. It is an important part of rewards management. There are four general approaches to learning—classical conditioning, operant conditioning, cognitive learning, and social learning. Of special importance here are cognitive learning, which relates to the motivational theories in Chapter 5, and operant conditioning, which is achieved when the consequences of behavior lead to changes in the probability of its occurrence.**

■ **Reinforcement is the means through which operant conditioning takes place. Its foundation is the law of effect, which states that behavior will be repeated or not, depending on whether the consequences are positive or negative. Applied behavior analysis uses four reinforcement strategies to change behavior. These are: positive reinforcement, avoidance, punishment, and extinction. Positive reinforcement, extinction, and punishment are of special significance to managers.**

■ **Positive Reinforcement** is used to encourage desirable behavior. It is the administration of positive consequences that tend to increase the likelihood of someone repeating a behavior in similar settings. Positive reinforcement should be contingent (administered only if the desired behavior is exhibited) and immediate (as close in time to the desired behavior as possible). It can be scheduled *continuously* or *intermittently* with somewhat different applications being better in each case.

■ **Extinction** is the withdrawal of the reinforcing consequences for a given behavior. It is often used to withhold reinforcement for a behavior that has previously been reinforced. This is done to weaken or eliminate that undesirable behavior. It is an especially powerful strategy when combined with positive reinforcement.

■ **Punishment** is the administration of negative consequences that tend to reduce the likelihood of repeating a given behavior in similar settings. Like extinction, it is used to weaken or eliminate undesirable behavior. There are a number of problems that can occur with punishment. Thus, one must be especially careful to follow appropriate reinforcement guidelines (including the laws of contingent and immediate reinforcement), when using it. Like extinction, punishment is likely to be more effective if combined with positive reinforcement.

■ **Reinforcement Perspectives: Research and Ethical Issues**, continue to be analyzed and debated. A number of success stories have been reported but many lack controlled scientific research designs. Some argue that these results may be due to variables other than reinforcement. Others point out that using the various reinforcement strategies may manipulate workers and lead to managerial abuse of power. The criticisms raise ethical considerations. Advocates of reinforcement approaches respond that all managerial strategies are manipulative in some sense and managers must be sensitive to the abuse of their power. Employees can also be encouraged to provide input into design of the reinforcement system and to use self-reinforcement wherever feasible.

■ **Managing Pay as an Extrinsic Reward** is particularly important because pay has multiple meanings—some positive and some negative. As a major and highly visible extrinsic reward, pay plays a role in reinforcement and in the motivation theories discussed previously. Its reward implications are especially important in terms of merit pay. Other pay practices that are increasing in importance and offer creative reward opportunities are: skill-based pay, gain-sharing plans, lump-sum pay increases, and flexible benefit plans.

## KEY TERMS

Applied Behavior Analysis
Classical Conditioning
Cognitive Learning
Continuous Reinforcement
Extinction
Extrinsic Rewards

Flexible Benefit Plans
Gain Sharing
Intermittent Reinforcement
Law of Contingent Reinforcement
Law of Effect
Law of Immediate Reinforcement
Learning
Lump-Sum Pay Increase
Merit Pay
Modeling
Negative Reinforcement
Operant Conditioning
Positive Reinforcement
Punishment
Shaping
Skill-Based Pay
Social Learning
Vicarious Learning

## REVIEW QUESTIONS

1. How do "operant conditioning" and "cognitive learning" differ from one another? Of what significance to managers are these differences?
2. What is "social learning theory"? How does it integrate the operant and cognitive approaches to learning and human behavior?
3. Explain "applied behavior analysis." Describe how one or more reinforcement strategies could be used to deal with an employee who is consistently late for work, but very productive once present.
4. Do you believe in the power of positive reinforcement when rewards other than pay are used as the potential reinforcers? Defend your answer.
5. When do you feel a manager is justified in using punishment as a reinforcement strategy? What guidelines should be followed when administering punishment?
6. Do you agree or disagree with those critics who claim that the systematic use of reinforcement strategies by managers is an unethical control of human behavior? Why or why not?
7. What is an "extrinsic" work reward? What are some examples of extrinsic rewards that managers might use to encourage high performance by subordinates? What does it mean to say that these rewards are best given on a "performance-contingent" basis?
8. Choose two of the creative pay practices discussed in this chapter. Do you feel the practices are valuable from the perspectives of (1) the managers who must implement them, and (2) their subordinates who participate in them? Explain your answers.

## AN OB LIBRARY

Edward E. Lawler, III, *Pay and Organization Development* (Reading, MA: Addison-Wesley, 1980).

Edward E. Lawler, III, *Strategic Pay: Aligning Organizational Strategies and Pay Systems* (San Francisco: Jossey-Bass, 1990).

Fred Luthans and Robert Kreitner, *Organizational Behavior Modification and Beyond* (Glenview, IL: Scott, Foresman, 1985).

Robert E. Quinn, Sue R. Faerman, Michael P. Thompson, and Michael R.

McGrath, *Becoming a Master Manager: A Competency Framework* (New York: John Wiley & Sons, 1990).

Anthony P. Raia, *Managing by Objectives* (Glenview, IL: Scott, Foresman, 1974).

EXERCISE

# ANNUAL PAY RAISES

*Objectives*

1. To provide an experience of choices faced by managers when they make pay raise decisions.
2. To help you review some of the theoretical issues involved in attempts to use pay as a motivator.
3. To apply these issues in a realistic and practical work setting.

*Total Time*

50 minutes

*Procedure*

1. Read the instructions on the accompanying Employee Profile Sheet and decide on a percentage pay increase for each of the eight employees.
2. Make salary increase recommendations for each of the eight managers that you supervise. There are no formal company restrictions on the size of raises you give, but the total for everyone should not exceed the $7000 (a 4-percent increase in the salary pool) which has been budgeted for this purpose. You have a variety of information upon which to base the decisions, including a "productivity index" (PI), which Industrial Engineering computes as a quantitative measure of operating efficiency for each manager's work unit. This index ranges from a high of "10" to a low of "1." Indicate the percentage increase *you* would give each manager in the blank space next to each manager's name. Be prepared to answer "why."

_______ *A. Alvarez* Alvarez is new this year and has a tough work group whose task is dirty and difficult. This is a hard position to fill, but you don't feel Alvarez is particularly good. The word around is that the other managers agree with you. PI = 3. Salary = $21,000.

_______ *B.J. Cook* Cook is single and a "swinger" who enjoys leisure time. Everyone laughs at the problems B.J. has getting the work out, and you feel it certainly is lacking. Cook has been in the job two years. PI = 3. Salary = $22,500.

_______ *Z. Davis* In the position three years, Davis is one of your best people even though some of the other managers don't agree.

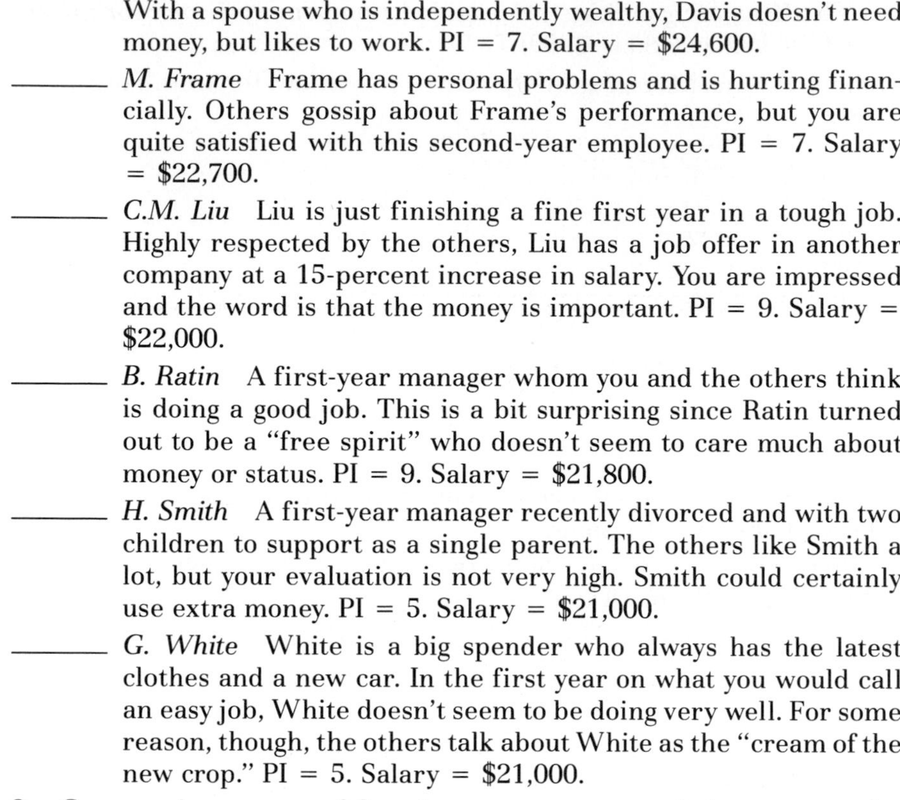

With a spouse who is independently wealthy, Davis doesn't need money, but likes to work. PI = 7. Salary = $24,600.

_______ *M. Frame* Frame has personal problems and is hurting financially. Others gossip about Frame's performance, but you are quite satisfied with this second-year employee. PI = 7. Salary = $22,700.

_______ *C.M. Liu* Liu is just finishing a fine first year in a tough job. Highly respected by the others, Liu has a job offer in another company at a 15-percent increase in salary. You are impressed and the word is that the money is important. PI = 9. Salary = $22,000.

_______ *B. Ratin* A first-year manager whom you and the others think is doing a good job. This is a bit surprising since Ratin turned out to be a "free spirit" who doesn't seem to care much about money or status. PI = 9. Salary = $21,800.

_______ *H. Smith* A first-year manager recently divorced and with two children to support as a single parent. The others like Smith a lot, but your evaluation is not very high. Smith could certainly use extra money. PI = 5. Salary = $21,000.

_______ *G. White* White is a big spender who always has the latest clothes and a new car. In the first year on what you would call an easy job, White doesn't seem to be doing very well. For some reason, though, the others talk about White as the "cream of the new crop." PI = 5. Salary = $21,000.

3. Convene in a group of four to seven persons and share your raise decision.
4. As a group, decide on a new set of raises and be prepared to report them to the rest of the class. Make sure that the group spokesperson can provide the rationale for each person's raise.
5. The instructor will call on each group to report its raise decisions. After discussion, an "expert's" decisions will be given.

## CASE

# HIGHVIEW STORES

Highview Stores is a convenience chain operating 14 small retail outlets in an eastern state.[36] Specializing in groceries, each store is run by a store manager (SM) during the day and night manager during the evening. Of the two, the night manager has little authority over decision-making and is mainly an evening "care-taker." The store manager employs one or two clerks, assisted once a week by an extra clerk, who stock shelves and handle bulk shipments and inventories.

The firm is headed by the president to whom a vice president and general manager (VP) reports. The VP directs the SMs of four stores, a day regional manager (RM) responsible for five stores, and night regional manager (NRM) responsible for another five.

At first, SMs were paid a flat salary that was adjusted by "headquarters" only when something significant had been done to improve store operations. There were no regular performance reviews, and salary adjustments were actually based more on length of service than performance accomplishments. In addition to base salary, the SMs were eligible for annual cash bonuses. These were distributed by the VP based on his personal evaluation of an SM's years of experience, overall value to the firm, and inventory shrinkage at the SM's store (i.e., the difference between actual inventory and projected inventory based on sales receipts). Most stores experienced shrinkage of one-half to one percent, and it was always discussed at what they called the VP's "regular weekly punishment" meetings. Nevertheless, the SM's jobs were quite secure and they had little fear of discharge.

One April, top management concluded the company was in trouble. Inventory shrinkage was high, 3.42 percent of sales, and growing; sales were down; stores looked sloppy; SMs were unhappy with their pay; SMs seemed unconcerned about supervising clerks and fulfilling management expectations. It was decided to test a new reward system in 10 of the 14 stores.

The plan was to pay the SMs on a commission plus annual bonus basis. The commission was negotiated with the VP and averaged 7 percent of a store's weekly sales. But, they had to pay a number of direct expenses out of this figure, including the clerk's wages, long distance phone calls, bad checks, and the like. Whatever was left after these expenses were deducted from the commission was the weekly income of the SM. The company covered things felt to be outside of the SM's control, such as insurance and electricity. The annual bonus was based on years service and inventory shrinkage. Another bonus based on store appearance was paid semiannually.

The SM's average weekly income rose 8.41 percent under the new system. The average store payroll for clerks dropped 3.33 percent. For the company as a whole, the new annual bonuses cost $4000 more than before, payroll expenses overall increased 3.56 percent, inventory shrinkage decreased an amazing 80.73 percent, and sales increased 5.3 percent. The new pay system was credited with a substantial portion of these positive results.

## *Questions*

1. Before the new pay system, what incentives existed for the SMs to improve store performance? Should these incentives have been sufficient to guarantee high-performance? Why or why not?
2. Analyze the new pay system in reinforcement terms. What reinforcement strategies did it involve? Why do they apparently work so well?
3. What is your evaluation, of the VP's as a manager? What suggestions do you offer, and why, to enhance the VP's effectiveness?

This study outline of major topics is meant to organize your reading now; it is repeated in the Summary to structure your review.

## STUDY OUTLINE

- Intrinsic Work Rewards
- Job Design in Theory
- Job Design in Practice

Job Simplification   Job Enlargement and Job Rotation   Job Enrichment
A Continuum of Job Design Strategies

- A Diagnostic Approach to Job Enrichment

The Theory   The Research   Implementing the Diagnostic Approach
Questions and Answers on Job Enrichment

- Goal Setting

Goal Setting Theory   Goal Setting and MBO

CHAPTER 7

# JOB DESIGN, GOAL SETTING, AND WORK SCHEDULING

# VISIONS 7

**Technology, the effective use of technology that is, reigns supreme at Mrs. Fields Cookies. The company's chairperson Randy Fields uses computers to keep headquarters in touch with stores, to keep store managers focused on goals, and to keep the organization chart as lean and trim as possible.**

**A computer in every Mrs. Fields store facilitates work in a variety of ways. To begin, electronic mail allows easy access to top management. Debbie Fields answers all inquiries—problems, suggestions, concerns—within 48 hours. In addition, store managers rely on their computers to set daily sales targets and guide a variety of operating decisions—including how much batter to mix and when. This goal-oriented computer support helps free up the store personnel for the work they do best, meeting and serving customers face-to-face. The result of Randy Fields's vision—using technology to help manage people—seems to be paying off. The company isn't selling just cookies anymore. Mrs. Fields software is now for sale to other retail chains.**

In the previous chapter we complemented our earlier internal focus on motivation with an external focus on reinforcement and extrinsic rewards. Here, we continue our emphasis on rewards but are concerned primarily with intrinsic rewards and the relation of job design (i.e., planning and specification of job tasks and the work setting for their accomplishment) to these rewards.

Thus, we first discuss the nature of intrinsic rewards and then concentrate on key job design and work setting aspects. We look at making jobs meaningful, interesting, and challenging, building goals, feedback, and incentives into jobs, and finally consider alternative work arrangements (focusing on different kinds of work schedules and telecommuting). And, of course, we look at guiding and facilitating work as did Randy Fields at Mrs. Fields Cookies. Our fast-changing society calls for a close look at all aspects of jobs, and alternative work arrangements are becoming increasingly important for dual-career families, single parents, those people who can't work traditional schedules, and those who do their work at home. Consistent with the individual emphasis in Part Two, we concentrate on these job aspects at the individual worker level. However, as we show in Part Three, group aspects of job design are also becoming more and more important. We examine these "creative work group designs" in Chapter 10.

# INTRINSIC WORK REWARDS

Intrinsic work rewards are those rewards received by an individual directly as a result of task performance. One example is the feeling of achievement that comes from completing a challenging project. Such feelings are individually determined and integral to the work itself. They are self-regulated in that a person is not dependent on an outsider, such as the manager, to provide them. In effect, people give these rewards to themselves. This is in direct contrast to the nature of extrinsic rewards such as pay, which, you should recall, are externally controlled. The following comments from people at work further highlight this unique nature of intrinsic rewards.[1]

**Intrinsic work rewards**

*Teacher:* "The money I earn as a teacher is nothing; but I really enjoy teaching a student a new idea."

*Machinist:* "The company doesn't give me a darn thing; but I take pride in producing a quality product."

*Social worker:* "My working conditions are bad and my co-workers are boring; but I get a real sense of satisfaction out of helping my clients."

When we discussed extrinsic rewards in the last chapter, we viewed the manager as responsible for allocating extrinsic rewards such as pay, promotion, and verbal praise to employees. To serve in this capacity, a manager must be good at evaluating performance, maintaining an inventory of valued work rewards, and giving these rewards to employees contingent upon work performance.

The management of intrinsic work rewards is an additional challenge for the manager. The manager still acts as an agent of the organization. Now, however, he or she must design jobs for individual subordinates so that intrinsic rewards become available to them as a direct result of working on assigned tasks. There is a natural tendency at this point to assume that every manager should design every job to provide every employee maximum opportunity to experience intrinsic work rewards. This is not a good assumption. Indeed, this chapter will help you to understand

- When people may desire intrinsic work rewards.
- How to design jobs for people who desire greater intrinsic work rewards.
- How to motivate those people who do not desire intrinsic work rewards.

# JOB DESIGN IN THEORY

Our investigation of the intrinsic sources of motivation begins with the job itself. What, really, is a "job"? We all have them, but can we define the term? A ***job*** is one or more tasks that an individual performs in direct support of the organization's production purpose. The key word in this definition is "tasks." In fact, ***intrinsic motivation*** is essentially task motivation, that is, a desire to work hard solely for the pleasant experience of

**Job**

**Intrinsic motivation**

task accomplishment. When a job is properly designed, both task performance and job satisfaction should be facilitated. Additional human resource maintenance aspects, such as absenteeism, commitment, and turnover, may also be influenced.

**Job design**

***Job design*** is the planning and specification of job tasks and the work setting in which they are to be accomplished. This definition includes both the specification of task attributes and the creation of a work setting for these attributes. The manager's responsibility is to design jobs that will be motivational for the individual employee. Figuratively speaking, this is properly done when

$$\text{Individual needs} + \text{task attributes} + \text{work setting} \xrightarrow[\text{to}]{\text{lead}} \text{performance and satisfaction}$$

The history of scholarly interest in job design traces in part to Frederick Taylor's work with "scientific management" in the early 1900s. As described in *Supplementary Module A* at the end of the book, Taylor and his contemporaries sought to increase the efficiency of people at work. Their approach was to increase job specialization by breaking a job into its basic components, and then establish exact time and motion requirements for each task to be done. These early efforts were forerunners of the industrial engineering approaches to job design that attempt to determine the best processes, methods, work-flow layouts, output standards, and person-machine interfaces for various jobs. For example,

> ***United Parcel Service*** More than a thousand industrial engineers use time study at UPS to set standards for a large number of tasks that are closely supervised. Drivers must walk to a customer's door at three feet-per-second and knock, without wasting time searching for a doorbell. UPS says that a mere 30 seconds wasted at each 120 or so stops can snowball into big delays at the end of the day. Some drivers cut their breaks to finish on time.

The Hawthorne studies of the 1920s, also described in *Supplementary Module A,* and the subsequent human relations movement of the 1950s and 1960s, further broadened job design issues to include other social and human factors. It is out of this historical context that the modern and comprehensive approaches to job design have emerged.

# JOB DESIGN IN PRACTICE

We can surely agree that job designs are important to the individual employee. Two questions, however, remain to be answered. What are some of the alternative strategies of job design? And which of these strategies provides more intrinsic work rewards for the employee? We'll use a continuing example of Metroma to develop answers to these questions and introduce four important job design strategies:

1. Job simplification.
2. Job enlargement.

3. Job rotation.
4. Job enrichment.

> ***Metroma*** At the Communications Division of Metroma, an assembly-line technology was formerly used to make small radio-paging devices. It consisted of 100 steps and people. Each person was responsible for a single operation. Breaks from the line consisted of lunch and a short morning and afternoon break. Sometimes it was possible for a person still to perform a single but different operation than his or her earlier one. Metroma was interested in considering job redesign. One alternative was to adjust the line so that each worker performed more than one operation. Another alternative, and the one chosen by Metroma, was to make a single person responsible for the assembling, testing, and packaging of a complete paging device.

## Job Simplification

***Job simplification*** involves standardizing work procedures and employing people in very clearly defined and specialized tasks. The initial job design at Metroma was simplified. The machine-paced automobile assembly line is also a classic example of this job design strategy.

**Job simplification**

Simplified jobs are highly specialized and usually require an individual to perform a narrow set of tasks repetitively. The potential advantages of this include increased operating efficiency. Simplified jobs can be staffed by low-skill and low-cost labor, they require little training, and production quantity is easily controlled. Possible disadvantages of this "de-skilling," on the other hand, include loss of efficiency due to low-quality work, high rates of absenteeism and turnover, and the need to pay high wages to get people to do unattractive jobs. For most people, simplified job designs tend to be low in intrinsic motivation. The jobs lack challenge and lead to boredom.

In today's high-technology age, a natural extension of job simplification is complete ***automation***—allowing a machine to do the work previously accomplished through human effort. This increasingly involves the use of robots, which are becoming ever more versatile and reliable.

**Automation**

## Job Enlargement and Job Rotation

The job enlargement and job rotation strategies seek to increase the "breadth" of a job by adding to the variety of tasks performed by a worker. Task variety is assumed to offset some of the disadvantages of job simplification and thereby increase job performance and satisfaction for the individual.

***Job enlargement*** increases task variety by combining into one job two or more tasks that were previously assigned to separate workers. The only change in the original job design is that a worker does more different tasks than previously. ***Job rotation*** increases task variety by periodically shifting workers among jobs involving different tasks. Job rotation can be arranged according to almost any time schedule, such as hourly, daily, or weekly.

**Job enlargement**

**Job rotation**

Job enlargement is illustrated in the Metroma example where each worker would perform more than one operation on the line. Job rotation would have them switching jobs with one another. Although both job rotation and job enlargement may lead to more intrinsic motivation than simplified jobs, they still fall short of *job enrichment.*

## Job Enrichment

Frederick Herzberg, whose two-factor theory we discussed in Chapter 5, feels that it is illogical to expect high levels of motivation from employees whose jobs are designed according to the rules of simplification, enlargement, or rotation. "Why," he asks, "should a worker become motivated when one or more 'meaningless' tasks are added to previously existing ones or when work assignments are rotated among equally 'meaningless' tasks?"[2] Rather than pursuing one of these job design strategies, therefore, he recommends that managers practice job enrichment.

**Job enrichment**

***Job enrichment*** is the practice of building motivating factors into job content. This job design strategy differs from the previous ones in that it seeks to expand job content by adding some of the planning and evaluating duties normally performed by the manager to the subordinates' job. These changes, which increase the "depth" of a job, are referred to by Herzberg as a ***vertical loading*** of the job tasks as opposed to the ***horizontal loading*** involved in enlargement and rotation.

**Vertical loading**
**Horizontal loading**

*TABLE 7.1*
HERZBERG'S PRINCIPLES OF JOB ENRICHMENT

| Principle | Motivators Involved |
|---|---|
| 1. Remove some controls while retaining accountability | Responsibility and achievement |
| 2. Increase the accountability of individuals for own work | Responsibility and recognition |
| 3. Give a person a complete natural unit of work (module, division, area, and so on) | Responsibility, achievement, and recognition |
| 4. Grant additional authority to an employee in his or her activity; provide job freedom | Responsibility, achievement, and recognition |
| 5. Make periodic reports directly available to the worker rather than to the supervisor | Recognition |
| 6. Introduce new and more difficult tasks not previously handled | Growth and learning |
| 7. Assign individuals specific or specialized tasks, enable them to become experts | Responsibility, achievement, and recognition |

*Source:* Copyright © 1968 by the President and Fellows of Harvard College; all rights reserved. Reprinted by permission of the *Harvard Business Review,* "One More Time: How Do You Motivate Employees?" by Frederick Herzberg, January–February 1968.

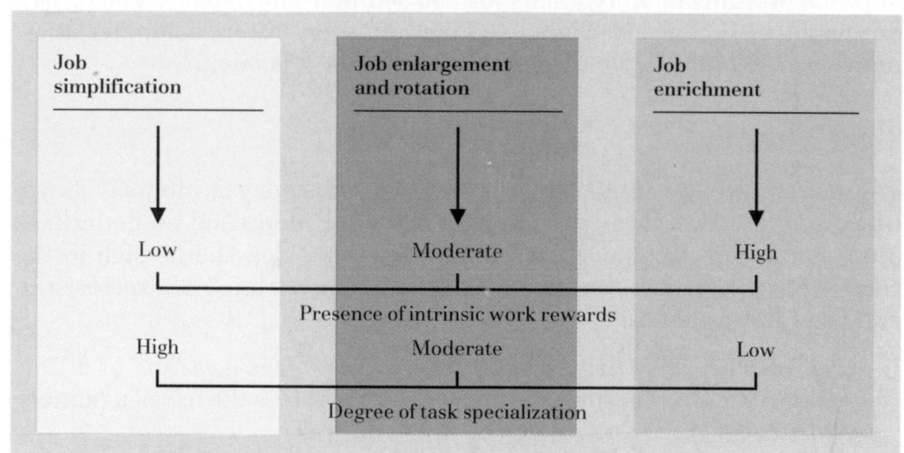


*FIGURE 7.1 A continuum of job design strategies.*

The final Metroma setup in the assembly situation contains elements of job enrichment. Making a given individual responsible for assembling, testing, and packaging the beepers provides examples of the vertical loading that Herzberg argues should increase intrinsic motivation. This, in turn, should increase satisfaction and performance. Basically this is what Metroma found.

The seven principles guiding Herzberg's approach to job enrichment are listed in Table 7.1. Note that each principle is an action guideline designed to increase the presence of one or more motivating factors in the content of a job. Remember, too, that in the job enlargement and rotation strategies managers retain all responsibility for work planning and evaluating. The job enrichment strategy, by contrast, involves vertical loading that allows subordinates to share in these planning and evaluating responsibilities, as well as to do the actual work.

## A Continuum of Job Design Strategies

The various strategies of job design are summarized on a continuum in Figure 7.1. This figure shows how the strategies differ in degree of task specialization and as sources of intrinsic work rewards. The availability of intrinsic rewards is lowest for task attributes associated with simplified jobs, and highest for enriched jobs. Task specialization, in turn, is higher for simplified jobs and lower for enriched ones.

# A DIAGNOSTIC APPROACH TO JOB ENRICHMENT

Herzberg's thinking implies that everyone's job should be enriched in order to improve job satisfaction and motivation to work. Although a natural extension of job enlargement and rotation, OB scholars were uncomfortable with job enrichment being universally applied to all types of people working in all types of jobs and settings. The diagnostic approach developed by Richard Hackman and his colleagues offers a popular alternative way to address job design in a contingency fashion.[3]

## The Theory

The current version of this "job characteristics" theory or model is shown in Figure 7.2. Five core job characteristics are identified as being task attributes of special importance to job designs. A job that is high in the core characteristics is said to be enriched. The core job characteristics and their definitions are

*Skill variety:* The degree to which a job requires a variety of different activities in carrying out the work and involves the use of a number of different skills and talents of the employee.

*Task identity:* The degree to which the job requires completion of a "whole" and identifiable piece of work, that is, one that involves doing a job from beginning to end with a visible outcome.

*Task significance:* The degree to which the job is important and involves a meaningful contribution to the organization or society in general.

*Autonomy:* The degree to which the job gives the employee substantial freedom, independence, and discretion in scheduling the work and determining procedures used in carrying it out.

*Feedback from the job itself:* The degree to which carrying out the work activities results in the employee obtaining direct and clear information on how well the job has been done.

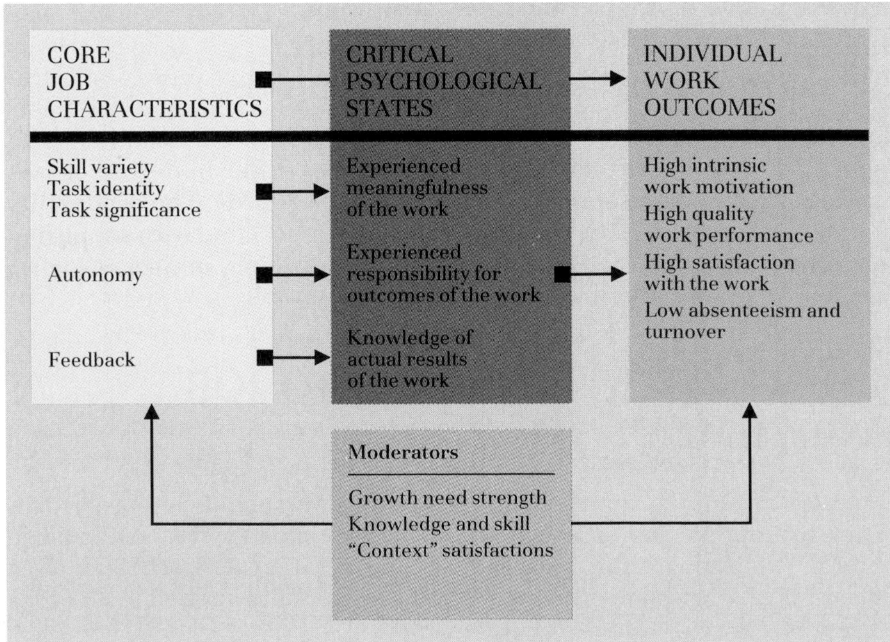


*FIGURE 7.2 Core job characteristics and individual work outcomes.* (Adapted from J. Richard Hackman and Greg R. Oldham, "Development of the Job Diagnostic Survey," *Journal of Applied Psychology,* Vol. 60, 1975, p. 161. Used by permission.)

Courtesy of Lands' End, Inc.

**SKILLS PERSPECTIVE**

## LANDS' END

**Lands' End, a specialty catalog retailer, is now up to $540 million plus in annual sales. Not bad for a company that started out selling hard-to-find sailboat fittings by mail order. Now new product development is a continuing goal for the firm, and new CEO Cary Comer is committed to making new ventures in the international area, home furnishings, and children's businesses successful. But all this requires that people work together in teams where different perspectives are brought to bear on a common goal—for example, creating a new line of children's clothing. Group and interpersonal skills are expected when the product manager meets in a final review with representatives of the merchandising and creative departments. Their teamwork helps build a competitive product for today's complex marketplace.**

Hackman and his colleagues state further that three critical psychological states must be realized for people to develop intrinsic work motivation: (1) experienced meaningfulness in the work, (2) experienced responsibility for the outcomes of the work, and (3) knowledge of actual results of the work activities. These psychological states represent intrinsic rewards that are believed to occur, and influence later performance and satisfaction, when the core job characteristics are present in the job design.

Consider the case of Christine Szczesniak who used to perform one job repetitively as a check processor for a bank.[4] Her job has been redesigned to include nearly all the tasks relating to checks received from the bank's clients. This includes receiving the checks, depositing them, calling customers with account information, and mailing the checks, depositing them, calling customers with account information, and mailing reports to them. About the new job design, Christine says: "I think it's exciting and different . . . it has cut down on the error ratio . . . I like it . . . you see the package from beginning to end . . . it's better to be part of the whole thing."

This theory recognizes that the five core job characteristics do not affect all people in the same way. Growth need strength, one of the moderators shown in Figure 7.2, is considered an important source of individual variation. The theory predicts that people with strong growth needs will respond positively to enriched jobs, whereas people low in growth need strength will have negative reactions and find enriched jobs a source of anxiety. An individual's knowledge and skill may also have a similar moderating effect. This point once again highlights how important a sense of competency can be to people at work. These relationships are summarized in Figure 7.3. People whose capabilities match the requirements of an enriched job are likely to experience positive feelings and perform well; people who are or who feel inadequate in this regard are likely to have difficulties.

## The Research

There is now considerable research on the diagnostic approach. It has been examined in a variety of work settings, including banks, dentists offices, corrections departments, telephone companies, and in such organizations as the federal government, IBM, and Texas Instruments. A comprehensive review shows:[5]

- On the average, job characteristics affect performance, but not nearly as much as they do satisfaction.
- It is important to consider growth need strength. Job characteristics tie to performance more strongly for high-growth need employees than for low-growth need employees. The relation is about as strong as with satisfaction.

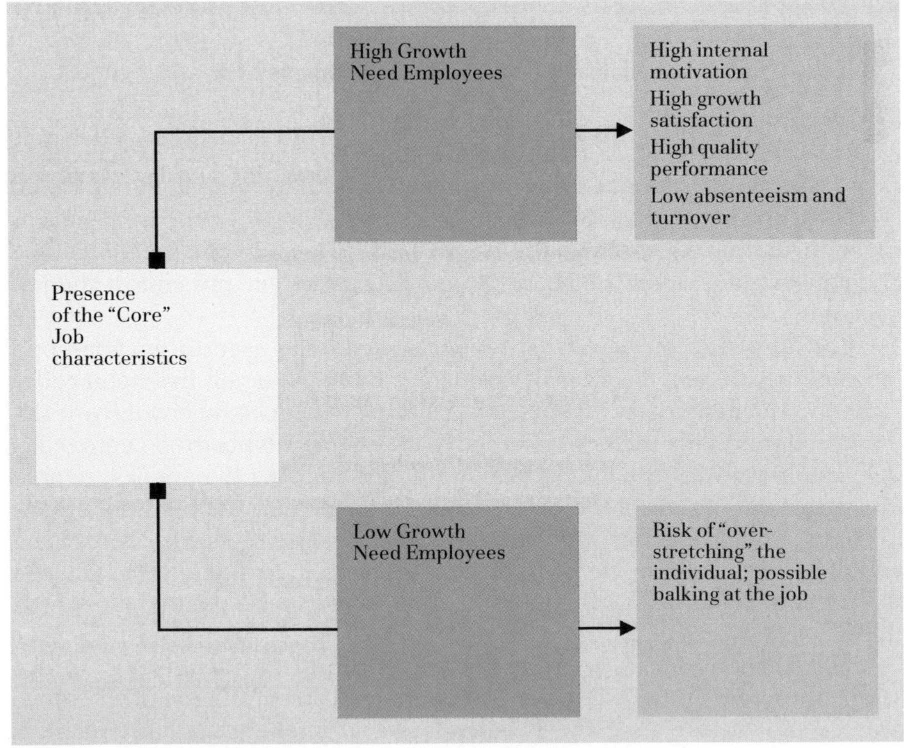


*FIGURE 7.3. Growth needs and the core job characteristics.* (From J. Richard Hackman, Greg Oldham, Robert Janson, and Kenneth Purdy, "A New Strategy for Job Enrichment." Copyright © 1975 by the Regents of the University of California. Reprinted from *California Management Review,* Vol. 17, p. 60 by permission of the Regents.)

- Employee perceptions of job characteristics are different from objective measures and those of independent observers.
- Positive results are strongest when an overall performance measure is used, rather than a separate measure of quality or quantity.

Experts generally agree that the job diagnostic approach is quite promising, but it is not a universal panacea for job performance and satisfaction problems. They also recognize that any job enrichment can fail when job requirements are increased beyond the level of individual capabilities and/or interests. In summary, remember that jobs high in core characteristics (especially as perceived by employees) tend to increase both satisfaction and performance, especially among high-growth need employees.

## Implementing the Diagnostic Approach

A diagnostic approach to job enrichment holds promise for the practicing manager. To make sure that you fully understand the concept, let's work through the following classic case from Traveler's Insurance.

### *Traveler's Insurance Company*

The company depends heavily on computerized information processing.[6] This information is provided by data entry clerks. They enter data from printed or written documents supplied by user departments.

Requests for data entry come from many departments within the company. These requests are received in the data entry unit by individuals who review the requests for accuracy, legibility, and so on. Rejected requests are sent to the unit supervisor, who corrects the problems through direct contact with the user departments. Accepted requests are parceled out to data entry clerks in small batches.

The clerks are supposed to punch exactly the information on the input documents, even when obvious coding mistakes exist. A verifier then checks all punching for accuracy as measured against the supporting documents. Any punching errors are randomly assigned back to the operators for correction.

1. Use the following scale to assess the data entry clerks' jobs on each of the five core job characteristics.

   | | | |
   |---|---|---|
   | Skill variety | low | high |
   | Task identity | low | high |
   | Task significance | low | high |
   | Autonomy | low | high |
   | Feedback | low | high |

2. Based on your analysis of the jobs, what do you predict in terms of the data entry clerks' job performance and satisfaction?

   | | | | |
   |---|---|---|---|
   | Job satisfaction: | low | moderate | high |
   | Job performance: | low | moderate | high |

## *Continuing On*

Travelers Insurance Company became concerned because the data entry clerks were apathetic and sometimes hostile toward their jobs. Error rates were high and absenteeism was frequent. If you predicted low performance and satisfaction, you were right.

The company next hired a professional consulting firm to look into the situation. The consultants concluded that the motivating potential of the data entry job was low. Specifically, they identified the following weaknesses.

*Skill variety:* There was none. Only a single skill was involved, the ability to punch the data recorded accurately on input documents.

*Task identity:* It was virtually nonexistent. Data entry batches were assembled to provide an even work load in the unit, but this did not create whole and identifiable jobs for the clerks.

*Task significance:* None was apparent. The data entry operation was a necessary step in providing service to the company's customers. The individual clerk, however, was isolated by an assignment clerk and a supervisor from any knowledge of what the operation meant to the user department let alone its meaning to the customers of the company.

*Autonomy:* There was none. The clerks had no freedom to arrange their daily tasks to meet production schedules, or to resolve problems with the user departments, or even to correct, while punching, information that was obviously wrong.

*Feedback:* There was none. Once a punching batch left the clerk's hands, he or she was not guaranteed feedback on its quality, since punching errors were randomly assigned back to the clerks.

## *Continuing On*

The consultants ultimately decided to enrich the job design. Initially, however, they did so only for some clerks. The jobs of the others were left unchanged to serve as a control group. This quasi-experimental procedure was followed by provide evaluative data as to whether or not the enriched job was beneficial for the company and the clerks. Thus, a decision could be made to abandon the program if it was not working or to revise it in a constructive fashion.

The actual changes made by the consultants to enrich the data entry clerk's job illustrate five implementation concepts central to the diagnostic approach to job enrichment. These concepts indicate that, to improve upon the five core job characteristics, a manager must be skilled at combining tasks, forming neutral work units, establishing client relationships, vertical loading, and opening feedback channels. The relationship between these implementation concepts and the core job characteristics is shown in Figure 7.4. Their use in the present case included:

1. *Forming natural units of work:* The random assignment of work batches was discontinued. Instead, each clerk was assigned continuing responsibility for certain accounts, either user departments or spe-

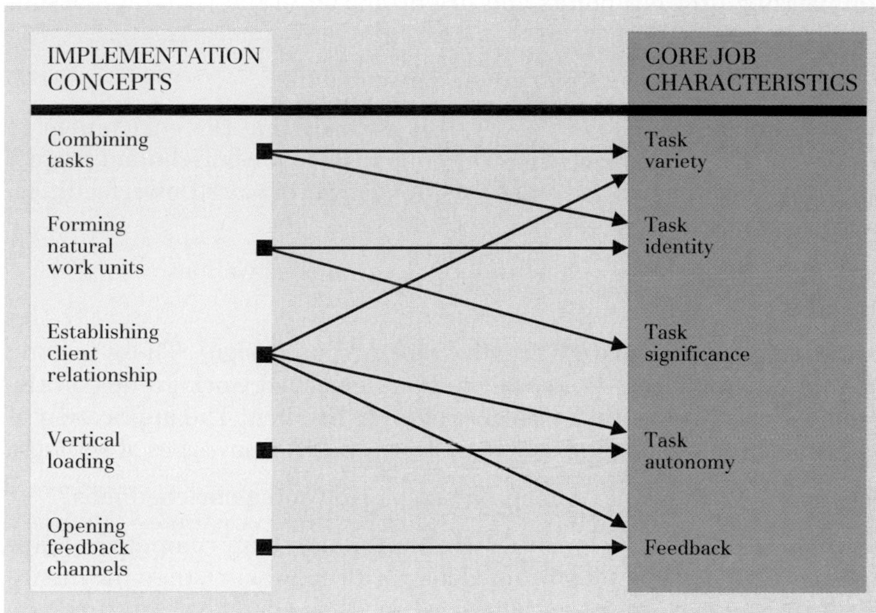


*FIGURE 7.4. Implementation concepts and the core job characteristics.* (Adapted from J. Richard Hackman et al., "A New Strategy for Job Enrichment." Copyright © 1975 by the Regents of the University of California. Reprinted from *California Management Review,* Vol. 17, p. 62 by permission of the Regents.)

cific recurring jobs. Now all work for a given account always goes to the same clerk.

2. *Combining tasks:* Some planning and evaluating duties were included along with the central task of data entry. These changes are elaborated upon as we discuss the additional changes undertaken.
3. *Establishing client relationships:* Each clerk was allowed direct contact with data entry clients. The clerks now inspect input documents for correctness and legibility. When problems arise, the clerk, not the supervisor, takes them up with the client.
4. *Opening feedback channels:* The clerks are provided with a number of additional sources of data about their performance. The computer department now provides feedback to the clerks and they correct their own errors. Each clerk also keeps a personal file of entry errors. These can be reviewed to determine trends in the frequency and types of errors being made. Each clerk receives a weekly computer printout summarizing errors and productivity. This report is sent directly to the clerk rather than to the supervisor.
5. *Vertical loading:* Clerks now have the authority to correct obvious coding errors on input documents. They also set their own entry schedules and plan their daily work, as long as they meet deadlines. Some especially competent clerks have been given the option of not having their work verified.

## Questions and Answers on Job Enrichment

Given the importance of job enrichment, there are probably a number of questions still in your mind. Answering these questions gives us a way of summarizing previous points and orienting you to the remaining issues to be covered in this chapter.

*Question:* "Is it expensive to do job enrichment?"

Job enrichment can be very costly. It is unlikely that the enrichment of the keypunch operator's job costs very much. But a job enrichment project can get expensive when it requires major changes in work flows, facilities, and/or equipment.

*Question:* "Can job enrichment apply to groups as well as individuals?"

Yes. In Chapter 9 we discuss creative work group designs. These include the innovative efforts that redesigned and enriched work groups on the automobile assembly line at a Volvo plant in Sweden. The application of job design strategies at the group level is growing in many types of settings.

*Question:* "Will people demand more pay for doing enriched jobs?"

Herzberg argues that if employees are being paid a truly competitive wage or salary (i.e., if pay dissatisfaction does not already exist), then the intrinsic rewards of performing enriched tasks will be adequate compensation for any increased labor required. Other researchers are more skeptical. One study reports that 79 percent of the people whose jobs were enriched in a company felt that they should have been paid more.[7] A manager must be cautious on this issue. Any job enrichment program should be approached with due consideration given to pay as an important program variable.

*Question:* "What do the unions say about job enrichment?"

It is hard to speak for all unions. Suffice it to say that the following comments made by one union official sound a note of caution for the manager.[8]

> better wages, shorter hours, vested pensions, a right to have a say in their working conditions, the right to be promoted on the basis of seniority, and all the rest. That's the kind of job enrichment that unions believe in. And I assure you that that's the kind of job enrichment that we will continue to fight for.

*Question:* "Should everyone's job be enriched?"

No, not everyone's job should be enriched. The informed manager will make very careful decisions when considering job enrichment as a way of promoting satisfaction and performance in the work unit. The logic of individual differences suggests that not everyone will want an enriched job. The people most likely to have positive reactions to job enrichment will be those who need achievement, those who hold middle-class working values, and/or those seeking higher-order growth need satisfactions at work. It also appears that job enrichment will be most advantageous when dissatisfiers are not found in the job context and when workers have the levels of ability required to do the enriched job. Costs, technological constraints, and work group or union opposition, furthermore, may make it difficult to enrich some jobs.[9]

*Question:* "What are some summary guidelines for doing job enrichment?"

The guidelines for implementing a program of job enrichment include:

1. Consider a job to be a candidate for job enrichment only when evidence exists that job satisfaction and/or performance is either deteriorating or open for improvement.
2. Use a diagnostic approach and proceed with actual job enrichment only when each of the following conditions is met:
   a. Employees view their jobs as deficient in one or more of the core job characteristics.
   b. Extrinsic rewards and job context are not causing dissatisfaction.
   c. Cost and other potential constraints do not prohibit the types of job design changes necessary to result in enrichment.
   d. Employees view the core job characteristics with high and positive valences.
   e. Employees have needs and capabilities consistent with the new job designs.
3. Whenever possible do a careful evaluation of the results of job enrichment. This gives the manager an opportunity to discontinue the job design strategy or to make constructive changes to increase its value.
4. Expect that enrichment will also affect the job of the supervising manager. He or she will normally be asked to delegate duties to subordinates. Some managers are threatened by this requirement, and they can become anxious or feel frustrated. These managers may need help to make the required personal work adjustments.

# GOAL SETTING

Without proper goals, employees may suffer a direction problem. Some years ago, for example, the Minnesota Vikings' Defensive End Jim Marshall gathered up an opponent's fumble. Then, with obvious effort and delight, he ran the ball some 50 yards into the *wrong* end zone. Clearly, Jim Marshall did not lack intrinsic motivation. Unfortunately, though, he failed to channel his work energies toward the right goal. Similar problems are found in many work settings. They can be eliminated, or at least reduced, by the proper setting and clarification of task goals.

## Goal Setting Theory

**Goal setting**

***Goal setting*** is the "process of developing, negotiating, and formalizing the targets or objectives that an employee is responsible for accomplishing."[10] Incorporating goal setting into job designs results in specific task objectives for each individual. The presence of these objectives is important because of the motivational consequences with which they may be associated.

Edwin A. Locke has developed a set of assertions as to the motiva-

INTERNATIONAL PERSPECTIVE

## FEDERAL EXPRESS

It's not all smooth sailing for Federal Express's journey into international markets. Founder and chairperson Frederick W. Smith keeps reminding everyone that success will only come with time and that the initial investment will be costly. Once again, though, he comes back to people as the key to the firm's past and future success. In fact, Federal Express recently received the Distinguished Service Award for strong leadership and effective human resource management. Smith claims to spend at least 25 percent of his time on personnel issues, and he stresses that everyone must understand the basic goal of having a 100 percent satisfied customer at the end of every transaction. When that is understood, he says, "it's a lot easier for that employee to answer the 'What's expected of me question.' " He further believes that clear expectations are needed to motivate employees—in the United States or anywhere else in the world.

Courtesy of Federal Express Corporation.

tional properties of task goals. Locke's research, and that of others, tends to support his predictions that[11]

1. Difficult goals are more likely to lead to higher performance than less difficult ones.
2. Specific goals are more likely to lead to higher performance than vague or very general ones (such as "do your best").
3. Task feedback, or knowledge of results, is likely to motivate people toward high performance when it leads to the setting of higher performance goals.
4. Goals are most likely to lead to higher performance when people have the abilities required to accomplish them.
5. Goals are most likely to motivate people toward higher performance when they are accepted.

This last finding is of special interest to managers. Unless your subordinates accept their task goals, you can't expect to receive a motivational advantage. Research suggests that people may be more inclined to accept goals when they have had the chance to participate in the goal-setting process. However, acceptance is the key and participation is not the only way for it to take place. Goal acceptance is also enhanced when people feel that the goals are reasonable (i.e., expectancy is high) and when they see a clear relationship between goal attainment and desirable work outcomes (i.e., high instrumentality).

Once again, as you can see, the basic tenets of expectancy theory prove useful in explaining work behavior. Indeed, ties such as these with expectancy theory sometimes have caused goal setting theory to be treated as a process motivation theory in addition to the equity theory and expectancy theory discussed in Chapter 5. Although goal setting's cognitive workings are not understood completely, we do know that it works. Indeed, one expert says that it has the most support to date of any of the work motivation theories.[12] There is one key point that *is* well understood and that you should not lose sight of as a manager: such factors as participation, feedback, and incentives have an effect in this approach *only* to the extent that they influence goal difficulty and goal acceptance or goal commitment.[13]

## Goal Setting and MBO

When we speak of goal setting and its potential to influence individual performance at work, the concept of ***management by objectives*** (or ***MBO***) comes immediately to mind. It has been used by such firms as Purex, Tenneco, and Black & Decker. The essence of MBO is a process of *joint* goal setting between a supervisor and a subordinate.[14] It involves managers working with their subordinates to establish performance goals that are consistent with higher-level work unit and organizational objectives. When this process is followed throughout an organization, MBO helps to clarify the hierarchy of objectives as a series of well-defined means–end chains—which we discussed in Chapter 1.

**Management by objectives**

Figure 7.5 shows a comprehensive view of MBO. The concept is consistent with the notion of goal setting and its associated principles just discussed. Notice how joint supervisor–subordinate discussions are

*FIGURE 7.5. The management by objectives (MBO) process.*

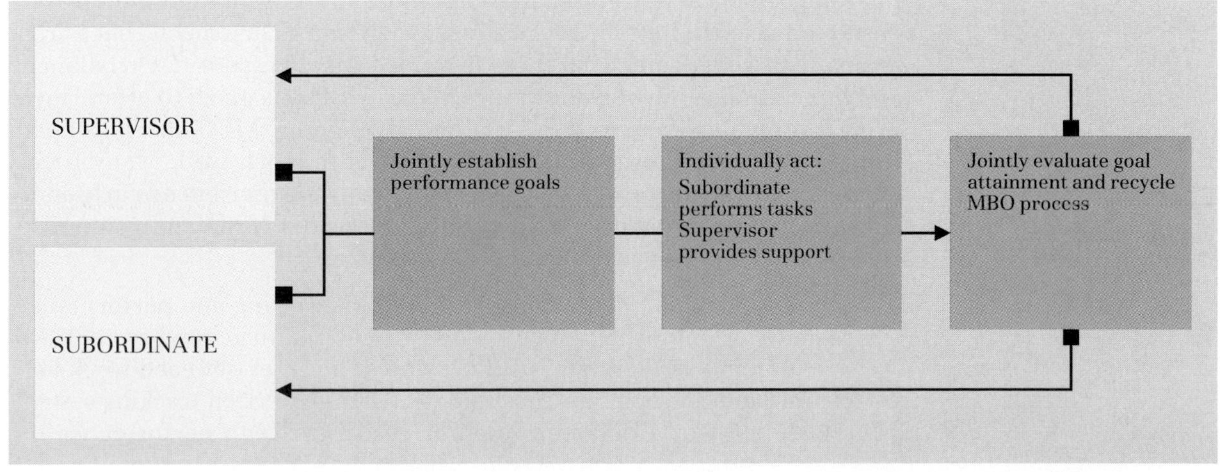

designed to extend participation from the point of initial goal establishment to the point of evaluating results in terms of goal attainment. Key issues for the mutual goal setting include:

- *What must be done?* Higher-level goals, job descriptions stating tasks to be performed, outcomes expected, necessary supplies and equipment, and so on, are useful starting points.
- *How will performance be measured?* Frequently time, money, or physical units may be used. Where the nature of the job is more subjective, behaviors or actions believed to lead to success may be emphasized.
- *What is the performance standard?* Previous performance or average performance of others doing this job is a reasonable starting point. Where these do not exist, then mutual supervisor–subordinate judgment and discussion is appropriate.
- *What are the deadlines for the goals?* Discuss these in terms of daily, weekly, or longer terms.
- *What is the relative importance of the goals?* Not all goals are equally important. The manager and subordinate should together decide on the goal ranking.
- *How difficult are the goals?* This topic is particularly tricky where the job is complex and where there are multiple goals. Again, it calls for a clearly agreed upon decision between the manager and subordinate.[15]

In addition to these initial goal setting steps, a successful MBO system calls for careful implementation. This means that the previous steps are translated into actions that will lead to goal accomplishment. Subordinates must have freedom to carry out the required tasks. Also, managers may have to do considerable coaching and counseling.

As with other applied OB programs, managers should be aware of MBO's potential costs as well as benefits. Some specific problems to be concerned about are: (1) an overemphasis on goal-oriented rewards and punishments; (2) too much paperwork from establishing goals and monitoring their accomplishments; (3) too much stress on goals from the top down; (4) goals that can be objectively stated may drive out important but harder to state ones; and (5) an overemphasis on individual as opposed to group goals. Furthermore, although there is a fair amount of research based on case studies of MBO success, there isn't very much that is rigorously controlled, and what there *is* reports mixed results.[16] On balance, and as an application of goal setting theory, MBO has much to offer. However, it is by no means easy to start and keep going. MBO also may need to be implemented organization-wide if it is to work well. Many firms have started and dropped it because of difficulties experienced early on.[17] However, some firms have successfully integrated MBO and computerized monitoring. For example,

> ***Cypress Semiconductor Corporation*** Goal setting and performance reviews are important parts of "no excuses" management system. All of the firm's 1400 employees have goals that they set each week and commit to achieving by a certain date. A computerized tracking system and supervisory follow-up monitor results to keep performance on

target. Monthly "completed goals reports" are issued for every person as a form of positive feedback.

# ALTERNATIVE WORK ARRANGEMENTS

Changing demographics and related societal trends are encouraging a number of alternative work arrangements that we need to consider as a third aspect of job design. These include the compressed work week, flexible working hours, job-sharing, part-time work, and telecommuting. Each of these shares a common concern for fitting work arrangements with individual needs. For example, dual-career families with children, part-time students, older workers retired or near retirement age, single parents with children at home, and others like them are all candidates for alternative work arrangements. In addition, these arrangements may offer more flexibility for employers as business expands or contracts, and they can mean energy and time savings for society.

## The Compressed Work Week

**Compressed work week**

A ***compressed work week*** is any scheduling of work that allows a full-time job to be completed in fewer than the standard five days. The most common form of compressed work week is the "4 – 40," that is, 40 hours of work accomplished in four 10-hour days. It is currently the least used of all the alternative work arrangements, although there are many possible benefits. Added time off is a major feature for the worker. The individual often benefits from increased leisure time, more 3-day weekends, free weekdays to pursue personal business, and lower commuting costs. The organization can benefit, too, in terms of reduced energy consumption during 3-day shutdowns, lower employee absenteeism, improved recruiting of new employees, and having extra time available for building and equipment maintenance.

The disadvantages may include increased fatigue from the extended workday and family adjustment problems for the individual, and increased work scheduling problems and possible customer complaints due to breaks in work coverage for the organization. Possible constraints on utilization of compressed workweek schedules include occasional union opposition and laws that require some organizations to pay overtime for work that exceeds 8 hours of individual labor in any one day.

Research results are mixed on the compressed work week. It sometimes has a positive effect on productivity, absenteeism, and the like, and sometimes does not. What seems to happen is that positive effects occur when the compressed work week is first implemented, and then these effects wear off.[18] This work schedule also can influence other aspects of the job design. For example, one study found that reaction to the compressed work week was most favorable for employees who had participated in the decision to compress the work week, who had had their jobs enriched as a result of the new schedule, and who had strong higher-order needs. The enrichment occurred because less employees were on duty at any one time and job duties were changed and enriched to accommodate this, since the organization was kept open the same number of days as before.[19]

## Flexible Working Hours

Would you believe that there is a work schedule loaded with advantages, but with few reported disadvantages? Examine these lists of potential benefits then read on.

| *Organizational Benefits* | *Individual Benefits* |
|---|---|
| Lower absenteeism | More leisure time |
| Reduced tardiness | Less commuting time |
| Reduced turnover | Higher job satisfaction |
| Higher work commitment | Greater sense of responsibility |
| Higher performance | Easier personal scheduling |

**Flexible working hours**

The work schedule to which these benefits are assigned is called ***flexible working hours***—defined as "any work schedule that gives employees daily choice in the timing between work and nonwork activities."[20] Nearly 25 percent of federal government workers are currently on a flexible working schedule and it is estimated that one-third to one-half of the work force may move to some form of flexible working time during the next 10 years.[21] A sample flexible working hour schedule is shown in Figure 7.6. Employees are required to work four hours of "core" time. They are then free to choose their remaining four hours of work from among flexible time blocks.

Flexible working hours, or "flextime," increases individual autonomy in work scheduling. Early risers may choose to come in early and leave at 4 P.M.; late sleepers may choose to start at 10 A.M. and leave at 6 P.M. In between these two extremes are opportunities to attend to such personal affairs as dental appointments, home emergencies, visiting the bank, and so on. Proponents of this scheduling strategy argue that the discretion it allows workers in scheduling their own hours of work encourages them to develop positive attitudes and increase commitment to the organization. Research tends to support this position. The reason for such positive impact may well trace to the ability of flexible working hours to help workers adjust themselves to the demands and opportunities of both work and nonwork involvements. For example,

*FIGURE 7.6 A sample flexible working hours scheme.*

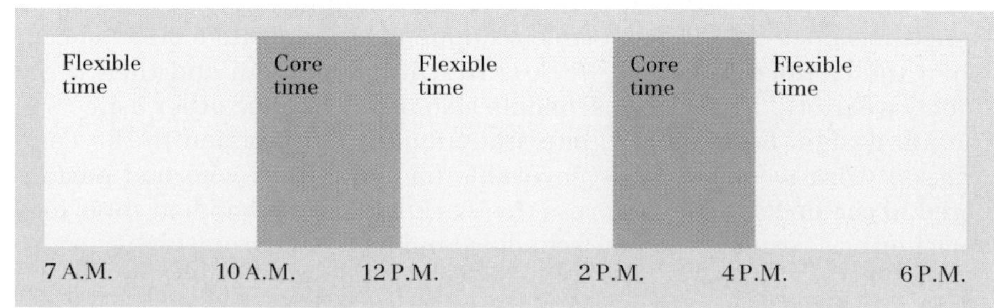

Courtesy of James River Corporation.

ETHICAL PERSPECTIVE

## JAMES RIVER

**A commitment to ethics stands at the top of James River Corporation's *Statement of Fundamental Values/Beliefs.* This commitment means: "Highest standards of integrity, ethics, and fairness must override in all transactions and relationships." A premier world-wide pulp, paper, packaging, and related products company, James River extends this ethical commitment to the treatment of its employees. In its vision for the future, the firm wants to have a challenged and motivated work force, but also one in which people "feel good about and have fun in their jobs." Operating with a clear sense of purpose and the highest standards of ethics, the firm is dedicated to being the most responsive and creative producer in the industry.**

*Aetna Life & Casualty Company* Some workers are allowed to do their jobs during any hours agreeable to both themselves and their supervisors at Aetna. The supervisor's manual states: "Conceivably, a person could work from 10 P.M. to 6 A.M. Wednesday through Sunday." An Aetna manager, commenting on the program, says: "We're not doing flexible work scheduling to be nice, but because it makes business sense."

Among the possible disadvantages of flextime approaches are difficulty in scheduling multiple persons, problems of interdepartmental communication during worker absences, and the potential for employees to become frustrated when problems occur in the absence of their supervisors.

## Job Sharing

**Job sharing**

Another alternative work schedule is ***job sharing.*** This occurs when one full-time job is assigned to two persons who then divide the work according to agreements made between themselves and with the employer.[22] Job sharing often occurs where each person works one-half day, although it can also be done on such bases as weekly or monthly sharing arrangements. It is still used by only a relatively small percentage of employers.[23]

Organizations can benefit from job sharing when they are able to attract talented people who would otherwise be unable to work. An example is the qualified schoolteacher who is also a parent. This person may feel unable to be away from the home a full day, but able to work a half-day. Through job sharing, two such persons can be employed to teach one class. Many other opportunities for job sharing exist. For example,

> ***Northeast Utilities Service Corporation*** Job sharing by both professional and hourly workers has met with positive results at Northeast Utilities. The firm employs 54 job-sharing pairs, but won't allow supervisors to share jobs. "Two job-sharers," says Mike Brown the director of employee relations, "each give four hours of 'full-bore' production."

## Part-Time Work

**Part-time work**
**Temporary part-time work**
**Permanent part-time work**

There is another work schedule of increasing prominence and controversy in the United States—***part-time work.*** There are two kinds of part-time work: ***temporary part-time*** (where an employee is classified as "temporary" and works less than the standard 40-hour work week) and ***permanent part-time*** (where a worker is considered "permanent" but works less than the standard work week). Note that employees involved in job sharing fit this latter category. Nearly one-quarter of the workers in Europe and the United States are on some kind of part-time schedule. As an example, about 20 percent of the work force at Federal Express is part time, most working the night shift.[24]

Temporary part-timers are usually easy to release and hire as needs dictate. Because of this, many organizations use part-time work to hold down labor costs and help smooth out peaks and valleys in the business cycle. This alternative work schedule can be a benefit to people who also hold full-time jobs, or want something less than a full work week for a variety of personal reasons. For someone who is holding two jobs, including at least one part-time, the added burdens can be stressful and may affect performance in either one or both work settings. Furthermore, part-timers often fail to qualify for fringe benefits such as health care, life insurance, and pensions, and they may be paid less than their full-time counterparts. Nonetheless, part-time work schedules are of growing practical importance because of the organizational advantages listed previously. They are likely to command additional attention from researchers in the future. For example,

> ***Corning, Inc.*** Janet McLaughlin, manager of strategic planning at Corning, is one of those "professionals" for whom part-time work is important. Originally hired as a part-timer, she asked to keep the status when first promoted to supervisor. "I told them that if it didn't work I'd gladly step down." It's now four promotions later and Janet's career is doing just fine.

## Telecommuting

High technology is influencing our final alternative work arrangement—telecommuting. ***Telecommuting*** is work done at home or in a remote location by using a computer linked to a central office or other employment location. Sometimes this arrangement is called "flexiplace" or "the electronic cottage."[25] It emphasizes place rather than scheduling, although working at home does allow flexible working hours.

**Telecommuting**

It is currently the most controversial of the alternative work arrangements. Nearly two million corporate employees are now telecommuting full time. And there are almost three times as many employees who do so one or two days a week. On the one hand, there are lots of reasons to pursue it. The Environmental Protection Agency recently approved a regulation requiring firms with more than 100 employees in four Southern California counties to present plans to cut commuter glut—part of these plans might involve telecommuting. And telecommuting also offers the potential advantages of flexibility, the comforts of home, and choice of locations consistent with one's lifestyle. On the other hand, firms such as Hartford Insurance have tried it and dropped it for most of its employees and a survey of 50 top employers in Pittsburgh showed that many were not supportive of it.[26] Managerial considerations in dealing with remote employees seem to be a prime reason. Other reasons are a sense of isolation from co-workers, decreased identification with the work team, and technical difficulties with computer linkages. Research is still needed to determine whether these disadvantages will overcome the advantages and appeal of telecommuting. Yet, it is a way of life for some already. For example,

> *Telecom USA* Salesperson Mike Saul of Telecom is among the growing number of Americans spending more time at home . . . while at work. He spends a few hours every day working out of his office at home. Recently the firm bought him a facsimile ("fax") machine to facilitate his work. He also has a telephone answering machine and separate business phone line.

## SUMMARY

■ **Intrinsic Work Rewards** **are those work rewards received by an individual directly as a result of task performance. They are self-motivating and do not require external reinforcement.**

■ **Job Design in Theory** **involves the planning and specification of job tasks and the work setting in which they are to be accomplished. The manager's responsibility is to fit individual needs with task attributes and** the work setting so that both performance and human resource maintenance are facilitated. The history of interest in job design traces to Taylor's scientific management movement—which emphasized job specialization—and to the Hawthorne studies—which emphasized human relations factors.

■ **Job Design Strategies** include three broad alternatives: job simplification, job enlargement and job rotation, and job enrichment. The first standardizes work procedures and employs people in very clearly defined and specialized tasks. Job enlargement increases task variety by combining two or more tasks previously assigned to separate workers. Job rotation increases task variety by periodically rotating work among jobs involving different tasks. Job enrichment builds motivating factors into job content by adding planning and evaluating duties. The intrinsic work rewards made available by these strategies range on a continuum from low (job simplification) to high (job enrichment).

■ **A Diagnostic Approach to Job Enrichment** has been developed by Richard Hackman and his associates. It does not assume that everyone wants an enriched job. Rather, it looks at the effect of five core job characteristics (ranging from skill variety to feedback from the job itself) on intervening critical psychological states that influence motivation, performance, and satisfaction. There is considerable research support for the job diagnostic approach. Questions and answers on job enrichment point out that it can be expensive, can apply to groups as well as individuals, may lead to demands for increased pay, may run into union opposition, and that not everyone's job should be enriched. People high in growth-need strength seem to respond best to the approach.

■ **Goal Setting** is an aspect of job design that emphasizes the building of goals, feedback, and incentives into the structure of the job. It emphasizes difficult, specific goals, knowledge of results, ability to accomplish the goals, and goal acceptance. Management by objectives (MBO) is a technique that applies goal setting theory. A manager and subordinate mutually agree on individual goals that are consistent with higher level ones. A process is then implemented to monitor and assist the subordinate in task accomplishment and the subordinate's performance is evaluated in terms of accomplished results. If implemented well, many positive aspects of goal setting theory can be realized from MBO; but effective MBO systems are difficult to establish and maintain.

■ **Alternative Work Arrangements** are becoming increasingly important in our rapidly-changing society. The compressed work week allows full-time work to be completed in less than five days. Flexible working hours allow employees a daily choice in timing between work and nonwork activities. Job-sharing occurs when two or more people divide one full-time job according to agreement between or among themselves and the employer. Part-time work is done on a schedule classifying the worker as temporary or permanent and requires less than a 40-hour work week. Telecommuting involves work done at home or at a remote location using a computer with linkage to the employment location.

## REVIEW QUESTIONS

1. Go back to the Metroma assembly-line job described earlier in the chapter. Write a profile of the type of person you feel would be satisfied and productive in this job. Defend your profile and describe its managerial implications.
2. Look back to the union official's comment in the section on questions and answers about job enrichment. Why do you think the official feels this way? Do you think this opinion would be shared by most union members? Why or why not?
3. How does growth need-strength influence employee reactions to job enrichment?
4. In what types of work situations would job enlargement and/or job rotation be preferred to job enrichment as job design strategies?
5. List and explain three of the conditions cited by Locke as creating motivational properties for task goals? What role should "participation" play in the goal-setting process?
6. In what ways does management by objectives (MBO) offer managers the opportunity to apply and benefit from the insights of Locke's goal-setting theory?
7. Why would (1) flexible working hours and (2) the compressed work week be attractive as alternative work schedules for some people? What difficulties might these schedules create for the managers of persons using them?
8. Extrinsic and intrinsic rewards present quite different challenges to managers who seek to make use of them. What are these differences and what are their implications for managers?

## KEY TERMS

Automation
Compressed Work Week
Flexible Working Hours
Goal Setting
Horizontal Loading
Intrinsic Motivation
Intrinsic Work Rewards
Job
Job Design
Job Enlargement
Job Enrichment
Job Rotation
Job Sharing
Job Simplification
Management by Objectives (MBO)
Permanent Part-Time Work
Telecommuting
Temporary Part-Time Work
Vertical Loading

## AN OB LIBRARY

Ramon J. Aldag and Arthur P. Brief, *Task Design and Employee Motivation* (Reading, MA: Addison-Wesley, 1979).

Allan R. Cohen and Herman Gadon, *Alternative Work Schedules: Integrating Individual and Organizational Needs* (Reading, MA: Addison-Wesley, 1978).

J. Richard Hackman and Greg R. Oldham, *Work Redesign* (Reading, MA: Addison-Wesley, 1980).

Richard E. Kopleman, *Managing Productivity in Organizations* (New York: McGraw-Hill, 1986).

Doug Stewart, *The Power of People Skills: A Manager's Guide to Assessing and Developing Your Organization's Greatest Resource* (New York: John Wiley & Sons, 1986).

# EXERCISE

## SETTING WORK GOALS

### *Objectives*

1. To help you develop and refine your skills for goal development and analysis.
2. To develop a realistic assessment framework for your personal goals.
3. To develop logical thinking and structure as a means of analysis.

### *Total Time*

45 to 70 minutes

### *Procedure*

1. Identify a specific goal that you would not mind sharing with others in the class. An appropriate goal might be targeted at something important for you during the current academic session (a short-range goal) or an important issue in your social, family, or career plans (a longer-range goal).
2. Next, you should identify three to five "objectives" or areas that are linked to the accomplishment of your goal.
3. For each objective, you should next develop three to five action steps, or "personal strategies," that would contribute to accomplishing the objective.
4. Briefly describe your goal statement with its objectives and strategies on one sheet of paper.
5. Pair up with a partner to evaluate each other's goal model:
   a. Is it achievable?
   b. Is it in an appropriate time frame?
   c. What resources are needed?
6. Discuss how items can be improved or better targeted.
7. Await direction from your instructor regarding class discussion.

CASE

# LECHMERE, INC.

Lechmere, Inc. is part of a 27-store retailing chain owned by the retailing giant Dayton Hudson.[27] Lechmere differs from many of the other stores, however, because it is located in Sarasota, Florida—an area with a very low unemployment rate of 4 percent. What this means is that there is a shortage of able workers.

Usually, as do other retailers, the company hires lots of entry-level part-timers, many of whom are housewives and teenagers. Then, it puts them into time slots as they are needed. That provides the necessary flexibility in a business where there is a big difference in customer traffic across departments. However, with a low unemployment rate, the company could not conduct business as usual—there simply weren't enough workers available.

Lechmere also has labor shortages at some of its other stores. So the Sarasota operation was allowed to try a way of dealing with an increasingly occurring labor shortage. It offered Sarasota workers raises based on the number of jobs they learned to perform. For example, sporting goods salespeople are taught to handle electronic equipment, while cashiers learn to sell tapes and records. Lechmere executives feel that by doing this they can quickly adjust to changes in staffing needs by moving employees around.

The pay incentives, in addition to creating a more varied and interesting workday, seemed to help with recruiting. In fact, the Sarasota store currently has a work force with 60 percent full-time employees versus half that percentage for the other stores in the chain. Paul Chadock, senior vice-president for personnel, says that the store is also considerably more productive than the others. Lechmere is in the process of using this approach in some of its other stores.

## *Questions*

1. What core characteristics of the employees' jobs are changed in this case? Explain.
2. Show how these characteristics and the other variables might operate in the Sarasota store in the context of the Hackman and Oldham model in Figure 7.2.
3. Discuss the case in terms of the various job-design strategies discussed in the chapter.

# PART THREE

# MANAGING GROUPS IN ORGANIZATIONS

This study outline of major topics is meant to organize your reading now; it is repeated in the Summary to structure your review.

## STUDY OUTLINE

### ■ The Usefulness of Groups

Groups and Task Performance   Groups and Individual Needs

### ■ Types of Groups in Organizations

Work Groups   Formal and Informal Groups   Psychological Groups

### ■ Group Effectiveness

What Is an Effective Group?   Groups as Open Systems

### ■ Input Foundations of Group Effectiveness

Organizational Setting   Nature of the Group Task
General Membership Characteristics   Group Size

# CHAPTER 8

# BASIC ATTRIBUTES OF GROUPS



## PHOTO ESSAYS

# VISIONS 8

**The Swedish automobile industry of the late 1960s and early 1970s was in trouble—quality and efficiency were down, absenteeism was rising, and it was hard to recruit new workers. Into this scene stepped Pehr Gyllenhammar, Chairperson of Volvo, and someone committed to offering workers something besides pay. It was his vision to build "a plant that, without sacrificing efficiency and financial result, provides the possibility for employees to work in groups, communicate freely, exchange jobs with each other, vary the rate of work, feel product identification . . . and also influence their own working environment."**

**In 1974 Volvo's new Kalmar plant introduced to the world a major step toward Gyllenhammar's vision. At Kalmar the assembly line is largely replaced by mobile assembly platforms that carry each car to various teams of 15 to 20 employees who share tasks and work together on large sections of a car. But still, Gyllenhammar wanted more. At Volvo's newest plant at Udevalla an even more dramatic change is seen. Teams of 10 employees, trained in all assembly jobs, work together to assemble four cars per shift. Says Gyllenhammar: "I want the people in a team to be able to go home at night and really say, 'I built that car.' " He seems to be doing that . . . and more. Absenteeism is low at the Udevalla plant, and worker morale is high.**

Pehr Gyllenhammar's vision of dramatic change in Volvo's approach to automobile manufacturing included the use of "teams" of workers as the focal point in designing the production process. Indeed, today more than ever before, we are witnessing a resurgence of interest in alternative ways of reorganizing the workplace. Organizations are adopting new forms in the quest for higher productivity and improvements in the quality of work life. They are growing smaller in size, flatter in structure, more flexible in operations, and—like the Kalmar and Udevalla plants that took shape under Pehr Gyllenhammar's vision—they are finding new and creative ways to use "groups" as cornerstones of performance improvements.

**Group**

Formally defined, a ***group*** is a collection of people who interact with one another regularly over a period of time and see themselves to be mutually dependent with respect to the attainment of one or more common goals. Managers are involved with groups of many types, and in this chapter we will talk about work groups, formal and informal groups, committees, task forces, self-managing work teams, and quality circles, to just name a few. In all cases, however, the managerial issue is the same—how to best utilize groups as human resources of organizations.

# THE USEFULNESS OF GROUPS

Groups are good for organizations and their members. Consider just a few examples of how this is increasingly being demonstrated in actual practice.

> *Aetna Life* The Rocky Hill, Connecticut office uses 12-person teams to do all claims handling functions previously assigned to different departments. The team members manage their own work flow, do their own scheduling, divide up overtime, and evaluate one another's performance.
>
> ***Corning Glass Works*** Linda Young works on a five-person team to inspect finished products in the firm's Blacksburg, Virginia plant. Team members together set goals and schedules and assign work. Linda has authority to decide if a piece she inspects will be shipped or thrown away. She is also training for other jobs. "The variety here makes you want to come to work," she says.

Examples of the prior types abound as managers increasingly recognize the usefulness of groups in organizations. It is time "to take groups seriously," says the noted scholar Harold J. Leavitt, who points out that:[1]

- Groups seem to be good for people.
- Groups seem to be useful in promoting innovation and creativity.
- Groups make better decisions than individuals in a wide variety of situations.
- Groups can gain commitment of members for carrying out decisions.
- Groups can control members in ways it is otherwise difficult to do.
- Groups help offset negative effects as organizations grow larger.
- Groups are natural phenomena in organizations.

## Groups and Task Performance

**Synergy**

***Synergy,*** as originally defined in Chapter 1, is the creation of a whole that is greater than the sum of its parts. When synergy occurs, groups accomplish more than the total of their members' individual capabilities. The prior examples at Aetna and Corning involved synergy being achieved through the effective utilization of groups as human resources of organizations.

Research shows, in particular, at least three performance advantages of groups.[2]

1. When the presence of an "expert" is uncertain, groups seem to make better judgments than would the average individual.
2. When problem solving can be handled by a division of labor and the sharing of information, groups are typically more successful than individuals.
3. Because of their tendencies to make more risky decisions than individuals, groups can be more creative and innovative in their task accomplishments.

On the other hand, it must be recognized that the term "group" raises both positive and negative reactions in the minds of most people. Although it is said that "two heads are better than one," we are also warned that "too many cooks spoil the broth." "A camel is a horse put together by a committee," admonishes the true group skeptic! At issue here is how well group members work together to accomplish a task. This includes a concern for ***social loafing,*** or something called the "Ringelmann effect," in groups. Ringelmann, a German psychologist, pinpointed this effect by asking people to pull as hard as they could on a rope, first alone and then in a group. He found that average productivity dropped as more people joined the rope pulling task.[3] Thus, the Ringelmann effect acknowledges that people may tend *not* to work as hard in groups as they would individually. This is because their contribution is less noticeable and because they like to see others carry the work load.

**Social loafing**

## Groups and Individual Needs

Groups are major influences on individual work attitudes and behaviors. To begin, they are mechanisms through which people learn relevant job skills and knowledge. Group members can model correct behaviors, offer feedback on performance, and provide direct instruction and assistance to one another. This helps group members acquire job competencies and may even make up for deficiencies in the formal training and education practices of the organization.

Group members also communicate expectations to one another regarding work performance, and influence one another's beliefs and predispositions about various aspects of the work setting. This may encourage or discourage high levels of effort. A new employee soon learns, for example, who the "bad" supervisors are or whom you cannot "trust" as a co-worker. These influences may even extend to how the individual should feel about his or her job and the organization. For example, a co-worker may indicate that "this is a good job to have and a great place to work" or "this is a lousy job and you are better off looking for something else."

Perhaps the most apparent function of groups is their ability to satisfy the needs of their members. Groups provide for social interactions and interpersonal fulfillments. A group can provide individual security in the form of direct work assistance and technical advice, or emotional support in times of special crisis or pressure. Groups also give their members a sense of identification and offer opportunities for ego involvement by assisting in group activities. In many ways, individuals can find from their group involvements the full range of need satisfactions discussed in Chapter 5.

# TYPES OF GROUPS IN ORGANIZATIONS

Groups appear in various forms in organizations. A useful managerial distinction is between work groups, formal and informal groups, and psychological groups.

## Work Groups

**Work group**

A ***work group*** is one created by the formal authority of an organization to transform resource inputs (such as ideas, materials, and objects) into product outputs (such as a report, decision, service, or commodity).[4] A good example is the *work unit* identified in Chapter 1 as consisting of a manager and his or her direct reports. You should also recall "the manager's challenge" faced by the head of a work unit. In the present case this means that the manager of a work group must fulfill an accountability for the group's performance while being dependent on group members to do the required work. It is popular to view organizations as interlocking networks of work groups, as shown in Figure 8.1. Notice the "linking-pin" function of the managers in such a network. Through managers, acting as superiors in one group and as subordinates in others, all work groups are interconnected to create a sense of totality for the organization as a whole.

Work groups may be permanent or temporary. *Permanent work groups* may appear on organization charts as departments (for example, market research department), divisions, (General Motors Oldsmobile Division),

*FIGURE 8.1 Likert's linking-pin model of an organization as a complex network of interlocking groups. (From* New Patterns of Management *by Rensis Likert. Copyright © 1961 McGraw-Hill. Used with the permission of McGraw-Hill Book Company.)*

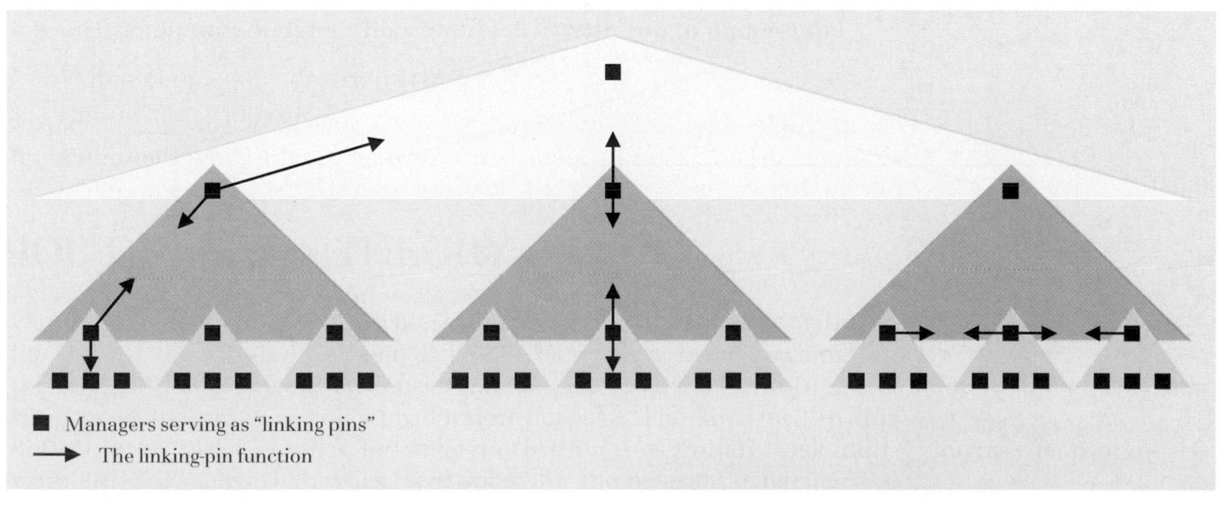

or teams (such as a product assembly team), among other possibilities. They can vary in size from very small departments or teams of just a few people to large divisions employing a hundred or more. In all cases, however, permanent work groups share the common characteristics of being officially created to perform a specific function on an ongoing basis. They continue in existence until a decision is made to change or reconfigure the organization for some reason.

*Temporary work groups,* by contrast, are created for a specific purpose and typically disband once that purpose has been accomplished. Good examples are the many temporary committees and task forces that are important components of any organization. Indeed, among the changes in today's organizations is the tendency to make more use of task forces for special problem-solving efforts. Usually, such temporary groups will have appointed chairpersons or heads who are held accountable for results much as is the manager of a work unit.

## Formal and Informal Groups

**Formal group**
**Informal group**

Social psychologists make an important distinction between ***formal groups*** or work groups created via formal authority for some purpose, and ***informal groups,*** which emerge unofficially and without being formally designated as parts of the organization. The key difference here is that whereas formal groups are officially defined in the organization structure, informal groups come into existence spontaneously and without formal endorsement. The latter are often found as subgroups or cliques within formal groups. You may find, for example, that the same people eat together, go on breaks together, or engage in other spontaneous activities on the job.

There are at least two reasons why informal groups emerge to coexist with formal groups in organizations. First, they help people to get their

*FIGURE 8.2 Informal groups and Likert's linking-pin model of an organization.*

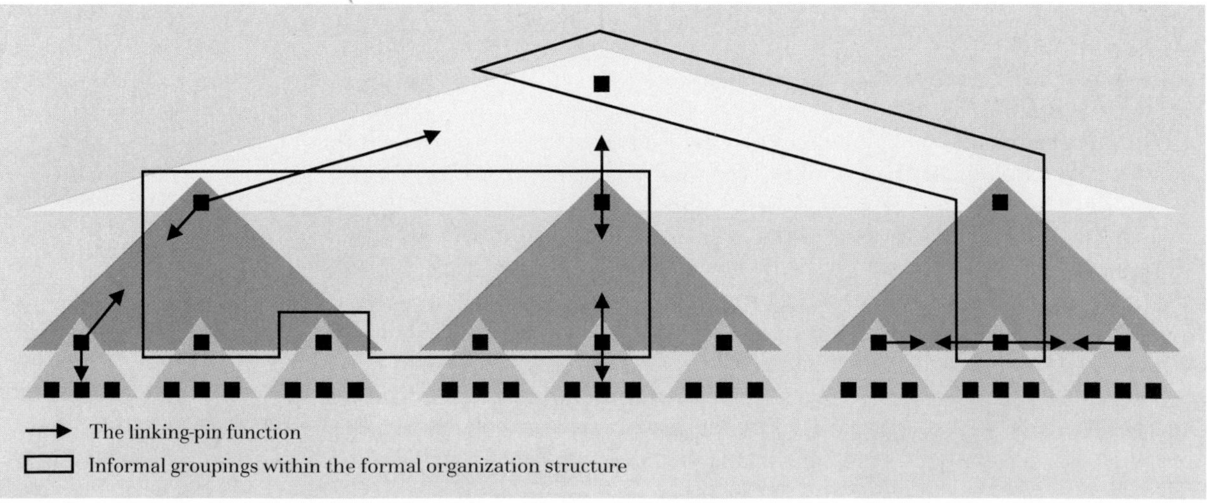

jobs done. Informal groups offer a network of interpersonal relationships with the potential to "speed up" the work flow or "gain favors" in ways that formal lines of authority fail to provide. Second, informal groups help individuals to satisfy needs that are thwarted or left unmet in a person's formal group affiliations. Among the things that informal groups can provide in this respect are:

- *Social satisfactions* Opportunities for friendships and pleasing social relationships on the job.
- *Security* Opportunities to find sympathy for one's feelings and actions, especially as they relate to friction with the formal organization; opportunities to find help or task assistance from persons other than one's superior.
- *Identification* Opportunities to achieve a sense of belonging by affiliating with persons who share similar values, attitudes, and goals.

Figure 8.2 illustrates how informal groups add complexity to the linking-pin model of organizations shown earlier. They create a vast array of informal, but very real, networks that further relate people from various parts of the organization to one another. Managers, accordingly, must be skilled at working with groups in both their formal and informal forms.

## Psychological Groups

**Psychological group**

Some people go further and talk about ***psychological groups.*** These are groups in which the members:[5]

- Truly interact with one another.
- Perceive themselves to be part of the group.
- Share a common sense of group purpose.
- Are psychologically aware of one another.

It is the final characteristic on this list that most sets a psychological group apart from others. Being "psychologically aware of one another" means that each member of the group is aware of every other member's needs and potential resource contributions. In other words, everyone knows a lot about one another and presumably uses that understanding in all aspects of group operations.

Not all groups are psychological groups. Most informal groups would qualify as psychological groups. However, many formal groups might not. Just being assigned to work together in the same department does not mean that group members will share and work toward common goals. Think of group projects you have worked on. Each project was designated as a formal group effort. But did all these groups meet the four criteria of psychological grouping? Perhaps group success and your satisfaction would have been higher if they all had.

Managers frequently wish that their formal work groups would act and think as psychological groups. Our study of group behavior in organizations should aid you, as a manager, to help your group make this transition.

# GROUP EFFECTIVENESS

Organizations, as complex networks of interlocking groups, depend—for their own longer run prosperity and well being—on how well these groups perform. Managers in organizations, accordingly, are concerned with creating "effective" groups that make real contributions to the continuing success of the total organization.

## What Is an Effective Group?

**Effective work group**

An ***effective work group*** is one that achieves high levels of *both* task performance and human resource maintenance over time. In respect to *task performance,* an effective group achieves its performance goals. In respect to *human resource maintenance,* an effective group is one whose members are sufficiently satisfied with their tasks, accomplishments, and interpersonal relationships to work well together on an ongoing basis. A classic listing of the characteristics of an effective group follows.[6]

- The members are loyal to one another and the leader.
- The members and leaders have a high degree of confidence and trust in each other.
- Group values and goals express relevant values and needs of members.
- All activities of the group occur in a supportive atmosphere.
- The group is eager to help members develop to their full potential.
- The group knows the value of "constructive" conformity, and knows when to use it and for what purposes.
- The members communicate fully and frankly all information relevant to the group's activity.
- The members feel secure in making decisions that seem appropriate to them.

## Groups as Open Systems

Generally stated, an effective group gets its job done and takes good care of its members in the process. Yet, the issue is still a bit broader than this view alone. Consider, for example, the open systems model of groups presented in Figure 8.3. This perspective is very similar to the one first advanced in Chapter 1 when organizations were also viewed as open systems. If you recall, an open system interacts with its environment to transform resource inputs into outputs.

For present purposes, the "environment" of a group can be considered other relevant individuals and groups from the larger organization within which it functions. To be truly effective in the broader context of the organization, a group should serve the needs of the total organizational system—not just its own. It should establish and maintain good input–output relations with other parts of the larger system, both individuals and groups. This helps the group gain the resource inputs it needs

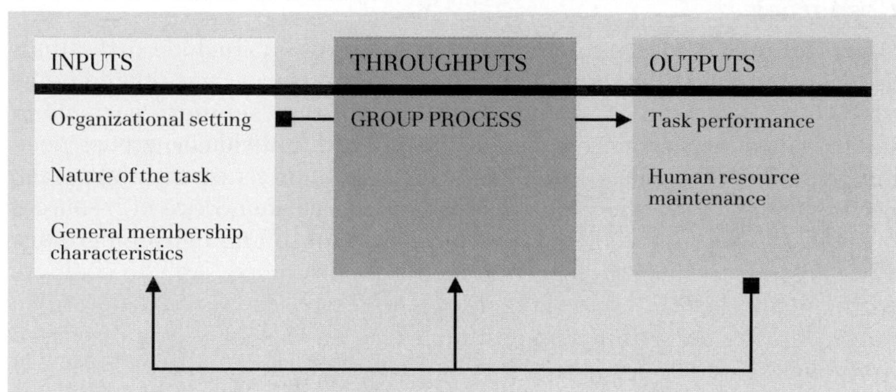


*FIGURE 8.3 A model of the work group as an open system.*

from the environment. It also helps the group perform in a manner that truly assists, rather than hinders, the performance efforts of other components of the organization.[7]

# INPUT FOUNDATIONS OF GROUP EFFECTIVENESS

A major influence on the effectiveness of any group is the nature of the inputs with which the group has to work. Inputs, as shown in Figure 8.3, are the initial "givens" in a group situation and they set the stage for all group action. If inputs are satisfactory, they can enhance efforts to achieve group effectiveness; if they are unsatisfactory, they can impede such efforts. Some of the major categories of group inputs that can make a difference in the work situation are—the organization setting, nature of the task, membership characteristics, and group size.

## Organizational Setting

The nature of the surrounding organization can affect the way a group operates and what it accomplishes. Specifically, research suggests that the organizational setting influences the degree to which group members get psychologically close to one another, the extent to which they cooperate and/or compete with one another, and the ways in which they communicate with one another.[8] Other things being equal, a "positive" organizational setting includes:

- Abundant resources.
- Appropriate technology.
- Spatial arrangements that make it easy to interact.
- Reward systems that emphasize the importance of group efforts.
- Goal systems that emphasize the importance of group efforts.
- Structure, size, and culture compatible with group operations.

### Resources

Organizational resources important to the work group include such things as technology, facilities, work methods and procedures, and related items of the kind discussed in Chapter 4 as a part of the "support" variable in the individual performance equation. Just as with individuals, groups need proper resource support if they are to achieve their true potential in task performance. Furthermore, the relative scarcity or abundance of resources in the organization can affect what happens within and between groups. When resources are scarce, group members are more likely to compete with one another to access them. Similarly, resource scarcity is often an antecedent to intergroup competition. More on this subject is discussed in the next chapter.

### Technology

Technology is the means through which work gets accomplished. The basic impact of technology on groups is the degree to which it facilitates or impedes interaction among group members. It is one thing, for example, for a group to work intensively on custom-crafted products tailor made to customer specifications; it is quite another to be part of a machine-paced assembly line. The former technology allows for more interaction among group members. It will probably create a closer-knit group that has a stronger sense of identity than the group formed around one small segment of an assembly line. This is part of the Volvo innovations described in the chapter opening *Visions.*

### Spatial Arrangements

The spatial or physical arrangements of the work setting can also influence what takes place in a group. Researchers recognize that differing spatial arrangements may affect the amount of interaction that occurs among group members, their attitudes toward their jobs and the organization itself, and their attitudes toward one another. Where people sit, who they sit next to, and the closeness of the seats in a meeting, for example, can easily affect what happens.

### Reward Systems and Goals

Like individuals, groups are influenced by the reward systems and goals characteristic of their work environment. Well-designed reward systems and appropriate goals help to establish and maintain proper levels and direction for group work efforts. Groups can suffer from reward systems that stress individual-level as opposed to group-level contributions and outcomes. They can also suffer from goals that are unclear, insufficiently challenging, or appear inappropriately imposed from the outside. We examined rewards and goals in Chapters 6 and 7. Many of the same insights can be applied to the group, in addition to the individual, level of analysis.

### Structure, Size, and Culture

The overall structure, size, and culture of the larger organization can affect a group's performance potential. A group whose internal structure

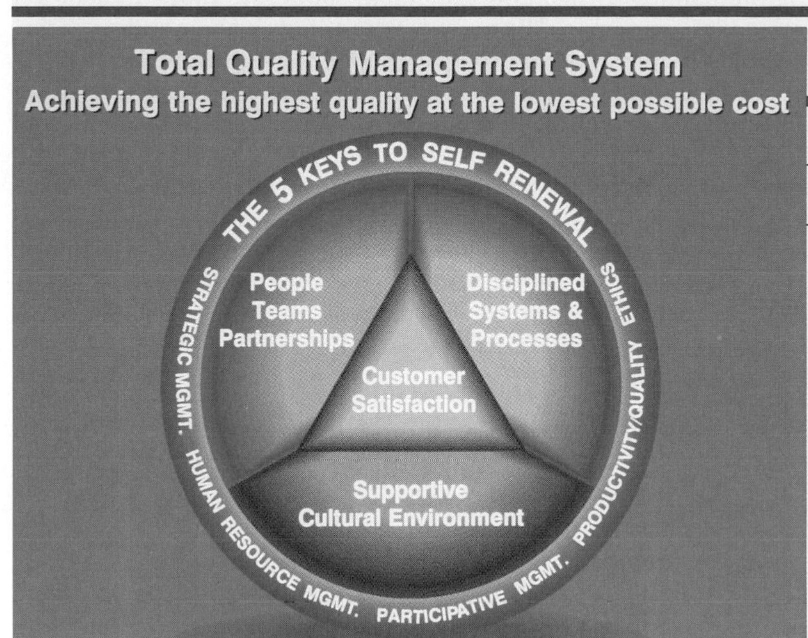


Courtesy of McDonnell Douglas Corporation.

SKILLS PERSPECTIVE

## MC DONNELL DOUGLAS

**Workers at McDonnell Douglas are hearing a lot about the company's commitment to quality—the Total Quality Management System (TQMS). They're also hearing about TQMS in their work teams—a key to achieving the company's performance quality goals. McDonnell employees work together in teams to determine the best ways of getting the jobs accomplished and mobilizing the skills needed to do them well. They experience a sense of empowerment from making decisions that affect them and their jobs. The company hopes that this will bring about a commitment to continuous improvement. The teams may even discover that work can be more enjoyable.**

is incompatible with that of the surrounding organization can experience difficulties as its members are forced to deal with different standards and procedures. A group that gets "lost" in the sheer size of the larger setting may experience confusion, loss of identity, and even a loss of accountability for results. Finally, a group that labors in an organizational culture that stresses individual performance and competition may find it hard to operate as an effective "team." Organizational structure and size are reviewed in Chapters 10 and 11, whereas organizational culture is the subject of Chapter 12.

## Nature of the Group Task

The nature of the task to be performed is an important group input. Different tasks place different demands on a group, and the challenges to group effectiveness increase with the degree of task complexity.[9] To master complex tasks group members must distribute their efforts more broadly than on simple tasks, and they must cooperate more to achieve high performance outcomes. When successful, however, member satisfaction is usually higher when a group works on more complex tasks.

Table 8.1 illustrates how task complexity varies on technical and social dimensions. In terms of *technical demands,* the key issues are task uniqueness, task difficulty, and information diffusion. Complex tasks are technically more unique and difficult and require more information processing than simple tasks. In terms of *social demands,* task complexity is affected by requirements for ego involvement and means–end agreement among group members. The most complex social demands arise when a group works on a task that is very ego involving but generates little means–end agreement. Some basic considerations here are:

1. *Ego involvement.* This refers to members' personal investment in the group's task and its outcomes. Tasks that engage deeply rooted values or beliefs, that affect important aspects of participants' lives, or that engage personally valued skills can all be considered high on the ego involvement dimension.
2. *Agreement on means.* This refers to agreements on *how* the group should go about performing its task. For some tasks there may be high agreement on the best approach to the task and on who should do what. For other tasks, different approaches will be favored by different group members.
3. *Agreement on ends.* This reflects group members' agreement on *what* they are trying to accomplish and what criteria will be used to

*TABLE 8.1*
**TECHNICAL DEMANDS OF A GROUP TASK—TASK UNIQUENESS, TASK DIFFICULTY, AND INFORMATION DIFFUSION**

| *Task Attributes* | *Characteristics of Simple Tasks* | *Characteristics of Complex Tasks* |
|---|---|---|
| Task Uniqueness | Single acceptable solution.<br>Solution easily verified.<br>Members have task experience.<br>Task remains constant. | Many alternative solutions.<br>Solution not easily verified.<br>Members do not have task experience.<br>Task requirements vary. |
| Task Difficulty | Little effort is required.<br>Few operations are required.<br>Involves low-level skills. | Great deal of effort required.<br>Many operations are required.<br>Involves complex skills. |
| Information diffusion | Knowledge is centralized.<br>Involves few areas of knowledge. | Knowledge widely distributed.<br>Involves several areas of knowledge. |

*Source:* Developed from David M. Herold, "The Effectiveness of Work Groups," in Steven Kerr, ed., *Organizational Behavior* (New York, John Wiley & Sons, 1979), p. 100. Adapted with permission from *Organizational Behavior* by Steven Kerr, John Wiley & Sons, Inc., New York, N.Y., 1979.

define success. For some tasks, it is very clear what the group is trying to achieve and one may expect wide agreement on the part of group members. For other tasks, the group may have considerable difficulty agreeing on what constitutes a satisfactory outcome.

## General Membership Characteristics

Individual attributes are an important input to any group. A group will be influenced by the demographic, competency, and psychological characteristics of its individual members. To the extent that the right competencies are present in the membership, group performance outcomes can be directly enhanced.

To take advantage of these competencies, however, group members must work well together. Whether they do so or not depends in part on how well individual attributes blend with characteristics of the membership as a whole. Important considerations include interpersonal compatibilities, membership heterogeneity, and status congruence.

### *Interpersonal Compatibilities*

FIRO-B (fundamental interpersonal orientation) theory helps to explain how people orient themselves toward one another.[10] It is based on how strongly people need to express and receive feelings of inclusion, control, and affection. These needs, along with descriptive statements adapted from an instrument (the FIRO-B Scale) designed to measure them, are the following.

- **Need for inclusion** Strive for prominence, recognition, and prestige.
  Try to be included in informal social activities.
  Like to be invited to things.
  Try to participate in group activities.
  Like to be asked to participate in discussions.
- **Need for control** Tendency to rebel and refuse to be controlled or tendency to be compliant and submissive
  Try not to let other people decide what I do.
  Try to influence strongly other people's actions.
  Try to be the dominant person when with people.
  Not easily led by people.
- **Need for affection** Desire to be friendly and seek close emotional ties with others.
  Try to have close, personal relationships with people.
  Try to be friendly with people.
  Like people to act close and personal.
  Do not like people to act distant toward me.

The FIRO-B theory argues that groups in which members have compatible needs will be most effective. Symptoms of harmful incompatibilities include withdrawn members, open hostilities, struggles over control, and domination of the group by a few members. The author of the FIRO-B theory states:[11]

> If at the outset we can choose a group of people who can work together harmoniously, we shall go far toward avoiding situations where a group's efforts are wasted in interpersonal conflicts.

### *Membership Homogeneity–Heterogeneity*

Homogeneous groups consist of members with similar backgrounds, interests, values, attitudes, and the like. Heterogeneous groups are diverse on these dimensions. Although membership heterogeneity can bring a variety of skills and viewpoints to bear on problems and thus facilitate task accomplishment, homogeneity increases the chances for harmonious working relationships among group members. The more heterogeneous the membership, furthermore, the more skilled the manager or group leader will have to be in facilitating a successful group experience.

The nature of the task is an important factor in determining whether membership homogeneity or heterogeneity is best for a group. Research shows a tendency for homogeneity to be more functional in simple as opposed to complex task situations. Managers, therefore, must exercise good judgment and try to balance the advantages of both homogeneity and heterogeneity when selecting members for their work groups.

### *Status Congruence*

**Status**

**Status congruence**

A person's ***status*** is an indicator of relative rank, worth, or standing on prestige and esteem within a group. This standing can be based on any number of characteristics, including age, work seniority, occupation, education, work accomplishments, or status in other groups. ***Status congruence*** occurs when a person's standing on each of these factors is consistent with his or her standing on the other factors. Status incongruity occurs when standings vary—for example,a senior member is not chosen to chair a committee, or a new college graduate without experience is hired to supervise a group of experienced production workers. When members of a group experience status incongruity stress, dissatisfaction, and frustration can all occur. Sometimes, attempts to reconcile the status incongruity may even be detrimental to group effectiveness (e.g., the senior committee member tries to take control anyway, or the experienced production workers refuse to help their new supervisor "learn the ropes").

## Group Size

Although it is difficult to pinpoint an ideal group size, it is known that in problem-solving groups of less than five members there are:[12]

- Fewer people to share task responsibilities.
- More personal discussions.
- More complete participation.

On the other hand, in a group of more than seven members there tend to be:

- Fewer opportunities to participate.
- More member inhibitions.

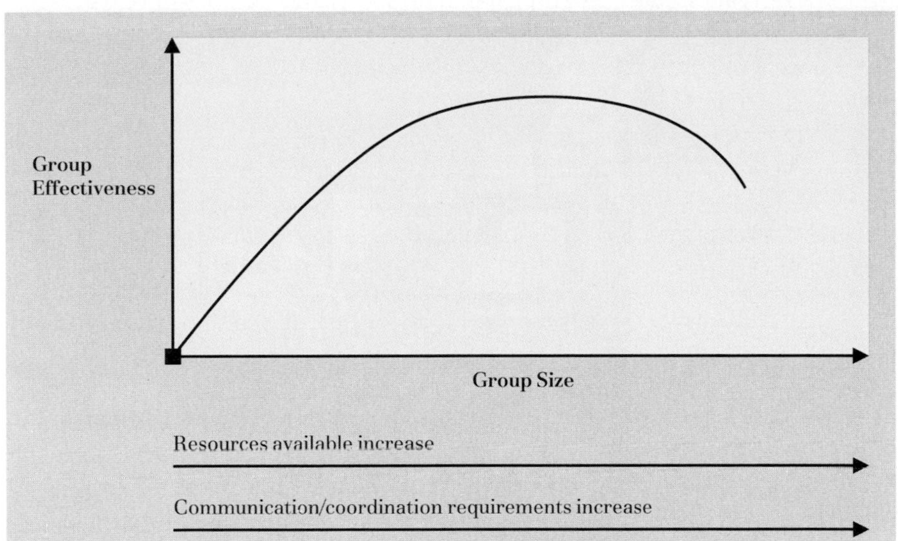


*FIGURE 8.4 Trade-offs between group size and group effectiveness.*

- Possible domination by aggressive members.
- Tendency to split into subgroups.

Figure 8.4 depicts some possible trade-offs between the size of a group and its effectiveness. As groups become larger, more potential human resources are available to divide the work and accomplish needed tasks—this can boost performance. But at the same time that the group grows larger, communication and coordination among members becomes more difficult. Research shows that turnover and absenteeism tend to increase with group size, as do opportunities for more social loafing. However, member satisfaction increases up to the size of about five members and decreases thereafter. Thus, it appears that problem solving groups should consist of about five to seven members.

Another issue in group size is its odd/even character. Groups with an even number of members tend to show more disagreement and conflict when performing tasks. These differences appear to occur because it is easier for members in odd-numbered groups to form coalitions and take majority votes to resolve disagreements. Where speed is required, this behavior is useful. Where careful deliberations are required, as for example in jury duty or very complex problem solving, even-numbered groups can be more effective *if* they do not deadlock.[13]

# PROCESS FOUNDATIONS OF GROUP EFFECTIVENESS

Group effectiveness always depends in part on how well groups utilize or "process" the available inputs as they work toward task accomplishment. Chapter 9 is devoted entirely to this issue. For now, an initial understand-

INTERNATIONAL PERSPECTIVE

## IBM

Courtesy of International Business Machines Corporation.

**IBM believes that the strength of its relationship with customers is the cornerstone of its business success. With a growing emphasis on global operations, the firm has made significant changes to support its key international customers better. Some, like Citicorp, now benefit from the coordinated attention of regional and branch offices specifically set up to handle their needs worldwide. IBM has also redeployed engineers and product developers from its laboratories to become part of branch office teams and assist in identifying customer problems and developing solutions. Team members are encouraged to build long-term relationships with their customers. They are supported by a special marketing education program designed to sharpen their skills in the customer's industry. A new financial training system based on artificial intelligence also gives the teams workstation access to financial strategies and information helpful to serving their customers' needs.**

ing of the process foundations of group effectiveness can be found in a classic model of group dynamics offered by George Homans.[14] He feels that it is useful to distinguish among the activities, sentiments, and interactions of group members, and to examine the required and emergent forms of each.

## Required and Emergent Behaviors

**Required behaviors**

**Emergent behaviors**

***Required behaviors*** are those contributions the organization formally requests from group members as a basis for continued affiliation and support. They may include such work-related behaviors as being punctual, treating customers with respect, and being helpful to co-workers. ***Emergent behaviors*** are what group members do in addition to, or in place of, what is formally asked of them by the organization. Whereas the required behaviors are formally designed with the group's purpose in mind, emergent behaviors exist purely as matters of individual and group choice. As shown in Figure 8.5, they exist as a "shadow" standing side-by-side with the required system.

You might think that the required behaviors in Homans' model are desirable and functional from a managerial viewpoint, while the emergent ones are not. This is incorrect. What is important is that the behaviors specified in the required/formal system and those found in the emergent/informal system complement rather than contradict one another in contributing to group effectiveness. Indeed, supportive emergent behaviors are necessary for almost any group or organization to achieve true effectiveness. Rarely, if ever, can the required behaviors be specified so perfectly that they meet all the demands of the work situation. This is especially true in dynamic and uncertain environments where job demands change over time. There are also times when the emergent work behaviors are more efficient than are those required by formal rules. We can illustrate this point in the reverse—that is, by giving an example of what happens when postal workers work strictly by the rules and do only what is required.[15]

> The U.S. postal system has many formal rules and policies that route delivery workers are supposedly required to follow. None of these men and women can perform their work satisfactorily while following all these rules to the letter. Complete conformity is so ridiculous that postal employees have chosen to follow rules perfectly only when they want to "strike" in opposition to federal law against "strikes." In such cases the "strike" is called a "work-by-the-rules strike." The deliverers leave in the morning, park on the opposite side of the street from their postal box (a rule), unlock their trucks, get their bags out, lock the trucks (a rule), go across the street, come back, unlock the trucks, put the mail in, lock their

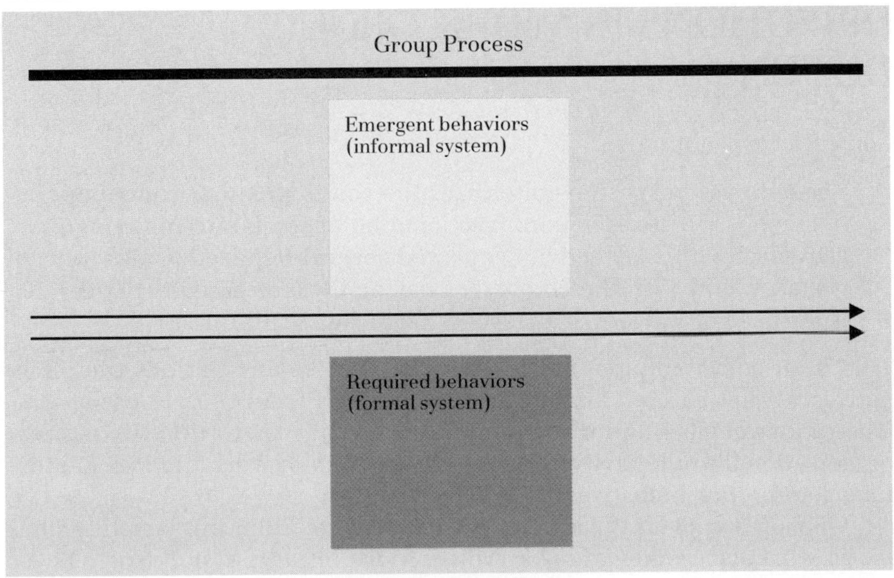


*FIGURE 8.5 Group process: Emergent behaviors and the informal system as a "shadow" for required behaviors and the formal system.*

trucks, and so on. Thus by following rules perfectly, the deliverers come in late from their daily activities with only half the mail delivered and free from any possible punishment.

## Activities, Interactions, and Sentiments

*Activities* are the verbal and nonverbal actions in which group members engage. They are the things people do in groups and include efforts directed toward the group task, social activities, and other forms of physical movement. The required activities of a work group member are often specified by the organization in a written job description. This document outlines the activities that the organization expects the individual to accomplish as a group member and in return for any inducements offered. Both required and emergent activities will be found in any group.

*Interactions* are communications and interpersonal contacts that occur between and among group members. The essence of any interaction is the sending and receiving of information. This occurs by oral conversation as well as in written (such as letters, memos, and signs) and nonverbal communication (such as facial gestures and hand signals). As with activities, required and emergent interactions can be positive or negative in their influence on group functioning and effectiveness.

*Sentiments* are the feelings, attitudes, beliefs, or values held by group members. These sentiments may be brought into a group from the outside by individual group members, or they may be learned as a result of becoming a group member. They are especially subject to emergent forces. Although it may be easy to require positive attitudes toward work such as a respect for authority and belief in company rules and procedures, it is more difficult to achieve these results in actual practice. When the goals of the emergent system support the required system, group process is also likely to facilitate rather than impede group effectiveness.

# DIRECTIONS IN WORK GROUP DESIGNS

Consider this comment.[16]

> The auto assembly line epitomizes the conditions that contribute to employee dissatisfaction: fractionation of work into meaningless activities, with each activity repeated several hundred times each workday, and with the employees having little or no control over work pace or any other aspects of working conditions.

This is an admittedly pessimistic view of work. But what are the alternatives? What can be done to protect workers from the alienation and frustrations of work under such conditions? What can be done to improve organizational productivity and raise the quality of work life in manufacturing and other industries?

One answer to all three prior questions is found in the *Visions* example of workplace innovations at Volvo. More broadly stated, the answer lies in the renewed emphasis on employee "participation" and "involvement" now found in many progressive organizations. All such approaches offer creative ways of making better use of groups as human resources of organizations. Good examples are self-managing work teams, quality circles, and worker involvement groups of various types. Among the advantages often associated with these current directions in workgroup design are:

- Improved production quality
- Improved production quantity.
- Lower employee absenteeism.
- Lower employee turnover.
- Improved work attitudes.
- Less need for "first-line" supervisors.

## Self-Managing Work Teams

**Self-managing work team**

***Self-managing work teams*** are autonomous work groups having substantial responsibility for a wide variety of decisions involved in the accomplishment of assigned tasks. Indeed, the very concept of the self-managing work team is that it takes on some duties previously performed by formal supervisors—that is, such things as quality control, work scheduling, and even performance evaluation. This is the process of ***empowerment,*** wherein individuals (or groups) are allowed to be responsible for making decisions about important things affecting them and their work. Members of self-managing work teams are typically empowered with substantial discretion in distributing tasks and determining work pace. They may even go so far as to establish pay grades and certify one another in required job skills. For example:

**Empowerment**

> *Volvo* Workers in the company's Uddevalla plant pretty much manage themselves. There are only two levels of management and no first-line supervisors. Each team of 7 to 10 hourly workers is responsible for scheduling, quality control, and hiring new members. They decide how long to work on each car and they fix their own defects. One worker comments: "This is the right way." The plant president says: "We've brought back craftsmanship to auto making."

An early U.S. experiment with this concept is also quite revealing.[17]

General Foods Corporation was planning to construct a new Gaines pet food plant in Topeka, Kansas. The company's existing plant was experiencing problems. Employees were indifferent and inattentive to their work, waste was high, shutdowns frequently occurred, and there were acts of worker violence and sabotage. General Foods wanted to avoid such problems in the new plant. Richard Walton, a noted social scientist, was asked to serve as a special consultant and evaluator.

Autonomous work groups were created in the new plant. Six teams of 7 to 14 workers were formed. Each included "operators" and a "team leader." The teams were individually responsible for a large part of the production process. Within teams, individuals were assigned work tasks by group consensus. These tasks were rotated

> and shared. The team was responsible for handling problems with other teams, covering of absentees, training members in equipment maintenance, product quality control, and maintenance of the work area. In addition, pay levels and raises for team members were based on the principle of job mastery; the guiding concept was "pay for learning." Individuals first mastered all jobs within their team and then within the plant. As they did so, their pay levels increased accordingly.
>
> Product quality and plant safety were high, employee attitudes were generally positive, and absenteeism was low. Prospects looked good for autonomous work groups in this facility.
>
> Yet, after careful and lengthy study, Walton noticed some difficulties as workers adjusted to the ways of this plant. The compensation scheme caused problems. Decisions regarding job mastery were sometimes controversial, and tensions appeared as team members began to qualify for different pay levels. Not all workers liked the increased responsibility of team membership and the atmosphere of mutual help. Some team leaders found their roles difficult.

Thus, Walton recognized that the introduction of autonomous work groups in organizations may have both pluses and minuses and that the whole process must be well managed for the full advantages to be realized.

As self-managing work teams have become more common and popular, Walton's conclusions that they can have profound effects on management have been confirmed. For those managers who have self-managing work teams reporting to them, it is a classic example of the "changing nature of managerial work." Especially those who are used to the "old" ways may require extra support in adapting to their new roles. Among the actions being taken by progressive organizations in this regard are:[18]

- Selection of managers with strong human and social skills, as well as good technical skills.
- Training managers to better understand group dynamics.
- Revising reward systems to emphasize managerial success at team development.
- Bringing managers together in mutual "support" groups of managers with similar responsibilities.
- Better utilizing managers by giving them higher-level planning and other management responsibilities.

## Quality Circles

One of the most popular attempts to utilize groups to solve problems and create opportunities in the workplace is the "quality circle."[19] A ***quality circle*** (QC for short) is a small group of persons who meet periodically (e.g., an hour or so once a week) to discuss and develop solutions for problems relating to quality, productivity, or cost. Members should receive special training in information gathering and problem analysis techniques. QC leaders should emphasize democratic participation in iden-

ETHICAL PERSPECTIVE

## AT&T

Reproduced with permission of AT&T.

**It hasn't been "business as usual" around AT&T for quite some time. Along with its company structure, its culture and strategy have changed dramatically since deregulation. Having undergone substantial downsizing (minus some 92,000 workers in six years), AT&T realizes it has to help employees adapt to the changes and explore new markets for its services. The firm offers its workers counseling for dealing with layoffs of colleagues, training in new job skills, rewards for making a smooth transition, and empowerment. Says an AT&T phone center manager, "I've been empowered to do whatever makes my customers happy."**

**Carrying the commitment to customers into its search for new business strategies, AT&T has recently entered a new business—Consumer Communications Services—which provides on-line translation of telephone calls in 136 possible languages. The service ranges from translation assistance to improve communication during emergencies, such as medical and police calls, to serving the communication needs of multinational corporations.**

tifying problems, analyzing problems, and choosing action alternatives. After proposed solutions are presented to management, implementation should be a joint effort between the QC and management. Here is an example.[20]

> "It's 9 o'clock, time for our meeting," announces one of the advertising specialists in the USAA Marketing Department. At that signal, several other employees leave their desks and head for the conference room. They start right to work on the problem they have been spending an hour a week on for the last two months. Then, regardless of how much or how little they accomplish, the meeting is adjourned exactly one hour later.
>
> Hardly typical of a business meeting, this is a quality circle in operation. Bob Gaylor coordinates and directs USAA's quality circle

> program. "The logic behind Quality Circles is that the people who do the work know the most about it, and are the best qualified to improve it," says Gaylor. "USAA's program has been successful largely because of the support of management. With that support and the enthusiasm of our employees, there's no limit to what we can accomplish."

Originally developed in Japan to promote employee involvement, encourage innovation, and improve efficiency, QCs are now very popular around the world. They cannot however, be looked upon as panaceas for all of an organization's ills. Indeed, a number of conditions must be met to keep them from becoming just another management "gimmick." These include the following requirements for QC success:

- An informed and knowledgeable work force.
- Managerial willingness to trust workers with necessary information.
- Presence of a "team spirit" in the QC group.
- Clear emphasis on quality in the organization's goals.
- An organization that encourages participation.

## Worker Involvement Groups

**Worker involvement group**

Participation and collaboration are the foundations of worker involvement. A ***worker involvement group*** is any group created in the organization to allow individuals to become more broadly included in workplace affairs. Such a group is a mechanism for participation that allows workers to gain influence over decisions affecting them and their work. It is also a mechanism for collaboration that provides managers with the benefit of worker know-how in problem-solving situations. Consider this short case.[21]

> Some time ago, Mahmood Mohajer, a production supervisor at Digital's Burlington, Vermont plant, realized that his work group was two weeks behind in an important production run. In the past, he would have immediately put everyone on an overtime schedule. This time he did things differently. He first met with the production teams and outlined the problem. He then asked them to come up with a solution. "It was a real risk," he says of the approach, "I was so nervous I had to trust them."
>
> The following Monday he got their response. Everyone decided to work the entire weekend to catch up on the production schedule. They had accepted responsibility for meeting the production goals, and came up with a way of doing so that would meet their needs as well as those of the firm. It was still an overtime schedule, but somewhat different from the one Mohajer might have set. Yet theirs would work also . . . perhaps even better than his. Because it was their idea, team members were highly motivated to make their solution a real success.
>
> Mohajer says that his new approach to worker involvement requires a "coaching" rather than a "policing" role. One of his

workers told him: "We wanted to tell you how to fix some problems before, but you wouldn't listen to us."

In order for worker involvement to succeed, managers like Mohajer must make sincere commitments to empowerment. Like the adjustments to self-managing teams and quality circles, this often requires new ways of managing. When accomplished, however, true worker involvement offers highly promising contributions in today's demanding work settings. For example,

*Federal Express* A work team at the company's Natick, Massachusetts facility engaged in problem-solving to shorten the time required in the daily package sort. They carefully monitored their daily routines, designed a new system, and established an incentive scheme to encourage everyone to follow through with recommended changes. Another group in Memphis, Tennessee, noticed and then solved a billing problem that cost the firm $2.1 million a year.

*Saturn* The new General Motors plant in Spring Hill, Tennessee, instructs management to stress worker involvement in decisions. This has been an important part of the new plant's concept right from the beginning. Workers sat on teams to help design factory processes, select dealerships, and find an ad agency, among other things. Now in their work groups, the unionized employees interview and hire new workers. In fact, the plant has no personnel department.

Clearly, the trend is for managers to adopt increasingly innovative ways for better using groups as human resources of organizations. Empowerment, participation, involvement, and collaboration are critical aspects of these new approaches. In addition, it is important to remember that many issues discussed elsewhere in this book are essential companions to these directions in work group designs. They include:[22]

- Flat and lean organizational structures.
- Enriched individual jobs
- Open information systems and shared performance data.
- Performance-based reward systems for individuals and groups.
- Responsive personnel policies creating loyalty and security.

## SUMMARY

**■ The Usefulness of Groups in Organizations extends to both the organization as a whole and the group's members. Group activity can facilitate organizational task accomplishment. Synergy—the creation of a whole greater than the sum of its parts—can greatly assist performance, but social loafing—wherein individual members do not work as hard as they otherwise might—can limit performance results. Groups can satisfy many individual needs and offer assistance in job training and task accomplishment.**

■ **Types of Groups in Organizations** include formal groups—such as work units, task forces, and committees—which are created by formal authority to achieve a specific purpose, and informal groups, which emerge spontaneously and exist in an unofficial capacity. All groups are collections of people who interact with one another to attain common goals. Members of psychological groups are also highly aware of one another's individual needs and potential resource contributions.

■ **Group Effectiveness** is achieved when a group displays both high levels of task accomplishment and human resource maintenance. This means that the group members work well enough together to accomplish long-run, not just short-run, performance results. When groups are viewed as open systems interacting with their environments, group effectiveness involves success in transforming a variety of inputs into outputs.

■ **Input Foundations of Group Effectiveness** include factors that set the stage for, or "arm," the group for action. Group inputs can directly influence group performance by how well they support group operations. Key group inputs of managerial significance include the organizational setting (e.g., resources, technology, reward and goal systems, structure, and size), nature of the task, general membership characteristics, and group size.

■ **Process Foundations of Group Effectiveness** represent the means through which group members work together to utilize available resources and achieve desired outputs. The Homans model of group dynamics identifies activities (things members actually do), interactions (interpersonal relationships among members), and sentiments (members' feelings, attitudes, or beliefs) as part of any group's internal operations. Each of these exists in both required forms (as specified by formal authority) and emergent forms (based on the group's informal system).

■ **Directions in Work Group Designs** are important foundations for the many changes taking place in today's organizations. Creative work group designs empower their members and expand participation in decision making. These include self-managing work teams that allow group members to plan, complete, and evaluate their work while performing many tasks for themselves previously done by first-line supervisors. They include the popular quality circles that facilitate problem-solving to improve the quality of goods and services produced. They also include a variety of worker involvement groups that utilize participative methods as a way of making better use of groups as human resources of organizations.

## ▶ KEY TERMS

Emergent Behaviors
Empowerment
Formal Group
Group
Group Process
Informal Group
Psychological Group
Quality Circle
Required Behaviors
Social Loafing

Self-Managing Work Team
Synergy
Status
Status Congruence
Task Activities
Work Group
Worker Involvement Group

## REVIEW QUESTIONS

1. State three reasons why groups are good for organizations. Are there any reasons why groups may *not* be good for organizations . . . and/ or their members?
2. What is the basic difference between a formal group and an informal group? Are informal groups good or bad for organizations? Explain your answer.
3. What is "group effectiveness" as defined in this chapter? What is "human resource maintenance" as a component of group effectiveness, and why is this concept important for a manager to understand?
4. Choose a group with which you are familiar. Diagram this group as an "open system." Identify and explain at least three "input foundations" that you consider essential to the effectiveness of this group.
5. Why is the size of a group important? What are some of the key "managerial" issues associated with group size, and what guidelines can you recommend for dealing with these issues?
6. Explain the difference between the "required" and "emergent" systems in Homan's model of group dynamics. Why is this difference important to our understanding of group behavior in organizations?
7. What is a "self-managing" work team? How does this approach to work design offer opportunities for improving the utilization of groups as human resources of organizations?
8. What is a "quality circle"? How can quality circles and other forms of worker involvement groups benefit organizations of all types and sizes?

## AN OB LIBRARY

Clyde W. Burleson, *Effective Meetings: The Complete Guide* (New York: John Wiley & Sons, 1990).

Andre L . Delbecq, Andrew H. Van de Ven, and David H. Gustafson, *Group Techniques for Program Planning: A Guide to Nominal Group and Delphi Processes* (Glenview, IL: Scott, Foresman, 1975).

Edward E. Lawler, III, *High-Involvement Management* (San Francisco: Jossey-Bass, 1986).

Glenn M. Parker, *Team Players and Teamwork: The New Competitive Strategy* (San Francisco: Jossey-Bass, 1990).

Alvin Zander, *The Purposes of Groups and Organizations* (San Francisco: Jossey-Bass, 1985).

# EXERCISE

## INTERPERSONAL RELATIONS IN GROUPS

### Objectives

1. To help you explore the typical ways that you interact with people.
2. To help you think about the meaning of power to you, in terms of your relations with other people.
3. To identify those individuals in the learning environment who have more or less power, and to understand how this power is derived.

### Total Time

60 minutes

### Procedure

1. Respond to the accompanying questionnaire[23] that targets the following items:
   a. *Expressed Inclusion* (your need to establish and maintain contact with other people).
   b. *Want Inclusion* (your need to have others express their need for contact to you).
   c. *Expressed Control* (the need to have influence or control over other people).
   d. *Want Control* (the need to have others influence or control you).
   e. *Expressed Affection* (the need to have a close, personal relationship with other people where you can comfortably express it).
   f. *Want Affection* (having others comfortably express their close, personal relationship to you).
2. You are to select a number from 0 (very low) to 9 (very high) for each of the 12 scales. Circle one number indicating your best estimate as to the strength of your need on that particular scale.
3. Find the average of your two scale scores for each of the six dimensions. Place this average score in the appropriate place on the questionnaire.
4. Form groups of three to four persons and compare your scores on each of the six dimensions. Also compare the discrepancy between your expressed scores and want scores. Finally, compare your total score (add all six scores together) as this is an indication of the relative importance of people in your life. The higher your total score, the more important your relations with people are.

*Expressed Inclusion*

| 0 | 1 | 2 | 3 | 4 | 5 | 6 | 7 | 8 | 9 |
|---|---|---|---|---|---|---|---|---|---|
| Most often try to be alone; not include others in activities and social events | | | | Sometimes; occasionally | | | Most often try to include others in activities and social events; not be alone | | |

| 0 | 1 | 2 | 3 | 4 | 5 | 6 | 7 | 8 | 9 |
|---|---|---|---|---|---|---|---|---|---|
| Most often don't include anybody in activities and social events; want to be by myself | | | | Some people; a few people | | | Most often try to include one or more people in activities and social events; want to be with someone | | |

Average score of two scales = ______

*Want Inclusion*

| 0 | 1 | 2 | 3 | 4 | 5 | 6 | 7 | 8 | 9 |
|---|---|---|---|---|---|---|---|---|---|
| Most often want to be alone; not included by others in activities and social events | | | | Sometimes; occasionally | | | Most often want others to include me in activities and social events; don't want them to leave me alone | | |

| 0 | 1 | 2 | 3 | 4 | 5 | 6 | 7 | 8 | 9 |
|---|---|---|---|---|---|---|---|---|---|
| Don't want anybody to include me in activities and social events; want to be alone | | | | Some people; a few people | | | Want most people to include me in their activities and social events; want to be included by a lot of people | | |

Average score of two scales = ______

*Expressed Control*

| 0 | 1 | 2 | 3 | 4 | 5 | 6 | 7 | 8 | 9 |
|---|---|---|---|---|---|---|---|---|---|
| Most often avoid influencing others; avoid trying to be dominant; avoid taking charge | | | | Sometimes; occasionally | | | Most often try to influence others; try to be dominant; try to take charge | | |

| 0 | 1 | 2 | 3 | 4 | 5 | 6 | 7 | 8 | 9 |
|---|---|---|---|---|---|---|---|---|---|
| Don't try to influence anybody; don't try to be dominant or take charge over most people | | | | Some people; a few people | | | Try to influence most people; try to be dominant of or take charge over most people | | |

Average of two scale scores = ______

*Want Control*

| 0 | 1 | 2 | 3 | 4 | 5 | 6 | 7 | 8 | 9 |
|---|---|---|---|---|---|---|---|---|---|
| Usually don't want to be influenced by others; don't want to be dominated; usually avoid others taking charge of me | | | | Sometimes; occasionally | | | Usually want to be influenced by others; want to be dominated; want others to take charge of me | | |

| 0 | 1 | 2 | 3 | 4 | 5 | 6 | 7 | 8 | 9 |
|---|---|---|---|---|---|---|---|---|---|
| Usually don't want anyone to influence me; don't want anyone to dominate me; don't want anyone to take charge of me | | | | Some people; a few people | | | Want lots of other people to influence me; dominate me; take charge of my activities | | |

Average of the two scales = ________

*Expressed Affection*

| 0 | 1 | 2 | 3 | 4 | 5 | 6 | 7 | 8 | 9 |
|---|---|---|---|---|---|---|---|---|---|
| Never want to act close and personal to others; usually want to act cool and distant to others | | | | Sometimes; occasionally | | | Usually want to act close and personal to others; never want to act cool and distant to others | | |

| 0 | 1 | 2 | 3 | 4 | 5 | 6 | 7 | 8 | 9 |
|---|---|---|---|---|---|---|---|---|---|
| Never want to act close and personal to anyone; want to act cool and distant to most people | | | | Some people; a few people | | | Want to act close and personal to most people; never want to act cool and distant to anyone | | |

Average of two scales = ________

*Want Affection*

| 0 | 1 | 2 | 3 | 4 | 5 | 6 | 7 | 8 | 9 |
|---|---|---|---|---|---|---|---|---|---|
| Never want people to act close or personal with me; usually want people to act cool and distant | | | | Sometimes; occasionally | | | Usually want people to act close and personal with me; never want people to act cool and distant | | |

| 0 | 1 | 2 | 3 | 4 | 5 | 6 | 7 | 8 | 9 |
|---|---|---|---|---|---|---|---|---|---|
| Don't want anybody to act close or personal with me; want most people to act cool and distant to me | | | | Some people; a few people | | | Want most people to act close and personal with me; never want anyone to act cool and distant to me. | | |

Average of two scales = ______

| | *Inclusion* | *Control* | *Affection* |
|---|---|---|---|
| You give (express to others) | $e^i$ = | $e^c$ = | $e^a$ = |
| You get (want from others) | $w^i$ = | $w^c$ = | $w^a$ = |

CASE

## WHERE TEAMWORK IS MORE THAN JUST TALK

Life inside a Cadillac engine plant in Livonia, Mich., is worlds apart from the atmosphere of a typical auto factory. Hourly workers and supervisors dress much the same and cooperate closely on "business teams" that organize the work and make other decisions normally left to management. "It makes you feel like a part of what's going on," says Gary L. Andrews, an hourly worker and assistant team coordinator (ATC). A 14-year Cadillac veteran, Andrews says he would return to a traditional auto plant "only if it was a choice between that and hitting the streets."

Livonia is one of nine General Motors Corp. plants that use the "pay-for-knowledge" team concept to make factory work less boring and more productive. This approach differs radically from the practice in most union shops, where workers perform narrow functions. At Livonia, production workers can learn all of the jobs in one section, giving management flexibility in assigning work and filling in for absent workers. Workers are paid according to the skills they acquire, giving them an incentive to learn new ones.

The system was introduced recently, when GM's Cadillac Motor Car Division closed its engine works in Detroit and moved to the western suburb of Livonia. About 95 percent of the Detroit workers transferred with Cadillac. Local 22 of the United Auto Workers was involved in planning the change from the start and even had a voice in choosing salaried employees who would function as the team coordinators. (ATCs such as Andrews, 32, are elected from the ranks.)

Livonia uses less labor per engine than the Detroit plant while producing higher-quality products. It hit the breakeven point after one year, instead of the anticipated two years. The scrap rate has fallen by 50 percent. In a recent year worker suggestions saved Cadillac more than $1.2 million.

The plant, which cranks out 1200 engines a day, is divided into 15 departments that are in turn subdivided into business teams of 10 to 20 workers each, consisting of production workers who assemble the engines and perform nonskilled maintenance duties. The engines are still produced on an assembly line, but the employees have varied routines and participate in decision making. Moreover, dress codes are passé: almost no one wears a tie, and some supervisors wear jeans. Managers and workers share the same cafeteria and compete for parking spots.

The teams meet weekly on company time to discuss issues such as safety and housekeeping. They decide when to award raises and rotate jobs, and they may even suggest redesigning the work flow. Recently, Andrews took it on himself to analyze every job on two teams that attach components to already-assembled engines. "I sat with pencil and paper and figured out how to make it easier," he recalls. His teammates accepted his idea of spreading the work more evenly along the lines. Within 15 minutes, Andrews says, the changes were made without any downtime or loss of production. His reward: election as ATC.

The 23 members of Andrews' team rotate among 12 or 13 jobs on the line, 6 engine-repair jobs, and 4 to 5 housekeeping and inspection jobs. As ATC, Andrews does a little of everything and helps the team coordinator plan work schedules.

In the old Detroit plant, there were 45 job classifications, each with its own wage rate. In Livonia, there are four wage levels for experienced workers, ranging from $9.63 an hour to a maximum of $10.08 for a "job setter"—a worker who sets up and changes tooling on the line. A worker reaches the top rate after learning all the skills on two business teams.

"In a traditional plant, you might have 90 to 100 job setters," says Peter J. Ulbrich, until recently Livonia's personnel administrator. "Here, you have the opportunity for 1200 to 1300 people to get there." This system can produce an expensive work force. "It is a neat way to get short-term productivity results," says one teamwork expert, "but you wonder what they will do when everybody reaches the top rate."

## *Questions*

1. Do the "business teams" described in this case appear to make good use of groups as human resources of organizations? Explain your answer by using the various concepts and ideas on group attributes found in this chapter.
2. What can be done by managers who have "business teams" reporting to them, to insure that the teams establish and maintain high levels of group effectiveness? Can team members ultimately be responsible for their own effectiveness or is this a distinctly "managerial" responsibility? Please explain.
3. Do you share the concern expressed in the last sentence in the case? Why or why not, and what can be done about it?

This study outline of major topics is meant to organize your reading now; it is repeated in the Summary to structure your review.

## STUDY OUTLINE

### Team Building and Group Development

The Team-Building Process　Stages of Group Development

### Individual Entry to Groups

Individual Problems upon Entering Groups　Clarifying Membership Expectations

### Group Norms and Cohesiveness

The Nature of Group Norms　Group Cohesiveness

### Roles and Communication Patterns in Groups

Group Task and Maintenance Roles　Group Communication Networks

CHAPTER 9

# GROUP AND INTERGROUP DYNAMICS

# VISIONS 9

**"Who needs a boss?" reads the headline of a *Fortune* magazine article. "Not the employees who work in self-managed teams," answers the first paragraph. And whether you call them autonomous work groups, high-performance teams, or self-managing work teams, the concept—as discussed in Chapter 8—is considered by many managers as the key to productivity improvement in the 1990s. Because of teams, General Mills' Lodi, California, plant no longer needs managers present during the night shift; a team at Ford's Romeo, Michigan, plant spotted and solved a problem with machine switches; a highly efficient Chaparral Steel plant uses machinery selected by workers. And this list could go on.**

**Yet like all groups in organizations, these teams require attention and support to achieve high effectiveness. Among the special problems that often occur in such teams are difficulty with direction, concerns about making decisions, handling disputes and internal conflicts, and dealing with the increased responsibilities of individual members. Says Donald Owen about his role as a team member at General Mills' Lodi plant: "I work a lot harder than I used to. You have to worry about the numbers." It's not enough, in other words, for visionary managers to implement creative work group designs. They must be prepared to do what is needed to help the groups properly develop and maintain themselves as "high performance systems" over time.**

If groups are to perform along such "visionary" lines, they must function well internally and in relationship to the organization as a whole. Good managers are able to positively influence groups as essential human resources of organizations. That is, they are able to understand and manage ***group dynamics***—the forces operating in groups that affect task performance and human resource maintenance. In the last chapter we described groups as open systems that transform resource inputs into task outputs. Group dynamics involve the "processes" through which members work together to accomplish their tasks.

Group dynamics

As our attention now shifts specifically to process considerations and group effectiveness, the managerial question becomes: What can be done to help a group best utilize its available inputs to achieve desired outputs?

To answer this question, we need to examine five key aspects of group dynamics—team building and group development, group norms and cohesion, roles and interaction patterns within a group, decision-making methods, and intergroup dynamics.

# TEAM BUILDING AND GROUP DEVELOPMENT

When we think of the word "teams," sporting teams come to mind. We know, too, that sporting teams have their problems. Members slack off or become disgruntled, and some get retired or traded to other teams as a result. Even world champion teams have losing streaks, and the most highly talented players are prone to lose motivation at times, quibble among themselves, and go into slumps. When these things happen, the owners, managers, and players are apt to examine their problems and take corrective action to "rebuild the team" and restore what we have been calling group effectiveness.

Work groups are teams in a similar sense. And like sporting teams, even the most mature work group is likely to experience problems over time. When difficulties occur, or as a means of preventing them from occurring, team building activities can help. ***Team building*** is a sequence of planned action steps designed to gather and analyze data on the functioning of a group and implement changes to increase its operating effectiveness.[1]

**Team building**

## The Team-Building Process

There are many team-building strategies, but they generally share the steps shown in Figure 9.1 and highlighted here.

- Someone notices that a group problem exists or might develop in the future.
- Group members work together to gather and analyze data relating to the actual or possible problem.
- The data are interpreted by the group and action plans are made.
- Action plans are implemented to achieve constructive change.
- Results are evaluated and any difficulties or new problems are reasons to recycle the process.

The team-building process just described is a collaborative one. Throughout the various steps it is expected that *all* members of the group work together to analyze the situation and decide what—if anything—needs to be done. Then, everyone shares in the responsibility for implementing the agreed-upon actions. In this way, team building is a highly *participative* way of assessing a work group's functioning and taking corrective action to improve its effectiveness. All this can be done with or without external consulting assistance. In any event, it can and should become a regular part of a group's continuing work routine.

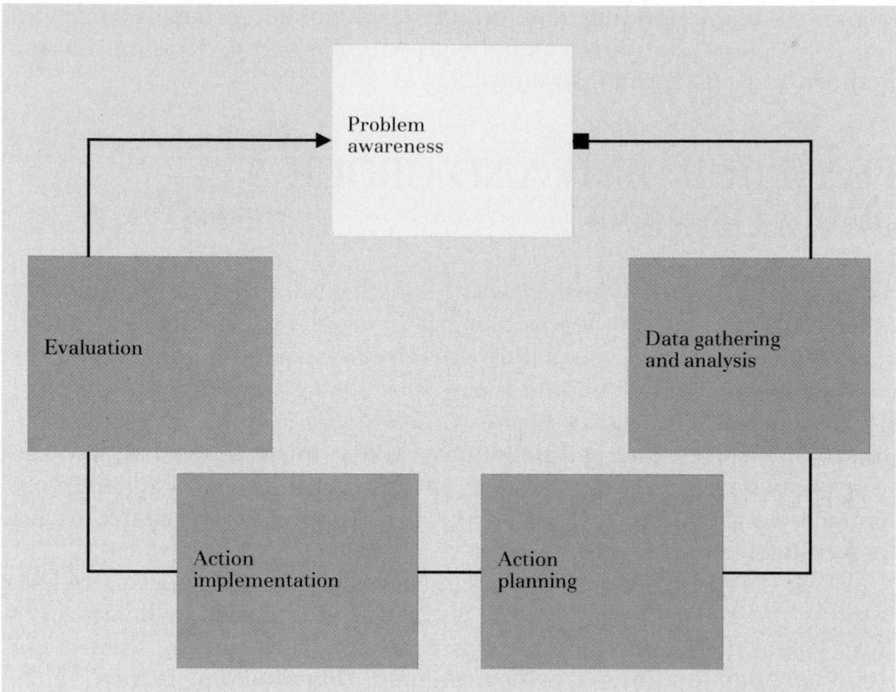


*FIGURE 9.1 Five steps in a typical team-building cycle.*

The gathering and analysis of data on group functioning is a key element in the team-building cycle. To be successful in this stage, group effectiveness must be carefully assessed. Questions such as—"How well are *we* doing in terms of task accomplishment?" and "How satisfied are we as individual members with the group and the way it operates?" must be asked . . . and answered in a collaborative and participatory fashion. Then group members can make plans and commit to actions designed to improve and/or maintain group effectiveness in the future. This may involve modification of one or more group input factors (previously examined in Chapter 8) and/or a change in the group process itself—the primary topic of the present chapter.

## Stages of Group Development

Newly formed groups show quite different behavior patterns from mature ones whose members have worked together for quite some time. A knowledge of group development can help you to predict the kinds of behavior most likely to occur and provide additional understanding of why one group acts one way and another quite differently. The four stages of group development and the key managerial or team-building challenges of each are:[2]

1. Forming stage—managing individual entry.
2. Storming stage—managing group norm development.
3. Initial integration stage—managing group cohesion.
4. Total integration stage—managing decision making.

In the *forming stage,* a primary concern is the initial entry of members to a group. At this point individuals ask a number of questions as they begin to identify with other group members and the group itself. These include: "What can the group offer me?" "What will I be asked to

A MATURE GROUP POSSESSES:

1. Adequate mechanisms for getting feedback:

| | 1 | 2 | 3 (Average) | 4 | 5 | |
|---|---|---|---|---|---|---|
| Poor feedback mechanisms | | | | | | Excellent feedback mechanisms |

2. Adequate decision-making procedure:

| | 1 | 2 | 3 (Average) | 4 | 5 | |
|---|---|---|---|---|---|---|
| Poor decision-making procedure | | | | | | Very adequate decision-making |

3. Optimal cohesion:

| | 1 | 2 | 3 (Average) | 4 | 5 | |
|---|---|---|---|---|---|---|
| Low cohesion | | | | | | Optimal cohesion |

4. Flexible organization and procedures:

| | 1 | 2 | 3 (Average) | 4 | 5 | |
|---|---|---|---|---|---|---|
| Very inflexible | | | | | | Very flexible |

5. Maximum use of member resources:

| | 1 | 2 | 3 (Average) | 4 | 5 | |
|---|---|---|---|---|---|---|
| Poor use of resources | | | | | | Excellent use of resources |

6. Clear communication:

| | 1 | 2 | 3 (Average) | 4 | 5 | |
|---|---|---|---|---|---|---|
| Poor communication | | | | | | Excellent communication |

7. Clear goals accepted by members:

| | 1 | 2 | 3 (Average) | 4 | 5 | |
|---|---|---|---|---|---|---|
| Unclear goals–not accepted | | | | | | Very clear goals–accepted |

8. Feelings of interdependence with authority persons:

| | 1 | 2 | 3 (Average) | 4 | 5 | |
|---|---|---|---|---|---|---|
| No interdependence | | | | | | High interdependence |

9. Shared participation in leadership functions:

| | 1 | 2 | 3 (Average) | 4 | 5 | |
|---|---|---|---|---|---|---|
| No shared participation | | | | | | High shared participation |

10. Acceptance of minority views and persons:

| | 1 | 2 | 3 (Average) | 4 | 5 | |
|---|---|---|---|---|---|---|
| No acceptance | | | | | | High acceptance |

*FIGURE 9.2 Schein's 10 criteria of group maturity.* (From Edgar H. Schein, *Process Consultation.* Vol. 1. Copyright © 1988. Addison-Wesley Publishing Company, Inc., Chapter 6, p. 81. Figure 6.1, "A Mature Group Process." Reprinted with permission.)

contribute?" "Can my needs be met at the same time I contribute to the group?" People are concerned to discover what is considered acceptable behavior, determining the real task of the group, and defining group rules. In a work group, this identification process is likely to be more complicated than in other settings. The work setting may consist of individuals who have been in the organization for substantial time periods. Such things as multiple group memberships and identifications, prior experience with group members in other contexts, and impressions or organization philosophies, goals, and policies may all affect newly formed work groups.

The *storming stage* of group development is a period of high emotionality and tension among the members. There may be periods of overt hostility and infighting. Typically, this period involves changes in the group. Required activities for members are further elaborated, and attention is shifted toward obstacles standing in the way of group goals. In work groups individuals begin to clarify one another's interpersonal styles. Efforts will be made to find appropriate ways to accomplish group goals while also satisfying individual needs. Outside demands create pressures. Coalitions or cliques may form as subgroups on an emergent and informal basis. Conflict may develop over authority as individuals compete to try to impose their preferences on the group and to achieve their desired position in the group's status structure.

The *initial integration stage* is where the group begins to come together as a coordinated unit. Probes and jockeying behaviors of the storming phase lead to a precarious balancing of forces. Group members strive to maintain this balance. The group will try to regulate individual behavior toward this end. Members are likely to develop a preliminary sense of closeness, and want to protect the group from disintegration. Holding the group together may become more important than successful task accomplishment. Minority viewpoints may be strongly discouraged.

The *total integration stage* sees the emergence of a mature, organized, and well-functioning group. The integration begun in the previous stage is completed. The group is able to deal with complex tasks and to handle membership disagreements in creative ways. Group structure is stable, and members are motivated by group goals and are generally satisfied. The primary challenges of this stage are to continue working together as an integrated unit, to remain coordinated with the larger organization, and to adapt successfully to changing conditions over time. A group that has achieved total integration will score high on the criteria of group maturity presented in Figure 9.2.

## INDIVIDUAL ENTRY TO GROUPS

The members of any group face many problems over time. But individual difficulties are especially likely to arise when a group is first convened or when the membership of an existing group changes as old members leave and new members join. Typical "entry" anxieties in such situations include concerns for *participation* ("Will I be allowed to participate?"), *goals* ("Do I share the goals of others?"), *control* ("Will I be able to influ-

INTERNATIONAL PERSPECTIVE

**TOYOTA**

Courtesy of Toyota Motor Corporation.

**When Toyota was ready to build its first U.S. plant in Georgetown, Kentucky, company executives were concerned about a new group of workers they would have to deal with—the Americans. They said: "A worker whose face we could not read—whose heart was a mystery to us . . . This was our greatest fear." They just weren't sure if this "foreign" worker would listen and learn Japanese ways of doing things. It turns out the problem wasn't too great to overcome. In fact, the Americans worked just as hard, just as proudly, and even more creatively sometimes than their Japanese counterparts. They also got the same "kicks" out of being part of a high performance team.**

ence what takes place?"), *relationships* ("How close do people get?"), and *processes* ("Are conflicts likely to be upsetting?").

## Individual Problems upon Entering Groups

Edgar Schein, a noted scholar and consultant, offers a set of profiles of individuals who encounter difficulties upon entering new groups.[3] The profiles, listed below, are often associated with coping responses that can include self-serving activities interfering with, rather than facilitating, group effectiveness.

1. *The Tough Battler:* Group members frustrated by identity problems may act aggressive and tend to resist the ideas and authority of others. These "tough battlers" are seeking answers to the question, "Who am I in this group?"
2. *The Friendly Helper:* Initial entry into a group can create tensions as people try to solve problems of control and intimacy. These ten-

sions may lead to showing support for others, acting dependent, and helping and forming supportive alliances. The "friendly helper" is trying to determine whether or not he or she will be liked by the other group members, and if he or she will be able to exert any control or influence over their behavior.

3. *The Objective Thinker:* Another anxiety that accompanies individual entry into a group is needs and goals. People join groups for various reasons and seek many types of need satisfactions from their group memberships. Initial passivity, indifference, or oneness of logic or reason in deliberations often characterize the "objective thinker." This person is trying to determine if group goals include opportunities to satisfy personal needs.

## Clarifying Membership Expectations

Problems experienced by individuals upon entering groups often reflect uncertainties regarding their expected roles. Similar concerns may emerge over time as a person grows and develops, when the membership of the

*FIGURE 9.3 Sample materials from a role negotiations exercise.* (From Roger Harrison, "When Power Conflicts Trigger Team Spirit," *European Business* (Spring 1972), pp. 61, 63. Used by permission.)

ROLE NEGOTIATIONS

**Issue Diagnosis Form**

Messages from Jim

to David

1. If you were to do the following things more or better, it would help me to increase my own effectiveness:

   *Be more receptive to improvement suggestions from the process engineers*

   *Give help on cost control (see 2)*

   *Fight harder with the G.M. to get our plan improved*

2. If you were to do the following things less, or were to stop doing them, it would help me to increase my own effectiveness:

   *Acting as judge and jury on cost control*

   *Checking up frequently on small details of the work*

   *Asking for so many detailed progress reports*

3. The following things which you have been doing help to increase my own effectiveness, and I hope you will continue to do them:

   *Passing on full information in our weekly meetings.*

   *Being available when I need to talk to you*

**Final agreement between Jim Farrell and David Sills**

*Jim agrees to let David know as soon as agreed completion dates and cost projections look as though they won't be met and also to discuss each project's progress fully with David on a bi-weekly basis.*

*In return David agrees not to raise questions about cost details and completion dates, pending a trial of this agreement to see if it provides sufficient information soon enough to deal with questions from above.*

group changes, and/or as the group is challenged by shifting external demands. At the heart of the matter in all such cases is a *psychological contract* issue. That is, the individual member is concerned about balance in his or her exchange of inducements and contributions with the group.

There is a continuing need in any group to establish and maintain healthy psychological contracts for all members—both at the point of someone's initial entry and then over time with their continuing membership. One strategy for accomplishing this is ***role negotiation***—a process through which individuals negotiate with one another to clarify expectations about what each should be giving and receiving as group members.

**Role negotiation**

Sample results from an actual role negotiation are shown in Figure 9.3. Note the presence of "give and take" in the final written agreements between negotiators. In general, the following five steps may be followed to accomplish role negotiations in groups.[4]

1. Individuals write lists of things they would like to see other group members (a) do more or do better, (b) do less or stop doing, and (c) keep doing or remain unchanged.
2. These lists are shared and discussed.
3. Individuals negotiate contracts with one another specifying action commitments that will help satisfy the other's needs and enhance group effectiveness.
4. The contracts are summarized in written form as a reminder to all members of their commitments.
5. The contracts are revised at regular intervals to update and further clarify group membership roles.

# GROUP NORMS AND COHESIVENESS

Two group process factors of major significance in any setting are *norms* and *cohesiveness.* Before we define and examine these terms in detail, consider the following incident as an illustration of their importance to managers.[5]

> Frank Jackson deftly soldered his last wires in the interconnection. That was 18 for the morning—not bad, he thought. He moved on to the next computer and began to string out the cable for the next job.
>
> "You're new here, aren't you?" The man was standing beside Frank, soldering iron in hand.
>
> "Yeah. I came over from Consumer Products Division—been with the company for 10 years."
>
> "I'm Jim Miller. Been working here in computer assembly for 5 years."
>
> The men shook hands. Jim walked back to the last job Frank did and looked it over. "Pretty good, Frank, pretty good." He looked back down the assembly floor. "How many have you done this morning?"
>
> "Eighteen."
>
> "Hey, you're quite a rate-buster, aren't you?" Jim laughed.

"Most of us here figure 15 interconnections a day is about par for the course."

"Well, these I'm doing are pretty easy."

Jim frowned. "Yeah, but look what happens. You do 20, maybe 25 easy ones, and the boys stuck with the hard jobs look bad. You wouldn't want that to happen, would you?"

"Well, no, of course not."

"That-a-boy!" Frank smiled. "You know, the boys here have a bowling team—kind of a company deal. Not everybody is on it—just the interconnection group. Even a few of them don't make it. You know, we like to keep it a friendly bunch." He paused. "Like to come next Wednesday?"

"Why, OK. Sure Jim, what does the foreman think about the number of jobs a day?"

"Him? He don't know the difference, and if he did, what difference would it make? You can't find good interconnection men right off the street. He goes along—the boys upstairs don't know how fast the work should go, and they don't bother him. So he don't bother us."

Frank looked over his next job. He was doing the toughest kind of interconnection, and he knew that any reasonably skilled person should be able to do at least 40 jobs a day on most of the other interconnections. Boy, this was going to be a relaxing job. He didn't like to goof off, but these people were going to be working with him every day—and he wasn't about to get off on the wrong foot with them. Besides, he liked to bowl.

"It's all cost plus anyhow," Jim said. "The company gets plenty from the government for the work. They've got nothing to worry about. Hey, come over to the latrine with me—we can have a smoke. We got plenty of time."

## The Nature of Group Norms

**Group norm**

A ***group norm*** is an idea or belief about behavior expected to be displayed by members of a group. Norms are often referred to as "rules" or "standards" of behavior that apply to group members.[6] When violated, norms may be enforced with reprimands and/or other sanctions such as expulsion from the group or social ostracism. In fact, it was just this concern that apparently caused Frank Jackson in the prior case to agree to the norm of restricted performance. Frank was clearly a highly capable and initially highly motivated worker. As a result of "pressure" from other group members, however, he accepted the norm and agreed to work at far less than his true performance potential.

Norms are among the sentiments that develop as group members interact with one another. They serve the group by allowing members to predict one another's behavior and, therefore, to be better able to select appropriate behaviors for themselves. Norms also help members gain a common sense of direction, and they reinforce a desired group or organizational culture. For example,

*Union Pacific* CEO Michael Walsh works very hard to communicate a high-performance culture. During a yearly meeting for the firm's top management group he engages in a "give-and-take" session to dramatically clarify and reinforce his performance themes. Highlights of the meeting are even videotaped and distributed to attendees for later viewing.

There are many types of norms. For a task force or project group, there may be norms regarding attendance at meetings, social behaviors, preparedness for meetings, willingness to challenge one another's ideas, and so on. Other common norms in the work setting deal with relationships with supervisors, colleagues, and customers, as well as honesty, security, personal development, and change. Table 9.1 shows examples of how such norms may emerge in both positive and negative forms. Of course, the Union Pacific example points out that one of the most important norms for any group is its performance norm—that is, the norm that governs how hard members work on the group task. As you might expect, work groups with more positive norms tend to be more successful in accomplishing their tasks than are groups with more negative norms.

Since group norms are essentially determined by the collective will of group members, it is very difficult for organizations and their managers

*TABLE 9.1*
**EXAMPLES OF THE *POSITIVE* AND *NEGATIVE* FORMS OF GROUP NORMS**

| Norms of . . . | Positive Form . . . | Negative Form . . . |
|---|---|---|
| Organizational and personal pride | It's a tradition around here for people to stand up for the company when others criticize it unfairly. | In our company they are always trying to take advantage of us. |
| Performance/excellence | In our company people always try to improve, even when they are doing well. | Around here there's no point in trying harder—nobody else does. |
| Teamwork/communication | Around here people are good listeners and actively seek out the ideas and opinions of others. | Around here it's dog-eat-dog and save your own skin. |
| Leadership/supervision | Around here managers and supervisors really care about the people they supervise. | In our company it's best to hide your problems and avoid your supervisor. |
| Profitability/cost effectiveness | Around here people are continually on the lookout for better ways of doing things. | Around here people tend to hang on to old ways of doing things even after they have outlived their usefulness. |

*Source:* Developed from Robert F. Allen and Saul Pilnick, "Confronting the Shadow Organization: How to Detect and Defeat Negative Norms," *Organizational Dynamics* (Spring 1973), pp. 6–10.

to dictate which norms a given work group will possess. Yet, the concerned manager must use a knowledge of group dynamics to help group members adopt norms supportive of organizational goals. Among the things a manager can do to help groups build and maintain positive norms are:[7]

- Act as a positive role model.
- Reinforce, via rewards, the desired behaviors.
- Control results by performance reviews and regular feedback.
- Train and orient new members to adopt desired behaviors.
- Recruit and select new members who exhibit the desired behaviors.
- Hold regular meetings to discuss group progress and ways of improving task performance and member satisfaction.
- Use group decision-making methods to reach agreement on appropriate behaviors.

## Group Cohesiveness

**Group cohesiveness**

The extent to which members of a group conform to its norms is strongly influenced by ***group cohesiveness***—the degree to which members are attracted to and motivated to remain part of a group.[8] Persons in a highly cohesive group value their membership and strive to maintain positive relationships with other group members. The work group that Frank Jackson joined was apparently cohesive. Other members of his team rallied together and restricted their work efforts. This sense of group belongingness apparently had a strong attraction for Frank. Perhaps it was a need for social affiliation that led him to accept this norm rather than to break it and run the risk of being ostracized from the group.

### *Sources of Group Cohesiveness*

Cohesion is an important group property. It tends to be high in groups where:

- Members are similar in age, attitudes, needs, backgrounds.
- Members respect one another's competencies.
- Members agree on group goals.
- Tasks require interdependent efforts.
- The group is of relatively small size.
- The group is physically isolated from other groups.
- The group is experiencing significant performance success.
- The group is experiencing a performance crisis *or* failure.

### *Results of Group Cohesiveness*

Cohesive groups are good for themselves and their members. Members of highly cohesive groups, whether formal or informal, are concerned about their group's activities and achievements. They tend—as opposed to persons in less cohesive groups—to be more energetic in working on group activities, less likely to be absent, happy about performance success, and sad about failures. Cohesive groups generally have stable memberships and foster feelings of loyalty, security, and high self-esteem among their members. They satisfy a full range of individual needs.

But, the critical remaining question is whether or not cohesive work groups are good for their host organization. The answer is quite clear: "It all depends on the group's performance norm!" A basic rule of group dynamics is that, the more cohesive the group, the greater the conformity of members to group norms. When the performance norm is positive, for example, high conformity has a very beneficial effect; when the norm is negative, however, high conformity has undesirable results.

Figure 9.4 shows the performance implications for various combinations of group cohesiveness and performance norms. Performance is highest in a very cohesive group with positive performance norms. In this situation, members encourage one another to work hard on behalf of the group. The worst situation for a manager is a highly cohesive group with negative performance norms. Once again members will be highly motivated to support one another. However, the organization will suffer as the group restricts its performance consistent with the negative norm. Between these two extremes are mixed situations where a lack of cohesion fails to ensure member conformity to the guiding norm. Thus the strength of the norm is less and the outcome is somewhat unpredictable, but most likely on the moderate or low side.

Given the implications of the last figure and discussion, there will be times when a manager will want to build cohesiveness in work groups—such as a group with positive norms but low cohesiveness. But there may be other times when the objective is to break down cohesiveness—such as a highly cohesive group with negative norms that are hard to change.

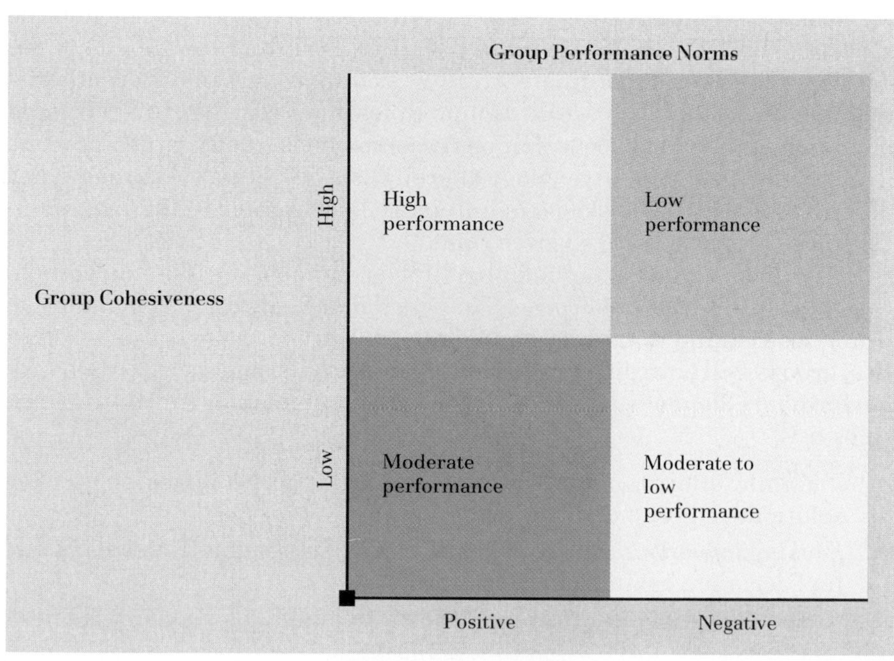


*FIGURE 9.4 How group cohesiveness and performance norms interact to influence group performance.*

*TABLE 9.2*
MANAGERIAL STRATEGIES FOR INCREASING AND DECREASING GROUP COHESIVENESS

| *Actions to Increase Cohesion:* | *Actions to Decrease Cohesion:* |
|---|---|
| Induce agreement on group goals | Induce disagreement on group goals |
| Increase membership homogeneity | Increase membership heterogeneity |
| Increase interactions among members | Restrict interactions among members |
| Decrease group size | Increase group size |
| Introduce competition with other groups | Allocate rewards to individuals rather than the group as a whole |
| Allocate rewards to the group rather than individuals | Remove physical isolation |
| Provide physical isolation from other groups | Introduce a dominating member |
| | Disband the group |

A number of things managers can do to increase and decrease group cohesion in these circumstances are listed in Table 9.2.

# ROLES AND COMMUNICATION PATTERNS IN GROUPS

The way in which group members interact with one another will have important consequences for group effectiveness. In the best groups members fulfill a variety of action roles and communicate in networks that facilitate, rather than impede, task accomplishment.

## Group Task and Maintenance Roles

**Role**

A ***role*** is formally defined as a set of activities expected of a person holding a particular office or position in a group or organization. "Leader/manager" or "follower/subordinate" are two common ways of differentiating membership roles in a work group. Roles may also be differentiated according to the kind of contributions a person makes to the group process. Research on the social psychology of groups suggests that two broad types of roles or activities—task and maintenance—are essential if group members are to work effectively over time.[9]

**Task activities**

***Task activities*** of group members focus on and contribute directly to the group's production purpose. They include efforts to define and solve problems relating to task accomplishment. Without relevant task activities, groups will have difficulty accomplishing their objectives. Group task performance depends on the willingness of members to fulfill such task roles as:[10]

- *Initiating:* offering new ideas or ways of defining problems, suggesting solutions to group difficulties.
- *Seeking information:* attempting to clarify suggestions in terms of factual accuracy, asking for ideas of others.
- *Giving information:* offering authoritative and relevant information and facts.

- *Clarifying:* clarifying relations among various suggestions or ideas, attempting to coordinate member activities.
- *Summarizing:* assessing group functioning, raising questions about logic and practicality of member suggestions.

***Maintenance activities*** support the emotional side of the group. They help to strengthen and perpetuate the group as an ongoing social system. They help to enhance member satisfaction and thereby contribute, along with the task activities, to group effectiveness. When maintenance activities are well performed, good interpersonal relationships should be achieved, and the ability of the group to stay together will be ensured. Examples include:[11]

**Maintenance activities**

- *Encouraging:* praising, accepting, agreeing with other members' ideas, indicating solidarity and warmth.
- *Harmonizing:* mediating squabbles within the group, reconciling differences, seeking opportunities for compromise.
- *Setting standards:* expressing standards for the group to achieve or use in evaluating group process.
- *Following:* going along with the group, agreeing to try out the ideas of others.
- *Gate-keeping:* encouraging participation of group members, trying to keep some members from dominating.

Both task and maintenance activities are required for groups to be effective over the long run. Every member can assist the group by performing these functions. Although a person in formal authority, such as chairperson or department head will do these activities, the responsibility for their occurrence should also be shared and distributed among all group members. Any and all group members should be able to recognize when task and/or maintenance activities are needed and properly respond to this need. This is sometimes called "distributed leadership" in group dynamics.

## Group Communication Networks

***Communication*** is discussed at length and defined in Chapter 14 as an interpersonal process of sending and receiving symbols with meanings attached to them. Communication is what allows group members to interact and complete their business. It enables members to get to know one another, learn norms, develop cohesiveness, and distribute information required to accomplish necessary tasks. Figure 9.5 depicts three common interaction patterns and communication networks found in groups.[12] ***Interacting groups*** display high interdependence among members in task performance. Each member interacts regularly with every other and close coordination is required to facilitate task performance. Interacting groups use ***decentralized communication,*** which allows all members of a group to communicate directly with one another.

**Communication**

**Interacting groups**

**Decentralized communication network**

Members of ***coacting groups*** work independently on common tasks. They divide up the required work and then labor individually to fulfill this responsibility. A central control point holds each member account-

**Coacting groups**

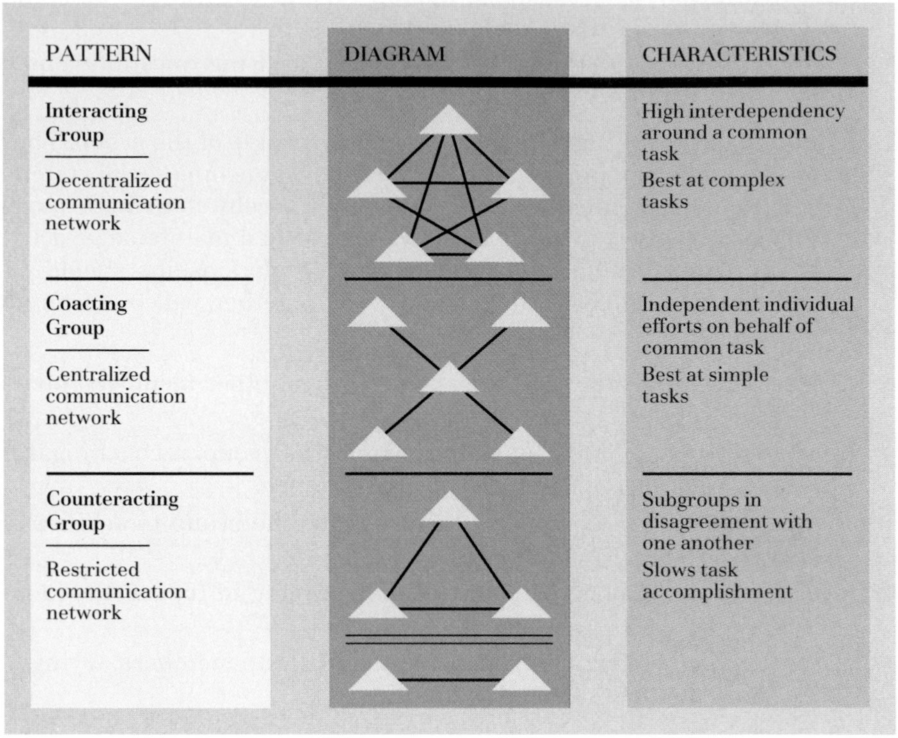

*FIGURE 9.5 Interaction patterns and group communication networks.*

| PATTERN | DIAGRAM | CHARACTERISTICS |
|---|---|---|
| Interacting Group<br>Decentralized communication network | | High interdependency around a common task<br>Best at complex tasks |
| Coacting Group<br>Centralized communication network | | Independent individual efforts on behalf of common task<br>Best at simple tasks |
| Counteracting Group<br>Restricted communication network | | Subgroups in disagreement with one another<br>Slows task accomplishment |

able and accumulates individual contributions into a final group product. In a coacting group all communication flows through this central person who serves as the "hub" of a ***centralized communication network.***

**Centralized communication network**

**Counteracting groups**

The presence of subgroups that disagree on some aspect of overall group operations characterizes ***counteracting groups.*** These may be issue-specific disagreements, such as temporary debate over the best means to achieve a goal. They may also be of longer-term duration, such as labor management disputes. In either case, the interaction pattern involves a ***restricted communication network*** in which polarized subgroups contest one another's positions and maintain sometimes antagonistic relations.

**Restricted communication network**

In general, people tend to be better satisfied in interacting groups using decentralized communication networks. This results from more opportunities to be involved in information flows associated with the group task. The central person in a coacting group or centralized network also tends to be highly satisfied. Again, this is because of this person's access to information.

Performance results of the networks also vary with the nature of the group task. Centralized communication networks work better on simple tasks requiring little creativity, information processing, and problem solving. Here, coacting groups will be faster and more accurate in task performance than will interacting groups. The reverse is true under more complex task conditions, where the decentralized network and interacting group is the top performer.

Communication within a counteracting group will be disjointed as subgroups form around different sides of an issue. The restricted communication network slows task accomplishment, but the underlying "conflict" can lead to creativity and critical evaluation which benefits the group. However, there are forces at work in the situation that make the manager's goal of achieving such benefits a most challenging one. Although the members of subgroups may relate effectively with one another, communication between them can suffer as emotions, antagonisms, and other biases intervene in the situation. This type of relationship is often typical of labor–management relations. However, new directions suggest improvements can work to both party's benefits. For example,

> *NUMMI* A California-based joint venture between General Motors and Toyota, NUMMI, relies on union–management cooperation to support the auto plant's extensive use of employee involvement and work teams. Cooperation has helped reduce employee grievances as many problems are worked out in face-to-face communications on the shop floor. It has also helped turn a once-failing operation into a productive one.

# DECISION MAKING IN GROUPS

One of the key activities in which group members engage is the making of decisions. The fundamentals of ***decision making*** as the process of choosing among alternative courses of action are discussed in Chapter 13. Our present interest is focused on the alternative ways in which groups make decisions as they communicate with one another to share information and work on tasks.

**Decision making**

## How Groups Make Decisions

Edgar Schein, a noted scholar and consultant, has worked extensively with groups to analyze and improve their decision-making processes. He observes that groups may make decisions through any of the six following methods.[13] As you read about them, think how often you encounter these methods in your group activities. Think, too, about the consequences resulting from each.

1. *Decision by lack of response.* One idea after another is suggested without any discussion taking place. When the group finally accepts an idea, all others have been bypassed and discarded by simple lack of response rather than by critical evaluation.
2. *Decision by authority rule.* The chairperson, manager, or some other authority figure makes a decision for the group. This can be done with or without discussion and is very time efficient. Whether the decision is a good one, however, depends on whether or not the authority figure had the necessary information and how well this approach is accepted by other group members.
3. *Decision by minority.* One, two, or three people are able to dominate

or "railroad" the group into making a decision they agree with. This is often done by providing a suggestion and then forcing quick agreement by challenging the group with—"Does anyone object? . . . Let's go ahead then."

4. *Decision by majority rule.* Groups can make decisions by majority rule, that is, by voting or polling members to find the majority viewpoint. This method parallels the democratic political system and is often used without awareness of its potential problems. Voting tends to create coalitions of "winners" and "losers." Those in the minority (i.e., the "losers") can easily feel left out or discarded without having a fair say. This can detract from the implementation of a decision since support for it is fragmented.

**Consensus**

5. *Decision by consensus.* ***Consensus*** is a state of affairs where a clear alternative appears with the support of most members, *and* even those who oppose it feel that they have been listened to and had a fair chance to influence the decision outcome. Consensus, therefore, does *not* require unanimity. What it does require is for any dissenting member to be able to say[14]

   I understand what most of you would like to do. I personally would not do that, but I feel that you understand what my alternative would be. I have had sufficient opportunity to sway you to my point of view but clearly have not been able to do so. Therefore, I will gladly go along with what most of you wish to do.

6. *Decision by unanimity.* All group members agree on the course of action to be taken. This is a "logically perfect" group decision method that is extremely difficult to attain in actual practice.

## Assets and Liabilities of Group Decision Making

The decision-making methods just discussed range from individual-oriented decisions at one extreme (e.g., authority rule) to more truly "group" decisions at the other (e.g., consensus). One of the reasons why groups sometimes turn to authority decisions, majority voting, or even minority decisions, is the difficulty of managing the group process to actually get consensus or unanimity. Table 9.3, for example, lists a number of guidelines for members in consensus-seeking groups. Success in achieving consensus requires discipline and support from everyone in the group. Breakdowns can and do occur in this process. As a result, there are both potential assets and liabilities to group decision making.[15]

> *Compaq Computer Corporation* "Consensus" is the key in a slow and methodical decision-making process which CEO Rod Canion thinks is a key to success in a company—and industry—driven by innovation. He indicates that Compaq's consensus management approach means that everyone gets a lot of facts, a lot of people get thinking, and everyone owns a decision when it's finally made.

Among the assets of group decision making are:

*TABLE 9.3*
ACTION GUIDELINES FOR ACHIEVING GROUP CONSENSUS

1. Avoid blindly arguing for your own individual judgments. Present your position as clearly and logically as possible, but listen to other members' reactions and consider them carefully before you press your point.
2. Avoid changing your mind just to reach agreement and avoid conflict. Support only solutions that you are able to agree with to at least some degree. Yield only to positions that have objectives and logically sound foundations.
3. Avoid "conflict-reducing" procedures such as majority vote, tossing a coin, averaging, or bargaining in reaching decisions.
4. Seek out differences of opinion. They are natural and expected. Try to involve everyone in the decision process. Disagreements can help the group's decision because a wide range of information and opinions improves the chances for the group to hit upon more adequate solutions.
5. Do not assume that someone must win and someone must lose when discussions reach a stalemate. Instead, look for the next most acceptable alternative for all members.
6. Discuss underlying assumptions, listen carefully to one another, and encourage the participation of all members—three important factors in reaching decisions by consensus.

*Source:* These guidelines are found in "Decisions, Decisions, Decisions," *Psychology Today* (November 1971), pp. 55, 56. Reprinted from *Psychology Today* magazine. Copyright © 1971 American Psychological Association.

- *Greater sum total of knowledge and information.* The involvement of more than one person increases the information that can be brought to bear on the problem.
- *Greater number of approaches to the problem.* The availability of several individuals means that more perspectives will be offered on a problem and the "tunnel vision" of a single perspective avoided.
- *Better understanding of final decision.* Because participants in group decision making are involved in all stages of discussion, comprehension of the decision is high.
- *Increased acceptance of final decision.* Participants in group decision making are more inclined to accept the final decision or feel a sense of responsibility for making it work.

On the other hand, the liabilities of group decision making include:

- *Social pressure to conform.* The desire to be a good member and go along with the group can lead people to conform prematurely to poor decisions.
- *Individual domination.* A dominant individual may emerge and control the group's decisions; this may be particularly true of the leader whose viewpoints may dominate group discussion.
- *Time requirements.* Groups are frequently slower to reach decisions than are individuals acting alone; groups can also delay decisions while individual members "play games" and/or "fight" with one another.

## "Groupthink"

There is another, very subtle side to group process that can work to a group's disadvantage. Let us consider an example from the world of business.[16]

> *The Ozyx Corporation* is a relatively small industrial company. The president of Ozyx has hired a consultant to help discover the reasons for the poor profit picture of the company in general and the low morale and productivity of the R&D division in particular. During the process of investigation, the consultant becomes interested in a research project in which the company has invested a sizable proportion of its R&D budget.
>
> When asked about the project by the consultant in the privacy of their offices, the president, the vice president for privacy of their offices, the president, the vice president for research, and the research manager each describe it as an idea that looks great on paper but will ultimately fail because of the unavailability of the technology required to make it work. Each of them also acknowledges that continued support of the project will create cash flow problems that will jeopardize the very existence of the total organization.
>
> Furthermore, each individual indicates he or she has not told the others about his reservations. When asked why, the president says he cannot reveal his "true" feelings because abandoning the project, which has been widely publicized, would make the company look bad in the press. In addition, it would probably cause his vice president's ulcer to kick up or perhaps even cause her to quit, "Because she has staked her professional reputation on the project's success."
>
> Similarly, the vice president for research says she cannot let the president or the research manager know her reservations because the president is so committed to it that "I would probably get fired for insubordination if I questioned the project."
>
> Finally, the research manager says he cannot let the president or vice president know of his doubts about the project because of their extreme commitment to the project's success.
>
> All indicate that, in meetings with one another, they try to maintain an optimistic facade so the others will not worry unduly about the project. The research manager, in particular, admits to writing ambiguous progress reports so the president and the vice president can "interpret them to suit themselves." In fact, he says he tends to slant them to the "positive" side, "given how committed the brass are."
>
> In a paneled conference room the project research budget is being considered for the following fiscal year. In the meeting itself, praises are heaped on the questionable project, and a unanimous decision is made to continue it for yet another year.

The Ozyx executives are having difficulty managing disagreement. Members of the group agree publicly with courses of action while privately having serious personal reservations. Simply put, its members strive to

Courtesy of Ford Motor Company.

## SKILLS PERSPECTIVE

## FORD

**"Employee involvement requires participative management" says Ford's CEO Donald E. Petersen. To build a sense of teamwork he established a corporate conference center where Ford managers from around the world meet to discuss strategies and share information. A variety of corporate-wide worker involvement efforts have helped the firm improve the quality and consumer appeal of its cars. Through these participative programs, Ford employees are encouraged to make decisions, individually and in groups, and apply their skills to solve important problems.**

maintain harmony and avoid the discomforts of disagreement. They change or suppress what they really believe in response to actual or perceived pressures from the group.

Groupthink

Social psychologist Irving Janis calls this phenomenon ***groupthink,*** the tendency of members in highly cohesive groups to lose their critical evaluative capabilities.[17] Because highly cohesive groups demand conformity, Janis believes that there is a tendency for their members to become unwilling to criticize one another's ideas and suggestions. Desires to hold the group together and to avoid unpleasant disagreements lead to an overemphasis on concurrence and an underemphasis on realistically appraising alternative courses of action. Poor decisions, like the one in the Ozyx case, are the result. A number of symptoms of groupthink are listed in Table 9.4. They can be used to help spot this phenomenon in practice. Then, when and if you ever do experience it, Janis suggests the following action guidelines for avoiding the negative consequences of groupthink.

*TABLE 9.4*
**SYMPTOMS OF "GROUPTHINK"—WHEN A GROUP MAY BE LOSING ITS CRITICAL EVALUATIVE CAPABILITIES**

**Illusions of group invulnerability** Members of the group feel that it is basically beyond criticism or attack.

**Rationalizing unpleasant and disconfirming data** Members refuse to accept contradictory data or to consider alternatives thoroughly.

**Belief in inherent group morality** Members of the group feel that it is "right" and above any reproach by outsiders.

**Stereotyping competitors as weak, evil, and stupid** Members refuse to look realistically at other groups.

**Applying direct pressure to deviants to conform to group wishes** Members refuse to tolerate a member who suggests the group may be wrong.

**Self-censorship by members** Members refuse to communicate personal concerns to the group as a whole.

**Illusions of unanimity** Members accept consensus prematurely, without testing its completeness.

**Mind guarding** Members of the group protect the group from hearing disturbing ideas or viewpoints from outsiders.

*Source:* Developed from Irving Janis, *Victims of Groupthink,* 2nd Ed. (Boston: Houghton Mifflin, 1982).

- Assign the role of critical evaluator to each group member; encourage a sharing of objections.
- Avoid, as a leader, seeming partial to one course of action.
- Create subgroups operating under different leaders and working on the same problem.
- Have group members discuss issues with subordinates and report back on their reactions.
- Invite outside experts to observe group activities and react to group processes and decisions.
- Assign one member to play a "devil's advocate" role at each meeting.
- Write alternative scenarios for the intentions of competing groups.
- Hold "second-chance" meetings after consensus is apparently achieved on key issues.

## Improving Group Decision Making

As you can see, group decision making is a complex and even delicate process. Its success depends on how well group process and individual contributions are balanced and integrated. Simply put:[18]

| Group decision effectiveness | = | sum of individual contributions | + | group process gains | − | group process losses |
|---|---|---|---|---|---|---|

In many respects, the goal of group decision making is to take advantage of the group as a decision resource while minimizing its potential disadvantages. Over the years social scientists have studied ways of avoiding some of the liabilities of open group meetings to improve decision making and enhance group creativity. Some examples include the brainstorming, nominal group, and Delphi techniques.[19]

## Brainstorming

In ***brainstorming,*** group members meet to generate ideas. Four rules typically govern the process:

**Brainstorming**

1. *All criticism is ruled out.* Judgment or evaluation of ideas must be withheld until the idea-generation process has been completed.
2. *"Freewheeling" is welcomed.* The wilder or more radical the idea, the better.
3. *Quantity is wanted.* The greater the number of ideas, the greater the likelihood of obtaining a superior idea.
4. *Combination and improvement are sought.* Participants should suggest how ideas of others can be turned into better ideas, or how two or more ideas can be joined into still another idea.

By prohibiting evaluation, brainstorming reduces fears of criticism or failure on the part of the individuals. Typical results include enthusiasm, involvement, and a free flow of ideas. Researchers consider brainstorming superior to open-group discussions as a basis for creative thinking and the generation of possible solutions to identified problems. Thus, this time-honored technique still has important practical applications. For example,

> *Hallmark Cards, Inc.* Brainstorming is used to come up with creative sayings for the company's Shoebox Greetings line of cards. Groups of writers meet weekly to share their weekly quotas of 50 potential "knee-slappers" per person. By the time the meeting is over, each has about three accepted for production. At Hallmark, it seems, almost any idea is valued in the search for a select few that are finally accepted.

## Nominal Group Technique

There will be times when group members have differing opinions and goals so that antagonistic argument can be predicted for a decision-making situation. In such cases where controversies may be dysfunctional, a nominal group technique could be more appropriate than either an open meeting or brainstorming. In a ***nominal group,*** the following rules apply:

**Nominal group technique**

- ▶ Participants work alone and respond in writing with alternative solutions to a stated problem.
- ▶ These ideas are then read aloud in round-robin fashion without any criticism or discussion.
- ▶ The ideas are recorded on large sheets of newsprint as they are read aloud.
- ▶ The ideas are then discussed individually in round-robin sequence for purposes of clarification only; evaluative comments are not allowed.

- A written voting procedure is followed; it results in a rank ordering of the alternatives in terms of priority.
- Steps 4 and 5 are repeated as desired to add further clarification to the process.

The final voting procedure allows alternatives to be explicitly evaluated under the nominal group technique, without risking the inhibitions, hostilities, and distorted outcomes that may accompany antagonistic or more open and unstructured meeting formats. Thus nominal grouping can improve group decision making under otherwise difficult circumstances.

### Delphi Technique

**Delphi technique**

A third approach, called the ***Delphi technique,*** was developed by the Rand Corporation to allow for the benefits of group decision making without members having to meet face to face. In fact, it allows group decision making to be accomplished over large distances and widely scattered members.

The Delphi procedure involves a series of questionnaires distributed over time to a decision-making panel. A typical approach works as follows: The first questionnaire states the problem and requests potential solutions. These solutions are summarized by the decision coordinator. The summary is returned to the panel in a second questionnaire. Panel members respond again and the process is repeated until a consensus is reached and a clear decision emerges. One of the problems with the Delphi technique relates to the complexity and cost of administering this series of questionnaires. However, it does make group decision making possible in circumstances when it is physically impossible to convene a meeting.

## INTERGROUP RELATIONS

**Intergroup dynamics**

Before leaving this discussion of group dynamics, we need to look once again at the organization itself as a complex network of many interlocking groups. In this setting, ***intergroup dynamics,*** that is, the dynamics that take place *between* as opposed to *within* groups, are especially important. Managers should strive to establish relationships among groups so that each works in harmony to help accomplish organizational goals. Unfortunately, the very nature of groups and organizations tends to create intergroup rivalries and antagonisms that can detract from rather than add to this desired synergy. In progressive organizations, however, managers are increasingly finding ways to build effective intergroup relations. For example,

> *Union Pacific* Cross-functional teams are used to solve customer problems and improve operations—they focus on breaking down internal barriers and developing cooperative solutions.
>
> *Ford* A special management development program brings together managers from different functional areas for common training. One

key concern is learning how the different functions view each other and how territoriality—short-sighted interest only in one's function—limits overall effectiveness.

## Factors Affecting Intergroup Relations

The nature of work-flow interdependencies, that is, the way work flows from one point to the next, affects intergroup relations in organizations. Figure 9.6 depicts how pooled, sequential, and reciprocal interdependencies affect the ways in which groups must work together to achieve their goals. Not much attention to intergroup relationships is needed where there is *pooled interdependence* since these groups seldom, if ever, meet. As long as each is familiar with overall organizational goals and the group's role in contributing to these, there should be little concern with the activities of other groups. The importance of managing intergroup relations increases when there is *sequential interdependence.* Here, one group's outputs become another group's inputs, and there are many possibilities for difficulties to arise. Things become even more complicated where there is *reciprocal interdependence.* In this case, multiple groups are sources of inputs and outputs for one another and the potential for breakdowns in working relationships is great.

Other factors affecting intergroup relations are found in the characteristics of the groups themselves. Just as people differ in *status,* relative standing, or prestige, compared with others within a group, groups can vary in status compared with others in the organization. Such differences are usually quite clear to the people involved, and they can influence intergroup relations. This is particularly true in sequential or reciprocal work flow interdependence when work passes from higher-status groups to lower-status ones. In this situation, there is less likely to be a problem than where the opposite is true.

Groups may also have different *time and goal orientations.* Time orientation is concerned with the length of time necessary to obtain information concerning task performance. A difference in time horizon can

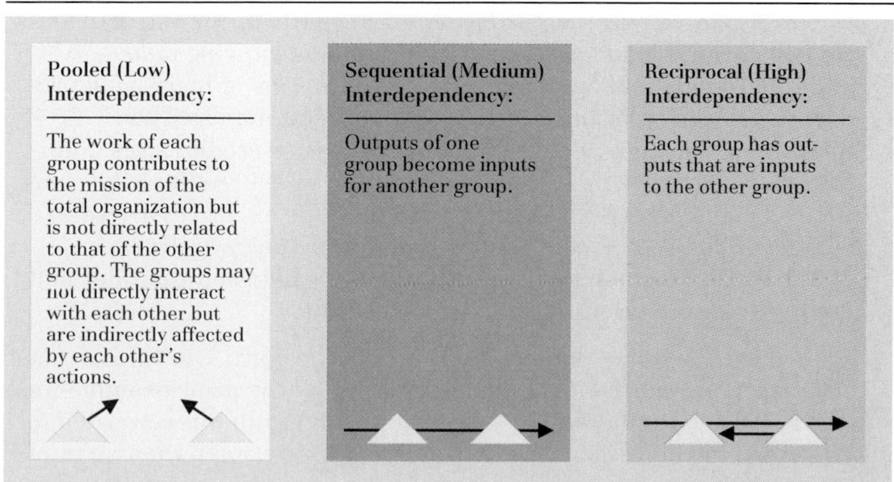


*FIGURE 9.6 Workflow interdependencies affecting intergroup relations in organizations.*

ETHICAL PERSPECTIVE

## SOUTHWEST AIRLINES

**How about an airline that formally states the goal of charging its customers the lowest possible fares? Southwest Airlines bills itself as America's low-fare, high customer satisfaction airline. Driven by a desire to keep things simple and customer-oriented, Chairperson Herb Kelleher says of this well-regarded carrier: "We're the product of 1000 small decisions, all designed to achieve simplicity." He also believes in the employees and teamwork. When officially designated a "major airline" by the Department of Transportation, Kelleher dedicated the annual report to . . . "our employees, the best team in the business, who made this milestone possible. And to the real winners, our customers."**

Courtesy of Southwest Airlines Co.

complicate intergroup relations where there is a high degree of work flow interdependence. The same is true for differences in goal orientations. One illustration follows.

> The sales manager of XYZ Company had just spent the last several weeks gearing up for increased sales during the upcoming quarter. He had carefully touched base with the manufacturing manager, and it looked as if all systems were "go" in terms of increasing production. However, at this same time, the credit manager had become increasingly concerned about excessive credit losses. She, therefore, developed a campaign to tighten up on credit at the same time as manufacturing and sales geared up for an aggressive sales campaign. Instead of sales increasing, they actually declined because of the tightening of credit Relations between the sales and credit groups deteriorated rapidly as a result.

The *reward systems* under which groups perform can have strong effects on intergroup relations. The sales group in the prior example was actually rewarded for increasing sales; the credit group was rewarded for holding down credit losses. Basic goal differences between the two interdependent groups were thus reinforced by the reward system. Difficulties in intergroup relations were also enhanced.

Groups differ in the amount of *resources* that have been allocated to them. If a "resource-rich" group has frequent dealings with one feeling "resource-deprived," problems in the intergroup relations may develop. In the previous example, if the credit group saw itself as receiving fewer resources to do its job than did sales, a potentially bad situation could become worse. Sometimes, too, groups need to share the same resources to get the job done. If resources are scarce and there is no clear agreement on how they are to be allocated, problems may develop as the groups jockey for position vis-a-vis one another.

## Dynamics of Intergroup Competition

An ideal conception of organizations views them as cooperative systems in which people and groups always work harmoniously together. The practical implications of our prior discussions, however, suggest a real world that is much less perfect. This is particularly true when groups begin competing with one another for such things as resources, rewards, and status. Under such conditions the dynamics depicted in Figure 9.7 are likely to occur.

Managers walk a thin line as they try to avoid the disadvantages of intergroup competition while still benefiting from some of its advantages. The latter, for example, include the possibilities of increased effort, greater task focus, more cohesion and satisfaction, and enhanced creativity in problem solving. On the negative side stand such things as a diversion of energies from important tasks, emergence of "grudges" and animosities, biased and selective viewpoints, and poor inter-unit coordination.

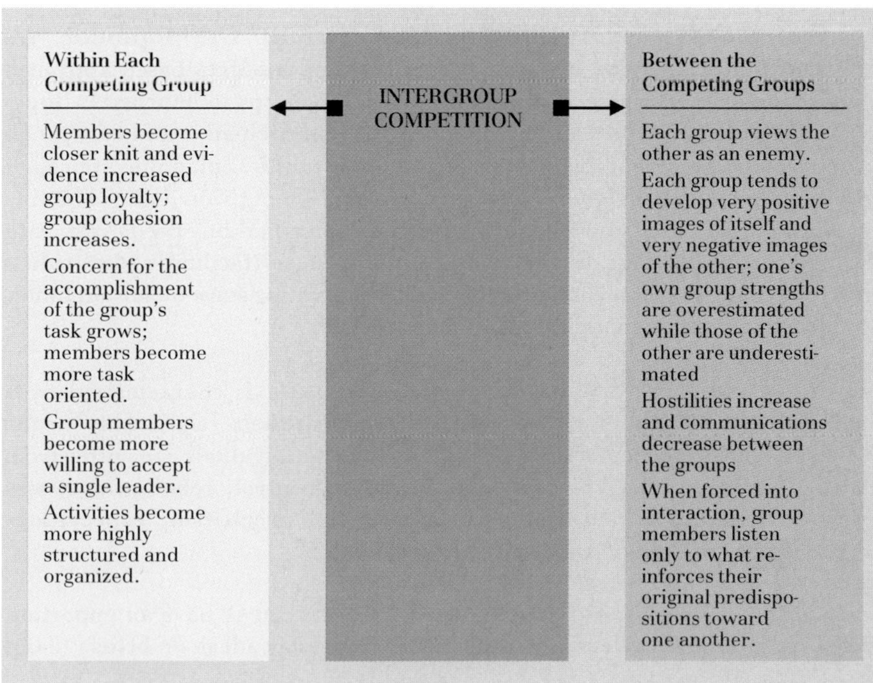


*FIGURE 9.7 Dynamics of intergroup competition: What happens* **within** *and* **between** *competing groups.*

There are two general approaches to managing intergroup competition.[20] The first is to deal with the competition after it occurs. The second is to take action that prevents its occurrence in the future. Strategies for controlling existing competition include:

- Identifying a common enemy.
- Appealing to a common goal.
- Bringing representative subgroups into direct negotiations with one another.
- Training members of the competing groups in group skills and then engaging them in structured interactions.

Additional guidelines for preventing intergroup competition in the future include:

- Rewarding groups on the basis of their contribution to the total organization rather than solely on individual group task accomplishment.
- Rewarding groups for the help they give one another.
- Stimulating frequent interaction between groups; avoiding tendencies for the groups to withdraw and become isolated from one another.
- Rotating members among the various groups whenever possible.
- Avoiding putting groups in positions of win–lose competition to obtain desired organizational rewards; emphasizing the sharing of resources for maximum benefit to the organization.

## SUMMARY

**Team Building and Group Development are important concerns of any manager. Team building is a data-based approach to analyzing the performance of a group and taking steps to improve its functioning in the future. The team-building process is participative and engages all group members in identifying problems and opportunities, planning appropriate actions, making individual commitments to implement them, and conducting appropriate evaluation and feedback activities. Team building needs vary with the four stages of group development—forming stage (facilitating individual entry), storming stage (norm building), initial integrating stage (cohesion building), and total integration stage (decision making).**

**Individual Entry to Groups is characterized by a number of possible problems as members establish their relationship to the group as a whole. Particularly in the forming stage, individuals can suffer from anxieties based on issues of participation, goals, control, relationships, and processes. Role negotiation is one way of clarifying membership expectations and facilitating individual entry into groups.**

**Group Norms and Cohesiveness have an important impact on group effectiveness. Group norms represent ideas or beliefs about**

what is appropriate behavior for group members, whereas group cohesiveness is the strength of attraction of a group for its members. Members of highly cohesive groups tend to conform to group norms. Thus, the most favorable position for any manager is to be in charge of a highly cohesive group with positive performance norms. Good managers are able to build positive norms and influence cohesion in desired directions.

■ **Roles and Communication Patterns in Groups** involve the ways members work with one another to accomplish tasks. In respect to group roles, both task and maintenance activities must be accomplished. Task activities, like initiating and summarizing, make direct contributions to task accomplishment. Maintenance activities, like encouraging and gatekeeping, help to maintain the social fabric of the group for long-term operations. In respect to communication, members of interacting groups are highly interdependent, form decentralized communication networks, and do best on complex tasks. Members of coacting groups are highly independent, form centralized communication networks, and do best at simple tasks.

■ **Decision Making in Groups** takes a variety of forms including lack of response, authority rule, decision by minority, decision by majority, decision by consensus, and unanimity. The potential assets of group decision making include more information and better member understanding and commitment. Liabilities include social pressures to conform and greater time loss. Managers must make good choices among the more individual and more group-oriented decision methods. They must also be aware of "groupthink," the tendency of highly cohesive groups to lose their critical evaluative capabilities. Techniques for improving creativity in group decision making include brainstorming, the nominal group technique, and the Delphi method.

■ **Managing Intergroup Relations** involves understanding the dynamics that take place between as well as within groups. Workflow interdependencies and differing group characteristics—status, time and goal orientations, reward systems, and resources—create the potential for problems in coordinating the activities of multiple groups. When groups compete with one another, they become internally more cohesive and task-oriented. They also develop perceptions of competitors as "enemies." The disadvantages of intergroup competition can be reduced through management strategies to direct, train, and reinforce groups to pursue cooperative instead of purely competitive actions.

## KEY TERMS

Brainstorming
Centralized Communication Network
Coacting Groups
Cohesiveness
Communication
Consensus
Counteracting Groups
Decentralized Communication Network
Decision Making
Delphi Technique
Groupthink
Group Cohesiveness

Group Dynamics
Interacting Groups
Intergroup Dynamics
Maintenance Activities
Nominal Group Technique
Norms
Restricted Communication Network
Role
Role Negotiation
Task Activities
Team Building

## REVIEW QUESTIONS

1. Describe the team-building process. Explain how this process could be used to benefit a special task force as it progresses through each of the four stages of group development.
2. What are three types of problems individuals may experience when joining a group? How could these problems best be dealt with to ensure group effectiveness?
3. What is a group "norm"? What kinds of norms might operate in a typical work group? What is group "cohesiveness"? Is cohesiveness good or bad for the members of a work group . . . for the organization as a whole? Why?
4. List at least four specific actions a manager might take to: (a) change the negative norms of a work group, (b) increase the cohesiveness of a work group, (c) decrease the cohesiveness of a work group.
5. Give examples of both "task" and "maintenance" activities that group members can provide to improve the effectiveness of a group during a long and involved meeting.
6. Explain the potential assets and liabilities of group decision making. In what ways can a group make decisions other than by consensus?
7. What is "groupthink" and why is it something a manager should be concerned about? What can be done to minimize groupthink in a decision-making situation?
8. Describe what can happen when two groups, for example a marketing group and a manufacturing group, become too competitive with one another in an organization. What can a concerned higher-level manager do to reduce destructive competition under such circumstances?

## AN OB LIBRARY

William G. Dyer, *Team Building: Issues and Alternatives,* Second Edition (Reading, MA: Addison-Wesley, 1987).

Jerry B. Harvey, *The Abilene Paradox and Other Meditations on Management* (Lexington, MA: Lexington Books, 1988).

Carl E. Larson and Frank M.J. LaFasto, *Teamwork: What Must Go Right/What Can Go Wrong* (San Francisco: Jossey-Bass, 1989).

Irving Janis, *Groupthink,* Second Edition (Boston: Houghton-Mifflin, 1982).

Edgar H. Schein, *Process Consultation: Volumes I and II* (Reading, MA: Addison-Wesley, 1988).

**EXERCISE**

# IDENTIFYING GROUP NORMS

*Objectives*

1. To help you determine the norms operating in an organization.
2. To assess the strength of response to particular norms.
3. To help clarify the importance of norms as influences on individual and group behavior.

*Total Time*

60 minutes

*Procedure*

1. Choose an organization you know quite a bit about.
2. Complete the questionnaire below, indicating your responses using one of the following:
   a. Strongly agree or encourage it.
   b. Agree with it or encourage it.
   c. Consider it unimportant.
   d. Disagree with or discourage it.
   e. Strongly disagree with or discourage it.

*Instrument*

*If* an employee in your organization were to . . . *Most other employees would:*

1. Show genuine concern for the problems that face the organization and make suggestions about solving them . . . _______
2. Set very high personal standards of performance . . . _______
3. Try to make the work group operate more like a team when dealing with issues or problems . . . _______
4. Think of going to a supervisor with a problem . . . _______
5. Evaluate expenditures in terms of the benefits they will provide for the organization . . . _______
6. Express concern for the well-being of other members of the organization . . . _______
7. Keep a customer or client waiting while looking after matters of personal convenience . . . _______
8. Criticize a fellow employee who is trying to improve things in the work situation . . . _______
9. Actively look for ways to expand his/her knowledge to be able to do a better job . . . _______
10. Be perfectly honest in answering this questionnaire . . . _______

*Scoring*

A = +2, B = +1, C = 0, D = −1, E = −2

1. Organizational/Personal Pride
   Score ______
2. Performance/Excellence
   Score ______
3. Teamwork/Communication
   Score ______
4. Leadership/Supervision
   Score ______
5. Profitability/Cost Effectiveness
   Score ______
6. Colleague/Associate Relations
   Score ______
7. Customer/Client Relations
   Score ______
8. Innovativeness/Creativity
   Score ______
9. Training/Development
   Score ______
10. Candor/Openness
    Score ______

## CASE

# THE CASE OF THE CHANGING CAGE

The voucher-check filing unit was a work unit in the home office of the Atlantic Insurance Company. The assigned task of the unit was to file checks and vouchers written by the company as they were cashed and returned. This filing was the necessary foundation for the main function of the unit: locating any particular check for examination on demand. There were usually eight to ten requests for specific checks from as many different departments during the day. One of the most frequent reasons checks were requested from the unit was to determine whether checks in payment of claims against the company had been cashed. Thus, efficiency in the unit directly affected customer satisfaction with the company. Complaints or inquiries about payments could not be answered with the accuracy and speed conducive to client satisfaction unless the unit could supply the necessary document immediately.

Nine workers staffed this unit. There was an assistant (a position equivalent to a supervisor in a factory) named Ms. Dunn, five other full-time employees, and three part-time workers.

The work area of the unit was well defined. Walls bounded the unit on three sides. The one exterior wall was pierced by light-admitting north windows. The west interior partition was blank. A door opening into a corridor pierced the south interior partition. The east side of the work area was enclosed by a steel mesh reaching from wall to wall and floor to ceiling. This open metal barrier gave rise to the customary name of the unit—"The Voucher Cage." A sliding door through this mesh gave access from the unit's territory to the work area of the rest of the company's agency audit division, of which it was a part, located on the same floor.

The unit's territory was kept inviolate by locks on both doors, fastened at all times. No one not working within the cage was permitted inside unless his or her name appeared on a special list in the custody of Ms. Dunn. The door through the steel mesh was generally used for departmental business. Messengers and runners from other departments usually came to the corridor door and pressed a buzzer for service.

The steel mesh front was reinforced by a rank of metal filing cases where checks were filed. Lined up just inside the barrier, they hid the unit's workers from the view of workers outside their territory, including Mr. Burke, the section head responsible for overall supervision of this unit according to the company's formal plan of operation.

On top of the cabinets, which were backed against the steel mesh, one of the male employees in the unit neatly stacked pasteboard boxes in which checks were transported to the cage. They were later reused to hold older checks sent into storage. His intention was less getting these boxes out of the way than increasing the effective height of the sight barrier so the section head could not see into the cage "even when he stood up."

The clerks stood at the door of the cage that led into the corridor and talked to the messengers. The workers also slipped out this door unnoticed to bring in their customary afternoon snack. Inside the cage, the workers sometimes engaged in a good-natured game of rubberband "snipping."

Workers in the cage possessed good capacity to work together consistently, and workers outside the cage often expressed envy of those in it because of the "nice people" and friendly atmosphere there. The unit had no apparent difficulty keeping up with its work load.

For some time, the controller's department of the company had not been able to meet its own standards of efficient service to the clients. Company officials felt the primary cause to be spatial. Various divisions of the controller's department were scattered over the entire 22-story company building. Communication between them required phone calls, messengers, or personal visits—all costing time. The spatial separation had not seemed very important when the company's business volume was smaller, but business had grown tremendously and spatial separation appeared increasingly inefficient.

Finally in November, company officials began to consolidate the controller's department by relocating two divisions together on one floor. One was the agency audit division, which included the voucher-check filing unit. As soon as the decision to move was made, lower-level supervisors were called in to help with planning. Line workers were not consulted, but were kept informed by the assistants of planning progress. Company officials were concerned about the problem of transporting many tons of equipment and some 200 workers from two locations to another single location without disrupting work flow. So the move was planned to occur over a single weekend, using the most efficient resources available. Assistants were kept busy planning positions for files and desks in the new location.

Desks, files, chairs, and even wastebaskets were numbered prior to the move and were relocated according to a master chart checked on the spot by the assistant. Employees were briefed as to where the new location was and which elevators they should take to reach it. The company successfully transported the paraphernalia of the voucher-check filing unit from one floor to another over one weekend. Workers in the cage quit Friday afternoon at the old stand and reported back Monday at the new.

The exterior boundaries of the new cage were still three building walls and the steel mesh, but the new cage possessed only one door—the sliding door through the steel mesh into the work area of the rest of the agency audit division. The territory of the cage had also been reduced in size. An entire bank of filing cabinets had to be left behind in the old location to be taken over by the unit moving there. The new cage was arranged so that there was no longer a row of metal filing cabinets lined up inside the steel mesh obstructing the view into the cage.

When the workers in the cage inquired about the removal of the filing cabinets from along the steel mesh fencing, they found that Mr. Burke had insisted that these cabinets be rearranged so his view into the cage would not be obstructed by them. Ms. Dunn had tried to retain the cabinets in their prior position, but her efforts had been overridden.

Mr. Burke disapproved of conversation. Since he could see workers conversing in the new cage, he "requested" Ms. Dunn to put a stop to all unnecessary talk. Attempts by clerks to talk to the messengers brought the wrath of Mr. Burke down on Ms. Dunn, who was then forced to reprimand her workers.

Mr. Burke also disapproved of an untidy work area, and any boxes or papers that were in sight were a source of annoyance to him. He did not exert supervision directly, but would "request" Ms. Dunn to "do something about those boxes." In the new cage, desks had to be completely cleared at the end of the day, in contrast to the work-in-progress piles left out in the old cage. Boxes could not accumulate on top of filing cases.

The custom of afternoon snacking also ran into trouble. Lacking a corridor door, the food-bringers had to venture forth and bring back their snack trays through the work area of the rest of their section, bringing a hitherto unique custom to the attention of workers outside the cage. The latter promptly recognized the desirability of afternoon snacks and began agitating for the same privilege. This annoyed the section head, who forbade workers in the cage from continuing this custom.

Mr. Burke later made a rule that permitted one worker to leave the new cage at a set time every afternoon to bring up food for the rest. This rigidity irked cage personnel, accustomed to a snack when the mood struck or none at all. Having made his concession to the cage force, Mr. Burke was unable to prevent workers outside the cage from doing the same thing. What had once been unique to the workers in the cage was now common practice in the section.

Although Ms. Dunn never outwardly expressed anything but compliance and approval of superior directives, she exhibited definite signs of anxiety. All the cage workers reacted against Burke's increased domination. When he imposed his decisions upon the voucher-check filing unit, he became "Old Grandma" to its personnel. The cage workers sneered at him and ridiculed him behind his back. Workers who formerly had obeyed company policy as a matter of course began to find reasons for loafing and obstructing work in the new cage. One of the changes that took place in the behavior of the workers had to do with their game of rubberband snipping. All knew Mr. Burke would disapprove of this game. It became highly clandestine and fraught with dangers. Yet shooting rubber bands increased.

Newly arrived checks were put out of sight as soon as possible, filed or not. Workers hid unfiled checks, generally stuffing them into desk drawers or unused file drawers. Since boxes were forbidden, there were fewer unused file drawers than there had been in the old cage. So the day's work was sometimes undone when several clerks hastily shoved vouchers and checks indiscriminately into the same file drawer at the end of the day.

Before a worker in the cage filed incoming checks, he or she measured the thickness in inches of each bundle to be filed. At the end of each day input was totaled and reported to Ms. Dunn. All incoming checks were measured upon arrival. Thus, Ms. Dunn had a rough estimate of unit intake compared with file input. Theoretically, she was able to tell at any time how much unfiled material she had on hand and how well the unit was keeping up with its task. Despite this running check, when the annual inventory of unfiled checks on hand in the cage was taken, a seriously large backlog of unfiled checks was found. To the surprise and dismay of Ms. Dunn, the inventory showed the unit to be far behind schedule, filing much more slowly than before the relocation of the cage.

### *Questions*

1. What specific management decisions led to the deterioration in group performance in the voucher-check filing unit?
2. Explain how (a) group *input* factors and (b) group *throughput* or *process* factors were affected by these management decisions. In what ways did they, in turn, specifically contribute to the deterioration of group performance? Be specific in supporting your answers with case details.
3. Given the situation as it now stands in the voucher-check filing unit, what can be done to help restore group effectiveness? Carefully explain and defend your improvement strategy based on chapter discussion and case details.

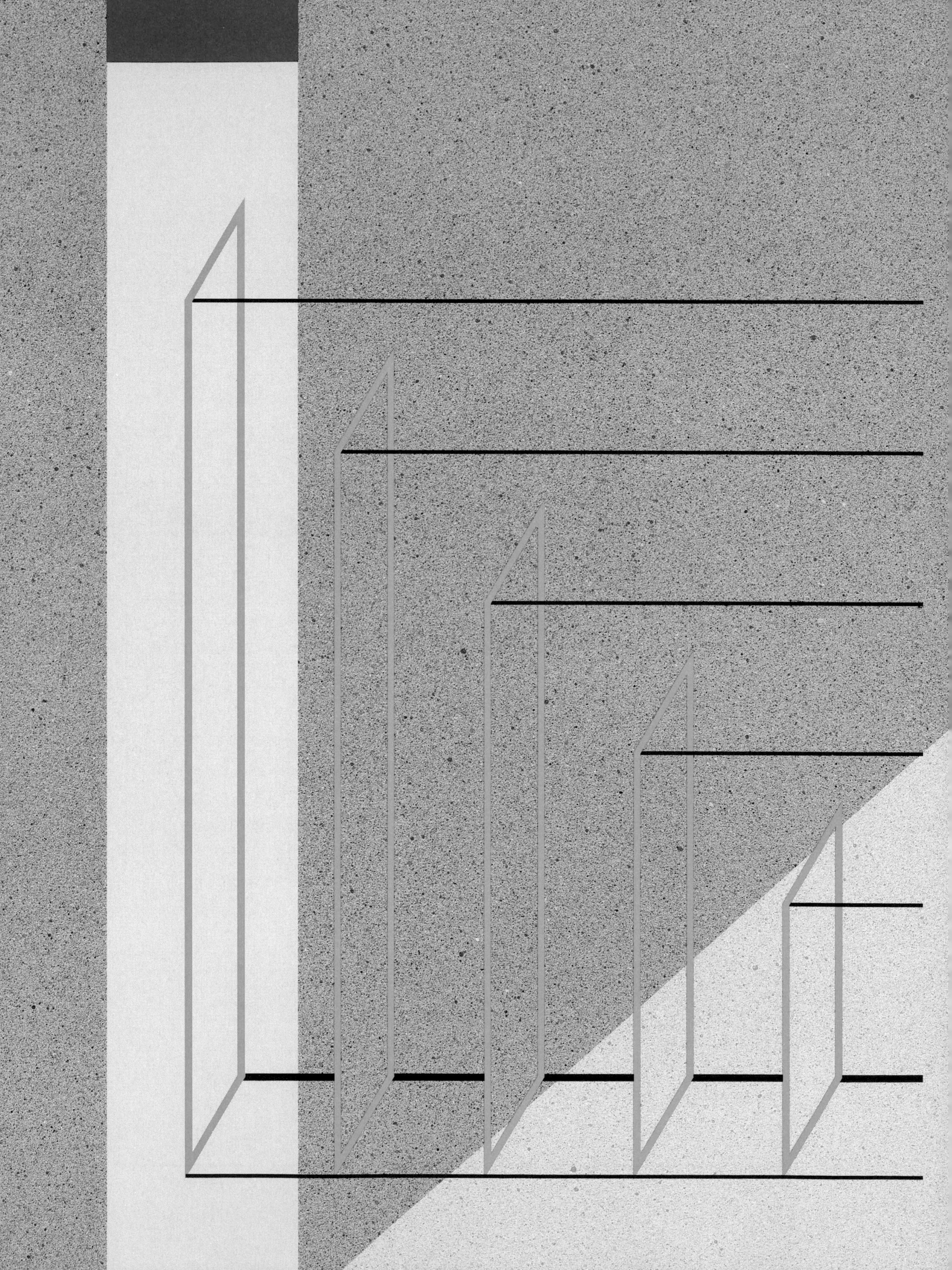

# PART FOUR

# MANAGING ORGANIZATIONS

This study outline of major topics is meant to organize your reading now; it is repeated in the Summary to structure your review.

## STUDY OUTLINE

■ **Organizational Goals**

Societal Contributions of Organizations    Systems Goals and Organizational Survival

■ **Formal Structures of Organizations**

■ **Vertical Specialization**

Chain of Command and the Span of Control    Line and Staff Units
Managerial Techniques

■ **Control**

Rules, Policies, and Procedures    Formalization and Standardization
Centralization and Decentralization

# CHAPTER 10

# BASIC ATTRIBUTES OF ORGANIZATIONS



## PHOTO ESSAYS

# VISIONS 10

**Among the "mini-mills" that have sprung up in the U.S. steel industry, Nucor Corporation has achieved considerable recognition for its streamlined organization. A visit to corporate headquarters gives immediate introduction to the unique vision of chairperson F. Kenneth Iverson.**

**The company's organization chart is one of Iverson's trademarks. There are only four levels of management from top to bottom. This contrasts with an industry norm of eight or nine in larger steel companies. Says Iverson: "I'm a firm believer in having the fewest number of management levels and in delegating authority to the lowest level possible." Each plant basically operates as a business of its own, headed by a general manager reporting directly to Iverson. There aren't many "staff" people either in the Nucor organization. The entire firm, with over 4000 employees and operations in several states, runs with a corporate staff of under 20 personnel. It's quite clear anywhere you go in Nucor that Kenneth Iverson believes in letting the people who know what's going on make the decisions.**

In Chapter 1 we defined an organization as a collection of people working together in a division of labor to achieve a common purpose. In this chapter we will expand on this definition to provide you with a working knowledge of organizational goals and the division of labor. We will devote one major section to the types of goals an organization appears to seek. After a brief overview of the division of labor, we will chart how organizations divide managerial duties and control both managers and units. The third major segment of this chapter will chart how work is assigned to different parts of the organization and how the efforts in different departments are linked together. Collectively, these three sections will provide a basic understanding of what the organization seeks and how it is organized.

## ORGANIZATIONAL GOALS

Organizations may be viewed as entities with goals.[1] They seek to improve themselves over time in many different ways. The goals pursued by organizations are multifaceted and often emerge in partial conflict with one another. These goals are common to individuals within the organization only to the extent that managers and other members see how their interests can be partially served by the organization. In this section we will examine two types of organizational goals. The first type centers on how the organization intends to serve society. The second focuses on its survival.

## Societal Contributions of Organizations

Jim Chan, executive vice president of Bion Engineering Research, had a problem. Key research staff were leaving. Exit interviews suggested that pay, work challenge, and supervision were rarely problems. Instead, researchers gave some vague reference to being unable to contribute to their discipline. They said that Bion was only interested in growing and making a profit. Merely making money or servicing a client was not enough. They wanted to contribute to their profession. And these researchers expected Bion to help them to contribute to society.

As this example illustrates, societal contribution forms a basis for claims many organizations make to control resources, hire individuals, and market products. Organizations seek both support from their environments and freedom from interference. When the appearance of self-interest in this relationship dominates, however, organizations may lose legitimacy. Their actions may be challenged by others. They may lose public trust and confidence. Employees may become demoralized. For instance, even though the United States will need electric energy from sources that do not make air pollution worse, it is difficult for U.S. utilities to propose construction of nuclear power plants. They have lost the public's confidence.

### *Societal Goals and the Organization's Mission*

Organizations that can effectively translate the character of their societal contribution for their members have an advantage. They have an additional set of motivational tools based upon a shared sense of noble purpose. Such a sense of purpose in a political party may be to generate and allocate power for the betterment of all U.S. citizens. A church attempts to instill values and protect the spiritual well-being of all. Our courts integrate the interests and activities of citizens. Finally, business firms provide economic sustenance and material well-being to society. Specifically, ***societal goals*** reflect the intended contributions of an organization to broader society.[2]

**Societal goals**

In sum, organizations normally serve a specific societal function or an enduring need of the society.[3] Astute top-level managers build upon the professed societal contribution of the organization by relating specific organizational tasks and activities to higher purposes.[4] ***Mission statements,*** that is written statements of organizational purpose, may incorporate these corporate ideas of service to the society. Furthermore, the type of societal contribution often establishes how we evaluate an organization.

**Mission statements**

### *Primary Beneficiaries*

While organizations may provide benefits to the society as a whole, most target their efforts toward a particular group.[5] In the United States we

**Primary beneficiaries**

often expect the ***primary beneficiaries*** of business organizations to be stockholders, that political organizations serve the common good, that many culturally oriented organizations serve their members, and that some social service organizations serve clients or customers.

While each organization may have a primary beneficiary, its mission statement may also recognize the interests of many other parties. Thus, business mission statements often include service to customers, their obligations to employees, and their intention to support the community.

### *What Business Are We in?—Output Goals*

Many larger organizations have found it useful to state very carefully which business they are in.[6] This statement can form the basis for long-term planning and help keep huge organizations from diverting too many resources to peripheral areas. For some corporations, answering this question may yield a more detailed statement concerning their products and services. These product and service goals provide an important basis for judging the quality of an organization's major contributions to society.

**Output goals**

In sum, ***output goals*** define the type of business an organization is in and begin to provide some substance to the more general aspects of mission statements. For instance, Zenith sold its very profitable personal computer business to concentrate on televisions. Zenith managers forsee a bright future in high-definition television (HDTV).

## Systems Goals and Organizational Survival

Many organizations face the immediate problem of just making it through the coming years. They do not have the luxury of concentrating on societal contribution or of worrying about who their prime beneficiary should be. For instance, fewer than 10 percent of the businesses founded in a typical year can be expected to survive to reach their twentieth birthday.[7] The survival rate for public organizations is not much better. Even for organizations where survival is not an immediate problem, one can ask, "What are the types of conditions needed to minimize the risk of demise?" "What types of conditions promote survival?"

**Systems goals**

To answer these questions executives may start by developing systems goals for their organizations. ***Systems goals*** are concerned with conditions within the organization that are expected to increase its survival potential. The list of systems goals is almost endless, since each manager and researcher links today's conditions to tomorrow's existence in a different way. For many organizations, however, the list includes growth, productivity, stability, harmony, flexibility, prestige, and, of course, human resource maintenance. For some businesses, analysts consider market share and current profitability. Other recent studies suggest that innovation and quality also might be considered important systems goals.[8]

In a very practical sense, systems goals represent near-term organizational characteristics that higher-level managers wish to promote. Systems goals must often be balanced against one another. For instance, a productivity and efficiency drive may cut the flexibility of an organization. Different parts of the organization may be asked to pursue different types of systems goals. As an example, higher-level managers may expect to see their production operations strive for efficiency, press for innovation from their R&D lab, and promote stability in their financial affairs.

The relative importance of different systems goals can vary substantially across various types of organizations. While we might expect a university such as Cal Tech to emphasize prestige and innovation, few would expect businesses such as Seimanns or AT&T not to emphasize growth and profitability.

# FORMAL STRUCTURES OF ORGANIZATIONS

**Formal structure**

To help accomplish their goals managers develop a ***formal structure*** that shows the intended configuration of positions (jobs), job duties, and the lines of authority among different parts of the enterprise. We emphasize the word "formal" simply because the intentions of organizational designers are never fully realized. Furthermore, no formal structure can provide all the detail needed actually to show the activities within a firm. Yet the

*FIGURE 10.1 A partial organization chart for a state university.*

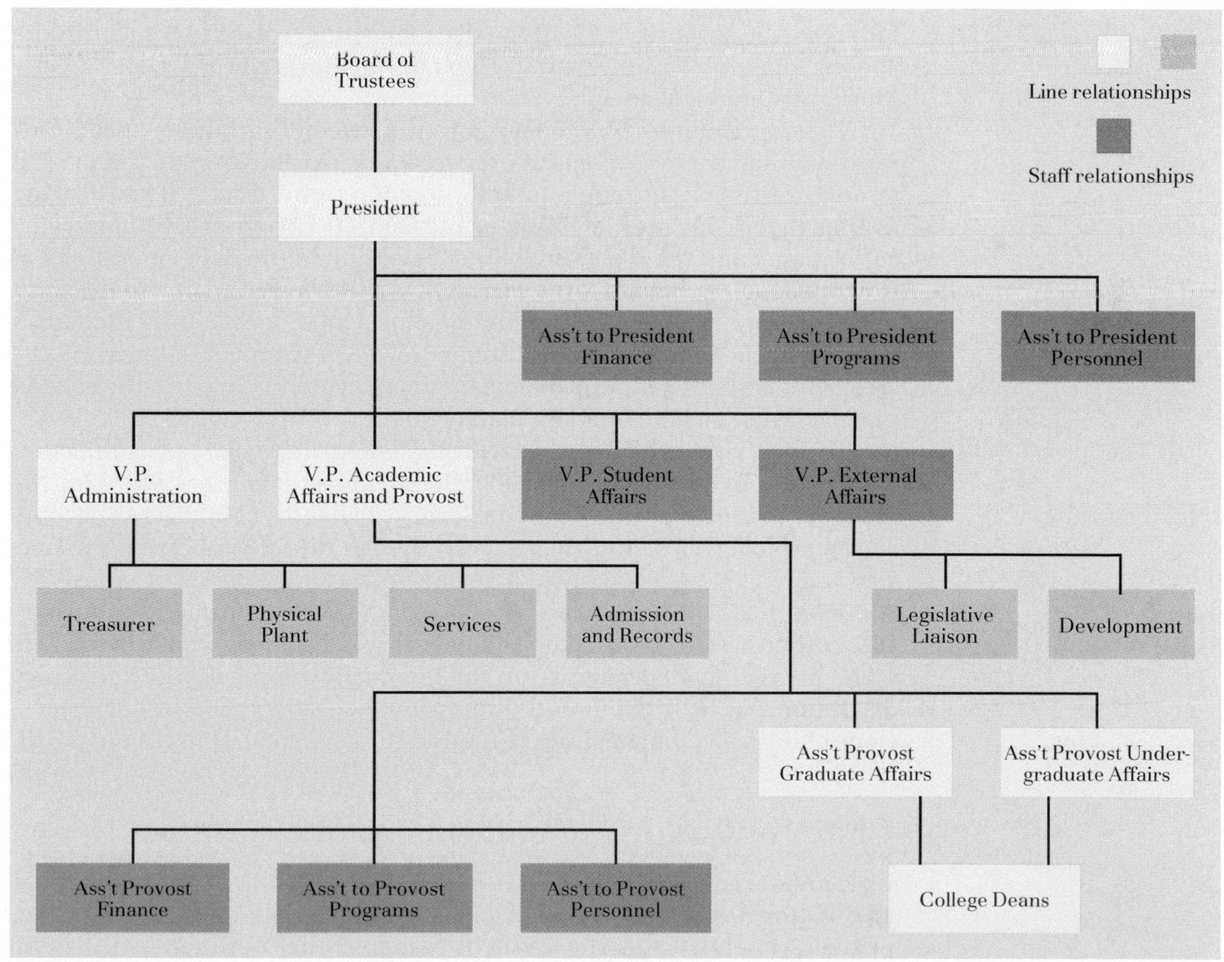

formal structure is still important because it provides the foundation for managerial action. It outlines the job to be done, who (in terms of position) is to perform specific activities, and how the total task of the organization is to be accomplished. It is the skeleton of the organization.

**Organization charts**

***Organization charts*** are diagrams that depict the formal structures of organizations. A typical chart shows the various positions, the position holders, and the lines of authority linking them to one another. Figure 10.1 is a partial organization chart for a large university. The total chart allows university employees to locate their positions in the structure and to identify the lines of authority linking them with others in the organization. For instance, in this figure the treasurer reports to the vice president of administration who in turn reports to the president.

# VERTICAL SPECIALIZATION

**Vertical specialization**

In most larger organizations, there is a clear separation of authority and duties by hierarchical rank. This separation represents ***vertical specialization,*** a hierarchical division of labor that distributes formal authority and establishes where and how critical decisions will be made. This creates a hierarchy of authority, an arrangement of work positions in order of increasing authority. One of the distinguishing features of Nucor in the chapter-opening *Visions* is a very short or flat hierarchy of authority. Only four levels of management exist.

The distribution of formal authority is evident in the responsibilities typical to managers. Top managers, or senior executives plan the overall strategy of the organization and plot its long-term future.[9] They also act as final judges for internal disputes and serve to certify promotions, reorganizations, and the like. Middle managers guide the daily operations of the organization, help to formulate policy, and translate top-management decisions into more specific guidelines for action. Lower-level managers supervise the actions of subordinates to ensure implementation of the strategies authorized by top management and compliance with the related policies established by middle management.

The description of managerial levels should alert you to two important considerations in vertical specialization. One, as managers move up the hierarchy, the scope of responsibility expands. Managers become accountable for more individuals even though they do not directly supervise their activities. You should recognize the importance of specifying common goals and emphasizing common values to ensure that unseen subordinates act as if the senior managers were directly supervising their work. Two, as managers move up the hierarchy they generally have more discretion. We will build on the importance of discretion in our discussions of organizational politics (Chapter 15) and leadership (Chapter 16).

## Chain of Command and the Span of Control

Executives, managers, and supervisors are hierarchically connected through the "chain of command." Individuals are expected to follow the decisions of their supervisors in the areas of responsibility outlined in the orga-

Courtesy of Nucor Corporation.

## SKILLS PERSPECTIVE

# NUCOR

**Nucor Corporation is one of the American steel industry's pioneer "minimills"—a segment that now represents some 40 to 50 percent of the industry. The firm is known for the "lean" management approach of its founding CEO Kenneth Iverson. Under Iverson's leadership, the company has experienced steady growth while operating with a structure of only four levels of management. "I'm a firm believer in having the fewest number of management levels and in delegating authority to the lowest level possible," says Iverson. What he doesn't say is that this approach can also bring out the best in people and allow a manager's skills to be fully utilized in a responsible and demanding day-to-day job. By the way, Nucor also operates without any corporate jets, company cars or limousines, or reserved parking spaces.**

nization chart. Traditional management theory suggests that each individual is to have one boss. Each unit is to have one leader. When this occurs there is "unity of command." Unity of command is considered necessary to avoid confusion, to assign accountability to specific persons, and to provide clear channels of communication up and down the organization. Without unity of command no single individual is "in charge." If mistakes occur, managers will naturally try to escape accountability and point the finger of responsibility at others.

The number of individuals a manager can directly supervise is obviously limited. Thus, in establishing vertical specialization the organization must limit the ***span of control***—that is, the number of persons reporting directly to one supervisor. Organizations tend to prefer broader spans simply because they reduce overhead expenses in terms of the required number of managerial personnel. While research does not suggest that there is an absolute minimum or maximum span of control, it does suggest some guidelines for establishing the average number of subordinates reporting to a manager[10].

**Span of control**

The span can be very broad if:

- Tasks are comparatively simple.
- Subordinates are experienced and well trained.
- Tasks to be performed do not call for a team effort.

## Line and Staff Units

**Line units**

**Staff units**

***Line units*** and personnel conduct the major business of the organization. The production and marketing functions are two examples. In contrast, ***staff units*** and personnel assist the line units by providing specialized expertise and services. Accounting and public relations are examples. The dashed lines on the organization chart previously shown in Figure 10.1 denote staff relationships, whereas the solid ones denote line relationships. For example, the vice president of administration heads a staff unit, as does the vice president of student affairs. All academic departments in the figure are line units since they constitute the basic production function of the university.

A useful distinction to be made for both line and staff units concerns the amount and types of contacts they maintain with outsiders to the organization. Some units are mainly internal in orientation: others are more external in focus. The following description briefly summarizes the differences between them.

| | | |
|---|---|---|
| *Line Units* | | |
| Internal (e.g., production) | Focus on → | Transforming raw material and information into products and/or services. |
| External (e.g., marketing) | Focus on → | Linking clients and/or suppliers to the organization. |
| *Staff Units* | | |
| Internal (e.g., accounting) | Focus on → | Assisting line units in the technical areas of budgeting and fiscal control. |
| External (e.g., public relations) | Focus on → | Linking the organization to its environment through the conveyance of a positive public image. |

The placement of staff units in the formal structure is particularly important. Figure 10.2 illustrates how placement of staff changes the look of the pyramid we visualize when we traditionally think of an organizational hierarchy. Grouping many staff units at the top reinforces the expertise and managerial scope of top-level decision makers. In effect, it expands top management capabilities. This tends to yield comparatively little vertical specialization. As an employee or lower-level manager, you are likely to think that formal authority is concentrated at the top.

When staff specialists are moved down into the organization, the action capacity of middle managers is expanded. Each can begin to operate more independently. Commensurate with the additional assistance available from staff specialists, we would expect middle managers to expand their range, scope, and depth of decision making.

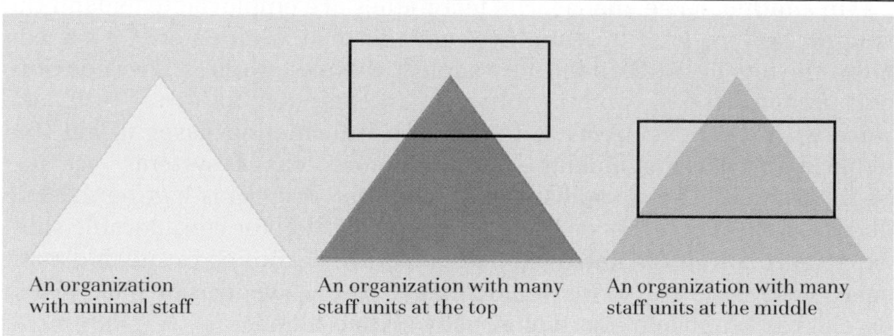


*FIGURE 10.2 How placement of staff changes the look of an organization.*

Rarely does an organization place all staff units at the top or bury them deep within the hierarchy. Most often some are elevated to the top while others remain farther down. Where the firm needs corporate-wide action to confront a specific threat or opportunity, staff specialists may be placed toward the top. But there may be secondary effects associated with staff units at the top. Staff personnel may use their high-level position to increase the attention given to their area. They may slow operations by requiring that operating managers obtain clearances before taking action. And some staff units become "empire builders" that keep detailed written records, routinize staff work via standardized forms, and improve their performance with more staff and a larger budget. Many organizations are now on guard against such trends. For example,

> ***Owens-Illinois*** The size of the corporate staff has been drastically reduced and the salaries of line managers raised at Owens-Illinois. CEO Robert Lanigan says: "There was a lot of time spent in exercising the power of the office through corporate staff." He adds that staff are now there as "consultants" to himself and other line personnel.

## Managerial Techniques

As we have seen, merely adding staff may not provide the organization with increased efficiency. In fact, one of the foremost trends in modern industry is to streamline operations and reduce staff in order to lower costs and raise productivity.[11] One way to facilitate this is to provide line managers with managerial techniques designed to expand upon their analytical and decision making capabilities, and thus eliminate the need for staff "experts." Good examples are the ever-increasing role of the computer and associated decision support software in all areas of management.

In one sense managerial techniques are substitutes for both line and staff managers and staff units.[12] They may be used to detect problems and opportunities, select among alternative courses of action, and monitor the progress of implementation. For instance, those studying financial management recognize the importance of financial planning models (in detecting problems), financial decision aids such as capital budgeting models and discounted cash-flow analyses (for selecting among alternatives) and, of course budgets (to monitor progress and ensure that managers stay within financial limits).

In another sense, managerial techniques are employed to expand the volume and scope of operations a manager can administer.[13] They can allow the manager to handle more sophisticated operations. Decision Support Systems (DSS) combine advances in computer hardware and software with the development of extensive information bases to aid line managers in decision making. More and more "expert systems" are also being created. These sophisticated computer programs can be used to duplicate the judgments of experts in areas calling for considerable skill, experience, intuition, and judgment. They are becoming invaluable managerial techniques allowing organizations to upgrade decision making and extend the scope and depth of already skilled managers.

Most organizations use a combination of line and staff units, plus managerial techniques to vertically specialize the division of labor (that is, to distribute formal authority). The most appropriate pattern of vertical specialization depends on the environment of the organization, its size, its technology, and its goals. Generally, as organizations grow, vertical specialization increases. We will return to this theme in the next chapter. For now, let us turn our attention to issues relating to control of the organization.

## CONTROL

**Control**

***Control*** is the set of mechanisms used to keep action and outputs within predetermined limits. Control deals with setting standards, measuring results versus standards, and instituting corrective action.

*TABLE 10.1*
SOME SIDE EFFECTS OF ORGANIZATIONAL CONTROLS

*Imbalance.* Concentrating on one goal neglects others. For example, rewards based on volume may lower quality. In emphasizing short-term efficiency, equipment maintenance, human resource maintenance, and research and development may be minimized.

*Lack of patience.* Managers attempt a "quick fix," and when that does not work, they try one short-term fix after another without allowing time for any to be successful.

*Across-the-board cuts.* Common in public institutions as politically acceptable, they don't focus on specific areas where cuts are needed most. The organization loses growth opportunities and may not reduce unnecessary expenditures.

*Confusing documentation with action.* Concern for performance may lead to a stack of impressive-sounding plans but no results.

*Vague and unrealistic expectations.* Chapter 6 indicated the problems of "do your best goals" in comparison with more specific ones. Also, goals asking for more than a 20 percent improvement are likely to lead to diminishing returns.

*Panic.* This often ensues when controls are suddenly established over a unit. Communication accompanied by participation helps avoid panic.

*Standard increasing.* Higher standards are set without increasing resources, changing methods, or giving better rewards. This often creates personnel problems.

A popular control technique is the planning-budgeting process. Corporations often develop five-year rolling plans where the latest year is used to develop a detailed budget. Businesses may also employ management by objectives (MBO) to ensure that managers set specific measurable goals, monitor progress toward these goals, and receive rewards based on their accomplishments. MBO, discussed in Chapter 7, is an example of *output controls*—that is, controls that focus on desired targets and allow managers to use their own methods for reacting to defined targets.[14] Organizations relying primarily on output controls can remain open to change and promote dialogue and discussion concerning how to take corrective action. Organizations may also institute a number of *process controls*—that is, controls that attempt to specify the manner in which tasks will be performed. Whereas managers may see these as attempts to gain uniform results, employees may view them as restrictive and limiting their direction. Organizations relying heavily on process controls can become inflexible.

Efforts to exert control in organizations can yield unfortunate side effects.[15] Some of these are summarized in Table 10.1. But, effective controls also bring a number of potential benefits to organizations. These include providing attainable standards, accurate measurement of performance, and a means of allocating rewards or sanctions based on performance and the discretion to institute corrective action. For example,

> ***Heinz*** David Sculley, senior vice-president of Heinz, says "we manage by exception generally." He notes the firm uses variance from projections to spot something that is going wrong. "There's a goal post that is clear for every member in the company—yearly and quarterly . . . When we see a problem developing, we jump on it."

## Rules, Policies, and Procedures

Most organizations of any size have a variety of rules, policies, and procedures. They may be used to help specify the goals of a worker, indicate the best method for performing a task, show which aspects of a task are the most important, and outline how an individual will be rewarded. Usually we think of a ***policy*** as a guideline for action that outlines important objectives and broadly indicates how an activity is to be performed. A policy allows for individual discretion and minor adjustments without direct clearance by a higher level manager. ***Rules and procedures,*** on the other hand, are more specific, rigid and impersonal. They typically describe in detail how a task or series of tasks are to be performed. They are designed to apply to all under specified conditions.

**Policy**

**Rules and procedures**

Rules, procedures, and policies are employed because they substitute for direct managerial supervision. With written rules and procedures the organization can specifically direct the activities of many individuals. It can ensure virtually identical treatment across even distant work locations. For example, a McDonald's hamburger and fries tastes much the same whether purchased in Hong Kong, Indianapolis, London, or New York simply because the ingredients as well as the cooking methods follow written rules and procedures.

**ETHICAL PERSPECTIVE**

**AICPA**

**The American Institute of Certified Public Accountants (AICPA) calls it the "measure of excellence." For the rest of us, it's a well-respected and rigorous ethical code of conduct to which all certified public accountants are supposed to subscribe. But the AICPA wants more. It's communicating its sense of ethical standards to business firms with the message that profits and ethical behavior can and should go hand-in-hand. They're calling for ethical standards to be set at the top and clarified for all levels. In this way, the AICPA says, a clear code of conduct can "raise morale and productivity, while reducing the potential for fraud and legal jeopardy."**

Rules, procedures, and policies also allow organizations to practice "management by exception." Managers need not concentrate on the routine activities or decisions. They can spend their time on more important, unusual, and unique conditions that may have a more direct impact on performance and/or satisfaction. Remember:

Rules, procedures, and policies —may seem→ impersonal and inflexible —but→ they free the manager for other choices

## Formalization and Standardization

Formalization

***Formalization*** refers to the written documentation of rules, procedures, and policies to guide behavior and decision making. Beyond substituting for direct management supervision, formalization is often used to simplify jobs. With written instructions individuals with less training may be able to perform comparatively sophisticated tasks. Written procedures may also be available to ensure that a proper sequence of tasks is executed even if it is only performed occasionally.

Standardization

Most organizations have developed additional methods for dealing with recurring problems or situations. ***Standardization*** is the degree to which the range of allowable actions in a job or series of jobs is limited. It involves the creation of guidelines so that similar work activities are repeatedly performed in a similar fashion. Such standardized methods may come from years of experience in dealing with typical situations. Or they may come from outside training. For instance, managers may be trained to handle crises by setting priorities and dealing with them at all costs. Obviously, such situations call for judgment and cannot be handled by written rules—no written rules could anticipate every possible crisis.

## Centralization and Decentralization

So far we have discussed rules, procedures, policies, formalization, and standardization as ways in which the organization can link the work efforts of individuals and units to goals. These methods minimize discretion and often eliminate choice in the attempt to integrate and focus work efforts. Organizations do run on routine, but they also face unusual situations that call for responsive decisions. While neither workers nor professionals are expected to question organizational goals or means–end linkages, managers may be given limited discretion in these areas.

The farther up the hierarchy of authority the discretion to spend money, hire people, and make similar decisions is moved, the greater the degree of ***centralization.*** The more such decisions are delegated, or moved down the hierarchy of authority, the greater the degree of ***decentralization.*** Generally speaking, greater decentralization provides higher subordinate satisfaction and a quicker response to problems. Decentralization also assists in the on-the-job training of subordinates for higher-level positions. Decentralization is now a popular approach in many industries. For instance, Union Carbide is pushing responsibility down the chain of command as are General Motors, Ford, and Chrysler.[16] In each case, the senior managers hope to improve both performance quality and organizational responsiveness.

**Centralization**
**Decentralization**

Closely related to decentralization is the notion of participation. Many people want to be involved in decisions affecting their work. Participation results when a manager delegates some authority for such decision making to subordinates. As we have discussed elsewhere, employees may want a say in both what the unit objectives should be as well as how they may be achieved.[17] Especially in recent years and with the challenge from the Japanese forms of participation, many firms are experimenting with new ways to decentralize parts of their operations. For example,

> ***General Motors*** The newspaper headlines announced "Stempel Cuts GM Bureaucracy" when Robert Stempel took over from Roger Smith as CEO. He unveiled to the press a new organization chart, which he said will cut levels of management and turn more responsibilities over to the firm's eight car and truck divisions.

# HORIZONTAL SPECIALIZATION

When dividing the total task into separate duties, management attempts to group similar people and resources together.[18] ***Horizontal specialization*** is a division of labor that establishes specific work units or groups

**Horizontal specialization**

within an organization; it is often referred to as the process of departmentation. Let us examine three basic forms of horizontal specialization: departmentation by function, division, and matrix.

## Departmentation by Function

**Functional departmentation**

Grouping by skill, knowledge, and action yields a pattern of ***functional departmentation.*** Figure 10.3 shows the organization chart for a nuclear power plant where each department has a technical speciality considered necessary for safe and efficient operation of the plant. In business, marketing, finance, production, and personnel are important functions. In many small firms, this functional pattern dominates. For instance, Apple Computer used this pattern early in its development.

*FIGURE 10.3 A functional pattern of departmentation for a nuclear power plant.*

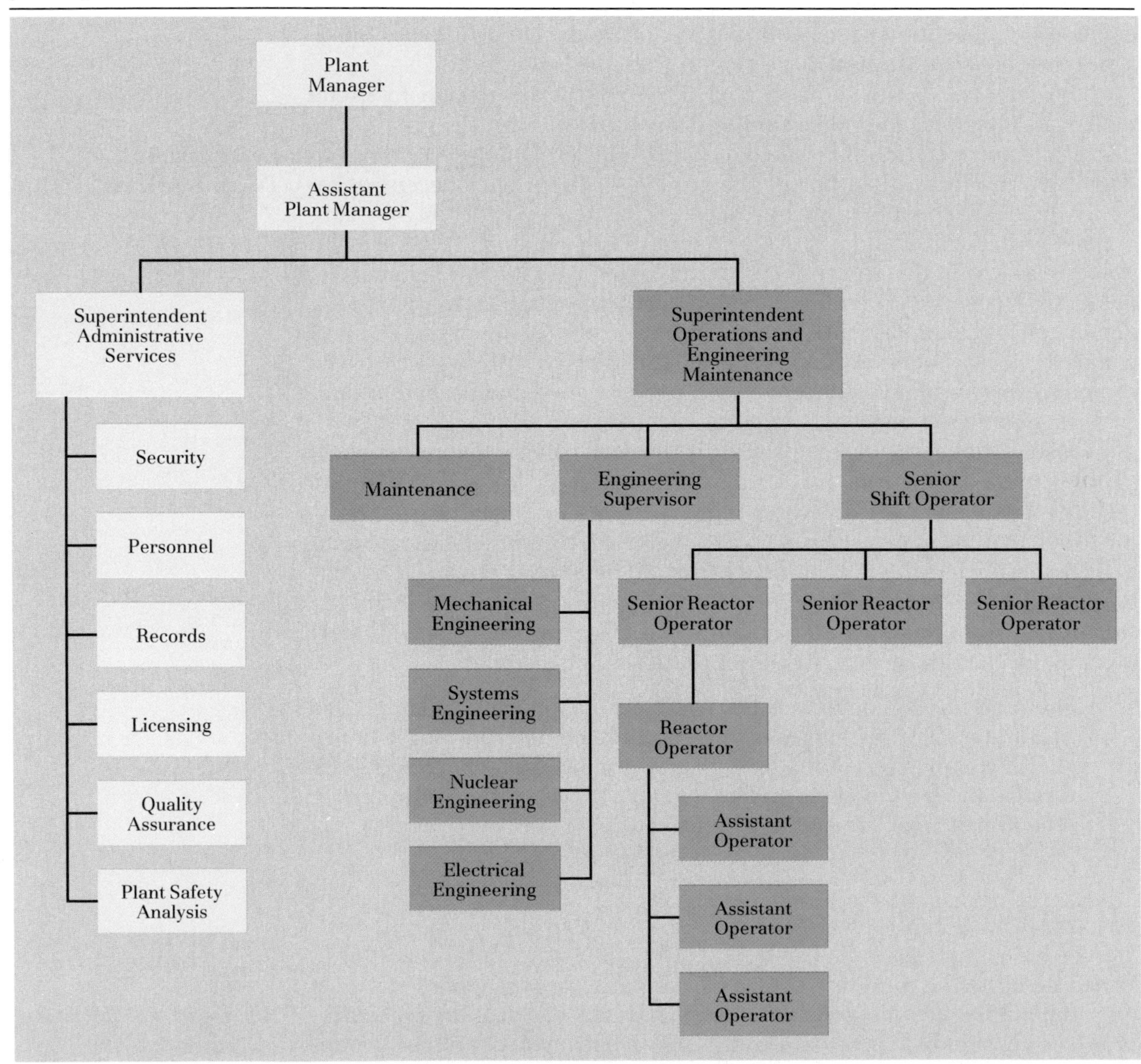

*TABLE 10.2*
**MAJOR ADVANTAGES AND DISADVANTAGES OF FUNCTIONAL SPECIALIZATION**

| Advantages | Disadvantages |
|---|---|
| 1. It can yield very clear task assignments that are consistent with an individual's training. | 1. It may reinforce the narrow training of individuals and lead to boring and routine jobs. Communication across technical areas is difficult and conflict between units may increase. Lines of communication across the organization can become very complex. |
| 2. Individuals within a department can easily build on one another's knowledge, training, and experience. Facing similar problems and having similar training facilitates communication and technical problem solving. | 2. Complex communication channels can lead to "top management overload." Top management may spend too much time and effort dealing with cross-functional problems. |
| 3. It provides an excellent training ground for new managers who must translate their academic training into organizational action. | 3. Individuals may look up the organizational hierarchy for direction and reinforcement rather than focus attention on products, services, or clients. Guidance is typically sought from functional peers or superiors. |
| 4. It is easy to explain. Most employees can understand the role of each unit, even though many may not know what individuals in a particular function do. | |

Table 10.2 summarizes the advantages of the functional pattern. With all these advantages, it is not surprising that the functional form is extremely popular. It is used in most organizations, particularly toward the bottom of the hierarchy. Of course, functional specialization also has some disadvantages, as also summarized in Table 10.2. Organizations that rely heavily on functional specialization may expect the following tendencies to emerge over time:

- An emphasis on quality from a technical standpoint.
- Rigidity to change, particularly if change within one functional area is needed to help other functional areas.
- Difficulty in coordinating the actions of different functional areas, particularly if the organization must continually adjust to changing external conditions.

## Departmentation by Division

The pattern of ***divisional departmentation*** groups individuals and resources by products, services, clients, and/or legal entities. Figure 10.4 shows a divisional pattern of organization grouped around products, regions, and clients for three divisions of a conglomerate. This pattern is often used to meet diverse external threats and opportunities.

**Divisional departmentation**

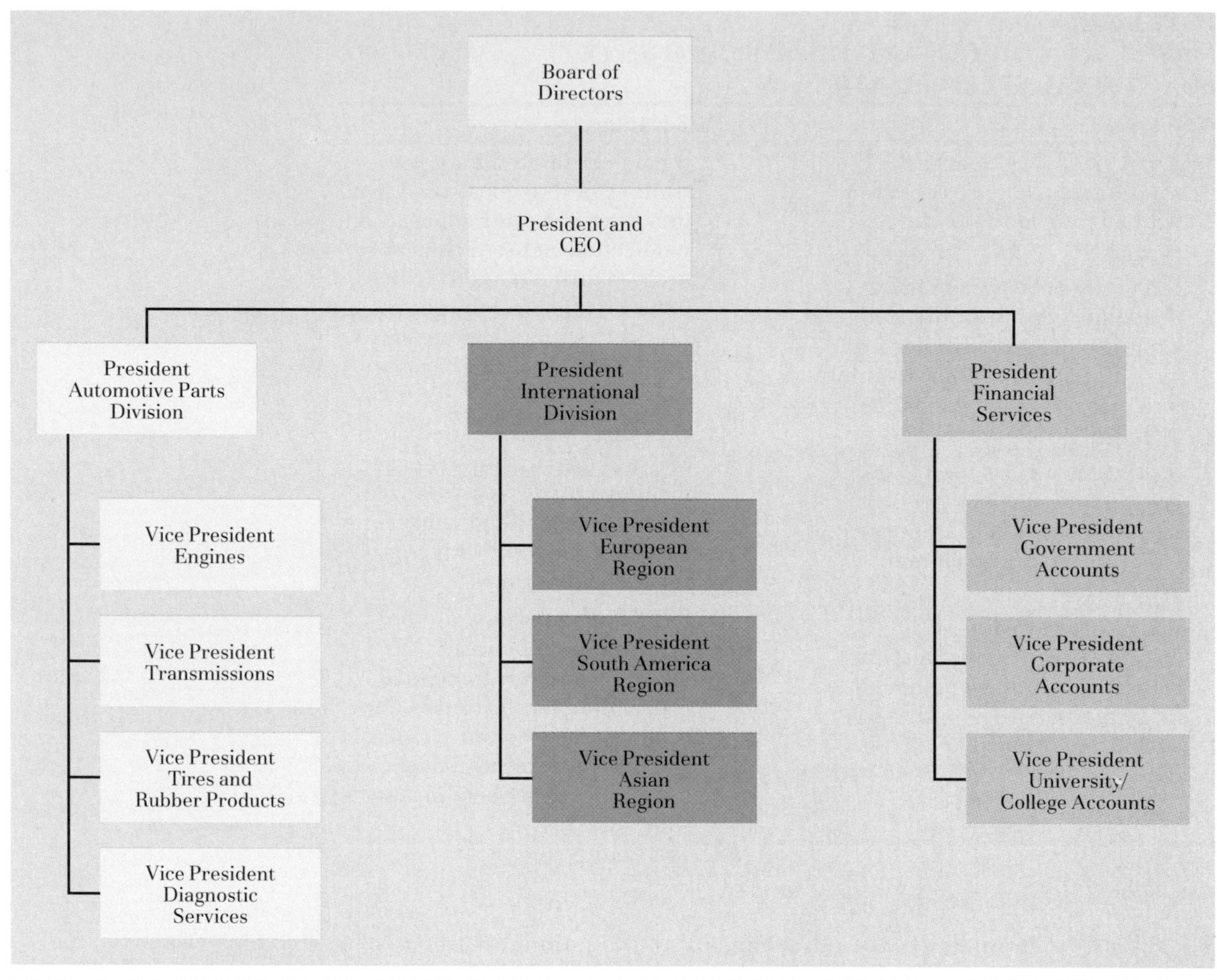


*FIGURE 10.4 A divisional pattern of departmentation for a conglomerate.*

Many larger, geographically dispersed organizations selling to national and international markets use departmentation by territory. The savings in time, effort, and travel can be substantial; and each territory can adjust to regional differences. Organizations that rely on a few major customers may organize their people and resources by client. Here, the idea is to focus attention on the needs of the individual customer. To the extent that customer needs are unique, departmentation by client can also reduce confusion, and increase synergy. Organizations expanding internationally may also divisionalize to meet the demands of complex host-country ownership requirements.

The major advantages and disadvantages of divisional specialization are summarized in Table 10.3. In organizations where satisfying the demands of outsiders is particularly important, the divisional structure may provide the desired capabilities. This pattern can help improve customer responsiveness for organizations that operate in many territories, produce quite different products and services, serve a few major customers, or operate internationally. Organizations that rely heavily on divi-

*TABLE 10.3*
**MAJOR ADVANTAGES AND DISADVANTAGES OF DIVISIONAL SPECIALIZATION**

| Advantages | Disadvantages |
|---|---|
| 1. It provides adaptability and flexibility in meeting the demands of important external groups. | 1. It does not provide a pool of highly trained individuals with similar expertise to solve problems and train new employees. |
| 2. It allows for spotting external changes as they are emerging. | 2. It can lead to a duplication of effort as each division attempts to solve similar problems. |
| 3. It provides for the integration of specialized personnel deep within the hierarchy. | 3. Divisional goals may be given priority over the health and welfare of the overall organization. Divisional organizations may have difficulty responding to corporatewide threats. |
| 4. It focuses on the success or failure of particular products, services, clients, or territories. | 4. Conflict problems may arise when divisions attempt to develop joint projects, exchange resources, share individuals or through "transfer pricing" charge one another for goods and services. |
| 5. To the extent that this pattern yields separate "business units," top management can pit one division against another. For instance, Procter & Gamble has traditionally promoted friendly competition among product groups. | |

sional specialization can generally expect the following tendencies to occur over time:

- An emphasis on flexibility and adaptability to the needs of important external units.
- A lag in the technical quality of products and services vis-à-vis functionally structured competitors.
- Difficulty in coordination across divisions, particularly where divisions must work closely or sell to each other.

## Departmentation by Matrix

**Matrix structure**

From the aerospace industry we developed a third unique form of departmentation now called ***matrix structure***[19]. In aerospace efforts projects are very technically complex and they involve hundreds of subcontractors located throughout the world. Precise integration and control is needed across many sophisticated functional specialties and corporations. This is often more than a functional or divisional structure can provide. Thus, *departmentation by matrix* uses both the functional and divisional forms simultaneously. Figure 10.5 shows the basic matrix arrangement for an aerospace program. Note the functional departments on one side and the project efforts on the other. Workers and supervisors in the middle of the matrix have two bosses—one functional and one project.

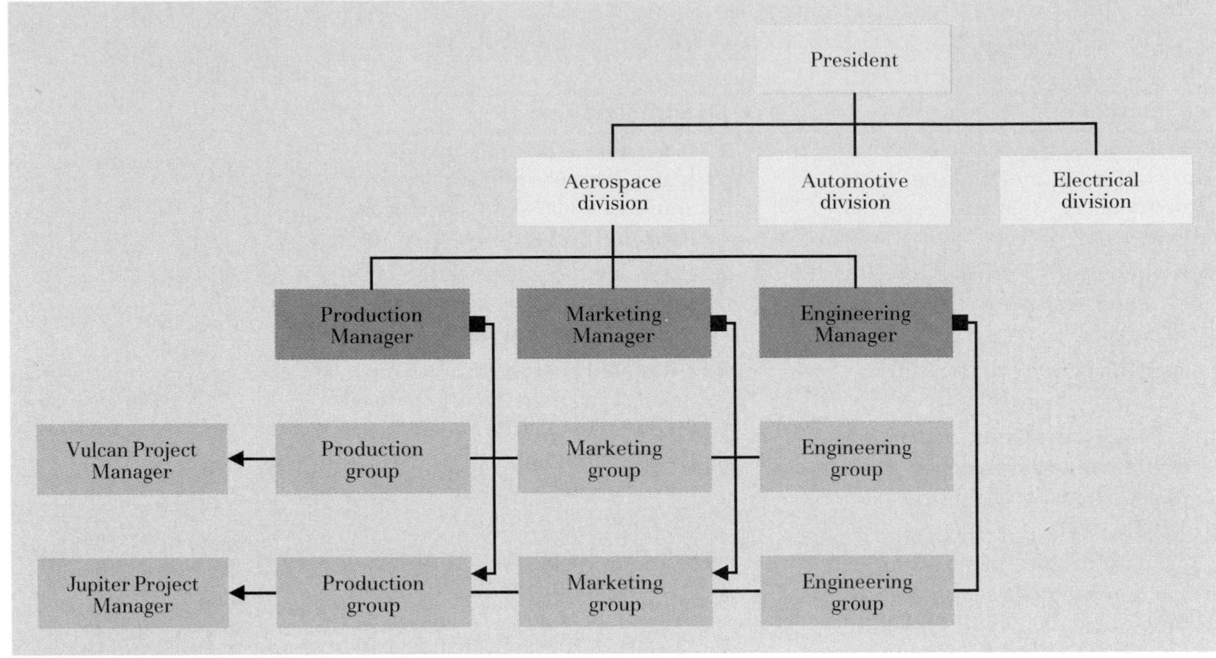


*FIGURE 10.5 A matrix pattern of departmentation in an aerospace division.*

The major advantages and disadvantages of the matrix form of departmentation are summarized in Table 10.4. The key disadvantage of the matrix method is the loss of unity of command. Individuals can be unsure what their jobs are, who they report to for specific activities, and how various managers are to administer the effort. It can also be a very expensive method since it relies on individual managers to coordinate efforts deep within the firm. Note that the number of managers almost doubles. Despite these limitations, however, the matrix structure provides a balance between functional and divisional concerns. Many problems can be

***TABLE 10.4***
**MAJOR ADVANTAGES AND DISADVANTAGES OF A MATRIX STRUCTURE**

| Advantages | Disadvantages |
|---|---|
| 1. It combines strengths of both functional and divisional departmentation. | 1. It is very expensive. |
| 2. It helps to provide a blending of technical and market emphasis in organizations operating in exceedingly complex environments. | 2. Unity of command is lost (individuals have more than one supervisor). |
| 3. It provides a series of managers able to converse with both technical and marketing personnel. | 3. Authority and responsibilities of managers may overlap causing conflicts and gaps in effort across units, and inconsistencies in priorities. |
| | 4. It is difficult to explain to employees. |

INTERNATIONAL PERSPECTIVE

## V. F. CORPORATION

Courtesy of V. F. Corporation.

**You may not have heard of V. F. Corporation directly, but surely you know some of the labels of this diversified international apparel company—Vanity Fair and Lee, to name just two. Staying in touch with a changing external environment and shifting consumer tastes is important at V.F. To develop quality market-responsive products, the firm is committed to consumer research and thorough analysis of trends. With interpretation and cooperation by design, plus review by manufacturing, sales and retail personnel, product lines are continually adapted to meet customer needs.**

resolved at the working level where the balance between technical, cost, customer, and organizational concerns can be rectified.

Many organizations also use elements of the matrix structure without officially using the term "matrix." For example, special project teams, coordinating committees, and task forces can be the beginnings of a matrix. Yet, these temporary structures can be used within a predominately functional or divisional form, and without upsetting the unity of command or hiring additional managers.

## Mixed Forms of Departmentation

Which form of departmentation should be used? As the matrix concept suggests, it is possible to departmentalize by two different methods at the same time. Actually, organizations often use a mixture of departmentation forms. In fact, it is often desirable to divide the effort (group people and resources) by two methods at the same time to balance the advantages and disadvantages of each. Consider this case:

> Northwest Manufacturing and Wholesale produces filters for autos and ships and, most recently, for the elimination of toxic and nuclear waste. Its plant in Tacoma, Washington, produces marine

filters. The Walla Walla, Washington, works specializes in nuclear and toxic waste filters. All auto filters are manufactured in Los Angeles. The firm is active in both the new equipment market for auto filters and the replacement market. Most auto filters are sold in the replacement market via discount stores and auto supply outlets. This is a highly competitive market in which success depends on providing inventory control and restocking for hundreds of retail outlets. Filters for toxic waste, nuclear applications, and marine use must be specifically tailored to individual customers. The president also sees substantial growth opportunities in Europe. Now European sales, mainly in the United Kingdom, account for 22 percent of total sales and 29 percent of gross profits.

Figure 10.6 shows a possible organization chart for this successful growing regional firm. It has three divisions, each of which is a separate legal entity. The largest division is Northwest Manufacturing, which produces all the filters and markets for industrial consumers. Note that it is functionally organized below the president with vice presidents of finance, personnel, R&D, and operations. Due to the close coordination required between manufacturing and industrial sales, both plant managers and the director of industrial sales report to the vice president of operations. As you might expect, both regional and product differences separate the plants. Note the technical thrust of this division, with its emphasis on a functional structure at the top and with product groups in sales and operations.

Eurofilter, a separate division, is structured to serve the European market. Note that the divisional form dominates. In a similar fashion, the wholesaling company is dominated by divisional departmentation, since the key to this business is service. Maintaining retailer inventories and ensuring prompt delivery are important. Thus, customers are grouped into territories, and the territories form regions headed by a regional manager.

## COORDINATION

**Coordination**

***Coordination*** is the set of mechanisms that an organization uses to link the actions of its units into a consistent pattern. Much of the coordination within a unit is handled by its manager. Smaller organizations may rely on their management hierarchy to provide the necessary consistency. But as the organization grows, managers become overloaded. The organization then needs to develop more efficient and effective ways of linking work units to one another.

A mix of personal and impersonal methods of coordination are used in organizations. Some of these methods are quite obvious: some are not. They are summarized in Table 10.5. As you review the table, remember that coordination is a dynamic and continual process.

Impersonal methods of control are extensions and refinements of formalization and standardization. In some cases, there are few provisions

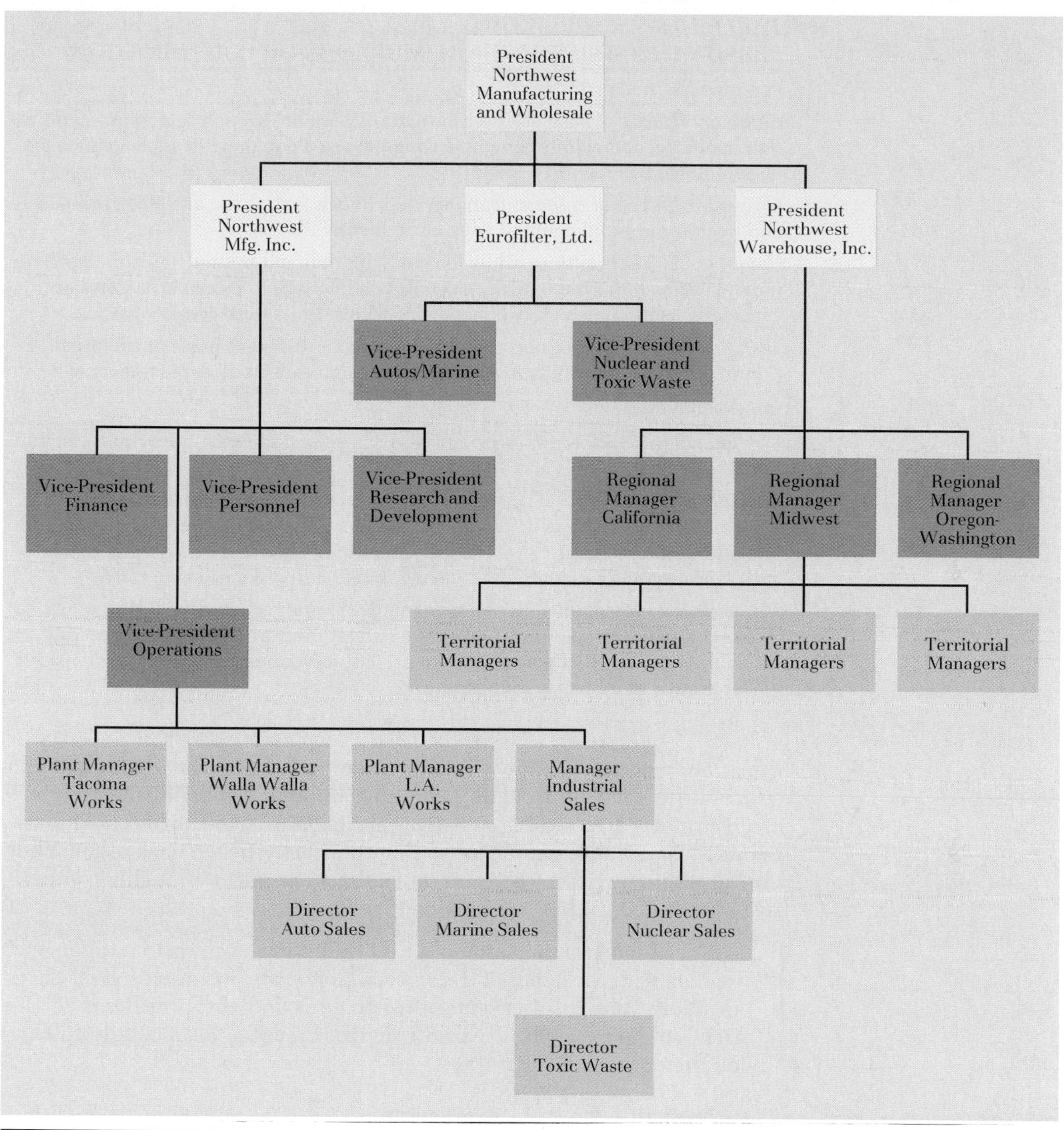


*FIGURE 10.6 A partial organization chart for Northwest Manufacturing and Wholesale.*

for dialogue and discussion among workers and managers. With some techniques, such as specialized staff units, the organization can promote dialogue and discussion. In general, however, organizations relying on impersonal control methods become more inflexible. By contrast, personal methods of coordination include common values, the grapevine, and committees. The key to making these techniques work to produce synergy lies in promoting dialogue and discussion among employees, man-

*TABLE 10.5*
**PERSONAL AND IMPERSONAL METHODS OF COORDINATION**

| Personal Methods |
|---|
| *Common values.* These are built into management through selection, socialization, training, and reinforcement. Examples are a company dress code or business philosophy. |
| *Grapevine/informal communications.* Although fast, these are often inaccurate and need to be supplemented with more formal means. |
| *Committees.* Committees allow for participation and mutual adjustment across units, are good for communicating complex, qualitative information, and are especially useful between two managers whose units must work together. |
| *Task forces.* Task forces bring individuals from different parts of the organization together to identify and solve problems cutting across departments. |
| **Impersonal Methods** |
| *Written rules, policies, and procedures.* These include schedules, budgets, and plans. |
| *Specialized staff units.* These units are often used to coordinate functions where there is divisional departmentation. An example is a personnel staff unit to ensure policy consistency across divisional units. In a matrix structure, the staff coordinating function often develops into a line decision center. |
| *Management information systems.* Originally, this included such things as suggestion systems, newsletters, and so on. Now it often refers to computerized information and record-keeping systems. These systems are particularly useful where timing of efforts is important. |

agers, and executives. These personal methods allow the organization to address the particular needs of distinct units and individuals. They are often preferred in situations where individuals from different departments must act as a team by adjusting their activities to each other. They are increasingly preferred in organizations operating in highly competitive environments. For example,

> *Heinz* Chairperson Anthony J.F. O'Reilly strives to maintain personal contact with the heads of Heinz's conglomerate businesses. He refuses to allow staff to intervene between him and the presidents of the firm's affiliates. With a worldwide work force of 50,000, only 150 are on the corporate staff.

# SUMMARY

**Organizational Goals include both societal concerns, which establish the basis for the organization's mission, and systems concerns (e.g., profit and innovation), which establish a basis for its survival and prosperity. As collections of people working together in a division of labor for a**

common purpose, it is convenient to think of organizations as goal-oriented social systems.

■ **Formal Structures of Organizations** are typically represented on an organization chart and stand distinct from the informal or emergent systems with which they coexist. It defines the basic division of labor within the organization and identifies the number of management levels in the hierarchy of authority.

■ **Vertical Specialization** is the hierarchical division of labor that specifies where formal authority is located for various decisions. Typically a chain of command exists to link lower-level workers with senior managers. The distinction between line and staff units also indicates how authority is distributed with some staff units having the capability to influence line operations. With managerial techniques such as decision support and expert computer systems, there is less need for staff experts. Many organizations today are reducing the number of staff personnel in the quest for increased operating efficiency.

■ **Control** is one of the basic management functions. It is facilitated in organizations by planning and goal-setting activities that define desired directions and standards by which to measure progress toward them. Output, goal-oriented controls are less restrictive on individual workers than process controls which describe how tasks are to be accomplished. In today's new-form organizations, more personal methods of control are being emphasized. In highly centralized organizations, control is concentrated at the top; in more decentralized ones, control is dispersed among workers at all levels.

■ **Horizontal Specialization** is the division of labor that results in various work units or groups in the organization. With different ways of achieving this "departmentation," three main types of organization structures are observed: functional, divisional, and matrix departmentation. Each of these structures has advantages and disadvantages. Organizations may successfully use any type, or a mixture, as long as the strengths of the structure match the needs of the organization. Divisionalized structures with product or geographical orientations are common in firms operating internationally.

■ **Coordination** is the means through which the behavior of multiple subgroups in an organization is linked together. Like the control process, coordination can be accomplished by a variety of personal and impersonal means. With a strong emphasis today on cross-functional task forces and teams in organizations, personal contact in groups is an increasingly important coordination mechanism.

## KEY TERMS

Centralization
Control
Coordination
Decentralization
Departmentation
Divisional Departmentation

Formal Structure
Formalization
Functional Departmentation
Horizontal Specialization
Line Units
Matrix Structure
Mission Statements
Organization Charts
Output Goals
Policy
Primary Beneficiaries
Procedure (or Rule)
Societal Goals
Span of Control
Staff Units
Standardization
Systems Goals
Vertical Specialization

## REVIEW QUESTIONS

1. What is the main difference between societal and systems goals of organizations? Give an example of goals in each category that you would like to find in an organization you might work for.
2. What is vertical specialization and how does it affect the way organizations operate?
3. Why is the size of the staff unit shrinking in many organizations today? What can staff personnel and departments do that are useful for organizations? In what ways can they become problems for organizations?
4. Draw an organization chart showing how a manufacturing concern, say a computer company, could operate on (a) a functional form of departmentation, and (b) a product divisional form of departmentation. What are the potential advantages and disadvantages of using these alternative types of structures?
5. What is a matrix structure? Why would an organization benefit by changing to a matrix structure? Under what conditions would you recommend that the possibility of switching to a matrix be considered?
6. What are some of the potential problems associated with matrix structures? Can organizations derive many of the benefits of matrix operations without switching to a formal matrix structure? Please explain.
7. Is there a difference between control and coordination as discussed in this chapter? Explain your answer by example.
8. Explain the difference between centralized and decentralized decision making. What advantages and disadvantages may surround decentralization (a) from a top manager's perspective and (b) from a lower-level manager's perspective?

## AN OB LIBRARY

Alfred D. Chandler, Jr., *Strategy and Structure: Chapters in the History of American Industrial Enterprise* (Cambridge, MA: MIT Press, 1962).

Stanley M. Davis, Paul R. Lawrence, Harvey Kolodny, and Michael Beer, *Matrix* (Reading, MA: Addison-Wesley, 1977).

Henry Mintzberg, *The Structuring of Organizations* (Englewood Cliffs, NJ: Prentice-Hall, 1986).

Gareth Morgan, *Images of Organizations* (Newbury Park, CA: Sage, 1986).

Thomas N. Peters and Richard A. Waterman, Jr., *In Search of Excellence: Lessons from America's Best-Run Companies* (New York: Harper Collins, 1982).

EXERCISE

# ORGANIZATIONAL ANALYSIS

### *Objectives*

1. To develop and refine your understanding of the basic attributes and characteristics of various organizations.
2. To explore differences and similarities among organizations.
3. To enhance your research and analysis skills.

### *Total Time*

60 to 90 minutes

### *Procedure*

1. Choose an organization you know quite a bit about. Develop a list of its basic attributes, including its: goals, culture, structure, specialization.
2. In groups of five members, select one organization and thoroughly assess its attributes. It is best to develop a matrix to record all discussion on each of the attributes.
3. Also address the five concerns listed below[20]:
   a. *Product:* Are its products of real social value? Are they critical elements in machines or elements of mass destruction?
   b. *Workplace:* Is the workplace safe? Is the business finding ways to involve workers in the decision-making process?
   c. *Environment:* If a manufacturer, does the business protect air, water, and so on. If a financial business, does it use environmental responsibility when investing or underwriting?
   d. *Community:* What kind of commitment does it have to local and national community? Does it apply some standards to overseas workers?
   e. *Ownership:* Are workers brought in to ownership through employee stock options?
4. In groups, discuss implications of what was observed in developing the matrix (i.e., similarities, differences, types of attributes common to a variety of organizations).
5. A group representative presents the highlights of their discussion and analysis to the entire class.

CASE

# THE MIDDLE STATES MANUFACTURING CASE

Jaccob Jaccober is the president of Middle States Manufacturing. The firm, while not particularly efficient, has been highly profitable, its emphasis being on innovation and maintaining the technical quality of its products at or above competitive levels. At the moment, Jaccob didn't feel much like a corporate tycoon as he sat slumped into the soft leather sidechair in his office overlooking the city. "How long will it be," he wondered, "before Susan Rice, my vice-president of finance, will call about the West Coast financing package?" The lights of the city glowed uniformly in the same neat grid of rows and columns some city planner had specified over a hundred years ago. "Oh, if only I could design such a logical, permanent structure for my rapidly growing organization," thought Jaccob.

His thoughts turned to a quick review of the hectic day of meetings. Opportunities were turning into problems. Each new piece of business seemed only to cloud further the distribution of roles and responsibilities among Middle States' managers. Orders were not getting processed promptly. Two important accounts were recently sent incomplete shipments, and both shipments were late at that! Of course, there were many new people in new jobs, and most were working long hours to overcome their inexperience. But nobody seemed able to agree with anybody on anything!

Joan Wood, vice president of production, for example, had argued convincingly that longer production runs were needed to reduce machine setup time, increase quality control, cut wear and tear on expensive machinery, and simplify the order delivery process. To provide these longer runs, a reduction in specialized orders was the key. Pat Vincent, vice president of marketing, however, strongly resisted this recommendation. Marketing, he explained, had carefully nurtured a company image of quick delivery of quality products engineered to the unique needs of major customers. Joan's recommendations would force marketing to sell a standardized product line. Pat foresaw immediate lost sales and a longer-term decline in market acceptance if this were done.

Then there was Howard Teebs, assistant to the vice president of finance. He was concerned over the financing of inventories. Howard had argued for a stricter budgeting process that stressed weekly targets for purchasing, in-process goods, and finished goods inventory. Variations over 10 percent of the plan would be subject to direct control by the assistant to the vice-president of production.

As the meeting of the executive committee droned on, it was apparent to Jaccob that the Middle States management team had numerous ideas for improving performance. Everyone seemed willing to recommend changes, particularly if the changes affected someone else's department.

As Jaccob stared out into the city lights, he argued to himself that the problems of growth had to be manageable. He reviewed things again. Business from three key customers—Chicago Distributing, Ohio Wholesalers, and Blake, Inc.—accounted for 50 percent of total sales and 75 percent of gross profits. Substantial new growth from these three appeared questionable. The potential lay with Profab. Profab was already used by the big three. It used slightly different production methods than current products and required a lot of handcrafting from a few highly skilled people. Longer production runs with a more flexible design could cut costs by 30 percent. This would increase the profitability of the existing market. Then, by starting a second shift and by using commission salespersons selling specialized lines related to Profab, new opportunities in the East and West Coast markets could be captured.

Yes, Profab was the future of the company. Yet the management staff was already overworked. Jaccob was already "passing off" direct daily relations with the "big three" to Pat. And the engineering requirements of the new direction might yield even more production problems in serving the big three. "How could Middle States capitalize on this opportunity without losing its major customers?"

Before Jaccob could try to answer his own question, the phone rang. It was an excited Susan Rice. She announced that within six months Middle States would have $2 million to market Profab and its derivatives nationally. Susan chided Jaccob that Middle States would no longer be an appropriate name. She suggested Profab National. Jaccob countered with Profab International.

Once again the grid of city lights, with neat rows and columns expanding to the horizon, caught Jaccob's eye as he congratulated Susan. It was time for a change—a change that would create the proper organization and establish the management team for Profab International.

### *Questions*

1. What is the current formal structure of Middle States Manufacturing?
2. What are the advantages and disadvantages of a divisional design for Middle States Manufacturing?
3. Describe the goals of Middle States Manufacturing as described by Jacob Jaccober.
4. Which coordination and control mechanisms appear most appropriate to Middle States Manufacturing?

This study outline of major topics is meant to organize your reading now; it is repeated in the Summary to structure your review.

## STUDY OUTLINE

- Designs for Smaller Organizations
- The Bureaucracy
- Mechanistic and Organic Designs

Mechanistic Designs and the Machine Bureaucracy
Organic Designs and the Professional Bureaucracy
Divisionalized Organizations   The Conglomerate

- Technology and Organizational Design

Technology   Where Technology Dominates: The Adhocracy
Developments in High Technology: Strategic Alliances

# CHAPTER 11

# ORGANIZATIONAL DESIGN



## PHOTO ESSAYS

# VISIONS 11

When Richard Nicolosi took over as head of Procter & Gamble's paper products division, he found a highly bureaucratic and very centralized organization. With a strong functional orientation, internal groups focused on separate and sometimes conflicting goals. The division was also losing market share in a newly competitive product environment. Nicolosi knew things had to become more market driven and integrated. "I had to make very clear," he says, "that the rules of the game had changed."

And change they did. With his vision and leadership a new focus on teamwork was initiated. The organization structure was changed to include more cross-functional groupings and encourage lower-level participation in decision making. With this came an increased emphasis on creativity and innovation. It paid off. Even though the competition got tougher, Nicolosi's division increased market share and experienced a 66 percent profit increase in a four-year period.

We all recognize that a Ford auto assembly plant and the Rolling Stones rock group are quite different. Auto assembly plants are organized to emphasize routine, efficient production. The rock group is loose, experimental, and organized for artistic expression even though the logistics of travel, the movement of the equipment, and the sale of the tickets are highly organized. In this chapter, we will discuss how you adjust the basic elements of organizational structure to fit the scale of the operation, the job to be done, the demands of outsiders, and how senior management intends to compete.

Organizational design

The process of choosing and implementing a structural configuration is what we refer to as ***organizational design.***[1] Our discussion of organizational design will emphasize how managers, like Richard Nicolosi in the chapter-opening *Visions*, should adjust the structural configuration of their organizations or work units to best meet the challenges faced at any given point in time.

## DESIGNS FOR SMALLER ORGANIZATIONS

Simple organizational designs resemble the "pyramid" description traditional to management thinking. They have few staff departments and formal procedures. All this is quite appropriate for a small organization and is popular in family businesses, retail stores, and thousand of other firms.[2] Strengths of the simple design are simplicity, flexibility, and responsiveness to the desires of a central manager—in many cases, the owner. Since a simple design relies heavily on the manager's personal leadership, this configuration is only as effective as the senior manager. Consider this case in point:

> B&A Travel is a comparatively small travel agency run by Helen Druse. Reporting to Helen are two staff members (Jane Bloon for accounting and finance and Ken Wiener for training and market development). The operations arm is headed by Joan Wiland who supervises 10 lead travel agents. While the lead travel agents each specialize in a geographic area, all but Sue Connely and Bart Merve take client requests for all types of trips. Sue is in charge of three major business accounts, while Bart heads a tour group. Each of the 10 lead agents head a group of five to seven associates. Coordination is by weekly meetings and a lot of personal contact by Helen and Joan. Control is enhanced by the computerized reservation system they all use. Helen makes sure each agent has a monthly sales target, and she routinely chats with important clients about their level of service. She realizes that developing participation from even the newest associate is an important tool in keeping the "fun" atmosphere.

## THE BUREAUCRACY

The simple design, like that used by B&A Travel, is a basic building block of all organizations. As the organization grows, it begins to add layers of management and more specialized departments. It quickly separates line and staff functions and may begin to expand its territorial scope. In this way, larger organizations become much more structurally complex than small ones.[3] The nature of the organization changes as layers of management increase, the division of labor and coordination mechanisms become more elaborate, and formal controls are established. Reliance upon a single senior manager is downplayed, and "levels" of management exercise varying degrees of authority.

Max Weber, the famous German sociologist, suggested that large organizations would thrive if they relied upon legal authority, logic, and order.[4] Weber argued that relying upon a division of labor, hierarchical control, promotion by merit with careers for employees, and administration by rule was superior to the simple design. He labeled the "ideal type" of organization the *bureaucracy*. What we have called the simple design, Weber called a "charismatic" organization because its success depends so much on the talents of one individual. Weber preferred the bureaucracy to the simple structure and expected it to be more efficient, to be fairer to employees, and to provide more freedom for individual expression. Weber predicted the bureaucracy, or some variation of his ideal form, would dominate modern society.

**Bureaucracy**

*TABLE 11.1*
**THE CHARACTERISTICS OF WEBER'S IDEAL BUREAUCRACY AND SOME ASSOCIATED DYSFUNCTIONS**

| Characteristics of Weber's Ideal Bureaucracy | Associated Dysfunctions Identified by Critics |
|---|---|
| Labor is specialized so each person has clear authority and responsibility. | Overspecialization stimulates a divergence of interests that lead to conflict. |
| Offices and positions are arranged in a hierarchy of authority. | A very formal hierarchy creates inflexibility in following "official" channels. |
| Members are selected and promoted on the basis of technical competence. | Bureaucracies become political systems serving an elite corps of managers. |
| Members have administrative careers and work on a fixed salary. | Conformity to the organization's ways can be detrimental to one's mental health. |
| Members are subject to rules and control that are strict and impersonal and are applied universally. | Rules become ends in themselves; rules can only specify minimum requirements. |

Weber was correct. If our society is one of organizations, the dominant organizations are bureaucracies. Table 11.1 summarizes the major characteristics of Weber's ideal bureaucracy. It also shows a number of dysfunctions in modern day bureaucracies.

Business firms in the Fortune 500, including such firms as GM, IBM, and Texaco are all bureaucracies. However, there are important but subtle differences in how each is designed to build on the strengths of the bureaucratic form while minimizing its weaknesses. Each of these very large organizations adjusts the bureaucratic form to "fit" external and internal requirements. No one design is preferred in all environments, for all technologies, and for all the strategies. The design is contingent upon the technologies of the firm, the nature of its environment, and the desires of senior management, among other factors.

# MECHANISTIC AND ORGANIC ORGANIZATIONAL DESIGNS

Some 30 years ago, British scientists Tom Burns and G.M. Stalker systematically investigated how bureaucracies might be designed to be more efficient and innovative.[5] Their investigation led them to propose that subtle variations in large bureaucratic organizations can be important. Specifically, they distinguished between "mechanistic" and "organic" organizational designs, whose major differences are summarized in Figure 11.1.

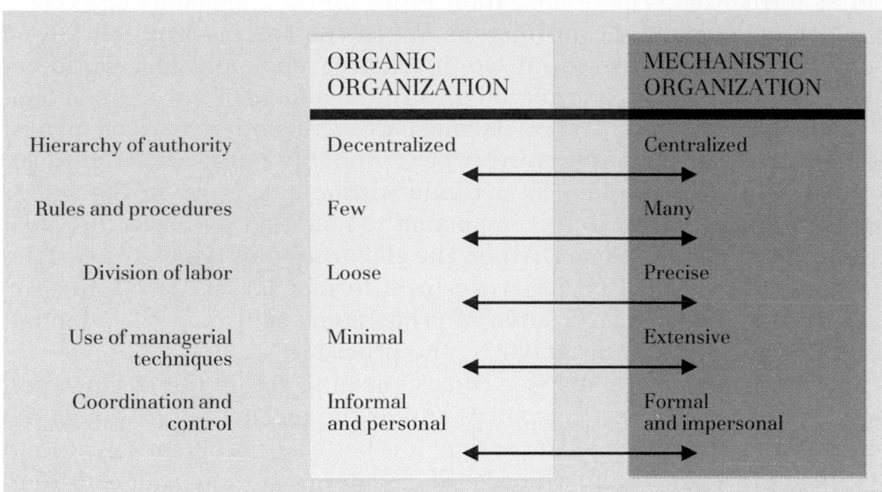


*FIGURE 11.1 A basic comparison of mechanistic and organic designs for organizations.*

## Mechanistic Designs and the Machine Bureaucracy

**Mechanistic design**

The ***mechanistic design,*** described in the figure, is a highly bureaucratic organization emphasizing vertical specialization and control. Organizations of this type stress rules, policies, and procedures; specify techniques for decision making; and emphasize developing well-documented control systems backed by a strong middle management and supported by a centralized staff. Where the entire organization is characterized in this manner, Henry Mintzberg calls it a machine bureaucracy.[6] Visually the machine bureaucracy resembles a tall thin pyramid with a bulge at the top for the centralized senior staff.

The mechanistic design results in a management emphasis on routine for efficiency. It is quite popular in basic industries with large-scale operations. Employees may not like such designs, however, when the organization is viewed as too rigid and centralized. In a strict hierarchy with most authority concentrated at the top, it is also not surprising to find that mechanistic designs can hinder an organization's capacity to adjust to external changes or new technologies. Facing stiff competition from the Japanese, the mechanistically-designed U.S. auto firms have attempted to change dramatically to become more participative, flexible, and innovative. Ford, GM, and Chrysler have all been in the news for cutting unnecessary rules and procedures, reducing centralized staff, and developing smaller more autonomous work teams.

## Organic Designs and the Professional Bureaucracy

**Organic design**

The ***organic design,*** described in Figure 11.1, is much less bureaucratic in appearance and functioning. Here the design strategy emphasizes horizontal specialization. Procedures are minimal and those that do exist are not as formalized. The organization relies on the judgments of experts and personal means of coordination. When controls are used, they tend to reinforce professional socialization, training, and individual reinforcement. Staff units tend to be placed toward the middle of the organization.

What Mintzberg calls a professional bureaucracy often relies on organic features in its design.[7] Your university is probably a professional bureaucracy looking like a broad flat pyramid with a large bulge in the center for the professional staff. It is important to note that power in this ideal type rests with knowledge. Further, the elaborate staff typically helps the line managers and often has very little formal power. Yet, control is enhanced by the standardization of professional skills and the adoption of professional routines, standards, and procedures.

The organic design stresses communication across the organization and focuses attention on customers and/or the technology. Although not as efficient as the mechanistic design, it is better for problem solving and serving individual customer needs. Since lateral relations and coordination are emphasized, centralized direction by senior management is less intense. Thus, this design is good at detecting external changes and adjusting to new technologies—but at the sacrifice of responding to central management direction.[8]

## Divisionalized Organizations

Many very large firms find that neither the mechanistic nor the organic designs are suitable for all their operations. To adopt a machine bureaucracy would overload senior management and yield too many levels of management.[9] Yet if they adopted an organic design, they would lose control and become too inefficient. Some firms find that while their businesses are related, some businesses call for an organic structure whereas others call for a mechanistic one. The solution is the ***divisionalized design*** where the firm establishes a separate structure for each business or division. The classic divisional organization was created by Alfred Sloan for General Motors when he divided GM's operations into divisions for designing and producing Chevys, Olds, Pontiacs, Buicks, and Cadillacs.[8] Each division was treated as a separate business. Each business competed against each other.

**Divisionalized design**

In the divisionalized organization, coordination across businesses is provided by a comparatively small centralized staff. The centralized staff provides support such as financial services and legal expertise. Senior line management provides direction and control over the presumably "autonomous" divisions. For very large organizations, this can free top management to establish strategy and concentrate on large, long-term problems. Divisional heads run their own businesses and compete for resources. Yet each enjoys the support (financial, personnel, legal, etc.) of the larger parent. While this form is expensive as redundant staff and support units must be developed for each division, it allows the firm greater flexibility to respond to different markets and customers. Yet, tension between divisional management and senior management is quite often apparent. It is very difficult for corporate executives and corporate staff to allow the divisions to operate as independent businesses. Over

Courtesy of Goodyear Tire & Rubber Company.

ETHICAL PERSPECTIVE

## GOODYEAR

**It's easy to find examples of corporations trying to be good citizens these days. But Goodyear, long interested in dealing positively with its environment, has taken a slightly different approach in one of its programs. This major tire manufacturer is trying to promote safe driving and roadside heroism by the nation's truckers. In its "Highway Hero" program, truckers are selected from each state based on their courage in rescuing highway accident victims from their cars. A nationwide panel of trucking industry leaders then selects one of these nominees as the grand award recipient, "America's National Highway Hero." The winner receives recognition for safe driving and is held as a role model for others. Of course, the trip to the Daytona 500 stock car race and $20,000 in bonds are pretty nice too.**

time senior staff may grow in size and force "assistance" on the divisions. Since they compete for common resources, coordination across divisions is often also quite difficult.

## The Conglomerate

In the 1960s a few organizations began to grow by buying unrelated businesses. On the surface these firms looked like divisionalized firms but the various businesses of the divisions were so unrelated that a new term had to be invented. They were called ***conglomerates.*** Pure conglomerates have not done particularly well in the United States mainly because substantive knowledge of the business is often needed for them to be successfully managed.[10]

**Conglomerates**

The line between the divisionalized form and the conglomerate can often be confusing. For us, the key question is whether there is synergy among the various businesses owned by the corporation. If there is, we would call it divisionalized. If there is little synergy, it is a conglomerate. For example, IBM and Ford are divisionalized, but General Electric and Beatrice are conglomerates. Of course with the wave of mergers and acquisitions in the 1980s, several corporations became conglomerates as raiders bought and sold various businesses. Here structure and organizational design, other than cost cutting, were not important. Financial manipulation was the key to short-term success.

Many state and federal entities are also, by necessity, conglomerates. For instance, a state governor is the chief executive officer of units concerned with higher education, welfare, prisons, highway construction/maintenance, police, and the like.

# TECHNOLOGY AND ORGANIZATIONAL DESIGN

So far our discussion has suggested that the design of the organization will be influenced by its size. A number of scholars argue that the size of an organization is the single most important factor influencing its structure.[11] As size increases, the organization's structure is predicted to become more complicated. On the other hand, a second group argues that there is a **technological imperative.** That is, successful organizations are said to arrange their internal structures to meet the dictates of their dominant "technologies" or work flows.[12] Some of the major issues in this debate are explained in the paragraphs that follow.

**Technological imperative**

## Technology

**Technology**

**Technology** is the combination of resources, knowledge, and techniques that creates a product or service output for an organization. The term is used in various ways in the OB literature. Thus, it will help you to become acquainted with two of the more common classification schemes used by theorists and managers to describe the technologies of organizations.

### *Thompson's View of Technology*

James D. Thompson classifies technologies as intensive, mediating, or long-linked. In the *intensive technology* there is uncertainty as to how to produce desired outcomes.[13] A group of specialists must be brought together to use a variety of techniques to solve problems. There is high interdependence among the members of such teams. Examples might be found in a hospital emergency room or a research and development laboratory. Standard operating procedures are difficult to develop for this technology, and coordination is achieved by mutual adjustment among those trying to solve the problem.

The *mediating technology* links parties desirous of becoming interdependent. Banks, for example, link creditors and depositors, and store money and information to facilitate such exchanges. While all depositors and creditors are interdependent, the reliance is pooled through the bank. Thus, if one creditor defaults on a loan, no one depositor is injured. Wholesalers, retailers, and insurance companies are other organizations that use a mediating technology.

The *long-linked technology* is also called mass production or industrial technology. Because it is known how to produce the desired outcomes, the task is broken down into a number of sequential and interdependent steps. A classic example is the automobile assembly line. Traditionally long-linked technology has been relatively inflexible and a high output volume was required to justify its use. Now we are entering an era of flexible manufacturing where mass production can be automated while the organization still maintains some flexibility for the future.

## *Woodward's View of Technology*

Joan Woodward divides technology into three categories: small-batch, mass production, and continuous-process manufacturing.[14] These are illustrated in Figure 11.2. In *small-batch production,* a variety of custom products are tailor made to fit customer specifications. The machinery and equipment used are generally not very elaborate, but considerable craftsmanship is often needed. In *mass production* the organization produces one or a few products with an assembly-line type of system. The work of one group is highly dependent on another, and the equipment is typically sophisticated and accompanied by very detailed instructions for workers. Mass production is similar to Thompson's long-linked technology. Organizations, using *continuous-process technology* produce a few products with considerable automation. Classic examples are automated chemical plants and oil refineries.

From her studies, Woodward concluded that the combination of structure and technology was critical in the success of the organizations. When technology and organizational design were properly matched, a firm was more successful. Specifically, successful small-batch and continuous-process plants had flexible structures with small work groups at the bottom; more rigidly structured plants were less successful. Successful mass production operations, by contrast, were rigidly structured and had large work groups at the bottom. This technological imperative has since been supported by some investigations.

*FIGURE 11.2 Examples of Woodward's three categories of technology: small batch, continuous process, and mass production.*

## Where Technology Dominates: The Adhocracy

More recent work on the role of technology in organizations has been much broader. Even though the technology may favor a particular pattern of specialization, other factors may not. The history of the firm, the attitudes of top management, and a host of economic and political factors may work against organizations that attempt to follow the technological imperative.[15]

The influence of technological considerations is most clearly seen in small organizations and in specific departments within large ones. In some instances, managers and employees simply do not know the appropriate way to service a client or produce a particular product. This is the extreme of Thompson's intensive type of technology and may be found in some small-batch processes where a team of individuals must develop a unique product for a particular client.

**Adhocracy**

Mintzberg suggests that at these technological extremes, the "adhocracy" may be an appropriate structure.[16] In an ***adhocracy*** there are:

- Few rules, policies, and procedures.
- Very decentralized, shared decision-making among members.
- Extreme horizontal specialization as each member of the unit may be a distinct specialist.
- Few levels of management.
- Virtually no formal controls.

The adhocracy places a premium on professionalism and coordination for problem solving. It is particularly suited to help professionals solve technical problems. As such, adhocracies are often used as a supplement to other designs to offset their dysfunctional effects.[12] Firms use temporary task forces, special committees, and even contract consulting firms to provide the creative problem identification and problem solving that the adhocracy promotes. For instance, Lotus Development Corporation creates autonomous new departments to encourage talented employees in developing new software programs. Allied Chemical and 3M also set up quasi-autonomous groups to work through new ideas.

## Developments in High Technology: Strategic Alliances

**Strategic alliances**

So far we have concentrated on the internal aspects of organizational design. In high-tech areas such as robotics, semiconductors, advanced materials (ceramics and carbon fibers), and advanced information systems, a single company does not often have all the knowledge necessary to bring new products to market. Often the firms with the knowledge are not even in the same country. Here, the organizational design must go beyond the boundaries of the organization into strategic alliances. ***Strategic alliances*** are announced cooperative agreements or joint ventures between two independent but technically related firms. Often these agreements involve corporations headquartered in different nations.[17]

INTERNATIONAL PERSPECTIVE

## HEWLETT-PACKARD

Courtesy of Hewlett-Packard Company.

**Hewlett-Packard, the American electronics firm, is a recognized leader in its industry. One of the key reasons for its success is its progressive management, which began with cofounders Bill Hewlett and Dave Packard. For example, the firm holds regular communication sessions that involve production people in planning, organizing, and controlling the work to be done. In addition, its investment in research and development is consistently among the tops in the industry. This strategy pays off on a large scale: HP is a global company whose organization structure must accommodate diverse operations and strategic alliances in many parts of the world. In the European Market, personal computers and terminals are produced in the Grenoble Personal Computer Division of HP, located in Grenoble, France. Recently, HP announced that it was moving its personal-computer headquarters to France to be run by a Frenchman, Jacques Clay. HP will still retain some operations in Silicon Valley.**

Strategic alliances are quite common in high technology industries, as firms not only seek to develop technology but to make sure their solutions become a standard across regions of the world. In some cases, the fight for a dominant design pits one nation against another. For instance, in high-definition television (HDTV), Zenith joined forces with AT&T to develop one system while Toshiba, Sony, and some 30 other Japanese firms formed a strategic network to develop their own system. The U.S. winner will likely get the lion's share of the estimated $20 billion HDTV market in North America. One of the largest and potentially most influential strategic alliances is the newly announced cooperation between West Germany's Daimler-Benz and Japan's Mitsubishi. They have agreed to share technology and will develop joint ventures, market-based cooperations, or high-tech consortia as the need arises.[18]

# ENVIRONMENT AND ORGANIZATIONAL DESIGN

If organizational design were merely dictated by size and technological concerns, it would be comparatively easy to specify a configuration for any particular organization. But an effective organizational design also reflects powerful external forces as well as the desires of employees and managers. Here we will focus more on the competitive elements that drive the selection and survival of a particular organizational design.

## The General and Specific Environment

Organizations, as open systems, need various inputs from their environment and need to sell outputs to their environment. Now we want to be more specific about what the environment is and what elements are likely to be important.[19]

**General environment**

**Specific environment**

The ***general environment*** is the set of cultural, economic, legal–political, and educational conditions in the areas in which it operates. The owners, suppliers, distributors, government agencies, and competitors with which an organization must interact to grow and survive constitute its ***specific environment***. Both the general and specific environments are depicted in Figure 11.3.

## Environmental Complexity

**Environmental complexity**

A basic question in analyzing the environment of the organization is its complexity. A more complex environment provides an organization with more opportunities and more problems. *Environmental complexity* is an estimate of the magnitude of the problems and opportunities in the organization's environment as evidenced by three main factors: the degree of richness, interdependence, and uncertainty.[17]

*FIGURE 11.3 Main components in the general and specific environments of organizations.*

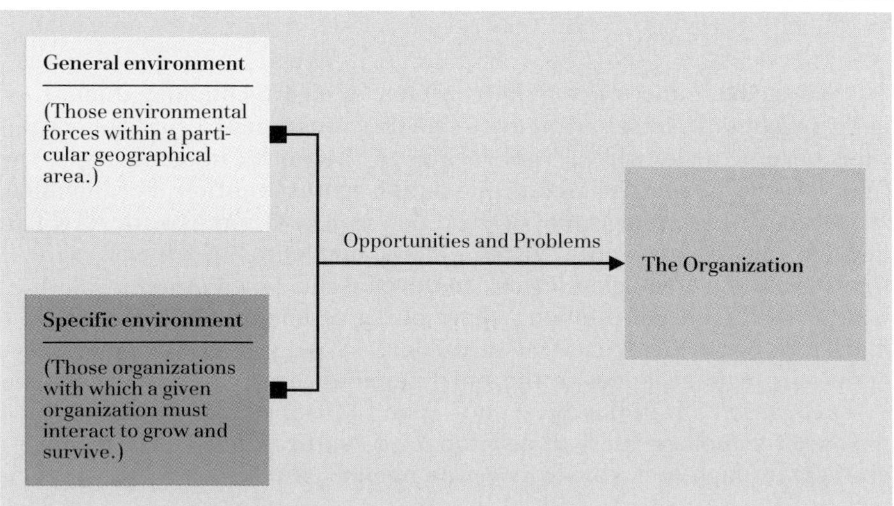

1. *Environmental richness.* The environment is richer when the economy is growing, individuals are improving their education, and others the organization relies on are prospering. For businesses, a richer environment means that economic conditions are improving, customers have more money, and suppliers (such as banks) see a bright future and are willing to invest in the organization. In a rich environment, more organizations survive even if they have poorly functioning organizational designs. But a richer environment is also filled with more opportunities. The organizational design will need the capability to recognize these opportunities and capitalize on them.
2. *Environmental interdependence.* The link between external interdependence and organizational design is often subtle and indirect. The organization may co-opt powerful outsiders by including them. For instance, many large corporations have financial representatives on their boards of directors. The organization may also adjust its overall design strategy to absorb or buffer the demands of a more powerful external element. Perhaps the most common adjustment is the development of a centralized staff department to handle an important external group. For instance, few large U.S. corporations are without some type of governmental relations group at the top. Where service to a few large customers is considered critical, we have suggested that the form of departmentation is likely to switch from a functional form to a divisionalized one.
3. *Uncertainty and volatility.* Environmental uncertainty and unpredictable volatility can be particularly damaging to large bureaucracies. In times of change, investments quickly become outmoded and internal operations no longer work as expected. The obvious organizational design response to uncertainty and volatility is to opt for a more organic form. At the extremes, movement toward an adhocracy may be important. However, these pressures may run counter to those from large size and technology. It may be too hard or too time consuming for some organizations to make the design adjustments. Thus, they continue to struggle while adjusting their design just a little bit at a time.

## Balancing Technological and Environmental Demands

As just suggested, technological imperatives and environmental demands can work at cross-purposes. In such cases, we often find that hybrid combinations of the mechanistic and organic designs may emerge along the two lines shown in Figure 11.4.

1. *An organic core with a mechanistic shell.* Earlier we suggested that the technology of the organization may call for an organic design to promote flexibility, creativity, and innovation. In reality, there may be organizational limits on the use of a purely organic design. For example, where environmental demands are backed up by powerful external groups, the organization may respond by developing a series of top-level and very mechanistic staff units. This strange design of

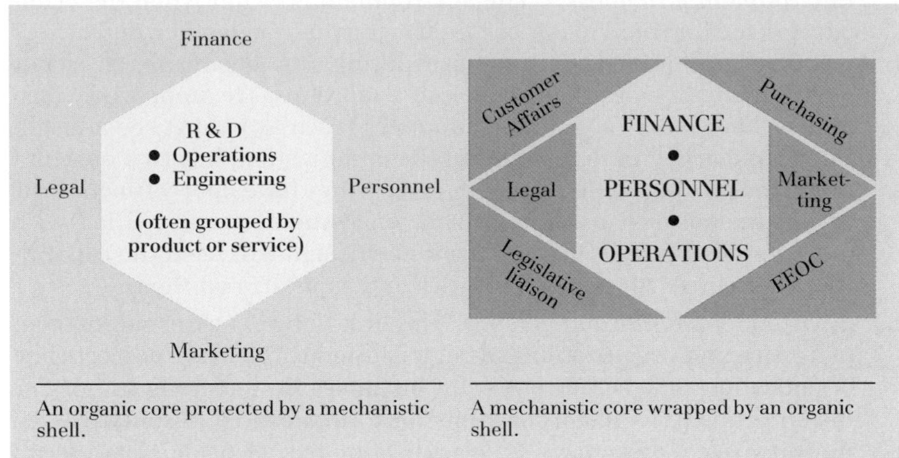


*FIGURE 11.4 Two mechanistic/organic design hybrids.*

mechanistic staff units at the top with very organic line units toward the middle and bottom of the organization can externally protect the organization while still allowing responsible internal operations.

2. *A mechanistic core with an organic shell.* Very large organizations with technologies calling for mechanistic designs and economies of scale are very vulnerable to environmental uncertainty and volatility. A partial solution to the problem is to wrap these inflexible cores with organic staff units. The staff units have two purposes. To the extent possible, they often attempt to change the external conditions by moderating the volatility in the specific environment. They can also attempt to absorb or buffer as many changes as possible. This option is found in firms that must balance efficient production coupled with flexible marketing and design operations. Although the assembly line is mechanistically structured, products may be designed by more organically structured teams.

# STRATEGY AND ORGANIZATIONAL DESIGN

**Organizational strategy**

***Organizational strategy*** is the process of positioning the organization in its competitive environment and implementing actions to compete successfully.[20] To develop a strategy, senior managers select those systems goals they believe should define organizational success, form this into a mission, select a target position within a specific environment, and decide how the firm can compete.

## Types of Strategies

Although there are as many types of strategies as firms, four "generic strategies" or types of strategies are common to many businesses.[20] They are:

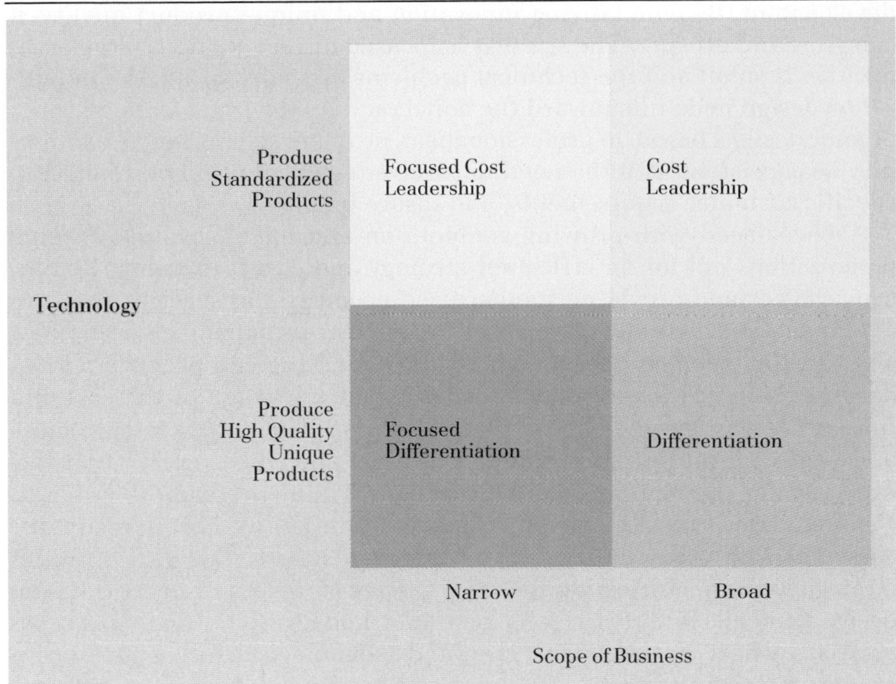


*FIGURE 11.5 Types of generic strategies as affected by the organization's scope of business and technology.*

1. Focused differentiation.
2. Focused cost leadership.
3. Differentiation.
4. Cost leadership.

The four strategic types as shown in Figure 11.5 are based on some simplified assumptions. The first assumption is that management must decide on the scope of its operations. If the firm is large and selects a broad range of customers and markets, it has breadth. If the choice is narrow, it has focus. The second assumption is that management selects technology to produce either comparatively inexpensive, standardized products or more expensive tailor-made products and services. If the firm competes by providing lower cost, standardized products, it relies on the economies of scale for cost leadership. If it produces higher quality, unique products (even if only in the minds of customers), it differentiates itself.

## Matching Strategy and Organizational Design

Table 11.2 shows some ideal combinations of size, technology, and design for each of the four strategy types. It essentially summarizes many of the points we have previously made in this chapter. As suggested in the table, no one strategy is always best. Rather, an organization has a better chance of prospering if it can "fit" its strategy and structure to environmental requirements.

Take the example of a small biotechnology firm. In a comparatively new and growing industry, the firm is on the leading edge of technological development. By emphasizing innovation and unique product quality, it can grow and prosper. The strategy is focused differentiation. If the organization is small and the technical problems are substantial, the organization design need tilts toward the adhocracy. As the organization grows, organic designs based on professionalism, problem solving, and flexibility may be consistent with the need to resolve technical problems, adjust to specific customer requirements, and insure quality.

When faced with growing competition and more customers, some organizations opt for an efficiency strategy and cost leadership. By limiting choices and providing standardized products and services they can cut production costs and offer lower prices. By capitalizing on economies of scale, for instance, McDonalds and Burger King can produce a standardized hamburger, milkshake, and fries for a fraction of the cost of a full-service restaurant. The cost leadership or efficiency strategy places a premium on routinization, standardization, and consistency. Thus, it is little wonder the more mechanistic designs will be preferred.

The various ideal forms of organization design we have already discussed can be used in different environments for firms with different strategies. Yet, modification to "ideal" types is the art of organizational design that calls for creativity, imagination, and foresight. Then too, organizations where environment, size, and technological forces are inconsistent with current strategy or structures are not helpless. They can alter technology. For instance, IBM is turning to flexible manufacturing systems. They can divisionalize and move resources from declining businesses and invest them in growing ones. Such is now the case with Kodak as it is moving away from silver-based films and toward the new age of electronic imaging. Organizations can change strategy or go back to an originally successful one[22].

As large organizations confront ever more complex environments, they will need to continually adjust their strategies and structures to

*TABLE 11.2*
EXAMPLES OF FIT AMONG ENVIRONMENT, SIZE, TECHNOLOGY, STRATEGY, AND ORGANIZATIONAL DESIGN

| | *Four Strategy Types* | | | |
|---|---|---|---|---|
| | Focused Differentiation | Focused Cost Leadership | Differentiation | Cost Leadership |
| Environment: | | | | |
| richness | rich | lean | rich | mixed |
| interdependence | high | high | high | low |
| violatility | high | stable | stable | mixed |
| Size | small | medium | large | very large |
| Technology | intensive | long linked | mediating intensive | mixed |
| Organization Design | adhocracy | machine bureaucracy | professional bureaucracy | divisionalized |
| Example | Bio-tech firm; | Steel Mill; Auto Parts Supplier | Prestigious research University; Regional Care Hospital | Exxon |

SKILLS PERSPECTIVE

## HELENE CURTIS

Courtesy of Helene Curtis Industries, Inc.

**"Leadership is our goal. . . . Innovation is our strategy" says the tag line on Helene Curtis Industries, Inc.'s annual report. Their success depends on the involvement of people throughout the organization in developing ideas and turning them into action. This lean organization respects open communication and the willingness to take risks. It also utilizes cross-functional task forces that bring people together from marketing, sales, operations, and research and development to develop and plan new product concepts. One of those task forces created the Helene Curtis Salon Selectives—recently chosen as the personal-care brand of the year. At this Chicago company, still controlled by the family of founder Gerald Gidwitz, President Ronald Gidwitz is leading the firm's current product-oriented strategy.**

survive. The modern U.S. corporation, for example, is becoming much more strategically innovative. It is moving beyond the traditional generic strategies toward increased innovation and less centralized direction by a remote senior manager. Some corporations, such as GM, are simultaneously moving production operations to lower-cost foreign plants, developing strategic alliances with foreign firms, and investing in new technologies with newly created divisions at home. Increasingly, we see such giants as IBM, AT&T, Ford, Dow, Chase, and Union Carbide readjusting how they formulate strategy. They are pushing the process further down the organization as senior executives recognize that middle- and lower-level managers and personnel can add important insights and assist with new strategic innovations. This is the level of action where strategy and design can turn into organizational performance.

# SUMMARY

■ **Designs for Smaller Organizations** tend to follow the traditional "pyramid" form of organizations, with heavy reliance on a single senior manager who is often the owner. They tend to be flexible and responsive.

As these organizations grow larger, their structures must be changed to adapt to new circumstances. Organizational design is the process of choosing and implementing a structural configuration.

■ **The Bureaucracy** was an "ideal" form of organization as originally conceived by Max Weber. Based on clear division of labor, rules, and procedures, strict hierarchy of authority, promotion by merit, and impersonality, it was expected to be an efficient and fair organization. In today's dynamic environments, rigid bureaucracies get into trouble as they are slow to adapt to new situations. Although all organization tend to have some bureaucratic characteristics, many blend this with other alternatives in design.

■ **Mechanistic and Organic Designs** represent two ends of an organizational design continuum. Mechanistic designs are very bureaucratic and work best in stable environments. Organic designs are much less bureaucratic and work best in dynamic and more uncertain environments. The classic mechanistic design is described as a machine bureaucracy; professional bureaucracies, such as the typical university, have some organic characteristics. Divisionalized organizations and conglomerates will involve a mixture of these designs.

■ **Technology and Organizational Design** are interrelated. Some argue that technology is the most important influence on organizational design—this position is called the technological imperative. Major distinctions in technology are the Thompson (intensive, long-linked, mediating) and Woodward (small batch, mass production, continuous processing) classification systems. In highly-intensive and small-batch technologies, organizational designs may tend toward the adhocracy, a very decentralized form of operation. In high-technology settings, more and more strategic alliances are appearing where organizations link with others for purposes of cooperation, often in international joint ventures.

■ **Environment and Organizational Design** are interrelated. It is recognized that environmental differences have a large impact on the type of organizational design that works best. In analyzing environments, both the general (background conditions) and specific (key actors and organizations) environment are important. The more complex the environment, the greater the demands on the organization. Organizations must respond with more complex designs that often blend mechanistic and organic forms with one another.

■ **Strategy and Organizational Design** are interrelated. The organizational design must support the strategy if it is to be able to prove successful. Strategy positions an organization in its competitive environment. Four generic strategies pursued by businesses are differentiation, focused differentiation, cost leadership, and focused cost leadership. The differentiation strategies are most consistent with organic structures and divisionalization. The cost leadership strategies emphasize routinization and efficiency and are most consistent with more mechanistic structures. Effective managers are able to "fit" structure and strategy in mutually supportive combinations.

## KEY TERMS

Adhocracy
Bureaucracy
Conglomerates
Divisionalized Design
Environmental Complexity
General Environment
Mechanistic Design
Organic Design
Organizational Design
Organizational Strategy
Specific Environment
Strategic Alliances
Technology
Technological Imperative

## REVIEW QUESTIONS

1. Explain Weber's concept of "bureaucracy." Do you think bureaucratic characteristics are necessary in organizations? Why or why not?
2. Explain the basic differences between mechanistic and organic organizational designs.
3. Describe an actual organization or subunit that you feel should function with an organic design. Do the same for a mechanistic design. Defend your choices in both cases.
4. What is a conglomerate? What organizational design challenges do conglomerates face as opposed to what the chapter previously called simple organizations?
5. Identify the types of technologies described in the classification schemes of (a) Thompson and (b) Woodward. Give examples of each, and suggest their organizational design implications.
6. What is the distinction between an organization's general and specific environment? If forces in the general environment are common to all organizations in a given geographical area, why should a manager even consider them?
7. Choose an organization with which you are familiar. Describe its environment in respect to the dimensions of "complexity" listed in the chapter. What are the organizational design implications for this organization?
8. In what way are strategy and organizational design interrelated? Are there any general organizational design guidelines available for firms following the generic business strategies?

## AN OB LIBRARY

Tom Burns and George Stalker, *The Management of Innovation* (London, Tavistock, 1961).

Jay Galbraith, *Designing Complex Organizations* (Reading, MA: Addison-Wesley, 1973).

Paul R. Lawrence and Jay W. Lorsch, *Organization and Environment* (Boston: The Division of Research, Graduate School of Business Administration, Harvard University, 1967).

William A. Pasmore, *Designing Effective Organizations: A Sociotechnical Systems Perspective* (New York: John Wiley & Sons, 1988).

Max Weber, *The Theory of Social and Economic Organization,* translated by A.M. Henderson and H.T. Parsons (New York: The Free Press, 1957).

# EXERCISE

## RATING ORGANIZATIONAL PERFORMANCE[23]

### *Objectives*

1. To reflect on the performance of an organization in relation to eight specific dimensions.
2. To compare different views regarding the strengths and weaknesses of various organizational units.

### *Procedure*

1. Select an organization (or unit of an organization) that you know quite a bit about.
2. Listed below are some statements that describe organizational performance. You should indicate how often you believe they occur in the organization you have selected. Using the scale below, place a number from 1 to 7 for each of the items to follow.

Very infrequently 1 2 3 4 5 6 7 Very frequently

_____ 1. The work process is coordinated and under control.
_____ 2. Participative decision making is widely and appropriately used.
_____ 3. Rules, procedures, and formal methods guide the work.
_____ 4. The goals are clearly understood by most members.
_____ 5. The work effort is usually intense.
_____ 6. There is a stable, predictable work environment.
_____ 7. Innovation is stressed.
_____ 8. There is a positive interpersonal climate.
_____ 9. Quantification and measurement are key parts of the work climate.
_____ 10. Consensual decision making is encouraged.
_____ 11. Outsiders perceive it as a vibrant, high-potential unit.
_____ 12. Creative insights, hunches, and innovative ideas are encouraged.

_____ 13. It is easy to explain the overall objectives of the unit.
_____ 14. There is a constant striving for greater accomplishment.
_____ 15. Employees feel as though they really belong to the unit.
_____ 16. The unit is clearly growing and improving over time.

3. Compute the rating for each performance dimension by summing scores as indicated below.

# 2 + # 10 = _____ Participation, Openness
# 8 + # 15 = _____ Commitment, Morale
# 7 + # 12 = _____ Innovation, Adaptation
# 11 + # 16 = _____ External Support, Growth
# 5 + # 14 = _____ Productivity, Accomplishment
# 4 + # 13 = _____ Direction, Goal Clarity
# 1 + # 6 = _____ Stability, Control
# 3 + # 9 = _____ Documentation, Information Management

Form groups of four to six persons and share your organizational performance assessments.

4. Discuss the differences found and be prepared to share your findings with the rest of the class. Special consideration should be given to "why" such differences in organizations exist.

CASE

## WHICH DESIGN PHILOSOPHY?

It had been five years since the major reorganization of the company had put all the once-separate division design groups into one design organization for three nameplates, yet Harry Stone, senior vice president of design for the auto group, was still as frustrated as ever. Each morning the group of design engineers discussed their "philosophy" of car design. Everyone had their own philosophy based on years of experience and hard-won rules of thumb. Those trained in car group C had a different view of designing a hood than those originally from division P or division O. Harry had partially solved this problem by grouping designers into teams assigned to specific "platforms." For instance, the old C division designers worked on the Z platform while the old division O personnel generally worked on the R platforms. Each platform was generally used as the basis for several cars.

Of course, there was still the ever-present problem of the politics between the stylists and engineers. The stylists worked on all platforms and they were generally a very unstable group. At times the firm got stylists from England, and then many came from Italy. In many cases, the styling was contracted out to specialized styling groups to get fresh ideas.

Engineers, on the other hand, were organized by function and section of the car. Some electrical engineers, for instance, would specialize in one aspect of the electrical aspects of autos such as starters, while others might specialize in suspension systems for passenger cars. They often complained that the design group was presenting them with costly engineering challenges. Rarely did the cars have the very latest engineering advances.

The debate between Pete Flag and Susan Haag was typical. Pete Flag, the new head designer for Z platforms, had over thirty years of design experience and he was convinced that the new computerized mathematical models were not helping. Auto designers should draw their two-dimensional models, based on the conceptions of the stylists, and have them systematically reviewed by the design group review committee. Only after review should the design group proceed to carefully construct a clay model. Only after constructing a clay model for higher management clearance should the design specifications be sent on to the engineering group. Based on the engineering specifications, prototypes could then be matched against the clay model to make sure the skin of the auto would appear precisely as it was modeled.

Susan Haag, a new transfer from the advanced technical group, made precisely the opposite arguments. It took months to get all the clearances necessary to start construction of a clay model. Even after senior management approval, the design often had to be modified when the engineering group could not craft specifications that met the requirements for cheap manufacturability. In several cases, the engineering group merely threw up their hands in disgust and asked the designers to start the process all over again. In several cases, modifications went all the way back to the styling group for a fresh conception. She suggested that the company use the new computer-aided design and computer-aided manufacturing systems developed by the engineering research group. Here the design could be mathematically modeled and pictured three-dimensionally on a computer screen. From the mathemetical model, a clay rendering could be made and subsequently modified, if the engineers decided a particular piece needed to be changed. The mathematical models were precise and could be sent directly to engineering. Any change in any part, such as where the hood mounts would be placed, could be trail analyzed by a computer simulation.

The debate seemed endless, and the process of design modification for a four-passenger car was taking over four years from styling, to design, to engineering, to cutting the final specifications for parts manufacturing. There were some sixteen to eighteen variations on a single "platform" given three "nameplates" and two-door and four-door models with and without station wagon modifications, as well as contingency designs if senior management approval was not forthcoming. And now they were being asked to consider a convertible option. There had to be a better way of styling, designing, and engineering a car that would cut the time for modifications and yet produce a technically excellent vehicle that could be easily manufactured.

*Questions*

1. What type of organizational design is now utilized in the design division?
2. What type of organizational design would you recommend for the division?
3. Can the design for the division be separated from that of engineering and styling?
4. If senior management wanted to emphasize technical excellence, would this change your design recommendation?
5. What changes in senior management would be important to developing a sound organizational design?

This study outline of major topics is meant to organize your reading now; it is repeated in the Summary to structure your review.

## STUDY OUTLINE

### The Concept of Organizational Culture

Levels of Cultural Analysis   Subcultures and Countercultures
Functions of Organizational Cultures

### Observable Aspects of Organizational Culture

Stories, Rites, Rituals, and Symbols   Shared Meanings   Cultural Rules and Roles

### Values and Organizational Culture

Linking Actions and Values   Values and National Culture
Values as a Competitive Advantage

### Managing Organizational Culture

CHAPTER 12

# ORGANIZATIONAL CULTURE

## Careers and Organizational Culture

Comparing Corporate Cultures   Matching Individuals and Corporate Cultures

## Ethics and Organizational Culture

## PHOTO ESSAYS

Skills Perspective   General Motors

International Perspective   UPS

Ethical Perspective   Northwestern Mutual Life

# VISIONS 12

**The credit card industry is increasingly crowded and competitive. When Lou Gerstner took over as head of Travel Related Services (TRS) at American Express over a decade ago, his vision brought change to a mature 130-year-old company. In doing so, he challenged a basic belief that only the "green card" was needed and he sought a more entrepreneurial culture for TRS that would serve the company well in a competitive marketplace.**

**Gerstner and his top managers hired people who would do well in the new culture, they rewarded risk taking, and they stymied the influence of entrenched bureaucracy. Special programs for high potential employees were established and great performers were singled out for recognition. At TRS, new products and services were introduced and new technology installed to facilitate operations. Oh yes, net income increased 500 percent—a compounded annual rate of 18 percent—over a ten-year period.**

As we approach the beginning of a new century, a transformation is occurring in many organizations—from the giants in the auto industry to the small software design firms. At all levels of operations, people are striving for productivity. Quality, innovation, and value are replacing the drive toward short-term efficiency. Managers are recognizing that they need to build viable organizations that stand for something. They are rediscovering the critical importance of human resources. The old methods of command and control are being replaced by new methods of participation and involvement. Managers are becoming facilitators, helpers, guides, and coaches.

Simply put, today's managers are beginning to change the very essence of what it means to work in the modern organization. In our terminology, they are changing their organization's "culture." As suggested in the opening *Visions* example, a strong and clear culture can be a distinct competitive advantage for an organization.

## THE CONCEPT OF ORGANIZATIONAL CULTURE

Organizational culture

In Chapter 3 we examined "culture" as it applies internationally and ethnically to the various nations and people of the world. Here, we are concerned with ***organizational culture***—the system of shared beliefs and values that develops within an organization and guides the behavior of its members.[1] In the business setting this is often referred to as the ***corporate culture.*** And just as no two individual personalities are the same, no two organizational cultures are perfectly identical. Most significantly, management scholars and consultants increasingly believe that cultural differences can have a major impact on the performance of organizations and the quality of work life experienced by their members. Edgar Schein, for example, singles out these two cases in point:[2]

**corporate culture**

> ***Digital Equipment Corporation*** A strong culture has emerged from the entrepreneurial approach of Digital Equipment's founder Ken Olsen. Generations of DEC managers have learned his way of seeing the world and the role of the firm in that world. Wherever you go in DEC, within the United States or in other countries, personnel share common assumptions about how the business should be run.
>
> ***Eastern Airlines*** The struggles of Eastern Airlines over the past few years have regularly been in the news—there is no strong and unifying culture. High turnover in the senior management ranks, in particular, has made it difficult for the firm to develop and sustain a distinctive culture that can be shared by its personnel. The company's financial performance has suffered and labor strife has been a nagging work force problem.

## Levels of Cultural Analysis

Figure 12.1 graphically depicts three important levels of cultural analysis in organizations: observable culture, shared values, and common assumptions. These may be envisioned as layers where the deeper one gets, the more difficult it is to discover the culture.

The first level concerns *observable culture* or "the way we do things around here."[3] These are the methods that the group has developed and teaches to new members. The observable culture often results from the

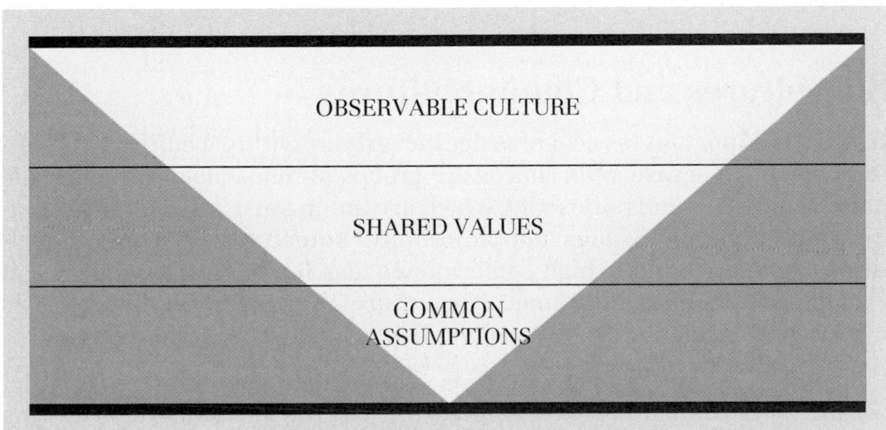


*FIGURE 12.1 Three levels of analysis in studying organizational culture.*

unique stories, ceremonies, and corporate rituals that make up the history of a successful work group. For example,

> ***Mary Kay Cosmetics*** Rituals and ceremonies are an important part of Mary Kay's motivational strategy. Salespeople attend rousing all-day pep talks where top performers enthusiastically share their success stories with others. To the applause of everyone, awards—including Mary Kay's famous pink luxury cars—are given to the highest achievers.

The second level of analysis recognizes that *shared values* play a critical part in linking people together and provide a powerful motivational mechanism for members of the culture. Many consultants suggest that organizations should develop a "dominant and coherent set of shared values."[4] The term *shared* in cultural analysis refers to the group as a whole. Each and every member may not agree with the shared values, but they have been exposed to them and have often been told they are important. For example,

> ***Hewlett-Packard*** "Quality" is part of everyone's vocabulary at Hewlett-Packard. The firm was founded with a belief that everyone could make a creative contribution to quality products. Given this shared sense of value, consultant Tom Peters said that getting quality circles started at Hewlett-Packard was like "falling off a log."

At the deepest level of cultural analysis are *common assumptions,* or the taken for granted truths that members share as a result of their collective experience. It is often extremely difficult to isolate these patterns, but doing so helps explain why culture invades every aspect of organizational life. For example,

> ***Mills College*** The board of trustees voted to admit men to the all-women Mills College in California. They claimed that changing to coeducation was an economic necessity. The board retreated, however, when students, alumnae, and administrators demonstrated the educational importance and unique contributions of an all women's liberal arts college. And these often separate constituencies united to develop a new plan to save the tradition and philosophy that they all believed to be fundamental to Mills.

## Subcultures and Countercultures

**Subcultures**

It is often important to recognize distinct groups within a culture—organizational or otherwise. ***Subcultures*** are groups of individuals with a unique pattern of values and philosophy which are not inconsistent with the organization's dominant values and philosophy.[5] Interestingly, strong subcultures are often found in high performance task forces, teams, and special project groups in organizations. The culture emerges to bind individuals working intensely together to accomplish a specific task. For example,

> ***Apple Computer, Inc.*** A strong and positive subculture developed at Apple in the team that created the MacIntosh computer. Working together in an isolated facility and free from operational constraints

SKILLS PERSPECTIVE

## GENERAL MOTORS

Courtesy of General Motors Corporation.

**It's a real fight these days in the automobile industry, and General Motors has taken its share of lumps—from both domestic and foreign competitors. But its new Saturn plant is now operating, and GM is betting that the technology-based operating strategy in place there will pay off—with the help of a capable and well-trained work force. GM believes the key to success is integrating people effectively with new technology, allowing both to work together to deliver quality products to customers. Training is a continuing commitment as GM prepares for the 21st century. A "learning culture" is being introduced to make employees aware that tomorrow's jobs can't be done with yesterday's skills. Employees are encouraged to commit to continuous learning of job skills. One major program—Skills 2000—itself uses high technology in the form of interactive videodisc and touch-sensitive computer screens for such training.**

of Apple's normal operations, the members of the team even flew a "Jolly Roger" flag over their building. New members were carefully selected and a spirit of creativity dominated. Everyone was proud to sign their names to the inside case of the final "Mac" prototype.

**Countercultures**

***Countercultures,*** on the other hand, have a pattern of values and a philosophy that rejects the surrounding culture.[6] The anti-apartheid counterculture in South Africa and the *Solidarity* movement in Poland of the 1980s are but two vivid examples on a national scale. Within an organization, mergers and acquisitions may produce countercultures. Employees and managers of an acquired firm may hold values and assumptions that are quite inconsistent with those of the acquiring firm. This is known as the "clash of corporate cultures."[7] For example,

***General Motors*** When GM bought EDS financial services, corporate cultures clashed. Billionaire H. Ross Perot, founder and once CEO of EDS, appeared to be the leader of this counterculture during his brief tenure at GM. His, and EDS's, individualistic, get-things-done culture had a tough time when confronted by GM's more bureaucratic and control-dominated culture.

## Functions of Organizational Cultures

According to Schein, the culture of an organization can help it deal with problems of both external adaptation and internal integration. Problems of *external adaptation* involve organizational (or work group) dealings with outside forces. As suggested by Table 12.1, a strong and positive culture helps develop the consensus needed for organizations to cope well with changing environments. Specifically, organizational culture can help develop shared understandings of:

- basic mission and strategy
- goals to be accomplished
- means to accomplish goals
- standards by which to measure progress toward goals
- correctve actions needed to improve goal accomplishment

Problems of *internal integration* deal with the creation of "togetherness," the internal force that makes members of organizations and/or work groups capable of achieving truly collective results. Organizational culture can facilitate internal integration by clarifying ways members can be expected to work together. As shown in Table 12.1, the organizational culture can help build a sense of "togetherness" through:

- developing a common language or jargon for members
- creating consensus on membership criteria
- clarifying power and status differentials
- setting standards for intimacy and friendship
- identifying how rewards and punishments are earned
- establishing ideology to give meaning to unexplainable events

*TABLE 12.1*
**THE FUNCTIONS OF ORGANIZATIONAL CULTURE: ANSWERING QUESTIONS REGARDING PROBLEMS OF EXTERNAL ADAPTATION AND INTERNAL INTEGRATION**

| *Problems of External Adaptation* | *Problems of Internal Integration* |
|---|---|
| • What are our core mission and strategy? | • How can be best communicate with one another? |
| • What specific goals are relevant to mission accomplishment? | • What are the criteria for organizational/group membership? |
| • What are the best means for achieving these goals? | • How are power and status to be differentiated? |
| • What criteria should be used to measure performance results? | • What are the standards for intimacy and friendship? |
| • What should be done if and when goals aren't being met? | • What are the standards for rewards and punishments? |
| | • How do we collectively explain uncontrollable events? |

*Source:* Developed from Schein, E. *Organizational Culture and Leadership.* Reading, MA: Addison-Wesley, 1985, pp. 52, 66.

# OBSERVABLE ASPECTS OF ORGANIZATIONAL CULTURE

Important parts of an organization's culture emerge from the collective experience of its members. These emergent aspects of the culture help make it unique and may well provide a competitive advantage for the organization when compared to others. Some of these aspects may be directly observed in day-to-day practices. Others may have to be discovered—for example, by asking members to tell stories of important incidents in the history of the organization. We often learn about the unique aspects of the organizational culture through descriptions of very specific events.[9] By closely observing employee actions, listening to stories, and asking knowledgeable members to interpret what is going on, you can begin to understand the culture.

## Stories, Rites, Rituals, and Symbols

Organizations are rich with stories of winners, losers, successes, and failures. Perhaps one of the most important stories concerns the founding of the organization. The ***founding story*** often contains the lessons learned from the heroic efforts of an embattled entrepreneur whose vision may still guide the firm. The story of the founding may be so embellished that it becomes a saga. ***Sagas*** are heroic accounts of accomplishments.[10] They are important because they are used to tell new members the real mission of the organization, how the organization operates, and how individuals can fit into the company.

**Founding story**

**Sagas**

If you have job experience, you may well have heard stories concerning the following topics. Is the boss human? How will the boss react to a mistake? Can someone move from the bottom to the top of the company? What will get me fired? These are common stories in many organizations.[11] Often the stories will provide valuable hidden information on who is more equal than others, whether jobs are secure, and how things are really controlled. In essence, the stories begin to suggest how organizational members view the world and live together. Of course, the stories are not necessarily true and may evolve into myths. ***Organizational myths*** are expressed, unproven beliefs that are accepted uncritically and used to justify current actions.

**Organizational myths**

Some of the most obvious aspects of organizational culture are ***rites*** and ***rituals***. Rites are standardized and recurring activities used at special times to influence the behaviors and understanding of organizational members, and rituals are systems of rites. It is common, for example, for Japanese workers and managers to start their work days together with group exercises and singing of the "company song." In other settings, such as the Mary Kay Cosmetics case introduced earlier, scheduled ceremonies are used to regularly spotlight positive work achievements and reinforce high performance expectations. Rituals and rites may be unique to particular groups within the organization. Subcultures often arise from the type of technology deployed by the unit, the specific function being performed, and the specific collection of specialists in the unit. The bound-

**Rites**

**Rituals**

aries of the subculture may well be maintained by a unique language. Often the language of a subculture and its rituals and rites emerges from the group as a form of jargon.

**Cultural symbol**

Of course, no discussion of corporate culture would be complete without mentioning the symbols found in organizations. A ***cultural symbol*** is any object, act, or event that serves to transmit cultural meaning. A good example is the corporate uniform, such as those worn by UPS and Federal Express delivery personnel. Although many such symbols are quite visible, their importance and meaning may not be.

## Shared Meanings

What you see as an outside observer may or may not be what organizational members see. You may see NASA personnel on television filling the tanks of a booster rocket for the space shuttle. If you could ask the workers directly what they were doing, you might be surprised by the answer. They are not just filling booster tanks; they are assisting with an important part of exploring space. Through interaction with one another and as reinforced by the rest of the organization, the workers have infused a larger ***shared meaning***—or sense of broader purpose—into their tasks. In this sense, organizational culture is a "shared set of meanings and perceptions that are created and learned by organizational members in the course of interactions."[12] For example

**Shared meaning**

> *Scandinavian Airlines Services (SAS)* The corporate values of on-time service are well known at SAS. When a business executive radioed ahead from his jet that he would be a few minutes late for his SAS flight to Stockholm, the crew knew immediately what to do. They didn't hold the plane—everyone knew it had to leave on time. But the businessman was met by an SAS representative who had rebooked him on a flight leaving just a short time later. Everyone also knew that customer service counts at SAS.

## Cultural Rules and Roles

Organizational culture often specifies when various types of actions are appropriate, and where individual members stand in the social system. These cultural rules and roles are part of the normative controls of the organization and emerge from its daily routines.[13] For instance, the timing, presentation, and methods of communicating authoritative directives are often quite specific to each organization. In one firm, meetings may be forums for dialog and discussion, where managers set agendas and then let others offer new ideas, critically examine alternatives, and fully participate. In another firm, the "rules" may be quite different—where the manager goes into the meeting with fixed expectations. Any new ideas, critical examinations, and the like are expected to be worked out in private before the meeting takes place. The meeting is a forum for letting others know what is being done and for passing out orders on what to do in the future.

Cultural rules and roles can become deeply ingrained in organizational behavior as they influence "the way things are done around here."

Courtesy of United Parcel Service.

### INTERNATIONAL PERSPECTIVE

## UPS

**The clean brown trucks and polite uniformed delivery people are familiar to most Americans. After all, United Parcel Service, self-proclaimed as "the tightest ship in the shipping business," has been diligently delivering packages around the country for over 80 years. It's now taking on the world by entering the global marketplace, and its culture is changing in the process. Not satisfied anymore to be secure in its traditional business, the firm has responded to the challenges of Federal Express and others to serve new and developing customer needs—in the United States and elsewhere in the world. Still dedicated to operating efficiency, it is now investing in new package-sorting technology and in expanded overseas operations. It's also helping employees master the new technologies and learning how to manage thousands of "foreign" workers. One thing top management has discovered is that, as Senior Vice-President Donald W. Layden says: "You can't impose the UPS culture on people outside the U.S. You have to let them assimilate at their own pace."**

Many times, these rules and roles must be revised in order for the organization as a whole to accomplish planned change. For example,

> *Xerox Corporation* The firm needed to improve a number of existing technologies and better integrate them with one another. To do this a new and more cooperative approach to product development had to be put in place. The corporate culture was reshaped as Xerox employees learned to work more closely with customers and software suppliers to accomplish their goals.

## VALUES AND ORGANIZATIONAL CULTURE

To describe more fully the culture of an organization it is necessary to go deeper than the observable aspects. To many researchers and managers, shared common values lie at the very heart of organizational culture.

Shared values

- Help turn routine activities into important actions.
- Tie the corporation to the important values of society.
- May provide a very distinctive source of competitive advantage.

## Linking Actions and Values

Individuals collectively learn (invent, discover, and develop) behaviors and concepts to help them deal with their problems. In organizations, what works for one person is often taught to new members as the correct way to think and feel. Important values are then matched to these solutions to everyday problems. By linking values and actions, the organization taps into some of the strongest and deepest realms of the individual. The tasks one performs are given not only meaning but value. What one does is not only workable but correct, right, and important.

## Values and National Culture

One can often trace corporate values to important national culture values. For instance, the difference between Sony's corporate emphasis on group achievements and Zenith's emphasis on individual engineering excellence can be traced to the Japanese values prizing collective action versus the U.S. emphasis on individualism.[14] To use Hofstede's cultural values framework (as introduced in Chapter 3), the national culture may provide guidelines on how the organization should:[15]

- Deal with uncertainty.
- Balance individual and collective interests.
- Allocate power up and across the organization.
- Encourage individuals to interact with one another.

Organizations operating internationally can easily find that the complications of national cultures can have an important impact on their performance. The background influence of national cultures must be considered, and appropriate adjustments in operating styles made. When organizations fail to take this into account, forces in the local situation can often cause misunderstandings that slow progress and prevent important objectives from being achieved. For example,

> *General Electric* A decision was made to try and increase morale at GE's newly-purchased French subsidiary, Cie. Generale de Radiologie. French and other European managers invited to a training seminar found in their hotel rooms colorful T-shirts printed with the GE slogan "Go for One"—a practice common in GE's American operations. The French resented having to wear the shirts, with one saying: "It was like Hitler was back, forcing us to wear uniforms. It was humiliating."

## Values as a Competitive Advantage

Some successful organizations share some common cultural characteristics. Table 12.2 provides a list suggested by two popular consultants—

*TABLE 12.2*
**ELEMENTS OF STRONG CORPORATE CULTURES**

*A widely shared philosophy.* This philosophy is not an abstract notion of the future but a real understanding of what the firm stands for, often embodied in slogans.

*A concern for individuals.* This concern often places individual concerns over rules, policies, procedures, and adherence to job duties.

*A recognition of heroes.* Heroes are individuals whose actions illustrate the shared philosophy and concerns of the company.

*A belief in ritual and ceremony.* Management understands that rituals and ceremonies are real and important to members and to building a common identity.

*A well-understood sense of the informal rules and expectations.* Employees understand what is expected of them.

*A belief that what employees do is important to others.* Networking, to share information and ideas, is encouraged.

*Source:* Developed from Terrence Deal and Allan Kennedy, *Corporate Cultures: The Rites and Rituals of Corporate Life* (Reading, MA: Addison-Wesley, 1982).

Terrence Deal and Allan Kennedy. As you can see from the table, organizations with "strong cultures" display many of the characteristics already noted in this chapter. In addition, however, they will possess a broadly and deeply shared value system. Increasingly, organizations are adopting values statements that express their commitments to such matters as customer service, product and service quality, creativity and innovation, and social responsibility.

A strong culture can, however, be a double-edged sword. Unique, shared values can provide a strong corporate identity, enhance collective commitment, provide a stable social system, and reduce the need for formal and bureaucratic controls. Conversely, a strong culture and value system can reinforce a singular view of the organization and its environment. If dramatic changes are needed, it may be very difficult to change the organization. Even though General Motors may have a "strong" culture, for example, the firm has faced enormous difficulty attempting to adapt its ways in a dynamic and highly competitive environment.

# MANAGING ORGANIZATIONAL CULTURE

In organizations with strong cultures, shared values and beliefs characterize a setting in which people are committed to one another and an overriding sense of mission. As just pointed out, this can be a source of competitive advantage for these organizations over their rivals. It is quite possible that the organization you work for now or will eventually work for does not have a strong and resilient culture. Like the conglomerate organizational design discussed in Chapter 11, it may be more a collection of separate units and people who don't seem to share much in common. It is also possible that the organization may have a strong culture, but that it is not one that meets the needs of a changing environment. It is also possible that the organization may be a mix of subcultures. Here, rivalries and value differences may create harmful conflicts.

For managers—especially top managers—in situations such as the latter three just described, managing organizational culture is a pressing issue. For managers in all organizations it should be considered as critical as structure and strategy in establishing the organizational foundations of high performance. Good managers are able to reinforce and support an existing strong culture; good managers are also able to help build resilient cultures in situations where they are absent. For example,

> ***Union Pacific*** CEO Mike Walsh of Union Pacific has brought a new and fresh approach to a firm with what *Fortune* magazine called an "introverted corporate culture." Cultural changes under Walsh's leadership include the empowerment of managers at all levels. Says one: "We were so elated the company was willing to give us new authority that we wanted it to work."

Managers can modify the visible aspects of culture such as the language, stories, rites, rituals, and sagas. They can change the lessons to be drawn from common stories and even encourage individuals to see the reality they see. Because of their positions, senior managers can interpret situations in new ways and adjust the meanings attached to important corporate events. They can create new rites and rituals. This takes time and enormous energy, but the long-run benefits can also be great. For example,

> ***Four Seasons Hotels*** All new employees are carefully screened at Four Seasons Hotels—with dishwashers interviewed up to four times—to make sure they understand the culture of the Toronto-based company. No one employed over five years can be dismissed without the CEO's permission. Turnover at Four Seasons, as you might expect, is less than half the industry average.

Top managers, especially, can set the tone for a culture—and for cultural change. Throughout the book we have opened the chapters with *Visions* sections illustrating how managers are shaping the corporate landscape of the 1990s. In most of these cases we see that managers are building on the shared values in the culture of their organizations. Managers at Aetna Life and Casualty Insurance built on its humanistic traditions to provide basic skills to highly motivated but underqualified individuals. Frances Hesselbein of the Girl Scouts stressed a clear mission of helping girls to reach their highest potential—in today's world, not yesterday's. Even in the highly cost-competitive steel industry, Chairperson F. Kenneth Iverson of Nucor built on basic entrepreneurial values in the U.S. society to halve the number of management levels. And at Procter and Gamble we saw that Richard Nicolosi evoked the shared values for greater participation in decision making to dramatically improve creativity and innovation.

We have witnessed, in these examples, the raw potential of tapping into the shared values of the corporation to build exciting, interesting, and innovative programs. In each case, the visionary manager knew the organization well enough to involve the keepers and holders of the culture and to build on what all members shared. Sometimes, however, managers attempt to revitalize an organization by dicating major changes rather than by building on shared values. While things may change a bit on the surface, a deeper look often finds whole departments resisting change and many key people who do not want to learn new ways. Such responses may indicate that the responsible managers are insensitive to the effects of their proposed changes on shared values. They fail to ask if their proposed changes are:

- Inconsistent with important values in the national culture, outside the firm.
- Contrary to important values that have emerged from participants within the firm.
- A challenge to historically important corporate-wide assumptions.

While reshaping shared values is an executive challenge of the first order, few executives are able to reshape common assumptions or "the taken for granted truths" in a firm without drastic, radical action. Rodger Smith of General Motors realized this and established a new division to produce the Saturn. At Harley Davidson a new senior management team had to replace virtually all of the company's middle managers to establish a new, unique, and competitive culture. At what was once U.S. Steel, now USX, executives sold the steel divisions and purchased a series of divisions with strong, resilient cultures. All too often, however, executives are unable to realize that they too can be captured by the broadly held common assumptions within their firms. Just as executives in Eastern European firms must reexamine the philosophical foundations of their firms as their countries adopt market economies, so must managers in the U.S. and other Western nations as they anticipate the exciting challenges of a new century.

# CAREERS AND ORGANIZATIONAL CULTURE

Management scholar Jeffrey Sonnenfeld suggests that individual careers may be affected by the degree to which one's personality matches the culture of the employing organization. He says: "We've taught managers how to assess their own abilities but not how to match those with the right company."[16] As a natural extension of our discussion of organizational culture, it is appropriate to consider his work and its career management implications.

## Comparing Corporate Cultures

Consider the four alternative "corporate cultures" described in Figure 12.2. They are:

1. *Academies*—in which new hires are carefully moved through a series of training programs and series of well-defined specialized jobs. IBM

| BASEBALL TEAMS | CLUBS | FORTRESSES | ACADEMIES |
|---|---|---|---|
| Value talent and performance, entreprenurial activity, and offer large financial rewards and individual recognition. | Stress loyalty, fitting in with the group, and getting to know right people. "Generalist" and step-by-step career progress. | Operate with survival in mind, but don't offer much job security; do offer "turn-around" opportunity. | Emphasize systematic career development, regular training, and gaining functional expertise. Offer long-term relationship. |

*FIGURE 12.2 Career opportunities in four categories of corporate cultures found in business today.* (*Source:* Developed from Carol Hymowitz, "Which Corporate Culture Fits You?" *The Wall Street Journal* (July 17, 1989), p. B1.)

is an "academy" that requires all managers to attend management training each year and carefully grooms fast-trackers to become functional experts.

2. *Fortresses*—in which corporate survival is an overriding concern. These firms are struggling in competitive markets and can't promise job security. What they do offer is the chance to participate in a "turn-around" and experience the sense of really making a difference.
3. *Clubs*—which are driven by seniority, loyalty, commitment, and working for the good of the group. Moving quickly up the ladder doesn't happen; in the "club" you're supposed to work your way up. It counts who you know, and people are concerned about "fitting in." Career progress often means becoming more of a generalist by working across functions in different jobs.
4. *Baseball Teams*—which are entrepreneurial, place a high premium on talent and performance, and reward people very well financially when they produce. Commitment isn't as important as daily performance, and job-hopping from one "baseball team" to the next is fairly common. They are common in such areas as advertising, software development, and consulting.

## Matching Individuals and Corporate Cultures

While we will discuss career planning in some detail in Chapter 18, it is worth pointing out here that achieving career success may be somewhat dependent on getting a good fit with the organizational culture. Whereas people who like to take risks in the prospect of large gains may thrive on a "baseball team," they would be out of place in a "club" where those who like being part of a group are more likely to do well. The "academy" is a good fit for someone who would like to settle in and develop systematically with one employer; the person who likes to move around and achieve a high-impact reputation may be better off in a "fortress."

Figure 12.2 identifies some characteristics associated with careers in the different types of cultures described by Sonnenfeld. They may give some indication of the type of career experiences that are likely for persons joining organizations with these cultures. The key thing, of course, is to try and achieve a good fit between individual desires and capabilities and what the culture may expect of the newcomer. Then, too, it should be remembered that cultures can and do change with time. Cultural tran-

ETHICAL PERSPECTIVE

## NORTHWESTERN MUTUAL LIFE

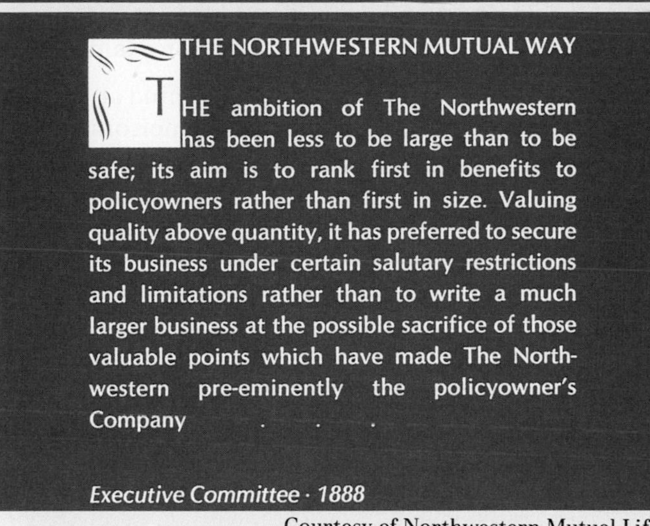

THE NORTHWESTERN MUTUAL WAY

THE ambition of The Northwestern has been less to be large than to be safe; its aim is to rank first in benefits to policyowners rather than first in size. Valuing quality above quantity, it has preferred to secure its business under certain salutary restrictions and limitations rather than to write a much larger business at the possible sacrifice of those valuable points which have made The Northwestern pre-eminently the policyowner's Company . . .

*Executive Committee · 1888*

Courtesy of Northwestern Mutual Life.

**Northwestern Mutual Life is the tenth largest life insurance company in the United States. Its force of 7000-member agents is guided by a company-wide quest for excellence and a corporate commitment to outstanding management practices. On center stage at Northwestern are values which stress a positive and respectful approach by all toward its mission, customers, products, employees, and representatives. This "Northwestern Mutual Way" is a great source of pride for those associated with the company. *Fortune* magazine, for the eighth year in a row, has called it the "most admired" among America's large insurance companies.**

sitions are not uncommon. And cultural diversity can often be found within one large employer. For example,

> *General Electric* The various corporations that exist within the GE conglomerate have a mix of internal cultures that tend to vary somewhat from one unit to the next. According to Sonnenfeld, NBC seems to have more of a "baseball team" character; the aerospace division is more of a "club;" electronics has "academy" aspects; and home-appliances is more like a "fortress."

# ETHICS AND ORGANIZATIONAL CULTURE

We have already talked quite a bit about ethics in this book and we'll continue to do so. For now, the issue is framed in a question: "Do organizations vary in the '*ethical* climates' they establish for their members?" The answer to this question is "yes," and it is increasingly clear that the ethical tone or climate of organizations is set at the top. What top managers do, and the culture they establish and reinforce, makes a big difference in the way lower-level personnel act and in the way the organization as a whole acts when ethical dilemmas are faced. What is needed in today's complicated times is for more organizations to step forward and operate with strong, positive, *and* ethical cultures. For example,

> ***Johnson & Johnson*** There was no doubt in anyone's mind at Johnson & Johnson what to do when the infamous Tylenol poisoning took place. Company executives immediately pulled their product from the marketplace—they knew that "the J & J way" was to do the right thing regardless of its cost. What they were implicitly saying was that the ethical framework of the company required that they act in good faith in this fashion.

**Ethical climate**

The ***ethical climate*** of an organization is the shared set of understandings about what is correct behavior and how ethical issues will be handled. This climate sets the tone for decision making at all levels and in all circumstances. Some of the factors that may be emphasized in different ethical climates of organizations are:[17]

- Personal self-interest.
- Company profit.
- Operating efficiency.
- Individual friendships.
- Team interests.
- Social responsibility.
- Personal morality.
- Rules and standard procedures.
- Laws and professional codes.

As suggested by the prior list, the ethical climate of different organizations can emphasize different things. In the Johnson & Johnson example just cited, the ethical climate supported doing the right thing due to social responsibility—regardless of the cost. In other organizations—perhaps too many—concerns for operating efficiency may outweigh social considerations when similarly difficult decisions are faced. Along with other aspects of organizational culture, therefore, the ethical climate will be an important influence on the behavior of individual members . . . and the organization as a whole. When the ethical climate is clear and positive, everyone knows what is expected of them when the inevitable ethical dilemmas occur. Then they can act with confidence knowing full well that they will be supported by top management and the entire organization.

## SUMMARY

**■ The Concept of Organizational Culture is as important to the management of an organization as strategy and structure. As the system of shared beliefs and values that guide and direct the behavior of members, culture can have a strong influence on day-to-day organizational**

behavior and performance. A strong culture can assist in responding to both internal and external problems. Organizations can also experience the strains of dealing with subcultures among various work units and subsystems, as well as possible countercultures, which can become the source of potentially harmful conflicts.

■ **Observable Aspects of Culture** include the stories, rites, rituals, and symbols that are shared by organization members. These are powerful aspects that can be important in helping to establish and maintain a certain culture. Shared meanings and understandings help everyone in a strong culture know how to act and expect others to act in various circumstances. They provide a common orientation to decision making and action that can facilitate performance. Cultural rules and roles similarly define expectations for behavior within an organization, and lend consistency to the behavior of its members.

■ **Values and Organizational Culture** are highly intertwined. Clearly articulated organizational values—such as quality, customer service, and innovation—help guide and direct action. Organizational values may be expressions, in part at least, of the surrounding national values. And as we already know, values can vary significantly from one national culture to another. When in place and understood, clear and positive values can create a competitive advantage for organizations. They can be a unifying force which brings efforts to bear on highly desirable outcomes.

■ **Managing Organizational Culture** is increasingly considered a top management task in the modern organization. As more and more senior executives realize that a strong culture can be a competitive advantage, they are trying to create such cultures where none previously existed and/or change existing cultures to more productive ones. In order to effectively manage organizational culture, the foundations must be established in the management of culture's observable aspects and in the belief systems that are sponsored from the top. Creating shared values among the membership is perhaps the biggest challenge, but it is also a task that must be successfully accomplished for the full benefit of a strong culture to be realized.

■ **Careers and Organizational Culture** are a relatively new, but important, area of discussion. Organizations of different cultural types—for example, the academies, baseball teams, clubs, and fortresses—can offer very different career opportunities to their members. Persons whose needs and goals fail to match the opportunities of the prevailing organizational culture may find themselves frustrated and limited in terms of career progress. By the same token, good "matches" between organizational culture and individuals can be a distinct career advantage.

■ **Ethics and Organizational Culture** must be considered in today's demanding times. The ethical climate of an organization is the shared set of understandings about what is correct behavior and how ethical issues will be handled. When properly established, a positive and clear ethical climate can help all organization members make good choices when facing ethical dilemmas. It can give them the confidence to act with the understanding that what they are doing is considered correct and will be supported by the organization.

## KEY TERMS

Corporate Culture
Cultural Symbol
Counterculture
Ethical Climate
Founding Story
Organizational Culture
Organizational Myth
Rite
Ritual
Saga
Shared Meaning
Subcultures

## REVIEW QUESTIONS

1. What is organizational culture? Why is it an important concept for managers to understand?
2. What is the difference between a subculture and a counterculture? Give an example of how each might be found in a large corporation.
3. In what ways can stories, myths, rites, and rituals become important for the creation and maintenance of a strong organizational culture? Give examples to support your answer.
4. What is the relationship between values and organizational culture? Can organizations have values? Please explain.
5. Can a strong culture be a competitive advantage for a business firm? Why or why not?
6. What can a new top manager or corporate CEO do to change the culture of an organization?
7. What difference to an individual's career can the culture of an employing organization make? Is it realistic to expect people to choose employment in organizations whose cultures are consistent with their individual needs and goals? Why or why not?
8. How can the ethical climate of an organization affect the behavior of its members? Use examples to support your answer.

## AN OB LIBRARY

Terrence E. Deal and Allen A. Kennedy, *Corporate Cultures* (Reading, MA: Addison-Wesley, 1982).

Susan Albers Mohrman and Thomas G. Cummings, *Self-Designing Organizations* (Reading, MA: Addison-Wesley, 1989).

Peter B. Smith and Mark F. Peterson, *Leadership, Organizations, and Culture* (Newbury Park, CA: Sage, 1988).

Edgar H. Schein, *Organizational Culture and Leadership* (San Francisco: Jossey-Bass, 1985).

James O'Toole, *Vanguard Organizations: Redesigning the Corporate Future* (Garden City, NY: Doubleday & Company, 1985).

EXERCISE

# THE "RATIONAL" ORGANIZATION

## *Objectives*

1. To assess an organization's ethical culture.
2. To understand the importance and relevancy of ethical issues in the modern business world.

## *Total Time*

60 to 75 minutes

## *Procedure*

1. Choose an organization you know.
2. Complete the following questionnaire as candidly as possible regarding that organization.

## *Instrument*[25]

Indicate whether you agree or disagree with each of the following statements about the company you have chosen. Use the rating scale below to represent your answer to what extent the following statements are true about your company.

| | | |
|---|---|---|
| 0 Completely False | 1 Mostly False | 2 Somewhat False |
| 3 Somewhat True | 4 Mostly True | 5 Completely True |

_____ 1. In this company, people are expected to follow their own personal and moral beliefs.
_____ 2. People are expected to do anything to further the company's interests.
_____ 3. In this company, people look out for each other's good.
_____ 4. It is very important here to follow strictly the company's rules and procedures.
_____ 5. In this company, people protect their own interests above all other considerations.
_____ 6. The first consideration is whether a decision violates any law.
_____ 7. Everyone is expected to stick by company rules and procedures.
_____ 8. The most efficient way is always the right way in this company.
_____ 9. Our major consideration is what is best for everyone in the company.
_____ 10. In this company, the law or ethical code of the profession is the major consideration.
_____ 11. It is expected that employees will always do what is right for the customer and the public.

3. Score your responses to the above statements by adding your totals on the grid below.

| | LEVELS OF ANALYSIS | | |
|---|---|---|---|
| | INDIVIDUAL | LOCAL | COSMOPOLITAN |
| EGOISM | Self-Interest<br>#5 Score ______ | Company Profit<br>#2 Score ______ | Efficiency<br>#8 Score ______ |
| ETHICAL CRITERIA BENEVOLENCE | Friendship<br>#3 Score ______ | Team Interest<br>#9 Score ______ | Social Responsibility<br>#11 Score ______ |
| PRINCIPLE | Personal Morality<br>#1 Score ______ | Rules and Standard Operating Procedures<br>#4 + #7 Score ______ | Laws and Professional Codes<br>#6 + #10 Score ______ |

4. In groups of three to five compare your results and share your reactions to the findings. Which of the criteria or levels of analysis do you believe is most revealing of your company?
5. Await further instruction from your instructor.

## CASE

# QUALITY PROBLEMS AT NIPPON ELECTRIC CORPORATION (NEC)

As the slow freight rumbled in front of her path to the plant, Izumi Koyo was getting frustrated.[19] Her group was in charge of the delicate machines used to produce semiconductors and their defect rate was far above that of other Nippon Electric Corporation (NEC) plants. Their group must be at fault and the fault must be corrected. Would this slow freight make her late to the early morning meeting the group had called to discuss the defect problem?

Izumi wondered if the vibration of the shaking train could be affecting the group's delicate machinery. Even though she could not feel the vibration in the plant, she decided to report her idea to the group. At the meeting, everyone was quite skeptical of Izumi's belief that the train vibration was the root cause of their defect problem. She was in the middle of the explanation when Shoichi Sango, the plant manager, joined the group. Immediately, Izumi bowed and formally greeted Sangosan. While the supervisor asked Sangosan to speak, Shoichi returned the bow and asked Izumi to continue. Izumi almost began to shake as if the train were passing, but with great courage she outlined her idea.

Shoichi Sango's response was immediate, "That could be it. But how could we be sure, and what could be done?" Yoshi Mauri, the senior worker, first suggested that the group could carefully monitor the timing of the defects and the passing of the trains. The group agreed Izumi should get the honor of making all the calculations. A few days of careful monitoring showed that the defects always occurred when a freight train was passing.

The group asked for the assistance of Motofusa Ito, a graduate of Tokyo University and well known within the plant as one of the best problem solvers in the firm. The supervisor was able to contact an old friend in Ito's group and Motofusa proposed digging a trench between the plant and the track and filling it with water. Itosan called an old friend from Tokyo University that was a retiree from NEC and now heading a small construction firm. Within two days the trench was completed and and filled with water.

Now that the defect rate problem was solved, Izumi's group turned to the challenge of increasing the production rate by five percent.

### *Questions*

1. How would you describe the organizational culture at NEC? Specifically, what observable aspects of culture do you see in this case, and what shared values?
2. How would you describe the subculture within Itosan's group? Would you consider this subculture as supporting or inhibiting NEC's competitive advantage in the marketplace? Why?
3. If this is a typical incident at NEC, what career implications might you derive from the case? In particular, do you note any special implications for a woman seeking to advance steadily up the corporate ladder? Please explain?

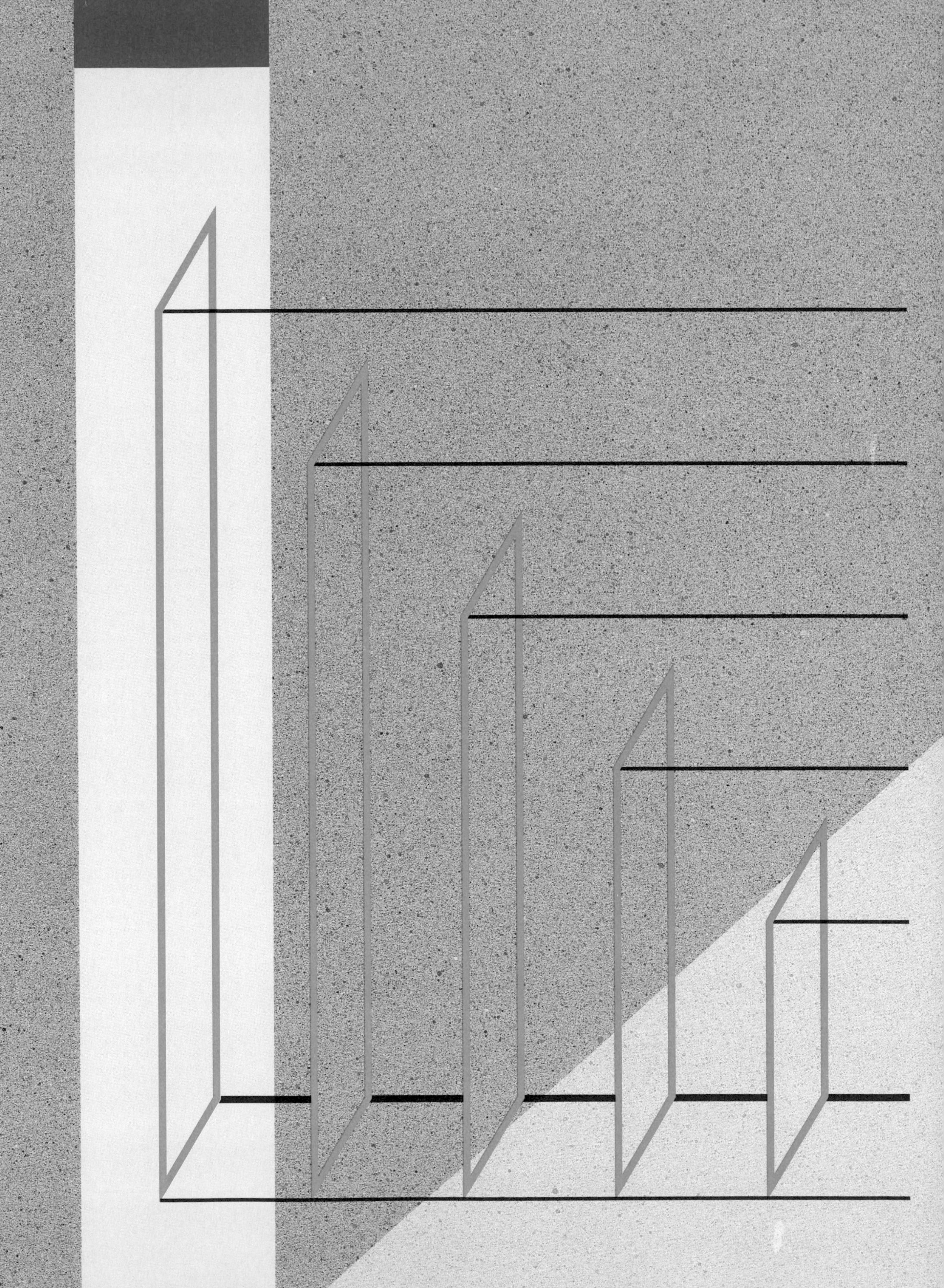

PART FIVE

# MANAGING THE PROCESSES OF ORGANIZATIONAL BEHAVIOR

This study outline of major topics is meant to organize your reading now; it is repeated in the Summary to structure your review.

## STUDY OUTLINE

### Decision Making in Organizations

Decision Environments of Managers   Types of Decisions Made by Managers
Ethical Aspects of Decision Making

### Intuition and Judgment in Managerial Decision Making

The Role of Intuition   Judgmental Heuristics   Escalating Commitments
Creativity Enhancement

### Managerial Issues in Decision Making

Deciding *to* Decide   Deciding *how* to Decide   Deciding *who* Should Decide
Managing Participation in Decision Making

# CHAPTER 13

# DECISION MAKING AND NEGOTIATION



## PHOTO ESSAYS

# VISIONS 13

Affirmative action has been around quite awhile now. But at Avon, a change in policies and practices in the mid-1980s brought a new vision to the program. Although minorities were being hired into the firm, they weren't advancing very fast. Marcia Worthing, corporate vice-president for human resources, says: "We really wanted to get out of the numbers game. We felt it was more important to have five minority people tied into the decision-making process than ten who were just heads to count."

Getting minorities involved in decision making was the goal. But to accomplish this goal, Worthing says: "We had to do more than change behavior. We had to change attitudes." Awareness training for managers at all levels was started. A Multicultural Participation Council was formed to oversee the firm's management of diversity program. Special networks were formed across the organization to help members of minority groups help one another, and provide advice to higher management on decisions relating to minority affairs. And at Avon, racially and ethnically diverse groups of managers meet regularly for three weeks of training designed to—as one executive says—help everyone come away as "disciples of diversity." These are Avon's new decision makers.

Organizations run on decisions made by managers and other persons who work in them. The quality of these decisions influences the longer-term success or failure of an organization, and the day-to-day "character" of the organization . . . in the eyes of employees, customers, and society at large. The commitment of Avon's senior management to improved opportunities for an increasingly diverse workforce, is but one example of the type of decisions which determine an organization's true potential in today's dynamic work environment.

## DECISION MAKING IN ORGANIZATIONS

**Decision making**

Formally defined, ***decision making*** is the process of choosing a course of action for dealing with a problem or opportunity.[1] The five basic steps in systematic decision making are:

1. Recognize and define the problem or opportunity.
2. Identify and analyze alternative courses of action.

3. Choose a preferred course of action.
4. Implement the preferred course of action.
5. Evaluate results and follow up as necessary.

Decision making in organizations takes place under various conditions and circumstances that make the process especially challenging. Here we will examine alternative environments for managerial decision making, the various types of decisions made by managers, and ethical aspects of decision making.

## Decision Environments of Managers

Problem-solving decisions in organizations are typically made under three different conditions or environments: certain, risk, and uncertain.[2] ***Certain environments*** occur when information is sufficient to predict the results of each alternative in advance of implementation. When one invests money in a savings account, absolute certainty exists about the interest that will be earned on that money in a given period of time. Certainty is an ideal condition for managerial problem solving and decision making. The challenge is simply to locate the alternative offering a satisfactory or even ideal solution. Unfortunately, certainty is the exception instead of the rule in managerial decision environments.

Certain environments

***Risk environments*** involve a lack of complete certainty regarding the outcomes of various courses of action, but some awareness of the probabilities associated with their occurrence. A ***probability,*** in turn, is the degree of likelihood that an event will occur. Probabilities can be assigned through objective statistical procedures or through managerial intuition. Statistical estimates of quality rejects in production runs can be made; a senior production manager, on the other hand, can make similar estimates based on past experience. Risk is a fairly common decision environment faced by managers.

Risk environments

***Uncertain environments*** exist when managers are unable to assign probabilities to the outcomes of various problem-solving alternatives. This is the most difficult of the three decision environments. Uncertainty forces managers to rely heavily on individual and group creativity to succeed in problem solving. It requires unique, novel, and often totally innovative alternatives to existing patterns of behavior. Responses to uncertainty are often heavily influenced by intuition, educated guesses, and hunches, all of which are heavily influenced by perception.

Uncertain environments

## Types of Decisions Made by Managers

The two basic types of managerial decisions apply to the presence of both routine and nonroutine problems in the work situation. ***Routine problems*** arise on a regular basis and can be addressed through standard responses. Called ***programmed decisions,*** these responses simply implement solutions already determined by past experience as appropriate for the problem at hand. Examples of programmed decisions are to reorder inventory automatically when stock falls below a predetermined level and to issue a written reprimand to someone who violates a certain personnel procedure.

Routine problems

Programmed decisions

**Nonroutine problems**

**Crafted decisions**

***Nonroutine problems*** are unique and new. Because standard responses are not available, they call for creative problem solving. These ***crafted decisions*** are specifically tailored to the situation at hand. Higher-level managers generally spend a greater proportion of their decision-making time on nonroutine problems. An example is the marketing manager faced with the problem of distributing a limited advertising budget between two important products. Although past experience may help, the immediate decision requires a solution based on the unique characteristics of the present market situation.

## Ethical Aspects of Decision Making

**Ethical dilemma**

The subject of managerial ethics cannot be overemphasized. Thus, it is appropriate to review once again the framework for ethical decision making first introduced in Chapter 1. If you recall, we defined an ***ethical dilemma*** as a situation in which a person must decide whether or not to do something that, although benefiting oneself or the organization, may be considered unethical and perhaps illegal. Most typically, ethical dilemmas involve risk and uncertainty, and nonroutine problem situations. Just how you handle the ones that will inevitably appear in your career may well be the ultimate test of your personal ethical framework. Consider this short case.[3]

> You are a new financial analyst for a small project engineering firm. Your job is to analyze competitive proposals for the electrical portion of a construction project supervised by your firm. Three have been received so far, and one is clearly the best. Your boss's assistant puts a copy of this proposal in an envelope and tells you to hand carry it to a "friend" of the boss's who runs an electrical contracting business. "He always gets a chance to look at the other bids before submitting one himself," the assistant says. Your boss is out of town for the next two days. *What should you do?*

What follows is a useful *seven-step decision making checklist for resolving ethical dilemmas* such as the one found in the prior case:[4]

1. Recognize and clarify the dilemma.
2. Get all possible facts.
3. List your options—all of them.
4. Test each option by asking: "Is it legal? Is it right? Is it beneficial?"
5. Make your decision.
6. Double check your decision by asking: "How would I feel if my family found out about this? How would I feel if my decision was printed in the local newspaper?"
7. Take action.

Remember, too, that people in organizations all too frequently use after-the-fact rationalizations to "excuse" or "explain" *un*ethical behavior. The common rationalizations to be guarded against include:[5]

- Pretending the behavior is not really unethical or illegal.

ETHICAL PERSPECTIVE

## THE KROGER COMPANY

Courtesy of the Kroger Co.

**Food safety is on everyone's minds these days. Like other supermarket chains, Kroger is concerned. But the company's commitment to food quality for customers goes beyond legal requirements alone. By using dependable suppliers, outside laboratories to test samples, and efforts to promote natural techniques for pest-free growing, the firm strives in everyday decision making to keep the customer's health and safety at the forefront of its concerns—just as they stand at the front of the customers' concerns.**

- Excusing the behavior by saying it's really in the organization's or your best interests.
- Assuming the behavior is acceptable because no one else would ever find out about it.
- Expecting your superiors to support and protect you if anything should go wrong.

# INTUITION AND JUDGMENT IN MANAGERIAL DECISION MAKING

This really happened.[6]

> Six teams of business-school students came from all over the country to participate in a contest as guests of General Foods Corporation. They were each secluded in a Connecticut hotel and given this task: create a marketing plan to stop the steeply declining sales of Sugar-Free Kool-Aid. The students worked for a full day. Then, neatly attired in dark business suits, they logically and articulately presented their solutions to the company's very real problem.
>
> The University of Pennsylvania team wanted to promote the product to young teens as well as to children, its existing target

market; Northwestern's wanted to target parents and stress increased parent–child interaction as a result of drinking the same beverage; Columbia's also wanted to promote the product as a "great drink for the whole family"; the University of Chicago's wanted to change the packaging to a cardboard container that could be filled with water; and Stanford's suggested developing a new low-calorie product to be called Super Kool that would serve the teen market. The University of Michigan team won with a plan to target adults and change part of the product label from "sugar-free" to "low-calorie."

These results, however, didn't really impress the judges who were from General Foods, advertising agencies, and a consulting firm. "There were a couple of ideas that were of interest," said a marketing manager, "but nothing we haven't looked at before." In fact, what was most striking about the presentations was their similarity . . . and their lack of originality. The marketing manager summed it up this way: Business schools "deal with the left side of the brain—with analysis and facts, but they don't help people much to use the other side, which is judging and intuitive."

## The Role of Intuition

A debate among scholars regarding how managers really plan nicely introduces the importance of intuition to our current discussion. On one side of the issue are those who believe planning can be taught and done in a systematic step-by-step fashion. On the other side are those who believe the very nature of managerial work makes this hard to do in actual practice. The ideas of Henry Mintzberg, whose research on managerial behavior was first introduced in Chapter 1, are illustrative here. He argues as follows.[7]

- *Managers favor verbal communications.* Thus, they are more likely to gather data and make decisions in a relational or interactive way, than in a systematic step-by-step fashion.
- *Managers often deal with impressions.* Thus, they are more likely to synthesize than analyze data as they search for the "big picture" in order to make decisions.
- *Managers work fast, do a variety of things, and are frequently interrupted.* Thus, they do not have a lot of quiet time alone to think, plan, or make decisions systematically.

**Intuition**

This reasoning leads Mintzberg and others to stress the role of personal "hunch" and "judgment" in managerial decision making. A key element is ***intuition,*** or the ability to know or recognize quickly and readily the possibilities of a situation.[8] Intuition adds an element of spontaneity to managerial decision making, and it offers the potential for greater creativity and innovation as a result. Especially in risk and uncertain environments, successful managers are probably using a good deal of intuition in problem solving. It is a way of dealing with situations where precedents are unclear, "facts" are limited or tenuous, and time is of the essence.

*TABLE 13.1*
**SUGGESTED WAYS TO ACTIVATE YOUR INTUITION**

*Relaxation Techniques*
- Drop the problem for a while
- Take some quiet time by yourself.
- Try to clear your mind.

*Mental Exercises*
- Use images to guide your thinking.
- Let your ideas run without a specific goal in mind.
- Practice accepting ambiguity and lack of total control.

*Analytical Exercises*
- Discuss problems with people having different viewpoints.
- Address problems at times of maximum personal alertness.
- Take creative pauses before making final decisions.

*Source:* Developed from Weston H. Agor, "How Top Executives Use Their Intuition to Make Important Decisions," *Business Horizons,* Vol. 29 (January–February 1986), pp. 49–53; see also Weston H. Agor, *Intuition in Organizations* (Newbury Park, CA: Sage, 1989).

One criticism of the MBA teams in the earlier example, in fact, was their lack of imagination in dealing with the Kool-Aid problem. Although very systematic and logical in their approaches, they were not very creative. Many executives argue that these students and others like them need help during their years of formal education to better develop their intuitive skills. A major and still lingering question at this point in time relates to how this can be done best. Suggestions like those listed in Table 13.1 should be considered as only a first-step toward developing your intuitive skills.

## Judgmental Heuristics

*Judgment,* or the use of one's intellect, is important in all aspects of decision making. When we question the ethics of a decision, for example, we are questioning the "judgment" of the person making it. Research shows that managers and other people are prone to make systematic errors and display biases that can interfere with the quality of any decisions made.[9] These biases trace to the use of ***heuristics,*** which are simplifying strategies or "rules of thumb" used to make decisions. They can make it easier for managers to deal with uncertainty and limited information, and prove helpful on certain occasions. But, they can also lead to systematic errors that affect the quality, and perhaps ethics, of any decisions made.

**Heuristics**

Any decision maker should be aware of three common judgmental heuristics. They are listed here along with an example of how each could bias managerial decision making.[10]

**Availability heuristic**

1. ***Availability heuristic.*** Assessing an event based on past occurrences that are easily available in one's memory. An example is the product manager who bases a decision *not* to fund a new product based on her recollection of the recent failure of a similar product. In this case, the existence of a past product failure has negatively, and perhaps inappropriately, biased the manager's judgment of the new product.

**Representativeness heuristic**

2. ***Representativeness heuristic.*** Assessing the likelihood of an event occurring based on the similarity of that event to one's stereotypes of similar occurrences. An example is the supervisor who hires a new employee not because of any special personal qualities, but only because that individual has a degree from a university known to have produced high-performers in the past. In this case, it is the individual's *alma mater* and not the individual's job qualifications that are the basis for a hiring decision.

**Anchoring and adjustment heuristic**

3. ***Anchoring and adjustment heuristic.*** Assessing an event by taking an initial value from historical precedent or other outside sources, and then incrementally adjusting it to make subsequent assessments. An example is the manager who arrives at salary increase recommendations for personnel by making adjustments to their base salary. In this case, the existing base salary becomes an "anchor" that affects subsequent salary increases.

In addition to using these judgmental heuristics, managers are prone to two more general biases in decision making. First is the *confirmation trap,* in which one seeks confirmation for what is already thought to be true and neglects opportunities to look for disconfirming information. Second is the *hindsight trap,* in which one overestimates the degree to which they really could have predicted an event that has already taken place.

## Escalating Commitments

**Escalating commitment**

Social psychologists recognize another common and potentially dysfunctional tendency of many decision makers. Called ***escalating commitment,*** this is the tendency for people to continue with a previously chosen course of action even though feedback indicates that it is not working.[11] For example,

> ***Compaq Computer Corporation*** Creativity and innovation are pursued at Compaq through effective decision making that doesn't accept the old ways as always being the right ways. Says CEO Rod Canion: "We're testing ideas, getting people to think in a different way, and asking questions. We're looking for the assumptions that aren't justified . . . It comes to the point where the more traditional a thing is the more you question it. If it's traditional, maybe you're just accepting it without really testing it."

Escalating commitment is encouraged by the popular adage, "If at first you don't succeed, try, try, again." Current wisdom in OB supports an alternative view represented in this quote attributed to the late W. C. Fields: "If at first you don't succeed, try, try, again. Then quit. No use being a damn fool about it."

Good decision makers know when to call it quits. They are willing to reverse previous decisions and commitments, and thereby avoid further investments in unsuccessful courses of action. The self-discipline required to admit mistakes and do this, however, is sometimes difficult to achieve. Often, the tendency to escalate commitments to previously chosen courses of action outweighs the willingness to disengage from them. This occurs as decision makers:[12]

- Rationalize negative feedback as simply a temporary condition.
- Protect their egos to avoid admitting the original decision was mistaken.
- Use the decision as a way of managing the impressions of others—such as a boss or peers.
- View the negative results as a "learning experience" that can be overcome with added future effort.

Escalating commitments are a form of decision entrapment that leads people to do things that are not justified based on the facts of the situation. Managers should be proactive in spotting "failures" and open to reversing decisions or dropping plans that don't appear to be working. For example,

> *Proctor & Gamble* Past decisions at Proctor & Gamble are being reconsidered in light of public concerns for more "environmentally friendly" products, as is the case at many other companies. Instead of going with more polyethelene jugs, P&G not too long ago switched to cardboard packaging for its Downy Refill.

Five guidelines for avoiding escalating commitments to previously chosen courses of action are:[13]

1. Try to set limits on your commitment to a decision ahead of time, and then stick to them.
2. Don't look at what others are doing as a cue to what you should be doing.
3. Stop to periodically assess exactly why you are continuing with a course of action.
4. Stop occasionally to accurately identify what it will cost to continue with a course of action.
5. Stay vigilant to avoid "creeping" commitments to previously chosen courses of action.

## Creativity Enhancement

Creativity

***Creativity*** in decision making involves the development of unique and novel responses to problems and opportunities of the moment. In a complex and dynamic environment, creativity in making "crafted decisions" often determines how well organizations and their members respond to important challenges. In Chapter 9 we pointed out that the group is an important resource for improving creativity in decision making. Indeed, managers who make good use of such techniques as brainstorming, nominal groups, and the Delphi method can greatly expand their creative potential. Here we look more specifically at the decision making implications of these four stages of creative thinking:[14]

1. *Preparation and problem definition*—Choosing good problems to solve and then framing them broadly to allow consideration of as many alternatives as possible.

SKILLS PERSPECTIVE

## NIKE

**What kid wants to be caught without a pair of Nike "Air Jordans" these days? Probably not many. But there are at least a few people who wish they'd never heard of them—Nike's competitors in the athletic shoe and apparel market. Nike—a company whose roots can be traced to a college term paper written by cofounder Phil Knight—has recently regained its position as industry leader with sales of $1.7 billion. Because an ability to anticipate and respond to shifting consumer taste is a key factor in its success, Nike places a premium on creativity and strong decision making. The company operates on the belief that "creative people need to work in a free, imaginative environment." Flexibility, creativity, loyalty, intensity, experience, and teamwork are the watchwords as Nike continually strives for success in response to a volatile marketplace.**

Courtesy of Nike, Inc.

2. *Incubation*—Looking at problems in diverse ways that allow for the consideration of unusual alternatives; avoiding tendencies toward purely linear and systematic problem solving.
3. *Illumination*—Responding to flashes of insight and recognizing when, "aha," all pieces to the puzzle suddenly fit into place.
4. *Verification*—Avoiding the tendency to relax after illumination occurs and, instead, proceeding with logical analysis to confirm that good problem-solving decisions have really been made.

The creative process in managerial decision making can be limited by a number of factors. *Judgmental heuristics*—like the availability, representativeness, and anchoring/adjustment heuristics just reviewed—can limit the search for alternatives in decision making. When attractive alternatives are left unconsidered, creativity can be limited. Tendencies toward *escalating commitments* also inhibit creativity. They tend to restrict future action possibilities to those in close proximity to ones already in place. Potentially creative responses may be foregone in deference to the continuation of existing courses of action. *Cultural and environmental blocks* can also limit creativity. This occurs when people are discouraged from considering alternatives that might be viewed as inappropriate by cultural standards or inconsistent with prevailing norms.

# MANAGERIAL ISSUES IN DECISION MAKING

Managers working at all levels, in all areas, and in all types and sizes of organizations aren't supposed to just make decisions. They are supposed to make *good* ones. Sometimes this means being willing to override previous commitments and discontinue a course of action that just isn't working out the way it should. Frequently, it means crafting a creative solution to a nonroutine problem. In all cases, successful managers make the right decisions in the right way at the right time. When it comes to managing the decision making process, we can say that an effective manager is one able to answer the following three questions for each and every problem situation he or she encounters.

1. Is a decision really required?
2. How should the decision be made?
3. Who should be involved in the decision?

## Deciding *to* Decide

Managers are too busy and have too many valuable things to do with their time to respond personally by making decisions on every problem or opportunity that comes their way. The effective manager knows when to delegate decisions to others, how to set priorities, and when not to act at all. When confronted with a problem, therefore, it is recommended that managers ask themselves the following questions.[15]

- *Is the problem easy to deal with?* Small and less significant problems should not get as much time and attention as bigger ones. Even if a mistake is made, the cost of decision error on small problems is also small.
- *Might the problem resolve itself?* Putting problems in rank order leaves the less significant for last . . . if any time remains. Surprisingly, many of these will resolve themselves or be solved by others before the manager gets to them. One less problem to solve leaves decision making time and energy for other uses.
- *Is this my decision to make?* Many problems can be handled by persons at lower levels in the hierarchy. These decisions should be delegated. Other problems can and should be referred to higher levels. This is especially true for decisions that have consequences for a larger part of the organization than under a manager's immediate control.

## Deciding *How* to Decide

OB theorists recognize the *two* alternative approaches to decision making shown in Figure 13.1—classical and behavioral. A discussion of each will help you to understand further the processes through which managers can and do make decisions.[16]

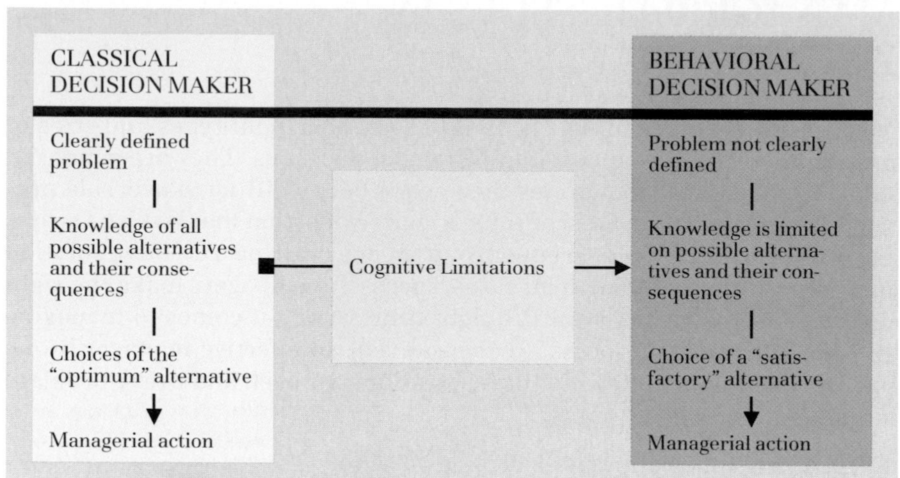


*FIGURE 13.1 Managerial decision making viewed from the classical and behavioral perspectives.*

## Classical Decision Theory

Classical decision theory

***Classical decision theory*** views the manager as acting in a world of complete certainty. The manager faces a clearly defined problem, knows all possible action alternatives and their consequences, and then chooses the alternative giving the best or "optimum" resolution of the problem. Clearly, this is an ideal way to make decisions. Classical theory is often used as a model for how managers *should* make decisions.

Behavioral scientists are cautious regarding classical decision theory. They recognize that the human mind is a wonderful creation, capable of infinite achievements. But they also recognize that we each have cognitive limitations. The human mind is limited in its information processing capabilities. Information deficiencies and overload both compromise the ability of managers to make decisions according to the classical model. As a result, it is argued that behavioral decision theory gives a more accurate description of how people make decisions in actual practice.

## Behavioral Decision Theory

Behavioral decision theory

***Behavioral decision theory*** says that people act only in terms of what they perceive about a given situation. Furthermore, such perceptions are frequently imperfect. Rather than facing a world of complete certainty, the behavioral decision maker is seen as acting under uncertainty and with limited information. Managers make decisions about problems that are often ambiguous; they have only a partial knowledge about the available action alternatives and their consequences; and, they choose the first alternative that appears to give a satisfactory resolution of the problem. This is referred to by Herbert Simon as a ***satisficing*** style of decision making. Simon and a colleague state:[17]

Satisficing

> Most human decision making, whether individual or organizational, is concerned with the discovery and selection of satisfactory alternatives; only in exceptional cases is it concerned with the discovery and selection of optimal decisions.

The key difference between a manager's ability to make an optimum decision in the classical style and the tendency to make a satisfying decision in the behavioral style is the presence of cognitive limitations and their impact on our perceptions. Cognitive limitations impair our abilities to define problems, identify action alternatives, and choose alternatives with ideal and predictable consequences.

## Deciding *Who* Should Decide

In practice, managers end up making decisions in any and all of the following ways:

- ***Individual decisions.*** The manager makes the final choice alone based on information that he or she possesses, and without the participation of other persons. Sometimes called an *authority decision,* this choice often reflects the manager's position of formal authority in the organization.

  **Individual decisions**

- ***Consultative decisions.*** The manager solicits inputs on the problem from other persons. Based on this information and its interpretation, the manager then makes a final choice.

  **Consultative decisions**

- ***Group decisions.*** The manager not only consults with other persons for information inputs but also asks them to participate in problem-solving discussions and in making the actual choice. Although sometimes difficult, the group decision is the most participative of the three methods of final choice and it seeks true *group consensus.*

  **Group decisions**

Good managers know when *and* how to use each of these methods. The basic goal, of course, is to always make a "good" decision. This is one high in quality, timely, and both understandable and acceptable to those whose support is needed for implementation. Good decisions, furthermore, can be made by each method—individual, consultative, or group—*if* the method fits the needs of the situation. Because each method has assets and liabilities, as shown in Figure 13.2, managers must be skilled at choosing among them when dealing with various problems.

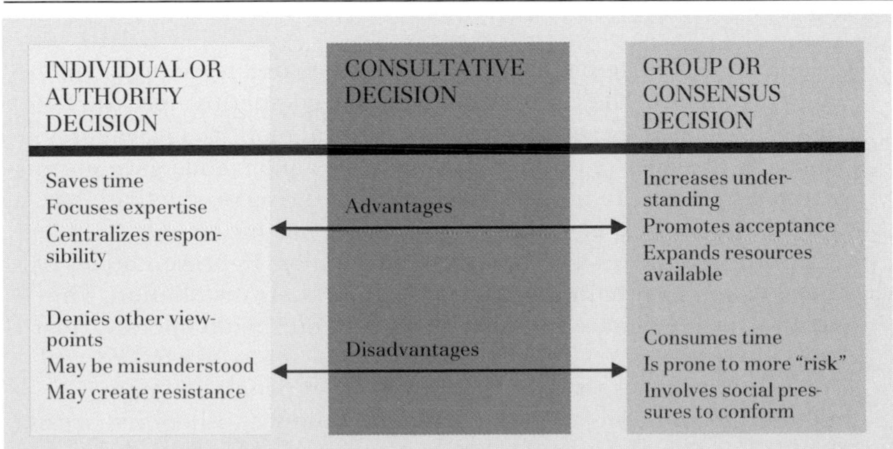


*FIGURE 13.2 A continuum of decision-making methods.*

## Managing Participation in Decision Making

Victor Vroom, along with Phillip Yetton and Arthur Jago, has developed a framework for helping managers choose which of the three decision-making methods is most appropriate for the various problem situations encountered in their daily work efforts.[18] Their framework begins by expanding the three basic decision-making methods into the five forms that follow:

1. AI *(first variant on the authority decision):* Manager solves the problem or makes the decision alone using information available at that time.
2. AII *(second variant on the authority decision):* Manager obtains the necessary information from subordinate(s) or other group members, then decides on the problem solution. The manager may or may not tell subordinates what the problem is before obtaining the information from them. The subordinates provide the necessary information but do not generate or evaluate alternatives.
3. CI *(first variant on the consultative decision):* Manager shares the problem with relevant subordinates or other group members individually, getting their ideas and suggestions without bringing them together as a group. The manager then makes a decision that may or may not reflect subordinates' influence.
4. CII *(second variant on the consultative decision):* Manager shares the problem with subordinates or other group members, collectively obtaining their ideas and suggestions. The manager then makes the decision that may or may not reflect subordinates' influence.
5. G *(the group or consensus decision):* Manager shares the problem with subordinates as a total group and engages the group in consensus seeking to arrive at a final decision.

The central proposition in the latest version—the Vroom and Jago model—is that the decision-making method used should always be appropriate to the problem being solved. The task is to know when and how to implement each of the possible decision methods as the situation requires. Consider how you would make a decision as the manager in this short case.[19]

> Nelida Lopez is vice-president for operations in a large high-technology company. The firm has been under competitive pressure to reduce costs and increase efficiency. Several months ago, the manufacturing manager requested new machines and Nelida gave permission to buy them. To her surprise, manufacturing productivity has not increased, whereas employee turnover has increased.
>
> Nothing appears wrong with the machines. Representatives of the company that built them have checked their installation. They say the machines were properly installed and should operate "just fine."
>
> Nelida suspects that changes in the ways people are now required to work might be the problem. But most other vice-presidents as well as the manufacturing manager and his first-line managers do not share this view. They think that production has

Courtesy of Phillips Petroleum Company.

## INTERNATIONAL PERSPECTIVE

# PHILLIPS PETROLEUM

**From the oilfields of Egypt to the North Sea and beyond, Phillips Petroleum Company has a long-term commitment to find capable people to staff its many operations. In today's fast-paced international oil industry, management styles are changing and the requirements for teamwork are being felt around the world. The company strives to have decisions made at lower levels where people have access to facts and know the work to be done. It strives to make more and more decisions at field locations and for fewer ones to find their ways to senior management. And through its Participative Action Teams, Phillips is trying to help employees motivate and support one another while solving business and technical problems.**

declined because of poor training, lack of financial incentives to increase production, and low morale. These are issues that affect the operation of the entire plant and over which Nelida and the others might be expected to disagree.

The president has just called Nelida into her office. She is displeased with the production figures for the last three months and asks Nelida to "get to the bottom of the work problem quickly." Both the quality and quantity of work have declined since the new machines were installed and the president indicates that the problem is Nelida's to solve.

Nelida shares the president's concern and knows that the manufacturing manager and his first-line managers are also upset. Nelida's problem is to decide what to do to correct the situation.

Vroom and Jago use the flowchart in Figure 13.3 to help managers analyze the unique attributes of a situation and choose a decision method most appropriate for the problem at hand. Key issues involve the quality

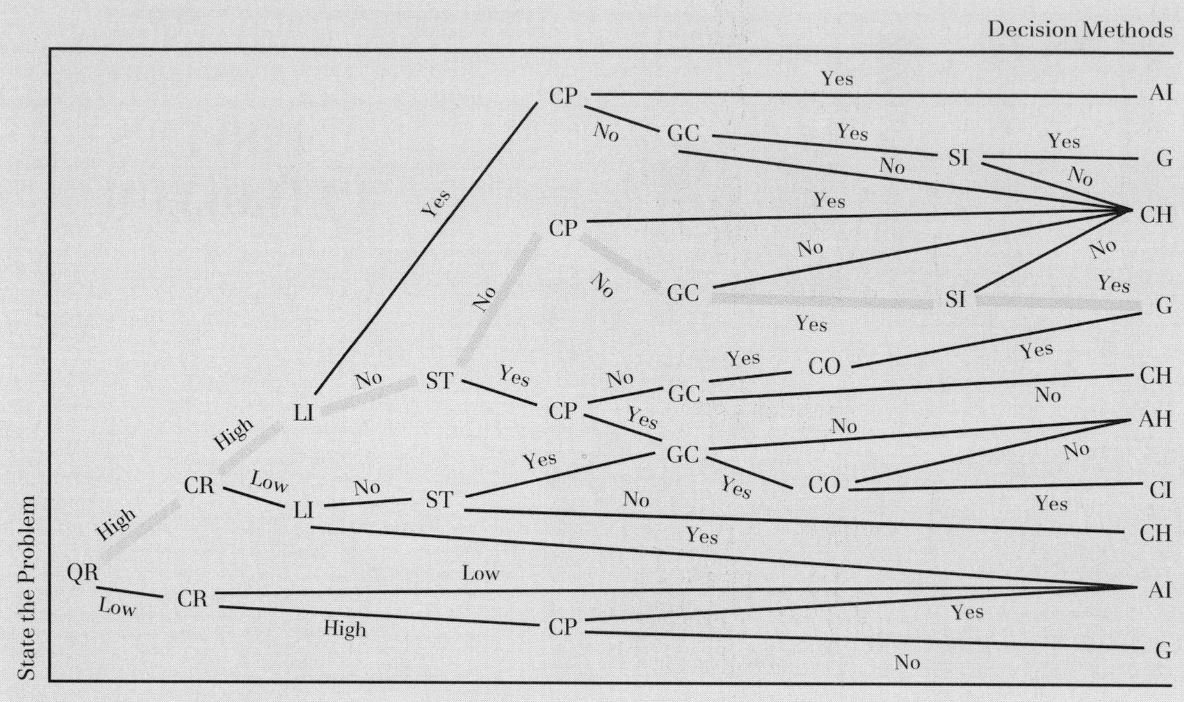


| Problem Attributes | | Manager's Questions |
|---|---|---|
| QR | Quality requirement | How important is the technical quality of this decision? |
| CR | Commitment requirement | How important is subordinate commitment to the decision? |
| LI | Leader's information | Do you have sufficient information to make a high-quality decision? |
| ST | Problem structure | Is the problem well structured? |
| CP | Commitment probability | If you were to make the decision by yourself, is it reasonably certain that your subordinate(s) would be committed to the decision? |
| GC | Goal congruence | Do subordinates share the organizational goals to be attained in solving this problem? |
| CO | Subordinate conflict | Is conflict among subordinates over preferred solutions likely? |
| SI | Subordinate information | Do subordinates have sufficient information to make a high-quality decision? |

*FIGURE 13.3 Selecting alternative decision-making methods: The Vroom and Jago decision process flow chart. (Source:* Reprinted from Victor H. Vroom and Arthur G. Jago, *The New Leadership* (Englewood Cliffs, NJ: Prentice-Hall, 1988), p. 184. Used by permission of the authors.)

requirements of a decision, the availability and location of the relevant information, the commitments needed for follow-through, and the amount of time available. In the present case, the darkened line in the figure indicates the problem is best handled via a "G" or group-decision method. That is, most managers should share the problem with subordinates and facilitate consensus decision.

The Vroom and Jago model shown in the figure seems complex and cumbersome. We agree, and certainly do not expect you to work through this figure for every problem faced. Yet there is a very useful discipline in the model. It helps you recognize how time, quality requirements, information availability, and subordinate acceptance issues can affect decision outcomes. It also helps you remember that all of the decision methods are important and useful. The key to effectively managing participation in decision making is evident: know how to implement each decision method in situations for which it is most suited, and then do it well.

# NEGOTIATION IN ORGANIZATIONS

Picture yourself trying to make decisions in the following situations. What would you decide to do?

*You* have been offered a new job and would really like to take it. But, the salary is lower than you expected.

*You* have been told by your boss that your merit salary increase for next year will be 5 percent of your base salary. You think you deserve more than that.

*You* are part of a cross-functional corporate task force. There is some possibility it may recommend a staff reduction in your department.

*You* have ordered one new state-of-the-art computer for your department. Two of your subordinates have each said they need the new computer to best do their work.

*You* are meeting with a quality circle active in your department. The group wants to try a new work method that may slow production, but increase quality.

The prior scenarios are but a sampling of *negotiation* situations that involve managers and other people in the workplace. ***Negotiation*** is the process of making joint decisions when the parties involved have different preferences. Stated a bit differently, negotiation can be considered a way of getting what you want from others in the process of making decisions.[20]

**Negotiation**

Negotiation is especially significant in today's work settings where more people are being offered opportunities to be involved in decisions affecting them and their work. As they do get involved, disagreements are likely over diverse matters such as wage rates, task objectives, performance evaluations, job assignments, work schedules, work locations, special privileges, and many other considerations. Since organizations are becoming more and more participative, a manager's familiarity with basic negotiation concepts and processes is increasingly important for dealing with such day-to-day affairs.

## Organizational Settings for Negotiation

Henry Mintzberg includes *negotiator* among the 10 roles performed by managers. In any organization, however, it is useful to recognize that the situations in which managers become involved in negotiations are varied. Figure 13.4 shows that managers should be prepared to participate in at least *four major action settings for negotiations.*

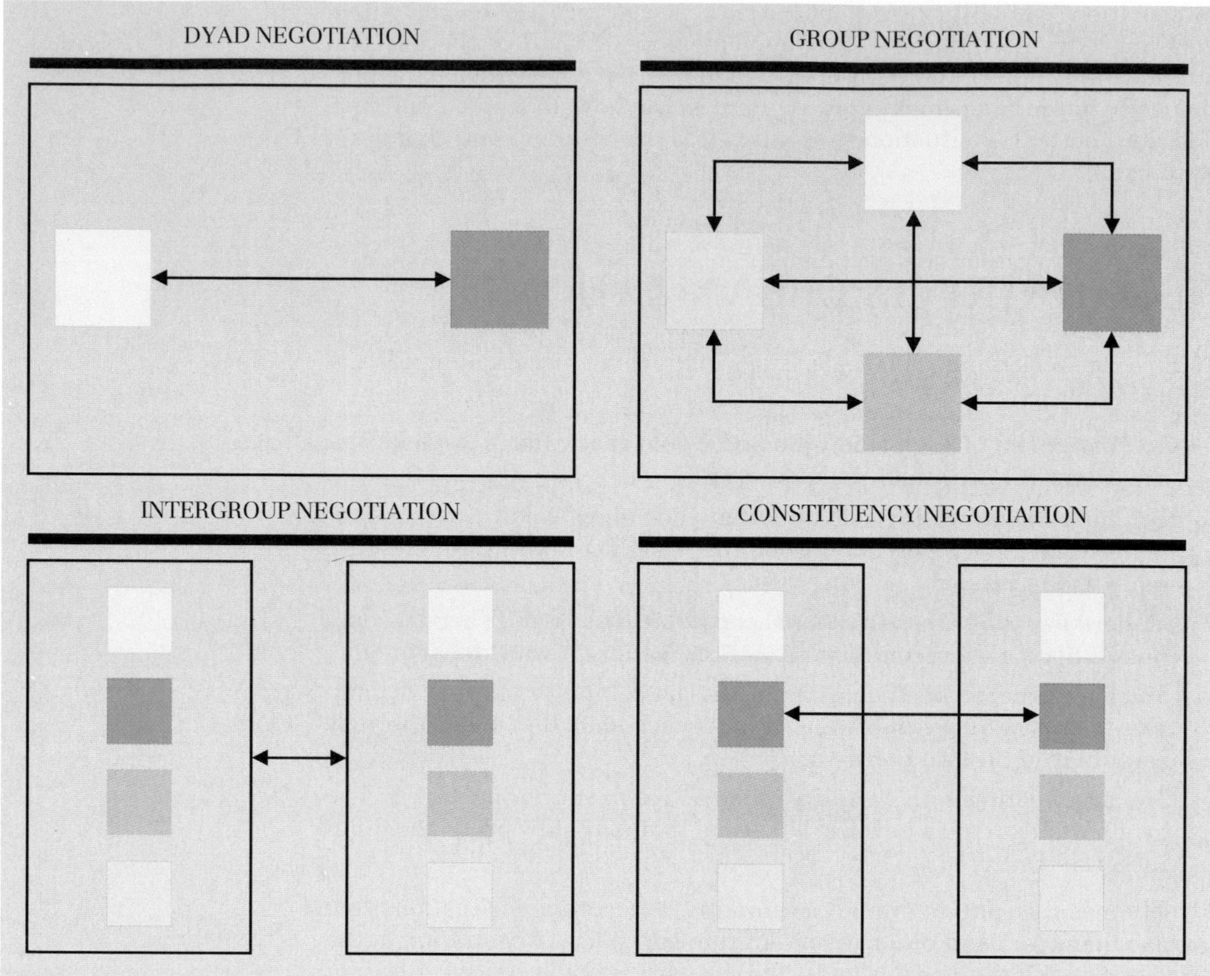


*FIGURE 13.4 Four types of negotiation situations for managers.*

1. *Two-party negotiation*—where the manager is negotiating directly with one other person. An example is the manager negotiating performance objectives with a subordinate.
2. *Group negotiation*—where the manager is part of a team or group whose members are negotiating to arrive at a common decision. An example is a task force that must reach agreement in order to make recommendations to higher management on a specific issue.
3. *Intergroup negotiation*—where the manager is part of a group that is negotiating with another group to arrive at a decision regarding a problem or situation affecting both. An increasingly common example is when management groups from two firms negotiate with one another to form a joint venture or strategic alliance.
4. *Constituency negotiation*—where the manager is involved in negotiation with other persons, and each individual party—the manager and others—represents a broad constituency. The most recognizable

example is a team representing "management" negotiating with a team representing "labor" to arrive at a collective bargaining agreement.

## Negotiation Goals and Outcomes

Two goals should be considered in any negotiation. ***Substance goals*** in negotiation are concerned with outcomes relative to the "content" issues at hand. ***Relationship goals*** are concerned with outcomes relating to how well people involved in the negotiation are able to work with one another once the process is concluded, and how well any constituencies they may represent are able to work together. Unfortunately, negotiation all too frequently results in a sacrifice of relationships as parties become preoccupied with substance goals and self-interests. ***Effective negotiation,*** by contrast, occurs when *both* substance issues are resolved *and* working relationships are maintained or even improved. Three criteria for identifying effective negotiation are:[21]

**Substance goals**

**Relationship goals**

**Effective negotiation**

1. The negotiation produces a "wise" agreement that is truly satisfactory to all sides.
2. The negotiation is "efficient" and no more time consuming or costly than absolutely necessary.
3. The negotiation is "harmonious" and fosters rather than inhibits good interpersonal relations.

*Impasse* in negotiation occurs when there are no overlapping interests and the parties fail to find common points of agreement. But *agreement* in negotiation can mean different things—and it may be an agreement "for the better" or "for the worse" for either or both parties to the process. Effective negotiation results in overlapping interests and joint decisions that are "for the better" of all parties. The trick is how to get there. Consider this classic example.

> Two people are alone in the reading room of a library. One wants the window open and the other wants it shut. They can't agree, become quite mad at each other, and arrive at a negotiating *impasse.* The observant librarian intervenes and asks each person "why?" they want the window open or closed. As it turns out, the person wanting the window open is seeking fresh air; the one wanting it closed wants to avoid a draft. When the librarian suggests that a window in the adjoining room could be opened to provide the fresh air without creating a draft, both parties are satisfied. The negotiated agreement is "for the better" of each.

## Ethical Aspects of Negotiation

Since any negotiation involves people with different preferences trying to reach a joint decision, ethical behavior is often an issue. Managers, like anyone involved in negotiation, should strive for high ethical standards even while personally involved in compelling negotiations where self-interests are paramount on one's mind. Indeed, the motivation to behave unethically in negotiations is often a function of:[22]

- *The profit motive* or the desire of each party to "get more" than the other from the negotiation.
- *A sense of competition* or belief among negotiating parties that there are insufficient resources to satisfy everyone's needs.
- *Concerns for justice* or the search by each party for outcomes defined as "fair" only from one's self-interested perspective.

When *un*ethical behavior does occur in negotiation, the people involved often try to rationalize or explain it away. This is indicated by comments like these: "It was clearly unavoidable," "Oh, it's harmless," "The results justify the means," or "It's really quite fair." Possible short-run gains from such after-the-fact rationalizations may be offset by long-run negative consequences. At the very least, the unethical party may be the target of "revenge" tactics by those who were disadvantaged. Once some people have behaved unethically in one situation, furthermore, they may become entrapped by such behavior and display it again in future circumstances.[23]

# DIFFERENT APPROACHES TO NEGOTIATION

Let's take another example. It's a simple case that illustrates an important point.

> Two sisters want an orange, but only one is available. They begin to negotiate over the orange.

For our purposes, the "orange" in this case represents any scarce organizational resource. It could be money, time, people, facilities, equipment, and so on. Like the two sisters, managers and other workers frequently negotiate with one another over access to scarce organizational resources. And the approach taken to the negotiation can have a major influence on its outcome. It is useful to discuss two alternatives—distributive negotiation and integrative negotiation.[24]

## Distributive Negotiation

**Distributive negotiation**

In ***distributive negotiation*** the focus is on "positions" staked out or declared by parties who, in turn, are each trying to "claim" certain portions of the available "pie." If we return to the short case, distributive bargaining asks the question: "Who is going to get the orange?"

Distributive negotiation usually unfolds in one of two directions—with neither one nor the other yielding optimal results. *"Hard" distributive negotiation* takes place when each party holds out to get its own way. Here, each party is trying to maximize its self interest. *"Soft" distributive negotiation* takes place when one party is willing to make concessions to the other to get things over with. Here, one party is trying to find ways to accommodate the other's desires. In our case, the "hard" approach

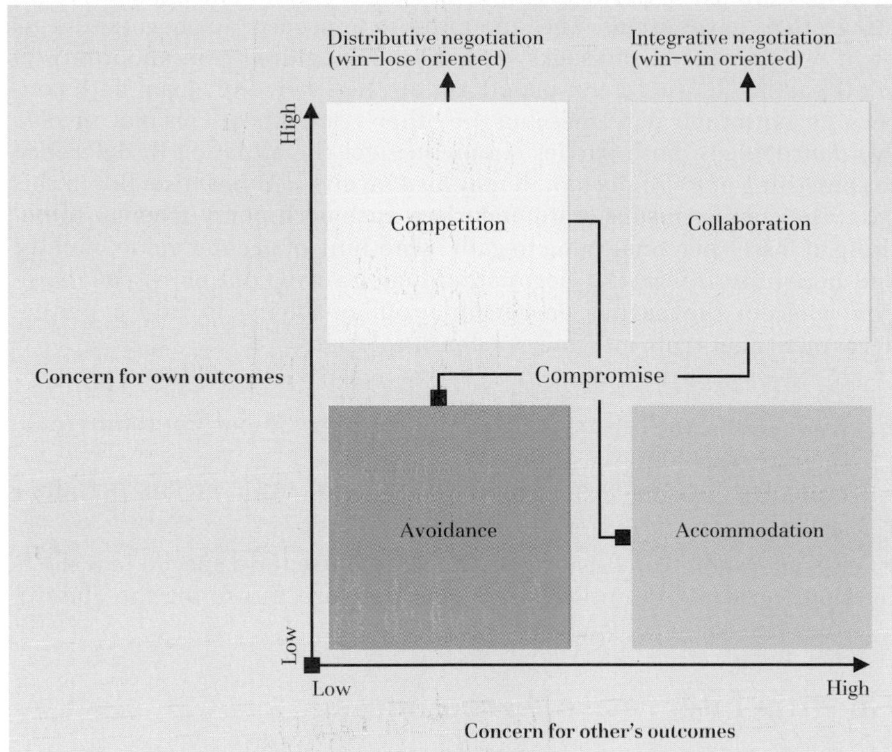


*FIGURE 13.5 Contrasts between the Distributive and Integrative styles of negotiation. (Source:* Suggested by a discussion in Roy J. Lewicki and Joseph A. Litteser, *Negotiation* (Glenview, IL: Irwin, 1985), pp. 103–106.)

may lead to an impasse where no one gets the orange; the "soft" approach may leave at least some latent dissatisfaction with one sister who agrees to give up the orange to the other.

Figure 13.5 depicts distributive negotiation on the unshaded diagonal. It tends to be "win–lose" oriented. A "hard" distributive approach leads to *competition* where each party seeks dominance over the other, whereas a "soft" approach leads to *accommodation* where one party gives in to the other. *Compromise* occurs when each party gives up something of value to reach agreement. Going back to our case, distributive negotiation could lead to:

- *Competition*—one sister takes the whole orange; the other sister gets none of it.
- *Compromise*—each sister gets one-half of the orange, but not as much as she really needs.
- *Accommodation*—one sister gives up and allows the other sister to have the orange.

## Integrative Negotiation

**Integrative negotiation**

In ***integrative negotiation,*** the focus is on the "merits" of the issues and everyone tries to enlarge the available "pie" rather than stake claims to certain portions of it. In the case, integrative negotiation asks the question: "How can the orange best be utilized?"

Figure 13.5 also shows essential differences between distributive and integrative negotiation. The integrative approach to negotiation is "win–win" oriented and seeks ways of satisfying the needs and interests of all parties. In the figure, people act on the shaded diagonal with concern for both their outcomes and the other's outcomes. This may involve *avoidance* where both parties simply neglect the situation in deference to something more important. It may also involve *compromise.* But in this case, the compromise is more enduring since each party gives up something of lesser personal value to gain something of greater value. Finally, and hopefully, integrative negotiation may involve continuing *collaboration* wherein the parties engage in problem-solving to find a mutual agreement that truly maximizes benefit to each.

In the case of the orange, integrative negotiation could lead to:

- *Avoidance*—each sister realizes she has more important things to do than worry about this orange.
- *Compromise*—one sister gets the orange this time, while the other sister gets the orange next time.
- *Collaboration*—one sister gets the skin to use for a special jam she is making, while the other sister gets the core to use for the glass of juice she wants to drink.

## Gaining Integrative Agreements

Some refer to integrative negotiation as *principled negotiation,* or negotiation based on the "merits" of the situation. The foundation for truly integrative agreements rests in three main areas—attitudes, information, and behaviors.[25]

The *attitudinal foundations of integrative agreements* involve each party approaching the negotiation with a willingness to:

- Trust the other party.
- Share information with the other party.
- Ask questions of the other party.

The *information foundations of integrative agreements* involve each party becoming familiar with:

- Their "best alternative to a negotiated agreement" (BATNA)—each must know what they will do if an agreement can't be reached.
- Their personal interests in the situation—each must know what is really important to them in the case at hand.
- The relative importance of the other party's interests—each must understand what the other party values, even to the point of determining their BATNA.

The *behavioral foundations of integrative agreements* involve each party being willing and able to:

- Separate the people from the problem, and not let emotional considerations affect the negotiation.

- Focus on interests and not positions, both one's own and those of the other party.
- Avoid making premature judgments, and keep the acts of alternative creation separate from evaluation.
- Judge possible agreements on an objective set of criteria or standards.

# MANAGERIAL ISSUES IN NEGOTIATION

Given the distinctions between distribute and integrative negotiation, it is appropriate to identify some negotiation issues of special relevance to managers. Specifically, we should consider classic two-party negotiation and individual problems in negotiation.

## Classic Two-Party Negotiation

Figure 13.6 introduces the case of the graduating senior.[26] In this case a graduating senior is negotiating with a corporate recruiter over a job offer. It illustrates the basic elements of classic two-party negotiation in many contexts.

To begin, look at the situation from the graduate's perspective. She has told the recruiter she would like a salary of $45,000—this is her *initial offer.* But she also has in mind a *minimum reservation point* of $35,000—the lowest salary that she will accept for this job. Thus she communicates a salary request of $45,000 but is willing to accept one as low as $35,000. Now, the situation is somewhat reversed from the recruiter's perspective. His *initial offer* to the graduate is $30,000 and his *maximum reservation point* is $40,000. This is the most he is eventually prepared to pay.

**Bargaining zone**

The ***bargaining zone*** is defined as the range between one party's minimum reservation point and the other party's maximum reservation point. In the figure the bargaining zone is $40,000–$45,000. It is a *positive* bargaining zone since the reservation points of the two parties overlap. Whenever a positive bargaining zone exists, bargaining has room to unfold. If the graduate's minimum reservation point was greater than the recrui-

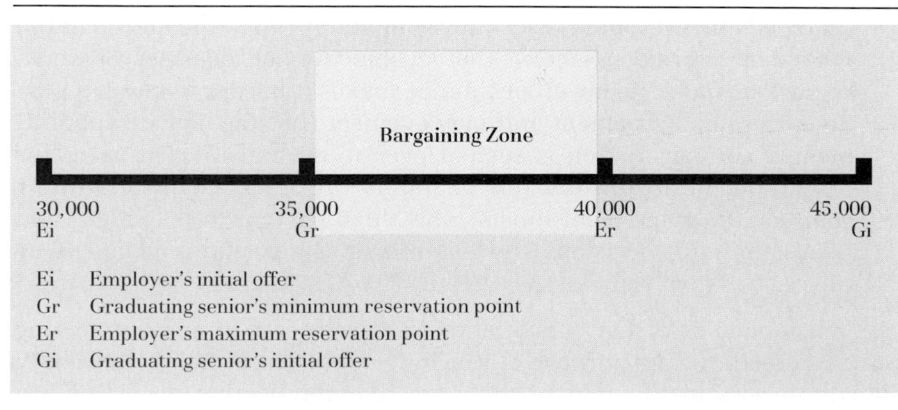


*FIGURE 13.6 Two-party negotiation and the bargaining zone: The case of the graduating senior.*

ter's maximum reservation point (for example, $42,000), no room would exist for bargaining.

Classic two-party bargaining always involves the delicate tasks of first discovering the respective reservation points (one's own and the other's), and then working to an agreement that is somewhere within the resulting bargaining zone and acceptable to each party. Impasse is likely unless each party becomes aware that a positive bargaining zone exists. Given that, the negotiation can proceed with each trying to achieve an agreement that is as close to the other party's reservation point as possible. When judgment errors are made, time and energies can be wasted as the parties fruitlessly pursue positions that are outside the reservation points. If positions are rigidly staked out and held, no negotiated agreement is likely.

## Communication Problems in Negotiation

The negotiation process is admittedly complex, and it is further characterized by all the possible confusions of sometimes volatile interpersonal and group dynamics. Individual negotiators, accordingly, need to guard against some common mistakes. These *negotiator pitfalls* include:[27]

1. *Falling prey to the myth of the "fixed pie"* It is too easy in negotiation to stake out your position based on the assumption that, in order to gain your way, something must be "subtracted" from the other party's way. This is a purely distributive approach to negotiation. The whole concept of integrative negotiation is based on the premise that the "pie" can sometimes be expanded and/or utilized to the maximum advantage of *all* parties, not just one.
2. *Nonrational escalation of conflict* Because parties to negotiations often begin by stating extreme demands, the possibility of escalating commitments is high. Once "demands" have been stated, people become committed to them and reluctant to back down. Concerns for "protecting one's ego" and "saving face" may enhance these tendencies. Self-discipline is needed to spot them in one's own behavior as well as other's.
3. *Overconfidence and ignoring other's needs* It is also common for negotiators to develop the belief that their positions are the only "correct" ones. In some cases they completely fail to see merits in the other party's position—merits that an objective outside observer would be sure to spot. Such overconfidence makes it harder to reach a positive common agreement and may even set the stage for disappointment if the negotiation is turned over to a neutral third-party for resolution. In ***arbitration*** (for example, the salary arbitration now common in professional sports), this third party acts as "judge" and issues a binding decision after listening to the positions advanced by the parties involved in a dispute.

**Arbitration**

It has been said that "negotiation is the process of communicating back and forth for the purpose of reaching a joint decision."[28] As we will shortly discuss in Chapter 14, however, communication problems are common in any organizational situation. In this respect, communication difficulties of two major types can foster negotiation pitfalls and compromise the quality of outcomes. First is the *"telling" problem.* That is, negotiation sometimes breaks down because the parties don't really "talk" to one another—at least in the sense of making themselves truly understood. Second is the "hearing" problem. In this instance, negotiation sometimes breaks down because the parties are unable or unwilling to "listen" well enough to understand what one another is saying. As a brief introduction to what we will be covering in the next chapter, remember that positive negotiation only occurs when:[29]

- Each party frequently asks questions to clarify what the other is saying.
- Each party "actively" listens and uses techniques such as paraphrasing to clarify what the other is saying.
- Each party occasionally "stands in the other party's shoes" and tries to view the situation from that party's perspective.

## SUMMARY

**Decision Making in Organizations is a continuing process of identifying problems and opportunities and then choosing among alternative courses of action for dealing successfully with them. Managers make many decisions in risky and uncertain environments where situations are ambiguous and the available information is limited. Some decisions can be programmed and used over and over again in routine situations. Many others must be created as unique and "crafted" responses to nonroutine situations. Ethical dilemmas are common in decision making in organizations. Dealing successfully with them requires an awareness of personal values and morals, and a special attempt to always ensure that one's decisions do not compromise ethical standards.**

**Judgment in Managerial Decision Making involves the use of cognitive skills to make choices among alternative courses of action. Intuition, the ability to quickly recognize the possibilities of a situation, is increasingly considered an important managerial asset. But judgmental heuristics, or simplifying rules of thumb, can potentially bias decision making. These include the availability, representativeness, and anchoring and adjustment heuristics. Escalating commitment to previously chosen courses of action can also bias decision making, and managers should be willing to call it quits when courses of action are not working. Creativity limitations can be overcome and decision making improved through individual awareness and a good use of groups as problem-solving resources.**

**Managerial Issues in Decision Making begin with differences between classical decision theory—which views managers as seeking "optimum" solutions—and behavioral decision theory—which views them as**

"satisficing" and accepting the first satisfactory alternative to come to mind. Managers must also know how to handle participation in decision making and choose among individual, consultative, and group decision methods. The Vroom–Yetton model identifies how decision methods can be varied to meet the unique needs of each problem situation. Key issues involve quality requirements, information availability, and time constraints.

■ **Negotiation in Organizations** occurs whenever two or more people with different preferences must make joint decisions. Managers may find themselves involved in various types of negotiation situations, including two-party, group, intergroup negotiation, and constituency negotiation. In all cases, both substance goals and relationship goals are at stake. Effective negotiation occurs when issues of substance are resolved and human relationships are maintained or even improved in the process. To achieve such results, ethical conduct must be carefully maintained even as negotiating parties represent viewpoints and preferences that differ greatly from one another.

■ **Different Approaches to Negotiation** can have very different results. In distributive negotiation, the focus of each party is on staking out positions in the attempt to claim desired portions of a "fixed pie." In integrative negotiation, sometimes called principled negotiation, the focus of each party is on determining the merits of the issues and finding ways to satisfy one another's needs. The distributive approach is often associated with individual styles of competition (the "hard" approach) or accommodation (the "soft" approach); the integrative approach ideally leads to some form of "collaboration" to achieve an integrated solution. The success of integrative negotiation depends on the parties being willing and able to communicate positive attitudes, share and obtain relevant information, and separate the "people" issues from the real "problem."

■ **Managerial Issues in Negotiation** include the importance of understanding the "bargaining zone" in two-party situations. This zone represents the overlap between one party's *minimum* reservation point—the "least" they are willing to accept—and the other party's *maximum* reservation point—the "most" they are willing to give. They include the special complexities of negotiation in groups, where complex group and interpersonal dynamics add further difficulties. They also include individual problems caused by misperceptions of negotiators and an inability to communicate well in the negotiation process.

## ▶ KEY TERMS

Anchoring and Adjustment Heuristic
Arbitration
Availability Heuristic
Bargaining Zone
Behavioral Decision Theory
Certain Environments
Classical Decision Theory
Consultative Decisions
Crafted Decisions
Creativity
Decision Making
Distributive Negotiation
Effective Negotiation

Escalating Commitment
Ethical Dilemma
Group Decisions
Heuristics
Individual Decisions
Integrative Negotiation
Intuition
Negotiation
Nonroutine Problems
Programmed Decisions
Relationship Goals
Representativeness Heuristic
Risk Environments
Routine Problems
Satisficing
Substance Goals
Uncertain Environments

## AN OB LIBRARY

Weston H. Agor, *Intuition in Organizations* (Newbury Park, CA: Sage, 1989).

Max H. Bazerman, *Judgment in Managerial Decision Making,* Second Edition (New York: John Wiley & Sons, 1990).

Roger Fisher and William Ury, *Getting to Yes: Negotiating Agreement without Giving In* (New York: Penguin, 1983).

Paul Nutt, *Making Tough Decisions* (San Francisco: Jossey-Bass, 1989).

Roger von Oech, *A Whack on the Side of the Head* (New York: Warner Books, 1983).

## REVIEW QUESTIONS

1. What, if any, is the role of intuition in the five-step process of managerial decision making described in this chapter? Is intuition something to be discouraged or encouraged? Why?
2. Give practical examples to explain how each of the following three judgmental heuristics can bias managerial decision making: (a) the availability heuristic, (b) the representativeness heuristic, and (c) the anchoring and adjustment heuristics.
3. Why is the concept of "escalating commitment" important to managers concerned about the quality of decision making in organizations? How can this phenomenon best be dealt with in actual practice?
4. What is the major distinction between "classical" and "behavioral" decision theory? Why is it important for a manager to understand this distinction?
5. Without drawing a complete decision tree, explain the major points of the Vroom–Yetton model of managerial decision making. Give an example of a circumstance in which you feel a problem should be resolved by (a) an individual decision, (b) a consultative decision, and (c) a group decision.
6. Why are both "substance" and "relationship" goals important in negotiation? How can a manager evaluate whether or not a given negotiation is effective?

7. Explain the major distinctions between "distributive negotiation" and "integrative negotiation." Use an example to show how the decision outcomes of each approach can vary.
8. Choose three negotiator pitfalls discussed in this chapter. Describe how each can limit the effectiveness of a manager involved in an important negotiation. What can be done to minimize the dysfunctional consequences of these pitfalls?

# EXERCISE

## THE FISHING TRIP

### *Objectives*

1. To help you experience both individual and group work when confronting an unstructured problem situation.
2. To show you the advantage of assessing and analyzing differences between individuals, groups, and processes of reaching decisions.

### *Total Time:*

60 to 75 minutes

### *Procedure*

1. Read the story "The Fishing Trip," which follows.[30]
2. Assume you are a member of the group in the story, and rank the items in order of importance under column A on the form provided.
3. Form groups of four to six people and rank the items again, this time placing your group rankings under column B.
4. Receive the ranking information of an experienced sea captain and follow further direction from your instructor.

### *The Fishing Trip*

It was the first week in August when four friends set out on an overnight fishing trip in the Gulf of Mexico. Everything went well the first day—the sea was calm, they caught fish, and later they camped out on a lovely little island. However, during the night a very strong wind pulled the anchor free and drove their boat ashore, and the pounding waves broke the propeller. Although there were oars in the boat, the motor was useless.

A quick review of the previous day's journey showed that the group was about 60 miles from the nearest inhabited land. The small deserted island they were on had a few scrub trees and bushes but no fresh water. They knew from their portable AM–FM radio that the weather would be hot and dry, with daytime temperatures expected to be over 100°F the rest of the week. They all were dressed in light clothing, but each had a windbreaker for the cool evenings. They agreed that whatever happened they would stick together.

The families back on shore expected the group to return from their trip that evening and would surely report them missing when they did not show up. They realized, however, that it might take time for someone to find them because they had gone out further than anyone might have expected.

While some members of the group were quite concerned about this predicament, there was no panic. To help keep the group calm, one member—Jim—suggested that, just to be safe, they inventory the food and equipment available to them. "It might be several days before we are safe," Jim said, "and I think we should prepare for that." Kate, Tom, and Ann agreed, and their effort produced the list of items that follows.

*After the list was complete, Jim suggested that every person independently rank each item according to its importance to the survival of the group.* They all agreed to do this.

| *Items Available* | *A* | *B* | *X* |
|---|---|---|---|
| Each person has: | | | |
| a. One windbreaker. | ____ | ____ | ____ |
| b. One poncho. | ____ | ____ | ____ |
| c. One sleeping bag. | ____ | ____ | ____ |
| d. One pair of sunglasses. | ____ | ____ | ____ |
| The boat contains: | ____ | ____ | ____ |
| e. A cooler with two bottles of soda per person and some ice. | ____ | ____ | ____ |
| f. One large flashlight. | ____ | ____ | ____ |
| g. One first-aid kit. | ____ | ____ | ____ |
| h. Fishing equipment. | ____ | ____ | ____ |
| i. Matches, rope, and a few tools. | ____ | ____ | ____ |
| j. One compass mounted on the boat. | ____ | ____ | ____ |
| k. Two rear-view mirrors that can be removed from the boat. | ____ | ____ | ____ |
| l. One "official" navigational map of the Gulf area where you are. | ____ | ____ | ____ |
| m. One salt shaker (full). | ____ | ____ | ____ |
| n. One bottle of liquor. | ____ | ____ | ____ |

CASE

# THE JIM DONOVAN CASE

Jim Donovan, 37, the new president and chief executive officer of Famous Products, was suddenly in the roughest spot in his life. Having just been selected by Omega Corporation, a huge conglomerate, to take over as president of its latest acquisition, he had been feeling very good about himself. Having grown up on "the wrong side of the tracks," worked his way through engineering college, earned an MBA from Harvard Business School, worked for 10 years as a management consultant and for two years as a successful president of a small company, he felt that he had arrived. The company he was going to manage was known throughout the world, had a good reputation, and would provide a good opportunity for visibility in the parent company. The pay would be the highest he had ever earned, and while the money itself was not that important (though he'd be able to assure his wife and four children financial security), he enjoyed the indicator of success a high salary provided. And Jim was eager to manage a company with over a thousand employees; the power to get things done on such a large scale was very attractive to him.

When Omega had selected him, he was told that Don Bird, the current president of Famous Products, was close to retirement and would be moved upstairs to chairperson of the board. Bird had been president of Famous for 22 years and had done reasonably well, building sales steadily and guarding quality. The top management group was highly experienced, closely knit, very loyal to the company, and its members had been in their jobs for a long time. As long-term employees, they all were reported to be good friends of Don Bird. They were almost all in their early sixties and quite proud of the record of their moderate-sized but successful company. Famous had not, however, grown in profits as rapidly as Omega expected of its operating companies, and Omega's president had told Jim that he wanted Jim to "grab a hold of Famous and make it take off."

With this challenge ringing in his ears, Jim flew out to Milwaukee for his first visit to Famous Products. He had talked briefly with Don Bird to say that he'd be arriving Thursday for half a day, then would be back for good after 10 days in New York at Omega. Bird had been cordial but rather distant on the phone, and Jim wondered how Bird was taking Jim's appointment. "I've only got a few hours here," thought Jim. "I wonder how I should play it."

When Jim pulled up to Famous Products headquarters in his rented car, he noticed the neat grounds and immaculate landscaping. To his surprise, Don Bird met him at the door. Bird had on a very conservative blue business suit, black tie, black shoes, and white shirt. He peered out at Jim through old-fashioned steel-rimmed glasses and said, "Welcome to our plant. You're just in time for our usual Thursday morning executive meeting; would you like to sit in on that and meet our people?" Jim thought that the meeting would give him a chance to observe the management group in action, and he readily agreed, planning to sit back and watch for as long as he could.

Jim was ushered into the most formal meeting room he could remember ever having seen. The dark-paneled room was dominated by a long, heavy table, with 12 high-backed chairs around it. Seven of the chairs were filled with unsmiling executives in dark suits.

Bird led Jim to the front of the room, indicated an empty chair to the left of the seat at the head of the table, then sat down in the place that was obviously his. Turning to the group, he said:

> Gentlemen, I want you to meet Mr. Donovan, but before I turn the meeting over to him, I want you to know that I do not believe he should be here; I do not believe he's qualified and I will give him no support. Mr. Donovan . . .

## *Questions*

1. Take the position of Jim Donovan as the situation exists at the end of the case. What decisions does he have to make right now? What do you see as his options in these decisions.
2. What do you recommend that Jim Donovan do now, and why? Should he react quickly and intuitively, or should he "buy time" to more systematically analyze and deal with the situation? In what ways might judgmental heuristics help or hurt him in this situation?
3. Assume that Jim wants to "work things out" with Don Bird. Describe a negotiation approach and strategy that you think could resolve matters in such a way that both Donovan and Bird will be able to work well together in the coming months. Explain and defend your recommendation.

**This study outline of major topics is meant to organize your reading now; it is repeated in the Summary to structure your review.**

## STUDY OUTLINE

### ■ The Communication Process

Effective and Efficient Communication
Formal and Informal Communication Channels  Nonverbal Communication
Barriers to Effective Communication

### ■ Guidelines for Effective Communication

Active Listening  The Art of Giving Feedback

### ■ Communication of Roles

Role Ambiguity  Role Conflict

### ■ Conflict

Levels of Conflict  Constructive and Destructive Conflicts

CHAPTER 14

# COMMUNICATION AND CONFLICT

# VISIONS 14

**Eastman Kodak's copy products group was in trouble when Chuck Trowbridge came in as general manager. But he and Bob Crandall, head of manufacturing, shared a vision: to make Kodak a world-class manufacturer and create a more decentralized and less bureaucratic organization. But, this vision required the acceptance of employees used to very different ways of operations.**

**"Communication" was the key to success. Crandall established an intense communication plan involving weekly meetings with his direct reports, monthly forums in which he met with employees from different groups, and quarterly meetings with supervisors to discuss progress and improvements. All managers held quarterly "state of the department" meetings with their personnel. An informative "Copy Products Journal" was sent to employees each month; employees were encouraged to send feedback in anonymous letters to top management; and wall charts throughout the facility reported performance in terms of quality, cost, and targets. In three years, productivity doubled.**

Communication

Communication is a word like "organization." Everyone knows what it means until asked to formally state its definition. It is useful to think of ***communication*** as an interpersonal process of sending and receiving symbols with meanings attached to them. The opening *Visions* example highlights the importance of this process to managers and the people who work with them. A major challenge for everyone in organizations is handling information exchanges and potential conflicts sometimes associated with them.

For managers, however, these tasks are especially important. The very nature of managerial work involves daily and almost continuous information giving, receiving, and sharing. This is the basis for effectiveness in the complex interpersonal networks through which managers enact a multitude of action agendas.[1] It is also the basis for potential conflicts—interpersonal and others—which may interfere with the manager's success in these efforts. For example,

> *Heinz* Interdepartmental task forces are considered a key to improved lateral communication at Heinz. In such groups, some temporary and some continuing employees share knowledge and form policy on diverse subjects from materials purchasing to media buying.

## THE COMMUNICATION PROCESS

The key elements in the communication process are diagrammed in Figure 14.1. They include a source, who is responsible for encoding an intended meaning into a message, and a receiver, who decodes the message into a perceived meaning. Feedback from receiver to source may or may not be given.

The information source is a person or group of persons with a reason for communicate with someone else, the receiver. The reasons for the source to communicate include changing the attitudes, knowledge, or behavior of the receiver. As a manager, for example, you may want to communicate with your boss to make him or her understand why your work unit needs more time to finish an assigned project.

To communicate with the receiver, the source translates his or her intended meaning into symbols. This translation is an encoding process that results in sending a message that may consist of verbal (such as written) or nonverbal (such as gestures) symbols, or some combination of both. The receiver receives the symbols and decodes the message into meaning. This process of translation may or may not result in the assignment of the same meaning intended by the source.

Frequently, in fact, the intended meaning of the source and the meaning as perceived by the receiver differ. How would you react, for example, to this well-intentioned road sign advertising a combination diner and gasoline station.[2]

EAT HERE AND GET GAS

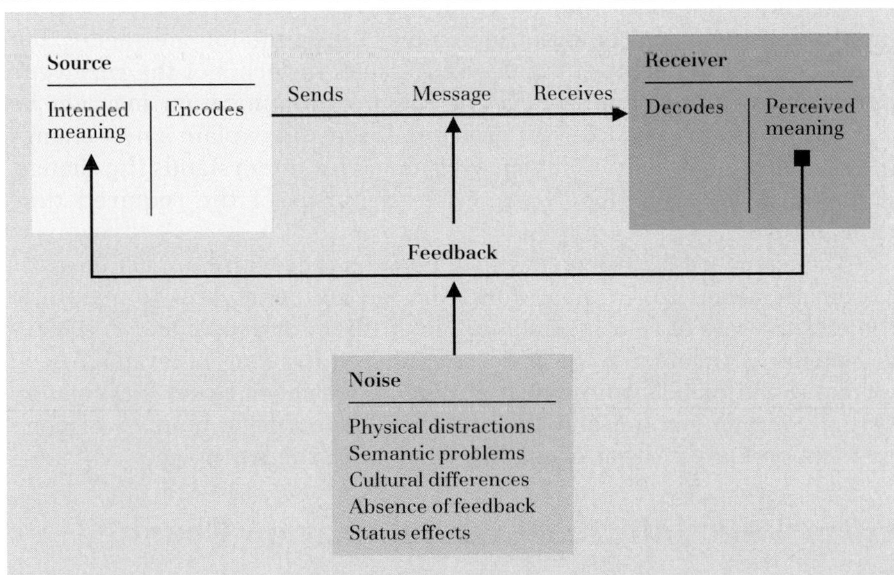


*FIGURE 14.1 The communication process and possible sources of "noise."*

Do not let the hilarity of this example fool you. It is a challenging task to communicate accurately. Managers, like owners of roadside diners, can make mistakes. A more specific look at the key elements in the communication process can help us analyze the causes of such communication errors.

## Effective and Efficient Communication

**Effective communication**

***Effective communication*** occurs when the intended meaning of the source and the perceived meaning of the receiver are one and the same. This should be the manager's goal in any communication attempt. It is not always achieved. Even now, we worry whether or not you are interpreting our written words as we intend. Our confidence would be higher if we were face-to-face in class together and you could ask clarifying questions. This opportunity to offer feedback and ask questions is one way of increasing the effectiveness of communication.

**Efficient communication**

***Efficient communication*** occurs at minimum cost in terms of resources expended. Time is an important resource in the communication process. Picture your instructor taking the time to communicate individually with each student. It would be virtually impossible to do. And even if it were possible, it would be very costly in terms of time. Managers often choose not to visit employees personally to communicate messages. Instead, they rely on the efficiency of memos, posted bulletins, group meetings, electronic (computer-transmitted) mail or videos. For example,

> *Colgate-Palmolive* No effort is spared at Colgate-Palmolive to keep employees informed about the company and its operations. The firm even distributes videotapes containing financial and technology reports, as well as updates on such matters as corporate policy toward South Africa and minority rights.

Efficient communications are not always effective. A low-cost communication such as a computer memo may save time for the sender, but it does not always achieve the desired results in terms of the receiver's perceived meaning. Similarly, an effective communication may not be efficient. For a manager to visit each employee and explain a new change in procedures may guarantee that everyone truly understands the change. It may also be prohibitively expensive in terms of the required time expenditure.

Managers are busy people who depend on their communication skills to remain successful in their work. You need to learn how to maximize the effectiveness of your communications with other people and to achieve reasonable efficiency in the process. This requires an understanding of formal and informal communication channels, a special awareness of nonverbal communication, and the ability to overcome a number of communication barriers that commonly operate in the workplace.

## Formal and Informal Communication Channels

**Formal communication channels**

***Formal communication channels*** follow the chain of command established by an organization's hierarchy of authority. An organization chart, for example, indicates the proper routing for official messages passing from one level or part of the hierarchy to another. Because formal communication channels are recognized as official and authoritative, it is typical for written communications in the form of letters, memos, policy statements, and other announcements to adhere to them.

Although necessary and important, the use of formal channels constitutes only one part of a manager's overall communication responsibilities. You should recall that in Chapter 2 we identified interpersonal "networking" as an essential activity for effective managers. In the present context, such networks represent the use of the formal channels just described *plus* a wide variety of ***informal communication channels*** that do not adhere to the organization's hierarchy of authority. They coexist with the formal channels, but frequently diverge from them by skipping levels in the hierarchy and/or cutting across vertical chains of command.

**Informal communication channels**

The importance of informal communication channels in organizations is highlighted in the best selling book *In Search of Excellence.*[3] Thomas J. Peters and Robert H. Waterman, Jr., the book's authors, report that, "The excellent companies are a vast network of informal, open communications. The patterns and intensity cultivate the right people's getting into contact with each other." Some of the interesting examples they cite include

*Walt Disney Productions.* Everyone from the president on down wears a tag with only his or her first name on it.

*Levi Strauss.* Management calls its open-door policy the "fifth freedom."

*Corning Glass.* Management installed escalators instead of elevators in a new engineering building to increase opportunities for face-to-face contact.

*3M.* The firm sponsors clubs for groups of 12 or more employees in hopes of increasing the probability of spontaneous problem-solving sessions.

Another informal channel we all know about is the "grapevine." Among the advantages of grapevines are their abilities to transmit information quickly and efficiently. Every experienced manager realizes that a message well placed in a grapevine can often travel faster and with greater impact than can the same message passed through formal channels. Grapevines also help to fulfill the needs of people involved in them. Being part of a grapevine can lead to a sense of security from "being in the know" when important things are going on. It also provides social support through the variety of interpersonal contacts involved in the give and take of communication.

The primary disadvantage of grapevines occurs when they transmit incorrect or untimely information. Rumors and prematurely released information can be dysfunctional. Astute managers get to know the grapevines operating in their work settings and try to use them to advantage. After all, one of the best ways of avoiding incorrect rumor is to make sure that key persons in a grapevine get the right information to begin with.

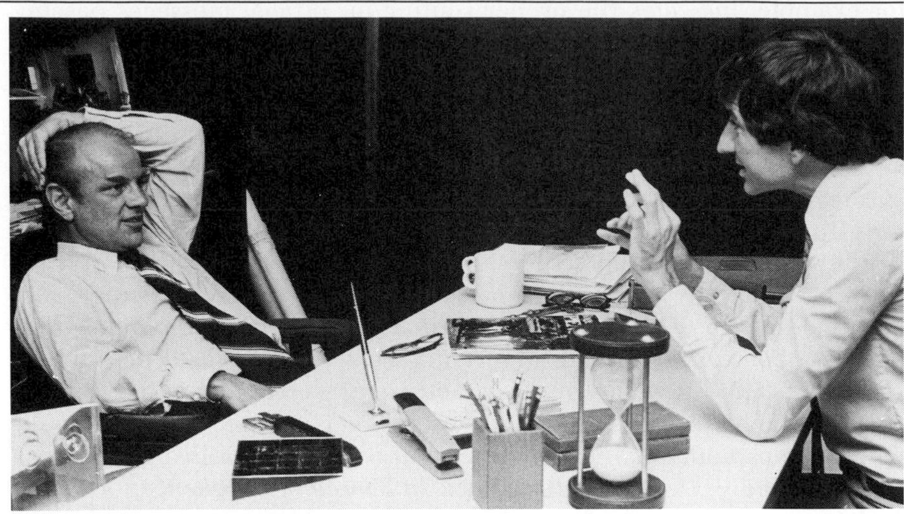

*FIGURE 14.2 Nonverbal communication.*

## Nonverbal Communication

A most interesting aspect of the communication process is its nonverbal form. Look at the photograph in Figure 14.2. Notice the facial expression of the man at the left; notice, too, the arm and hand position of the man at the right. Each person appears to be communicating something, but without a spoken word of their conversation being known to us!

**Nonverbal communication**

***Nonverbal communication*** is communication through facial expressions, body position, eye contact, and other physical gestures rather than written or oral expression. Although it is widely recognized that there is a nonverbal side to communication, we often underestimate its importance. A second look at the photograph should sensitize you to the managerial significance of this issue. Consider, too, the fact that nonverbal communication affects the impressions we make on other persons. It is

*FIGURE 14.3 Furniture placement and nonverbal communication in the office.*

known, for example, that interviewers respond more favorably to job candidates whose nonverbal cues (such as eye contact and erect posture) are positive than to those displaying negative nonverbal cues (such as looking down and slouching). Impression management, as introduced in Chapter 2, requires attention to one's nonverbal as well as verbal communications.

Nonverbal communication can also take place through the physical arrangement of space, such as that found in various office layouts. Figure 14.3 shows three different office arrangements and the messages they may communicate to visitors. Check the diagrams against the furniture arrangement in your office, your instructor's, or that of a manager with whom you are familiar. What are you/they saying to visitors by the choice of furniture placement?

Research confirms that office designs do in fact communicate[4]. It is known that visitors tend to be uncomfortable in offices where a desk is placed between them and the person to whom they are speaking. Other things that also seem to make a difference are the selection of artwork and decorations found in an office, as well as its neatness.

## Barriers to Effective Communication

**Noise**

***Noise*** is anything that interferes with the effectiveness of a communications attempt. Six special sources of noise are physical distractions, semantic problems, cultural differences, mixed messages, the absence of feedback, and status effects. Each of these sources of noise should be recognized and subjected to special managerial control. They are included in Figure 14.1 (shown earlier) as potential threats to any communication process.

### *Physical Distractions*

Any number of physical distractions can interfere with the effectiveness of a communications attempt. Some of these distractions are evident in the following conversation between an employee, George, and his manager.[5]

> Okay, George, let's hear your problem (phone rings, boss picks it up, promises to deliver the report, "just as soon as I can get it done"). Un, now, where were we—oh, you're having a problem with your secretary. She's (. . . secretary—the manager's—brings in some papers that need immediate signature, so he scribbles his name where she indicates; secretary leaves) . . . you say she's depressed a lot lately, wants to leave . . .? I tell you what, George, why don't you (phone rings again, lunch partner drops by) . . . uh, take a stab at handling it yourself . . . I've got to go now.

Besides what may have been poor intentions in the first place, George's manager was suffering from physical distractions that created information overload. He was letting too many requests for information processing occur at once. As a result, the communication with George suffered.

The mistake of processing too much information at once can be eliminated by setting priorities and planning. If George has something to say, his manager should set aside adequate time for the meeting. In addition, interruptions such as telephone calls, secretarial requests, and drop-in visitors should be prevented. All these things physically distracted both parties in their attempt to communicate in the example. Each distraction, in turn, could have been avoided by proper managerial attention.

## *Semantic Problems*

Semantic barriers to communication occur as encoding and decoding errors and as mixed messages. They involve symbols being poorly selected by the source and the message being subsequently misinterpreted by the receiver. Communications will be effective only to the extent that the source makes good choices when creating messages.

We generally do not realize how easily semantic errors occur. They abound.

The following illustrations of the "bafflegab" that once tried to pass as actual "executive communication" are an additional case in point.[6]

**A.** "We solicit any recommendations that you wish to make, and you may be assured that any such recommendations will be given our careful consideration."

**B.** "Consumer elements are continuing to stress the fundamental necessity of a stabilization of the price structure at a lower level than exists at the present time."

One has to wonder why the messages weren't more simply stated as: (A) "Send us your recommendations. They will be carefully considered," and (B) "Consumers want lower prices."

**Mixed messages**

Another semantic problem is the conflict between verbal and nonverbal communications. ***Mixed messages*** result when a person's words communicate one message while their actions or "body language" communicate something else.

## *Cultural Differences*

Managers and other persons must always exercise caution when involved in cross-cultural communication. This was a major point in Chapter 3 on the international dimensions of OB. Managers must understand that different cultural backgrounds between senders and receivers can cause breakdowns in the communication process. This includes communications between persons of different geographical or ethnic groupings from within one country, as well as between persons of different national cultures.

**Ethnocentrism**

A common problem in cross-cultural communications is ***ethnocentrism,*** the tendency to consider one's culture and its values as being superior to others. Very often such tendencies are accompanied by an unwillingness to try and understand alternative points of view and take seriously the values they represent. This can be highly disadvantageous when trying to conduct business and maintain effective working relationships with persons from different cultures.

The difficulties with cross-cultural communication are perhaps most obvious when it comes to language differences among people. A convenient illustration is the case of advertising messages that work well in one country but encounter difficulty when translated into the language of another. Consider these international business mistakes.

Courtesy of Texas Instruments.

INTERNATIONAL PERSPECTIVE

## TEXAS INSTRUMENTS

**Communication is a worldwide challenge for the computer giant Texas Instruments. For more than 30 years the company has been marketing advanced electronics and computers outside the United States. Today it has more than 50 manufacturing facilities and 75,000 employees worldwide. Global operations are integrated in sophisticated and computerized communication networks. These networks allow TI employees from various locations to share knowledge with one another. They allow the firm to utilize the experience of some of the world's best experts for longer-term research and development and for shorter-term problem solving. They also help TI take good care of its customers—from Buenos Aires to Central Lakes, Canada and from Lubbock, Texas to Singapore.**

*Coca-Cola Company* They once lost sales in some Asian markets when consumers were confused over the ad, "Coke Adds Life." They translated the message to mean "Coke Brings You Back From the Dead."

*General Motors* Chevrolet's "Nova" model translated into Spanish as "Chevrolet no go." This is exactly what happened to sales of the car in Latin America.

## *Absence of Feedback*

In one-way communications like the written memo there is no direct and immediate feedback from receiver to source. Two-way communications include such feedback and are characterized by the normal interactive conversations in our daily experiences. Figuratively speaking, two-way communication is of the form:

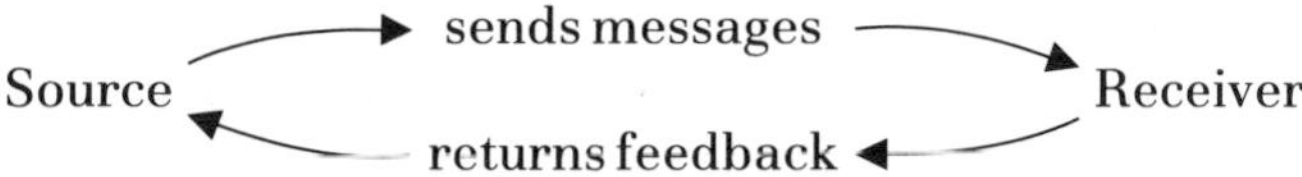

Research indicates that two-way communication is more accurate and effective than one-way; it is also more costly and time consuming.[7] Yet the more efficient one-way forms of communication—memo, letter, electronic mail, and the like—are frequently used in work settings. Because it avoids immediate feedback, it can be less threatening to the sender although very frustrating for the receiver. In particular, the recipient of a one-way message is often unsure of just what the sender wants done.

### *Status Effects*

The hierarchy of authority in organizations can create another barrier to effective communication. Communication is frequently biased when flowing upward in organizational hierarchies.[8] Status differentials create special barriers between managers and their subordinates. Given the authority of their positions, managers may be inclined to do a lot of "telling" but not much "listening." Subordinates, on the other hand, may tell their superiors only what they expect the boss wants to hear. Whether the reason is a fear of retribution for bringing bad news, an unwillingness to identify personal mistakes, or just a general desire to please, the result is the same. The manager ends up making poor decisions because of a biased and inaccurate information base.

To avoid such problems, managers must develop trust in their working relationships with subordinates and take advantage of all opportunities for face-to-face communications. "Management by wandering around" is now popularly acclaimed as one way to do this. It simply means getting out of the office and talking regularly to people as they do their jobs. Managers who spend time walking around can greatly reduce the perceived "distance" between themselves and their subordinates. They can also create an atmosphere of open and free-flowing communication, which makes more and better information available for decision making, as well as increases the relevancy of decisions to the needs of lower-level personnel. Of course, the wandering around must be a genuine attempt to communicate. It should not be perceived as just another way to "check up" on employees.

## GUIDELINES FOR EFFECTIVE COMMUNICATION

Effective communicators not only understand and are able to deal with communication barriers, they are also exceptionally good at active listening and feedback delivery. Each of these skills is frequently called upon during a manager's daily work routines.

### Active Listening

The ability to listen well is a distinct asset to managers whose jobs, as noted earlier, involve such a large proportion of time spent "communicating" with other people. After all, there are two sides to the communication process—sending a message or "telling," and receiving a message or "listening." There is legitimate concern, however, that too many managers may emphasize the former and neglect the latter—especially in their relationships with subordinates.[9] One solution is for managers to develop better ***active listening*** skills, an ability to help the source of a message say what he or she really means. The concept comes from counselors and therapists who are highly skilled at helping people express themselves and talk about things that are important to them. You should be familiar with active listening as a technique for improving the effectiveness of communications in organizations. Five guidelines are especially useful in this regard.[10]

**Active listening**

1. *Listen for message content:* Try to hear exactly what is being said in the message.
2. *Listen for feelings:* Try to identify how the source feels in terms of the message content. Is this something pleasing or displeasing to the source? Why?
3. *Respond to feelings:* Let the source know that his or her feelings, as well as the message content, are recognized.
4. *Note all cues, verbal and nonverbal:* Be sensitive to the nonverbal communications as well as the verbal ones; identify mixed messages that need to be clarified.
5. *Reflect back to the source, in your own words, what you think you are hearing:* Paraphrase and restate the verbal and nonverbal messages as feedback to which the source can respond with further information.

One of the two conversations below involves active listening by the supervisor. Read each and think through how you would feel as the group leader in the case.

## Example 1

*Group leader:* Hey, Al, I don't get this production order. We can't handle this run today. What do they think we are?

*Supervisor:* But that's the order. So get it out as soon as you can. We're under terrific pressure this week.

*Group leader:* Don't they know we're behind schedule already because of that press breakdown?

*Supervisor:* Look, Kelly, I don't decide what goes on upstairs. I just have to see that the work gets out and that's what I'm gonna do.

*Group leader:* The group isn't gonna like this.

*Supervisor:* That's something you'll have to work out with them, not me.

## Example 2

*Group leader:* Hey, Ross, I don't get this production order. We can't handle this run today. What do they think we are?

*Supervisor:* Sounds like you're pretty sore about it, Kelly.

*Group leader:* I sure am. We were just about getting back to schedule after that press breakdown. Now this comes along.

*Supervisor:* As if you didn't have enough work to do, huh?

*Group leader:* Yeah, I don't know how I'm gonna tell the group about this.

*Supervisor:* Hate to face 'em with it now, is that it?

*Group leader:* I really do. They're under a real strain today. Seems like everything we do around here is rush, rush.

*Supervisor:* I guess you feel like it's unfair to load anything more on them.

*Group leader:* Well, yeah, I know there must be plenty of pressure on everybody up the line, but—well, if that's the way it is . . . guess I'd better get the word to 'em.

The supervisor in Example 2 possesses active listening skills. He responded to the group leader's communication attempt in a way that increased the flow of information. The supervisor ended up receiving important information about the work situation and should be able to use this information for constructive results. The group leader also feels better after having been able to really say what he felt, and after being heard!

## The Art of Giving Feedback

Managers frequently give feedback to other people, often in the form of performance appraisals. There is an art to giving feedback in such a way that it is accepted and used constructively by the receiver. Feedback poorly given can be threatening and become a basis for resentment and alienation.

**Feedback**

***Feedback*** is the process of telling someone else how you feel about something they did or said, or about the situation in general. The first requirement in giving feedback is to recognize when it is intended to truly benefit the receiver and when it is purely an attempt to satisfy a personal need. A manager who berates the secretary for typing errors, for example, may actually be mad about personally failing to give clear instructions in the first place.

Given that the sender's intent is to give helpful feedback to the receiver, a manager should recognize that constructive feedback is[11]

- Given directly and with real feeling, ideally based on a foundation of trust.
- Specific rather than general, with good clear examples.
- Given at a time when the receiver appears most ready to accept it.
- Checked with others to support its validity.
- In respect to things that the receiver can really do something about.
- Not more than the receiver can handle at any particular time.

Giving criticism is certainly one of the most difficult of all communication situations faced by managers. What is intended to be polite and constructive can easily end up being unpleasant and even hostile. This risk is particularly evident in the performance appraisal process discussed in Supplementary Module C. A manager must be able to do more than complete an appraisal form and document performance for the record. In order to serve the developmental needs of the subordinate, the results of the appraisal—both the praises and the criticisms—must be well communicated. As a supervisor, it often helps to make criticism more productive if you:[12]

- Get to the point.
- Describe the situation in specific terms.
- Mutually agree on the sources of the problem and the solution.
- End by having the subordinate summarize the meeting and the solution.

# COMMUNICATION OF ROLES

One of the most important communications in which managers become involved is the sending and receiving of role expectations. A ***role*** is a set of activities expected of a person holding a particular office or position in a group or organization.[13] The various people who have these expectations regarding the behavior of someone in a role are considered members of the ***role set.*** Managers are part of the role sets of their subordinates. For a subordinate, the role expectations communicated by the manager are likely to include instructions about desired behavior and behavior to be avoided, intentions regarding the allocation of rewards, and evaluations about past performance. At the organizational level, a key issue in establishing a unified sense of mission and culture is the communication of a shared role orientation for all members. For example,

**Role**

**Role set**

> ***Progressive*** As one of America's fastest growing property and casualty insurers, Progressive, located in Mayfield, Ohio, faces the challenge of communicating company values to thousands of new employees. The watchwords of an introductory training program are integrity, aspiration, excellence, respect for all people, and profits.

When the communication of role expectations is distorted by barriers such as those discussed earlier, role ambiguity and role conflict may occur. These role dynamics deserve your attention as one of the many reasons why every manager should work hard at interpersonal communication skills.

## Role Ambiguity

***Role ambiguity*** occurs when the person in a role is uncertain about the role expectations of one or more members of the role set. To do their jobs well, people need to know what is expected of them. Sometimes these expectations may be unclear because the manager has not tried to communicate them to the subordinate or has done so inadequately. Or it may be a failure of the subordinate to listen that creates the lack of understanding. In either case, the resulting role ambiguity can be stressful for the individual. Research indicates that it may cause a loss of confidence in the role sender, lowered self-confidence, and/or decreased job satisfaction.

**Role ambiguity**

## Role Conflict

Role conflict

***Role conflict*** occurs when the person in a role is unable to respond to the expectations of one or more members of the role set. The role expectations are understood, but for one reason or another, they cannot be complied with. Role conflict is another source of potential tension that may result in a loss of job satisfaction, decreased confidence in one's boss, and/or a tendency to avoid the unpleasant work situation.

Role overload

A common form of conflict is ***role overload.*** This is a situation in which there are simply too many role expectations being communicated to a person at a given time. There is too much to be done and too little time to do it. Managers may create role overload for their subordinates, especially when they rely on one-way communication. When cut off from valuable feedback, it is hard for these managers to learn when or why a subordinate is experiencing stress.

Role conflicts also occur when the expectations of one or more members of the role set are incompatible. The four basic types are intrasender, intersender, person–role, and interrole conflicts. A definition and example of each follows.

1. *Intrasender Role Conflict:* The same role-set member sends conflicting expectations.
   *Example*—A purchasing agent is asked by the boss to buy materials unavailable through normal channels; the boss also says company procedures should not be violated.
2. *Intersender Role Conflict:* Different role-set members send conflicting expectations.
   *Example*—A manager's boss expects her to be very direct and to exercise close control over subordinates; the subordinates want more freedom in their work.
3. *Person–Role Conflict:* The values and needs of the individual conflict with the expectations of the members of the role set.
   *Example*—There is growing pressure on a senior executive to agree secretly to fix prices with competing firms; this violates the personal ethics of the executive.
4. *Interrole Conflict:* The expectations of two or more roles held by the same individual become incompatible.
   *Example*—As work load increases, a manager spends evenings and weekends at work; the family is upset because they feel home obligations are not being met.

Role ambiguities and conflicts such as these can create tensions that reflect adversely on individual work attitudes and behaviors. The informed manager will seek to minimize these negative consequences by opening and maintaining effective two-way communications with all members of his or her role sets. This same manager will use active listening to solicit feedback from others on their understandings of any reactions to role expectations.

# CONFLICT

Our review of roles and role dynamics introduces the ability to deal with conflict as another key aspect of a manager's interpersonal skills. ***Conflict*** occurs whenever disagreements exist in a social situation over issues of substance and/or emotional antagonisms.[14] ***Substantive conflicts*** are natural in organizations and center on disagreements over ends and means. Different views of such things as group and organizational goals, the allocation of resources, distribution of rewards, policies and procedures, and the assignment of roles are the every day life of the manager. ***Emotional conflicts*** involve feelings of anger, mistrust, dislike, fear, resentment, and personality clashes. Since organizations are hierarchies of unequal power, it is often difficult for the manager to separate substantive and emotional conflict and to deal with each on its own merits. Further, unresolved substantive conflicts can result in sustained emotional conflict and escalate into dysfunctional relationships between individuals and work units. Although conflict is a fact in organizations, it need not degenerate to open warfare.

**Conflict**

**Substantive conflicts**

**Emotional conflicts**

Managers are known to spend up to 20 percent of their time dealing with conflict.[15] These include conflicts in which the manager is a principal party, one of the persons actively in conflict with one or more others. They also include conflicts in which the manager acts as a mediator, or third party, to try and resolve the conflicts between other people to the benefit of the organization and the individuals involved. In all cases, the manager must be a skilled participant in the dynamics of interpersonal conflict. He or she must be able to recognize situations that have the potential for conflict. Then the manager should be capable of diagnosing the situation and taking action through communications to ensure that the goals of the organization are best served.

## Levels of Conflict

People at work encounter conflicts at each of four levels: (1) intrapersonal or conflict within the individual, (2) interpersonal or individual-to-individual conflict, (3) intergroup conflict, and (4) interorganizational conflict. The relevant question becomes, "How well prepared are you to encounter and deal successfully with each level of conflict in your experiences?"

### *Intrapersonal Conflict*

Among the significant conflicts affecting behavior in organization are those that involve the individual alone. We call these *intra*personal conflicts, and one example is person–role conflict previously discussed. They also often include actual or perceived pressures from incompatible goals or expectations of the following types.

- *Approach–approach conflict.* A situation requiring a person to choose between two positive and equally attractive alternatives. An example is having to choose between accepting a valued promotion in the organization and taking a desirable new job offer with another firm.

- *Avoidance–avoidance conflict.* A situation requiring a person to choose between two negative and equally unattractive alternatives. An example is being asked to accept a job transfer to another town in an undesirable location or have one's employment with an organization terminated.
- *Approach–avoidance conflict.* A situation requiring a person to make a decision regarding an alternative that has both positive and negative consequences associated with it. An example is being offered a promotion carrying much higher pay but also carrying unwanted and greatly increased job responsibilities.

## *Interpersonal Conflict*

Interpersonal conflict occurs among one or more individuals. It can be substantive or emotional, or both. Everyone has experience with interpersonal conflict; it is a major form of conflict faced by managers given the highly interpersonal nature of the managerial role itself. We will address this form of conflict in detail when conflict management strategies are discussed in a later section of this chapter.

## *Intergroup Conflict*

Another level of conflict in organizations occurs among groups. This topic was first introduced in our look at intergroup relations in Chapter 9. Intergroup conflict is common in organizations, and it makes the coordination and integration of task activities difficult. A classic example is the contrast in the working relationships between sales and production personnel observed in two plants of the same manufacturing company.[16] In the Elgin plant, a conflict relationship existed between the two departments; in the Bowie plant the working relationship was collaborative. These differences are most apparent in two respects to how group goals and orientation toward information handling affected decision making in each setting.

- Differences over group goals.
  At Elgin: Each department emphasized its own needs and tasks.
  At Bowie: Each department stressed common goals and cooperation.
- Differences over information handling.
  At Elgin: Each department ignored the other's problem and distorted its communications with the others.
  At Bowie: Each department sought to understand the other's problems and communicated accurate information to the other.

Managers stand at the interface of intergroup relationships and any conflicts they may entail. At times, the manager acts as a liaison directly linking his or her work unit with one or more others. At other times the manager is a higher level of authority to whom multiple subunits report. In each case, intergroup relations must be properly managed to maintain collaboration and avoid dysfunctional consequences from any conflicts that occur. For example,

SKILLS PERSPECTIVE

## ESPRIT

Courtesy of Esprit de Corps.

**Everything hasn't been "coming up roses" for a while at Esprit, the popular woman's clothier. Conflict between cofounders Susie and Doug Tompkins had been bogging down the firm and a "buy-out" by an outside firm was imminent. Finally a deal was struck and the conflict resolved. Susie bought the company, and Doug got $325 million and some continuing control over international operations. Susie also gained the freedom to take Esprit in the direction she thinks is necessary for success in the 1990s—going beyond the youth market and catering to career women. Doug's opposition had been slowing this shift in strategy. An industry consultant says: "In a business that depends on change for survival, Doug was not willing to change."**

*American Express* A program called "One Enterprise" encourages collaboration across divisions at American Express. Communication is essential as peers work together on internal joint ventures involving purchasing, marketing, and innovation. Their individual rewards are tied in part to their efforts on the One Enterprise teams.

### *Interorganizational Conflict*

Conflict also occurs between organizations. This conflict is most commonly thought of in terms of the competition that characterizes firms operating a private enterprise. But interorganizational conflict is really a much broader issue. Consider, for example, disagreements between unions and organizations employing their members, between government regulatory agencies and organizations subject to their surveillance, and more generally between organizations and others that supply them with raw materials. In each setting, the potential for conflict involves individuals who represent total organizations, not internal subunits or groups.

Although participation in interorganizational conflict is frequently the province of higher-level managers, middle-level and lower-level managers can represent their organizations in such relationships with others. Typical examples are a purchasing agent's relationships with suppliers and a supervisor's relationships with union representatives. Again, any resulting conflicts should be managed to the benefit of the organizations and individuals concerned. When accomplished, the benefits can be quite substantial. For example,

> *IBM* There is a new emphasis on communication and customer partnerships at IBM. Efforts are being made to increase communication between company employees and customers. Engineers and customers may work together on joint development teams where they share proprietary data to develop a better product.

## Constructive and Destructive Conflicts

Conflict in organizations can be upsetting to the persons directly involved and to others who may observe or who are affected by its occurrence. A fairly common byproduct is stress, a topic we address in considerable detail in Chapter 18. It can be quite uncomfortable, for example, to be in an environment where two co-workers are continually hostile toward one another. There are two sides to conflict, however, as it relates to organizational outcomes. Conflict that results in positive benefits to the group or organization is constructive; conflict that works to the group's or organization's disadvantage is destructive.

*Destructive* conflict occurs, for example, when two employees are unable to work together due to interpersonal hostilities (a destructive emotional conflict) or when the members of a committee fail to act because they cannot agree on group goals (a destructive substantive conflict). Destructive conflicts reduce group effectiveness by decreasing work productivity and member satisfaction and increasing absenteeism and turnover. Managers must be alert to destructive conflicts and be quick to take action that prevents or eliminates these conflicts or at least minimizes their resulting disadvantages. But conflict can also be beneficial. *Constructive* conflict offers individuals and groups a chance to identify otherwise neglected problems and opportunities. Creativity and performance can improve as a result. Indeed, an effective manager is able to stimulate constructive conflict in situations where satisfaction with the status quo inhibits needed change and development. He or she is comfortable dealing with both sides of the conflict dynamic—the constructive and the destructive.

# CONFLICT SITUATIONS IN ORGANIZATIONS

The very nature of the manager's position and responsibilities in an organization guarantees that conflict will be a part of his or her work experience. To help you better fulfill the challenges of achieving a constructive balance in conflict outcomes, we now examine the types of conflict situations experienced by managers, a way to understand these situations, and the various stages of conflict they may involve.

## Types of Conflict Situations

Among the many conflict situations in organizations, four basic types exist. An effective manager is able to recognize these situations for their potential to create conflict.[17]

1. *Vertical conflict.* Occurs between levels in an organization's hierarchy of authority. A common example is conflict between a supervisor and subordinate over such things as task goals, deadlines, and performance accomplishments.
2. *Horizontal conflict.* Occurs between persons or groups operating at the same level in the hierarchy. It may trace to such things as goal incompatibilities, resource scarcities, or purely interpersonal factors.
3. *Line–staff conflict.* Occurs when line and staff representatives disagree over issues of substance in their working relationships. Because staff personnel (e.g., an internal auditor) often have the potential for major impact on certain areas of line operations, line–staff conflict can and does appear with some frequency in organizations.
4. *Role conflict.* Occurs when the communication of task expectations from role-set members proves inadequate or incompatible for the role holder. Earlier in this chapter we identified four specific types of role conflicts: intrasender, intersender, interrole, and person–role.

Conflict becomes more likely in each of the prior situations when certain antecedent conditions exist. These include the following characteristics of working relationships among individuals and groups in organizations.[18]

- *Work-flow interdependence.* As discussed in Chapters 10 and 11, an organization exists and must be managed as a system of interdependent parts performing distinct but coordinated functions in a division of labor. When work-flow interdependence is such that a person or group must rely on task contributions from one or more others to achieve *its* goals, the circumstances are ripe for occasional conflict.
- *Asymmetry.* Work relationships are asymmetrical when one party differs substantially in power, values, and/or status from another with whom he or she regularly interacts. Conflict due to asymmetry is prone to occur, for example, when a low-power person needs the help of a high-power person who will not respond, when people of dramatically different values are forced to work together on a task, or when a high-status person is required to interact with and perhaps be dependent on someone of lower status. A common example of the latter case occurs when a manager is forced to deal with another manager only through his or her secretary.
- *Role ambiguity or domain ambiguity.* As discussed earlier, a lack of adequate direction or clarity of goals and tasks for persons in their work roles can create a stressful and conflict-prone situation. At the

group or department level, this often materializes as ambiguity of domains or jurisdictions. That is, two groups are ripe for conflict when either one or both fails to understand just who is responsible for what.

- *Resource scarcity.* Actual or perceived needs to compete for scarce resources makes working relationships among individuals and/or groups conflict-prone. This is especially relevant for individuals or groups in declining as opposed to growing organizations. Resources are usually scarce in times of decline, with the result that cutbacks commonly occur. As various persons or groups try to position themselves to receive maximum shares of the shrinking resource pool, others are likely to resist or employ countermeasures to defend their respective interests. Resources are essential to the survival and prosperity of individuals and groups in organizations. As a result, resource scarcity often breeds conflict.

## The Stages of Conflict

It is useful to recognize that conflict develops in stages, as shown in Figure 14.4. These stages include antecedent conditions, perceived and felt conflict, manifest conflict, conflict resolution or suppression, and conflict aftermath.[19] Some of the antecedents that establish conditions from which conflict can develop are role ambiguities, competition for scarce resources, communication barriers, unresolved prior conflicts, and individual differences in needs, values, and goals. In effect, when these conditions exist,

*FIGURE 14.4 The stages of conflict.*

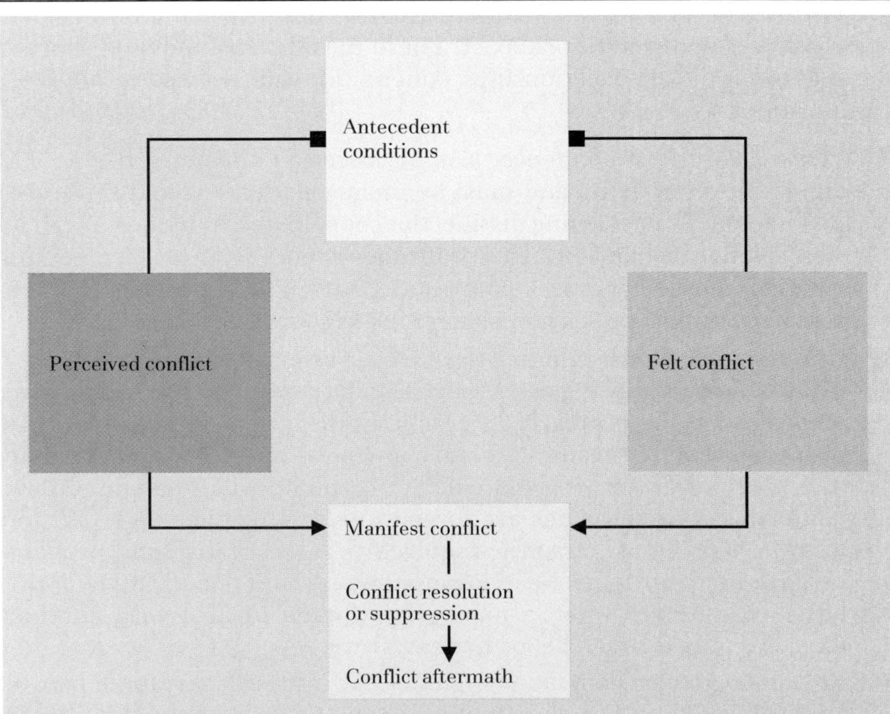

the stage is set for conflict to develop. Any person who works in a situation characterized by one or more of these conditions, therefore, should be sensitive to the conflict potential they represent.

When the antecedents are viewed as a basis for substantive or emotional differences, perceived conflict exists. Of course, this perception may be held by only one of the conflicting parties. There is also a difference between perceived and felt conflict. When conflict is felt, we give it meaning in the sense that a tension exists that creates motivation to reduce feelings of discomfort. Sometimes we feel conflict, but cannot pin down its source or cause.

For conflict to be resolved, all parties should both perceive and feel the need to do something about the conflict. When conflict is openly expressed in behavior it is said to be manifest. A state of manifest conflict can be resolved in the sense that its antecedent conditions are corrected. It can also be suppressed in that, although no change in antecedent conditions occurs, the manifest conflict behaviors are controlled.

Finally, the way in which a given conflict is handled can affect future conflicts. Unresolved conflicts continue to fester and promote future conflicts over similar issues. Truly resolved conflicts may establish conditions that reduce future conflicts of a similar nature and that help other eventual conflicts to be resolved in a constructive fashion. Thus, any manager should be sensitive to the influence of conflict aftermath on future conflict episodes.

# CONFLICT MANAGEMENT

Conflict in organizations is inevitable. You should recognize that the process of conflict management can be subtle, active, and exceedingly difficult. Always, the goal should be true ***conflict resolution***—that is, when the underlying reasons for conflict are eliminated.

**Conflict resolution**

## Indirect Conflict Management

Indirect conflict management techniques are quite common and potentially useful. They include appeals to common goals, hierarchical referral, organizational redesign, and the use of mythology and scripts.

### *Appeal to Common Goals*

An appeal to a common organizational goal can focus the attention of potentially conflicting parties on one mutually desirable conclusion. By elevating the potential dispute to a common framework where the parties recognize their mutual interdependence, petty disputes can be put in perspective. However, this can be difficult when prior performance is poor and individuals or groups disagree over how to improve performance. In this negative situation, the manager needs to remember the attributional tendency of individuals to blame poor performance on others and external conditions. Here, conflict resolution begins by making sure the parties take personal responsibility that the situation will improve.

## Hierarchical Referral

Hierarchical referral makes use of the chain of command for conflict resolution—problems are simply referred up the hierarchy for a higher-level manager to deal with. Senior managers who are the common bosses of subordinates have the formal authority to resolve disputes. If conflict is severe and recurring, however, continual use of hierarchical referral may have some undesirable consequences. For instance, a common tendency is to consider conflicts as caused by poor interpersonal relations. Senior managers may seek harmony as evidence of their good management or act quickly to simply replace one of the subordinate managers.[20] In such cases they don't really delve into the problem and subordinates may learn that it is best not to refer any conflict upward. They may sweep legitimate disputes under the rug and allow them to fester into major problems.

## Organizational Redesign

Where the organizational design allows groups, units, and departments to operate in relative isolation from one another, conflict tends to be muted. At points where work needs to be coordinated and units share resources, however, conflicts often arise. Managers have a number of options to reduce conflicts by adjusting the organizational design at the points of friction.

*Decoupling* the groups by redesigning the organization is one option. The tasks of the units can be adjusted to reduce the number of required points of coordination. The conflicting units can then be separated from one another and each can be provided separate access to valued resources. While reducing conflict, decoupling may yield duplication and a poor allocation of valued resources. Often the question is whether the conflict costs more than the inefficiencies of resource allocation.[21]

*Buffering* is often used where two groups must integrate the pace of their work. The classic buffering technique is to build an inventory between units that depend on one another's outputs to maintain their work flows. Although it reduces conflict, this technique is increasingly out of favor because it may dramatically increase inventory costs and the ability of the organization to respond rapidly to change.

*Linking pins* are individuals and units designed to increase the flow of communication between the members of the conflicting groups.[22] Linking pin individuals, such as project managers and liaisons, are expected to get to know each unit's operations, its members, and their social norms. With this knowledge they are to work with unit members to develop creative solutions to the overall question of mutual adjustment. The diplomatic skills of such managers are often severely tested as they span the boundaries of the two groups. Although expensive, this technique is often used where different specialized groups—such as engineering and sales—must closely coordinate their efforts.

A variation of the linking pin is to create a department of several members to coordinate units and prevent clashes. Unlike liaison managers who are individually assigned to coordinate groups, liaison departments may be given formal authority to resolve technical disputes, claims to common resources, or disagreements over who should perform specific

ETHICAL PERSPECTIVE

## TEXACO

Courtesy of Texaco Inc.

**The four-year legal battle between Texaco and Pennzoil was called by a senior executive "the biggest disruption in any corporate history." It left Texaco with Chapter 11 bankruptcy and a $3 million judgment to Pennzoil. It also left them with employees who wondered just what was happening with their company. Texaco is back—with a strong commitment to employee communication. It is striving to keep employees informed about the company and to help get them the information they need to act quickly in their jobs. This commitment to open channels of communication extends to the firm's relationships with shareholders, suppliers, customers, and the community at large.**

work. While this may eliminate conflict, it can also stifle the development of creative solutions to potential conflicts by group members.

### *Mythology and Scripts*

In far too many organization conflict management is done poorly. Instead of dealing directly with the conflicts among groups and individuals, conflict is hidden by scripts or repeated behavior routines that become a part of the organization's culture.[23] The scripts become rituals that allow the conflicting parties to vent their frustrations, and to recognize that they are mutually dependent on one another via the larger corporation. An example is a scripted, monthly "department heads" meeting for purposes of coordination and problem solving.[24] Managers know their roles and the impossibility of resolving any real conflicts, yet the script allows them to say and act as if they are working on the problem while avoiding the more difficult task of dealing with it directly.

Conflict may also be hidden by *myths* that deny the necessity to make trade-offs. For example, in complex dangerous technologies, safe operations may come at some sacrifice to efficiency. Some organizations hide this by proclaiming that "an efficient operation is a safe one." Analyses of operating statistics on safety and efficiency suggest otherwise. Such myths may become "social facts." People may begin to act them out. To continue our example, managers may begin to stress efficiency and say they are also improving safety. The result could be a serious accident.

Scripts and myths are most likely to hide conflict in organizations simply when:

- Managers have a limited capability for managing conflict.
- Managing conflict is perceived as time-consuming and expensive.
- There are irreconcilable differences among individuals, units, and organizational stakeholders.

## Direct Conflict Management Techniques

Generally, consultants and academics agree that true conflict resolution can occur when the underlying substantive and emotional reasons are identified, and a solution that allows both conflicting parties to *win* is developed.[25] From the perspective of the individual participants, let's examine conflict from the perspective of who wins.

### *Lose–Lose Conflict*

**Lose–lose conflict**

***Lose–lose conflict*** occurs when nobody really gets what they want. This is often a result of managing conflict by avoidance, smoothing, and/or compromise. No one achieves his or her true desires, and the underlying reasons for the conflict remain unaffected. Future conflict of a similar nature is likely to occur.

*Avoidance* is an extreme form of nonattention. Everyone pretends that conflict does not really exist and hopes that it will simply go away. *Smoothing* plays down differences among the conflicting parties and highlights similarities and areas of agreement. Peaceful coexistence through a recognition of common interests is the goal. Smoothing may ignore the real essence of a given conflict.

"Let's compromise" is a phrase frequently heard in a group setting. The classic example occurs whenever representatives of unions and management meet to prepare new labor contracts. *Compromise* occurs when each party gives up something of value to the other. As a result, neither party gains its full desires, and the antecedent conditions for future conflicts are established. Although a conflict may appear to be settled for a while through compromise, it may well reappear again at some future time.

### *Win–Lose Conflict*

**Win–lose conflict**

In ***win–lose conflict,*** one party achieves its desires at the expense and to the exclusion of the other party's desires. This may result from *competition,* where a victory is achieved through force, superior skill, or domination. It may also occur as a result of *authoritative command* wherein a formal authority simply dictates a solution and specifies what is gained and lost by whom. When the authority is a party to the conflict, it is easy to predict who will be the winner and who the loser. Each of these strategies also fails to address the root causes of the conflict and tends to suppress the desires of at least one of the conflicting parties. As a result, future conflicts over the same issues are likely.

### *Win–Win Conflict*

**Win–win conflict**

***Win–win conflict*** is achieved by *confrontation* of the issues and the use of *problem solving* to reconcile differences. This positive approach to conflict involves a recognition by all conflicting parties that something is wrong and needs attention. When success is achieved in problem solving, true conflict resolution has occurred. Win–win conditions eliminate reasons for continuing or resurrecting the conflict, since nothing has been avoided or suppressed. All relevant issues are raised and openly discussed. The ultimate test for a win–win solution is whether or not the conflicting parties are willing to say to each other,[26]

> "I want a solution that achieves your goals and my goals and is acceptable to both of us."
>
> "It is our collective responsibility to be open and honest about facts, opinions, and feelings."

## Conflict Management Styles

The five conflict management styles of avoidance, authoritative command, smoothing, compromise, and problem solving are depicted on the conflict management grid in Figure 14.5. The grid classifies each style as some combination of a person's.[27]

Cooperative

**Smoothing or Accommodation**
Letting the other's wishes rule; smoothing over differences to maintain superficial harmony.

**Problem Solving**
Seeking true satisfaction of everyone's concerns by working through differences; finding and solving problems so everyone gains as a result.

**Compromise**
Working toward partial satisfaction of everyone's concerns; seeking "acceptable" rather than "optimal" solutions so that no one totally wins or loses.

Cooperativeness (attempting to satisfy the other party's concerns)

**Avoidance**
Downplaying disagreement, failing to participate in the situation, and/or staying neutral at all costs.

**Competition or Authoritative Command**
Working against the wishes of the other party, fighting to dominate in win-lose competition, and/or forcing things to a favorable conclusion through the exercise of authority.

Uncooperative

Unassertive — Assertive

Assertiveness
(attempting to satisfy one's own concerns)

*FIGURE 14.5 The conflict management grid.*

- *Cooperativeness:* Desire to satisfy the other party's concerns
- *Assertiveness:* Desire to satisfy one's own concerns

As you would expect, only the problem-solving style scores high on both dimensions. This is one reason why theorists argue that only problem solving strategies lead to real conflict resolution.

Once again, it requires an attempt by the manager to locate and treat the causes of conflict, not merely to suppress them temporarily. True problem solving involves bringing conflicting parties together to discuss the situation. Through direct communication, attempts are made to identify where fact, values, methods, and/or goal differences contribute to the conflict. Then, reasons for the conflict in terms of such things as information, goals, and perceptions are identified. Once these reasons are clear, steps can be taken to eliminate or minimize them as sources of conflict.

Each of the five conflict-management styles has some potential value to the practicing manager. Although only problem solving results in true conflict resolution, there may be times when the other styles will yield adequate outcomes. The following are sample situations in which the chief executives of several large organizations report using conflict-management styles other than problem solving.[28]

- *Avoidance is used:* When an issue is trivial or more important issues are pressing; and to let people cool down and regain perspective.
- *Authoritative command is used:* When quick, decisive action is vital, e.g., in emergencies; and on important issues where unpopular actions, such as cost cutting, enforcing unpopular rules, and discipline need implementing.
- *Accommodating or Smoothing is used:* When issues are more important to others than yourself; and to build social credits for later issues.
- *Compromising is used:* To achieve temporary settlements to complex issues; and to arrive at expedient solutions.

# SUMMARY

**■ The Communication Process is effective when both sender and receiver interpret a message in the same way. It is efficient when messages are transferred at low cost. Managers use a variety of formal and informal communication channels in their work, and they use both verbal and nonverbal forms of communication. Semantic problems, physical distractions, cultural differences, and status effects are examples of "noise" or "barriers" that can interfere with the effectiveness of a communication attempt.**

**■ Guidelines for Effective Communication include developing your active listening and feedback delivery skills. Active listening is a "sender-oriented" approach to communication which encourages a free and**

complete flow of communication from someone else to you. It is non-judgmental and encouraging. Managers must give feedback to others, and the performance appraisal interview is but one example. It, however, often occurs under difficult and stressful conditions. In order to be constructive, feedback must be given directly and specifically and at a time when the recipient may be most prepared to accept it.

■ **Communication of Roles** is essential to daily life in organizations. Through communication, people at work send and receive job expectations. A variety of role dynamics can result from this particular form of communication. Role ambiguity occurs when a person is unclear about the expectations of others. Role conflicts occur when an individual receives expectations which, for one reason or another, he or she cannot fulfill. This commonly occurs when expectations sent by different sources are mutually exclusive, or when too many expectations exist and "overload" occurs.

■ **Conflict** can be emotional (e.g., based on personal feelings) or substantive (e.g., based on work goals). Both forms can be harmful in organizations if they result in individuals and/or groups being unable to work constructively with one another. When kept within tolerable limits, conflict can be a source of creativity and performance enhancement. It becomes destructive when these limits are exceeded.

■ **Conflict Situations in Organizations** occur in vertical and lateral working relations, and in line–staff relations. Often they result from work-flow interdependencies and resource scarcities. Most typically, conflict develops through a series of stages beginning with such antecedent conditions and progressing into manifest conflict. This may or may not be entirely "resolved" in the sense that the underlying reasons for the emotional and/or substantive conflict are eliminated. Unresolved prior conflicts set the stage for future conflicts of a similar nature.

■ **Conflict Management** should always proceed with the goal of true conflict resolution. Indirect forms of conflict management are common and useful in organizations. They include appeal to common goals, hierarchical referral, organizational redesign, and the use of mythology and scripts. Direct conflict management proceeds with different combinations of assertiveness and cooperativeness on the part of conflicting parties. Win–win conflict is achieved through collaboration and problem-solving most associated with high assertiveness and high cooperation. Win–lose conflict occurs through direct competition or authoritative command. Lose–lose conflict is typically found with avoidance, smoothing, and compromise approaches.

## KEY TERMS

Active Listening
Communication
Conflict
Conflict Resolution
Effective Communication
Efficient Communication
Emotional Conflicts
Ethnocentrism

Feedback
Formal Communication Channels
Informal Communication Channels
Lose–Lose Conflict
Mixed Message
Noise
Nonverbal Communication
Role
Role Ambiguity
Role Conflict
Role Overload
Role Set
Substantive Conflicts
Win–Lose Conflict
Win–Win Conflict

## REVIEW QUESTIONS

1. Make a list of the communication barriers that might limit the effectiveness of a manager's communications with subordinates. Give examples of each barrier as it might be found in the work setting in which you expect to practice as a manager.
2. Analyze the communication skills of a person for whom you work. (Your instructor is one possible choice.) What does he or she do well as a communicator? What could he or she do to improve communications with other persons?
3. Describe the difference between formal and informal communication channels in organizations. Why are both important to managers?
4. What is "active listening"? What is its significance in terms of achieving effectiveness in managerial communications?
5. Diagram the role set for a managerial position with which you are familiar. Identify where role ambiguities and conflicts might develop in this situation. What could be done by (a) the person and (b) his or her supervisor to minimize the negative consequences of these role dynamics?
6. Select an interpersonal conflict in which you have recently been involved. Adopt a diagnostic approach to identify the reasons for this conflict. How could problem solving have been used to resolve the conflict?
7. When would a manager want to promote conflict within the work unit? How can this be done in a way that ensures a constructive rather than destructive result?
8. Identify three major alternatives for managing conflict by altering structural variables in a situation. What are the implications of each in terms of operating efficiencies?

## AN OB LIBRARY

Alan C. Filley, *Interpersonal Conflict Resolution* (Glenview, IL: Scott, Foresman, 1975).

William M. Fox, *Effective Group Problem Solving: How to Broaden Participation, Improve Decision Making, and Increase Commitment to Action* (San Francisco: Jossey-Bass, 1987).

Neal Q. Herrick, *Joint Management and Employee Participation: Labor and Management at the Crossroads* (San Francisco: Jossey-Bass, 1990).

Bradford D. Smart, *The Smart Interviewer: Tools and Techniques for Hiring the Best* (New York: John Wiley & Sons, 1990).

Richard E. Walton, *Managing Conflict: Interpersonal Dialogue and Third-Party Roles,* Second Edition (Reading, MA: Addison-Wesley, 1987).

EXERCISE

# CONFLICT MANAGEMENT STRATEGIES

## *Objectives*

1. To assess your personal propensity to rely on different conflict management strategies.
2. To examine your personal propensity and compare it with those of others in the class.

## *Total Time*

60 minutes

## *Procedure*

1. Complete the personal and case assessments below.
2. Form groups of four to five members and link the responses on the three assessment instruments below to the following categories of conflict management behavior:
   a. *Forcing*—getting your own way.
   b. *Avoiding*—Avoiding having to deal with conflict.
   c. *Compromising*—Reaching an agreement quickly.
   d. *Accommodating*—Not upsetting the other party.
   e. *Collaborating*—Solving the problem together.
3. Discuss your rankings and reach consensus as to the most appropriate behavior for each of the two cases.
4. Be prepared to share the results of your group work with the rest of the class, including rationale.

## *Personal Assessment*[30]

Rank the following five approaches according to your relative use of each, using 1 = most frequent to 5 = least frequent.

_____ 1. I am generally firm in pursuing my personal goals. I try to show others the logic and benefits of my positions. If they are equally committed to their position, I make a strong effort to get my way by stressing my points. I give in reluctantly.

_____ 2. I try to avoid the debilitating tensions associated with conflict by letting others take responsibility for solving the problem. If possible, I try to postpone dealing with the problem until I can cool off and take time to think it over. To reduce the likelihood of conflicts, I often avoid taking controversial positions and I try not to get uptight when others express positions different from my own.

_____ 3. I try to find a middle-ground solution. I am willing to give up some points if it will lead to a fair combination of gains and losses for both parties. To expedite the resolution, I generally suggest that we search for a compromise, instead of stubbornly holding on to my position.

_____ 4. I try to soothe the other's feelings so the disagreement doesn't damage our relationship. I try to diffuse the conflict by focusing on points of agreement. If the other person's position seems very important to him or her, I will likely concede my own to maintain harmony.

_____ 5. I attempt to get all the concerns and issues out in the open. I frankly describe my position and ask that the other person do the same. I favor a direct discussion of disagreements as a way of forging an agreement. It is not always possible, but I try to satisfy the wishes of both parties.

### *Case Assessments*

Rank the five alternative courses of action under each of the two cases below using 1 = most desirable and 5 = least desirable.

### *Case One*

Pete is lead operator of a production molding machine. Recently he has noticed that one of the men from another machine has been coming over to his machine and talking to one of his men (not on break time). The efficiency of Pete's operator seems to be falling off, and there have been some rejects due to his inattention. Pete thinks he detects some resentment among the rest of the crew. *If you were Pete, you would:*

_____ a. Talk to your man and tell him to limit his conversations during on-the-job time.

_____ b. Ask the manager to tell the lead operator of the other machine to keep his operators in line.

_____ c. Confront both men the next time you see them together (as well as the other lead operator, if necessary), find out what they are up to, and tell them what you expect of your operators.

_____ d. Say nothing now; it would be silly to make something big out of something so insignificant.

_____ e. Try to put the rest of the crew at ease; it is important that they all work well together.

### *Case Two*

Sally is the senior quality-control (Q-C) inspector and has been appointed group leader of the Q-C people on her crew. On separate occasions, two of her people have come to her with different suggestions for reporting test results to the machine operators. Paul wants to send the test results to the supervisor and then to the machine, since the supervisor is the person ultimately responsible for production output. Jim thinks the results should go directly to the lead operator on the machine in question, since he is the one who must take corrective action as soon as possible. Both ideas seem good, and Sally can find no ironclad procedures in the department on how to route the reports. *If you were Sally, you would:*

_____ a. Decide who is right and ask the other person to go along with the decision (perhaps establish it as a written procedure).

_____ b. Wait and see; the best solution will become apparent.

_____ c. Tell both Paul and Jim not to get uptight about their disagreement; it is not that important.

_____ d. Get Paul and Jim together and examine both of their ideas closely.

_____ e. Send the report to the supervisor, with a copy to the lead operator (even though it might mean a little more copy work for Q-C).

CASE

# CONFLICT AT BURGER MART

It was not a typical March day at Burger Mart as Lynn Baker, the manager, thought about the day's events. Should she fire both Janice and Jane? What should she do? She reviewed the situation.

Janice, the assistant night manager, had been an excellent worker at Burger Mart for over three years. She worked thirty hours a week while completing high school and saving for a new car. Lynn had hoped that Janice would start in the Burger Mart managerial training program and enter West Side Community College. Even though Janice was only eighteen and earning $4.50 an hour, Lynn could always count on her. Normally Janice was bubbly, enthusiastic, and always cracking jokes, but lately Lynn had noticed a change in her. Perhaps Janice's change in attitude was due to Burt. He was going to State, while Janice's application had been contingent upon completing two math courses in summer school. Lynn really did not want to see Janice go to State, and she knew that Burt was just a passing phase.

Jane was another matter. Quiet, almost sullen at times, she was probably the brightest student employee in the group. In the four years she had worked at Burger Mart, she always wanted more hours but she was habitually late and just did not fit into the group. Perhaps it was because of her parents' recent divorce. Perhaps it was because Jane was a nerd and off to Hollymount with a full scholarship. Anyway, Jane just did not fit in. She was now the only holdover from before Lynn was appointed as manager.

In a way, the incident had been almost funny. As Lynn was returning from checking the inventory in the freezer, she saw that Janice was talking to Jane. From around the corner she heard Janice say something to Jane about being late again and about failing to clean the french fry slots properly before putting on more fries. Jane called Janice a slob because the top button on her uniform was missing.

Since orders were backing up and some of the customers were beginning to grumble about where their food was, Lynn started to see why there was a hold-up. She saw Janice point her finger in Jane's face and poke her shoulder. Jane turned slowly, picked up a five-gallon container of vegetable oil, and poured it over Janice's head. As Janice grabbed Jane, both slipped on the greasy floor. It took the crew ten minutes to clean up the mess after Lynn sent both of them home.

### *Questions*

1. What are the antecedent conditions underlying the conflict between Jane and Janice?
2. Besides the conflict between Jane and Janice, what other types of conflict may be present?
3. What conflict management style would you suggest for Lynn, and why?
4. What actions would you recommend to Lynn to minimize conflict between employees in the future?
5. How would you evaluate the patterns of communication between Lynn and the two student workers?

This study outline of major topics is meant to organize your reading now; it is repeated in the Summary to structure your review.

## STUDY OUTLINE

### POWER

Position Power Personal Power Authority

### Power, Authority, and Obedience

The Milgram Experiments Obedience and the Zone of Indifference Obedience and the Acceptance of Authority

### Managerial Perspectives on Power and Influence

Acquiring Managerial Power Turning Power into Influence Empowering Others

### Organizational Politics

The Two Traditions of Organizational Politics The Double-Edged Sword of Organizational Politics

# CHAPTER 15

# POWER AND POLITICS



## PHOTO ESSAYS

# VISIONS 15

There's a new view of power at work these days at Johnsonville Foods. This family-owned $100 million and rapidly growing Sheboygan, Wisconsin specialty foods maker has given up on "pyramid power" and is seeking the advantages of a flatter and more streamlined organization structure. The visions of CEO Ralph Stayer are quite clear. "Flattening pyramids doesn't work if you don't transfer the power too," he says. "Real power is getting people committed. Real power comes from giving it up to others who are in a better position to do things than you are."

They're serious about sharing power at Johnsonville Foods. There is no personnel department anymore—but there is a Personal Development and Lifelong Learning Department to help people meet their goals and dreams. Each year volunteers from the shop floor write the manufacturing budget, to help the sales department reach 40 percent higher sales goals the manufacturing group set its own goals of adding the output but keeping cost increases to only 20 percent. CEO Stayer wants goals like these set as far down in the organization as possible. The company's growth curve indicates the process is working.

Power

"Power is America's last dirty word"—so begins an article in the *Harvard Business Review*.[1] The implication is that we are uncomfortable with the concept of power, that we are perhaps even somewhat offended by it. But the author of this provocative sentence then goes on to explore power in organizations and to suggest how managers can act to ensure that they have the power required to be successful in their jobs. Increasingly, as well, managers are realizing that they must share power with others and help them develop the power needed to function effectively in their jobs. This is the message behind the chapter-opening *Visions,* and it is a decidedly positive view of power. This is the view of power we will explore in the present chapter. In addition, we will examine the link between power and politics in organizations, with a special concern for ethics.

## POWER

In OB, power is the ability to get someone else to do something you want done or the ability to make things happen in the way you want. The essence of power is control over the behavior of others.[2] One of the interesting things about ***power*** is that it has no verb form. You do not "power" something. You can, however, "influence" something. Power is the force that makes things happen in an intended way. ***Influence*** is a behavioral response to the exercise of power. It is an outcome achieved through the use of power. People are "influenced" when they act in ways consistent with the desires of someone else. Managers use power to achieve influence over other people in the work setting.

**Influence**

Figure 15.1 summarizes the link between power and influence. It also identifies the key bases of power managers can use to influence the behavior of other people at work. Managers derive power from both organizational and individual sources. We call these sources position power and personal power, respectively.[3]

## Position Power

Three bases of power are available to a manager because of his or her position in the organization: reward, coercive, and legitimate power. ***Reward power*** is the extent to which a manager can use extrinsic and intrinsic rewards to control other people. Examples of such rewards include money, promotions, compliments, or enriched jobs. These types of rewards are discussed in detail in Chapters 6 and 7. Although all managers have some access to rewards, success in accessing and utilizing them to achieve influence varies according to the skills of the manager.

**Reward power**

Power can also be founded on punishment instead of reward. A manager may, for example, threaten to withhold a pay raise, transfer, demote or even recommend the firing of a subordinate who does not act as desired. Such ***coercive power*** is the extent to which a manager can deny desired rewards or administer punishments to control other people. The availability of coercive power also varies from one organization and manager to another. The presence of unions and organizational policies or on employee treatment can weaken this power base considerably.

**Coercive power**

The third base of position power is ***legitimate power.*** It stems from the extent to which a manager can use subordinates' internalized values or beliefs that the "boss" has a "right of command" to control their behavior. It is legitimate power, for example, that allows a manager to approve—or deny—such employee requests as job transfers, equipment purchases, personal time off, or overtime work.

**Legitimate power**

*FIGURE 15.1 Power sources and the influence process.*

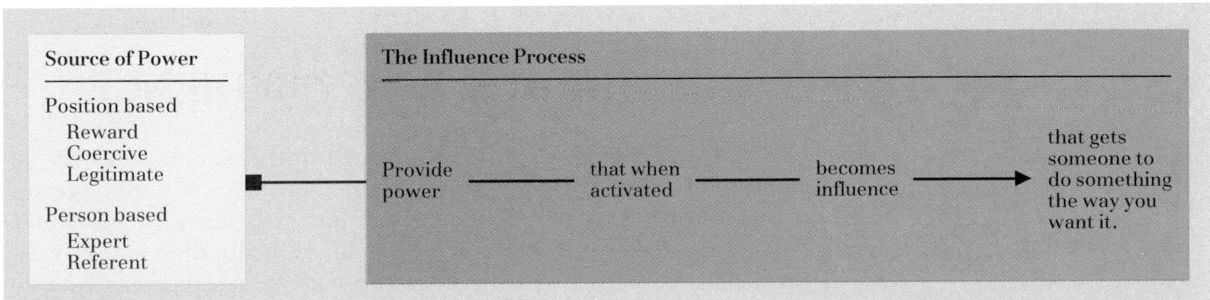

## Personal Power

Expert power

Two bases of personal power are expertise and reference. ***Expert power*** is the ability to control another's behavior through the possession of knowledge, experience, or judgment that the other person does not have but needs. In the case of a supervisor having expert power, a subordinate would obey because the boss is felt to know more about what is to be done or how it is to be done than the subordinate. Access to or control over information is an important element in this particular power base. Access to key organizational decision makers is another. A person's ability to contact key persons informally can allow for special participation in the definition of a problem or issue, alteration in the flow of information to decision makers, and lobbying for use of special criteria in decision making.

Referent power

***Referent power*** is the ability to control another's behavior because of their wanting to identify with the power source. In this case, a subordinate would obey the boss because he or she wants to behave, perceive, or believe as the boss does. This may occur, for example, because the subordinate likes the boss personally and therefore tries to do things the way the boss wants them done. In a sense, the subordinate behaves in order to avoid doing anything that would interfere with the pleasing boss-subordinate relationship.

## Authority

Authority

Formal ***authority*** and legitimate power are one and the same. The two terms represent a special kind of power that a manager has because subordinates believe it is legitimate for a person occupying the managerial position to have the right to command. In practice it is often hard to separate authority, or legitimate power, from the use of reward and coercive power. This is because persons with authority usually have special access to rewards and punishments and can thereby alter their availability to subordinates. Although not always in evidence, it is top management authority that lies behind the mandated changes that are restructuring many of today's large corporations. For example,

> ***Torchmark*** Chief-Executive Ronald K. Richey eliminated layers of management at Torchmark, consolidated sales territories, and automated the insurance company's back office. He used his authority to initiate the desired changes. The company has since experienced a 20 percent higher earnings growth.

# POWER, AUTHORITY, AND OBEDIENCE

Power is the potential to control the behavior of others, and authority is the potential to exert such control through the legitimacy of a managerial position. Yet we also know that people who seem to have power don't always get their way. This leads us to the subject of obedience. Why do some people obey directives, while others do not? More specifically, why should subordinates respond to a manager's authority or "right to command"? Furthermore, given that they are willing to obey, what determines the limits of obedience?

## The Milgram Experiments

These last questions point directly toward Stanley Milgram's seminal research on obedience.[4] Milgram designed an experiment to determine the extent to which people obey the commands of an authority figure, even if believing that they are endangering the life of another person. The subjects were 40 males, ranging in age from 20 to 50, representing a diverse set of occupations (engineers, sales people, school teachers, laborers, and others). They were paid a nominal fee for participation in the project, which was conducted in a laboratory at Yale University.

The subjects were falsely told that the purpose of the study was to determine the effects of punishment on learning. They were to be the "teachers," and the "learner," a confederate of Milgram's, was strapped to a chair in an adjoining room with an electrode attached to his wrist. The "experimenter," another confederate of Milgram's, was dressed in a gray laboratory coat. Appearing impassive and somewhat stern, he instructed the "teacher" to read a series of word pairs to the learner and then to reread the first word along with four other terms. The learner was supposed to indicate which of the four terms was in the original pair. This was accomplished by pressing a switch that caused a light to flash on a response panel in front of the teacher.

The teacher was instructed to administer a shock to the learner each time a wrong answer was given. This shock was to be increased one level of intensity each time the learner made a mistake. The teacher controlled switches that ostensibly administered shocks ranging from 15 to 450 volts. The voltage and degree of shock were labeled on the switches. In reality, there was no electric current in the apparatus, but the learners purposely "erred" often and responded to each level of "shock" in progressively distressing ways. A summary of the switch markings and the learner's fake responses to the various levels of shock is shown in Figure 15.2.

| Switch Voltage Marking | Switch Description | "Learner's" Responses | "Teachers" Refusing to Go on |
|---|---|---|---|
| 15–60 | Slight | No sound | ________ |
| 75–120 | Moderate | Grunts and moans | ________ |
| 135–180 | Strong | Asks to leave | ________ |
| 195–240 | Very strong | Can't stand the pain | ________ |
| 255–300 | Intense | Pounds on wall | ________ |
| 315–360 | Extreme intensity | No sound | ________ |
| 375–420 | Danger: severe shock | No sound | ________ |
| 435–450 | XXX | No sound | ________ |

*FIGURE 15.2 Shock levels and set learner responses in the Milgram experiment.*

If a teacher proved unwilling to administer a shock, the experimenter used the following prods to get him or her to perform as requested: (1) "please continue" or "please go on," (2) "the experiment requires that you continue," (3) "it is absolutely essential that you continue," and (4) "you have no choice, you must go on." Only when the teacher refused to go on after the fourth prod would the experiment be stopped. When do you think the "teachers" would refuse to go on?

Milgram asked some of his students and colleagues the same question. Most felt that few, if any, of the subjects would go beyond the "Very strong shock" level. In actual fact, 26 subjects (65 percent) continued to the end of the experiment and shocked the "learners" to the XXX level! None stopped prior to 300 volts, the point at which the learner pounds on the wall. The remaining 14 subjects refused to obey the experimenter at various intermediate points.

Most people, as was Milgram, are surprised by these results. They wondered just why other people would have a tendency to accept or comply with authoritative commands under such extreme conditions. Milgram conducted further experiments to try to answer these questions. Things that appeared to make a difference in subjects' tendencies toward obedience were: the building in which the experiment took place (university laboratory or run-down office), proximity of subject and victim, proximity of subject and the experimenter, and the observed behaviors of other subjects.

## Obedience and the Zone of Indifference

Milgram's experiments provide a dramatic example of people's tendency to obey the directives of higher authority figures in organizational settings. A useful way to bring this issue and its implications into focus lies with the psychological contract—introduced in Chapter 2 as a set of expectations held by the individual that specify what the individual and the organization expect to give and to receive from each other in the course of their working relationship. Most people seek a balance between what they put into an organization (contributions) and what they get from an organization in return (inducements). Within the boundaries of the psychological contract, therefore, employees will agree to do many things in and for the organization because they think they should. That is, in exchange for certain inducements, they recognize the authority of the organization and its managers to direct their behavior in certain ways. Chester Barnard, a former president of the New Jersey Bell Telephone Company and a renowned management scholar, calls this area in which directions are obeyed the "zone of indifference."[5]

**Zone of indifference**

A ***zone of indifference*** is the range of authoritative requests to which a subordinate is willing to respond without subjecting the directives to critical evaluation or judgment, hence to which he or she is indifferent. Directives falling within the zone are obeyed. Requests or orders falling outside the zone of indifference are not considered legitimate under terms of the psychological contract. Such "extraordinary" directives may or may not be obeyed. This link between the zone of indifference and the psychological contract is shown in Figure 15.3.

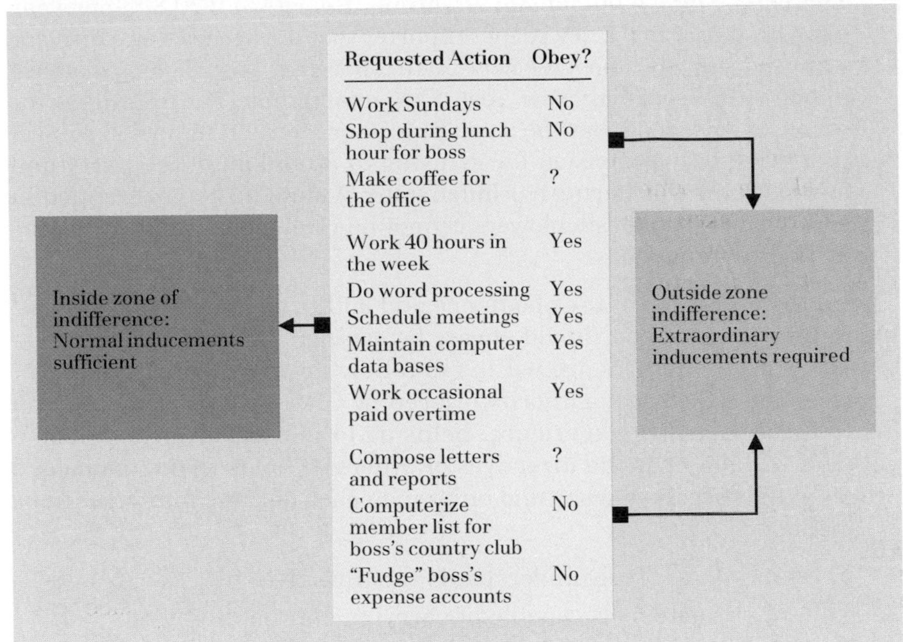


*FIGURE 15.3 Hypothetical psychological contract for a secretary.*

The secretary whose psychological contract is shown in the figure may be expected to perform with no questions asked a number of activities falling within the zone of indifference. There may be times, however, when the boss would like the secretary to do things falling outside the zone. This requires efforts to enlarge the zone to accommodate additional behaviors. In these attempts the boss will most likely have to use more than pure position power. In some instances, such as Sunday work and "fudging" expense accounts, no power base may be capable of accomplishing the desired result.

## Obedience and the Acceptance of Authority

Before leaving this discussion, there is another side to power, authority, and obedience with which you should be familiar as a manager. That side is your own zone of indifference and tendency to obey. When will you say "no" to your boss? When should you be willing to say "no"? At times, this may even reach the extreme of involving ethical dilemmas where one is asked to do things that are illegal, unethical, or both. Research on ethical managerial behavior, for example, shows that supervisors are singled out by their subordinates as sources of pressure to do such things as support incorrect viewpoints, sign false documents, overlook their wrongdoing, and do business with their friends.[6]

Most of us will occasionally face such ethical dilemmas during our careers. In Chapters 1 and 13 our look at ethical aspects of decision making offers some advice on how to best handle these matters. For now, we must simply remind you that saying "no" or "refusing to keep quiet" can be difficult and potentially costly . . . as many *whistleblowers* find out. But it may still be the *right* thing to do. For example,

***The Ohio State Employment Relations Board*** A $20,800-per-year word processor told a newspaper reporter that the agency's vice director was conducting business for her $59,010-per-year post via long distance phone calls from her New York City apartment. The vice director eventually resigned, but the word processor later found herself subject to a three-day suspension for refusing to attend an office party and awards ceremony during her lunch hour. A state inspector stepped in and warned that whistleblowers cannot be retaliated against for aiding official investigations.

On the other side of the obedience and authority issue is the "boss's" point of view. He or she should always be asking: "What do I need to do to make sure that others are willing to follow my directive or request?" An acceptance theory of authority offered by Chester Barnard, based on his years of executive experience, helps us to understand when people will and will not obey the directives of others. It holds that a manager's orders will be accepted when and only when each of these four conditions is satisfied:[7]

1. The subordinate truly understands the directive.
2. The subordinate feels capable of carrying out the directive.
3. The subordinate sees the directive in the organization's best interests.
4. The subordinate believes the directive to be consistent with personal values.

# MANAGERIAL PERSPECTIVES ON POWER AND INFLUENCE

A considerable portion of any manager's time will be directed toward what is called "power-oriented" behavior. This is "behavior directed primarily at developing or using relationships in which other people are to some degree willing to defer to one's wishes."[8] Figure 15.4 shows three basic dimensions of power and influence with which a manager will become involved in this regard: downward, upward, and lateral. Also shown in the figure are some preliminary ideas on achieving success along each of these dimensions. When facing upward, managers must rely on the use of personal power to achieve influence over higher-level superiors. When facing downward, by contrast, both position and personal power can be mobilized in dealing with subordinates. In lateral relations with peers and outsiders, the manager must again emphasize personal power to achieve the desired influence.

## Acquiring Managerial Power

The effective manager is one who succeeds in building and maintaining high levels of both position and personal power over time. Then and only then will sufficient power of the right types be available when a manager needs to exercise influence on downward, lateral, and upward dimensions.

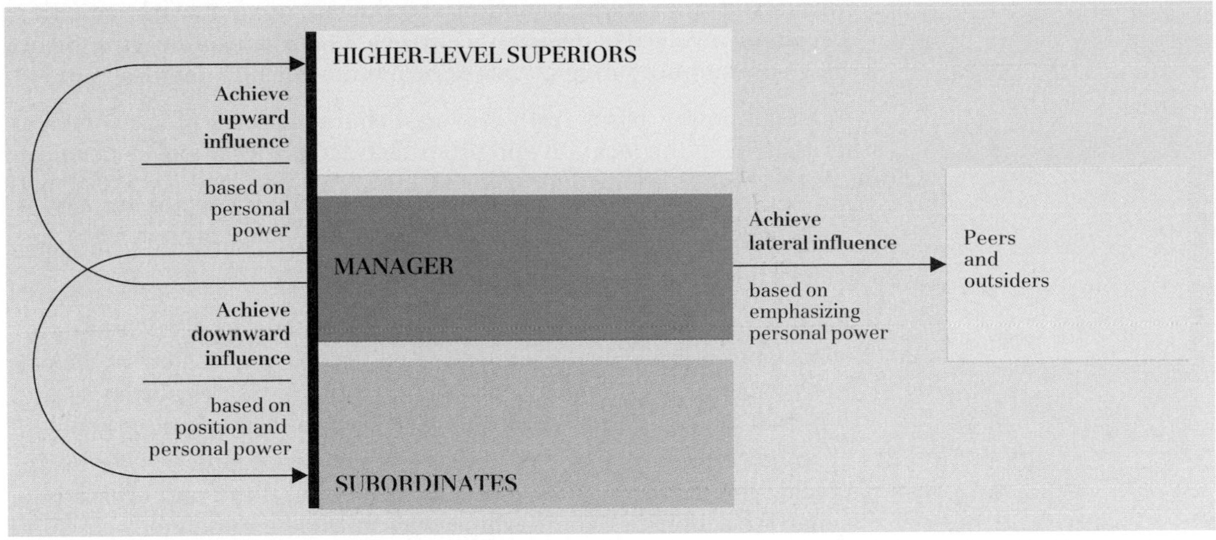


*FIGURE 15.4 Three dimensions of managerial power and influence.*

Position power is based on formal authority and the legitimacy of a manager's location in the organization's hierarchy of authority. Position power can be enhanced when managers are able to demonstrate to others that their work units are highly relevant to organizational goals and able to respond to urgent organizational needs. In addition, there are five general guidelines for enhancing one's position power:[9]

1. *Increase your centrality and criticality in the organization* by acquiring a more central role in the work flow, having information filtered through you, making at least part of your job responsibilities unique, expanding your network of communication contacts, and occupying an office convenient to main traffic flows.
2. *Increase the personal discretion and flexibility of your job* by getting rid of routine activities, expanding task variety and novelty, initiating new ideas, getting involved in new projects, participating in the early stages of the decision-making process, and avoiding "reliable performance criteria" for judging your success on the job.
3. *Build tasks that are difficult to evaluate into your job* by creating an ambiguous job description, developing a unique language or set of labels in your work, obtaining advanced training, becoming more involved in professional associations, and exercising your own judgment.
4. *Increase the visibility of your job performance* by expanding the number of contacts you have with senior people, making oral presentations of written work, participating in problem-solving task forces, sending out notices of accomplishment that are of interest to the organization, and seeking additional opportunities to increase personal name recognition.
5. *Increase the relevance of your tasks to the organization* by becoming an internal coordinator or external representative, providing services and information to other units, monitoring and evaluating activities

within your own unit, expanding the domain of your work activities, becoming involved in decisions central to the organization's top-priority goals, and becoming a trainer or mentor for new members.

Personal power arises from personal characteristics of the manager rather than from the location and other characteristics of his or her position in the organization's hierarchy of authority. We discussed two primary bases of personal power as resting in expertise and reference. Three personal characteristics are singled out for their special potential to enhance someone's personal power in an organization.[10]

1. *Knowledge and information.* A manager can enhance his or her personal power through the expertise gained by possession of special knowledge (e.g., gained by education, training, and experience) and information (e.g., gained through special access to data and/or people).
2. *Personal attractiveness.* A manager's reference power will be increased by characteristics that enhance "likability" and create personal attraction in relationships with other people. These include pleasant personality characteristics, agreeable behavior patterns, and attractive personal appearance.
3. *Effort.* The demonstration of sincere hard work in behalf of task performance can also increase personal power by enhancing both expertise and reference. A person perceived to try hard may be expected to know more about the job and thus be sought out for advice; a person who tries hard is also likely to be respected for the attempt and even become depended on by others to maintain that effort. For example,

> ***Sara Lee*** It is recognized that power flows from consistent high performance. Sara Lee top executive John Bryan observes that performance leads to an ability to "take on" and "argue" with superiors and more easily "resist" staff people. A high performer, he says, "becomes a star, and over time comes to seem indispensable."

## Turning Power into Influence

The acquisition of power is certainly an important task for any manager. Using this power well actually to achieve the desired influence over other people, however, is yet another challenge. Consider the following examples of how some managers attempt to exercise influence.

"I voice my wishes loudly."

"I offer a quid pro quo; that is, I offer to do for them if they do for me."

"I keep at it and reiterate my point over and over again until I get my way."

"I have all the facts and figures ready, and I use them as necessary."

"I go over the boss's head to higher levels when I get turned down."

Practically speaking, there are many useful ways of exercising influence. These strategies involve managers attempting to get their ways by:[11]

- *Reason.* Using facts and data to support a logical argument.
- *Friendliness.* Using flattery, goodwill, and favorable impressions.
- *Coalition.* Using relationships with other people.
- *Bargaining.* Using the exchange of benefits as a basis for negotiation.
- *Assertiveness.* Using a direct and forceful personal approach.
- *Higher authority.* Gaining higher level support for one's requests.
- *Sanctions.* Using organizationally derived rewards and punishments.

Actual research on these strategies for achieving managerial influence suggests that *reason* is the most popular strategy overall.[12] In addition, friendliness, assertiveness, bargaining, and higher authority are used more frequently to influence subordinates than supervisors. This pattern of influence attempts is consistent with our earlier contention that downward influence will generally include mobilization of both position and personal power sources, while upward influence will more likely draw on personal power.

There is not much research available on the specific subject of upward influence in organizations. This is unfortunate since a truly effective manager is one who is able to influence his or her boss as well as subordinates. One study reports that reason or the logical presentation of ideas is viewed by both supervisors and subordinates as the most frequently used strategy of upward influence.[13] When queried on reasons for success and failure, however, both similarities and differences are found in the viewpoints of the two groups. Table 15.1 shows that the perceived causes of success in upward influence are similar for both supervisors and subordinates. These reasons involve the favorable content of the influence attempt, a favorable manner of its presentation, and the competence of the subordinate. Where the two groups disagree is on the causes of failure. Subordinates view failure in upward influence as caused by closemindedness of the supervisor, unfavorable content of the influence attempt, and unfavorable

*TABLE 15.1*
**PERCEIVED CAUSES OF SUCCESS AND FAILURE IN UPWARD INFLUENCE ATTEMPTS**

| | Supervisor's Views | Subordinate's Views |
|---|---|---|
| Causes of success | Favorable content of influence attempt; favorable manner in which attempt made; competency of subordinate | Agreement with supervisor's views |
| Causes of failure | Unfavorable content of influence attempt; lack of competence of subordinate; poor manner in which attempt made | Unfavorable content of influence attempt; closemindedness of supervisor; poor interpersonal relations with supervisor |

*Source:* Developed from Warren K. Schilit and Edwin A. Locke, "A Study of Upward Influence in Organizations." *Administrative Science Quarterly,* Vol 27 (1982), pp. 304–316.

interpersonal relationships with the supervisor. Supervisors, by contrast, view failures as due to unfavorable content of the attempt, the unfavorable manner in which it was presented, and lack of competence of the subordinate.

## Empowering Others

**Empowerment**

***Empowerment*** is the process through which managers help others to acquire and use the power needed to make decisions affecting themselves and their work. More than ever before, managers in progressive organizations are expected to be good at and highly comfortable at empowering the people with whom they work. Rather than considering power as something only to be held at higher levels in the traditional "pyramid" of organizations, this view considers power as something that can be shared by everyone working in flatter and more collegial structures.

The concept of empowerment is part of sweeping change being witnessed in today's industry. Corporate staff is being cut back; layers of management are being cut back; the number of employees is being cut back. What is left is a leaner and trimmer organization staffed by fewer people who *share* more power as they go about daily tasks. It may well be, as suggested by Corning's Chairperson John R. Houghton, that "the age of the hierarchy is over."[14] Indeed, empowerment is a key foundation of the increasingly popular self-managing work teams and other creative worker involvement groups discussed in Chapter 8 and elsewhere in the book. This is well evidenced, for example:

> *Pillsbury Company* Advertising for workers at its Westerville, Ohio plant, Pillsbury said that applications were being accepted for jobs as "team" members. Listed as characteristics of the "team" environment in which successful applicants would be working were: Solving problems, learning and performing a variety of jobs, assisting and coaching others, and working well with little supervision.

Clearly, the implications in the prior example are that successful candidates for the Pillsbury jobs will be *empowered.* This should mean not only that they are given the opportunity to develop and use power in their jobs—but that they will be expected to use it responsibly and actively for high performance. At Johnsonville Foods, cited in the chapter-opening *Visions* for its empowerment program, the CEO says: "No one gets a raise unless they take on more responsibility."[15]

Not everyone is comfortable assuming power in their work. Although the concept may seem very attractive to us, it can be quite threatening when newly introduced into a work setting where most people have learned through experience *not* to exercise personal discretion and judgment in their jobs. In such cases, special support may be needed to help people become acquainted with their potential power and learn to use it responsibly.

When all goes well, everyone can gain from empowerment. To keep their organizations competitive, top management must attend to a variety of challenging and strategic forces in the external environment. While

SKILLS PERSPECTIVE

## MONTGOMERY WARD

Courtesy of Montgomery Ward.

**Empowerment of workers is one of the keys to Montgomery Ward's future success, believes Chairperson Bernard F. Brennan. He has authorized the retailer's 7700 salesclerks to exercise more personal discretion in decisions affecting their customers. For example, salesclerks can now make decisions to approve checks and handle merchandise return problems. Previously, only the store managers could make these decisions. Customer service is enhanced, and worker skills are better utilized with this shift in emphasis toward sharing power in the firm.**

they concentrate on decisions about strategy and dynamic change, others throughout the organization must be ready and willing to make critical operating decisions. By providing these opportunities, empowerment increases the total power available in an organization. In other words, the top levels don't have to give up power for the lower levels to gain it. The same basic argument holds true in any manager–subordinate relationship.

Among the trends in managerial efforts at empowering others are these emerging guidelines:

- *Delegation of authority to lower levels should be clear and unambiguous*—people must know what they are empowered to do and what they are being held accountable for.
- *Planning must be integrated and participative at all levels*—people must be involved in planning if they are to understand plans and goals, and have the commitments needed to implement them effectively.
- *Managers at all levels, but especially the top, should exercise strong communication skills*—information is the key to understanding goals and responsibilities, and for understanding the "big picture" within which they become meaningful.

# ORGANIZATIONAL POLITICS

Any study of power and influence inevitably leads to the subject of "politics." This word may conjure up thoughts of illicit deals, favors, and special personal relationships in your mind. Perhaps this image of shrewd, often dishonest, practices of obtaining one's way is reinforced by Machiavelli's classic fifteenth-century work *The Prince,* which outlines how to obtain and hold power via political action. It is important, however, to adopt a perspective that allows for politics in organizations to function in a much broader capacity.[16]

## The Two Traditions of Organizational Politics

There are two quite different traditions in the analysis of organizational politics. One tradition builds on Machiavelli and defines politics in terms of self-interest and the use of non-sanctioned means. In this tradition

**Organizational politics**

***organizational politics*** may be formally defined as the management of influence to obtain ends not sanctioned by the organization or to obtain sanctioned ends through non-sanctioned influence means.[17] Managers are often considered political when they seek their own goals or use means not currently authorized. It is also important to recognize that where there is uncertainty or ambiguity it is often extremely difficult to tell whether a manager is being political in this self-serving sense.[18]

The second tradition treats politics as a necessary function resulting from differences in the self-interests of individuals. Here organizational politics is viewed as the art of creative compromise among competing interests. In a heterogeneous society individuals will disagree on whose self interests are most valuable and whose concerns should therefore be bounded by collective interests. Politics arise since individuals need to develop compromises, avoid confrontation, and live together. The same holds true in organizations where individuals join, work, and stay because their self-interests are served. Further, it is important to remember that the goals of the organization and the acceptable means are established by organizationally powerful individuals in negotiation with others. Thus, organizational politics is also the use of power to develop socially acceptable ends and means that balance individual and collective interests.

## The Double-Edged Sword of Organizational Politics

These two different traditions of organizational politics are reflected in how executives describe their effects on managers and their organizations. In one survey some 53 percent interviewed indicated that organizational politics enhanced the achievement of organizational goals and survival.[19] Yet, some 44 percent suggested that it distracted individuals from organizational goals. In this same survey 60 percent suggested that organizational politics was good for career advancement; 39 percent reported that it led to a loss of power, position, and credibility.

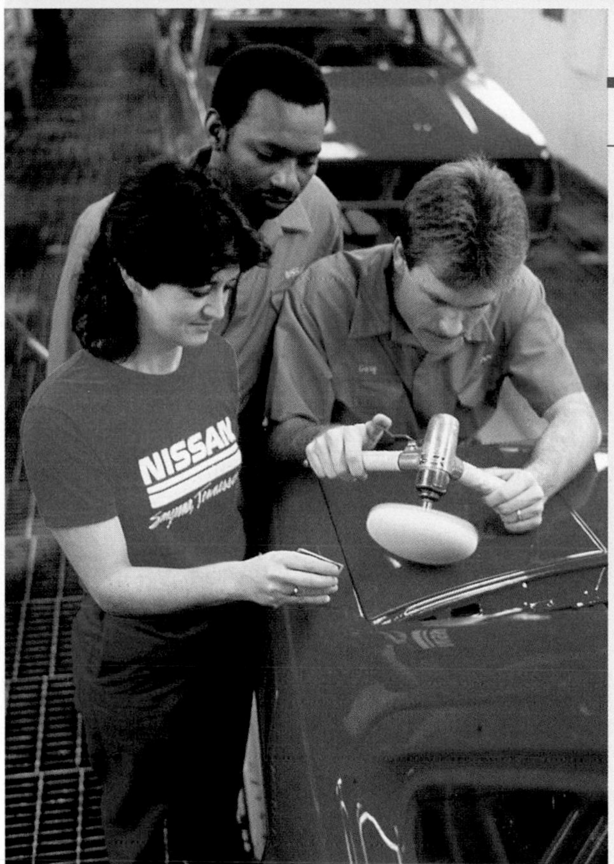

Courtesy of Nissan Motor Co., Ltd.

**INTERNATIONAL PERSPECTIVE**

## NISSAN

**Workers at Nissan's 782 acre Smyrna, Tennessee, plant are steeped in "teamwork"—one of the keys to the plant's successful Japanese-oriented approach to manufacturing. Participative management, in which workers are allowed to share authority and be involved in decisions affecting them and their work, is facilitated by Nissan's management approach. Minimum organizational layering has kept the plant to only five levels of management between the company president and line workers. There are only four job categories, and within each area workers learn multiple skills. In their teams, workers also share tasks and rotate responsibilities regularly. Members go through months of extensive training, and they together learn such techniques as *kanban,* for regulating production flow, and *kaizen,* a system of always looking for better ways of doing things. Of course, they also check their own quality. It takes work to maintain a spirit of *togetherness* on these teams. But that's all part of the challenge when you have the sense of purpose these groups of American workers seem to have found.**

Organizational politics is not automatically good or bad. It can serve a number of important functions, including helping managers to:

- *Overcome personnel inadequacies.* As a manager, you should expect some mismatches between people and positions in organizations. Even in the best managed firms, mismatches arise among managers who are learning, burned out, lacking in needed training and skills, overqualified, or lacking resources needed to accomplish their assigned duties. Organizational politics provides a mechanism for circumventing these inadequacies and getting the job done.
- *Cope with change.* Changes in the environment and technology of an organization often come more quickly than an organization can restructure. Even in organizations known for detailed planning, unanticipated events occur. To meet unanticipated problems, people and resources must be moved into place quickly before small headaches become major problems. Organizational politics can help to identify

such problems and move ambitious, problem-solving managers into the breach.

- *Channel personal contacts.* In larger organizations, it is all but impossible to know the persons in every important position. Yet managers need to influence individuals throughout the organization. The political network of the organization can provide the necessary access.
- *Substitute for formal authority.* When a person's formal authority breaks down or fails to apply to a situation, political actions can be used to prevent a loss of influence. Managers may use political behavior to maintain operations and achieve task continuity in circumstances where the failure of formal authority may otherwise cause problems.

# POLITICAL ACTION IN ORGANIZATIONS

Political action is a part of organizational life and it is best to view organizational politics for its potential to contribute to managerial and organizational effectiveness. It is in this spirit that we now examine political action in organizations from the perspectives of managers, subunits, and chief executives.

## Political Action and the Manager

Managers may gain a better understanding of political behavior by placing themselves in the positions of other persons involved in critical decisions or events. Each action and decision can be seen as having benefits and costs to all parties concerned. Where the costs exceed the benefits, the manager may act to protect his or her position.

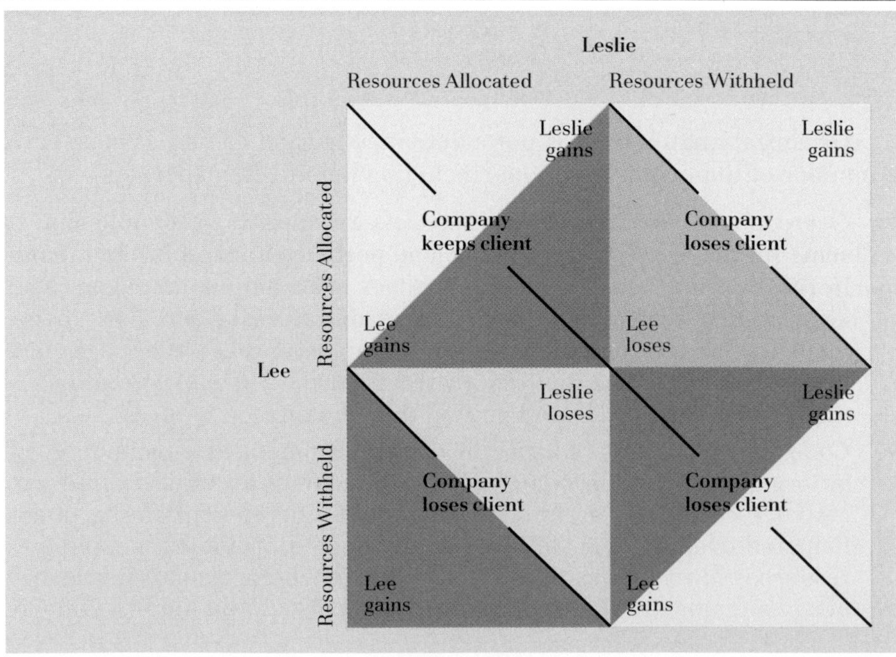


*FIGURE 15.5 Political payoff matrix for the allocation of resources on a sample project.*

Figure 15.5 shows a sample payoff table for two managers, Lee and Leslie, in a problem situation involving a decision whether or not to allocate resources to a special project. If both authorize the resources, the project gets completed on time and their company keeps a valuable client. Unfortunately, by doing so both Lee and Leslie will overspend their budgets. Taken on its own, a budget overrun would be bad for their performance record. Assume that the overruns will be acceptable only if the client is kept. Thus, if both act, both they and the company win. This is the upper left block in the figure. Obviously, it is the most desirable outcome for all parties concerned.

Assume that Leslie acts, but Lee does not. The company loses the client and Leslie overspends the budget in a futile effort, but Lee ends up within budget. While the company and Leslie lose, Lee wins. This is the lower left block of the figure. The upper right block shows the reverse situation, where Lee acts but Leslie does not. Leslie wins, and the company and Lee lose. Finally, if both fail to act, they each stay within the budget and therefore gain, but the company loses the client.

The company clearly wants both Lee and Leslie to act. But will they? Would you take the risk of overspending the budget, knowing that your colleague may refuse? The question of trust is critical here, but building trust among co-managers and other workers takes time and can be difficult. The involvement of higher-level managers may be needed to set the stage better. Yet, we would predict that in many organizations both Lee and Leslie would fail to act. Why? Because the "climate" or "culture" too often encourages people to maximize their self-interest at minimal risks. What we need are more settings where people are willing to take a chance and be rewarded for doing so.

## Political Action and Subunit Power

Another level of political action links managers more formally to one another as representatives of their work units. In Chapter 9, we examined the group of dynamics associated with such intergroup relationships. Table 15.2 highlights five of the more typical lateral and intergroup relations in which you might engage as a manager—work flow, service, advisory, auditing, and approval. The table also shows how lateral relationships challenge even further the political skills of a manager—each example requires the manager to achieve influence through some other means than formal authority.

To be effective in political action, managers should understand the politics of subunit relations. Line units are typically more powerful than staff groups, and units toward the top of the hierarchy are often more powerful than are those toward the bottom. Units gain power as more of their relations with others are of the approval and auditing types. Work-flow relations are more powerful than are advisory associations, and both are more powerful than service relations. Units can also increase power by incorporating new actions that tackle and resolve difficult problems. Certain strategic contingencies can often govern the relative power of subunits. For a subunit to gain power vis-à-vis others, it must increase its control over such strategic contingencies as:[20]

*TABLE 15.2*
**TYPICAL LATERAL RELATIONS ENGAGED IN BY MANAGERS AND THEIR ASSOCIATED INFLUENCE REQUIREMENTS**

| *Type of Relationship* | *Sample Influence Requirements* |
|---|---|
| *Work flow*—contacts with units that precede or follow in a sequential production chain. | An assembly-line manager informs another line manager responsible for a later stage in the production process about a delay that must be taken. |
| *Service*—contacts with units established to help with problems. | An assembly-line manager asks the maintenance manager to fix an important piece of equipment on a priority basis. |
| *Advisory*—contacts with formal staff units having special expertise. | A marketing manager consults with the personnel manager to obtain special assistance in recruiting for a new salesperson. |
| *Auditing*—contacts with units having the right to evaluate the actions of others. | A marketing manager tries to get the credit manager to retract a report criticizing marketing's tendency to open bad-credit accounts. |
| *Approval*—contacts with units whose approval must be obtained before action may be taken. | A marketing manager submits a job description to the company affirmative action officer for approval before recruiting for a new salesperson can begin. |

*Source:* Developed from James L. Hall and Joel L. Leidecker, "Lateral Relations in Organizations," pp. 213–223 in Patrick E. Connor, ed., *Dimensions in Modern Management* (Boston: Houghton Mifflin, 1974), which was based in part on Leonard Sayles, *Managerial Behavior* (New York: McGraw-Hill, 1964).

- *Scarce resources.* Subunits gain in power when they obtain access to or control scarce resources needed by others.
- *Ability to cope with uncertainty.* Subunits gain in power when they are able to cope with uncertainty and help solve problems that uncertainty causes for others.
- *Centrality in the flow of work.* Subunits gain in power when their position in the work flow allows them to influence the work of others.
- *Substitutability of activities.* Subunits gain in power when they perform tasks or activities that are nonsubstitutable, that is, when they perform essential functions that cannot be completed by others.

## Political Action and the Chief Executive

From descriptions of the 1890s robber barons such as Jay Gould to the popular JR of "Dallas," Americans have been fascinated with the politics of the chief executive suite. An analytical view of executive suite dynamics may lift some of the mystery behind the political veil at the top levels in organizations.

## *Resource Dependencies*

Executive behavior can sometimes be explained in terms of resource dependencies—the firm's need for resources that are controlled by others.[21] Essentially, the resource dependence of an organization increases as (1) needed resources become more scarce, (2) outsiders have more control over needed resources, and (3) there are fewer substitutes for a particular type of resource controlled by a limited number of outsiders. Thus, one political role of chief executives is to develop workable compromises among the competing resource dependencies facing the organization—compromises that enhance the executive's power. To create such compromises, executives need to diagnose the relative power of outsiders and craft strategies that respond differently to various external resource suppliers.

For larger organizations, many strategies may center on altering the firm's degree of resource dependence. Through mergers and acquisitions, a firm may bring key resources within its control. By changing the "rules of the game," a firm may also find protection from particularly powerful outsiders. For instance, markets may be protected by trade barriers, or labor unions may be put in check by "right to work" laws. Yet, there are limits on the ability of even our largest and most powerful organizations to control all important external contingencies. International competition has narrowed the range of options for chief executives. They can no longer ignore the rest of the world. Some may need to fundamentally redefine how they expect to conduct business. For instance, once U.S. firms could go it alone without the assistance of foreign corporations. Now chief executives are increasingly leading them in the direction of more *joint ventures* and *strategic alliances* with foreign partners from around the globe. Such "combinations" can allow for access to scarce resources and technologies among partners, as well as provide new markets and shared production costs. For example,

> *Corning Inc.* Corning is involved in more than 40 joint ventures with U.S. and foreign firms—many from Europe and Japan. CEO James R. Houghton believes the joint venture is an idea whose time has come. He says Corning's competitors these days "aren't merely companies but combinations of companies, or entire nations and even combinations of nations. No one's strong enough to go it alone, to bend all others to its will."

## *Organizational Governance*

**Organizational governance**

***Organizational governance*** refers to the pattern of authority, influence, and acceptable managerial behavior established at the top of the organization. This system of an organization establishes what is important, how issues will be defined, who should and should not be involved in key choices, and the boundaries for acceptable implementation. Those studying organizational governance suggest that a "dominant coalition" comprised of powerful organizational actors is a key to its understanding.[22]

ETHICAL PERSPECTIVE

## RYDER

**For some firms, the idea of a "hostile" takeover wouldn't even be questioned. But for Ryder, a growing and increasingly international transportation and aviation services firm, this type of power-play is never considered. "There are enough tugs and pulls and challenges to operating a business in this changing environment," says M. Anthony Burns, Ryder's Chairperson and CEO, "that you don't want to introduce the element of confrontation." Of course, it's not just an ethical issue: there are practical business advantages to the approach also. Through "friendly" acquisition, Ryder's Caledonian Airmotive Division in Scotland operates with all the benefits of many of its experienced managers.**

Courtesy of Ryder System, Inc.

While one expects many top officers within the organization to be members of this coalition, it occasionally includes outsiders with access to key resources. Thus, analysis of organizational governance builds on the resource dependence perspective by highlighting the effective control of key resources by members of a dominant coalition.

This view of the executive suite recognizes that the daily practice of organizational governance is the development and resolution of issues. Via the governance system, the dominant coalition attempts to define reality. By accepting or rejecting proposals from subordinates, by directing questions toward the interests of powerful outsiders, and by selecting individuals who appear to espouse particular values and qualities, the pattern of governance is slowly established within an organization. This pattern, furthermore, rests in part at least upon very political foundations.

Whereas in the past organizational governance was an internal and rather private matter, it is now becoming more public and openly controversial in many instances. This was evidenced to some extent in the many well-publicized hostile take-overs of the 1980s. While some argue that senior managers don't represent shareholder interests well enough, others are concerned that too little attention is given to public concerns—especially among those running organizations with high-risk technologies like chemical process, integrated oil refinery, and nuclear power. Even the ability to compete on a global scale can be controversial. While senior managers may lend blame to such externalities as unfavorable trade laws and a "weak" dollar, their critics suggest that it's just a lack of global operating savvy that limits the corporations these managers are supposed to be leading.[23]

# THE ETHICS OF POWER AND POLITICS

No treatment of power and politics in organizations is complete without consideration of related ethical issues. We can begin this task by clarifying the distinction between the nonpolitical and political uses of power.[24] Power is nonpolitical in its use when it remains within the boundaries of formal authority, organizational policies and procedures, and job descriptions, and when it is directed toward ends sanctioned by the organization. When the use of power moves outside the realm of authority, policies, procedures, and job descriptions, or is directed toward ends not sanctioned by the organization, that use of power is political.

When the use of power moves into the realm of political behavior, important ethical issues emerge. It is in this context that a manager, for example, must stop and consider more than a pure "ends justify the means" logic. This issues are broader and involve distinctly ethical questions as the following example shows.[25]

> Chan is the production manager of a work group responsible for meeting a deadline that will require coordinated effort among her subordinates. Believing that the members of the work group will pull together and meet the deadline if they have a little competition, Chan decides to create the impression that members of the sales department want the group to fail to meet the deadline so that sales can gain an edge over production in upcoming budgetary negotiations.

Think about what Chan's decision means. On the one hand, the action may seem justifiable if it works and the group gets its assigned job done on time. On the other hand, there may be side-effects. What about the possibility that the sales and production departments will lose trust in one another and thus find it difficult to work together in the future? Then, too, consider the fact that Chan was "creating an impression" to achieve her goal. Isn't this really "lying"? And, if it is, can we accept lying as an ethical way for a manager to get his or her job done?

Work in the area of ethical issues in power and politics suggests the usefulness of the integrated structure for analyzing political behavior depicted in Figure 15.6. This structure suggests that a person's behavior must satisfy the following criteria to be considered ethical.[26]

1. *Criterion of utilitarian outcomes.* The behavior results in optimization of satisfactions of people inside and outside the organization; that is, it produces the greatest good for the greatest number of people.
2. *Criterion of individual rights.* The behavior respects the rights of all affected parties; that is, it respects basic human rights of free consent, free speech, freedom of conscience, privacy, and due process.
3. *Criterion of distributive justice.* The behavior respects the rules of justice; that is, it treats people equitably and fairly as opposed to arbitrarily.

The figure also indicates that there may be times when a behavior is unable to pass these criteria but can still be considered ethical in the given situation. This special case must satisfy the *criterion of overwhelming factors,* in which the special nature of the situation results in (1) con-

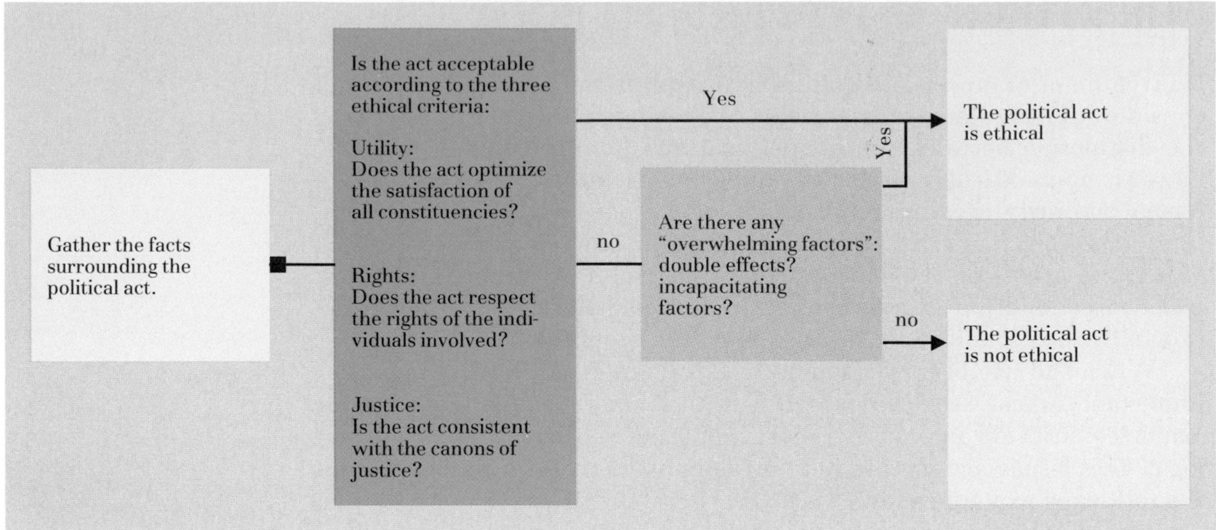


*FIGURE 15.6 An integrated structure for analyzing political behavior in organizations.*
*Source:* Manuel Velasquez, Dennis J. Moberg, and Gerald F. Cavanagh, "Organizational Statesmanship and Dirty Politics. Ethical Guidelines for the Organizational Politician," *Organizational Dynamics,* Vol. 11 Autumn 1982, p. 73. Used by permission.

flicts among criteria (e.g., a behavior results in some good and some bad being done), (2) conflicts within criteria (e.g., a behavior uses questionable means to achieve a positive end), and/or (3) incapacity to employ the criteria (e.g., a person's behavior is based on inaccurate or incomplete information).

Choosing to be ethical often involves considerable personal sacrifice. Four rationalizations are often used to justify unethical choices: (1) individuals feel that the behavior is not really illegal and thus could be moral; (2) the action appears to be in the firm's best interests; (3) it is unlikely the action will ever be detected; and (4) it appears that the action demonstrates loyalty to the boss or the firm. While these rationalizations appear compelling at the moment of action, each deserves close scrutiny. The individual must ask, "how far is too far," "what are the long term interests of the organization," "what will happen when (not *if*) the action is discovered," and "do individuals, groups or organizations that ask for unethical behavior deserve my loyalty?"[27]

All managers use power and politics to get their work done. But every manager also bears a responsibility to do so in an ethical and socially responsible fashion. By recognizing and confronting ethical considerations such as those just discussed, each of us should be better prepared to meet this important challenge.

# SUMMARY

■ **Power is an essential managerial resource. It is the ability to get someone else to do what you want them to do. Power vested in managerial** positions derives from three sources: rewards, punishments, and legitimacy. Legitimacy is the same as formal authority and is based on the manager's position in the hierarchy of authority. Personal power is based on one's expertise and reference. It allows a manager to extend his or her power beyond that available in the position alone.

■ **Power, Authority and Obedience** are interrelated. Obedience is what happens when one individual responds to the request or directive of another person. In the Milgram experiments it was shown that people may have a tendency to obey directives coming from people who appear powerful and authoritative—even if these directives seem contrary to what the individual would normally consider "right." A zone of indifference defines the boundaries within which people in organizations will let others influence their behavior. Ultimately, power and authority only work if the individual "accepts" them.

■ **Managerial Perspectives on Power and Influence** must include the practical considerations of how to get the power needed to get the job done. Managers can pursue various ways of acquiring both position and personal power. They can also become skilled at using various tactics such as reason, friendliness, ingratiation, and bargaining to influence superiors and peers, as well as subordinates. They are also increasingly called upon to be skilled at empowering others—that is, helping others to acquire and utilize power so that their jobs can be done with the highest performance and satisfaction.

■ **Organizational Politics** are inevitable. Managers must become comfortable with political behavior in organizations and then use it responsibly and to good advantage. Politics involves the use of power to obtain ends not officially sanctioned; it is a use of power to find ways of balancing individual and collective interests in otherwise difficult circumstances.

■ **Political Action in Organizations** can be examined at the managerial, subunit, and chief executive levels. For the manager, politics often occurs in decision situations where the interests of another manager or individual must be reconciled with one's own. In such circumstances, "trust" is the key word. With mutual trust, "win–win" outcomes can often be realized. Politics also involves subunits as they jockey for power and advantageous positions vis-à-vis one another. For chief executives, politics come into play as resource dependencies with external environmental elements must be strategically managed, and as organizational governance is transacted among the members of a "dominant coalition."

■ **The Ethics of Power and Politics** are common to those found in any decision situation. Managers can easily slip into questionable territory as they resort to power plays and politics to get their way in situations where resistance exists. While this behavior may be "rationalized" as acceptable, it may not meet the personal test of ethical behavior established earlier in Chapter 1. When political behavior is ethical it will satisfy the criteria of utilitarian outcomes, individual rights, distributive justice, and/or overwhelming factors.

## KEY TERMS

Authority
Coercive Power
Empowerment
Expert Power
Influence
Legitimate Power
Organizational Governance
Organizational Politics
Power
Referent Power
Reward Power
Zone of Indifference

## REVIEW QUESTIONS

1. What is "power" and why is it an essential resource of any manager? Use an example to explain your answer.
2. Explain how the various bases of position and person power do or do not apply to a managerial situation with which you are familiar. What sources of power do lower-level participants in this situation have over their supervisors?
3. Consider the Milgram experiments on obedience. Write a short essay describing whether or not the "lessons" of this experiment have any implications at all for people at work in organizations today.
4. Identify and explain at least three guidelines for how managers may acquire: (a) position power and (b) personal power.
5. What is empowerment? Why is this concept considered so important in today's "changing" organizations? Use specific examples to explain your answer.
6. Identify and explain at least four influence tactics used by managers. Give examples of how each tactic may or may not work when exercising influence (a) downward and (b) upward in organizations.
7. Define "organizational politics" and give an example of how it can operate in both functional and dysfunctional ways.
8. Explain when political behavior in organizations can be considered ethical. Defend your answer.

## AN OB LIBRARY

Peter Block, *The Empowered Manager* (San Francisco: Jossey-Bass, 1987).

Kenneth E. Boulding, *Three Faces of Power* (Newbury Park, CA: Sage, 1989).

Michael Korda, *Power: How to Get It, How to Use It* (New York: Random House, 1975).

Allan R. Cohen and David L. Bradford, *Influence without Authority* (New York: John Wiley & Sons, 1990).

John P. Kotter, *A Force for Change: How Leadership Differs from Management* (New York: The Free Press, 1990).

EXERCISE

# MACHIAVELLIANISM

*Objectives*

1. To assess individual Machiavellianism (Mach) scores.
2. To explore the dynamics of power in a group environment.
3. To develop an understanding of the rewards and frustrations of held power.
4. To analyze behaviors of various Mach personality types.

*Total Time*

45 to 60 minutes

*Procedure*

1. Complete the 10-item Mach Assessment Instrument below.[29]
2. Follow directions for scoring your instrument individually.
3. Form a group of five to seven persons and designate one individual as the official group "observer." The observer will not participate in any of the discussion but will take notes on the activities of the group and later report to the class.
4. Your instructor will announce the topic to be discussed. The topic should be highly controversial, stimulating, and one that encourages different viewpoints.
5. The observer will begin by handling a specific textbook or magazine to one member of the group. Only that member of the group may speak. The textbook or magazine will be held by that person until another member of the group signals, *nonverbally,* that he or she wishes to have it. The person with the textbook or magazine may refuse to relinquish it even when signaled. A time limit of 15 minutes should be placed on the group discussion.
6. Following the controversial discussion period, the group observer should lead a group discussion on what they observed and learned: power phenomena, frustrations, feedback, and so on.
7. Each group observer will then present what their group has learned to the entire class.

*Mach Assessment Instrument*

For each of the following statements, circle the number that most closely resembles your attitude.

| | *Disagree* | | | *Agree* | |
|---|---|---|---|---|---|
| *Statement* | *A lot* | *A little* | *Neutral* | *A little* | *A lot* |
| 1. The best way to handle people is to tell them what they want to hear. | 1 | 2 | 3 | 4 | 5 |
| 2. When you ask someone to do something for you, it is best to give the real reason for wanting it rather than reasons that might carry more weight. | 1 | 2 | 3 | 4 | 5 |
| 3. Anyone who completely trusts someone else is asking for trouble. | 1 | 2 | 3 | 4 | 5 |
| 4. It is hard to get ahead without cutting corners here and there. | 1 | 2 | 3 | 4 | 5 |
| 5. It is safest to assume that all people have a vicious streak, and it will come out when they are given a chance. | 1 | 2 | 3 | 4 | 5 |
| 6. One should take action only when it is morally right. | 1 | 2 | 3 | 4 | 5 |
| 7. Most people are basically good and kind. | 1 | 2 | 3 | 4 | 5 |
| 8. There is no excuse for lying to someone else. | 1 | 2 | 3 | 4 | 5 |
| 9. Most people forget more easily the death of their father than the loss of their property. | 1 | 2 | 3 | 4 | 5 |
| 10. Generally speaking, people won't work hard unless forced to do so. | 1 | 2 | 3 | 4 | 5 |

### *Scoring Key and Interpretation*

This assessment is designed to compute your Machiavellianism (Mach) score. Mach is a personality characteristic that taps people's power orientation. The high-Mach personality is pragmatic, maintains emotional distance from others, and believes that ends can justify means. To obtain your Mach score, add up the numbers you checked for questions 1, 3, 4, 5, 9, and 10. For the other four questions, reverse the numbers you have checked, so that 5 becomes 1, 4 is 2, and 1 is 5. Then total both sets of numbers to find your score. A random sample of adults found the national average to be 25. Students in business and management typically score higher.

The results of research using the Mach test have found: (1) men are generally more Machiavellian than women; (2) older adults tend to have lower Mach scores than younger adults; (3) there is no significant difference between high Machs and low Machs on measures of intelligence or ability; (4) Machiavellianism is not significantly related to demographic characteristics such as educational level or marital status; and (5) high Machs tend to be in professions that emphasize the control and manipulation of people—for example, managers, lawyers, psychiatrists, and behavioral scientists.

CASE

# POLITICAL BEHAVIOR ANALYSIS

The following two incidents involve the use of power and politics in organizations.[28] Read each incident and carefully analyze the actions being described.

### *Incident 1: New Product Development at General Rubber*

Sam and Bob are highly motivated research scientists who work in the new product development lab at General Rubber. Sam is by far the most technically competent scientist in the lab, and he has been responsible for several patents that have netted the company nearly $6 million in the past decade. He is quiet, serious, and socially reserved. In contrast, Bob is outgoing and demonstrative. While Bob lacks the technical track record Sam has, his work has been solid though unimaginative. Rumor has it that Bob will be moved into an administrative position in the lab in the next few years.

According to lab policy, a $300,000 fund is available every year for the best new product development idea proposed by a lab scientist in the form of a competitive bid. Accordingly, Sam and Bob both prepare proposals. Each proposal is carefully constructed to detail the benefits to the company and to society if the proposal is accepted, and it is the consensus of other scientists from blind reviews that both proposals are equally meritorious. Both proposals require the entire $300,000 to realize any significant results. Moreover, the proposed line of research in each requires significant mastery of the technical issues involved and minimal need to supervise the work of others.

After submitting his proposal, Sam takes no further action aside from periodically inquiring about the outcome of the bidding process. In contrast, Bob begins to wage what might be termed an open campaign in support of his proposal. After freely admitting his intentions to Sam and others, Bob seizes every opportunity he can to point out the relative advantages of his proposal to individuals who might have some influence over the decision. So effective is this open campaign that considerable informal pressure is placed on those authorized to make the decision on behalf of Bob's proposal. Bob's proposal is funded and Sam's is not.

### *Incident 2: Chemical Disposal at American Semiconductor*

Lee, age 61, has been director of engineering for American Semiconductor for 14 years. He is very bright and a fine supervisor, but he has not kept abreast of new developments in technology.

American Semiconductor's manufacturing process creates substantial quantities of toxic materials. Lee's casual attitude toward the disposal of these chemicals has resulted in a number of environmental citations. The firm is now tied up in court on two cases and will probably be forced to pay a considerable amount in damages. Yet Lee still does not perceive the disposal problem as urgent. For three years, Charlie, the executive vice president, has tried to persuade Lee to make this a priority issue but has failed. Charlie has reluctantly concluded that Lee must be taken out of his position as director of engineering.

Charlie recognizes that it would demoralize the other managers if he were to fire Lee outright. So Charlie decides that he will begin to tell selected individuals that he is dissatisfied with Lee's work. When there is open support for Lee, Charlie quietly sides with Lee's opposition. He casually lets Lee's peers know that he thinks Lee may have outlived his usefulness to the firm. He even exaggerates Lee's deficiencies and failures when speaking to Lee's co-workers. Discouraged by the waning support from his colleagues, Lee decides to take an early retirement.

### *Questions*

1. Can Bob's behavior in the first incident be justified on ethical grounds? Why or why not?
2. Can Charlie's behavior in the second incident be justified on ethical grounds? Why or why not?
3. What would you consider to be the most appropriate courses of action that Bob and Charlie should have taken in their respective situations? Defend your answer.

This study outline of major topics is meant to organize your reading now; it is repeated in the Summary to structure your review.

## STUDY OUTLINE

- Leadership and Managerial Activities
- Leader Traits and Behaviors

Great Man/Trait Theory    Leadership Behaviors
Leader Reward and Punishment    Charismatic/Transformational Theories
Bass's Transformational/Transactional Approach
Trait/Behavior Research and Applications

- Situational Contingencies and Leadership

Fiedler's Leadership Contingency Theory    House's Path–Goal Leadership Theory
Situational Leadership Theory    Competing Values Framework
Situational Contingencies and Applications

# CHAPTER 16

# LEADERSHIP



## PHOTO ESSAYS

# VISIONS 16

**For more than 100 years PPG Industries, the Pittsburgh glass, paint, and chemical manufacturer, shared the fate of other rustbelt firms: It was dependent on construction and autos. When Vincent A. Sarni became the CEO he reshaped the old firm's culture and made this glass company into a model of modern leadership.**

**What did he do? European sales have tripled in five years and productivity is increasing. PPG now runs the paint shops in several GM plants and they are building their second minimill for glass. Costs are low and quality is so high Sarni is supplying coatings to Japanese auto plants. How did he do it: With a vision based on his "Blueprint for the Decade."**

**The blueprint is an eight-page paper with a mission statement, corporate goals, and performance objectives. Everything would have to do 20 percent better than long-range projections. Sarni trudged from plant to plant extolling his vision based on his blueprint. Now the vision has been absorbed all the way down to the shop floor. Says Sarni: "This little mundane, nonglamorous commodity business is very exciting and challenging. And we're going to do a better job. And have fun doing it too."**

Vincent Sarni, in the opening vignette, captures, for many, what is the essence of leadership—the vision to make things happen. Some think of leadership as an almost mystical quality that some have and others don't. For them, they can't define it, but they know it when they see it. Others think of it as something more specific, such as being considerate to your subordinates.

Even though they don't always view leadership in the same way, probably most people agree that leadership makes a difference. However, there are some who also argue just as strongly that leadership doesn't matter—it isn't important. For them, leaders are so bound by constraints in what they can do, that they just don't have much impact. Furthermore, people often give credit to leaders for happenings that were caused by something else. In this chapter we cover all these views and more in our look at where leadership fits in the organization.

# LEADERSHIP AND MANAGERIAL ACTIVITIES

In Chapters 1 and 2 we touched on the functions, roles, and activities of managers. Most often, leadership is seen as narrower than management—it is but one of the four functions (leading) or one of Mintzberg's 10 roles (leader role). Less often, it is seen as anything done by a person occupying a managerial position. Recently, there have been strong arguments that those, such as Vincent Sarni, who are visionary and exciting, are leaders, whereas those who handle the mundane everyday activities of management are managers.[1] For them, the former ITT head, Harold Geneen, whose forte was quantitative analysis, would be called a manager and not a leader.[2]

Leadership

For our purposes, we can think of ***leadership*** as a special case of interpersonal influence that gets an individual or group to do what the leader (or manager) wants done. It is related to the various forms of power and influence discussed in the previous chapter and is treated as a special case because it has long been a topic of special interest and has developed its own literature. The various approaches that we examine in this chapter are consistent with our definition and, as you will see, some more than others separate leadership from management.

Formal leadership

Informal leadership

Leadership appears in two forms: ***formal***—exerted by persons appointed to or elected to positions of formal authority in organizations—and ***informal***—exerted by persons who become influential because they have special skills that meet the needs and resources of others. Both are important in organizations. However, most of our emphasis in this chapter is on formal leadership. In Table 16.1 we categorize a number of useful leadership approaches into a four-cell matrix. The theories grouped

*TABLE 16.1*
**LEADERSHIP APPROACHES CATEGORIZED BY EXTENT TO WHICH THEY ARE SEEN AS HAVING PRIMARY IMPACT ON PERFORMANCE/HUMAN RESOURCE MAINTENANCE**

| | |
|---|---|
| *I. Leader traits and behaviors*<br>Great man/trait theory<br>Leadership behavior theory<br>Leader reward and punishment theory<br>Charismatic/transactional theories | *III. Symbolic leadership* |
| *II. Leader situational contingencies*<br>Fiedler's leadership contingency and cognitive resource theories<br>House's path–goal theory<br>Situational leadership theory<br>Competing values framework | *IV. Substitutes for leadership* |

*Source:* The general idea for this table was suggested by James C. McElroy, "Alternative Schemes for Teaching Leadership," *The Organizational Behavior Teaching Review,* Vol. II, No. 2, 1986–87, p. 91.

together in each cell share some common ground in seeking to explain how leadership has a primary impact on performance or human resource maintenance.[3]

Leader traits and behaviors are featured in Cell I. Here the leader is seen as the key determinant in causing performance and human resource maintenance outcomes. Situational contingencies and leadership are the focus of Cell II. Here the leader is still seen as having a strong impact on outcomes, but only in combination with various situational contingencies. In other words, the nature of the leader's impact varies depending on the particular situational aspects that are operating.

Symbolic leadership is in Cell III. Rather than leadership *causing* outcomes, outcomes are seen as causing leadership or leadership is used to explain positive or negative outcomes only after fact. A common example is the almost ritualistic firing of a top manager when things are going badly for the organization. In such cases, failure has been attributed to the manager in a symbolic way after the fact. For example, when Frederick A. Wang was forced out of Wang Laboratories by his father, Dr. Wang and Fred decided together that the company was making a dramatic statement that it was no longer business as usual at Wang Laboratories.[4] Substitutes for leadership, in Cell IV, assume many individual, task, and organizational characteristics are able substitutes for hierarchical leadership. At Hewlett-Packard, for instance, experienced engineers with lots of expertise don't need much leadership since their experience and expertise are a leadership substitute.

# LEADER TRAITS AND BEHAVIORS

All the leader traits and behaviors approaches make the assumption that, in one way or another, selected personal traits or behaviors have a major

*TABLE 16.2*
**EXAMPLES OF TRAITS ILLUSTRATING DIFFERENT ASPECTS OF LEADERSHIP**

| *With respect to others* |
|---|
| Personal integrity |
| Cooperativeness |
| Sociability |
| *Predisposition to be influential* |
| Dominance |
| Need for influence |
| *With respect to task/organizational goals* |
| Need for achievement |
| Initiative |
| Desire to excel |
| Task-related ability |

*Source:* Developed from Robert J. House, in James G. Hunt, B. R. Baliga, H. Peter Dachler and Chester A. Schriesheim (Eds.), *Emerging Leadership Vistas* (Lexington, MA: Lexington Books, 1988), Chapter 14.

Courtesy of Time–Warner Inc.

INTERNATIONAL PERSPECTIVE

### TIME-WARNER INC.

**Not only has Time–Warner Inc. broken traditions with its highly stylized and unusual annual report, the international entertainment and communications giant was founded on controversy. When Time Inc. and Warner Communications Inc. merged, people wondered "Why?" The new firm's leadership is quite clear in its response—"globalization." In a world of profound political and economic changes, executives at Time and Warner each concluded that long-term success required global competitiveness. They started out talking about a joint venture, and they ended up in a merger. The corporate leaders are convinced, though, that in the end they've created the foundation to meet the challenge.**

impact on leadership outcomes. Other variables are considered to be relatively less important. However, among the various approaches, there are differences in terms of the explanations for leadership results.

## Great Man/Trait Theory

This approach is the earliest used to study leadership and dates back at least to the turn of the century. The early studies attempted to identify those traits that differentiated the great person in history from the masses.[5] This led to a research emphasis that tried to identify traits that would separate leaders from nonleaders or more effective from less effective leaders. The argument is that certain traits may be related to leadership success in a given unit or organization and once they are identified, they can be used to select a leader for a particular position.

Table 16.2 lists examples of traits illustrating three different aspects of what leaders must do in their leadership role. They must maintain relations with others, want to be influential, and be oriented toward task or organizational goals. Traits such as those in the table have been argued to be useful in carrying out these responsibilities. As an example, William Gates, CEO of Microsoft Computer is described as having technical sharpness, intellectual breadth, and business savvy, among other characteristics.[6]

## Leadership Behaviors

The leadership behavior approach, like the great man/trait approach, again assumes that the leader is the primary cause of performance/human resource maintenance. This time, however, instead of dealing with underlying traits like those shown in Table 16.2, behaviors or actions are used. Two classic research programs at the University of Michigan and Ohio State University provide useful insights into leadership behaviors.

### *Michigan Studies*

These researchers divided leader behaviors into employee-centered and production-centered. Employee-centered supervisors are those who place strong emphasis on the welfare and motivation of subordinates. Production-centered supervisors tend to place a stronger emphasis on getting the work done than on the welfare and motivation of the employees. In general, employee-centered as opposed to production-centered supervisors were found to have more productive work groups.[7]

These behaviors may be viewed on a continuum, with employee-centered at one end and production-centered at the other. Sometimes the more general terms human relations-oriented and task-oriented are used to describe these alternative leader behaviors.

### *Ohio State Studies*

Another important research program at Ohio State University investigated two dimensions of leader behavior similar to those above—consideration and initiating structure.[8] A highly considerate leader is sensitive to people's feelings and, much like the employee-centered leader, tries to make things pleasant for followers. A leader high in initiating structure is concerned with spelling out task requirements and clarifying other aspects of the work agenda and might be seen as similar to a production-centered supervisor. These dimensions and those above are related to what people sometimes refer to as socioemotional and task leadership, respectively. They also encompass what we discussed in Chapter 8 as group maintenance and task activities.

At first, it looked to the Ohio State researchers as if being high on consideration or socioemotional warmth resulted in a leader having more highly satisfied and/or better performing subordinates. Later results, however, indicated that leaders should be high on both consideration and initiating structure behaviors.

### *Managerial Grid*

In contrast to traits, leader behaviors are dynamic. Thus, training becomes important. One of the more popular outgrowths of this perspective is the managerial grid concept developed by Robert Blake and Jane Mouton.[9] They measure a manager's concern for people and concern for task and then plot the results on a 9-position grid with concern for people on the vertical axis and concern for task on the horizontal axis similar to the plot above. A person with a 1/9 score is a "country club manager" (1 on concern for task, 9 on concern for people). Some other positions are 1/1 impoverished management style and 9/1 task management style. A 5/5 style, in the middle of the grid, is a middle-of-the-road style. The ideal position is a 9/9 "team manager" (high on both dimensions). The leader behavior approaches above have in common an emphasis on the importance of people-oriented and task-oriented behaviors in determining outputs. A timely question is: how well do these behaviors transfer internationally? Recent work in the United States, Britain, Hong Kong, and Japan showed that although the behaviors seem to be generally important, they must be carried out in different ways in alternative cultures. For instance, British leaders were seen as considerate if they showed subordinates how to use equipment, whereas in Japan the highly considerate manager helped subordinates with personal problems.[10]

## Leader Reward and Punishment

Leader reward and punishment theory is based on the reinforcement concepts discussed in Chapter 6, where the leader is seen as someone who manages reinforcements for subordinates.[11]

Recent research examines the following four leader behavior dimensions in this context:

1. *Performance-contingent reward behavior.* The degree to which a leader administers positive reinforcers such as acknowledgements, recognition, and so on, contingent on high subordinate performance.
2. *Contingent punishment behavior.* The extent to which a leader administers punitive measures such as reprimands and disapproval contingent on poor subordinate performance.
3. *Noncontingent reward behavior.* The extent to which a leader rewards a subordinate regardless of how well the subordinate performs.
4. *Noncontingent punishment behavior.* The degree to which a leader uses punitive measures, regardless of how well a subordinate performs.

Results indicate that performance-contingent reward behavior is generally associated with higher levels of subordinate performance and satisfaction. Results for contingent punishment and noncontingent reward behavior are mixed, and, as you probably predicted, noncontingent punishment behavior is often negatively associated with performance and satisfaction. It has also been found that subordinates strongly dislike seemingly discretionary or arbitrary punishment.[12] In summary, performance-contingent leader rewards are most strongly related to performance and satisfaction; discretionary punishment is strongly disliked.

## Charismatic/Transformational Theories

The charismatic/transformational approaches are concerned essentially with elevating the goals of the followers so that they have the confidence to go beyond their performance expectations. Vincent Sarni did this in the chapter opener with his vision of a new PPG. Often seen as mystical and mysterious, charisma was not seriously studied in OB until the last few years. This recent work owes much to those below.

House developed a charismatic approach that uses both traits and

**Charismatic leaders**

behaviors. He defines ***charismatic leaders*** as those "who by force of their personalities are capable of having a profound and extraordinary effect on followers." Such people have the traits of self-confidence, dominance, and conviction in the moral rightness of their beliefs. These traits influence leader behaviors like role modeling, image building, goal articulation (emphasizing simple and dramatic goals), emphasizing high expectations, showing confidence, and arousing motives.[13]

Conger and Kanungo have summarized some key leader characteristics that differentiate charismatic from noncharismatic leaders:[14]

- *Self-confidence.* They are completely confident in their ability and judgment.
- *Vision.* They have an idealized goal that proposes a future beyond the status quo.
- *Strong conviction in the vision.* They are strongly committed to the vision and willing to take great risks for it.
- *Out of the ordinary behavior.* They engage in novel, unconventional behavior.
- *Change agent.* They are perceived as catalysts to radical change moving beyond the status quo.

## Bass's Transformational/Transactional Approach[15]

**Transactional leadership**

Building on the ideas of House and others, Bass has developed an approach focusing on transformational and transactional leadership. The high points of this approach are summarized in Figure 16.1. Let's start by discussing Bass's transactional category first. ***Transactional leadership*** involves daily exchanges between leaders and subordinates and is nec-

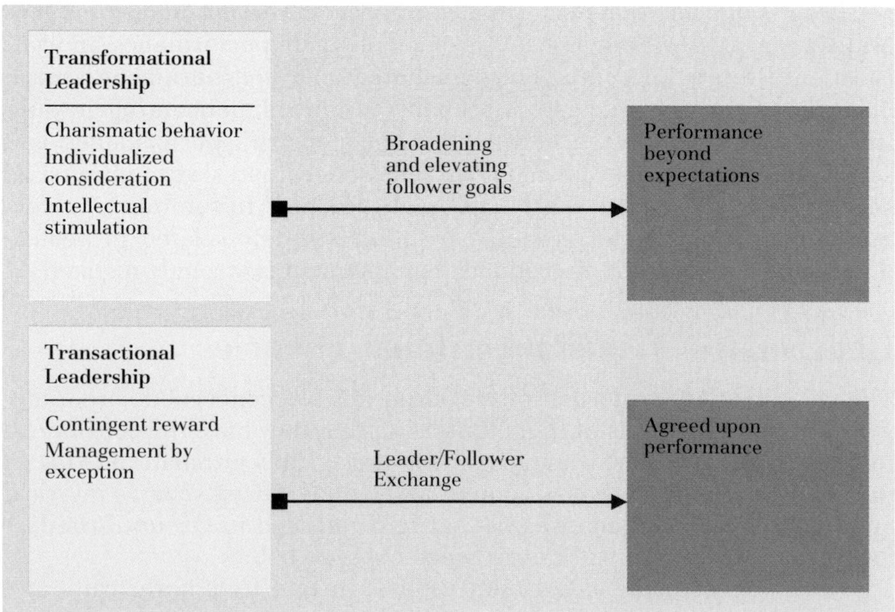


*FIGURE 16.1 High-points of Bass's transformational/transactional leadership approach.*

essary for routine performance agreed upon between leaders and subordinates. These exchanges involve ***contingent rewards*** and management-by-exception. Essentially, contingent rewards provide rewards in exchange for mutually agreed upon performance accomplishment. ***Management-by-exception*** involves leaving subordinates alone if the old ways are working or if subordinates are meeting mutually accepted performance goals.

**Contingent rewards**

**Management-by-exception**

Bass sees transactional leadership as appropriate for effective daily performance. However, transformational leadership is needed to go beyond this routine accomplishment. ***Transformational leadership*** broadens and elevates the goals of subordinates and gives them confidence to go beyond their expectations. It has three dimensions: charismatic behavior, individualized consideration, and intellectual stimulation. For example,

**Transformational leadership**

> *Disney* CEO Michael Eisner occasionally admits that he's been "driving people crazy" at Disney. Described as a hands-on leader, he also strives to encourage and induce creativity in others. He says: "I'll use meetings, company anniversaries, anything, to create some kind of catalyst to get us all going." He also believes people must be free of constraints if they are to develop the entrepreneurial spirit.

***Charismatic behavior*** instills pride, faith, and respect and spells out a sense of vision. An illustration of this kind of behavior is where Cray Research disregarded Steven S. Chin's plea to build a supercomputer and 40 colleagues followed him out the door after he told them that his vision of a supercomputer must be built because, "The future of technology in this country is at stake."[16] ***Individualized consideration*** delegates tasks to stimulate learning and emphasizes the individual needs of each subordinate and is based on respecting each as an individual. ***Intellectual stimulation*** introduces and encourages developing new ideas and rethinking old ones with an emphasis on the many angles in performing a job. Charismatic leadership transforms subordinate expectations but individualized consideration and intellectual stimulation are needed to provide the necessary follow-through.

**Charismatic behavior**

**Individualized consideration**

**Intellectual stimulation**

Bass concludes that transformational/charismatic leadership is likely to be strongest at the top management level—that is, where there is the greatest opportunity for proposing and communicating a vision. Second, transformational or charismatic leadership operates *in combination with* the other kinds of traits or behaviors discussed in this chapter. We can think of these traits or behaviors as similar to Bass's transactional leadership. Finally, rather than being a mystical gift rarely seen, charismatic leadership is something that is both necessary and possible to develop.

## Trait/Behavior Research and Applications

While the very earliest approaches to examining traits gave largely inconsistent results, there is evidence supporting the kinds of traits shown in Table 16.2. The most promising of the leader behavior approaches, in terms of research evidence, is the leader reward and punishment perspective.

Among the charismatic perspectives, Bass's work has begun to attract much research. Basically, the results show that transformational leaders:

**SKILLS PERSPECTIVE**

## CIBA-GEIGY

Courtesy of Ciba-Geigy Corporation.

**Ciba-Geigy Corporation is a wholly-owned subsidiary of Ciba-Geigy Limited in Basel, Switzerland. The company is a major developer and manufacturer of pharmaceuticals, plastics, and vision care products, among others. In a diversified industry and competitive environment, leadership at all levels in the firm is important. Training plays an important role in leadership development. At the Ardsley, N.Y., headquarters, groups of employees work together in a corporate training program to examine and discuss the nature of leadership and develop their personal skills and capabilities.**

(1) have higher performing work teams and are rated as having more advancement potential; (2) are rated more often as "world class" leaders; (3) take greater risks and have more satisfied subordinates who report more extra effort and superior performance; and (4) have subordinates who themselves demonstrate transformational leadership.[17]

In terms of applications, since traits are considered to be relatively stable, we can use them for leader selection and placement. Traits are a kind of individual attribute, as discussed in Chapter 4, here applied specifically to leadership. We can use the kinds of traits shown in Table 16.1. Also, following Chapter 4, we can try to fit the traits to the job or organizational requirements in hiring or placing leaders.

In contrast to traits, leader behaviors are dynamic. Thus, training becomes important. One example is the Managerial Grid training program developed by Blake and Mouton. Once it is determined where on the grid the leader stands, the training program is used to shift his or her behavior toward the 9/9 team manager style.[18] Another example is provided by Bass, who developed a training program to try to develop transformational leadership behaviors.[19]

# SITUATIONAL CONTINGENCIES AND LEADERSHIP

In Cell II of Table 16.1, leader traits and behaviors are seen as acting in conjunction with *situational contingencies* (that is, other important aspects of the leadership situation) to determine outcomes. The major contributions to this perspective include the work of Fred Fiedler, Robert House, Paul Hersey and Kenneth Blanchard, and Robert Quinn.

## Fiedler's Leadership Contingency Theory

The first situational contingency approach we consider is one by Fred Fiedler, since his work essentially started the situational contingency era.[20] His theory clearly demonstrates the discipline of situational thinking. Such thinking is very important if you are to be able to make the most of what situational contingency approaches have to offer.

Fiedler's object is to predict work-group task performance or effectiveness. His theory holds that group effectiveness depends on a successful match between the leader's style and the demands of the situation. Specifically, Fiedler is interested in the amount of control the situation allows the leader. ***Situational control*** is defined as the extent to which a leader can determine what the group is going to do, and what the outcomes of its actions and decisions are going to be. For example, where there is high control, leaders can predict with a great degree of certainty what will happen when they want something done.

**Situational control**

### *Leadership Style, Situational Control, Behavior and Performance*

Fiedler uses an instrument called the least preferred co-worker (LPC) scale to measure a person's basic leadership style. The people completing the scale are asked to describe the person with whom they have been able to work least well (least preferred co-worker or LPC). Fiedler argues that leaders with high LPC scores have a relationship motivated style and leaders with low LPC scores have a task-motivated style.

He considers this task- and relationship-motivation to be a trait that leads to different leadership behaviors (directive or nondirective) depending on the amount of situational control the leader has. In turn, the match between these directive and nondirective behaviors and situational control influences group performance. Figure 16.2 summarizes Fiedler's predictions of the effective style in high, moderate, and low-control situations. In general, task-motivated leaders perform best in situations of high leadership control and low leadership control. Relationship-motivated leaders are at their best in *moderate* control situations.

In emphasizing task completion, the task-motivated leaders tend to act nondirectively where there is high control and directiveness is not needed and act directively where there is low control and directiveness

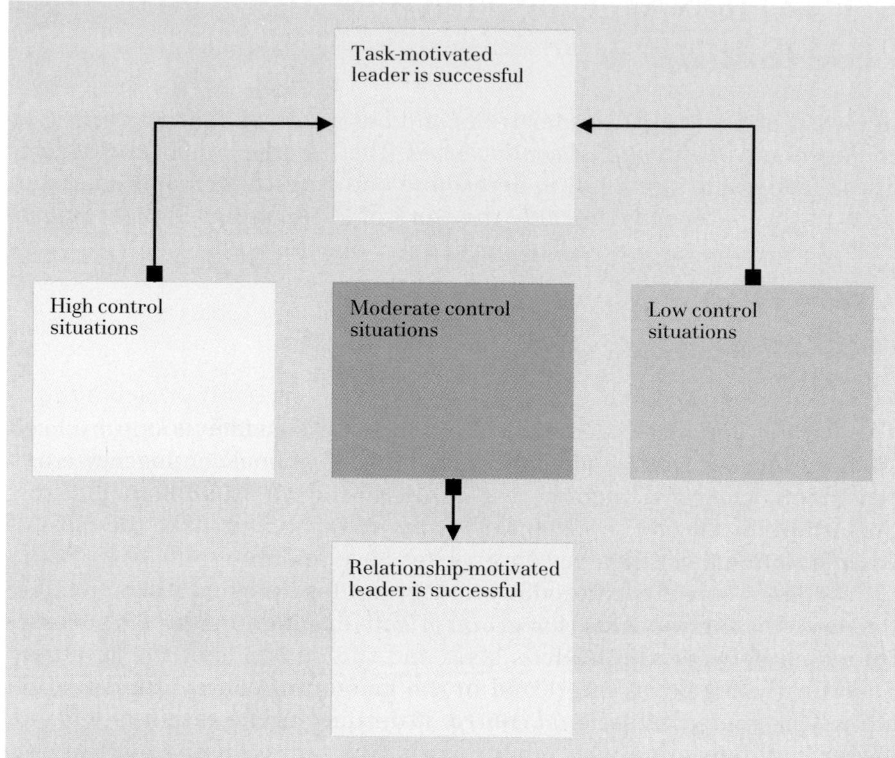


*FIGURE 16.2 Predictions from Fiedler's contingency theory of leadership.*

is needed (so performance is helped). In moderate control situations they tend to be too directive and performance suffers. In emphasizing good relations, the relationship-motivated leaders tend to behave directively where there is high control and directiveness is not needed and the opposite in low control situations so performance suffers. In moderate control situations their nondirectiveness fits well and enhances performance.

## *Diagnosing Situational Control*

While the prior discussion is a useful summary of Fiedler's theory, the question remains how we diagnose or measure the amount of situational control. Fiedler emphasizes three dimensions: leader–member relations, task structure, and position power. *Leader–member relations* (good/poor) is concerned with the extent that group members support the leader. *Task structure* (high/low) is concerned with the degree that task goals, procedures, and guidelines the leader is responsible for in the group are spelled out (the what and how of the task). *Position power* (strong/weak) is concerned with the leader's task knowledge and the extent to which the position gives the leader authority to reward and punish group members.

Figure 16.3 shows how these three variables relate to one another in eight combinations to create different amounts of situational control for a leader. The earlier mentioned characteristics of high-, moderate-, and low-control situations are now presented along with examples also highlighted in the figure.

## High-Control Situations

During high-control situations, the leader has a great deal of control illustrated by good leader–member relations, a highly structured task, and strong position power. An experienced supervisor of a production line with nonunion, highly supportive workers serves as an example. Supportive subordinates mean good leader–member relations. The structure of the task is high, and the leader has considerable experience so there is high task structure. Likewise, the nonunion nature of the job tends to provide the leader with the authority to reward and punish and hence provides high position power.

## Moderate-Control Situations

During moderate-control situations, the leader is typically presented with mixed problems—perhaps good relations with subordinates *but* a low structured task *and* weak position power; or the opposite, poor relations but a structured task and strong position power. An example might be a well-liked university department head with a high proportion of tenured faculty and responsible for enhancing the teaching, research, and service missions of the department. There are good leader–member relations, but task structure is low since the "how" of the task is not very clear. The leader's position power also is not very strong vis-à-vis the tenured faculty members.

## Low-Control Situations

During low-control situations, the leader encounters poor leader–member relations and *neither* the task nor position provide control for the leader—a challenging situation indeed. An example might be the chair of a student council committee of volunteers who are not happy about this particular person being the chair. The committee is to organize a "Parents' Day" program to improve university–parent relations. The "what" is clear, but the "how" is not. Who can say exactly which activities will improve relations? Because the volunteers can readily quit, the leader also has weak position power.

*FIGURE 16.3 Summary of Fiedler's situational variables and their preferred leadership styles.*

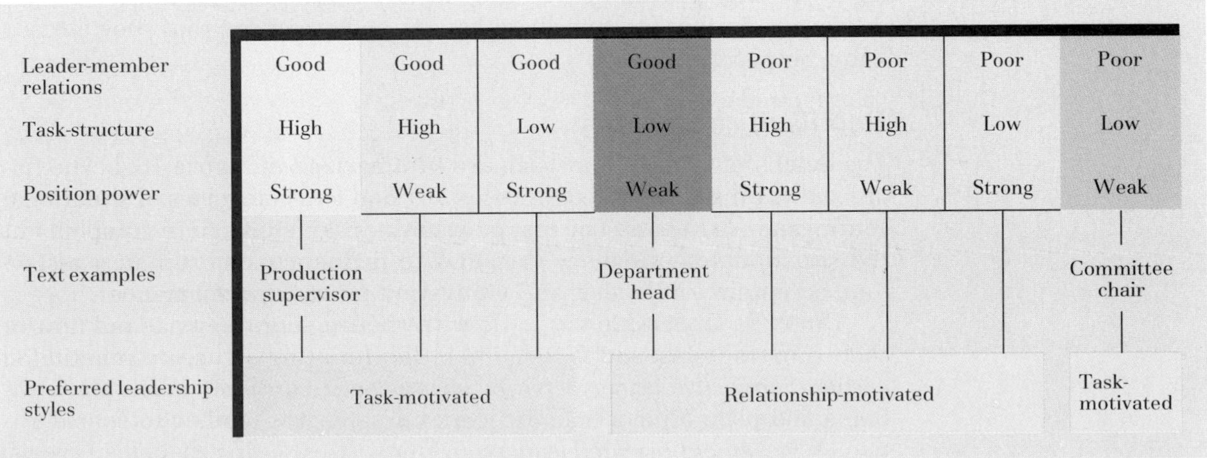

### Fiedler's Cognitive Resource Theory[21]

Fiedler has recently moved beyond his contingency theory by developing the cognitive resource theory. Cognitive resources are abilities or competencies. In this approach, whether a leader should use directive or nondirective behavior depends on the situational contingencies of: leader or subordinate group member ability/competency, stress, experience, and group support of the leader. Basically, cognitive resource theory is most useful because it directs us to leader or subordinate group member ability, an aspect not typically considered in other leadership approaches.

The theory views directiveness as most helpful for performance when the leader is competent, relaxed, and supported. The group is ready and directiveness is the clearest means to communicate. When the leader feels stressed, then he or she is diverted and experience is more important than ability. If support is low, then the group is less receptive and the leader has less impact. Group-member ability becomes most important when the leader is nondirective and there is strong support. If support is weak, then task difficulty or other factors have more impact than either the leader or subordinates.

## House's Path–Goal Leadership Theory

Another well-known approach to situational contingencies is one developed by Robert House; based on the earlier work of others.[22] This theory has its roots in the expectancy model of motivation that we discussed in Chapter 5. The term "path–goal" is used because of its emphasis on how a leader influences subordinates' perceptions of work goals and personal goals, and the links or paths found between these two sets of goals.

The theory assumes that a leader's key function is to adjust his or her behaviors to complement situational contingencies, such as those found in the work setting. House argues that when the leader is able to compensate for things lacking in the setting, subordinates are likely to be satisfied with the leader. Performance should benefit as the paths by which effort leads to performance (expectancy) and performance leads to valued rewards (instrumentality) become clarified. Redundant behavior by the leader will not help and may even hinder performance. People do not need a boss telling them how to do something that they already know how to do!

### Details of the Theory

The details of House's approach are summarized in Figure 16.4. The figure shows four types of leader behaviors and two categories of situational contingency variables. The leader behaviors are adjusted to complement the situational contingency variables to influence subordinate satisfaction, acceptance of leader, and motivation for task performance.

*Directive leadership* has to do with spelling out the what and how of subordinates' tasks and is much like the initiating structure mentioned earlier. *Supportive leader behavior* focuses on subordinate needs and well-being and promoting a friendly work climate. It is similar to consideration. *Achievement-oriented leadership* emphasizes setting challenging goals, emphasizing excellence in performance, and so on. *Leader participative-*

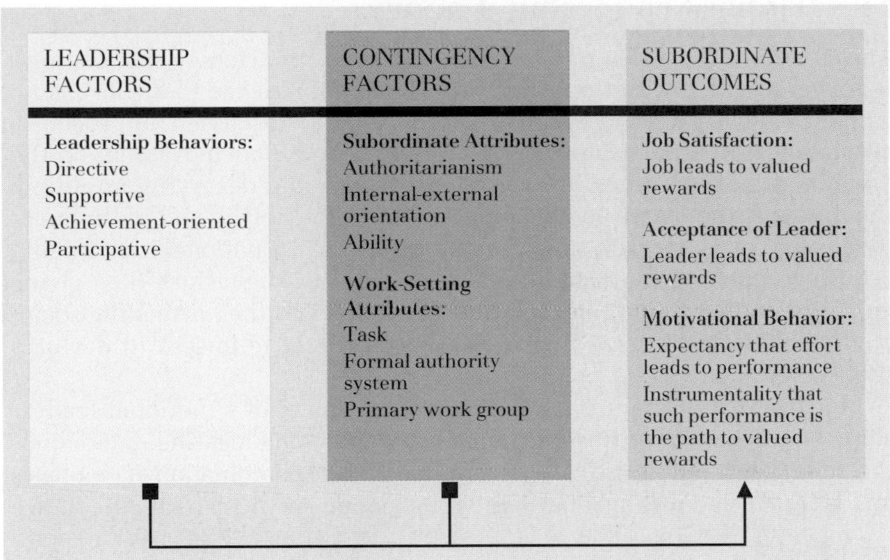


*FIGURE 16.4 Summary of major path–goal relationships in House's leadership approach.* (Adapted from Richard N. Osborn, James G. Hunt, and Lawrence R. Jauch, *Organization Theory: An Integrated Approach.* New York: John Wiley & Sons, 1980, p. 464.)

*ness* focuses on consulting with subordinates and seeking and using their suggestions.

The contingency variables include subordinate attributes and work setting attributes. Important subordinate characteristics are authoritarianism (close-mindedness, rigidity), internal–external orientation, and ability. The key work setting factors are the nature of the subordinates' tasks, the formal authority system, and the primary work group.

## *Predictions from the Theory*

*Leader directiveness* is predicted to have a positive impact on subordinates when the task is ambiguous and to have just the opposite effect for clear tasks. When task demands are ambiguous, leader directiveness is needed to compensate for the lack of structure. When task clarification is otherwise available, directiveness is seen as a hindrance by subordinates. In addition, the theory predicts that ambiguous tasks being performed by highly authoritarian and close-minded subordinates call for even more directive leadership than do ambiguous tasks alone.

*Leader supportiveness* is predicted to increase the satisfaction of subordinates who work on highly repetitive tasks or on tasks considered to be unpleasant, stressful, or frustrating. The leader's supportive behavior helps to compensate for these adverse conditions.

*Leader achievement orientedness* is predicted to cause subordinates to strive for higher performance standards and to have more confidence in their ability to meet challenging goals. For subordinates in ambiguous nonrepetitive jobs, achievement-oriented leadership should increase subordinates' expectancies that effort will lead to desired performance.

*Leader participativeness* is predicted to promote satisfaction on nonrepetitive tasks which allow for the ego involvement of subordinates. On repetitive tasks, open-minded or nonauthoritarian subordinates will also be satisfied with a participative leader.

## Situational Leadership Theory

The situational leadership theory developed by Paul Hersey and Kenneth Blanchard agrees with the other situational approaches that there is no single best way to lead[23] and, like the earlier discussed approaches, emphasizes situational contingencies. Hersey and Blanchard focus on the "readiness" of followers as a contingency variable deserving attention. Readiness is the extent to which people have the ability and willingness to accomplish a specific task. They argue that "situational" leadership requires adjusting the leader's emphasis on task behaviors (i.e., giving guidance and direction) and relationship behaviors (i.e., providing socio-emotional support) according to the readiness of followers to perform their tasks.

Figure 16.5 displays the essence of this model of situational leadership. The figure identifies four leadership styles: delegating, participating, selling, and telling. Each represents a different combination of emphasis on task and relationship behaviors by the leader. As you can see, the figure

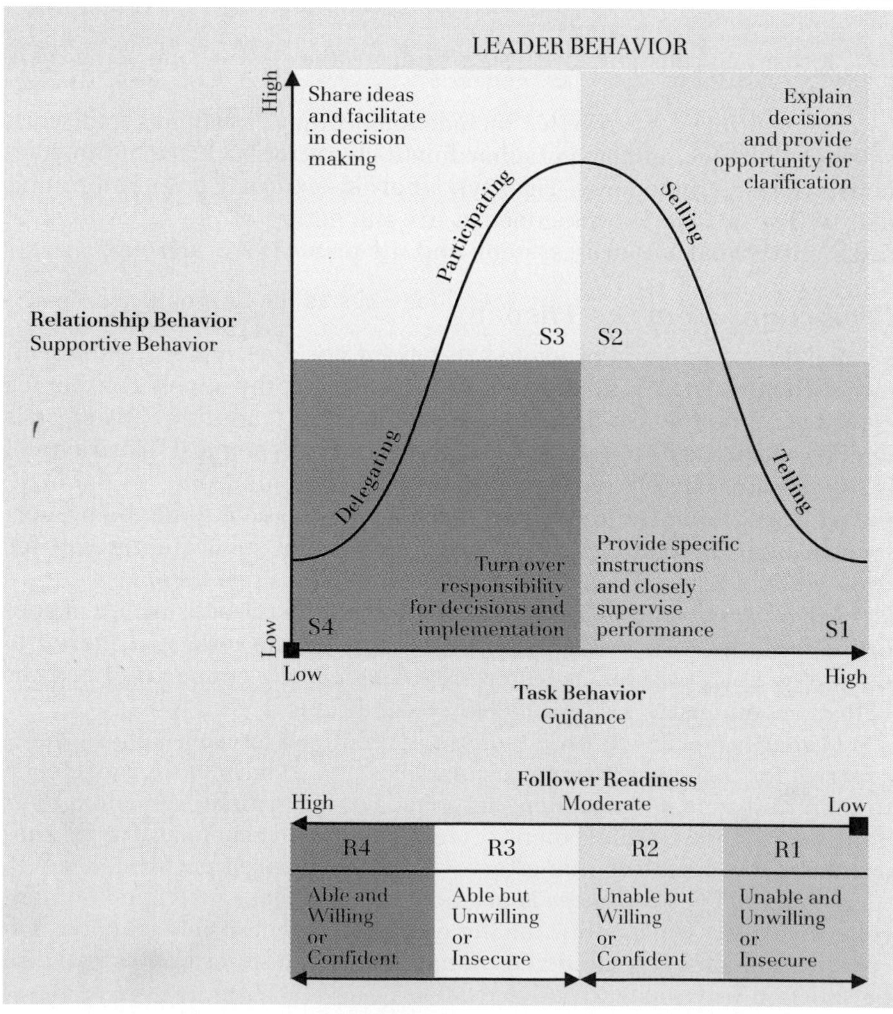


*FIGURE 16.5 Hersey and Blanchard model of situational leadership.* (From Paul Hersey and Kenneth H. Blanchard, *Management of Organizational Behavior,* Prentice–Hall, Englewood Cliffs, N.J., 1988, p. 171. Used by permission.)

ETHICAL PERSPECTIVE

## XEROX

Courtesy of Xerox Corporation.

**Leadership sets the tone at Xerox Corporation, where "equal opportunity" isn't just another company program—it's a way of life. Xerox is dedicated to working toward a world of one race . . . the human race. Since the late 1960s the company has been a frontrunner in American industry for minority programs that affect all phases of the firm's structure, from pre-entry to upper management. It has received the Department of Labor Exemplary Voluntary Effort Award for affirmative action. In the process, Xerox believes it's creating an employee team free from the constraints of prejudice—making them even stronger in their ability to serve clients. As they're proud to say at Xerox: "A team that has no prejudice has no limits."**

also suggests the following situational matches as the best choice of leadership style for followers of each of four readiness levels.

*A "telling" style is best for low follower readiness.* The direction provided by this style defines roles for people who are unable and unwilling to take responsibility; it eliminates any insecurity about the task that must be done.

*A "selling" style is best for low to moderate follower readiness.* This style offers both task direction and support for people who are unable but willing to take task responsibility; it involves combining a directive approach with explanation and reinforcement to maintain enthusiasm.

*A "participating" style is best for moderate to high follower readiness.* Able but unwilling followers require supportive behavior to increase their motivation; by sharing in decision making, this style helps to enhance the desire to perform a task.

*A "delegating" style is best for high readiness.* This style provides little in terms of direction and support for the task at hand; it allows able and willing followers to take responsibility for what needs to be done.

This approach requires that a leader develop the capability to diagnose the demands of situations, and then to choose and implement the appropriate leadership response. The theory gives specific attention to followers and their feelings about a task or job to be done. It also suggests that an effective leader reassess situations over time, with special attention being given to emerging changes in the level of "readiness" among people involved in the work. Again, Hersey and Blanchard advise that leadership style should be adjusted as necessary to remain consistent with actual levels of follower readiness. They suggest that effectiveness should improve as a result.[24]

## Competing Values Framework[25]

The most recent situational contingency perspective is the competing values framework developed by Robert Quinn and his colleagues. The leadership aspects of this approach are summarized in Figure 16.6. The capital letter labels inside the circle indicate eight leader roles, which are quite similar to Mintzberg's 10 roles reviewed in Chapter 2. For each role there are three numbered competencies (i.e., knowledge and skills necessary to perform the role). For example, the first competency for the innovator role is "living with change." And the roles are tied to four models—the human relations, open systems, internal process, and rational goal models—each of which emphasizes a different approach to management. Finally, the whole scheme is reinforced by eight different orientations or values also shown in the figure.

Note that each of the four management models has a different emphasis, and that each is still important. Because of this different emphasis, Quinn describes the models and their values orientations as "competing." For example, we want our organizations to be adaptable and flexible but we want them also to be stable and controlled. We want growth, resource acquisition, and external support; however, we also desire tight information management and formal communication. The competing values framework argues that over time we must be able to deal with all of these different orientations. Thus, we must be able to think in terms of competing values and competing aspects of leadership.

Even though a leadership situation may call for a given set of roles, the performance of these roles alone is not enough. To maintain the necessary balance, the other roles, especially the competing ones in the opposite quadrant, must be used. The intent is that, over time, people will work toward being able to balance the various roles as necessary. Those leaders who are able to do this are called "master managers" according to Quinn's framework.

## Situational Contingency Research and Applications

The roots of Fiedler's contingency approach go back more than 25 years and have been thoroughly researched. There are both pro and con results. One example of controversy concerns exactly what Fiedler's LPC instrument measures. Some question Fiedler's behavioral interpretation. To help answer these and other questions, Fiedler and others have conducted extensive research, making the contingency theory the most thoroughly researched of all leadership approaches. In contrast, Fiedler's cognitive

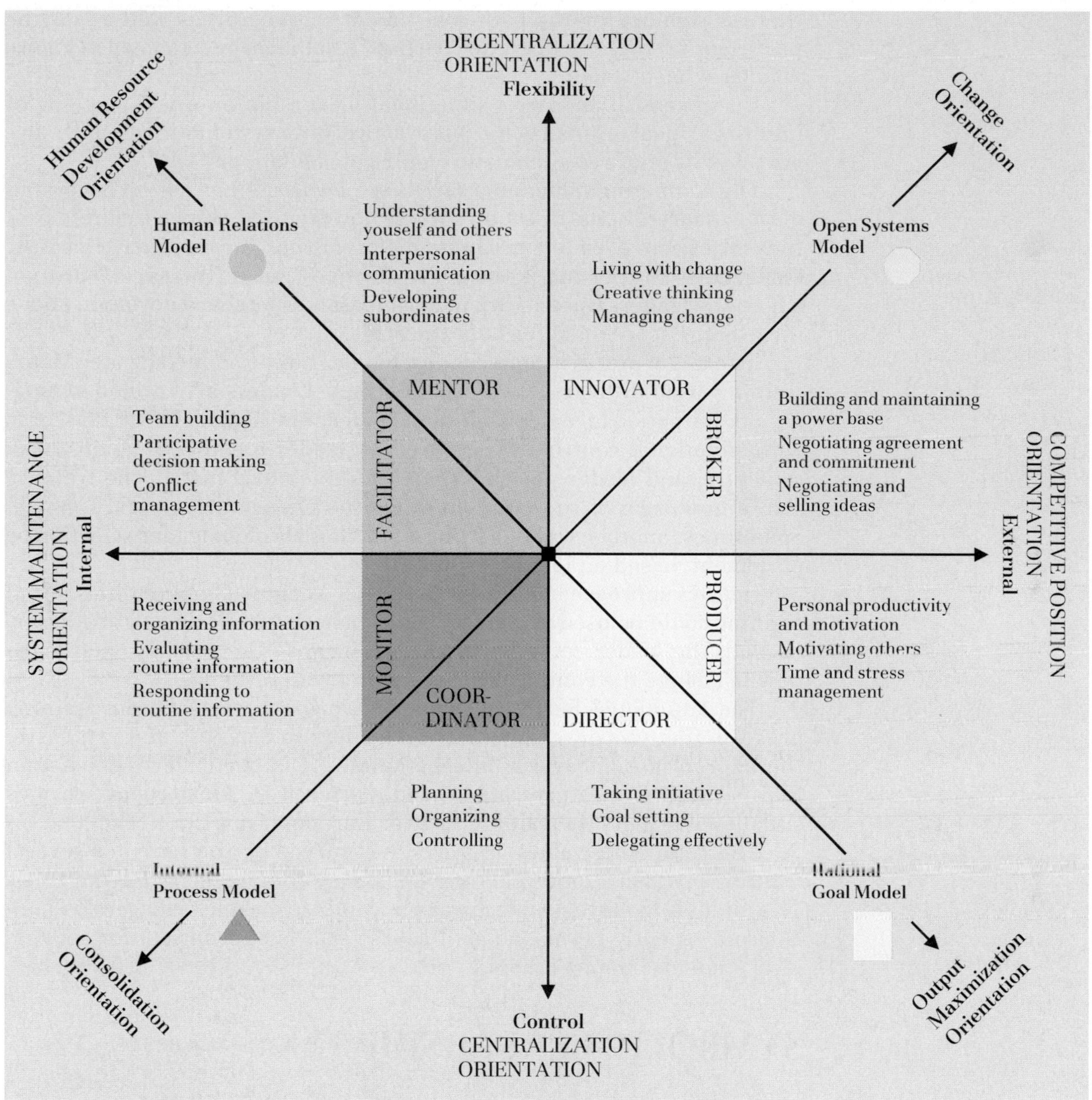


*FIGURE 16.6 The competencies and the leadership roles in the competing values framework. Note: Each of the eight leadership roles in the competing values framework contains three competencies. They, like the values or orientations, complement the ones next to them and contrast with those opposite to them.* (Adapted from Robert E. Quinn, Sue R. Faerman, Michael P. Thompson, and Michael R. McGrath, *Becoming a Master Manager,* New York: John Wiley & Sons, 1990, p. 15.)

resource theory is so new that there has not yet been time for much research to develop.[26]

House's path-goal approach has attracted quite a bit of research, and there is support for the path-goal theory in general, as well as for the particular predictions discussed earlier.[27] Not all aspects shown in Figure 16.5 have been tested.

Hersey and Blanchard's situational leadership approach has lots of intuitive appeal for managers, but practically no systematic research support. It still requires systematic empirical validation.[28]

The competing values approach is so new that it has not yet generated much research. Some of Quinn's work, however, has shown that role profiles for effective leaders are quite different than for ineffective leaders. Particularly interesting is the very effective "master manager" profile, where the leaders were shown to be at least one standard deviation above the average score on all eight of the roles.[29]

In terms of practical applications, Fiedler has developed Leader Match training, used by Sears Roebuck and others. Leaders are trained to diagnose the situation to match their or other leaders' high and low LPC scores with situational control as measured by leader-member relations, task structure, and leader power. Where there is not a match, the training shows how each of these variables can be changed to obtain a match. Sometimes, another way of getting a match is through leader selection or placement, based on LPC.[30]

House's approach lends itself to at least a couple of possibilities. First, training could be used to change leader behavior to fit the contingencies. Second, the leader could be taught to diagnose the situation and learn how to change the contingencies, as with Leader Match.

The situational leadership approach has a very elaborate training program that was developed to train leaders to diagnose and emphasize the appropriate behaviors. Internationally, it is particularly popular in Europe, where an organization headquartered in Amsterdam provides situational leadership training all over Europe, if not the world.

The competing values approach has served as the basis for several training programs to develop the necessary competencies for the roles. The intent is to move people toward becoming "master managers." There is also a recently developed skill course that is appropriate for college-level students, among others.[31]

# SYMBOLIC LEADERSHIP

In contrast to the leader traits and behaviors and the situational contingencies approaches, stands a third category of theorizing we call *symbolic leadership.* This perspective recognizes that leadership may have very little to do with causing performance/human resource maintenance. Rather, leadership may be a result instead of a cause of performance/human resource maintenance. Or, it may be used symbolically to explain outcomes after the fact.

With regard to the former, there is a fair amount of evidence suggesting that leader behavior is influenced by outcomes.[32] For example, a leader would be more supportive and do less structuring for high performing as opposed to low performing subordinates. This evidence raises the question of whether leadership is a necessary prerequisite for performance/human resource maintenance at all.

Several recent studies illustrate the symbolic aspects of leadership. Jeffrey Pfeffer argues that a major part of what leaders do is to develop explanations to legitimize various actions that were taken.[33] Some have called this the "romance of leadership." For these people leadership is used, after the fact, to explain very complex matters that are not clearly understood. For example, who can say what really caused a major firm or sporting team to perform well or poorly? Was it the environment, the people, the way the organization was structured, or was it merely luck? In complicated situations like this, it is almost impossible to explain what really caused the performance. However, people don't like to admit that, so they often attribute the results or lack thereof to "leadership" or to a given leader or coach. Thus, they romanticize leadership as a kind of symbol to make sense out of a situation that is otherwise complex and confusing.[34]

Here, people use leadership as a symbol to help maintain the social order. Leadership becomes an attribution used to explain things after the fact. Thus, successful leaders can attach themselves to successes and attempt to separate themselves from failures.

Let us briefly look at how a subordinate might attribute leadership to his or her boss.[35] Subordinates may use actual observations, "hearsay" descriptions, or "inferred" observations. For example, if a manager responds quickly to a message left by you, this may be inferred as "decisive" behavior. As a subordinate you might then use this observation as evidence of "leadership" on the part of your supervisor.

Subordinates may also make inferences about whether the causes of observed behaviors are internal (e.g., the leader is basically a considerate person) or external (e.g., the leader is considerate because the boss requires it) to the leader. If these causes coincide with the subordinates' implicit views about what makes a good leader or ways in which "real leaders" would act in a given situation, then the supervisor will be seen as exhibiting "leadership." Whether the person in a leadership role is seen in this way or not can have a substantial impact on his or her relations with subordinates and key outcomes in the work unit. This perception sometimes has been described as an *implicit leadership theory*. Alternatively it has been called a *leadership prototype,* where people have a picture in their minds of what the image of a model leader should look like.[36]

## Symbolic Leadership Research and Applications

Unlike the other perspectives, we haven't pinpointed a series of specific approaches that have led to research. Rather, we summarized some of the more interesting work in our just-completed symbolic leadership discussion. In terms of application, we can say that the perspective lends itself to training. The training would involve making people sensitive to the impact of attributions and symbols. Leaders would be taught such things as impression management and related ideas.

# SUBSTITUTES FOR LEADERSHIP

**Substitutes for leadership**

Standing in contrast to all three of the prior categories of leadership approaches, is the ***substitutes for leadership*** perspective of Steven Kerr

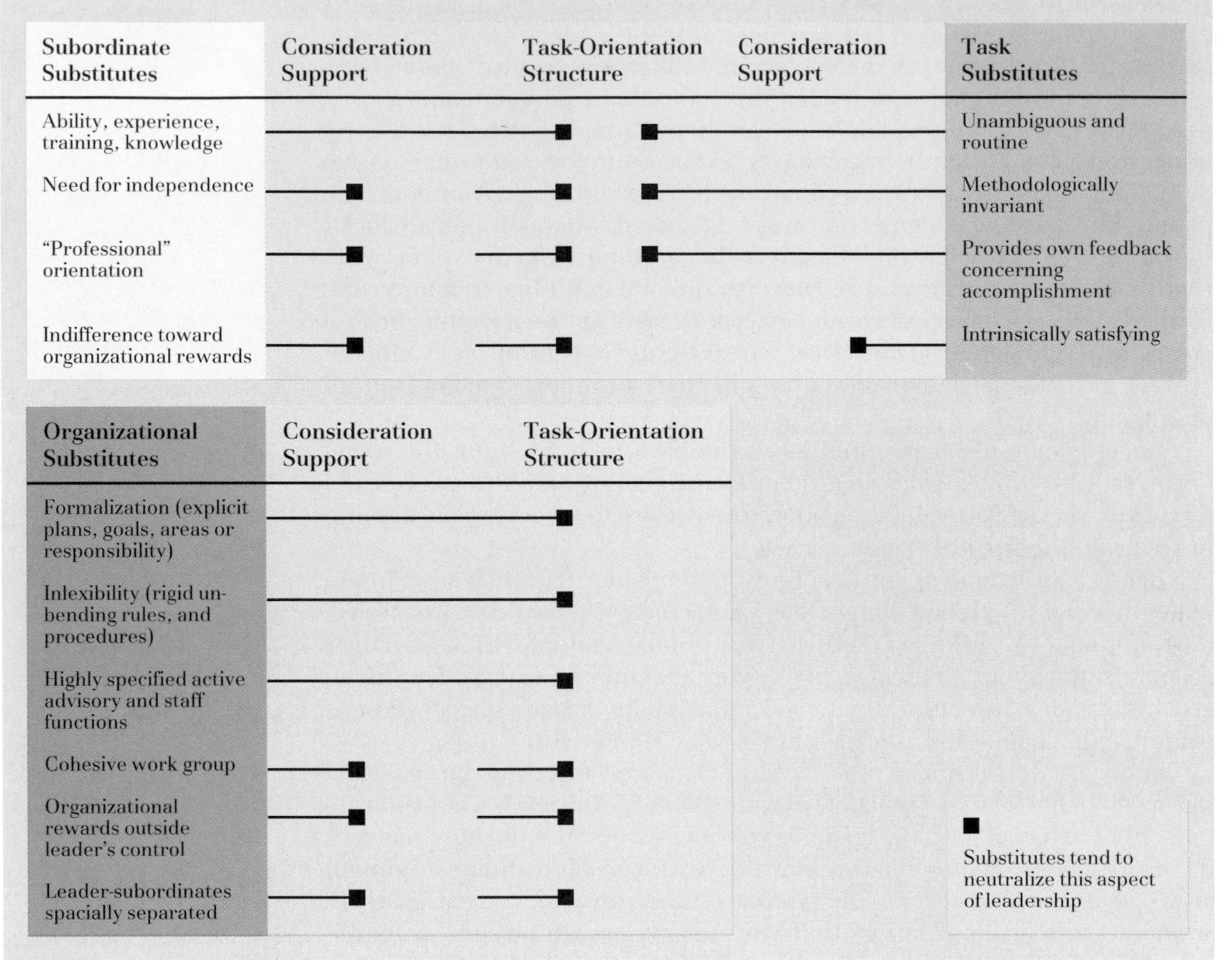


*FIGURE 16.7 Substitutes for leadership.* (Suggested by Steven Kerr and John Jermier, "Substitutes for Leadership: Their Meaning and Measurement," *Organizational Behavior and Human Performance,* Vol. 22 (1978), p. 387.)

and John Jermier.[37] They argue that frequently organizational and/or individual or task situational variables substitute for leadership in causing performance/human resource maintenance. Figure 16.7 shows several elements in this leadership approach.

Let us briefly discuss some of these substitutes as represented in the figure. In terms of the subordinate—ability, experience, training, and knowledge can be at a high enough level so that a person needs very little if any task-oriented leadership. Even here, however, relationship-oriented leadership is expected to be important. For example, a highly skilled tool and die maker does not need much task-oriented leadership, though he or she would still like a pat on the back. If someone has a strong professional-orientation, that person will probably tend to rely heavily on his or her education, training, peers, and outside people and organizations for much of his or her job guidance. That person is also likely to look at these same sources for much of the interpersonal comfort that supportive leaders provide.

In terms of the task, machine paced work (such as that found on traditional automotive assembly lines) possesses the methodologically invariant characteristic shown in the figure. Work on an assembly line does not require much direction from a leader. However, the tedium of the task is likely to make leader supportiveness important for most people. Again looking at task substitutes for leadership, performance feedback from the work itself can operate to minimize feedback needed from a task-oriented leader. Remember the impact of feedback as part of job enrichment in Chapter 7. Similarly, an intrinsically satisfying task can mean that leader supportiveness may not be needed. In terms of the organization, cohesive, interdependent work groups and active advisory and staff personnel can also reduce the need for a leader's performance feedback. Recall, especially from Chapters 9 and 10, the powerful impact that norms and cohesion can have on work guidance and performance.

## Substitutes for Leadership Research and Applications

Recent research on leadership substitutes tends to support the general approach. There has been some work comparing Mexican and U.S. workers that suggests both similarities and differences in the effects of various substitutes, and there is work that has proposed additional substitutes, such as "face saving," that may operate as substitutes in Asia and other parts of the Far East.[38] Perhaps the most important practical development lies with the emergence of self-managing work teams and more enriched job designs—all of which empower workers and provide substitutes for leadership.

# SUMMARY

■ **Leadership and Managerial Activities** are sometimes seen as similar and sometimes not. Most often leadership is seen as narrower than management—it is but one of four functions or only one of Mintzberg's roles. Less often, it is seen as anything done by a person occupying a managerial position. Some argue that those who are visionary and exciting are leaders, whereas those who handle routine, everyday managerial activities are managers. Leadership can be thought of as both formal—that is, exerted by persons granted formal authority in organizations—and informal—that is, exerted by persons who become influential because of special resources or skills.

■ **Leader Traits and Behaviors** summarize the emphasis of those approaches in this cell. Included are: great man/trait theory, leadership behavior theory, reward and punishment theory, and the charismatic/transformational approaches of House, Bass, and Conger and Kanungo.

■ **Situational Contingencies and Leadership** approaches include: Fiedler's leadership contingency theory and his cognitive resource theory; House's path–goal theory; situational leadership theory; and the competing values framework.

■ **Symbolic Leadership** connotes leadership treated as either a result of outputs or symbolically to explain outputs in a complex situation, after the fact.

■ **Substitutes for Leadership** consider various kinds of subordinate, task, and organizational aspects as substitutes for considerate or structured leadership. Where these substitutes are operating, a given aspect of leadership is not needed.

## KEY TERMS

Charismatic Behavior
Charismatic Leaders
Contingent Reward
Formal Leadership
Individualized Consideration
Informal Leadership
Intellectual Stimulation
Leadership
Management-by-Exception
Situational Control
Substitutes for Leadership
Symbolic Leadership
Transactional Leadership
Transformational Leadership

## REVIEW QUESTIONS

1. Describe how leadership is related to the broader concepts of power and politics treated in Chapter 15.
2. Think of a work situation and describe at least one instance of informal leadership.
3. Describe the difference between leadership traits and behaviors and the implication of these differences for understanding current leadership theories.
4. Compare and contrast the assumptions regarding leadership underlying each of the Cells in the four-cell matrix categorizing leadership and its relation to maintenance.
5. Explain the basic elements in: (1) Fiedler's leadership contingency theory and (2) Fiedler's cognitive resource theory. Give examples of good leader situation matches for persons with strong relationship-motivation and task-motivation, respectively.
6. Describe a situation you experienced where leadership was inferred from performance/human resource maintenance, or where it was used attributionally after the fact to explain good or poor performance/human resource maintenance.
7. Show the similarities and differences in Fiedler's contingency theory, House's path–goal theory, situational leadership theory and the competing values framework.
8. Think of a work situation, apply one of the leadership theories and briefly explain how you would use selection/placement, training, or some combination to enhance performance/human resource maintenance.

## AN OB LIBRARY

Bernard M. Bass, *Bass & Stogdill's Handbook of Leadership* (New York: The Free Press, 1990).

Max DePree, *Leadership Is an Art* (East Lansing, Mich.: Michigan State University Press, 1987).

John W. Gardner, *On Leadership* (New York: The Free Press, 1989).

James M. Kouzes and Barry Z. Posner, *The Leadership Challenge* (San Francisco: Jossey-Bass, 1989).

Noel M. Tichy and Mary Anne DeVanna, *The Transformational Leader* (New York: John Wiley & Sons, 1986).

# EXERCISE

## YOUR LEADERSHIP STYLE

### *Objectives*

1. To assess your personal propensity for transformational or transactional leader style.
2. To develop an understanding of leadership characteristics and what makes a person a leader.
3. To aid your understanding of the similarities and differences in leadership styles and types of leaders.
4. To provide a broad perspective of current and historical leaders.
5. To develop and enhance your research and analytical skills and abilities.

### *Total Time*

30 to 60 minutes

### *Procedure*

1. You should begin by individually completing and scoring the leadership questionnaire below.[39]
2. Next, choose a leader (current or historical) whom you know something about.
3. Now, develop a listing of the key characteristics of this particular leader. Write these characteristics down on a piece of paper.
4. Form a group of five to seven persons and share key characteristics of your individual leaders in a round-robin fashion. Designate one member of the group to serve as group reporter, who will later present your findings to the rest of the class.
5. As a group, rank the strongest characteristics (i.e., the characteristics that appeared most frequently on people's lists), and discuss overall generalizations and ideas about leadership.
6. Discuss whether there is any relationship between your personal

transformational/transactional score and your evaluation of the leaders above.

7. The group reporter shares results in general class discussion.

### *Leadership Questionnaire*

For each of the following 10 pairs of statements, divide five points between the two according to your beliefs, perceptions of yourself, or according to which of the two statements characterizes you better. The five points may be divided between the A and B statements in any way you wish with the constraint that only whole positive integers may be used (i.e., you may not split 2.5 points equally between the two). Weigh your choices between the two according to the one that better characterizes you or your beliefs.

_____ 1. A. As leader I have a primary mission of maintaining stability.
_____ B. As leader I have a primary mission of change.

_____ 2. A. As leader I must cause events.
_____ B. As leader I must facilitate events.

_____ 3. A. I am concerned that my followers are rewarded equitably for their work.
_____ B. I am concerned about what my followers want in life.

_____ 4. A. My preference is to think long range: What might be.
_____ B. My preference is to think short range: What is realistic.

_____ 5. A. As a leader I spend considerable energy in managing separate but related goals.
_____ B. As a leader I spend considerable energy in arousing hopes, expectations, and aspirations among my followers.

_____ 6. A. While not in a formal classroom sense, I believe that a significant part of my leadership is that of teacher.
_____ B. I believe that a significant part of my leadership is that of facilitator.

_____ 7. A. As leader I must engage with followers at an equal level of morality.
_____ B. As leader I must represent a higher morality.

_____ 8. A. I enjoy stimulating followers to want to do more.
_____ B. I enjoy rewarding followers for a job well done.

_____ 9. A. Leadership should be practical.
_____ B. Leadership should be inspirational.

_____ 10. A. What power I have to influence others comes primarily from my ability to get people to identify with me and my ideas.
_____ B. What power I have to influence others comes primarily from my status and position.

### *Scoring Key*

| *Transformational* | *Your Point(s)* | *Transactional* | *Your Point(s)* |
|---|---|---|---|
| 1. B | ________ | 1. A | ________ |
| 2. A | ________ | 2. B | ________ |
| 3. B | ________ | 3. A | ________ |
| 4. A | ________ | 4. B | ________ |
| 5. B | ________ | 5. A | ________ |
| 6. A | ________ | 6. B | ________ |

| | | | |
|---|---|---|---|
| 7. B | ______________ | 7. A | ______________ |
| 8. A | ______________ | 8. B | ______________ |
| 9. B | ______________ | 9. A | ______________ |
| 10. A | ______________ | 10. B | ______________ |

*Column Totals:* ____ ____

*Note:* The higher column total indicates that you agree more with, and see yourself as more like, either a transformational leader or a transactional leader.

CASE

## THREE LEADERS

Read and think about the leaders and leadership situations described in each of the following examples.[40]

### *Quality Circle Chair*

There are 10 people in the chairperson's quality circle (QC). The QC chair is also a supervisor within a department. He chooses the QC members by placing the names of volunteers into piles, by department, so that there will be a cross-section from all departments. Then he draws one name from each pile. Thus, he has his own plus other people in the QC.

The QC chair makes sure things keep moving rather than getting bogged down. He does not want to call himself a QC supervisor because he does not want to impose his feelings on the circle. He likes to think of himself as a member like the others. He wants decisions to be made by the QC, not by him, and if the circle wants his recommendations he wants members to ask for them because of his experience and expertise.

The leader and members work with the QC facilitator who sits in on all the meetings. The facilitator is a liaison with other units and helps obtain cooperation when necessary.

To develop members, the QC chair uses an alphabetical system to assign a new session leader from the members every week. Then the chair sits back and watches the circle move. If the group gets bogged down, he intercedes to keep it moving. He also serves as a mediator, suggesting ways to deal with problems. He wants members to solve problems with their own techniques rather than to use his to please him.

When the circle makes presentations to management, the chair introduces the presentation and the rest of the members are present. There are many practice runs first. The chair feels the circle is helping people grow by giving them experience in problem solving and decision making. The chair feels the circle broadens him and exposes him to technical areas he previously knew little about. He also feels that he deliberately gives up much of his supervisory power in the circle. He spends many unpaid hours at night working with the members on presentations.

The chair indicates that he can be freer in the QC than in his regular group, since there are no deadlines in the QC and almost constant ones in the regular group.

However, he feels some of his QC kind of leadership has carried over to his regular group. Now, when time is available and there is a question he asks his people what they think.

The QC chair sees QCs as having an impact on the leadership of those above him. He claims his superiors have become more participative. In summary, he thinks both his and his superiors' styles have changed.

### *Airline Field Manager*

The airline field manager is a walking, talking ball of fire perhaps in her mid-thirties in age. She dresses professionally in what is not quite a uniform. She works for a major airline and is responsible for her firm's ticket counter, sky captains in the airport, and security.

Her performance is judged on delays. Do late passengers delay the plane? If her loading times are too late, she is called on the carpet. If there is one delay, it backs up other flights. Everything is supposed to be on time.

Her boss goes through monthly computerized charts showing lateness statistics and then gives her feedback. Lots of paperwork from above causes her additional stress. She would rather be with her people on the floor than doing paperwork but the paperwork is required.

She also gets lots of pressure from below. She must make sure her lines run as fast as feasible. Thus, she has to get enough staffing to handle passengers for a given time of day. She always tries to be out front as a visible member of management—especially when there are weather delays and missing connections. When there is a long line at the ticket counter she moves in and helps out.

Sometimes men do not like taking orders from her. She typically says something like, "you can spend eight hours a day being miserable or you can spend the time doing your job."

If a baggage belt breaks she will be right in the middle straightening out the bags. She frequently is dependent on other airports to deal with late passengers. Thus, she has to try to get cooperation when she has no direct authority over these airports.

She does not want to be too friendly with subordinates. She is their boss, not their buddy. If there is a passenger an agent cannot deal with, she handles the passenger. If the agent was correct she tells the passenger that. If the agent was wrong she apologizes for the agent's behavior and talks to the agent later. She also arbitrates between skycaps and passengers and skycaps and agents. She works hard to train agents to be polite to customers.

### *Heart Transplant Surgeon*

This heart transplant surgeon directs between one and three assistant surgeons, two cardiac anesthesiologists, a scrub nurse, a circulating nurse, a profusionist (operates the heart-lung machine), and an intensive care team of physicians and nurses. About 98% of this teams' patients' health has been improved and about 85% have been cured.

The surgeon meets the patient and relatives after a cardiologist has diagnosed the problem. Then, if called for, either a transplant or less extensive surgery is done. Once the patient and family have made a decision to have the surgery, and the operating room is scheduled, the surgeon has conferences with his surgical team, the cardiologist, and the intensive care people. He tries to make sure everything is thoroughly planned and potential problems anticipated. He also has tests conducted to make sure there are no contraindictaions for conducting the operation. Again, he goes over the operation with the patient and family and yet again with the patient immediately before the operation.

The patient is then taken to the operating room, put to sleep, and inserted with catheters for fluids, medications, and monitoring. The patient is then hooked up to a heart–lung machine.

The surgeon monitors what is happening: in the operating field—with the anesthesiologists at the head of the table, at the heart–lung machine, and with the circulating and scrub nurses. This monitoring involves coordination and the reduction of stress. He anticipates the next moves and makes sure his team is ready for them.

After the operation is completed, the patient is taken to intensive care. Those helping the patient there are under the surgeon's direction. He then discusses the operation with the relatives. He debriefs the team and asks each member how he or she thinks the operation went. He also tells team members how he thinks it went. He goes beyond depending on their professionalism to provide positive feedback and provides it himself.

By and large, team members are aware of mistakes and will work to correct them. The surgeon tries to get the most competent person on a given task to correct the error. He does not criticize in front of others. After the operation he talks with the person making the mistake and they try to work out procedures to keep it from happening again. The surgeon also encourages feedback on his own errors. He uses the team's mistakes as a foundation for improvement. Whenever possible, he allows team members to draw conclusions rather than imposing his own. He tries to lower the level of stress in the operating room. He encourages healthy patients after the operation to visit his team and the team in intensive care so that these people can see how well the patient is doing.

When there is a heart transplant, there are additional logistics to which the surgeon must attend. For example, he must obtain a donor heart and the like.

Death is a constant possibility that can affect the morale of his team. He reminds the team of its good record and he and its members carefully assess what happened to see if it was avoidable or not. In spite of his team always doing its best, deaths sometimes do occur.

### *Questions*

1. Using three of the theories discussed in the text, compare and contrast the leader behaviors or leadership styles of the three leaders.
2. Discuss the extent to which you think the described leader behaviors are appropriate for the situations faced by each of the leaders. How would you go about deciding such appropriateness?
3. Describe how you might use the leadership applications discussed in the chapter to provide the appropriate leadership for each of these positions.

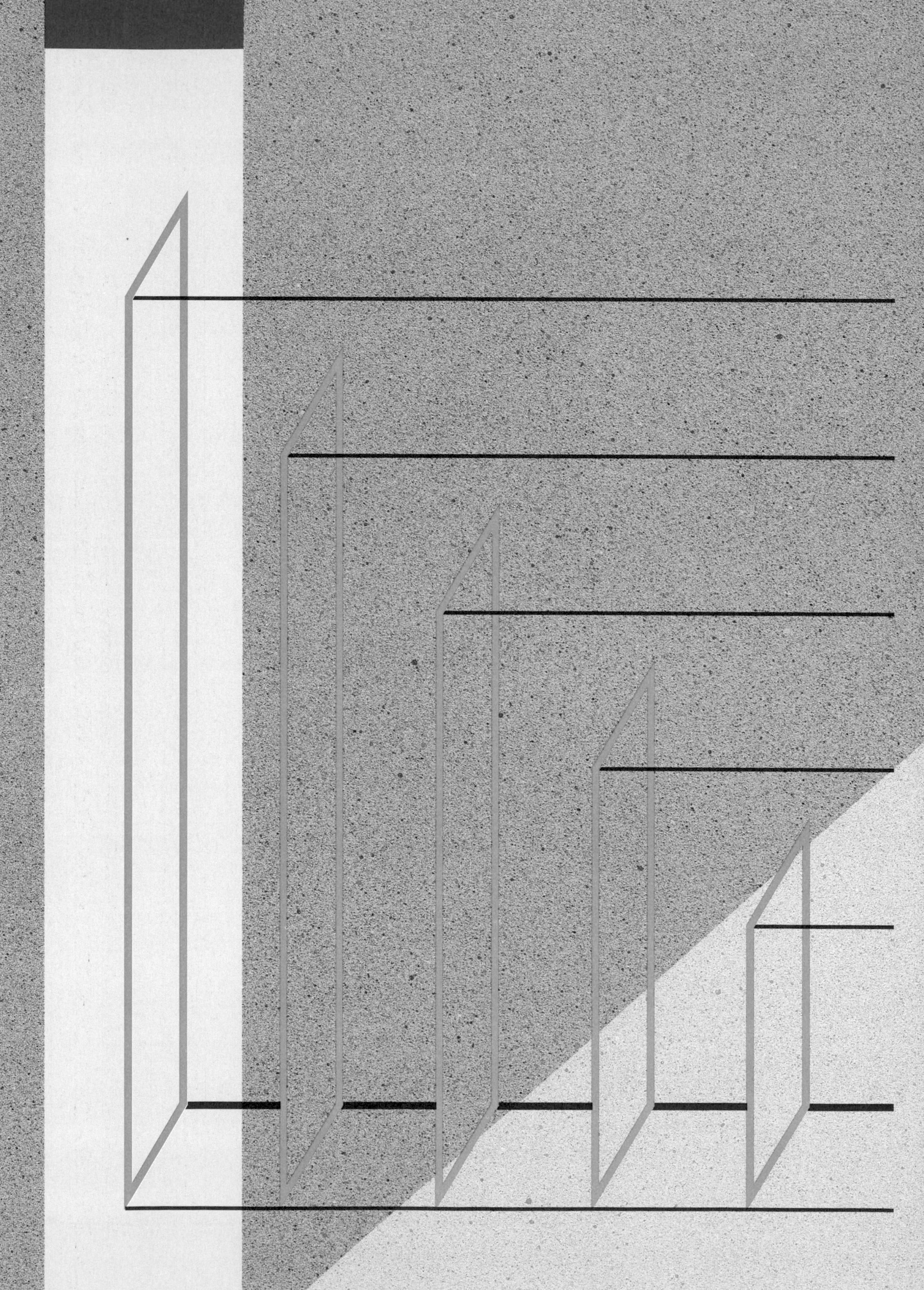

# PART SIX

# MANAGING IN A DYNAMIC ENVIRONMENT

This study outline of major topics is meant to organize your reading now; it is repeated in the Summary to structure your review.

## STUDY OUTLINE

### ■ The Nature of Organizational Change

Planned and Unplanned Change   Organizational Targets for Change
Phases of Planned Change

### ■ Planned Change Strategies

Force-Coercion   Rational Persuasion   Shared Power

### ■ Resistance to Change

Why Do People Resist Change?   Dealing with Resistance to Change

### ■ Organization Development

Goals of Organization Development   Principles Underlying Organization Development
Ethical Aspects of Organization Development

CHAPTER 17

# PLANNED CHANGE AND ORGANIZATION DEVELOPMENT



## PHOTO ESSAYS

# VISIONS 17

**Maybe it doesn't seem like much, but DuPont CEO Edgar Woolard shows great *vision* when he says: "Employees have been underestimated. You have to start with the premise that people at all levels want to contribute and make the business a success." This vision is real at the company's Towanda, Pennsylvania plant where employees work in self-managing work teams, and the plant's managers call themselves "facilitators" rather than "bosses." And in the space of four-years time, productivity rose 35 percent at the facility.**

**Part of the new culture at DuPont involves managers accepting responsibilities to "coach" workers and help them understand the market and competitive forces to which the company, and its employees, must respond. Mark Suwyn, one of the firm's vice presidents, clearly rejects the notion that only the white-collar and management employees have something to contribute. He says: "These people manage their lives well outside the factory. They sit on school boards or coach Little League. We have to create a culture where we can bring that creative energy into the work force."**

Many of the ideas discussed earlier in this book represent potential changes that can be made to improve organizational performance and the quality of work life of their members. Along with the DuPont example just provided, highly *progressive* organizations today are pursuing change and developing themselves in a shift toward new ways of managing people and organizations. Among the observable trends are:[1]

*On who makes the decisions:*

*Old way* Managers maintain control and spend time directing and controlling the work of subordinates.

*New way* Managers empower others, and seek ways to support the self-directed work of individuals and groups.

*On what managers assume about workers:*

*Old way* Workers want nothing but pay, dislike responsibility, must be closely controlled.

*New way* Workers want challenge on the job, will seek autonomy and responsibility if allowed.

*On how jobs are defined:*

*Old way* Work is deskilled and narrow, focusing on individuals who do, but don't think.

*New way* Work is multiskilled and team oriented. Doing and thinking are combined.

*On how wages are determined:*

*Old way* Pay based on the job not the person, and determined by job evaluations.

*New way* Pay is based on skills acquired, and includes group evaluations and incentives.

*On how organizations are structured:*

*Old way* Strict hierarchy with many levels, and top-down use of authority.

*New way* Flatter structures with fewer levels, and room for lower-level participation.

*On the nature of labor relations:*

*Old way* Incompatible interests emphasized, leads to more conflict.

*New way* Mutual interests are emphasized, leads to more cooperation.

Regardless of how attractive and appropriate such developments appear, change and continuous improvement in dynamic environments are sometimes hard to achieve. Tendencies toward the status quo dominate a situation even though new circumstances call for change. As the following historical examples suggest, it just isn't that easy to change the behavior of people or organizations.[2]

First,

*From the history of England*

The Royal Artillery was giving a demonstration to some visiting Europeans on Salisbury Plain in the 1950s. Visitors were most impressed with the speed and precision of the light artillery crew, but one asked about the duty of the man who stood at attention throughout the demonstration.

"He's number six," the adjutant explained.

"I, too, can count. But why is he there?"

"That's his job. Number six stands at attention throughout."

"But why then do you not have five?"

No one knew. It took a great deal of research through old training manuals, but finally they discovered his duty. He was the one who held the horses.

Second,

*From the American automobile industry*

H. Ross Perot left the board of directors of General Motors Corporation in late 1986 after a stormy relationship with CEO Roger Smith. A frustrated Perot once remarked, "It takes five years to develop a new car in this country. Heck, we won World War II in four years."

# THE NATURE OF *ORGANIZATIONAL* CHANGE

**Change agent**

A ***change agent*** is a person or group taking responsibility for changing the existing pattern of behavior of another person or social system. It only makes sense, therefore, that part of every manager's job in today's dynamic times is to act as a change agent in the work setting. This means being alert to situations or people needing change, open to good ideas, and able to support the implementation of new ideas into actual practice. For example,

> ***3M Corporation*** CEO Allen Jacobson makes sure that continuous innovation is a trademark of 3M. He gives technical people all the resources they need to come up with new ideas. He also encourages managers to give their subordinates the freedom and time to think. "You've got to sponsor your people's ideas," he says. "You've got to help them along."

## Planned and Unplanned Change

**Unplanned change**

Not all change in organizations happens at a change agent's direction. ***Unplanned change*** occurs spontaneously or at random and without a change agent's attention. These changes may be disruptive, such as a wildcat strike that results in a plant closure, or beneficial, such as an interpersonal conflict that results in a new procedure or rule being established to guide interdependent relations. The appropriate goal in managing unplanned change is to act immediately once the change is recognized to minimize any negative consequences and maximize any possible benefits.

**Planned change**

**Performance gap**

We are particularly interested in ***planned change*** that happens as a result of specific efforts by a change agent. Planned change is a direct response to someone's perception of a ***performance gap***—that is, a discrepancy between the desired and actual state of affairs. Performance gaps may represent problems to be resolved or opportunities to be explored. It is useful to think of most planned changes as efforts initiated by managers to resolve performance gaps to the benefit of the organization and its members. For example, consider the following analysis of a change situation reported in a *Wall Street Journal* article.[3]

> *Scene*—Jerry Hathaway and his family are driving their camper toward a weekend outing in the country. But it's a Friday and Jerry is supposed to be at work at a New Hampshire packaging plant—his wife called in "sick" for him so they could all get away early.
>
> *Performance gap*—The plant at which Jerry works suffers an abnormally high absenteeism rate.
>
> *Significance*—In its legitimate and not-so-legitimate forms, absenteeism annually costs U.S. industry over $20 billion in lost pay alone. Another $10 billion or more gets spent in sick pay; $5+ billion goes for benefits which continue in the workers' absences. Once when Jerry and his co-workers failed to report for their evening shift, his plant lost 20 percent on its targeted production run.

*Manager's response*—The plant manager Eli Kwartler initiated a problem-solving and planned change effort in response to the perceived performance gap. Workers were surveyed to determine their feelings about work schedules. The data showed clear preferences among evening workers for a four-day week of 10-hour shifts Monday through Thursday instead of the 8-hour shifts. The company changed work schedules to a "4 – 40" compressed work week on the evening shifts.

*Results*—Absences fell and shift production climbed 9 percent. Even Jerry took fewer days off . . . he no longer had to skip work on Fridays to make a long weekend with his family.

## Organizational Targets for Change

Planned change can modify any of the various components reviewed in Chapters 10 and 11 as that constituting the essence of an organization. These targets of change, as shown in Table 17.1 include organizational purpose and objectives, culture, strategy, tasks, technology, people, and structure. These targets are sometimes addressed mistakenly by management "fads," offered by consultants and adopted by managers without much thought for the real situation and/or people involved. The logic of truly *planned* change, by contrast, requires a managerial willingness and ability to address problems concretely and systematically, and to avoid tendencies toward an easy but questionable "quick fix."[4] Furthermore, you must recognize that the various targets of planned organization change are highly intertwined. For example,[5]

A change in the basic *tasks* performed by an organization—that is, a modification in what it is the organization does—is almost inevit-

*TABLE 17.1*
**ORGANIZATIONAL TARGETS FOR CHANGE AND METHODS FOR DEALING WITH THEM**

| Targets | Possible Change Methods |
|---|---|
| Purpose and objectives | Clarify overall mission; modify existing objectives; use management by objectives |
| Culture | Clarify, modify, and/or create core beliefs and values to help shape behavior of individuals and groups |
| Strategy | Modify strategic plans; modify operational plans; modify policies and procedures |
| Tasks | Modify job designs; use job enrichment and autonomous work groups |
| Technology | Improve equipment and facilities; improve methods and workflows |
| People | Modify selection criteria; modify recruiting practices; use training and development programs; clarify roles and expectations |
| Structure | Modify job descriptions; modify organizational design; adjust coordination mechanisms; modify distribution of authority |

ably accompanied by a change in *technology*—that is, a modification in the way in which tasks are accomplished. Changes in tasks and technology usually require alterations in the *structure* of the organization, including changes in the patterns of authority and communication as well as in the roles of members. These technological and structural changes can, in turn, necessitate changes on the part of *members*—the basic components of the organization. For example, members may have to acquire additional knowledge and develop new skills to perform their modified roles and to work with the new technology.

## Phases of Planned Change

Kurt Lewin. a famous psychologist, recommends that any change effort be viewed as a three-phase process: unfreezing, changing, and refreezing.[6] This process is diagrammed in Figure 17.1.

*Unfreezing* is the stage of preparing a situation for change. It involves disconfirming existing attitudes and behaviors to create a felt need for something new. Unfreezing is facilitated by environmental pressures, declining performance, the recognition of a problem, and awareness that someone else has found a better way, among other things. Many changes are never tried or fail simply because situations are not properly unfrozen to begin with. Ross Perot, in an earlier example, was citing the difficulty of getting the industrial giant GM moving at a time when change was desperately needed. Large systems seem particularly susceptible to the so called "boiled frog phenomenon."[7] This refers by analogy to a classic physiological experiment, which demonstrated that a live frog will immediately jump out when placed in a pan of hot water. When placed in cold water that is then heated very slowly, the frog will stay until it boils to death. Organizations, too, can fall victim to similar circumstances. When managers fail to monitor their environments, don't recognize the important trends, and sense no need to change, their organizations may slowly suffer and lose their competitive edge.

The *changing* stage involves an actual modification in people, task, structure, and/or technology. Lewin feels that many change agents enter this stage prematurely, are too quick to change things, and therefore end up creating resistance to change in a situation that is not adequately unfrozen.

*FIGURE 17.1 Lewin's three phases of the planned change process.*

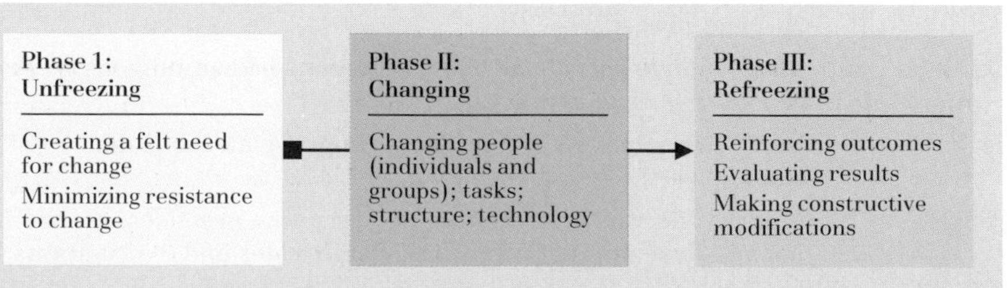

ETHICAL PERSPECTIVE

## J. C. PENNEY

Courtesy of J.C. Penney Company, Inc.

**Any change can be hard on people, but large-scale organizational restructuring can be really difficult. J.C. Penney recently went even further in moving 3800 job functions halfway across a continent when shifting its corporate headquarters from New York to Texas. To assist employees in handling the stresses of change, the company established a Relocation Steering Committee to guide the effort and a J.C. Penney Relocation Center to provide employee support. As center director Pam MacIntyre once said: "Our goal is to have a relocated J.C. Penney Company filled with satisfied, involved associates and their families."**

*Refreezing* is the final stage in the planned change process. Designed to maintain the momentum of a change, refreezing positively reinforces desired outcomes and provides extra support when difficulties are encountered. Evaluation is a key element in this final step. It provides data on the costs and benefits of a change and offers opportunities to make constructive modifications in the change over time. Improper refreezing results in changes that are abandoned or incompletely implemented.

## PLANNED CHANGE STRATEGIES

Managers and other change agents use various means for mobilizing power, exerting influence over other people, and getting them to support planned change efforts. Three major strategies are force-coercion, rational persuasion, and shared power.[8] As described in Figure 17.2, each of these strategies builds from different foundations of social power, as discussed in Chapter 15, and each has somewhat differing implications for the planned change process.

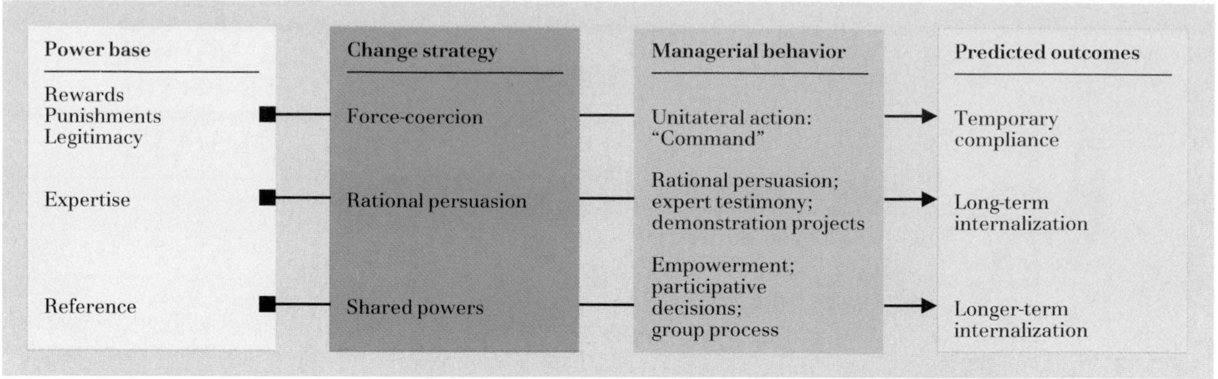


*FIGURE 17.2 Power bases, change strategies, managerial behavior, and predicted outcomes.*

## Force-Coercion

**Force-coercion strategy**

A ***force-coercion strategy*** uses legitimacy, rewards, and punishments as primary inducements to change. The change agent acts unilaterally to try to "command" change through the formal authority of his or her position, to induce change via an offer of special rewards, or to bring about change via threats of punishment. People respond to this strategy mainly out of the fear of punishment or desire for reward. Compliance is usually temporary in nature and will continue only so long as the change agent remains visible in his or her legitimate authority, or so long as the opportunity for rewards and punishments remains obvious. *If* you as change agent were to use the *force-coercion strategy* for bringing about planned change, the following profile might apply:[9]

> You believe that people who run things are basically motivated by self-interest and what situations offer in terms of potential personal gains or losses. Since you feel that people change only in response to such motives, you try to find out where their vested interests lie and then put the pressure on. If you have formal authority you use it; if not, you resort to whatever possible rewards and punishments you have access to and do not hesitate to threaten others with these weapons. Once you find a weakness, you exploit it and are always wise to work "politically" and by building supporting alliances wherever possible.

## Rational Persuasion

**Rational persuasion strategy**

Change agents using ***rational persuasion strategy*** attempt to bring about change by special knowledge, empirical support, and rational argument. Use of this strategy assumes that rational people will be guided by reason and self interest in deciding whether or not to support a change. Expert power is mobilized to convince others that the cost–benefit value of a proposed change is high; that the change will leave people better off than before. When successful, this strategy results in a longer-lasting more internalized change than does the force-coercion strategy. *If* you as change

INTERNATIONAL PERSPECTIVE

## RAMADA

Courtesy of Ramada International Hotels & Resorts.

**At Ramada International, a "grassroots" approach is aimed at making the hotel company the most environmentally responsive in the industry. Says a senior vice-president: "We want to become the hotelier of environmental integrity." To achieve success with this goal, total organizational commitment from all employees is essential. And instead of coming down with the standard corporate mandates, Ramada turned to its 22,000 employees in 40 countries—the people whose efforts would mean success or failure—for ways to make the environment around Ramada hotels better than the competitors'. The result is an employee-driven effort called "Hotels of the New Wave." The program is aimed at finding new ways of recycling waste, conserving energy, reducing water usage, using biodegradable products, and using organically grown foods.**

agent use a *rational persuasion strategy* for bringing about planned change, the following profile might apply:

> You believe that people are inherently rational and are guided by reason in their actions and decision making. Once a specific course of action is demonstrated to be in a person's self-interest, you assume that reason and rationality will cause the person to adopt it. Thus you approach change with the objective of communicating through information and facts the essential "desirability" of change from the perspective of the person whose behavior you seek to influence. If this logic is effectively communicated, you are sure that the person(s) will adopt the proposed change.

## Shared Power

**Shared power strategy**

A ***shared power strategy*** actively and sincerely involves other people who will be affected by a change in planning and making key decisions in respect to it. Sometimes called a *normative-reeducative approach,* this strategy seeks to establish directions and social support for change through the empowerment of others. It builds essential foundations such as personal values, group norms and shared goals so that support for a proposed change naturally emerges. Managers using normative-reeducative approaches emphasize personal reference and share power by allowing other persons to participate in change planning and implementation. Given this high level of involvement, the strategy is likely to result in a longer lasting and internalized change. *If* you as change agent use a *shared power strategy* for bringing about planned change, the following profile might apply:

> You believe that people have complex motivations. You feel that people behave as they do as a result of sociocultural norms and commitments to these norms. You also recognize that changes in these orientations involve changes in attitudes, values, skills, and significant relationships, not just changes in knowledge, information, or intellectual rationales for action and practice. Thus when seeking to change others, you are sensitive to the supporting or inhibiting effects of any group pressures and norms that may be operating. In working with people, you try to find out their side of things and to identify their feelings and expectations.

# RESISTANCE TO CHANGE

"Resistance" is usually viewed by change agents as something to be overcome in order for change to be successful. It is better to view resistance to change as feedback that can be used constructively by the astute change agent.[10] The essence of this notion is to recognize that when people resist change, they are defending something important that appears threatened by the change attempt.

## Why Do People Resist Change?

Shown in Table 17.2 are examples of why people might resist the introduction of a new management practice. A manager's subordinates, for

*TABLE 17.2*
**POTENTIAL SOURCES OF RESISTANCE TO A NEW MANAGEMENT PRACTICE AND SUGGESTED CHANGE AGENT RESPONSES**

| Sources of Resistance | Suggested Response |
|---|---|
| Fear of the unknown | Offer information and encouragement |
| Need for security | Clarify intentions and methods |
| No felt need to change | Demonstrate the problem or opportunity |
| Vested interests threatened | Enlist key people in change planning |
| Contrasting interpretations | Disseminate valid information and facilitate group sharing |
| Poor timing | Delay change and await a better time |
| Lack of resources | Provide supporting resources and/or reduce performance expectations |

example, might resist the introduction of advanced personal computers at their work stations because

- They had never before used the computer's operating system and were apprehensive that they could learn to use it successfully.
- They sensed the manager was forcing the computers on them without discussing their feelings on the matter first.
- They felt they were doing their jobs fine and didn't need the new computers.
- They were really busy at the present time and didn't want to try something new until the work slackened a bit.
- They weren't sure "why" the change was being made and wondered if the manager just wanted to "get rid" of them.

These and other viewpoints often create resistance to even the best and most well-intended planned changes. To better deal with these forces, managers often find it useful to separate such responses into resistance to change directed toward the change itself, the change strategy, and the change agent as a person.

People may reject a change because it does not appear as something worth their time, effort, and/or attention. To minimize such resistance, you should be careful to ensure that any changes that you sponsor as a manager satisfy four criteria.

1. Have a positive relative advantage; that is, their benefits are clearly apparent to the persons you are asking to change.
2. Are compatible with existing values and experiences.
3. Are not too complex, that is, they are easy to understand and to learn how to use.
4. Can be tried on an incremental or experimental basis before a total commitment has to be made.

Resistance is sometimes focused on the strategy rather than on the change itself. Attempting change via force-coercion, for example, may create resistance among persons who resent management by "command" or the use of threatened punishment. People may also resist an empirical-rational strategy in which the data are suspect or expertise is not clearly demonstrated, and a normative-reeducative strategy that appears manipulative and insincere.

Resistance may also reflect inadequacies in the personality of the change agent. Change agents who are isolated from other persons in the change situation, who appear self-centered, and who have a high emotional involvement in the changes are especially prone to such problems. Research also indicates that change agents who are different from other key persons on such dimensions as age, education, and socioeconomic factors are likely to experience greater resistance to change.[11]

## Dealing with Resistance to Change

Table 17.3 also shows that an informed change agent can take steps to constructively deal with such resistance, *if* it is recognized early enough

*TABLE 17.3*
**METHODS FOR DEALING WITH RESISTANCE TO CHANGE**

| *Approach* | *Commonly Used* | *Advantages* | *Drawbacks* |
|---|---|---|---|
| Education and communication | Where there is a lack of information or inaccurate information and analysis. | Once persuaded, people will often help with the implementation of the change. | Can be very time consuming if lots of people are involved. |
| Participation and involvement | Where the initiators do not have all the information they need to design the change, and where others have considerable power to resist. | People who participate will be committed to implementing change, and any relevant information they have will be integrated into the change plan. | Can be very time consuming if participants design an inappropriate change. |
| Facilitation and support | Where people are resisting because of adjustment problems. | No other approach works as well with adjustment problems. | Can be time consuming, expensive, and still fail. |
| Negotiation and agreement | Where someone or some group will clearly lose out in a change, and where that group has considerable power to resist. | Sometimes it is a relatively easy way to avoid major resistance. | Can be too expensive in many cases if it alerts others to negotiate for compliance. |
| Manipulation and co-optation | Where other tactics will not work, or are too expensive. | It can be a relatively quick and inexpensive solution to resistance problems. | Can lead to future problems if people feel manipulated. |
| Explicit and implicit coercion | Where speed is essential, and the change initiators possess considerable power. | It is speedy, and can overcome any kind of resistance. | Can be risky if it leaves people mad at the initiators. |

*Source:* Reprinted by permission of the *Harvard Business Review*. Excerpt from "Choosing Strategies for Change" by John P. Kotter and Leonard A. Schlesinger, Vol. 57 (March–April 1979), p. 111. 

in the change process. All things considered, *six general approaches for dealing with resistance to change* can be identified.[12]

1. *Education and communication.* Use of one-on-one discussions, presentations to groups, memos, reports, and demonstrations to educate people beforehand about a change and to help them see the logic of the change.
2. *Participation and involvement.* Allowing others to help design and implement the changes; asking individuals to contribute ideas and advice, or forming task forces or committees to work on the change.
3. *Facilitation and support.* Providing socioemotional support for the hardships of change, actively listening to problems and complaints, providing training in the new ways, and helping to overcome performance pressures.
4. *Negotiation and agreement.* Offering incentives to actual or potential

resistors; working out trade-offs to provide special benefits in exchange for assurance that the change will not be blocked.

5. *Manipulation and co-optation.* Use of covert attempts to influence others; selectively providing information and consciously structuring events so that the desired change receives maximum support.
6. *Explicit and implicit coercion.* Use of force to get people to accept change; threatening resistors with a variety of undesirable consequences if they do not go along as planned.

The advantages and disadvantages of these approaches are further described in the table. Managers using them must understand that resistance to change is something to be recognized and constructively addressed instead of feared. The presence of resistance typically suggests that something can be done to achieve a better "fit" among the change, the situation, and the people the change will affect. A manager should "listen" to such feedback and act accordingly.

# ORGANIZATION DEVELOPMENT

**Organization development**

***Organization development (OD)*** is a comprehensive approach to planned change that is designed to improve the overall effectiveness of organizations. Formally defined, OD is the application of behavioral science knowledge in a long-range effort to improve an organization's ability to cope with change in its external environment and increase its internal problem-solving capabilities.[13]

Organization development is used to improve performance in organizations of all types, sizes, and settings. Perhaps the best way to become acquainted with the concept is through example. Let's look at just one part of an OD program conducted in a large federal agency.[14]

> A new district director of a large federal agency was appointed following the retirement of the previous director. The new director found that operations appeared inefficient and lethargic, with low performance. After discussion and diagnosis using an outside consultant, the director felt that team building directed toward improving task accomplishment might be helpful.
>
> The first step was to hold a three-day meeting with all 36 managers of the district. The meeting objectives were to identify current operating processes, identify desired ways of operating, and develop improvement plans. The first day was primarily devoted to preparing general written procedures for the conduct of future performance reviews to be used as one way of motivating subordinates. The next day groups met to identify additional issues and problems facing the district, including the development of specific action plans for specific problems. The third day of the meeting, the district director and group members discussed recent administrative actions and the reasoning behind them. The discussion was open and candid.
>
> Six months later, a one-day followup conference was held to review progress and to deal with new items. The groups discussed

> what action had been taken on the issues raised in the first meeting, and shared reports on improvement plan achievements. Some action had been taken on all issues, but they agreed that there was considerable room for improvement in working in a collaborative mode and in further problem solving.
>
> Additional problems mentioned by the group were listed on the blackboard. Subgroups each took two of the listed problems, analyzed them, and proposed alternative courses of action. The total group reviewed these analyses and alternatives, and agreed on plans to resolve the problems. Although considerable progress had already been made during the previous six months, the group decided to meet again in three months to report on the implementation of action plans and decide upon further action.
>
> The director had begun a continuing series of collaborative problem-identification and problem-solving activities. Not only were better operating procedures developed, but all of the district managers were involved in a team effort to revitalize district operations. The director was convinced that productivity and efficiency had improved to a satisfactory level.

As the prior example indicates, OD is an exciting application of behavioral science theory to management practice. It includes a set of tools with which any manager concerned about achieving and maintaining high levels of productivity will want to be familiar. Because of its comprehensive nature and scientific foundations, OD is frequently done with the aid of an external consultant or internal professional staff member. But, its basic concepts can and should be routinely used by managers. Just as "human resource development" must be a continuing management concern, so too must "organizational development." There are times when every organization or subunit needs to reflect systematically on its strengths and weaknesses—and on the problems and opportunities it faces. The concepts and ideas of OD can assist managers to do just that.

## Goals of Organization Development

OD is *not* a panacea or surefire cure for all that ails an organization and/or its members. What OD does offer, however, is a systematic approach to planned change in organizations that addresses both:

**Process goals**

1. ***Process goals*** include achieving improvements in such things as communication, interaction, and decision making among an organization's members. They focus on how well people work together.

**Outcome goals**

2. ***Outcome goals*** include achieving improvements in task performance. They focus on what is actually accomplished through individual and group efforts.

OD is designed to help organizations and their members better achieve process and outcome goals by[15]

- Creating an open problem-solving climate throughout an organization.

- Supplementing formal authority with that of knowledge and competence.
- Moving decision-making to points where relevant information is located.
- Building trust and maximizing collaboration among individuals and groups.
- Increasing the sense of organizational "ownership" among members.
- Allowing people to exercise self-direction and self-control at work.

## Principles Underlying Organization Development

The strong human resource focus of OD is evident in the prior list. As a framework for planned change, OD is designed to improve the contributions of people to organizational goals. But, it seeks to do so in ways that respect them as mature adults who need and deserve high-quality experiences in their working lives. The foundations for achieving change in this manner rest with a number of well-established behavioral science principles shared with the field of OB as described in this book.[16]

The principles regarding individuals include:

- Individual needs for growth and development are most likely to be satisfied in a supportive and challenging work environment.
- Most people are capable of assuming responsibility for their own actions and of making positive contributions to organizational performance.

The principles regarding groups include:

- Groups help people satisfy important needs.
- Groups can be either helpful or harmful in supporting organizational objectives.
- People can increase the effectiveness of groups in meeting individual and organizational needs by working in collaboration.

The principles regarding organizations include:

- Changes in one part of an organization will affect other parts as well.
- The culture of the organization will affect the nature and expression of individual feelings and attitudes.
- Organizational structures and jobs can be designed to meet the needs of individuals and groups as well as the organization.

## Ethical Aspects of Organization Development

Since organization development involves OD practitioners (consultants and managers) working with people and organizations to achieve planned change, the ethical aspects of OD are an important consideration. Presumably, OD practitioners are trying to "help" a client system—group or organization—and its members accomplish positive change. In any helping relationship, however, ethical dilemmas may arise and the risk exists that the relationship may be abused or misused in some way.

The principles underlying OD implicitly foster high ethical standards among OD practitioners. As just described, they represent a basic and fundamental concern for human dignity and the quality of worklife, as well as for system improvement and high performance. In addition, groups of OD practitioners have been concerned about developing ethical standards to guide members of this emerging profession.[17] Among the most common ethical dilemmas that arise in OD are those involving the following four decision situations:[18]

1. *The choice of "intervention" or ways of bringing about change in the client system.* It is not considered ethical to use an intervention that the OD practitioner is not skilled in the practice of, and/or to use an intervention the client system does not want to use.
2. *The use of information that arises during the OD process.* It is not considered ethical to use data to manipulate the client system or to give one individual or group within the system special advantage over another.
3. *The management of client system dependency.* It is not considered ethical to build and maintain prolonged dependency of the client system on the OD practitioner; rather, the goals of OD include making the client system independent and capable of managing its own self-renewal and continuous improvement.
4. *Freedom of choice in regard to participation in the OD process.* It is not considered ethical to conduct OD activities in situations where the participants do not have full information about what is taking place, and where they are not allowed to exercise free choice in respect to their continued involvement.

# THE PROCESS OF ORGANIZATION DEVELOPMENT

Figure 17.3 depicts a general model of OD and shows its relationship to the phases of planned change. The OD process begins with *diagnosis,* that is, gathering and analyzing data to assess a situation and set appropriate change objectives. From a planned-change perspective, good diagnosis helps to unfreeze an existing situation as well as pinpoint appropriate action directions. Diagnosis leads to active *intervention* wherein change objectives are pursued through a variety of specific activities. This equates to the changing phase of the planned-change process. In the *reinforcement* stage of OD, changes are monitored, reinforced, and evaluated. Refreezing of change occurs at this point, and the foundations for future replication of similar diagnosis–intervention–reinforcement cycles are set. For one business firm these stages evolved as follows:

1. *Diagnosis.* Management perceived a performance gap and hired a consultant. The consultant interviewed key people and planned a

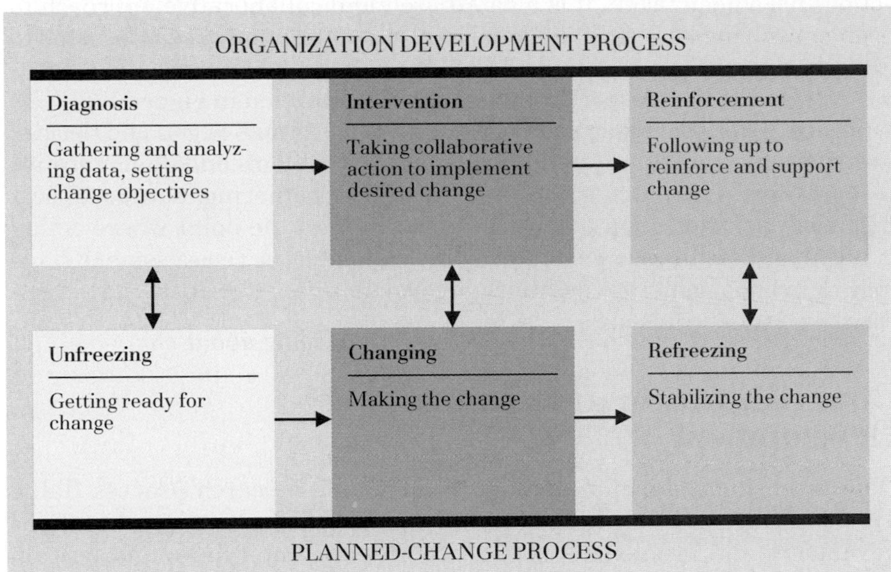


*FIGURE 17.3 A comparison of the organization development and planned change processes.*

workshop where managers could analyze the interview results in a problem-solving format.

2. *Intervention.* The workshop was held. Participants were coached on how to analyze the data and determine appropriate action directions; they also received advice on the effectiveness of the group process.
3. *Reinforcement.* The consultant continued to meet periodically with the group to review progress; additional help was given when things "bogged down"; problem-solving workshops became annual events for the firm.

Although OD is a planned-change process, the example suggests that it is also something more. Think of OD as "planned change *plus*" if you'd like. That *plus* is the goal of creating change in a way that organization members develop a capacity for continual self-renewal by learning how to implement similar diagnosis–intervention–reinforcement cycles in the future. True OD, therefore, seeks more than the successful accomplishment of one planned change. OD seeks to achieve change in such a way that organization members become more active and confident in taking similar steps to maintain longer-run organization effectiveness. A large part of any OD program's success in this regard rests with the strength of its action-research foundations.

## Action Research and Organization Development

**Action research**

***Action research*** is a process of systematically collecting data on an organization, feeding it back to the members for action planning, and evaluating results by collecting and reflecting on more data after the planned actions have been taken. It is a data-based and collaborative approach to problem solving and organizational assessment. Action research helps to identify action directions that may enhance organization effectiveness.

A typical action-research sequence is diagrammed in Figure 17.4. The sequence is initiated when someone senses a performance gap and decides to analyze the situation systematically for the problems and opportunities it represents. The process continues with data gathering, data feedback, data analysis, and action planning. It continues to the point where action is taken and results are evaluated. The evaluation or reassessment stage may or may not generate another performance gap. If it does, the action-research cycle begins anew.

## Data Utilization in Organizational Development

Data gathering is a major element in the action-research process. Table 17.4 describes several methods available for this, including the major advantages and problems associated with each. Interviews and written questionnaires are common means of gathering data in action research. Formal written surveys of employee attitudes and needs are growing in

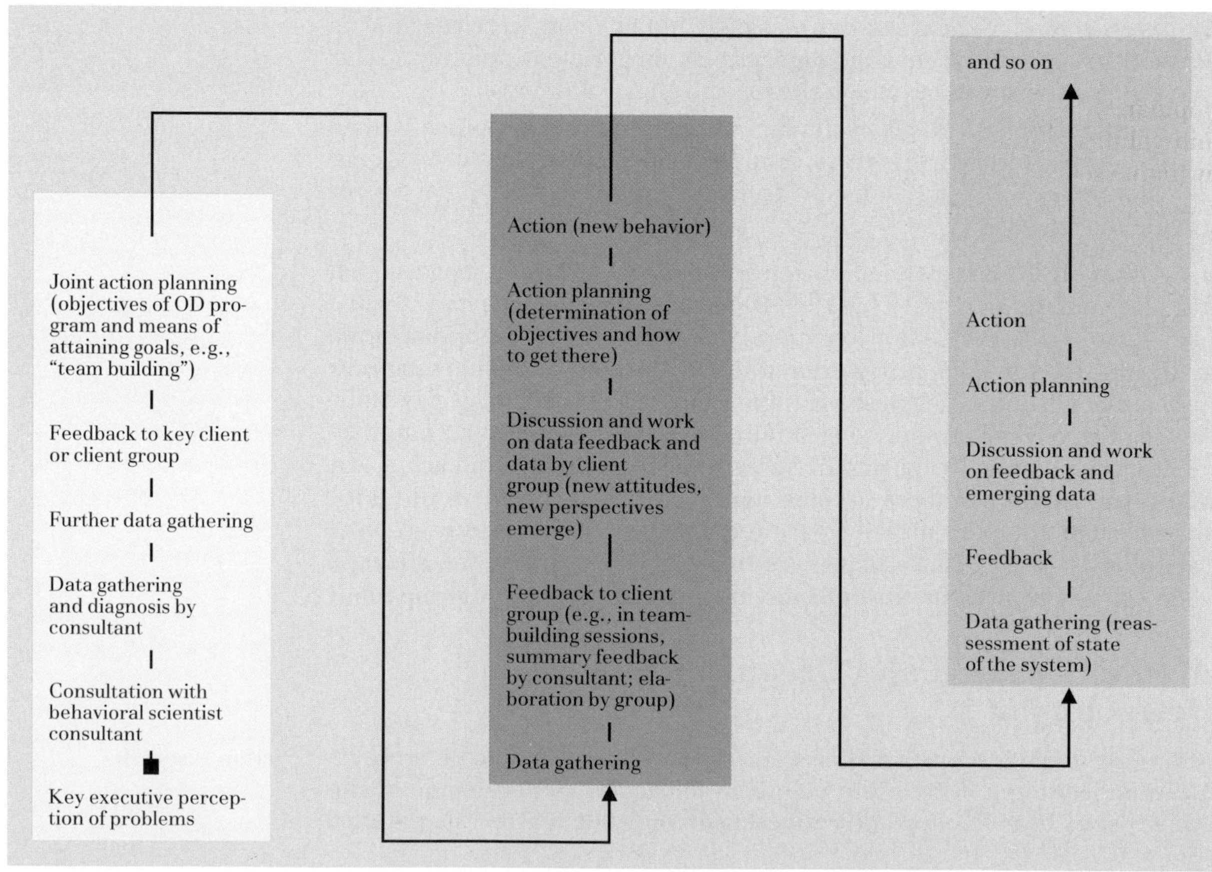


*FIGURE 17.4 An action-research model for organization development.* (*Source:* Copyright 1969 by the Regents of the University of California. Reprinted from the *California Management Review,* Vol. XII, No. 2, p. 26, Figure 1, by permission of the Regents.)

*TABLE 17.4*
A COMPARISON OF DIFFERENT METHODS OF DATA COLLECTION

| Method | Major Advantages | Major Potential Problems |
|---|---|---|
| Interviews | 1. Adaptive—allow data collection on a range of possible subjects<br>2. Source of "rich" data<br>3. Empathic<br>4. Process of interviewing can build rapport | 1. Can be expensive<br>2. Interviewer can bias responses<br>3. Coding/interpretation problems<br>4. Self-report bias |
| Questionnaires | 1. Responses can be quantified and easily summarized<br>2. Easy to use with large samples<br>3. Relatively inexpensive<br>4. Can obtain large volume of data | 1. Nonempathic<br>2. Predetermined questions may miss issues<br>3. Data may be overinterpreted<br>4. Response bias |
| Observations | 1. Collect data on behavior rather than reports of behavior<br>2. Real-time, no retrospective<br>3. Adaptive | 1. Interpretation and coding problems<br>2. Sampling is a problem<br>3. Observer bias/reliability<br>4. Costly |
| Secondary data/ unobtrusive measures | 1. Nonreactive—no response bias<br>2. High face validity<br>3. Easily quantified | 1. Access/retrieval possibly a problem<br>2. Potential validity problems<br>3. Coding/interpretation |

*Source:* David A. Nadler, *Feedback and Organizational Development: Using Data-Based Methods,* p. 119. Copyright © 1977 Addison-Wesley, Reading, MA. Reprinted with permission.

popularity, and many of those available have been tested for reliability and validity. Some have even been used to the extent that "norms" are available so that one organization can compare its results with those from a broader sample of organizations.

## Diagnostic Foundations of Organization Development

Action research and data collection can only facilitate the OD process *if* they are directed toward the right concerns and targets. Thus it is essential for managers and consultants to understand the basic diagnostic foundations of OD—that is, the frameworks for gaining useful understanding of what is happening in the client system. In the field of organization development, these diagnostic foundations are needed to help understand the behavior of the organization as a whole, of groups or major subunits within the organization, and of individual members of the groups and organization.

Figure 17.5 identifies one set of frameworks that can assist OD practitioners in accomplishing the required diagnoses. These foundations apply the open systems framework and OB concepts you are already familiar with from earlier parts of this book. At the organizational level, the figure indicates that effectiveness must be understood in respect to forces in the external environment and major organizational aspects such as strategy, technology, structure, culture, and management systems. At the group

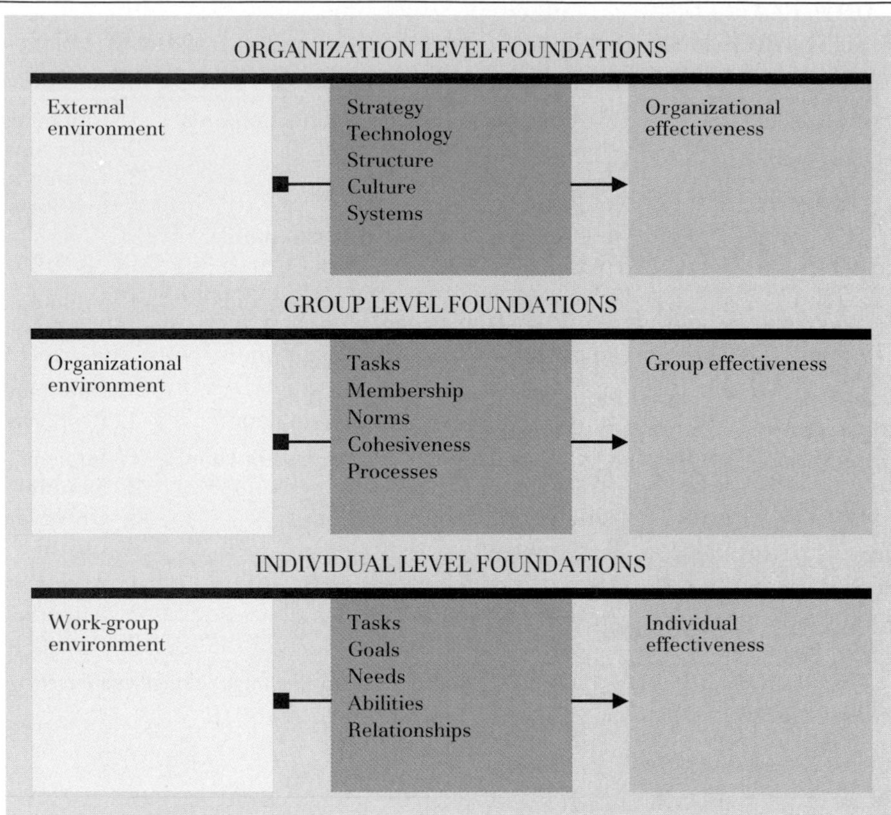


*FIGURE 17.5 Diagnostic foundations of organization development: concerns for individual, group, and organizational effectiveness.*

level, effectiveness is viewed in a context of forces in the internal environment of the organization and major group aspects such as tasks, membership, norms, cohesiveness, and group processes. At the individual level of analysis, effectiveness is considered in relationship to the internal environment of the work group and such individual aspects as tasks, goals, needs, and interpersonal relationships.

# ORGANIZATION DEVELOPMENT INTERVENTIONS

OD interventions

The basic responsibility of the OD practitioner is to engage members of the client system in activities designed to accomplish the required diagnoses and develop and implement plans for constructive change. Action research, data collection, and the diagnostic foundations should blend together through the OD practitioner's choice and use of ***OD interventions.*** These are activities initiated by the consultant or manager to facilitate planned change and assist the client system in developing its own problem-solving capabilities. As with the diagnostic frameworks just presented, the major OD interventions can be categorized in respect to their major impact at the organizational, group, and individual levels of action.[19]

Before we present the major OD interventions in each category, it is important to recognize that many of them have already been discussed. Terms such as job design, management by objectives, team-building, and role negotiation, are already part of your OB vocabulary. At this point, we are simply showing that these concepts can be used in the larger context of a comprehensive organization development program.

It is also important to understand that a comprehensive OD program usually involves more than one of these interventions being used in conjunction with one another. Indeed, the typical OD program might see various interventions being used in sequence in a "building-block" approach to the desired change. One such approach is illustrated in Figure 17.6. Note the involvement of all organizational levels along with the use of survey feedback, T-groups, team building, and management training sessions. As this example shows, organization development is an important integrating resource for managers interested in working comprehensively, collaboratively, and regularly over time to introduce planned changes and improve organizational productivity.

## Organization-Wide Interventions

An *effective organization* is one that achieves its major performance objectives while maintaining a high quality of work life for its members. OD interventions designed for system-wide application in the attempt to

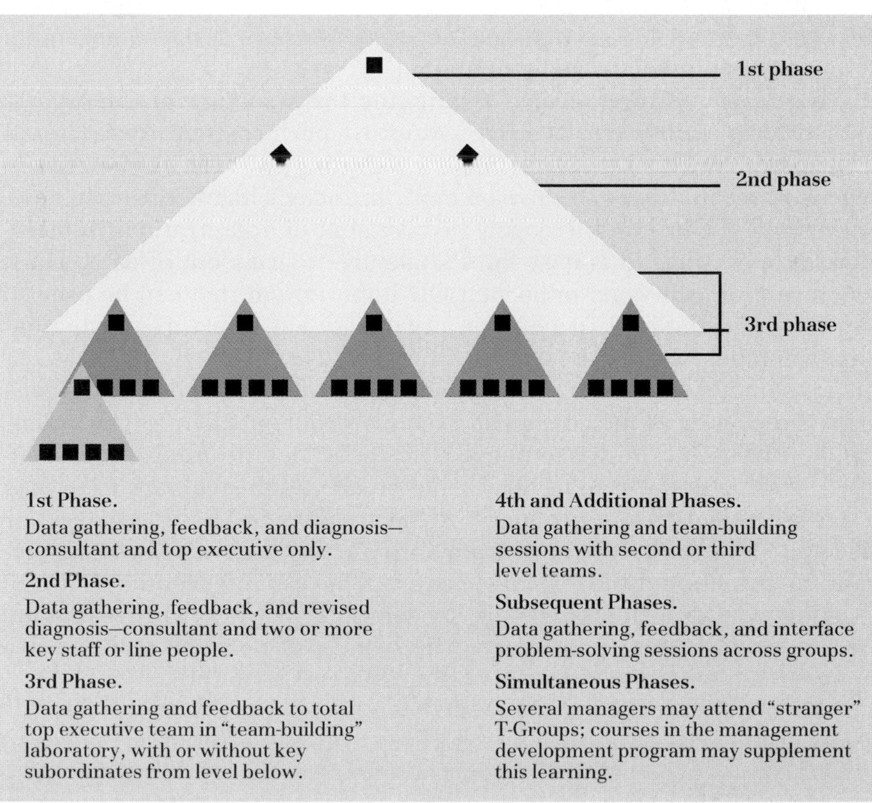


*FIGURE 17.6 Different levels and types of organization development interventions in a hypothetical setting.* (*Source:* Copyright 1969 by the Regents of the University of California. Reprinted from the *California Management Review,* Vol. XII, No. 2, p. 27, by permission of the Regents.)

improve the effectiveness of an organization or one of its major subsystems include:

- Survey feedback.
- Confrontation meeting.
- Structural redesign.
- Collateral organization.
- Management by objectives.

**Survey feedback**

***Survey feedback*** is a popular intervention that begins with the collection of data via questionnaire from organization members, or a representative sample of them. The data are then presented to or "fed back" to the members, and they are engaged in a collaborative process to interpret the data's and develop action plans in response. The role of the OD practitioner is to collect the data and manage the feedback sessions; the role of the client system is to assume responsibility for collaboratively analyzing the data and taking constructive action to improve organizational effectiveness based on the data's implications.

**Confrontation meeting**

The ***confrontation meeting*** intervention was refined by Richard Beckhard, and is designed to help determine quickly how an organization might be improved and to take initial actions to improve things.[20] The intervention involves a one-day meeting conducted by an OD facilitator for a representative sample of organizational members including top management. In a structured format the consultant asks participants to make individual lists of what they feel could be done to improve things. Then, through a series of small group work sessions and sharing of results, these ideas are refined into a tentative set of actions that top management endorses for immediate implementation.

**Structural redesign**

***Structural redesign*** involves realigning the structure of the organization or major subsystem in order to improve performance. As suggested in Chapters 10 and 11, this includes examining the best "fit" between structure, technology, and environment. In today's highly dynamic environments and with the increasing involvement of organizations in international operations, it is easy for a structure to grow out of date. Thus, structural redesign is an important OD intervention that can be used to help maintain the best fit between organizational structures and situational demands.

**Collateral organization**

It is sometimes difficult for organizations with intense day-to-day performance pressures to accomplish creative problem-solving. The ***collateral organization*** is designed to make this possible by pulling a representative set of members out of the formal organization structure to engage in periodic small-group problem-solving sessions.[21] These collateral or "parallel" structures are temporary in nature and exist only to supplement the activities of the formal structure. This OD intervention is useful for allowing the formal structure to continue to work with maximum efficiency while also experiencing the benefit of periodic and creative support from members working in the collateral structure.

**Management by objectives**

***Management by objectives*** (MBO) can be used as a system-wide OD intervention. In this case, the joint goal-setting process between managers and subordinates is formalized throughout an organization and across all hierarchical levels. The intention is to try to link the activities of all individuals and subunits into meaningful means–end chains that will ensure the accomplishment of major organizational performance objectives.

## Group and Intergroup Interventions

OD interventions at the group level are designed to improve *group effectiveness.* As defined in Chapter 8, this involves enhancing both task performance and human resource maintenance within a group. The major interventions at this level include:

- Team building.
- Process consultation.
- Intergroup team building.

We described ***team building*** in Chapter 9. As you should recall, it essentially involves a manager or consultant engaging the members of a group in a series of activities designed to help them examine how the group functions and how it might function better. Like survey-feedback at the organizational level, team-building involves some form of data collection and feedback. The key element, however, is a collaborative assessment of the data by all members of the group and the achievement of consensus regarding what might be done to improve group effectiveness. Team building is often done at "retreats" or "off-site" meetings where group members spend two to three days working intensely together on this reflection–analysis–planning process.

**Team building**

***Process consultation*** is related to team building in that it involves structured activities facilitated by the OD practitioner and designed to improve group functioning. Process consultation has a more specific focus than team building, however, with its attention being directed toward the key "processes" through which members of a group work with one another. As discussed in Chapter 9 on group dynamics, the process consultant is concerned with helping a group function better on such things as norms, cohesiveness, decision-making methods, communication, conflict, and task and maintenance activities.

**Process consultation**

***Intergroup team building*** is a special form of team building. It is designed to help two or more groups improve their working relationships with one another and, hopefully, to experience improved group effectiveness as a result. Here, the OD practitioner engages the groups or their representatives in activities which increase awareness of how each group perceives the other *and* is perceived by the other in return. Given this understanding, collaborative problem-solving can take place to improve coordination between the groups and make them more mutually supportive of one another as important components in the total organization.

**Intergroup team building**

## Individual Interventions

Task performance and job satisfaction are important concerns in respect to improving *individual effectiveness* in the workplace. OD interventions at this level of attention range from those addressing very personal issues to those dealing more with specific job and career considerations. Individual-level OD interventions include:

- Sensitivity training (T-groups).
- Management training.
- Role negotiation.
- Job redesign.
- Career planning.

**Sensitivity training**

***Sensitivity training*** is an OD intervention designed to increase the self-awareness of individuals and their "sensitivity" toward other people. It involves a number of persons—usually strangers—working together with a professional trainer in a small group, called a *T-group*. In this setting, T-group participants are encouraged to share feelings and concerns, and to listen to those expressed by others. Since the opportunity exists for people to get very personal—both in exposing their emotions and responding to others—this is a controversial type of intervention. It must only be exercised under the guidance of a highly-skilled group facilitator.

**Management training**

A most common and useful individual intervention is ***management training.*** This can be a formal "classroom" style training, or less formal training that takes place on the job. In all cases, the goal is to improve people's management skills and thereby improve their effectiveness. Management training is important, in part, because managers exert such important influence on the performance and satisfaction of other workers. Thus, improvements in management skills have the capacity for extended positive impact throughout an organization. Management training covers all the topics presented in this book and is a most useful professional development activity.

**Role negotiation**

***Role negotiation*** was formally introduced in Chapter 9 as a means for clarifying what individuals expect to give and receive of one another in their working relationship. Because roles change over time and with any changes of personnel, role negotiation can be an important means for maintaining task understandings among individuals in an organization. It is quite easily accomplished by helping people who must work together to clarify what they need from each other in order to do their jobs well.

**Job redesign**

In Chapter 7 we discussed various approaches to job design, and emphasized the importance of achieving a good "fit" between task demands and individual capabilities. ***Job redesign,*** as an OD intervention, is the process of adjusting task demands to achieve and maintain this fit. A good example is the Hackman, et al., diagnostic approach to job enrichment. When used as an OD intervention, this would involve: (1) analyzing the "core" characteristics of a job or group of jobs, (2) analyzing the "needs" and capabilities of workers in those jobs, and (3) taking action to adjust the core job characteristics to either enrich or simplify the job to best match individual preferences.[22]

**Career planning**

***Career planning*** will be discussed in the next chapter as an important way of achieving long-term congruence between individual goals and organizational career opportunities. As an OD intervention, it takes the

SKILLS PERSPECTIVE

## KNIGHT-RIDDER

Courtesy of Knight-Ridder, Inc.

**At Knight-Ridder, one of the world's leading publishing and information companies, people are expected to achieve and utilize their full potential. The in-house Knight-Ridder Institute of Training, with a full-time staff of over 50 training experts and leaders from within the firm, helps employees meet this challenge. In an increasingly pluralistic workplace and changing environment, the company recognizes the need for managers with strong commitments to leadership and human resource development. Organization development workshops bring together executives and middle-level managers for team-building and vision sharing. This is important to continuing success in service driven customer markets. Says one recent workshop participant: "We can't be a customer-driven company unless we are honest and clean inside."**

form of structured opportunities for individuals to work with their managers and/or staff experts from a personnel or human resources department on career issues. They may "map" career goals, "assess" personal development needs, and actively "plan" possible short-term and longer-term career moves. Increasingly, career planning is becoming a major part of the support provided by highly progressive organizations for their members.

## SUMMARY

■ **The Nature of Organizational Change** involves the activities of *change agents* who seek to bring about change in people and/or systems. Managers are responsible for serving as change agents with a special concern for resolving any *performance gaps* that indicate discrepancies between desired and actual states of affairs. Organizational targets for change include strategies, structures, people, tasks, and technologies. The three phases of successful planned change include unfreezing, changing, and refreezing.

■ **Planned Change Strategies** are the means used by change agents to implement desired change. *Force-coercion strategies* utilize aspects of a manager's position power to try to "command" that change will take place as directed. Temporary compliance is a common response of persons who are "forced" to change in this manner. *Rational persuasion strategies* use logical arguments and appeal to knowledge and facts to convince people to support change. When successful, this method can lead to more commitment to change. *Shared power strategies* seek to involve other persons in change planning and implementation. Of the three strategies, shared power creates the longest-lasting and most internalized commitments to the change.

■ **Resistance to Change** is to be expected. Dealing successfully with resistance begins with an awareness that it represents "feedback" that can be used by a change agent to increase the effectiveness of a change effort. People sometimes resist because they do not find value or believe in the change. They sometimes resist because they find the change strategy offensive or inappropriate. And they sometimes resist because they do not like or identify positively with the change agent as a person. Successful change agents are open to resistance, and capable of responding to it in ways that create a better "fit" between the change, the situation, and all the people involved.

■ **Organization Development in Concept** is a special application of behavioral science knowledge to create a comprehensive effort to improve organizational effectiveness. OD has both outcome goals, in respect to improved task accomplishments, and process goals, in respect to improvements in the way organization members work together. With a strong commitment to collaborative efforts and human values, OD utilizes basic behavioral science principles in respect to individuals, groups, and organizations. Ethical aspects of OD require a commitment to working with client systems in such a way that the OD facilitator does not act beyond the boundaries of his/her expertise, allows free and informed choice on the part of all affected parties, and avoids the creation of unnecessary dependencies.

■ **The Process of Organization Development** is a special form of planned organizational change. The OD phases of diagnosis, intervention, and reinforcement correspond to the unfreezing, changing, and refreezing phases of planned change. OD uses *action research* to develop a data base for collaborative problem solving and action planning by members of the client system. The diagnostic foundations of OD rest with basic models of organizational behavior at the organizational, group, and individual levels of analysis. Data collection methods in OD include use of surveys, interviews, and other creative techniques.

■ **Organization Development Interventions** are undertaken to improve organizational, group, and individual effectiveness. Very

**often, more than one intervention is used as the OD process proceeds in building-block fashion and with ongoing identification of problems to be resolved. Organization level, or system-wide interventions, include survey-feedback, management by objectives, confrontation meetings, collateral organization, and structural redesign. Group level interventions include team building, process consultation, and intergroup team building. Individual level interventions include sensitivity training, role negotiation, job redesign, management training, and career planning. All OD interventions involve applications of basic concepts and understandings from the field of organizational behavior.**

## KEY TERMS

Action Research
Career Planning
Change Agent
Collateral Organization
Confrontation Meeting
Force-Coercion Strategy
Intergroup Team Building
Job Redesign
Management by Objectives
Management Training
Organization Development (OD)
OD Intervention
Outcome Goals
Performance Gap
Planned Change
Process Consultation
Process Goals
Rational Persuasion Strategy
Role Negotiation
Sensitivity Training
Shared Power Strategy
Structural Redesign
Survey Feedback
Team Building
Unplanned Change

## REVIEW QUESTIONS

1. What is a change agent? In what ways might change agent responsibilities vary among (a) first-level, (b) middle-level, and (c) top-level managers? Use examples to explain your answers.
2. List and define the three phases of planned change as identified by Kurt Lewin. Give an example of how a planned organizational change could "fail" at each phase in the process if the responsible change agent fails to do his or her job properly.
3. What is the difference in the "ways" the force-coercion, rational persuasion, and shared power strategies seek to bring about planned change? What is the difference in the "results" that are likely to follow the use of each strategy?
4. Identify what you consider to be the five most important sources of resistance to change as discussed in this chapter. State at least one way that managers can deal successfully with each type of resistance to change.
5. Explain the difference between the "process" and "outcome" goals of OD. How does this distinction help to explain the difference between "organization development" and "planned change?"

6. Describe how action research is used as a framework for the OD process. What diagnostic models might an OD facilitator use to guide action research when addressing issues at the organizational, group, and individual levels of analysis?
7. List and explain three ethical considerations that managers and consultants should be aware of when they facilitate OD efforts in organizations.
8. Choose two interventions from each of the following categories and describe why you feel they could be used in certain situations to help improve organizational functioning: (a) organization-level interventions, (b) group-level interventions, and (c) individual-level interventions.

## AN OB LIBRARY

Rosabeth Moss Kanter, *The Change Masters* (New York: Simon & Schuster, 1983).

Ralph R. Kilmann, *Beyond the Quick Fix: Managing Five Tracks to Organizational Success* (San Francisco: Jossey-Bass, 1984).

Tom Peters, *Thriving on Chaos* (New York: Alfred A; Knopf, 1988).

Gordon Pinchot, *Intrapreneuring* (New York: Harper Collins, 1985).

Robert H. Waterman, Jr., *The Renewal Factor: How the Best Companies Get and Keep the Competitive Edge* (New York: Bantam Books, 1987).

# EXERCISE

## FORCE FIELD ANALYSIS

### *Objectives*

1. To improve your analytical skills for addressing complex situations.
2. To assist you in understanding how force field analysis can aid understanding change.

### *Total Time*

30 to 60 minutes

### *Procedure*

1. Choose a situation that you have high personal stakes in (for example: how to get better grade in course X; how to get a promotion; how to obtain a position).

2. Using the Force Field Analysis Form below, apply the technique to your situation.
   a. Describe the situation as it now exists.
   b. Describe the situation as you would like it.
   c. Identify those "driving forces"—the factors that are presently helping to move things in the desired direction.
   d. Identify those "restraining forces"—the factors that are presently holding things back from moving in the desired direction.
3. Try to be as specific as possible in terms of the above in relation to your situation. You should attempt to be exhaustive in your listing of these forces. List them all!
4. Now go back and classify the strength of each force as weak, medium, or strong. Do this for both the driving and restraining forces.
5. At this point you should rank the forces regarding their ability to influence or control the situation.
6. In groups of three to four persons share your analyses. Discuss the usefulness and drawbacks to using this method for personal situations and its application to organizations.
7. Be prepared to share the results of your group's discussion with the rest of the class.

*Force Field Analysis Form*

| *Current Situation* | *Situation as You Would Like it To Be* |
|---|---|
| ____________________ | ____________________ |
| ____________________ | ____________________ |
| ____________________ | ____________________ |

| *Driving Forces* | *Restraining Forces* |
|---|---|
| ____________________ | ____________________ |
| ____________________ | ____________________ |
| ____________________ | ____________________ |
| ____________________ | ____________________ |
| ____________________ | ____________________ |
| ____________________ | ____________________ |
| ____________________ | ____________________ |
| ____________________ | ____________________ |
| ____________________ | ____________________ |

# CASE

## WARNER MANUFACTURING COMPANY

For the past year Pat Lee had been acquainted with Ron Carbone, Director of Human Resources for the Warner Manufacturing Company. Ron once attended a seminar on the management of planned change and organization development for which Pat served as the instructor. Since then he called several times seeking Pat's advice on some new training and development programs being developed for the company. Most recently, Ron asked Pat to conduct a six-day management training workshop for the top management team and key middle managers of the company, a total of 14 persons.

The workshop was held a week ago. From all reports, it was well received by the participants. During the six sessions, Pat covered such topics as motivation, job design, group dynamics, perception, decision making, communication, conflict, leadership, and management by objectives. The last topic seemed to really turn the group on. Several persons spontaneously brought up their beliefs that the company suffered from a lack of clear-cut objectives. After some discussion, but without reaching any consensus on the issues, the group moved on to another workshop topic.

During the final session, Pat asked the participants to consider what follow-up activities, if any, were in order. They asked to meet once again in two weeks to review the workshop further with Pat and develop more specific ideas about future actions.

Yesterday Ron called and asked Pat to a meeting over lunch. At that time he expressed his concern that many of the persons attending the workshop felt the company's overall management practices could be changed for the better. However, he also indicated that an informal poll of the group showed that most of the dissatisfaction was felt by the middle managers. They felt, in turn, that nothing really constructive could happen until top management agreed with them that something must be done. "Finally," Ron said, "the problem is best summed up this way. The President (Marc Wilson) thinks the only problem facing the company is the inability of the Operations Vice President (Everett Morgan) to meet production schedules. Everett thinks the problem is Mark's lack of leadership. And, the Director of Finance (Alice Yates) doesn't seem to think there's any problem at all."

The day-long evaluation session with the entire top and middle management group is scheduled one week from now. Ron is looking toward you for suggestions on how to initiate a long-term planned change and organization development program for the company.

### *Questions*

1. How do Lewin's three phases of planned change apply to this case? What are the implications for Pat Lee as a potential change agent?
2. To what extent is resistance to change an important issue for Pat to consider? What resistance might be expected for any comprehensive change effort and what might be done in advance to minimize this resistance?
3. How should Pat approach this situation in order to accomplish true organization development? Be specific and complete in addressing the full range of OD issues relevant to this situation.

**This study outline of major topics is meant to organize your reading now; it is repeated in the Summary to structure your review.**

## STUDY OUTLINE

### The Dynamics of Stress

What Is Stress? Stress and Performance Stress and Health

### Stress in the Workplace

Work-Related Stressors Nonwork Factors and Stress Personal Factors and Stress

### Effective Stress Management

Strategies for Coping with Stress Personal Wellness and Stress Management

### Career Planning and Development

A Career Planning Framework Initial Entry to a Career
Adult Life Cycles and Career Stages Career Plateaus
Family Responsibilities and Careers

# CHAPTER 18

# STRESS MANAGEMENT AND CAREER PLANNING



## PHOTO ESSAYS

# VISIONS 18

**The average annual company cost per employee for illness attributed to smoking, hypertension and poor diet is $430 according to the National Center for Health Promotion. A little more than half these costs are attributable to employees over the age of 54.**

**"Wellness programs" are increasingly in the visions of progressive employers. Johnson & Johnson, for one, subscribes to the concept. For the past 11 years the firm has been trying to convince its employees on healthful living—and saving some money for itself. Of course, like all business endeavors, one has to invest money to make money. J & J's investments in personal wellness include a program called "Live for Life." It tries to get employees to exercise, watch their diets, lose weight, quit smoking, and do whatever else may be needed to live healthier. Facilities like the gym at company headquarters, "healthy heart" foods offered in the cafeteria, and top-management commitment reinforce the program's goals.**

Yes, we live and work at a time when "pressures" abound in the workplace . . . and in the world-at-large. People are being asked to adjust to competitive pressures, organizational restructuring, new technologies, and the ever-present push for improved productivity. In broader society we face the uncertainties of geo-politics, environmental worries, social change . . . and more. Indeed, as we look ahead to your "career" and the inevitable stress it will entail, one has to wonder if these old and famous words—penned by Charles Dickens to describe his world of 1775—might not still ring true today.[1]

> It was the best of times, it was the worst of times, it was the age of wisdom, it was the age of foolishness, it was the epoch of belief, it was the epoch of incredulity, it was the season of Light, it was the season of Darkness, it was the spring of hope, it was the winter of despair, we had everything before us, we had nothing before us.

## THE DYNAMICS OF STRESS

Change of any sort in organizations is often accompanied by increased stress for the people involved. It is time now to develop a further understanding of "stress" as something with which all managers must successfully cope. Read and think about the following experiences of three people—Mary, Bob, and Ray. Although working in different managerial jobs and organization settings, each shares the problem of accommodating high levels of job-related stress.[2]

1. *Mary.* Mary, a recent Wharton MBA holder, spent a sleepless night contemplating her first presentation before the executive committee of her new employer. She had spent much of the last six months preparing the report for her presentation and felt that it was the first real test of her managerial potential. Mary's presentation lasted 5 minutes and was followed by about 10 minutes of questions from committee members. Mary was thanked for making a fine presentation and dismissed from the meeting by the firm's president. She quickly went to the nearest lounge and in a release of tension shook uncontrollably.
2. *Bob.* Bob's wife, Jane, is becoming increasingly worried about her husband. Several months ago Bob was passed over for a promotion to plant supervisor that he felt he deserved after 15 years of loyal service to the company. Bob used to come home from work tired but cheery and would spend an hour or so playing with their two boys. Lately, however, Bob walks into the house, grabs a can of beer, and plops down in front of the television. Except for dinner, he spends his evenings watching television and drinking beer. He has little to do or say to either Jane or the kids. Jane is at her wit's end. She has begged Bob to go to the doctor, but he says, "Nothing is wrong with me. It's your imagination."
3. *Ray.* Ray, a successful advertising account executive, was finishing his typical "two-martini" lunch with a potential client, but Ray's mind was not on business as usual. He was thinking about the pain in his stomach and the diagnosis the doctor had given him yesterday. Ray's doctor had told him he had a spastic colon induced by his life-style. Ray, recently divorced, knows that his gin consumption, smoking habit, and 12-hour workdays are not good for him, but his job is now the most important thing in his life, and the advertising business just happens to be highly stressful. He decides not to worry about his health and to concentrate on selling his luncheon partner one fantastic contract.

## What Is Stress?

***Stress*** is a state of tension experienced by individuals facing extraordinary demands, constraints, or opportunities.[3] In Mary's case, stress resulted from an opportunity to make an important presentation. Bob's stress emerged from a constraint—inability to gain promotion. Ray is torn between the demands of a doctor's advice and the potential opportunity of a successful business luncheon. Stress, again, is the result.

Stress

Any look toward your managerial future would be incomplete without confronting stress as something you are sure to encounter along the way.[4] For a start, think about this statement by a psychologist who works with top-level managers having severe drinking problems: "All executives deal with stress. They wouldn't be executives if they didn't. Some handle it well, others handle it poorly." If you understand stress and how it operates in the work setting, you should be more likely to handle it well. This goes both for the personal stress you may experience and for the stress experienced by persons you supervise.

## Stress and Performance

This preliminary discussion and even your personal views may give the impression that stress always acts as a negative influence on our lives. There are actually two faces to stress, as shown in Figure 18.1—one constructive and one destructive.[5] ***Constructive stress,*** or ***eustress,*** acts in a positive way for the individual and/or the organization. The figure shows that low to moderate levels of stress act in a constructive or energizing way. Moderate stress can increase effort, stimulate creativity, and encourage diligence in one's work. You may know such stress as the tension that causes you to study hard before exams, pay attention in class, and complete assignments on time. The same positive results of stress can be found in the workplace.

**Constructive stress**

**Destructive stress**

***Destructive stress,*** or ***distress,*** on the other hand, is dysfunctional for the individual and/or the organization. Whereas low to moderate levels of stress can enhance performance, excessively high stress can overload and break down a person's physical and mental systems. Performance can suffer as people experience illness brought on by very intense stress and/or react to high stress through absenteeism, turnover, errors, accidents, dissatisfaction, and reduced performance.

Managers seek the positive performance edge offered by constructive stress. But, they must also be concerned about destructive stress and its

*FIGURE 18.1 The relationship between stress intensity and individual performance: constructive versus destructive stress.*

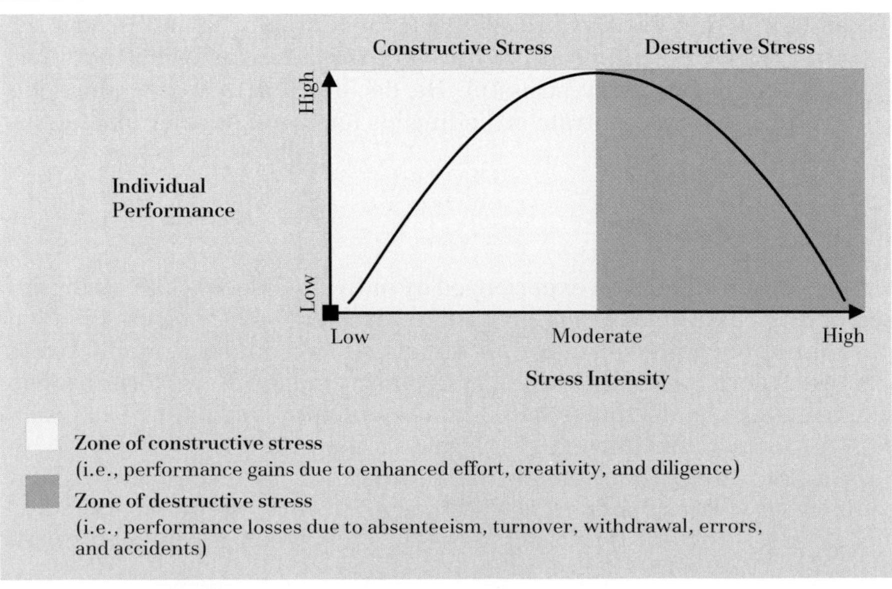

potential to impact people and their work performance adversely. One of the most difficult tasks here is to find the optimum stress points for yourself and for the persons you supervise.

## Stress and Health

There is no doubt that stress impacts the health of an individual. Stress is a potential source of both anxiety and frustration, each of which, in turn, is capable of breaking down the body's physiological and/or psychological well-being over time.[6] Excessive stress can lead to several health problems in the form of heart attack, stroke, hypertension, migraine headache, ulcers, drug–alcohol–tobacco abuse, overeating, depression, and muscle aches, among others.

Managers should be alert to signs of excessive stress in themselves and persons with whom they work. The symptoms are multiple and varied. When it comes to habits and feelings, here are some things to watch for.[7]

- Change in eating habits.
- Unhealthy feeling—aches and pains.
- Restlessness, inability to concentrate.
- Tense, uptight, fidgety, or nervous feelings.
- Increase in drinking or smoking.
- Feelings of being disoriented or overwhelmed.
- Sleeping problems.
- Depression or irritability.
- Upset stomach.
- Dizziness, weakness, lightheadedness.

When it comes to observable work behaviors the key things to look for are *changes* from normal patterns. These may involve:

| *Changes from . . .* | *to . . .* |
|---|---|
| regular attendance | absenteeism |
| punctuality | tardiness |
| diligent work | careless work |
| positive attitude | negative attitude |
| openness to change | resistance to change |
| being cooperative | being hostile |

The prior emphasis on being alert to behaviors indicating excessive stress for you *and* others is deliberate and important. It is increasingly the case, and rightly so, that modern managers are asked to display greater concern and accept more responsibility for job-related influences on the health of their colleagues and subordinates. This position is defended on the basis of the following arguments.[8]

1. *Humanitarianism.* To the extent that managerial awareness and action can enhance employee health, managers have a humanitarian responsibility to do so.

2. *Productivity.* Healthy employees are absent less, make fewer errors, and must be replaced less frequently than less healthy ones.
3. *Creativity.* Persons in poor health are less creative and less prone to take reasonable risks than are their healthy counterparts.
4. *Return on investment.* Organizations invest substantial amounts of time and money in the development of employees; poor health decreases the return on this human resource investment.

# STRESS IN THE WORKPLACE

**Stressors**

***Stressors*** are the things that cause stress. For example, one study of stress experienced by executives around the world reports that:[9]

- Managers in mature industrialized countries worry about—
  Losing their jobs
  Family and social pressures
  Lack of autonomy
  Poorly trained subordinates
- Managers in developing and recently industrialized countries worry about—
  Work overloads
  Interpersonal relations
  Competition for promotion
  Lack of autonomy

It is important for a manager to understand and be able to recognize these and other potential stressors. They are root causes of job-related stress which, in turn, influences work attitudes and behavior. Figure 18.2 shows three categories of stressors that can act in this fashion—work, nonwork, and personal factors.

## Work-Related Stressors

Of the stressors depicted in the figure, work factors have the most obvious potential to create stress. For example:

> *U.S. Postal Service* Union officials complain about the stress caused by automated equipment and restrictive rules at the U.S. Postal Service. "There's a rule for everything," says one shop steward, "if a supervisor wants to get you, he'll get you." In response to new equipment requiring mail sorters to work faster, another union official says, "The stress is tremendous."

Work-related stress arises from many sources. It can result from excessively high or low task demands, role conflicts or ambiguities, poor interpersonal relations, or career progress that is too slow or too fast. A look back to the examples of Mary, Bob, and Ray shows how these factors can act alone or in combination to cause job stress. Common work-related stressors are:

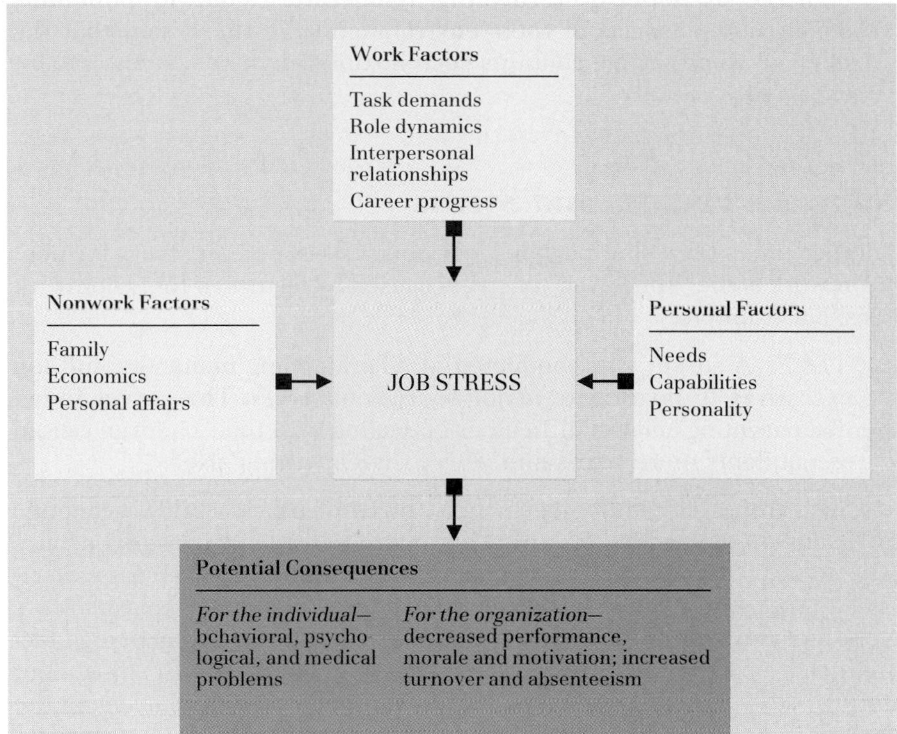


*FIGURE 18.2 Three categories of stressors and their potential consequences for individuals and organizations.*

1. *Unrealistic task demands.* People asked to do too much for available time and/or for their abilities may suffer role overload. This can result in anxiety and high stress. Role underload, having too little to do or having insufficient challenge, may also be stressful.
2. *Role ambiguities.* Not knowing what you are expected to do and/or not knowing the standards by which your work will be evaluated can be stressful. People with low tolerances for ambiguity are most prone to such reactions.
3. *Role conflicts.* Feeling that you are unable to satisfy the multiple and potentially conflicting performance expectations of other people can create stress. Facing a situation where two or more people are expecting you to do different things at the same time is one example.
4. *Interpersonal conflicts.* Conflicts caused by emotional antagonisms and personality conflicts can be very upsetting to the people involved. Negative side effects may even occur for other people who have to work with them.
5. *Career developments.* Career progress that comes too fast can bring the pressures of having to work extra hard to perform up to expectations. Lack of progress can also be stressful for those who want to advance in their career but are blocked for some reason.
6. *Physical aspects of the work environment.* People are sometimes

bothered by noise, overcrowding, temperature, and air pollutants among other aspects of their environments. To the extent that the physical work setting contains such noxious elements, stress can be expected.

## Nonwork Factors and Stress

Another important—but perhaps less obvious—source of stress for people at work is the "spill-over" of stress caused by factors in their nonwork lives. For example:

> *AT&T* A survey was conducted at AT&T among managers and top executives to investigate major sources of stress. The survey found that parenting and the difficulties of dealing with their children caused respondents more stress and worry than anything else.

Such things as family events (e.g., birth of a new child), economic difficulties (e.g., sudden loss of a big investment), and personal affairs (e.g., facing a divorce) can add substantially to the overall stress experienced by a person. Since it is often difficult to completely separate one's work and nonwork lives, stress of this sort can affect the way people feel and behave on the job as well as away from it. The Social Readjustment Rating Scale presented in Table 18.1 is a popular way of measuring the amount of stress experienced by people from their basic life circumstances.

You might like to complete the scale for yourself or a person familiar to you. If so, circle the mean value for each event that has affected you or the other person. Total them to obtain a final stress score. Research suggests that life event stress totals of 150 or less indicate generally good health, scores of 150 to 300 indicate a 35–50 percent probability of stress-related illness, and scores of 300+ indicate an 80 percent probability. An understanding of the potential impact of such "life" events on the individual's overall well-being can help to moderate and even control their harmful consequences.

## Personal Factors and Stress

The final set of stressors includes personal factors such as individual needs, capabilities, and personality. These are properties of the individual that influence how one perceives and responds to stress emanating from work and nonwork sources. Stress can reach a destructive state more quickly, for example, when experienced by highly emotional people and those having low self-esteem. People who perceive a good fit between job requirements and personal skills have a higher tolerance for stress than those who feel less competent because of a person–job mismatch.[10]

Basic aspects of personality also cause some people to experience more stress than others in similar situations. The achievement orientation, impatience, and perfectionism of individuals with Type A personalities, for example, often creates stress in work circumstances that other persons find relatively stress-free. Type A's in this sense, bring stress on

*TABLE 18.1*
THE SOCIAL READJUSTMENT RATING SCALE

| Life Event | Mean Value |
|---|---|
| 1. Death of spouse | 100 |
| 2. Divorce | 73 |
| 3. Marital separation from mate | 65 |
| 4. Detention in jail or other institution | 63 |
| 5. Death of a close family member | 63 |
| 6. Major personal injury or illness | 53 |
| 7. Marriage | 50 |
| 8. Being fired at work | 47 |
| 9. Marital reconciliation with mate | 45 |
| 10. Retirement from work | 45 |
| 11. Major change in the health or behavior of a family member | 44 |
| 12. Pregnancy | 40 |
| 13. Sexual difficulties | 39 |
| 14. Gaining a new family member | 39 |
| 15. Major business readjustment | 39 |
| 16. Major change in financial state | 38 |
| 17. Death of a close friend | 37 |
| 18. Changing to a different line of work | 36 |
| 19. Major change in the number of arguments with spouse | 35 |
| 20. Taking out a mortgage or loan for a major purchase | 31 |
| 21. Foreclosure on a mortgage or loan | 30 |
| 22. Major change in responsibilities at work | 29 |
| 23. Son or daughter leaving home | 29 |
| 24. In-law troubles | 29 |
| 25. Outstanding personal achievement | 28 |
| 26. Wife beginning or ceasing work outside the home | 26 |
| 27. Beginning or ceasing formal schooling | 26 |
| 28. Major change in living conditions | 25 |
| 29. Revision of personal habits | 24 |
| 30. Troubles with the boss | 23 |
| 31. Major change in working hours or conditions | 20 |
| 32. Change in residence | 20 |
| 33. Changing to a new school | 20 |
| 34. Major change in usual type and/or amount of recreation | 19 |
| 35. Major change in church activities | 19 |
| 36. Major change in social activities | 18 |
| 37. Taking out a mortgage or loan for a lesser purchase | 17 |
| 38. Major change in sleeping habits | 16 |
| 39. Major change in number of family get-togethers | 15 |
| 40. Major change in eating habits | 15 |
| 41. Vacation | 13 |
| 42. Christmas | 12 |
| 43. Minor violations of the law | 11 |

*Source:* T. H. Holmes, and R. H. Rahe, "The Social Readjustment Rating Scale," *Journal of Psychosomatic Research,* Vol. 11 (1967), pp. 213–18. Reprinted with permission of Pergamon Press and Thomas H. Holmes, M.D. Copyright 1967, Pergamon Press, Ltd.

Type A orientation

themselves. You should recall from Chapter 3 that the ***Type A orientation*** is one for which stressful behavior patterns like the following are commonplace.[11]

- Always moves, walks, and eats rapidly.
- Feels impatient with the pace of things, hurries others, dislikes waiting.
- Does several things at once.
- Feels guilty when relaxing.
- Tries to schedule more and more in less and less time.
- Uses nervous gestures such as clenched fist, banging hand on table.
- Does not have time to enjoy life.

There are some interesting issues regarding the relative advantages and disadvantages of Type A orientations in the workplace. On the one hand, the Type A characteristics may be beneficial for early and mid-career managerial success. That is, the characteristics and perhaps the performance edge gained by stress associated with Type A individuals may help people to advance through the ranks to the senior executive levels in organizations. When it comes to success at the top, however, the implications may change and Type A characteristics could lose their beneficial impact. Top managers with these orientations may lack the patience required to exhibit balanced reasoning, satisfy multiple or even conflicting performance demands, and deal with inevitable time delays. Their success, in turn may depend on being able to modify or at least control their Type A behavior to meet the different requirements of a chief executive role. The ability to manage stress is certainly critical to this flexibility. It is also essential to the maintenance of personal health and perormance accomplishment at all steps in a managerial career.

# EFFECTIVE STRESS MANAGEMENT

You can see that the role of stress in the work setting is complex. We know that constructive stress may facilitate individual task performance, but it is also true that destructive stress can reduce performance and even impair a person's health. Thus a good manager will find a healthy fit among the individual, the work environment, and the amount of job stress it involves. A *healthy fit* is one that stimulates productivity without damaging health. It is achieved through effective stress management, which includes the ability to (1) prevent stress, (2) cope with stress, and (3) maintain personal wellness.

## Strategies for Coping with Stress

Stress prevention

***Stress prevention*** is the best first-line strategy for dealing with stress. This involves taking action for yourself or for other persons to avoid having stress reach destructive levels in the first place. In particular, stressors emerging from personal and nonwork factors must be recognized so that action can be taken to prevent them from adversely affecting the work experience. Persons with Type A orientations, for example, may exercise self-discipline; managers of Type A employees may try to model a lower-key, more relaxed approach to work. At another level, family difficulties may be relieved by a change of work schedule, or the anxiety they cause may be reduced by knowing that one's supervisor understands. Work stressors such as role ambiguities, conflicts, and overloads can be prevented by good supervisor–subordinate communication, a willingness of subordinates to "speak up" when role dynamics are creating difficulties, and sensitivity by supervisors to behaviors or other symptoms indicating that subordinates are experiencing problems.

**Stress management**

Once stress has reached the point of causing difficulty, special techniques of ***stress management*** can be used to maintain the desired "healthy fit." This process begins with recognition of some of the symptoms of excessive stress noted earlier. These include such things as uncharacteristic irritability, nervousness or hostility, complaints of spontaneous illnesses, as well as any deviation from customary behavior patterns. When these symptoms are recognized, it is time to take action to maintain the desired healthy fit. Five useful guidelines for managing excessive stress follow:[12]

1. *Control the situation.* Avoid unrealistic deadlines. Do your best, but know your limits. You cannot be everything to everyone. Learn to identify and limit your exposure to stressors that trigger a strong stress response within you.
2. *Use time management techniques.* Avoid the trap of trying to do too many things at once—and subsequently failing to accomplish much, if anything at all. Set realistic goals, and plan and manage your day in line with the time available. Effective supervisory behavior can be successful in preventing or, at least, minimizing these sources of stress. A good manager is supportive in setting a climate of trust and respect, but also provides goal clarification and adequate task directions to alleviate uncertainty and confusion in performance expectations.
3. *Free yourself.* Plan your day on a flexible basis. Do not try to do two or more things at the same time. Counter unproductive haste by forcing yourself to slow down. Think before reacting to negative situations or people. Live on a day-to-day basis instead of a minute-by-minute basis.
4. *Open up to others.* Freely discuss your problems, fears, frustrations, and sources of uptightness with those who care about you. When in doubt, smile! A sincere smile can often defuse emotion and build a bridge of goodwill.
5. *Exercise and relax.* Engage in regular noncompetitive physical activity such as jogging, swimming, riding a bike, or playing tennis, handball, or racquetball. (See your doctor when in doubt about your physical condition.) When feeling uptight, practice the "relaxation response." Relax for a few minutes by following these simple steps: (a) sit comfortably with eyes closed in a quiet location, (b) slowly repeat a peaceful word or phrase over and over to yourself in your mind, (c) take complete but comfortable breaths, inhaling through the nose and exhaling through the mouth, and (d) avoid distracting thoughts by keeping a passive mental attitude.

SKILLS PERSPECTIVE

## JOHNSON & JOHNSON

Courtesy of Johnson & Johnson.

**Johnson & Johnson is quite clear on its priorities. The company's annual report states: "We believe our first responsibility is to the doctors, nurses, and patients, to mothers and all others who use our products." But don't forget for a minute that the company's employees count too. The report goes on to state: "We are responsible to our employees, the men and women who work with us throughout the world." Nowhere is this commitment to employees more apparent than in the J&J "Live for Life" program. Here, employees are helped to develop personal wellness skills. The goal is to help the employees maintain and improve their physical health and general well-being. It covers such areas as improved nutrition, weight control, alcohol and drug abuse, stress management, and quitting smoking.**

## Personal Wellness and Stress Management

Personal wellness

***Personal wellness*** is a term used to describe the pursuit of one's physical and mental potential through a personal health promotion program.[13] The concept recognizes individual responsibility to enhance and maintain wellness through a disciplined approach to physical and mental health. This requires attention to such things as smoking, weight, diet, alcohol use, and physical fitness. The essence of personal wellness is a life-style that reflects a true and comprehensive commitment to health.

Because stress has the potential to impact health, personal wellness makes a great deal of sense as a preventive stress management strategy. The manager who aggressively maintains his or her health should be better prepared to deal with the inevitable stressors that accompany the managerial role. This manager should also be able to take constructive advantage of stress that would otherwise take on destructive characteristics.

More generally, however, the managerial role also includes responsibility for the personal wellness of subordinates. A supervisor can impact personal wellness within the work unit through positive example, encouragement, and sensitivity and by practicing the basic concepts and techniques of human resource management presented throughout this book. When the manager is successful in creating a "healthy" work climate and environment, everyone should benefit from the increased capacity of people in this environment to handle successfully the change and stress that inevitably accompanies their lives at work. The chapter-opening *Visions* shows how Johnson & Johnson employees benefit from such progressive practices.

# CAREER PLANNING AND DEVELOPMENT

If you think back to the three examples used to introduce our discussion of stress, you'll recognize that they deal with people in an early and "stressful" stage of their careers. Now, we can bring your initial study of OB to conclusion in the context of some basic career planning and development issues.[14] And, as you certainly realize, people's careers are an important component of their total life experience. The following quotes from a study about people and their careers should cause you to think about your career, as well as the careers of those persons who will some day become your subordinates.[15]

> "Years ago I made a bad mistake, and now I'm paying for it; I'm trapped in this job."
>
> "I should have found out how this firm was run before taking their offer. I had other good prospects at the time."
>
> "They led me down the garden path, and I was damn fool enough to be taken in."

## A Career Planning Framework

Figure 18.3 summarizes a basic framework for formal career planning. It has a lot in common with the process of decision making covered in Chapter 13. The five steps in the career planning framework begin with per-

*FIGURE 18.3 Five steps in formal career planning.*

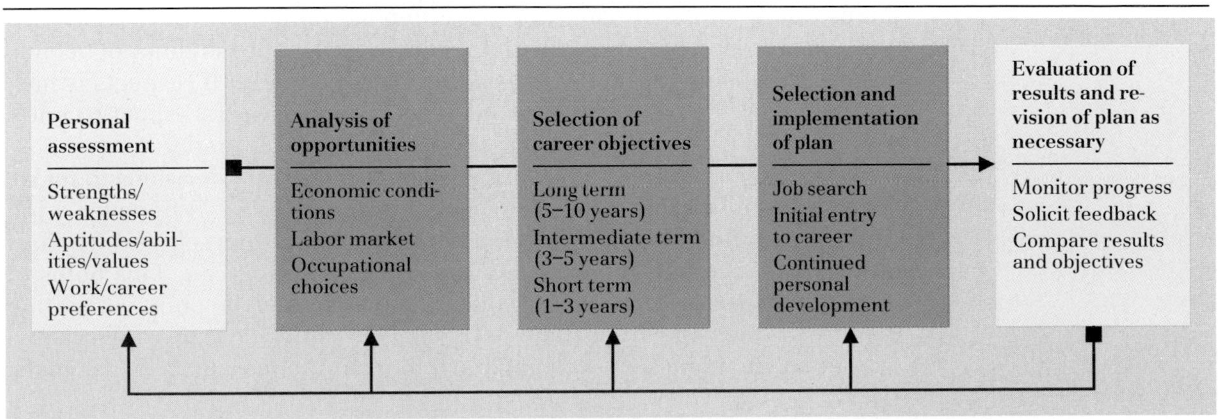

sonal assessment and then progress through analysis of opportunities, selection of career objectives, and implementation of strategies, until the point of evaluation of results is reached. The process is recycled as necessary to allow constructive revision of the career plan over time. Success in each of these steps entails a good deal of self-awareness and frank assessment. The message is clear—a successful career begins with sufficient insight to make good decisions about matching personal needs and capabilities with job opportunities over time.

The manager's responsibility in respect to career planning is twofold. It includes both (1) planning and managing a personal career *and* (2) assisting in the career planning and development of subordinates. To take charge of his or her personal career, a manager should:[16]

- Establish a personal career plan; be willing to modify this plan as opportunities develop.
- Take and maintain a personal skills inventory; try to match job responsibilities and skills.
- Set specific personal development objectives.
- Maintain a career-oriented dialogue with higher-level managers.
- Take advantage of all training and development opportunities.
- Evaluate and constructively modify personal development efforts over time.

To assist in the career planning and development of subordinates, a manager should:

- Establish a human resource plan for the work unit.
- Take and maintain a human resource inventory for the work unit.
- Establish human resource development objectives for the work unit.
- Maintain a career-oriented dialogue with subordinates.
- Encourage and support subordinates' participation in training and development activities.
- Evaluate and constructively modify all efforts to meet the development needs of subordinates over time.

## Initial Entry to a Career

Many issues will command your attention as you grapple over time with personal career planning and with the managerial responsibilities of helping others with their careers. Of special importance in both respects is how initial entry to a career is handled. This issue arises in respect to one's first job and it arises again whenever a job change is made.

Choosing a job and a work organization are difficult decisions to make. They inevitably exert a lot of influence over our lives. Whenever a job change is contemplated, the best advice is to know yourself and learn as much about the new job and new organization as you can. This helps to ensure the best person–job–organization match. It is the point where one begins to form the important psychological contract that we first discussed in Chapter 2. By working hard to examine personal needs, goals,

*TABLE 18.2*
**SAMPLE ITEMS FOR A "NEW JOB" BALANCE SHEET**

| *What are the tangible gains and losses for* myself? | *Gain?* | *Loss?* |
|---|---|---|
| • salary and fringe benefits | ______ | ______ |
| • work hours and schedules | ______ | ______ |
| • use of skills and competencies | ______ | ______ |
| • development of skills and competencies | ______ | ______ |
| • status inside the organization | ______ | ______ |
| • status outside the organization | ______ | ______ |
| • out-of-town travel requirements | ______ | ______ |
| • chances for further advancement | ______ | ______ |
| *What are the tangible gains and losses for* others *who are important to me?* | | |
| • income available for family needs | ______ | ______ |
| • time available for family/friends | ______ | ______ |
| • spill-over effects of my work stress | ______ | ______ |
| • pride in my accomplishments | ______ | ______ |
| • personal development opportunities | ______ | ______ |
| • leisure time activities | ______ | ______ |
| • overall life styles | ______ | ______ |

and capabilities, gather relevant information, share viewpoints, and otherwise make the recruitment process as *realistic* as possible, you can help get a new job started on the best possible note. Table 18.2 is a sample checklist of things to be considered when contemplating a possible job change. Giving such careful and thoughtful attention to the critical joining-up decision can help in the successful implementation of a career plan.

## Adult Life Cycles and Career Stages

As people mature, they pass through an adult life cycle involving many different problems and prospects. It is helpful for you to recognize this cycle and to prepare to face its implications over the course of a career. It is also useful to recognize the effects of this cycle on other people with whom you work. Understanding their special problems and pressures can help you to work with them better in a managerial capacity.

Daniel Levinson's ideas about personality development as a series of life stages were introduced in Chapter 4. You should recall his basic point that life unfolds with a number of ***adult transitions*** having quite different implications for work and personal aspects of one's life.[17] Three transitions relevant to our present interest in careers are: early adulthood, midlife, and later adulthood. Each transition involves special challenges as described in the following list.

**Adult transitions**

| | |
|---|---|
| Young adulthood | This is a period of completing one's education, entering an occupation, and becoming married. Parenthood follows, with new family and job responsibilities. It is a time of vitality, self-determination, and perhaps one or more job changes. |

| | |
|---|---|
| Adulthood and mid-life transition | In the late thirties and early forties, the career is all important. Family complications stress this orientation, and personal crisis can occur. Some frustration in the career may occur and bring with them added questions of confidence, goals, and identity. For the first time health and age become relevant concerns. |
| The move to later adulthood and senescence | Settling in begins here, with a knowledge of the "system" and a mellowing of goals. Concerns turn toward making a real impact at work, being a mentor to others, and balancing goals and reality. This is a time of consolidating personal affairs and accepting career limitations. The next step is retirement and, perhaps, a new career. |

**Career stages**

As suggested in Figure 18.4, adult transitions and their special attributes can be linked to various ***career stages*** through which people move over the course of their lives. These are often referred to as the establishment, advancement, maintenance, and withdrawal career stages.[18]

Initial entry to a career is part of the *establishment stage.* Here, the individual develops skills and abilities through initial work experiences. For example,

> *Citicorp* A formal mentorship program allows senior "volunteers" to coach junior "mentorees" at Citicorp on how to refrain from major corporate mistakes and to learn how to do things such as ask the boss for more responsibility. One vice-president says: "If we can help newcomers avoid pitfalls, we all benefit."

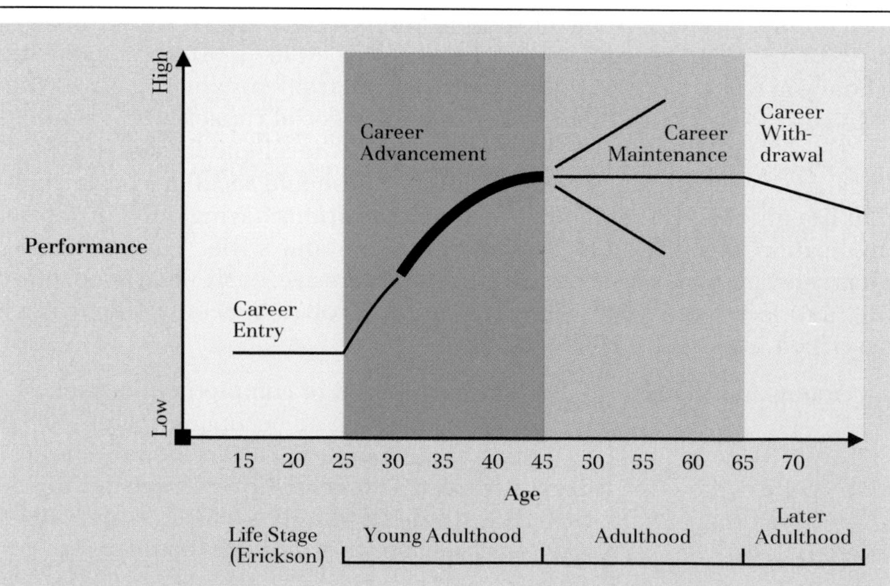


*FIGURE 18.4 Career stages, individual performance, and the adult life cycle. (Source:* From *Careers in Organizations* by Douglas T. Hall. Copyright © 1976 by Scott, Foresman and Company. Reprinted by permission.)

INTERNATIONAL PERSPECTIVE

## RUBBERMAID

Courtesy of Rubbermaid Incorporated.

**For five consecutive years Rubbermaid has been selected as one of *Fortune* magazine's 10 "most admired" American corporations. Begun some 70 years ago in Wooster, Ohio as a small business, the firm now has close to $1350 million in sales and has achieved growth with a commitment to its employees and customers. An ambitious expansion plan has resulted in international growth now exceeding that of the domestic market. Rubbermaid is currently reorganizing to explore even further international opportunities. With the exception of the Far East operations, the management of Rubbermaid businesses, sales, and marketing around the world are now the responsibility of the U.S. operating companies. Thus, even U.S.-based employees at Rubbermaid can plan to have their careers take on a global character.**

In the *advancement stage* the individual seeks growth and increased responsibility through the continued development and utilization of these skills. Advancement may be pursued through internal career paths within a given organization, or through external career paths that involve taking advantage of opportunities that require a change of employers. In either case, advancement is an exciting stage that must be balanced by the skills of the individual. For example,

> ***Chubb Corporation*** Experience has shown at Chubb that "fast trackers" don't always have time to develop the competencies they really need to perform well at higher levels. A senior vice-president suggests that up-and-coming managers need to be slowed down at times to allow their self-confidence to develop and avoid dropping to the bottom when they do get placed in the "deep end" of the pool.

During the *maintenance stage* individuals can experience continued growth of performance and accomplishments or, by contrast, they can encounter career stability. Sometimes a further change in employers is necessary to sustain advancement, but often the individual loses career flexibility. This may be due to personal considerations such as limited interest in learning new skills; organizational considerations such as a basic lack of opportunity; and/or family considerations which simply make it difficult to either change jobs or take on added work responsibilities. Finally, the *withdrawal stage* signifies the approach and acceptance of retirement. Depending upon the individual, this can be a very positive or highly upsetting stage of one's career. More and more employers now provide training and support to help people make a positive transfer from the routines of regular employment to the flexibility of retirement.

## Career Plateaus

**Career plateau**

A ***career plateau*** is a position from which someone is unlikely to move to advance to a higher level of responsibility. This phenomenon is typically encountered during the maintenance stage of one's career. Career plateaus occur for one or more of the following three reasons:[19]

1. *Personal choice:* In this case, the individual basically decides he or she no longer wants to advance in responsibility. This can occur due to satisfaction with one's job, lack of confidence in being able to do higher-level work, and/or simply being hesitant to undergo change.
2. *Limited ability:* Some people plateau in their careers because they have reached the limits of their abilities. Whether because they are incapable of further learning or simply unwilling to put in the needed effort, they do not qualify for further advancement.
3. *Lack of opportunity:* As organizations become "slimmer" and fewer jobs are made available at higher levels, more persons are limited in advancement *not* by personal choice, but by the availability of openings. Thus, lack of opportunity for promotion or transfer is an increasingly common source of career plateauing.

Managers must be able to deal with career plateaus, both personally and as their subordinates are affected. It can be difficult to maintain job satisfaction and a high-performance edge when caught in a career plateau that is due to something other than individual choice. In such cases, it can be very easy to drift into low or at best marginal performance levels. Thus, this is a case where a manager's ability to understand and respect individual needs can help in developing appropriate responses.

In many organizations, in fact, progressive human resource managers are taking note of declining promotion opportunities. They are trying to help employees find satisfaction in "lateral" job changes that increase variety and challenge. They are trying to temper ambition through orientation and training programs that emphasize more realistic career expectations. For example:

> *P. G. & E.* In San Francisco, the director of career management for P. G. & E., one of America's largest utilities, says: "We're trying to get out in front of this before we have tons and tons of people who are dissatisfied." To do so, she adds: "We're trying to tell people what plateauing is, what it is not, and that it's O.K. We're saying . . . it's okay to move laterally."

ETHICAL PERSPECTIVE

**WELLS FARGO**

Courtesy of Wells Fargo & Company.

**Wells Fargo Bank was one of the first companies to make a "personal growth leave" available to its employees. Under this program, someone who has been an employee for 10 or more years can take up to three months paid time off to pursue a personal interest. An employee-based committee screens applications and selects employees with interests that could not normally be carried out unless the leave were made available. Not only is this good for the employee, the community can benefit from services performed by people on these volunteer leaves. The volunteers, says an administrator of the Wells Fargo program, "have these business and technical skills that they use everyday in a corporate environment. When they go into a nonprofit environment, they are able to make tremendous contributions."**

## Family Responsibilities and Careers

**Dual-career couple**

The ***dual-career couple***—that is, a family or household in which both adult partners are members of the work force—is an increasingly important force in contemporary society.[20] And as individuals experience the stresses caused by difficulties of satisfying both career interests and family responsibilities, organizations and their managers are being asked to respond.[21] Although both partners in a dual-career couple can face problems, the woman often experiences special difficulties. For example,

> *Ford* Vernal Brown works in a St. Louis Ford auto plant in what used to be an all-male job—making front car bumpers. Even though she started working to help pay the bills, she complains that her husband "expected the same as if I was a housewife" and recommended she quit if she "couldn't take care of the needs at home and have his food ready." She quit her marriage instead.

Vernal Brown's problem isn't uncommon among two-career families. One study found that 75 percent of the wives typically came home and worked another shift—doing the housework. The author of the study charges: "Men are trying to have it both ways. They're trying to have their wives' salaries and still have the traditional roles at home."[22]

An important and related dual-career issue is the *trailing spouse problem,* or need to find employment for the partner of a person being newly recruited or asked to transfer to a new location. Without extra assistance for the trailing spouse, many people are unwilling to commit to new opportunities that may result in a career sacrifice for their partners.

In the United States, traditional households where the husband works and the woman stays at home are down to five percent of all married couples. In addition, more than half of new mothers have jobs.[23] Thus, another family-related career issue of growing significance relates to the care of the children of working parents. This problem is especially acute for single parents, many of whom are women. More and more employers are taking action to try and minimize the cost and inconvenience of child care for their employees. As a further sign of the times, many are also recognizing the pressures and demands some employees face for taking care of elderly parents. Again, the need is the same—some form of opportunity for the elderly parent or child to be well taken care of while the responsible adult is at work. For example,

> ***IBM*** Twenty-five million dollars was recently allocated to improve child care and elder care programs in communities in which IBM's employees live. CEO John Akers justified the program by saying IBM wanted to give people the flexibility to "advance their careers while minimizing the impact on their personal lives."
>
> ***Stride Rite*** Having made headlines by opening an onsite childcare center in 1971, Stride Rite is now back in the news by combining eldercare and childcare. The shoe manufacturer's Stride Rite Intergenerational Day Care Center helps its employees meet family responsibilities. It also brings together the seniors and juniors in a positive and mutually beneficial environment.

# MANAGING A MANAGERIAL CAREER

Throughout this book we have focused on managers as persons to whom others report in organizations. While performing *four management functions*—planning, organizing, leading, and controlling—an *effective manager* facilitates high levels of both task performance and human resource maintenance in the workplace. Success in a managerial career is predicated on your ability to accomplish such results.

## Mastering the Manager's Challenge

The field of "OB" is and should be considered a knowledge base that can be used by managers to achieve high performance. For one last time, let

**Organizational behavior**

us define ***organizational behavior*** as the study of individuals and groups

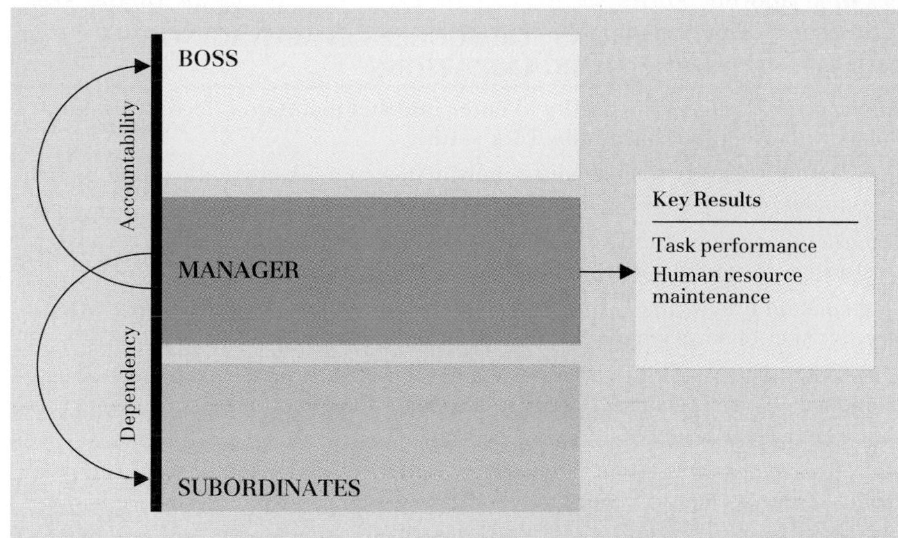


*FIGURE 18.5 The manager's challenge: an action framework for understanding and applying the insights of organizational behavior.*

in organizations. And let us recognize that good human resource utilization by managers is a major key to managerial success and organizational productivity.

As we now bring your initial study of OB to closure, think once again about the situation depicted in Figure 18.5—what we have referred to as ***the manager's challenge.*** In order to master this challenge—that is, to fulfill an accountability to higher levels for the accomplishment of work one is dependent upon subordinates to produce—a manager must be able to work well with other people inside and outside of the work unit.

**The manager's challenge**

At this point we are confident that you have been exposed to the major OB concepts, theories, and applications that can help you master this challenge. Yet, it is important to point out that this is but the beginning. You must continue to learn from your experience and continue to improve your requisite managerial skills and competencies over the entire course of your career. Table 18.3 offers a final "checklist," illustrating the types of concerns that should always be on your mind as you pursue success in managing human behavior in organizations.

## Final Career Advice

Without any doubt, many opportunities await you in a managerial career. As you look ahead to this exciting future, however, remember the insights from this initial study of OB *and* remember these *six career commandments.*[24]

1. *Perform.* The basic foundation of success in any job is good performance. A record of high performance will please your superiors, earn respect from your peers and subordinates, and call attention to you as a person of high potential.
2. *Stay visible.* Do not hesitate to make sure that others recognize your hard work and the performance results achieved. This is a public

*TABLE 18.3*
**SELECTED FOUNDATIONS FOR SUCCESS IN MANAGING HUMAN BEHAVIOR IN ORGANIZATIONS**

*Interpersonal relations*—Ability to enter into and maintain effective relationships with other persons in the work setting.

*Leadership*—Ability to deal with subordinates, to motivate and train, to help, and to deal with authority and dependency problems.

*Conflict-resolution*—Ability to mediate between conflicting parties, resolve disturbances, and negotiate differences with others.

*Information processing*—Ability to collect information, organize information for decision-making purposes, and disseminate information.

*Decision making*—Ability to know when a decision is needed, diagnose situation, plan an approach, search for solutions, evaluate potential consequences, and select an alternative.

*Resource allocation*—Ability to distribute physical, financial, human, and personal resources among competing demands.

*Entrepreneurism*—Ability to recognize problems, implement solutions, and take advantage of opportunities for constructive change.

*Introspection*—Ability to understand one's job and staff and to learn through self-study and awareness.

*Source:* Developed from Henry Mintzberg, *The Nature of Managerial Work* (New York: Harper & Row, 1973), pp. 188–193; and Robert L. Katz, "Skills of an Effective Administrator," *Harvard Business Review*, Vol. 42 (September–December 1974), pp. 90–102.

relations task to be done in a professional manner and without becoming known as a braggart. When the performance record is there, project memos, progress reports, and even requests for more frequent evaluation and feedback sessions with superiors can enhance the visibility of your success.

3. *Be willing to move.* Do not get locked into a job that you have already mastered and/or that is narrow and limited in the visibility or opportunity it offers. Take advantage of promotion opportunities within the organization. Be willing to change organizations for similar reasons. Do not be afraid to nominate yourself when appropriate for new and challenging changes of assignment.
4. *Find a mentor.* It is always beneficial to have a senior executive who acts as a mentor from whom you can learn and who sponsors your career interests. Ideally, this will be a person who can create mobility and opportunity for you as his or her own career progresses over time.
5. *Manage your career.* Stay active in thinking seriously and systematically about your career. Prepare and maintain a career plan even if it is only a broad frame of reference for directing your efforts and evaluating opportunities as they arise. Do not let success at any one stage distract you from taking advantage of new appointments with further growth potential. Take charge of your career, and stay in charge.
6. *Continue your education.* Life-long learning is both a responsibility and a prerequisite of long-term managerial success. In today's dynamic

and challenging environment, the manager who fails to continue to learn and develop appropriate skills will not succeed. Maintain the "yearn to learn"—that is, make a commitment to take advantage of all opportunities for continuing education and personal managerial development that come your way.

## SUMMARY

■ **The Dynamics of Stress** emerge when people experience tensions caused by extraordinary demands, constraints, and/or opportunities in their work situations. Moderate levels of stress can be constructive and facilitate performance, but too much stress can be destructive and inhibit performance. Stress can create frustrations and adversely impact both a person's mental and physical health. A wide variety of stress symptoms can be observed, and good managers are constantly alert for these symptoms in their behavior and that of others.

■ **Stress in the Workplace** traces to a variety of work, nonwork, and personal factors. In the immediate work situation, such issues as task demands, interpersonal relationships, and career progress can be a source of stress for the individual. On the other hand, what happens to people in their nonwork lives can also create stress that "spills over" to affect their behavior at work. Nonwork stressors include family situations, economics, and personal affairs. Personality, needs, and values are additional individual factors that make a difference in how stressful different people find the same situations.

■ **Effective Stress Management** begins with an awareness of potential sources of stress. Stress can be prevented by making appropriate adjustments in work and nonwork factors, as well as by being aware of how individual personality may affect responses in various situations. When under stress, a variety of coping mechanisms—including both exercise and relaxation techniques—can be used to keep things under control. In the long run, everyone is better off with a commitment to "personal wellness" and ongoing efforts to maintain a healthy body and mind capable of withstanding the inevitable stress in all aspects of our lives.

■ **Career Planning and Development** is complicated in today's often stressful work environments. Managers must be able to successfully manage their personal careers and assist in the career planning and development of their subordinates. Formal career planning involves a systematic process of self-assessment, analysis of opportunities, establishment of career objectives, implementation of strategies, and evaluation of outcomes. Among the special career planning issues in our dynamic environment are concerns for individual entry to a job and/or organization, adult transitions over the life of a career, and the increasing burdens of family responsibilities for members of the work force.

■ **Managing a Managerial Career requires a personal commitment to life-long learning and personal development, as well as willingness to utilize the available understandings of organizational behavior to best perform in managerial assignments. OB, as the study of individuals and groups in organizations, can be a great asset for managers who conscientiously strive to facilitate high performance outcomes for their organizations and high-quality work environments for their members. Among the guidelines for personal career success to concentrate on are: achieving high performance in all job assignments, finding a mentor to help and guide you, and always continuing your education by attending seminars, workshops, and formal courses in the many important areas of organizational behavior and management.**

## KEY TERMS

Adult Transitions
Career
Career Plateau
Career Path
Career Stages
Constructive Stress
Destructive Stress
Dual-Career Couple
Organizational Behavior
Personal Wellness
Stress
Stress Management
Stress Prevention
Stressors
The Manager's Challenge
Type A Personality

## REVIEW QUESTIONS

1. What symptoms should a manager be on guard for as indicators of excessively high levels of stress being experienced by a subordinate? Can such stress ever be "constructive?" Why or why not?
2. Identify and give examples of (a) work-related and (b) nonwork stressors that can affect individual behavior. Explain why the nonwork stressors may be as important for a manager to understand as the work-related stressors.
3. What is a "Type A" orientation? In what ways can a Type A orientation affect individual behavior in the workplace? What can a manager do to best deal with a subordinate with Type A characteristics?
4. Whose responsibility is it to "manage" your career—yours or, for example, your supervisor or a career specialist in the human resource department? Please explain.
5. What is the relationship between adult life cycles and the typical career stages experienced by someone during a lifetime of work? Why is this relationship important for a manager to understand?
6. What is a "career plateau?" If this were to happen to you, is it necessarily bad . . . (a) for you, and (b) for your employer? Explain and defend your answer.
7. In what ways are family responsibilities important concerns as management struggles to attract and maintain a high-quality work force?

What should progressive organizations be doing in response to these concerns?

8. Of the six steps listed in this chapter as "final career advice," which *three* do you consider most important, and why? Is there anything missing from this list? If so, what additional career guidelines would you add and why?

## AN OB LIBRARY

Joseph F. Coates, Jennifer Jarratt, and John B. Mahaffie, *Future Work: Seven Critical Forces Reshaping Work and the Work Force in North America* (San Francisco: Jossey-Bass, 1990).

Arlie Hochschild (with Ann Machung), *The Second Shift: Working Parents and the Revolution at Home* (New York: Viking, 1989).

Uma Sekaran, *Dual Career Families* (San Francisco: Jossey-Bass, 1985).

Edgar H. Schein, *Career Dynamics: Matching Individual and Organizational Needs* (Reading, MA: Addison-Wesley, 1978).

Gail Sheehy, *Passages: Predictable Crises of Adult Life* (New York: Dutton, 1976).

**EXERCISE**

## ASSESSING PERSONAL STRESS

### *Objectives*

1. To help you identify the personal emotional impact of various events.
2. To assess and analyze chronic (or ongoing) sources of stress in your life.
3. To differentiate between events within and outside your control.

### *Total Time*

30 to 60 minutes

### *Procedure*

1. Consider events that you have experienced during the past month or so which you feel to be emotionally unsettling and indicate your emotional impact score, using 1 = low impact to 10 = major impact. Place your assessed score in column A (events beyond my power to change) or column B (events within my power to change). You may divide the score for one event between column A and column B if that is appropriate. Only score events that occurred—skip items that did not occur or are not applicable to you.

## *Emotional Impact Assessment*[25]

| *Events beyond my power to change* A | *Events within my power to change* B | |
|---|---|---|
| _______ | _______ | a. My course load or study requirements feel excessive. |
| _______ | _______ | b. I find some instructors boring, or I feel inadequately challenged. |
| _______ | _______ | c. I haven't enough quiet for study, or have too many distractions. |
| _______ | _______ | d. My outside commitments conflict with school work. |
| _______ | _______ | e. My class schedule creates problems. |
| _______ | _______ | f. I feel too much peer or parent pressure. |
| _______ | _______ | g. I question what value I get from going to school. |
| _______ | _______ | h. My procrastination or cramming creates excessive pressure. |
| _______ | _______ | i. I have continuing problems with one or more teachers, teaching assistants, or the administration. |
| _______ | _______ | j. I am uncertain about my career objectives, or future plans. |
| _______ | _______ | k. I don't find school socially rewarding, or my standards and preferences conflict with other activities. |
| _______ | _______ | l. I miss social support from a relationship, family, or roommate. |
| _______ | _______ | m. I don't have adequate privacy. |
| _______ | _______ | n. My budget is too tight. |
| _______ | _______ | o. Transportation creates problems for me (e.g., parking, commuting, mobility). |
| _______ | _______ | p. I am concerned with security on or off campus. |
| _______ | _______ | q. Getting the kind of food I prefer is a problem. |
| _______ | _______ | r. I don't have any easy access to my preferred forms of recreation. |
| _______ | _______ | s. School facilities, such as the library, heath care, or the computer center, are inadequate. |
| _______ | _______ | t. I feel self-conscious about a personal problem (such as weight, pimples, social ease). |
| _______ | _______ | u. other ______________________ |
| _______ | _______ | v. other ______________________ |
| _______ | _______ | Totals for Emotional Impact Score |

2. Total your scores for each column and place them in the columns above. Your scores highlight areas of your life that may be contributing as ongoing sources of stress.
3. Form groups of three to four persons and share any personal insights you have made as a result of having completed the assessment.
4. Discuss what implications this information has on the future of such stressors in your life. What can you do to reduce the stress? Who can you go to for help?
5. Be prepared to share your conclusions with the rest of the class.

CASE

## JOURNEY TO THE TOP

When he became chief executive of a newly independent International Playtex, Inc., Joel E. Smilow also became his own boss. This marked the end of a journey originally charted in a career path he had set upon graduation from the Harvard Business School. The chart identified the positions and salaries he wanted to achieve by certain ages. The last entry showed him as chief executive of an independent company. Twenty-eight years later, on August 5, he finally "checked" it off as a mission accomplished!

Joel's drive for success was evident in his college years at Yale. He spent summers working as a sales clerk in a department store to help pay his way. After graduating, he married, did a two-year stint in the U.S. Navy, and then went to Harvard. There he earned an MBA "with distinction" and accepted an offer to join Procter & Gamble in Cincinnati. He says he learned "strategy" at Harvard and "execution" at P&G.

One thing the brash young marketer kept in mind was his career plan. Whenever he felt he was slipping behind, he let his superiors know. Colleagues from his early days at P&G describe him as "incredibly smart" and very ambitious. He rose quickly and became brand manager for a number of winning products, and a couple of losers. But he felt limited by the institutional pace and the nature of the job. With a tendency to be "short" with people less capable than he, his personality wasn't a great fit with the brand manager's job of little authority but lots of responsibility. After being passed over for a promotion he quit to join a small consulting firm. From there he was asked to join Playtex as a vice president—an offer he rejected as beneath his abilities. The company hired him as president four years later. Overnight, Joel went from supervising 18 people at the consulting firm to managing 12,000 at Playtex.

Joel thrived under the freedom to run his own show. He acquired rights to promising new products, and diversified the product lines. He also built a reputation as a no-nonsense demanding boss about whom one observer says: "He wants people to work seven days a week, or at least a solid six." Some of his top managers quit along the way. One comments:

"It's not his intellect I fault . . . it's the human dimension—or lack of it." Joel responds by stressing his honesty in dealing with others. "I've never in my life misled an executive as to his future. Maybe when you tell them the truth, you're considered tough."

When Playtex was bought by Beatrice, Joel quit in just four months. After spending the next 18 months looking at, but always refusing, a variety of top jobs, he joined a group seeking to take Beatrice private. Ultimately, he and a group of executives bought Playtex for $1.25 billion.

### *Questions*

1. Analyze the potential benefits and risks of the career planning approach taken by Joel Smilow. Do you think this approach would be good for you to follow or not? Please explain.
2. Do you think Joel is an "effective" manager as was originally discussed in Chapters 1 and 2? Does he seem to have a good feel for OB as a knowledge base that managers can use to fully utilize the potential of an organization's human resources? Why or why not?
3. Would you want to work for Joel Smilow? Why or why not?

SUPPLEMENTARY MODULE A

# HISTORICAL FOUNDATIONS OF ORGANIZATIONAL BEHAVIOR

One of the delightful aspects of contemporary society is a reawakening interest in our past. Many people are investigating their ancestries and trying to learn as much as possible about their "roots." To understand better what OB is today, it is also useful to identify its roots from the past. The significance of this historical inquiry is well expressed by Paul Lawrence in an introduction to his recent overview of the discipline.[1]

> Organizational behavior is a young and rapidly growing area of systematic inquiry. It is therefore not surprising that professionals in the field are often preoccupied with its present and future, and seldom reflect on its past. Yet an understanding of that past and an awareness of how knowledge and expertise have gradually accumulated can enrich the field's identity and add meaning to current efforts.

## SCIENTIFIC MANAGEMENT

In 1911, Frederick W. Taylor published a short book called *The Principles of Scientific Management.*[2] This classic book is one you will still find to be provocative (and quick) reading today. The book begins with the following statement.

> The principle object of management should be to secure maximum prosperity for the employer, coupled with the maximum prosperity for the employee.

**Scientific management**

Taylor goes on to offer managers four principles of ***scientific management*** as guidelines for meeting this managerial responsibility.

1. Develop a "science" for every job. This science should include such things as rules of motion, standardized work implements, and proper working conditions.
2. Carefully select workers who have the right abilities for the job.
3. Carefully train these workers to do the job; then offer them proper incentives to cooperate with the job science.
4. Support the workers by taking responsibility for work planning and by smoothing the way as they go about their jobs.

## Taylor's Pig Iron Study

Taylor reported a pig iron study conducted at the Bethlehem Steel Company to illustrate these principles. The year was 1899, and the company had a problem. There were 80,000 tons of iron to be loaded on freight cars for shipment. This iron was in the form of 92-pound "pigs" that workers hand carried up inclined planes to freight cars. A worker typically loaded 12½ tons of pig iron to earn a daily wage of $1.15. There were 75 persons in the loading gang available to do the work.

Taylor determined that it was possible for one worker to load 47½ tons per day if the principles of scientific management were followed. To prove his point, a study was conducted.

The principal actor was a man Taylor called "Schmidt." He was described as a person

> observed to trot back home for a mile or so after his work in the evening about as fresh as when he came trotting down in the morning . . . upon wages of $1.15 a day he had succeeded in buying a small plot of ground, and he was engaged in putting up the walls of a little house for himself in the morning before starting work and at night after leaving . . . he also had a reputation of . . . placing a high value on a dollar."

Taylor reports that under scientific management, Schmidt earned $1.85 per day while loading 47 tons and never failed to work at the new pace during a three-year period. One worker after another was picked out of the gang and similarly trained.

## Implications

Over the years Taylor's work has been expanded, modified, and criticized, even to the point of questioning whether or not Taylor's reported data were really fiction or fact.[3] Edwin A. Locke, however, has offered a very thorough analysis of Taylor's basic arguments and the criticisms commonly lodged against them.[4]

Locke begins by noting that an essential element of Taylor's philosophy of management was the "scientific approach." By this, Taylor meant that something must be based on proven fact rather than on tradition, rule of thumb, guesswork, precedent, personal opinion, or hearsay. Locke considers this philosophical foundation for Taylor's thinking directly consistent with the trend of modern management theory that emphasizes similar scientific rigor. He goes on to critique several of the major techniques recommended by Taylor. For your convenience, each of the techniques is briefly reviewed here in terms of Locke's evaluation.

1. *Time and motion study.* Taylor advocated breaking work down into its constituent elements or motions to eliminate inefficiencies and wasted effort. What we now know as "time study" is used routinely in industrial settings. Even though worker resistance to time study continues to exist, the methodology is generally accepted as standard management practice today.
2. *Standardized tools and procedures.* Taylor advocated standardization in the design and use of tools. This principle is also accepted today and includes the science of human engineering.
3. *The task.* Taylor felt that workers should be assigned specific amounts of work based on time study. This assigned quota he called a "task"; it is the equivalent of what we now refer to as a work "goal." Locke notes that virtually every contemporary theory or approach to motivation, including organizational behavior modification and management by objectives, includes goal setting as an important component.
4. *The money bonus.* Taylor felt that money was a significant incentive to workers. Although money continues to be attacked by some social scientists for the primacy of its role in the latter sense, Locke acknowledges that the large variety of monetary incentive schemes have been developed since Taylor's time.
5. *Individualized work.* Taylor advocated individual as opposed to group tasks. He believed that group work and group rewards would undermine individual productivity. Locke quotes Taylor as writing, "Personal ambition always has been and will remain a more powerful incentive to exertion than a desire for the general welfare." This view of Taylor's is in some opposition to the current trend of management theory that emphasizes group tasks. Locke notes that this trend exists even though the evidence is not conclusive one way or the other that the group or individual level of task and reward is superior. He leaves this issue for future research to resolve and suspects that outcomes will depend on such situational factors as the nature of the task.
6. *Management responsibility for training.* Taylor was concerned that workers should not learn their skills haphazardly from other cohorts in the work setting. Rather, he felt that they should learn the proper way in which to perform the task from management experts. Management theory and practicing managers of today accept training as a substantial supervisory responsibility.
7. *Scientific selection.* Taylor advocated the selection of only "first-class" persons as defined in terms of high aptitude. Contemporary manage-

ment theory emphasizes rigorous and scientific employee selection techniques as a means of ensuring that persons of correct ability are hired to fill jobs. Locke feels that Taylor's work was a substantial impetus to what are now known as the fields of industrial psychology and personnel management.

Managerially speaking, Locke is redirecting the attention of theorists and practitioners back to Taylor's work as one initial impetus to what we now know and respect as contemporary management theory. He cautions against premature dismissal of Taylor's ideas and/or preoccupation with criticisms that he feels are largely unjustified or misdirected. Locke concludes his paper with a statement that seems an appropriate summary to this brief look at Taylor's place among the historical roots of OB.[5]

> Considering that it has been over 65 years since Taylor's death and that a knowledge explosion has taken place during these years, Taylor's track record is remarkable. The point is not, as is often claimed, that he was "right in the context of his time" but is now outdated, but that *most of his insights are still valid today*. The present authors agree with those who consider Taylor a genius.

# THE HAWTHORNE STUDIES

Not long after Taylor's book was published, in 1924 to be exact, the Western Electric Company began a study of individual productivity in its Cicero (a suburb of Chicago) plant known as the Hawthorne Works.[6] The company was interested in the effects of physical working conditions on output. This concern reflects a direct interest in Taylor's first principle of scientific management.

## Illumination Studies

Between 1924 and 1927, a series of studies was conducted to determine how various levels of illumination affected the output of workers. After varying the intensity of light for different work groups, measuring changes in output, and then analyzing the results, the researchers were disappointed. They failed to find any relationship between level of illumination and production. In some groups, output moved up and down at random; in others it increased steadily; and in one, it increased even as illumination was reduced to the level of moonlight! Perplexed by these results, the researchers concluded that unforeseen "psychological factors" had somehow interfered with the experiments.

## Relay Assembly Test Room Studies

In 1927, a new group of researchers from Harvard University led by Elton Mayo began another series of studies. Their objective was to establish the effects of worker fatigue on productivity. Care was taken to design a test of this relationship that would be free of the "psychological effects" thought to have confounded the illumination studies.

Six operators who assembled relays were isolated for intensive study in a special test room. The operators were subjected to various rest pauses, lengths of workday, and lengths of workweek, while their production was regularly measured.

Once again, the Hawthorne researchers were unable to find any direct relation between changes made in physical working conditions and worker outputs. Overall, the productivity of the relay assemblers increased over time and regardless of the specific changes made in the work setting by researchers.

Mayo and his colleagues concluded that the new "social setting" created in the test room accounted for the increased productivity. Two factors were singled out as having special importance in this regard. First, there was a positive group development in the test room. The operators shared both good social relations with one another and a common desire to do a good job. Second, supervision was more participative than that otherwise experienced by the operators. Operators in the test room were made to feel important, given a lot of information, and frequently consulted for their opinion on what was taking place. This was not the case in their normal work situation.

## Further Studies

Until worsening economic conditions forced their termination in 1932, Mayo and his group of researchers continued their Hawthorne studies. After the relay assembly test room experiments, however, their interest shifted from physical working conditions to such aspects of the "social setting" of work as employee attitudes, interpersonal relations, and group relations.

Two further studies were conducted. In one, 21,126 Western Electric employees were interviewed to learn what they liked and disliked about their work. The researchers felt that this knowledge could help management to make changes that would improve productivity. The interviews also yielded "complex" and "baffling" results that led researchers to conclude that the same thing (e.g., work conditions, wages) can be sources of satisfaction for some people and dissatisfaction for others. In other words, people are different! Interestingly enough, a variation of this thesis was also advanced by Frederick Taylor.

The second of the final Hawthorne studies was conducted in the Bank Wiring Room. This time the researchers specifically set out to examine the behavior of the work group. One of their "surprises" was to find individuals willing to sacrifice pay that could be earned by increasing output, that is, to restrict their output, to avoid the displeasure of the group. This finding complemented the earlier relay assembly study and suggested that the work group can have strong negative, as well as positive, influences on individual productivity.

## Implications

The Hawthorne studies shifted the attention of managers and researchers away from physical work planning and the application of monetary incentives toward the social setting of workers and their individual attitudes. They gave birth to a body of literature now referred to as the "Human Relations Movement," a movement characterized by its concern for the creation of good human relationships between managers and their subordinates.[7] Many of the more humanistically oriented writers whose theories are well studied in the management fields received stimulation from this time in OB's history. They include Abraham Maslow, Chris Argyris, Douglas McGregor, Rensis Likert, and Frederick Herzberg, among others.

**Hawthorne effect**

The Hawthorne studies have been criticized for their scientific methods.[8] A common concern is summarized in the ***Hawthorne effect,*** a term now used to describe situations in which persons who are singled out for special attention end up performing as anticipated only because of the expectancies created by the special situation. This term is a constant reminder that Mayo's test room operators may have improved their performance, not because of any subtle group dynamics or supervisory practices, but simply because they felt increased output was what the researchers and the company wanted.

Like Taylor's work, it is what the Hawthorne studies led to in terms of future research rather than what they actually achieved as research, that counts most. They represent an important historical turning point that allowed the field of management a new way of thinking about people at work. They extended the thinking of researchers beyond concerns for physical and economic considerations alone, and clearly established the managerial significance of the psychological and sociological aspects of people as *human* beings. As a result, the Hawthorne studies have had a major impact on what we study as part of OB. This legacy includes an interest in

- ▶ The group as an important force in the work setting.
- ▶ The sources of individual job satisfaction and dissatisfaction.
- ▶ Different "styles" of supervision, with a special emphasis on employee participation.
- ▶ The need for good interpersonal skills of managers.
- ▶ The importance of social relationships as a determinant of individual behavior at work.

# THE MANAGEMENT FUNCTIONS

Perhaps you have already had a course or done some reading in an area called "management" or "administrative theory." If so, you are familiar with the classical axiom: good managers will do five things well: planning, organizing, staffing, directing or leading, and controlling. These "functions" of management derive from another important root of OB. This root includes a body of early literature that does not pretend to rigorous scientific foundations but is derived from the systematic reflections of practicing managers on their work experiences. This "grass-roots" approach to management is often criticized for being based on "armchair" rather than scientific evidence. We have discussed this problem more generally in a section on scientific thinking in Chapter 1. Nonetheless, the ideas of

*TABLE A.1*
**HENRI FAYOL'S RULES FOR MANAGERS AND THEIR RELATIONSHIP TO THE FUNCTIONS OF MANAGEMENT**

| *Fayol's Rules* | *Management Function* |
|---|---|
| *Foresight.* To complete a plan of action; to scheme for the future. | Planning |
| *Organization.* To provide the resources needed to implement the plan; to mobilize effort in support of the plan. | Organizing |
| *Command.* To get the best out of people working toward the plan; to lead; to properly select and evaluate workers. | Leading |
| *Coordination.* To ensure that the efforts of subunits fit together properly; that information is shared and any problems solved. | Controlling |
| *Control.* To verify progress; make sure things happen according to plan; take any necessary corrective action. | Controlling |

*Source:* Developed from M. B. Brodie, *Fayol on Administration* (London: Lyon, Grant, and Green, 1967), pp. 12–14.

these early writers on management and administration have also had a significant impact on OB.

The classics among these works were written by Henri Fayol, Mary Parker Follett, James Mooney, and Lyndall Urwick.[9] We will limit our attention to Fayol, a successful executive in French industry.[10] In 1916, he published *Administration Industrielle et Generale* outlining his reflections on the proper management of organizations and the people within them.[11] His book offered the five "rules" listed in Table A.1. These rules, as shown in the table, have led to the formulation of what are now known as functions of management—planning, organizing, staffing, directing or leading, and controlling.

# OB AND THE BEHAVORIAL SCIENCES

The three components of science deal with physical, biological, and behavioral phenomena, respectively. The behavioral sciences are particularly concerned with the study of human behavior. They would like to predict how people will behave in various settings. OB is an applied behavioral science that has a special interest in human behavior in organizations.

Figure A.1 shows that OB is closely related to three behavioral sciences: psychology and its concern for the individual, sociology and its concern for people in interaction with one another, and anthropology and its concern for people in their respective cultural settings. The Hawthorne studies, for example, can be viewed from the perspective of each of these disciplines. A psychologist would look at the relay assembly test room and be most interested in the feelings and behavior of the individual operators; a sociologist would be studying the group of six operators as they interacted and worked with one another; an anthropologist would be look-

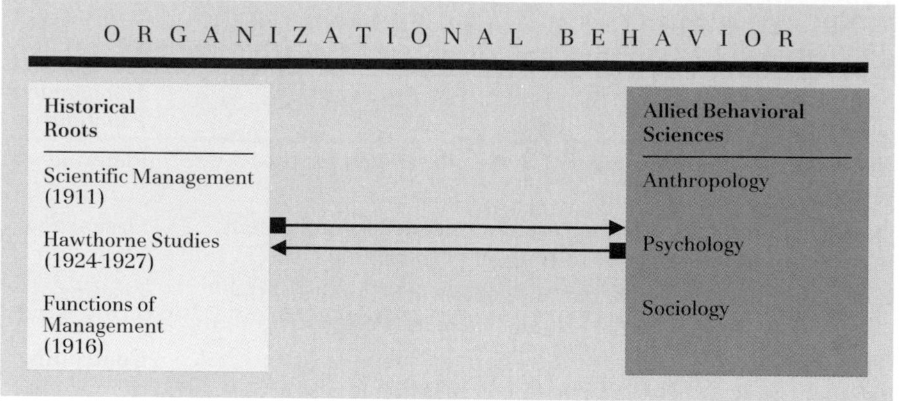


*FIGURE A.1 The Heritage of OB as an Academic Discipline.*

ing at the social system created by the test room environment and the behaviors of the operators and observers within it.

There is a natural bridge between OB and these behavioral sciences, as well as other allied social sciences like economics and political science. As a result, OB is an interdisciplinary body of knowledge that draws insights from many scientific sources and vantage points. OB is unique, however, in applying and integrating these diverse insights to better understand human behavior in organizations.

## KEY TERMS

Hawthorne Effect
Scientific Management

## REVIEW QUESTIONS

1. It is possible to criticize the work of Frederick W. Taylor and the Hawthorne studies. What impact do you feel these criticisms of OB's "roots" have had on the field of OB as it exists today?
2. How would you differentiate among the responses Frederick Taylor, Elton Mayo, and Henri Fayol would give to the question: "What should a manager do to ensure a high level of work unit performance?"

EXERCISE

# THE GREAT OB HISTORY DEBATE

*Purpose:*

To increase your understanding of the historical "roots" of OB and to provide an opportunity to examine critically these roots for their managerial implications.

*Time:*

50 minutes.

*Procedure:*

1. Form work groups as assigned by your instructor.
2. Each group will be assigned or allowed to choose one of the following responses to the question: What should a manager do to ensure a high level of work unit performance?

   *Response A:* "Frederick Taylor offers the best insight into this question. His advice would be to . . ." (advice to be filled in by the group).
   *Response B:* "The Hawthorne studies are the true source of insight into this question. They suggest that a manager should . . ." (advice to be filled in by the group).
   *Response C:* Henri Fayol is the best source of insight into this question. His advice would be to . . ." (advice to be filled in by the group).

3. Each group will have 20 minutes to prepare a 5-minute response for oral presentation to the rest of the class.
4. The instructor will reconvene the class and a debate will take place according to the following format:
   a. Each group makes an opening statement.
   b. Each group is allowed to ask questions and/or offer rebuttals to the other groups.
   c. Each group makes a final 1-minute closing statement.
5. After time is called, the instructor will lead an open discussion on the three responses. This discussion will end with confrontation of the question: "Where does OB go from here?"

## SUPPLEMENTARY MODULE B

# SCIENTIFIC FOUNDATIONS OF ORGANIZATIONAL BEHAVIOR

The field of OB takes care to ensure that the knowledge base from which you will derive managerial applications is built by acceptable scientific methods.

## THE SCIENTIFIC METHOD

Scientific method

The ***scientific method*** involves four steps:[1]

1. Observations are made regarding real-world events and occurrences.

   *Example* Company officials become concerned that productivity in a plant is not as high as possible.

2. An explanation for the events and occurrences is formulated.

   *Example* These officials agree that productivity probably suffers because the physical working conditions are not as conducive to high production as they could be. One aspect that seems especially important is the level of illumination in the work place.

3. Statements are made that use the explanation to predict future events and occurrences.

   *Example* Company officials and a team of researchers predict that changes made in levels of illumination will directly affect work output. As illumination increases, output should increase; as illumination decreases, output should decrease.

4. The predictions are verified by an examination conducted under systematic and controlled conditions.

   *Example* Two groups of workers are selected for study and their existing levels of output measured. In one group, light intensity is increased; in the other, it is held constant. Output is measured again for both groups. The prediction that illumination will directly affect output is tested against the data.

The previous example shows how the scientific method was followed as company officials moved from an initial observation that a problem may exist, to the point of eventually testing a plausible explanation for the problem and/or a means of resolving it. In actual practice, OB research is sometimes criticized because of the inability of researchers to completely meet the requirements set forth in step 4. It is very difficult to conduct a true experiment when the subjects are people working in organizations. Consequently, when you evaluate an OB research study and the managerial insights it claims to offer, you must have a basic understanding of the strengths and weaknesses of various research designs.

# RESEARCH DESIGNS

A ***research design*** is the step-by-step approach used to study systematically a phenomenon in question.[2] The three basic research designs are experimental, quasi-experimental, and nonexperimental. Through good choice and use of a given research design, a researcher seeks to gather and interpret data in a scientifically defensible fashion. Two very important criteria in the selection of a research design are:[3]

1. *Internal validity* the strength of the design in establishing a definitive test of the research question (e.g., does X cause Y?).
2. *External validity* the strength of the design in its ability to generate findings generalizable to other people and situations (e.g., will X cause Y somewhere else?).

## Experimental Research

The best way to verify an explanation of the type "an increase in illumination will cause an increase in productivity" is to perform a true experiment. A ***true experiment*** exists when the subjects of a research investi-

True experiment

gation are randomly assigned to one or more treatment and control groups. The key to the prior statement is the word "random." Unless a subject has an equal chance of being assigned to the treatment group (for example, the one where light intensity is varied) and the control group (for example, the one where light intensity remains the same), a variety of explanations alternative to the one advanced by researchers could account for any changes observed. Randomization equalizes the chances and simplifies the process of drawing conclusions.

Consider the following diagrammatic example of a true experiment. In the diagram the "R" stands for random assignment of subjects, "O" for measures taken (e.g., production output), and "X" for the treatment being investigated (e.g., increased illumination).

| | | | | |
|---|---|---|---|---|
| R | O | X | O | treatment |
| R | O | | O | control |

Most true experimental research in OB is accomplished in the laboratory setting. Because it is hard to randomize subjects in the real-world work situation, "field" studies are most often not true experiments. This lack of true experimentation can lead to problems in drawing research conclusions and establishing "cause–effect" relationships.

In the illumination study discussed earlier there was no randomization in the assignment of subjects to treatment and control groups. Suppose in the study that output actually increased only in the treatment group as the researchers originally predicted. Would that have meant that increased light intensity caused an increase in productivity? Not necessarily. In addition to the possibility that the results were due to increased illumination, one or more of the following explanations could have accounted for the observed differences in productivity.

- The workers in the treatment group might have been better workers than those in the control group to begin with.
- Something may have occurred in the treatment group that facilitated higher output—for example, new workers added, change in machinery, salary increased, and so on.
- Something may have occurred in the control group that inhibited higher output—for example, loss of workers, change in machinery, salary decrease, and so on.

Whenever a true experiment is not done, alternative explanations such as those just given should always be carefully ruled out. Then, and only then, can observed support for the original explanation be accepted as a basis for decision making and action.

## Quasi-Experimental Research

It is possible to approximate true experimental conditions in field settings. In the illumination studies, for example, nonrandom treatment and control groups were formed, measures were taken before and after the treatment was administered, and the results were then analyzed systematically. This is a good research approach, but its strength relies very heavily on the ability of researchers to deal with alternative explanations.

A typical quasi-experimental design is diagrammed next. Although treatment and control groups exist, they are not created by randomization. This lack of random assignments makes them easier to do in work settings than true experiments. With good attention given to rival explanations, the quasi-experimental design can make a fine contribution to OB knowledge.

| | | | |
|---|---|---|---|
| O | X | O | treatment |
| O | | O | control |

## Nonexperimental Research

The least rigorous research designs are nonexperimental. In them, researchers simply observe events or occurrences of interest and then draw conclusions from the results. Still, nonexperimental designs are a source of OB knowledge. They exist in the form of case studies, questionnaire surveys, and reports on systematic interviews. When well accomplished and interpreted, nonexperimental research can be as insightful as research accomplished with the more rigorous designs. The burden of proof, however, is on the investigator to demonstrate that truly logical and defensible interpretations are being made from the research.

One of the most common of the nonexperimental designs is for data to be gathered from a number of persons. Then correlational statistics are used to establish the empirical relationships in the data. In such cases, researchers rely on the strength of statistical argument to overcome the built-in weaknesses of the research design. Much OB research is conducted using this method.

# THE VOCABULARY OF SCIENCE

The previous discussion sets up the necessary groundwork for you to understand the OB research we discuss throughout the book. To further help you to become comfortable with the scientific vocabulary of OB, the following terms are introduced with clarifications as to how we use them.[4]

### *Variable*

A measure used to describe a real-world phenomenon.

> *Example* Researchers counted the number of parts produced by workers in a week's time as a measure of their individual productivity.
>
> *Clarification* How well variables are measured is an important criterion of good research. Measures are often criticized and debated; good measures get used repeatedly by many researchers. You need to be able to judge how well researchers have measured their variables. It is far easier to count the number of parts produced and call that productivity than it is to measure how the worker feels about the job and call that job satisfaction.

## *Hypothesis*

A tentative explanation about the relationship between two or more variables.

*Example* One historical hypothesis of OB researchers was that an increase in the number of rest pauses allowed workers in a workday would increase productivity. Confirmation of this hypothesis would lead to the action implication: If you want to increase individual productivity in a work unit, give the subordinates more frequent rest pauses. This hypothesis has not been confirmed by scientific research.

*Clarification* An hypothesis is what becomes formulated during step 3 of the scientific method. Hypotheses are "predictive" statements. Once verified through empirical research, an hypothesis can be a source of direct action implications. Hypotheses are sometimes called "propositions."

## *Dependent Variable*

The event or occurrence expressed in an hypothesis that indicates what the researcher is interested in explaining.

*Example* In OB research, individual performance is often the dependent variable of interest; that is, researchers try to determine what factors cause increases in performance. One hypothesized relationship between a causal factor and this dependent variable is

increased rest periods ⟶ lead to ⟶ increased performance (*dependent variable*)

## *Independent Variable*

An event or occurrence that is presumed by hypothesis to affect one or more other events or occurrences as dependent variables.

*Example* In the previous example, increased rest periods was the independent variable.

## *Intervening Variable*

An event or occurrence that provides the linkage through which an independent variable is presumed to affect a dependent variable.

*Example* It is sometimes hypothesized that participative supervisory practices (independent variable) improve worker satisfaction (intervening variable) and therefore increase performance (dependent variable). This relationship would be depicted as

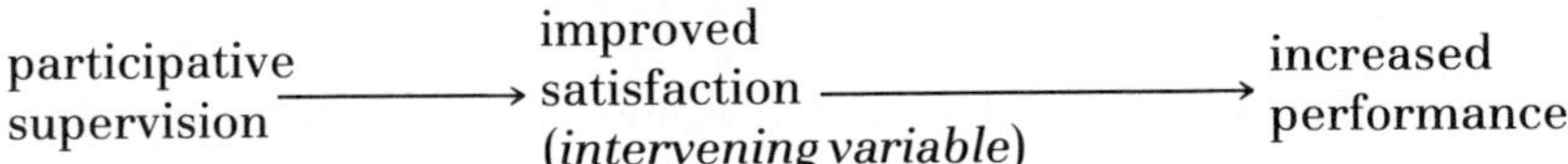


## *Moderator Variable*

An event or occurrence that specifies the condition under which an independent variable affects a dependent variable.

*Example* The previous example hypothesizes that participative supervision would lead to increased productivity. It may well be that this relationship will hold only when the employees feel their participation is real and legitimate (a moderator variable). This role of a moderator variable can be diagrammed as

participative supervision ⟶ increased performance
↑
participation viewed as real and legitimate (*moderator variable*)

### *Theory*

A set of systematically interrelated concepts, definitions, and hypotheses that are advanced to explain and predict phenomena.[5]

*Example* One current theory of leadership effectiveness argues that task-oriented leaders will have more effective work groups when the leader has very much or very little situation control, and that relationship-oriented leaders will have more effective work groups when the situation affords the leader an intermediate amount of control.[6]

*Clarification* Theories tend to be abstract and to involve multiple variables. They usually include a number of hypotheses, each of which would be based on clearly articulated concepts and definitions. Most, if not all, of the previously discussed kinds of variables would probably be involved. We should also note that many things called "theories" in OB do not strictly meet the definition above. Actually, they represent viewpoints, explanations, or perspectives that have logical merit and that are in the process of being scientifically verified. Theories are frequently referred to as "models" in OB.

### *Empirical Research*

The use of objective measurements of research variables as a basis for investigating and verifying theories and hypotheses.

*Example* Researchers collected data on the output of a work unit on a daily basis. These were objective "facts" because the same results would have been obtained by anyone who used the same measuring procedures. These "facts" are quite different from the "opinion" of an observer who may have watched the workers perform and then made a purely personal judgment regarding their accomplishments.

## SCIENTIFIC RESEARCH IN REVIEW

The scientific method as depicted in Figure B.1 is an important criterion used to evaluate research contributions to OB. Ultimately you need to become a good consumer of other people's research. A familiarity with the scientific method, alternative research designs and the vocabulary of

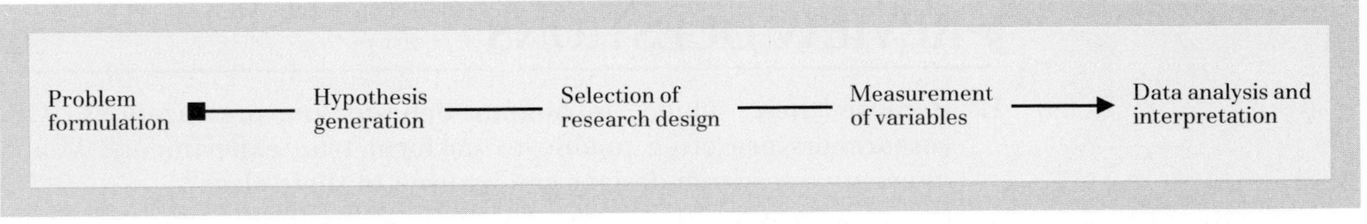


*FIGURE B.1 The Scientific Research Process.*

science are helpful first steps on the way. Important, too, is an awareness of increasing attention within the field of OB to the practicality of research.

Five dimensions of research relevance have been proposed to represent the key needs of practitioners with respect to the utilization of organizational science knowledge.[7] These five dimensions or properties of relevant research are briefly summarized as follows:

1. *Descriptive relevance* is the accuracy of research findings in capturing phenomena encountered by the practitioner in his or her organizational setting.
2. *Goal relevance* is the correspondence of outcome or dependent variables in a theory to things the practitioner actually wishes to influence.
3. *Operational validity* is the ability of the practitioner to implement action implications of a theory by manipulating its causal or independent variables.
4. *Nonobviousness* is the degree to which a theory meets or exceeds the complexity of common sense theory already used by a practitioner.
5. *Timeliness* is the requirement that a theory be available to practitioners in time to use it to deal with problems.

For managers to benefit in actual practice from OB research, theories must be high in practical relevance. To achieve this goal, organizational scientists are increasingly recognizing their responsibility to make research relevant, that is, to make sure that the work they do satisfies the five dimensions just described—descriptive relevance, goal relevance, operational validity, nonobviousness, and timeliness. You should find a good correspondence between these criteria and the various theories and findings discussed in this book. You should also find that the emerging OB research as reported in the scholarly literature is responsive to similar tests of practicality and meaningfulness for managers and people at work.

## KEY TERMS

Dependent Variable
Empirical Research
External Validity
Hypothesis
Independent Variable
Internal Validity
Intervening Variable
Moderator Variable
Research Design
Theory
True Experiment
Variable

# REVIEW QUESTIONS

1. Because their subject is human behavior in organizations, OB researchers are often unable to perform true experiments. What alternative research designs can be used in their place?
2. Use each of the terms in The Vocabulary of Science section as they might be found in a work conversation between two managers.

## CASE

# TRAINING SUPERVISORS AND CONVINCING MANAGEMENT

Shane Alexander is the personnel director of the Central State Medical Center. One of her responsibilities is to oversee the hospital's supervisory training programs. Recently, Shane attended a professional conference where a special "packaged" training program was advertised for sale. The "package" includes a set of videotaped lectures by a distinguished management consultant plus a workbook containing readings, exercises, cases, tests, and other instructional aids. The subjects covered in the program include motivation, group dynamics, communication skills, leadership effectiveness, performance appraisal, and the management of planned change.

In the past, Shane felt that the hospital had not lived up to its supervisory training goals. One of the reasons for this was the high cost of hiring external consultants to do the actual instruction. This packaged program was designed, presumably, so that persons from within the hospital could act as session coordinators. The structure of the program provided through the videotapes and workbook agenda was supposed to substitute for a consultant's expertise. Because of this, Shane felt that use of the packaged program could substantially improve supervisory training in the hospital.

The cost of the program was $3500 for an initial purchase of the videotapes plus 50 workbooks. Additional workbooks were then available at $8 per copy. Before purchasing the program, Shane needed the approval of the senior administrative staff.

Upon returning from the conference, Shane proposed such a purchase at the next staff meeting. She was surprised at the response. The hospital president was noncommittal, the vice president was openly hostile, and the three associate administrators were varied in their enthusiasm. It was the vice president's opinion that dominated the discussion. He argued that to invest in such a program on the assumption that it would lead to improved supervisory practices was unwise. "This is especially true in respect to the proposed program," he said. "How could such a package possibly substitute for the training skills of an expert consultant?"

Shane argued her case and was left with the following challenge. The administrators would allow $1000 to be spent to rent the program with 30 workbooks. It would be up to Shane to demonstrate through a trial program that an eventual purchase would be worthwhile.

There were 160 supervisors in the hospital. The program was designed to be delivered in eight 2½-hour sessions. It was preferred to schedule one session per week, with no more than 15 participants per session.

Shane knew that she would have to present very strong evidence to gain administrative support for the continued use of the program. Given the opportunity, she decided to implement a trial program in such a way that conclusive evidence on the value of the "packaged" training would be forthcoming.

### *Questions*

1. If you were Shane, what type of research design would you use to test this program? Why?
2. How would the design actually be implemented in this hospital setting?
3. What would be your research hypothesis? What variables would you need to measure to provide data that could test this hypothesis? How would you gather these data?
4. Do you think the administrator's request for "proof before purchase" was reasonable? Why or why not?

SUPPLEMENTARY MODULE C

# PERFORMANCE APPRAISAL FOUNDATIONS OF ORGANIZATIONAL BEHAVIOR

A concern for performance, a key result of the efforts of people at work, underlies a manager's interest in the field of Organizational Behavior.[1] Accordingly, one major responsibility shared by all managers is to facilitate high levels of individual and group performance accomplishment. It is in this action context that our study of OB, and its many concepts and theories, takes meaning.

An important foundation for the managerial application of OB in the workplace is the process of performance appraisal. Formally defined, ***performance appraisal*** is a process of formally evaluating performance and providing feedback on which performance adjustments can be made. Essentially, performance appraisal works on the basis of the equation: Desired performance − actual performance = need for action. To the extent that desired levels exceed actual levels, a performance variance requiring special attention exists. And only when actual performance is accurately measured is a manager well prepared to apply a knowledge of OB to analyze the performance situation, identify problems and/or opportunities involved, and take appropriate action.

**Performance appraisal**

Although most managers will be involved with performance appraisal at the individual and group levels, we'll restrict our attention here to the appraisal of individual performance. Many of the issues, problems, and principles that can be identified at this level of action also apply at the group level. It is useful in this respect to recall our Chapter 1 discussion of means–end chains. This logic suggests that each person should perform tasks that are the "means" for higher-level objectives (i.e., "ends") to be achieved. When such means–end linkages are made throughout an organization and across all levels, organizational performance in the form of mission accomplishment should be facilitated.

Beginning with this notion of interlocking means–end chains, we can say (1) that jobs are created to fulfill specific purposes within the framework of organizational objectives, (2) those specific job duties/responsibilities that define each of the many jobs that get created should point to what is expected of people at work, and (3) that these specific duties/responsibilities become the focus of evaluating one's performance. Performance appraisal, therefore, plays a key role in completing the means–end linkages of work activities and goals throughout an organization.

# PURPOSES OF PERFORMANCE APPRAISAL

Any performance appraisal system is central to an organization's human resource management activities. The major functions of performance appraisal are to:[2]

1. *Define* the specific job criteria against which performance will be measured.
2. Accurately *measure* past job performance.
3. *Justify* the rewards given to individuals, thereby discriminating between high and low performance.
4. *Define* the development experiences the employee needs to both enhance performance in the current job and prepare for future responsibilities.

These four functions include two general purposes served by good performance-appraisal systems: evaluation and development. For the manager this means that fulfilling both judgmental (serving evaluation purposes) and counseling (serving developmental purposes) roles are essential to the performance-appraisal process. From an evaluative perspective, performance appraisal lets people know where they stand relative to objectives and standards. As such it is an input to decisions that allocate rewards and otherwise administer the personnel function of the organization. From a counseling perspective, performance appraisal facilitates decisions relating to planning for and gaining commitment to the continued training and personal development of subordinates.

## Administrative Decisions

Administrative decisions are concerned with such issues as promotions, transfers, terminations, and salary increases. Where these decisions are made on performance criteria as opposed to some other basis (e.g., seniority), some sort of performance appraisal system is necessary. Performance appraisal information is also useful for making selection and placement decisions, where performance results are matched against individual attributes and selection dimensions to determine which are most related to performance. Also, if one were to identify specific aspects of performance which are inadequate, the performance appraisal process may lead to improved training and development programs. Then, too, appraisals form the basis of any performance-contingent reward system. As discussed in Chapter 6, such systems depend on good performance appraisals to make them work.

Managers make a wide variety of these and other administrative decisions relating to the performance of people at work. The quality of these decisions depends directly on the quality of the performance information collected. Therefore, effective management action requires good performance appraisal information.

## Employee Feedback and Development Decisions

Another use of performance appraisals is to let employees know how they stand in terms of management expectations and performance objectives. Performance appraisal feedback should involve a detailed discussion of the employee's job-related strengths and weaknesses. This feedback can then be used for developmental purposes. In terms of the expectancy motivational approach in Chapter 5, feedback can help to clarify the individual's sense of both instrumentality and expectancy.

Performance appraisal feedback can also be used as a basis for individual coaching or training by the manager to help the employee overcome performance deficiencies. In one recent survey, approximately 65 percent of the sampled firms were found to be using performance appraisals for developmental purposes.[3]

# DIMENSIONS AND STANDARDS OF PERFORMANCE APPRAISAL

The ease or difficulty of establishing performance dimensions and standards makes a difference in the way performance appraisal systems are established. In addition to performance outcomes, the behaviors or activities that result in these outcomes are frequently important to performance appraisal. Thus, it is essential to discuss both output measures and activity measures as key components of the performance appraisal process.

## Output Measures

A number of production and sales jobs provide ready measures of work output. For example, an assembler may have a goal of 50 completed units of a product per hour. The number of assembled units is easily measurable, and it is possible for the organization to set standards concerning how many units should be completed per hour. Here, the performance dimension of interest is a quantitative one—50 completed units per hour. However, the organization may also introduce a performance quality dimension as well. The employee may be evaluated not only in terms of the number of units per hour but the number of units that pass a quality control inspection per hour. Now, *both* quantity and quality are important, and the worker cannot trade one for the other. In other words, assembling 60 units per hour will not do if only 40 pass inspection. Neither will having a larger proportion of units pass inspection if only 35 units are assembled per hour.

In addition, management may also be interested in other performance dimensions, such as downtime of the equipment used for assembling. Thus, a worker would be evaluated in terms of the performance dimensions of quantity and quality of assembly output and equipment downtime. In this way, management could make sure not only that a desirable product was assembled at a desirable rate but that the worker was careful with the equipment.

## Activity Measures

In the preceding example, the output measures were straightforward as was the measure of equipment downtime. Often, however, output measures are difficult, if not impossible, to obtain for a single individual over a period of time and unsuitable for providing appropriate appraisal and feedback. Rather than using output measures, activity or behavioral measures may be called for. For a sales representative, for example, number of units sold during a given time period represents output, whereas techniques used to obtain sales, such as number of calls made, would be activity measures of performance.

Activity measures are typically obtained by some sort of observation and rating on the part of the evaluator. Output measures, on the other hand, are often directly obtained from written records or documents (e.g., production records). While difficulty of obtaining output measures may be one reason for using activity measures, some activity measures are more useful for employee development and counseling than are output measures alone.

Where jobs lend themselves to systematic analysis, the activities can be inferred from a job analysis. Job analyses typically result in written descriptions of job duties and responsibilities (job descriptions) and specification of personal requirements to perform the duties (job specifications).[4] These documents are used in many organizations as the basis for selection and training, as well as for other aspects of wage and salary administration.[5]

# MEASUREMENT ERRORS IN PERFORMANCE APPRAISAL

In addition to concern with the purpose of the appraisal system and its dimensions and standards, it is important to be concerned about those things that can threaten the reliability and validity of a performance appraisal system. To be meaningful, an appraisal system must be both ***reliable*** (i.e., provide consistent results each time it is used) and ***valid*** (i.e., actually measure people on relevant job content). A number of measurement errors can threaten performance appraisals from each perspective.[6]

**Reliable**
**Valid**

## *Deficiency and Contamination Errors*

Systematic job analyses define the domain of key job duties/responsibilities, and as a result, help prevent two common errors in measuring performance—*deficiency* and *contamination.* Deficiency occurs where elements important to job success are left out. For example, a job description for a secretary that failed to consider "dealing with others" would be a deficiency in most such jobs. Careful job analysis would help avoid such deficiencies, and thus help ensure that the performance evaluation would cover *all* relevant dimensions of work.

The opposite of deficiency is contamination. Here, dimensions extraneous to job success are included in the performance measure. This might take several forms, from measuring specific behaviors that are not truly a part of the job to having the measures reflect common judgmental errors or even bias as a part of the evaluation. Thus, a measure of "leadership" might be a contaminating dimension for a salesperson. However, it would not be a contaminating factor for a managerial job. This is why systematic analysis is so important. In like manner, raters often commit one or more judgmental or rating errors (described below) that are reflected in their evaluations of others. This important source of contamination must be guarded against if useful performance information is to be collected.

## *Halo Errors*

Halo error results when a person rates another person on each of several different dimensions and gives a similar rating for each dimension. Here, a sales representative considered to be a "go-getter" (and thus rated high on "dynamism") would also be rated high on dependability, tact, and whatever other performance dimensions were used. The rater fails to discriminate between the person's strong and weak points, and thus a "halo" carries over from one dimension to the next. As you can see, this can create a problem where each of the performance dimensions is considered to be an important and relatively independent aspect of the job.

## *Leniency/Strictness Errors*

Just as some professors are know as easy "A's," some managers tend to give relatively high ratings to virtually everyone under their supervision. Sometimes the opposite also occurs, where some raters tend to rate everyone low. A key problem is that there is very little discrimination between the good and poor performers. Leniency errors involve a tendency to lump them all together.

## *Central Tendency Errors*

In contrast to a tendency to rate all subordinates as very good or very bad, central tendency errors occur when the manager lumps them together around the "average" or middle category. This gives the impression that there are no very good or very poor performers on the dimension being rated. No true performance discrimination is made.

### *Recency Errors*

A different kind of error from those just noted occurs when a rater lets recent events influence a performance rating more than earlier ones. Take, for example, the case of an employee who is usually on-time but shows up one hour late for work the day before a performance rating is made. She is rated low on "promptness" because the one incident of tardiness overshadows her usual promptness. Recency errors can easily occur in the performance appraisal process.

### *Personal Bias Errors*

In addition to the preceding kinds of errors, raters sometimes allow specific biases to enter into performance evaluations. For example, a given rater may intentionally give higher ratings to white than nonwhite ratees, thereby having the performance appraisal reflect a racial bias. Managers must reflect carefully on their personal biases and guard against their interference with ratings of subordinates that are supposed to be performance based.

# PERFORMANCE APPRAISAL METHODS

A number of methods are commonly used in performance appraisal. As a part of the discussion, we include a brief treatment of some strengths and weaknesses of these methods in terms of purpose, dimensions and standards, and rating errors. The methods are divided into two general categories: comparative methods and absolute methods.[7]

## Comparative Methods

Comparative methods of performance appraisal seek to identify the relative standing among those being rated. That is, they would like to establish that Bill is better than Mary who is better than Leslie on a performance dimension. Comparative methods can indicate that one person is better than another on a given dimension, but not how much better. They also fail to indicate whether the person receiving the better rating is "good enough" in an absolute sense. It may well be that Bill in our example is merely the best of a bad lot. Three comparative performance appraisal methods are ranking, paired comparison, and forced distribution.

### *Ranking*

Ranking is the simplest of all the comparative techniques. It consists of merely rank ordering each individual from best to worst on each performance dimension being considered.

### *Paired Comparison*

In a paired comparison method, each person is directly compared with every other person being rated. The frequency of endorsement across all pairs determines one's final ranking. Every possible paired comparison within a group of ratees is considered as shown here. (Underlines indicate the person rated better in each pair):

<u>Bill</u> vs Mary    <u>Mary</u> vs Leslie    <u>Leslie</u> vs Tom<br>
<u>Bill</u> vs Leslie    <u>Mary</u> vs Tom<br>
<u>Bill</u> vs Tom

Number of times Bill is better = 3<br>
Number of times Mary is better = 2<br>
Number of times Leslie is better = 1

Overall, the best performer in this example is Bill, next comes Mary, then Leslie, and last of all is Tom. The paired comparison method becomes tedious when there are lots of people to compare.

### *Forced Distribution*

Here a small number of performance categories are used (e.g., very good, good, adequate, poor, very poor). Each rater is instructed to rate a specific proportion of employees in each of these categories (e.g., 10 percent must be rated very good, 20 percent must be rated good, etc.). This *forces* the rater to use all the categories and not to rate everyone as outstanding or poor or average or the like.

### *Summary*

Comparative methods force the evaluator to differentiate among ratees. A halo error can still occur since comparisons may be similar across all dimensions, although this is less likely with paired comparisons. These methods are not especially good for individual feedback or counseling since they do not reveal much about how close to standard a given employee is. Comparing one employee unfavorably with another is also likely to make the person receiving this feedback defensive. Finally, it may be hard to anchor the performance in terms of expected standards and to compare employees in one group with those of another. It is hard to determine, for example, if the highest ranked person in one group is an equivalent performer to the highest ranked persons in other groups.

On balance, then, comparative techniques are primarily useful for administrative purposes. Two strengths are the forced discrimination they provide and their relative simplicity. A key shortcoming is the lack of an absolute performance standard for comparison purposes.

## Absolute Methods

Absolute methods of performance appraisal specify precise measurement standards. For example, tardiness might be evaluated on a scale ranging from "Never tardy" to "Always tardy." Four of the more common absolute rating procedures are (1) graphic rating scales, (2) critical incident diary, (3) behaviorally anchored ratings scales, and (4) management by objectives approach.

### *Graphic Rating Scales*

This method lists a variety of dimensions thought to be related to high-performance outcomes in a given job, and that the individual is accordingly expected to exhibit. The scales allow the manager to assign the individual scores on each dimension. These ratings are sometimes given point values to allow a summary numerical rating of performance to be given. An example is shown in Figure C.1 found in the case at the end of this module.

The primary appeal of graphic rating scales is that they are relatively easy to do, are efficient in the use of time and other resources, and can be applied to a wide range of jobs. Unfortunately, they are also subject to halo errors and because of generality may not be linked to job analysis or other specific aspects of a given job. This can be corrected by ensuring that only relevant dimensions of work based on sound job analysis procedures are rated.

### *Critical Incident Diary*

In this method, supervisors record incidents of each subordinate's behavior that led to either unusual success or failure in a given performance aspect. These are typically recorded in a diary-type log kept daily or weekly under predesignated dimensions. In a sales job, for example, followup of sales calls and communicating necessary customer information might be two of the dimensions. Descriptive paragraphs can then be used to summarize each salesperson's performance for each dimension as they are observed.

This approach is excellent for employee development and feedback. Since it consists of qualitative statements rather than quantitative information, however, it is difficult to use for administrative decisions. To provide for such information, the critical incident technique is sometimes combined with one of the other methods.

### *Behaviorally Anchored Ratings Scales (BARS)*

This is a performance appraisal approach that has received increasing attention. The procedure for developing this type of scale starts with the careful collection of descriptions of observable job behaviors. These descriptions are typically provided by managers and personnel specialists and include both superior and inferior performance. Once a large sample of behavioral descriptions is collected, each is evaluated to determine the extent to which it describes good-versus-bad performance. The final step is to develop a rating scale where the anchors are specific critical behaviors, each reflecting a different degree of performance effectiveness. An example of a BARS is shown in Table C.1 for a retail department manager. Note the specificity of the behaviors and the scale values for each. Similar behaviorally anchored scales would be developed for other dimensions of the job.

Employee: Jayne Burroughs Supervisor: Dr. Cutter
Department: Pathology Date: 11-28-91

| Work Quantity | | Work Quality | | Cooperation | |
|---|---|---|---|---|---|
| Far below average | | Far below average | | Far below average | |
| Below average | ✓ | Below average | | Below average | ✓ |
| Average | | Average | ✓ | Average | |
| Above average | | Above average | | Above average | |
| Far above average | | Far above average | | Far above average | |

Employee: John Watson Supervisor: Dr. Cutter
Department: Pathology Date: 12-24-91

| Work Quantity | | Work Quality | | Cooperation | |
|---|---|---|---|---|---|
| Far below average | | Far below average | | Far below average | |
| Below average | | Below average | | Below average | |
| Average | ✓ | Average | | Average | |
| Above average | | Above average | ✓ | Above average | |
| Far above average | | Far above average | | Far above average | ✓ |

*FIGURE C.1 Sixth-Month Performance Reviews for Burroughs and Watson.*

As you can see, the BARS approach is detailed and complex. It requires much time and effort to develop. A separate BARS is required for each job, and thus the method is most cost efficient where there are many similar jobs subject to the same appraisal.

The BARS provides specific behaviors useful for counseling and feedback combined with quantitative scales useful for administrative comparative purposes. Initial results with BARS suggested that they were less susceptible to common rating errors than more traditional scales. Later evidence suggests that the scales may not be as clearly superior as originally thought, especially if an equivalent amount of developmental effort is put into other types of measures. Nevertheless, these scales are likely to have a lower level of contamination and deficiency than most other methods. They represent state-of-the-art notions concerning appraisal procedures, and there is strong rationale supporting their use.[8]

## *Management by Objectives*

Of all the appraisal methods, the management by objectives (MBO) procedure is most directly linked to means–end chains and goal setting.[9] Where an MBO system is used, subordinates work with their supervisor to establish specific task-related objectives that fall within their domains and serve as means to help accomplish the supervisor's higher-level objec-

*TABLE C.1*
**EXAMPLE OF A BEHAVIORALLY ANCHORED RATING SCALE DIMENSION**

*Supervising Sales Personnel*

Gives sales personnel a clear idea of their job duties and responsibilities; exercises tact and consideration in working with subordinates; handles work scheduling efficiently and equitably; supplements formal training with his or her own "coaching"; keeps informed of what the sales people are doing on the job; and follows company policy in agreements with subordinates.

| | | |
|---|---|---|
| Effective | 9 | Could be expected to conduct full day's sales clinic with two new sales personnel and thereby develop them into top sales people in the department. |
| | 8 | Could be expected to give his or her sales personnel confidence and strong sense of responsibility by delegating many important jobs to them. |
| | 7 | Could be expected *never* to fail to conduct training meetings with his or her people weekly at a scheduled hour and to convey to them exactly what is expected. |
| | 6 | Could be expected to exhibit courtesy and respect toward his or her sales personnel. |
| | 5 | Could be expected to remind sales personnel to wait on customers instead of conversing with each other. |
| | 4 | Could be expected to be rather critical of store standards in front of his or her own people, thereby risking their development of poor attitudes. |
| | 3 | Could be expected to tell an individual to come in anyway even though he or she called in to say he or she was ill. |
| | 2 | Could be expected to go back on a promise to an individual whom he or she had told could transfer back into previous department if he or she did not like the new one. |
| Ineffective | 1 | Could be expected to make promises to an individual about his or her salary being based on department sales even when he or she knew such a practice was against company policy. |

*Source:* J.P. Campbell, M. D. Dunnette, R. D. Arvey, and L . V. Hellervik, "The Development and Evaluation of Behaviorally Based Rating Scales," *Journal of Applied Psychology,* Vol. 57 (1973), pp. 15–22. Copyright 1973 by the American Psychological Association. Reprinted/adapted by permission of the publisher and author.

tives. Each set of objectives is worked out between a supervisor and subordinate for a given time period. The establishment of objectives is similar to a job analysis, except that it is directed toward a particular individual in his or her job rather than toward a particular job type alone. The increased discretion of the MBO approach means that each specific person is likely to have a custom tailored set of work goals, while still working within the action context of organizational means–end chains.

MBO is the most individualized of all the appraisal systems and tends to work well for counseling if the objectives go beyond simply desired outputs and focus on important activities as well. In comparing one employee with another, a key concern is the ease or difficulty of achieving the goals. If one person has an easier set of objectives to meet than another, then comparisons are unfair. Since MBO tends to rely less heavily on ratings than do the other appraisal systems, rating errors are less likely to be a problem. Contamination is less likely and deficiency can also be low, depending on the comprehensiveness of the objectives.

# IMPROVING PERFORMANCE APPRAISALS

The prior section summarizes a number of strong and weak points for various performance appraisal methods. As with most other issues in organizational behavior, there are trade-offs that managers must recognize in setting up and implementing a performance appraisal system. In addition to the pros and cons already mentioned for each method, some specific things to keep in mind to reduce errors and improve appraisals include[10]

1. Train supervisors so that they understand the evaluation process rationale and can recognize the various sources of measurement error.
2. Make sure that supervisors observe subordinates on an ongoing, regular basis or do not try to limit all their evaluations to the formally designated evaluation period (e.g., every six months or every year).
3. Do not have the supervisor rate too many subordinates. The ability to identify performance differences drops and fatigue sets in when the evaluation of large numbers of people is involved.
4. Make sure that the performance dimensions and standards are clearly stated and that the standards are as noncontaminating and nondeficient as possible.
5. Try to avoid terms such as "average" and the like since different evaluators tend to react differently to the terms.
6. Remember that appraisal systems cannot be used to discriminate against employees on the basis of age, sex, race, and so on. To help provide a legally defensible system in terms of governing legislation, the following recommendations are useful.[11]

   - Appraisal must be based on an analysis of job requirements as reflected in performance standards.
   - Appraisal is appropriate only where performance standards are clearly understood by employees.
   - Clearly defined individual dimensions rather than global measures should be used.
   - Dimensions should be behaviorally based and supported by observable evidence.

- If rating scales are used, avoid abstract trait names (e.g., loyalty) unless they can be defined in terms of observable behaviors.
- Rating scale anchors should be brief and logically consistent.
- The system must be validated and be psychometrically sound as must the ratings given by individual evaluators.
- There must be an appeal mechanism if the evaluator and ratee disagree.

## REVIEW QUESTIONS

1. Define and give examples of two types of (a) comparative performance appraisal methods and (b) absolute performance appraisal methods, as they might be applied to jobs with which you are familiar.
2. Explain steps you might take as a manager to improve the performance appraisal process and help ensure that it is legally defensible.

## KEY TERMS

Behaviorally Anchored Rating Scales (BARS)
Contamination Error
Critical Incident Diary
Deficiency Error
Forced Distribution
Halo Error
Leniency/Strictness/Central Tendency Errors
Management by Objectives (MBO)
Paired Comparison
Performance Appraisal
Personal Bias Error
Ranking
Recency Error
Reliability
Validity

## CASE

# ALLEGED SEX DISCRIMINATION IN PERFORMANCE APPRAISAL

Jayne Burroughs and John Watson are both employed as technicians in the pathology lab of Central Catholic Hospital, a major medical center in the core of a major city. They both hold specialist degrees and are licensed pathologist's assistants. Both have been employed in their jobs for five years.[12]

Last month, Dr. Clarence Cutter, the chief pathologist and supervisor of the lab, decided to reorganize his operation. He decided that supervising the work of both assistants was taking up too much of his time. He reasoned that if he were to promote one of them to a midlevel supervisory position, he could reduce the time he spent in direct supervision. Dr. Cutter presented his argument to Fred Wunderlich, the hospital's director of personnel. Wunderlich agreed and added that Dr. Cutter could probably use even more help in the lab. He suggested that either Burroughs or Watson be promoted to a new job titled Administrative Assistant to the Pathologist and that a new person be hired to fill the vacated lab technician position. Thus, a new structure was developed for the department in which two lab technicians reported to an administrative assistant, who in turn reported to the chief pathologist.

The next task for Dr. Cutter was to decide which of his lab technicians to promote to the new position. In order to make the decision, he pulled the latest six-month performance evaluations he had made on Burroughs and Watson. Figure C.1 reproduces their performance review results. On the basis of the performance reviews, he promoted John Watson to the administrative assistant position.

Upon learning of Watson's promotion, Burroughs went to Dr. Cutter and demanded that he justify why he promoted Watson instead of her. His explanation did not satisfy Burroughs, and she filed a formal complaint alleging sex discrimination in a promotion decision, both with Mr. Wunderlich, the personnel manager, and Robyn Payson, the Hospital's Equal Employment Opportunity officer.

A hearing was scheduled by Wunderlich to resolve the issues. Wunderlich and Payson constituted the review board at the hearing, and Cutter and Burroughs were invited to present their cases. In the hearing, Burroughs opened the case by presenting her formal complaint: Both she and Watson have identical credentials for their jobs and have equal tenure on the job (five years). In addition, it is her belief that she and Watson have performed equivalently during this period of time. He told her that he was not obligated to present a justification to her; that he was perfectly within his rights as chief pathologist to make such a decision and that she should rest assured that his decision was made on grounds that were fair and equitable to her and Watson. Therefore, according to her charge, the only reason Dr. Cutter could possibly have had for promoting Watson over her would be her sex. She noted that a decision of that nature is in clear violation of Title VII of the Civil Rights Act of 1964, which reads in part:

> It shall be an unlawful employment practice for an employer to fail or refuse to hire or to discharge, or otherwise to discriminate against any individual with respect to his compensation terms, conditions, or privileges of employment because of such individual's race, color, religion, sex, or national origin. (Title VII, Sec. 703, Par. a-1 of the Civil Rights Act of 1964, as amended by P.L. 92-261, effective March 24, 1972.)

Dr. Cutter countered by justifying his decision on the basis of actual performance review data. He argued that sex had nothing whatsoever to do with his decision. Rather, he presented to the board the latest six-month performance evaluations, which showed Watson to be performing better than Burroughs on three performance dimensions: (1) work quantity; (2) work quality; and (3) cooperation (see Figure C.1).

The performance results served to anger Burroughs further. She requested that the hearing be adjourned and reconvened after she had had a chance to review the results and prepare her case further. Wunderlich and Payson agreed and rescheduled a second hearing two weeks later.

At the second hearing, Burroughs presented the following list of grievances with regard to the promotion decision and the information on which it was based:

1. The decision is still in violation of Title VII of the Civil Rights Act because the way the performance evaluation was carried out discriminated against her on the basis of sex. Her reasoning on this point included the following charges:
   (a) Dr. Cutter is biased against females, and this factor caused him to rate males in general above females in general.
   (b) Dr. Cutter and Mr. Watson are in an all-male poker group that meets on Friday nights, and she has systematically been excluded. Thus, ties of friendship have developed along sex lines, which created a conflict of interest for Dr. Cutter.
   (c) Dr. Cutter has said to her and to others on several occasions that he doubts females can carry out managerial tasks because they must constantly be concerned with duties at home and they get pregnant.
2. The measuring device itself failed to include a number of activities she carries out that are critical to the functioning of the lab. For example, while Dr. Cutter and Watson are talking over coffee, she is frequently cleaning up the lab. She says that, although Mr. Watson's work is good, he tends to concentrate only on visible work outcomes, and leaves much of the "invisible work," like cleaning up, to her.
3. The timing of the performance review was bad. She charged that it was unfair to her to base the decision on only one six-month evaluation. Dr. Cutter has a total of 10 performance reviews for each of them. Why didn't he base his decision on all 10, rather than on just the latest review?
4. Also with respect to timing, Ms. Burroughs pointed out that her review has been made a month earlier than Mr. Watson's. She charged that December 24 was Christmas Eve and the day of the lab's office party. She charged that the spirits of the occasion (liquid and other) tended to shade Dr. Cutter's judgment in favor of Watson.

### *Questions*

Put yourself in the position of Mr. Wunderlich and Ms. Payson. Decide whether there is any justification to Ms. Burroughs' charges, or if Dr. Cutter is justified in his decision. In making your decision, address yourself to the following questions:

1. Are issues of reliability, validity, and measurement error involved in this case? If so, what sources of error must you consider in making a judgment?

2. Is the measuring instrument itself at issue in this case? Why or why not? What recommendations would you make for changing the instrument?
3. What general changes would you recommend in this case? Why?

# GLOSSARY

## A

Ability The capacity to perform the various tasks needed for a given job.

Absenteeism The failure of people to attend work on a given day.

Action Research The process of systematically collecting data on an organization, feeding it back for action planning, and evaluating results by collecting and reflecting on more data.

Active Listening Communication (verbal and nonverbal) by the receiver that helps the source of a message articulate what she or he really means.

Adult Transitions Major stages in the adult life cycle in which different responsibilities and concerns are important.

Anchoring and Adjustment Heuristic Assessing an event by beginning with an initial value taken from historical precedent or other outside sources, and then making subsequent assessments based only on incremental adjustments to that value.

Applied Behavior Analysis The systematic reinforcement of desirable work behavior and the nonreinforcement or punishment of unwanted work behavior.

Aptitude The capability to learn something.

Arbitration Where a neutral third party acts as judge and issues a binding decision affecting parties at a negotiation impasse.

Attitude A predisposition to respond in a positive or negative way to someone or something in one's environment.

Attribution The tendency to understand behavior or events by interpreting them as caused by certain factors; the attempt to explain "why" something happened the way it did.

Attribution Error The attributional tendency to underestimate the influence of situational factors and overestimate the influence of internal or personal factors in evaluating someone else's behavior.

Attribution Theory The attempt to understand the cause of an event, assess responsibility for outcomes of the event, and assess the personal qualities of people involved.

Availability Heuristic Assessing an event based on instances of occurrences of that event that are easily available in one's memory.

Authoritarianism/Dogmatism Traits Focusing on the rigidity of a person's beliefs.

Authority The right to act and to command other persons.

Automation A job design that allows machines to do work previously accomplished by human effort.

## B

Bargaining Zone In negotiating situations, the zone between one party's minimum reservation point and the other party's maximum reservation point.

Brainstorming A group decision technique in which members contribute ideas in an open and "freewheeling" format, and without criticizing one another.

Bureaucracy An ideal form of organization whose characteristics were defined by the German sociologist Max Weber.

## C

Career A sequence of jobs and work pursuits representing what a person does for a living.

Career Path A sequence of jobs held over time during a career.

Career Planning An organization development intervention that creates opportunities for achieving long-term congruence between individual goals and organizational career opportunities.

Career Plateau A position from which someone is unlikely to move to advance to a higher level of responsibility.

Career Stages Different points of work responsibility and achievement through which people pass during the course of their work lives.

Centralization The degree to which the authority to make decisions is restricted to higher levels of management.

Centralized Communication Network A group communication network where all communication flows through a central person who serves as the "hub" of the network.

Certain Environment A decision environment in which information is sufficient to predict the results of each alternative in advance of implementation.

Change Agent An individual or group that takes responsibility for changing the existing pattern of behavior of a person or social system.

Charismatic Leaders Those leaders who by force of their personal abilities are capable of having a profound and extraordinary effect on followers.

Classical Conditioning A form of learning through association that involves the manipulation of stimuli to influence behavior.

Coacting Groups Groups whose members work independently on common tasks.

Coercive Power The extent to which a manager can deny desired rewards or administer undesirable outcomes to control other people.

Cognitive Dissonance A state of perceived inconsistency between a person's expressed attitudes and actual behavior.

Cognitive Learning A form of learning achieved by thinking about the perceived relationship between events and individual goals and expectations.

Cohesiveness The degree to which members are attracted to and motivated to remain part of a group.

Collateral Organization An organization development intervention designed to improve creative problem solving by pulling a representative set of members out of the formal organization structure to engage in periodic small-group, problem-solving sessions.

Communication An interpersonal process of sending and receiving symbols with meanings attached to them.

Compressed Work Week Any scheduling of work that allows a full-time job to be completed in fewer than the standard five days.

Conceptual Skill The ability to view the situation as a whole and solve problems for the benefit of everyone concerned.

Conflict When two or more people disagree over issues of organizational substance and/or when they experience some emotional antagonisms with one another.

Conflict Resolution Occurs when the reasons, substantial, and/or emotional, for a conflict are eliminated.

Confrontation Meeting An organization development intervention refined by Richard Bechard that is designed to quickly help determine how an organization might be improved and start action toward such improvement.

Consensus A group decision-making method wherein a clear alternative is supported by most members and even those who oppose it feel they have been listened to and had a fair chance to influence the decision outcome.

Constructive Stress Stress that acts in a positive way for the individual and/or the organization.

Consultative Decision A decision made by an individual after seeking input from or consulting with members of a group.

Content Theories Theories that offer ways to profile or analyze individuals to identify the needs that motivate their behavior.

Contingency Approach The attempt by OB scholars to identify how situations can be understood and managed in ways that respond appropriately to their unique characteristics.

Continuous Reinforcement This schedule administers a reward each time a desired behavior occurs.

Contributions Individual work efforts of value to the organization.

Control The set of mechanisms used in an

organization to keep actions and outputs within predetermined limits.

Controlling The process of monitoring performance, comparing actual results to objectives, and taking corrective action as necessary.

Coordination The set of mechanisms used in an organization to link the actions of its subunits into a consistent pattern.

Corporate Social Responsibility The obligation of organizations to behave in ethical and moral ways as institutions of the broader society.

Counteracting Groups Groups that include the presence of subgroups that disagree on some aspect of overall group operations.

Counterculture The pattern of values and philosophy that outwardly rejects those of the larger organization or social system.

Crafted Decision A decision created to deal specifically with a situation at hand.

Culture The learned and shared ways of thinking and doing things found among members of a society.

Culture Shock Feelings of frustration and confusion resulting from the continuing challenge of living in an unfamiliar foreign country.

## D

Decentralized Communication Network A group communication network where all members communicate directly with one another.

Decentralization The degree to which authority to make decisions is given to lower levels in an organization's hierarchy.

Decision Making The process of identifying a problem or opportunity and choosing among alternative courses of action.

Delphi Technique A group decision technique in which a series of questionnaires is used to help geographically dispersed members reach a decision.

Demographic Characteristics Background variables (e.g., age, sex) that help to shape what a person becomes over time.

Departmentation The process of dividing duties and grouping jobs and people together to form administrative units; horizontal specialization.

Destructive Stress Stress that acts in a dysfunctional way for the individual and/or the organization.

Distributive Negotiation Where the focus is on "positions" staked out or declared by the parties involved who are each trying to claim certain portions of the available "pie."

Division of Labor The process of breaking work to be done by individuals or groups into small components that serve the organization's purpose.

Divisional Departmentation Grouping individuals and resources by product, service, client, territory, or legal entity.

Domestic Multiculturalism The presence of cultural diversity among people living in a particular town or city locale or other geographical region within one country.

Dual-Career Couple A family in which both adult partners are part of the work force.

## E

Efficient Communication Communication at minimum cost in terms of resources expended.

Effectance Motive The stimulation to work hard based on a feeling of competency or mastery over one's environment.

Effective Communication When the intended meaning of the source and the perceived meaning of the receiver are one and the same.

Effective Manager A manager whose work unit achieves high levels of *both* task performance *and* human resource maintenance.

Effective Negotiation When issues of substance are resolved without any harm to the working relationships among the parties to the negotiation.

Empowerment Allowing individuals or groups to make decisions affecting them or their work.

Environmental Complexity The magnitude of the problems and opportunities in the organization's environment as evidenced by the degree of richness, interdependence, and uncertainty.

Escalating Commitment The tendency to continue with a previously chosen course of action even when feedback suggests that it is failing.

Esteem Needs Desires for ego gratification in the forms of self-esteem and reputation.

Ethical Behavior That which is morally accepted as "good" and "right" as opposed to "bad" and "wrong" in a particular social context.

Ethical Climate The shared set of understandings in an organization about what is correct behavior and how ethical issues will be handled.

Ethical Dilemma A situation in which a person must decide whether or not to do something that—although benefiting oneself or the organization or both—may be considered unethical and perhaps illegal.

Ethical Managerial Behavior Managerial behavior that conforms not only to the mere dictates of law but also to a broader moral code common to society as a whole.

Ethnocentrism The tendency to consider one's culture and its values as being superior to others.

Existence Needs Desires for physiological and material well-being.

Expatriates Persons who take employment and live in foreign countries.

Expectancy The tendency to create or find in another situation or individual that which one expected to find in the first place.

Expert Power The ability to control another's behavior due to the possession of knowledge, experience, or judgment that the other person does not have but needs.

Extinction Withdrawal of the reinforcing consequences for a given behavior.

Extrinsic Rewards Positively valued work outcomes that are given to the individual by some other person in the work setting.

## F

Feedback The process of telling someone else how one feels about something the person did or said or about the situation in general.

Felt Inequity A work situation in which the individual feels that his or her rewards received in return for work contributions made are relatively less (felt negative inequity) or relatively more (felt positive inequity) than those received by others.

Flexible Working Hours Any work schedule that gives employees daily choice in the timing between work and nonwork activities.

Force–Coercion Change Strategy A strategy that uses legitimacy, rewards, and punishments as primary inducements to change.

Foreign Direct Investment Involves the purchase of domestic or local assets by foreign investors.

Formal Authority Legitimate power; the right of command vested in a managerial position.

Formal Communication Channels Communication channels that follow the chain of command established by the organization's hierarchy.

Formal Leadership Exercising influence from a position of formal authority in an organization.

Formal Structure The intended configuration of positions, job duties, and lines of authority among the component parts of an organization.

Formalization The written documentation of work rules, policies, and procedures.

Functional Departmentation Grouping individuals and resources by skill, knowledge, and action.

## G

Gain Sharing A pay system that links pay and performance by giving workers the opportunity to share in productivity gains through increased earnings.

General Environment The set of cultural, economic, educational, and legal–political forces common to organizations operating within a given geographical area.

Glass Ceiling Effect A hidden barrier limiting the advancement of minorities in some occupations and employment settings.

Global Geographic Division Structure Where a firm engaged in extensive international business uses a geographic breakdown for operations beneath the corporate staff level.

Global Manager Someone who knows how to do business across borders.

Global Product Division Structure Where a firm engaged in extensive international business uses a product breakdown for operations in foreign countries.

Goal Setting The process of developing, negotiating, and formalizing the targets or objectives that an employee is responsible for accomplishing.

Group Decision A decision made by all members of the group, ideally with consensus being achieved.

Group Dynamics The forces operating in groups that affect group performance and member satisfaction.

Groupthink A tendency for highly cohesive groups to lose their critical evaluative capabilities.

Growth Needs Desires for continued personal growth and development.

## H

Halo Effect When one attribute of a person or situation is used to develop an overall impression of the person or situation.

Heuristics Simplifying strategies or "rules of thumb" that people use when making decisions.

Hierarchy of Authority The arrangement of work positions in order of increasing formal authority.

Higher-order Needs Esteem and self-actualization needs in Maslow's hierarchy.

Horizontal Specialization A division of labor through the formation of work units or groups within an organization; the process of departmentation.

Human Resource Maintenance The attraction and continuation of a viable work force.

Human Skill The ability to work well in cooperation with other persons.

## I

Impression Management The systematic attempt to behave in ways that create and maintain desired impressions of oneself in the eyes of others.

Individual Decision A decision made by one individual on behalf of the group.

Inducements Things that the organization gives to the individual in return for contributions.

Inducements–Contributions Balance When the exchange of values in the psychological contract is felt to be fair.

Influence A behavioral response to the exercise of power.

Informal Communications Channels Communication channels that do not adhere to the organization's hierarchy.

Informal Leadership Exercising influence through special skills or resources that meet the needs of other persons.

Instrumental Values Values that reflect a person's beliefs about the "means" for achieving desired ends.

Instrumentality The probability assigned by the individual that a given level of achieved task performance will lead to various work outcomes.

Integrative Negotiation A negotiation where the focus is on the merits of the issues and parties involved try to enlarge the available "pie" rather than stake claims to certain portions of it.

Interacting Groups Groups with high interdependence among members such that when violated the standards may be enforced with reprimands and/or other group sanctions.

Intergroup Dynamics The dynamics that take place between as opposed to within groups.

Intergroup Team Building A special form of team building and organization development intervention designed to help two or more groups improve their working relationships with one another and, hopefully, experience improved group effectiveness.

Intermittent Reinforcement This schedule rewards behavior only periodically.

International Organizational Behavior The study of individuals and groups in organizations operating in an international setting.

Intrinsic Motivation A desire to work hard solely for the pleasant experience of task accomplishment.

Intrinsic Rewards Positively valued work outcomes that are received by the individual directly as a result of task performance.

Intuition The ability to quickly and readily know or recognize the possibilities of a situation.

## J

Job One or more tasks that an individual performs in direct support of the organization's production purpose.

Job Commitment The degree to which a person strongly identifies with his or her job and feels a part of the organization.

Job Design The planning and specification of job tasks and the work setting in which they are to be accomplished.

Job Enlargement Increasing task variety by combining into one job tasks that were previously assigned to separate workers.

Job Enrichment The practice of building motivating factors into job content.

Job Involvement The willingness of a person to work hard and apply effort beyond normal job expectations.

Job Redesign An organization development intervention that creates opportunities for achieving long-term congruence between individual goals and organizational career opportunities.

Job Rotation  Increasing task variety by periodically shifting workers among jobs involving different tasks.

Job Sharing  The assignment of one full-time job to two persons who divide the work according to agreements made between themselves and the employer.

Job Simplification  Standardizing work procedures and employing people in very clearly defined and specialized tasks.

Joint Ventures (or Strategic Alliances)  Where two firms—often from different countries—make joint investments in an operation to accomplish certain objectives.

## L

Law of Contingent Reinforcement  The view that for a reward to have maximum reinforcing value, it must be delivered only if the desired behavior is exhibited.

Law of Effect  Thorndike's observation that "behavior that results in a pleasing outcome will be likely to be repeated; behavior that results in an unpleasant outcome is not likely to be repeated."

Law of Immediate Reinforcement  The more immediate the delivery of a reward after the occurrence of a desirable behavior, the greater the reinforcing effect on behavior.

Leadership  A special case of interpersonal influence that gets an individual or group to do what the leader wants done.

Learning  A relatively permanent change in behavior that occurs as a result of experience.

Legitimate Power  The extent to which a manager can use the internalized values of a subordinate that the "boss" has a "right of command" to control other people.

Lifelong Learning  Continuous learning from the full variety of one's actual work and life experiences.

Line Units  Work groups that conduct the major business of the organization.

Locus of Control  The internal–external orientation that is the extent to which people feel able to affect their lives.

Lower-order Needs  Physiological, safety, and social needs in Maslow's hierarchy.

Lump-Sum Pay Increase  A pay system in which people elect to receive their annual wage or salary increase in one or more "lump-sum" payments.

## M

Machiavellian  A person who views and manipulates others for purely personal gain.

Maintenance Activities  Activities that support the emotional life of the group as an ongoing social system.

Management by Objectives (MBO)  A process of joint goal setting between a supervisor and subordinate.

Management Training  An organization development intervention involving formal "classroom" style training, or a less formal training that takes place on the job, with the goal of improving someone's management skills.

Manager  A person in an organization who is responsible for the performance of one or more subordinates.

Managerial Ethics  Standards and principles that guide the actions and decisions of managers and determine if they are "good" or "bad" in a moral sense.

Managerial Techniques  The analytical methods, procedures, and tools organizations use to supplement managerial judgment.

Managerial Work  Influencing the activities of other people so that organizational performance objectives are well served and so that the people themselves experience personal satisfaction from their work.

Matrix Departmentation or Matrix Structure  A combination of functional and divisional patterns wherein an individual is assigned to more than one type of unit.

Means–End Chains  The linking of the work efforts of individuals and groups to an organization's purpose.

Mechanistic Organization  An organizational structure that emphasizes vertical specialization and control, an extensive use of managerial techniques, impersonal coordination and control, and a heavy reliance on rules, policies, and procedures.

Merit Pay  A compensation system that bases an individual's salary or wage increase on a measure of the person's performance accomplishments during a specified time period.

Mission Statements  Written statements of organizational purpose.

Mixed Messages  Messages that appear mixed when a person's words communicate one message while the individual's actions or nonverbal language communicate another.

Modeling (or Vicarious Learning) Learning new behaviors by directly observing and imitating their demonstration by others.

Motivation to Work The forces within an individual that account for the level, direction, and persistence of effort expended at work.

## N

Need A physiological or psychological deficiency that the individual feels some compulsion to eliminate.

Need for Achievement (nAch) The desire to do something better, solve problems, or master complex tasks.

Need for Affiliation (nAff) The desire to establish and maintain friendly and warm relations with other persons.

Need for Power (nPower) The desire to control other persons, influence their behavior, and be responsible for other people.

Negative Reinforcement Withdrawal of negative consequences that tend to increase the likelihood of repeating the behavior in similar settings.

Noise Anything that interferes with the effectiveness of a communication attempt.

Nominal Group Technique A group decision technique that uses structured rules for minimizing interactions to facilitate decision making on potentially controversial subjects.

Nonprogrammed Decisions Decisions that implement new and creative solutions to problems that have not been encountered before.

Nonverbal Communication Communication that takes place through facial expressions, body position, eye contact, and other physical gestures.

Norms Rules or standards that apply to group members such that when violated the standards may be enforced with reprimands and/or other group sanctions.

## O

Open Systems Transform human and physical resources received as inputs from their environments into goods and services that are then returned to the environment for consumption.

Operant Conditioning The process of controlling behavior by manipulating its consequences.

Organic Organization An organizational structure that emphasizes horizontal specialization, an extensive use of personal coordination, and loose rules, policies, and procedures.

Organization A collection of people working together, in a division of labor, to achieve a common purpose.

Organization Charts Diagrams that depict the formal structures of organizations.

Organization Development (OD) The application of behavior science knowledge in a long-range effort to improve an organization's ability to cope with change in its external environment and increase its internal problem-solving capabilities.

Organization Development (OD) Interventions Activities initiated in support of an OD program and designed to improve the work effectiveness of individuals, groups, or the organization as a whole.

Organizational Behavior The study of individuals and groups in organizations.

Organizational Culture The system of shared beliefs and values that develops within an organization or within its subunits and that guides the behaviors of members (sometimes called the corporate culture).

Organizational Design The process of choosing and implementing a structural configuration for an organization.

Organizational Governance The pattern of authority, influence, and acceptable managerial behavior established at the top of the organization.

Organizational Politics The management of influence to obtain ends not sanctioned by the organization or to obtain sanctioned ends through nonsanctioned means of influence.

Organizational Purpose The goal of producing a good or service.

Organizing The process of dividing up the work to be done and then coordinating results to achieve a desired purpose.

Outcome Goals Goals of organization development that focus on improvements in what people accomplish in organizations.

Output Goals The goals that define the type of business an organization is in.

## P

Part-Time Work Work done on a schedule that requires less than the standard 40-hour work week.

Perception The process through which people receive, organize, and interpret information from their environment.

Performance A summary measure of the quantity and quality of task contributions made by an individual or group to the work unit and organization.

Performance-Contingent Reward A reward whose size and value varies in proportion to someone's work accomplishments.

Performance Gap A discrepancy between an actual and a desired state of affairs.

Personal Wellness A term used to describe the pursuit of one's physical and mental health through a personal health program.

Personality The overall profile or combination of traits that characterize the unique nature of a person.

Physiological Needs The basic desire for biological maintenance.

Planned Change Change that happens as a result of specific efforts on its behalf by a change agent.

Planning The process of setting performance objectives and identifying the actions needed to accomplish them.

Positive Reinforcement Administration of positive consequences that tend to increase the likelihood of repeating the behavior in similar settings.

Power The ability to get someone else to do something you want done; the ability to make things happen or get things done the way you want.

Primary Beneficiaries Particular groups expected to benefit from the efforts of specific organizations.

Problem-solving style The way in which a person goes about gathering and evaluating information in solving problems and making decisions.

Process Consultation An organization development intervention concerned with helping a group improve on such things as norms, cohesiveness, decision-making methods, communication, conflict, and task and maintenance activities.

Process Goals The goals of organization development that focus on improvements in the way people work together in organizations.

Process Theories Seeking to understand the thought processes that take place in the minds of people and that act to motivate their behavior.

Productivity A summary measure of the quantity and quality of work performance with resource utilization considered.

Programmed Decisions Decisions that implement specific solutions determined by past experience as appropriate for the problems at hand.

Projection The assignment of personal attributes to other individuals.

Psychological Characteristics Psychological factors that predispose an individual to behave in predictable ways.

Psychological Contract The set of expectations held by the individual specifying what the individual and the organization expect to give and to receive from one another in the course of their working relationship.

Punishment Administration of negative consequences that tend to reduce the likelihood of repeating the behavior in similar settings.

## Q

Quality Circle A group of workers who meet periodically to discuss and develop solutions for production problems relating to quality, productivity, or cost.

Quality of Work Life QWL for short; a term indicating the overall quality of human experiences in the workplace.

## R

Rational Persuasion Change Strategy A strategy that attempts to bring about change through persuasion by special knowledge and rational argument.

Realistic Job Previews Give perspective employees as much pertinent information—both good and bad—about the job as possible and without distortion.

Referent Power The ability to control another's behavior because of the individual's wanting to identify with the power source.

Relatedness Needs Desires for satisfying interpersonal relationships.

Relationship Goals A goal of organizational development concerned with how well people involved in a negotiation are able to work with one another once the process is concluded and how well any constituencies they may represent are then able to work together.

Representativeness Heuristic Assessing the likelihood of an event occurring based on the similarity of that event to one's stereotypes of similar occurrences.

Restricted Communication Network One in which polarized subgroups contest one another's positions, restrict interactions, and maintain sometimes antagonistic relations.

Reward Power The extent to which a manager can use extrinsic and intrinsic rewards to control other people.

Risk Environment A decision environment involving a lack of complete certainty but one that includes an awareness of probabilities associated with the possible outcomes of various courses of action.

Role A set of activities expected of a person holding a particular office or position in a group or organization.

Role Ambiguity The uncertainty of a person in a role about the role expectations of one or more members of the role set.

Role Conflict The inability of a person in a role to respond to the expectations of one or more members of the role set.

Role Negotiation A process through which individuals negotiate with one another to clarify expectations about what each should be giving and receiving as group members.

Role Overload A situation in which there are simply too many role expectations being communicated to a person at a given point in time.

Role Set The various people who hold expectations regarding the behavior of someone in a role.

Routine Problems Problems that arise on a routine basis and which can be addressed through standard responses.

## S

Safety Needs The desire for security, protection, and stability in daily life.

Satisficing Choosing the first satisfactory rather than the optimal decision alternative.

Selective Perception The tendency to single out for attention those aspects of a situation or person that reinforce or emerge and are consistent with existing beliefs, values, and needs.

Self-actualization Needs The desire to fulfill one's self, to grow, and to use one's abilities to their full and most creative extent.

Self-managing Work Teams (or Autonomous Work Groups) Work groups having substantial responsibility for a wide variety of decisions involved in the accomplishment of assigned tasks.

Self-serving Bias The attributional tendency to deny personal responsibility for performance problems but to accept it for performance success.

Sensitivity Training An organization development intervention designed to increase the self-awareness of individuals and their "sensitivity" toward other people (sometimes called a "T-group").

Shaping The creation of a new behavior by the positive reinforcement of successive approximations to the desired behavior.

Shared Power Change Strategy A strategy that attempts to bring about change by identifying or establishing values and assumptions such that support for the change naturally emerges.

Situational Constraints Factors in the workplace that give inadequate support to individual performance.

Situational Control The extent to which leaders can determine what their group is going to do and what the outcomes of their actions and decisions are going to be.

Skill-based Pay A pay system that rewards people for acquiring and developing job-relevant skills in number and variety relevant to organizational needs.

Social Learning Learning that is achieved through the reciprocal interaction between people and their environments.

Social Needs The desire for love and affection and a sense of belongingness in one's relationships with other persons.

Societal Goals Goals reflecting the intended contributions of an organization to broader society.

Specialization The division of labor within an organization that groups people and resources together in order to accomplish important tasks.

Specific Environment The set of suppliers, distributors, competitors, and government agencies with which a particular organization must interact to survive and grow.

Staff Units Groups that assist the line units by performing specialized services to the organization.

Standardization The degree to which the range of actions in a job or series of jobs is limited.

Stereotype Assigning an individual or event to a group or category and then ascribing to that individual or event the attributes commonly associated with the group or category.

Stress A state of tension experienced by individuals facing extraordinary demands, constraints, or opportunities.

Stress Management Taking action to reduce existing stress from potentially destructive levels.

Stress Prevention Taking action to avoid having stress reach destructive levels.

Stressors Things that cause stress (e.g., work, nonwork, and personal factors).

Structural Redesign An organization development intervention that involves realigning the structure of the organization or major subsystem in order to improve performance.

Subculture A unique pattern of values and philosophy within a group that is not consistent with the dominant culture of the larger organization or social system.

Substance Goal A goal of organization development concerned with outcomes tied to the "content" issues at hand in a negotiation.

Substitutes for Leadership Organizational-, individual-, or task-situational variables that substitute for leadership in causing performance/human resource maintenance.

Survey Feedback An organization development intervention that begins with the collection of data via questionnaires from organization members or a representative sample of them.

Symbolic Leadership Leadership may be a result, rather than a cause, of performance/human resource maintenance, or may be used symbolically as an attribution to explain outcomes after the fact.

Synergy The creation of a whole that is greater than the sum of its parts.

Systems Goals Goals concerned with conditions within the organization that are expected to increase its survival potential.

## T

Task Performance The quality and quantity of work produced.

Team Building A sequence of planned action steps designed to gather and analyze data on the functioning of a group and implement changes to increase its operating effectiveness.

Technical Skill The ability to use a special proficiency or expertise relating to a method, process, or procedure.

Technology The combination of resources, knowledge, and techniques that creates a product or service output for an organization.

Technological Imperative The idea that if an organization does not adjust its internal structure to the requirements of the technology, it will not be successful.

Telecommuting Work done at home using a computer and/or facsimile ("fax") machine as links to the central office or other places of employment.

Terminal Values Values that reflect a person's beliefs about "ends" to be achieved.

Transactional Leadership Where the leader exerts influence during daily leader–subordinate exchanges without much emotion.

Transformational Leadership Where the follower's goals are broadened and elevated and where confidence is gained to go beyond expectations.

Turnover Decisions by workers to terminate their employment.

Type A Orientation An orientation characterized by impatience, desire for achievement, and perfectionism.

Type B Orientation An orientation characterized by being easy going and less competitive in daily life.

## U

Uncertain Environment A decision environment in which managers are unable to assign probabilities to the possible outcomes of various courses of action.

Unplanned Change Change that occurs at random or spontaneously and without a change agent's direction.

## V

Valence The value attached by the individual to various work outcomes.

Value-added Managers Managers whose efforts clearly improve "bottom-line performance" for the organization as a whole.

Values Global beliefs that guide actions and judgments across a variety of situations.

Vertical Loading Increasing job depth by adding responsibilities like planning and controlling previously done by supervisors.

Vertical Specialization A hierarchical division of labor that distributes formal authority and establishes how critical decisions will be made.

Vicarious Learning (or Modeling) Learning new behaviors by directly observing and imitating their demonstration by others.

## W

Whistleblower Someone who exposes organizational wrongdoings in order to preserve ethical standards and protect against wasteful, harmful, or illegal acts.

Work An activity that produces value for other people.

Work-force Diversity A work force consisting of a broad mix of workers from different racial and ethnic backgrounds, of different ages and genders, and of different domestic and national cultures.

Work Unit A task-oriented group in an organization that includes the manager and his or her immediate subordinates.

## Z

Zone of Indifference The range of authoritative requests to which a subordinate is willing to respond without subjecting the directives to critical evaluation or judgment, hence to which the subordinate is indifferent.

# NOTES

## CHAPTER 1

[1]For a good overview of the OB discipline, see Jay W. Lorsch, ed., *Handbook of Organizational Behavior* (Englewood Cliffs, NJ: Prentice Hall, 1987).

[2]David A. Kolb, "On Management and the Learning Process," in David A. Kolb, Irwin M. Rubin, and James M. McIntyre, eds., *Organizational Psychology: A Book of Readings,* 2nd ed. (Englewood Cliffs, NJ: Prentice Hall, 1974), pp. 27–42.

[3]Adapted from "The Second Book of Moses, Called Exodus," Chapter 18, *The Holy Bible* (Philadelphia: A. J. Holman Company, 1942), pp. 88–89.

[4]See, for example, John Naisbitt and Patricia Aburdene, *Megatrends 2000: Ten New Directions for the 1990s* (New York: William Morrow, 1990).

[5]For data reported in this section, see *Workforce 2000: Work and Workers for the 21st Century* (Indianapolis: The Hudson Institute, 1987); "Business: Gone Fishing," *The Economist* (January 6, 1990), pp. 61–62; "Education Mismatch," special issue of *The Wall Street Journal* (February 9, 1990); "Census '90: Mirror Image," special issue of *The Wall Street Journal* (March 9, 1990).

[6]See Steven N. Brenner and Earl A. Mollander, "Is the Ethics of Business Changing," *Harvard Business Review,* Vol. 55 (January–February 1977), pp. 50–57; Saul W. Gellerman, "Why 'Good' Managers Make Bad Ethical Choices," *Harvard Business Review,* Vol. 64 (July–August 1986), pp. 85–90; Barbara Ley Toffler, *Tough Choices: Managers Talk Ethics* (New York: John Wiley, 1986); Justin G. Longnecker, Joseph A. McKinney, and Carlos W. Moore, "The Generation Gap in Business Ethics," *Business Horizons,* Vol. 32 (September–October 1989), pp. 9–14; John B. Cullen, Vart Victor, and Carroll Stephens, "An Ethical Weather Report: Assessing the Organization's Ethical Climate," *Organizational Dynamics,* Winter 1990, pp. 50–62.

[7]Developed in part from Alan L. Otten, "Ethics on the Job: Companies Alert Employees to Potential Dilemmas," *The Wall Street Journal* (July 14, 1986), p. 17. See also the discussion in John R. Schermerhorn, Jr., *Management for Productivity* (New York: John Wiley, 1989), pp. 603–610.

[8]Based on Gellerman, op. cit.

[9]Examples from *The Wall Street Journal* (December 31, 1984), p. 11; *Business Week* (July 25, 1988), p. 38; *Time* (July 16, 1990), p. 49.

[10]See David A. Nadler and Edward E. Lawler III, "Quality of Work Life: Perspectives and Directions," *Organizational Dynamics,* Vol. 11 (1983), pp. 22–36; the discussion of "QWL" in Thomas G. Cummings and Edgar F. Huse, *Organization Development and Change* (St. Paul: West, 1990).

[11]Quoted from Studs Terkel, *Working* (New York: Avon Books, 1973), p. 7.

## CHAPTER 2

[1]Andrew Grove, *High Output Management* (New York: Random House, 1983; (Henry Mintzberg,

*The Nature of Managerial Work* (New York: Harper & Row, 1973).

[2]Abridged and adapted from p. 30 of *The Nature of Managerial Work* by Henry Mintzberg (New York: Harper & Row, 1973), p. 30. Copyright © 1973 by Henry Mintzberg. Reprinted by permission of Harper & Row, Publishers, Inc.

[3]See Mintzberg, op. cit.; Morgan W. McCall, Jr., Ann M. Morrison, and Robert L. Hannan, *Studies of Managerial Work: Results and Methods,* Technical Report No. 9 (Greensboro, NC: Center for Creative Leadership, 1978; John P. Kotter, *The General Managers* (New York: Free Press, 1982a); Robert E. Kaplan, *The Warp and Woof of the General Manager's Job,* Technical Report No. 27 (Greensboro, NC: Center for Creative Leadership, 1986).

[4]Fred Luthans, "Fifty Years Later: What Do We Really Know About Managing and What Managers Do?" *Academy of Management Newsletter,* Vol. X (1986), pp. 3, 9–10; Fred Luthans, Stuart Rosenkrantz, and Harry Hennessey, "What Do Successful Managers Really Do?" *The Journal of Applied Behavioral Science,* Vol. 21 (No. 2), 1985, pp. 255–270; Fred Luthans, "Successful versus Effective Real Managers," *The Academy of Management Executive,* Vol. II (No. 2), 1988, pp. 127–132.

[5]Allen I. Kraut, Patricia R. Pedigo, D. Douglas McKenna, and Marvin D. Dunnette, "The Role of the Manager: What's Really Important in Different Management Jobs," *Academy of Management Executive,* Vol. III, No. 4, 1989, pp. 286–293.

[6]Kotter, op. cit. (1982a), pp. 67–69.

[7]John P. Kotter, "What Effective General Managers Really Do," *Harvard Business Review,* Vol. 60 (November–December 1982b), p. 161. See also Robert E. Kaplan, "Trade Routes: The Manager's Network of Relationships," *Organizational Dynamics,* Vol. 12 (Spring 1984), pp. 37–52.

[8]Data from Lester B. Korn, "How the Next CEO Will be Different," *Fortune* (May 22, 1989), pp. 157–158.

[9]Robert L. Katz, "Skills of an Effective Administrator," *Harvard Business Review,* Vol. 52 (September–October 1974), p. 94. See also Richard E. Boyatzis, *The Competent Manager: A Model for Effective Performance* (New York: John Wiley, 1982).

[10]See Ann M. Morrison, Randall P. White, and Ellen Van Velsor, *Breaking the Glass Ceiling* (Reading, MA: Addison-Wesley, 1987). For a controversial commentary, see Felice N. Schwartz, "Management Women and the New Facts of Life," *Harvard Business Review,* Vol. 67 (January–February 1989), pp. 65–76. For status reports on work-force diversity and age/gender/ethnic stereotypes, consult recent issues of *The Wall Street Journal, Fortune,* and *Business Week.* For data on the pay gap between men and women managers, see *The New York Times* (August 21, 1989), p. 8, and *The Wall Street Journal* (November 17, 1989), p. B1.

[11]Dewitt C. Dearborn and Herbert A. Simon, "Selective Perception: A Note on the Departmental Identification of Executives," *Sociometry,* Vol. 21 (1958), pp. 140–144.

[12]J. Sterling Livingston, "Pygmalion in Management," *Harvard Business Review,* Vol. 47 (July–August 1969).

[13]See Terence R. Mitchell, S. G. Green, and R. E. Wood, "An Attribution Model of Leadership and the Poor Performing Subordinate," pp. 197–234, in Barry Staw and Larry L. Cummings, eds., *Research in Organizational Behavior* (New York: JAI Press, 1981); John H. Harvey and Gifford Weary, "Current Issues in Attribution Theory and Research," *Annual Review of Psychology,* Vol. 35 (1984), pp. 427–459.

[14]For a good overview, see B. R. Schlenker, *Impression Management: The Self-Concept, Social Identity, and Interpersonal Relations* (Monterey, CA: Brooks/Cole, 1980).

[15]The Job Descriptive Index (JDI) is available from Dr. Patricia C. Smith, Department of Psychology, Bowling Green State University; the Minnesota Satisfaction Questionnaire (MSQ) is available from the Industrial Relations Center and Vocational Psychology Research Center, University of Minnesota.

[16]For job satisfaction trends, see *Work in America: Report of a Special Task Force to the Secretary of Health, Education and Welfare* (Cambridge, MA: MIT Press, 1973); George H. Gallup, *The Gallup Poll, 1972–77 (V.1)* (Wilmington, DE: Scholarly Resources, 1978); Charles N. Weaver, "Job Satisfaction in the United States in the 1970s," *Journal of Applied Psychology,* Vol. 65 (1980), pp. 364–367; "Employee Satisfaction," *Inc.* (August, 1989), p. 112; Alan Farnham, "The Trust Gap," *Fortune* (December 4, 1989), pp. 56–78.

[17]Barry M. Staw, "Organizational Psychology and the Pursuit of the Happy/Productive Worker," *California Management Review,* Vol. XXVIII (Summer 1986), pp. 40–53.

[18]See Fred Luthans, *Organizational Behavior,* Fifth Edition (New York: McGraw-Hill, 1989), pp. 181–184.

[19]Farnham, op. cit.

[20]Examples from "The End of Corporate Loyalty," *Business Week* (August 4, 1986), pp. 42–49; "The Boss that Never Blinks," *Business Week* (July 28, 1986), pp. 46–47; Marlene C. Piturro, "Employee Performance Monitoring ... or Meddling?" *Management Review* (May 1989), pp. 31–33.

[21]Barry M. Staw, "The Consequences of Turnover," *Journal of Occupational Behavior,* Vol. 1 (1980), pp. 253–273.

[22]John P. Wanous, *Organizational Entry* (Reading, MA: Addison-Wesley, 1980).

[23]Charles N. Greene, "The Satisfaction–Performance Controversy," *Business Horizons,* Vol. 15 (1972), p. 31. Michelle T. Iaffaldano and Paul M. Muchinsky, "Job Satisfaction and Job Performance: A Meta-Analysis," *Psychological Bulletin,* Vol. 97 (1985), pp. 251–273; Greene, op. cit., pp. 31–41; Dennis Organ, "A Reappraisal and Reinterpretation of the Satisfaction-Causes-Performance Hypothesis, *Academy of Management Review,* Vol. 2 (1977), pp. 46–53; Peter Lorenzi, "A Comment on Organ's Reappraisal of the Satisfaction-Causes-Performance Hypothesis," *Academy of Management Review,* Vol. 3 (1978), pp. 380–382.

[24]Lyman W. Porter and Edward E. Lawler III, *Managerial Attitudes and Performance* (Homewood, IL: Richard D. Irwin, 1968).

## CHAPTER 3

[1]Shawn Tully, "The Hunt for the Global Manager," *Fortune* (May 21, 1990), pp. 140–144.

[2]"The Global Giants," *The Wall Street Journal* (September 22, 1989), pp. R13–R23.

[3]This and subsequent example from Lennie Copeland and Lewis Griggs, *Going International* (New York: New American Library, 1985), p. xvi.

[4]*Workforce 2000* (Indianapolis: The Hudson Institute, 1987). For a recent update, see Gilbert Fuchberg, "Many Businesses Responding Too Slowly to Rapid Work Force Shifts, Study Says," *The Wall Street Journal* (July 20, 1990), pp. 31, 33.

[5]For a good overview, see Nancy J. Adler, *International Dimensions of Organizational Behavior* (Boston: Kent, 1986).

[6]See Chapter 19, "Managing in an International Arena," in John R. Schermerhorn, Jr., *Management for Productivity,* Third Edition (New York: John Wiley, 1989).

[7]Alvin Toffler, *The Third Wave* (New York: William Morrow, 1980), p. 320.

[8]Sonia Nazario, "Boom and Despair," *The Wall Street Journal* (September 22, 1989), pp. R26–R27.

[9]Adler, op. cit., p. 10).

[10]Joann S. Lublin, "Grappling with the Expatriate Issue," *The Wall Street Journal* (December 11, 1989), p. B1.

[11]Adler, op. cit., pp. 192–194. See also Rosalie Tung, "Expatriate Assignments: Enhancing Success and Minimizing Failure," *Academy of Management Executive* (May 1987), pp. 117–126.

[12]Adler, op. cit., pp. 198–212; Nancy J. Adler, "Reentry: Managing Cross-Cultural Transitions," *Group and Organization Studies,* Vol. 6, No. 3 (1981), pp. 341–356.

[13]A classic work here is Benjamin Lee Whorf, *Language, Thought and Reality* (New York: John Wiley, 1956), p. 116.

[14]The classic work here and the source of our examples is Edward T. Hall, *The Silent Language* (New York: Anchor Books, 1959).

[15]Once again, Edward T. Hall's book *The Hidden Dimension* (New York: Anchor Books, 1969) is a classic reference and the source of our examples.

[16]The classic work is Max Weber, *The Protestant Ethic and the Spirit of Capitalism* (New York: Scribner, 1930).

[17]Geert Hofstede, *Culture's Consequences: International Differences in Work-Related Values,* abridged edition (Beverly Hills: Sage, 1984).

[18]Geert Hofstede and Michael H. Bond, "The Confucius Connection: From Culture Roots to Economic Growth," *Organizational Dynamics,* Vol. 16 (1988), pp. 4–21.

[19]Adler, op. cit.

[20]Adler, op. cit., p. 63.

[21]Adler, op. cit, p. 67.

[22]David A. Ricks, *Big Business Blunders* (Homewood, IL: Dow Jones-Irwin, 1983).

[23]See Geert Hofstede, "Motivation, Leadership and Organization: Do American Theories Apply Abroad?" *Organizational Dynamics* (Summer 1980), pp. 42–63; Nancy Adler, op. cit., pp. 123–148.

[24]Fritz Rieger and Durhane Wong-Rieger, "Strategies of International Airlines as Influenced by Industry, Societal and Corporate Culture," *Proceedings of the Administrative Sciences Association of Canada,* Vol. 6, Part 8 (1985), pp. 129–141.

[25]Adler, op. cit., pp. 135–136.

[26]Based on Arvind Phatak, *International Dimensions of Management* (Boston: Kent, 1983), pp. 67–87, and Roen, op. cit., pp. 307–343.

[27]William Ouchi, *Theory Z: How American Businesses Can Meet the Japanese Challenge* (Reading, MA: Addison-Wesley, 1981); Richard Tanner and Anthony Athos, *The Art of Japanese Management* (New York: Simon & Schuster, 1981).

[28]Jerry Sullivan and Richard B. Peterson, "Japanese Management Theories: A Research Agenda," pp. 255–275, in Benjamin A. Prasad, *Advances in International Comparative Management,* Vol. 4 (Greenwich, CT: JAI Press, 1989).

[29]James R. Lincoln, "Employee Work Attitudes and Management Practice in the U.S. and Japan: Evidence from a Large Comparative Survey," *California Management Review,* Vol. XX (Fall 1989), pp. 89–106.

## CHAPTER 4

[1]Melvin Blumberg and Charles D. Pringle, "The Missing Opportunity in Organizational Research: Some Implications for a Theory of Work Performance," *Academy of Management Review,* Vol. 7 (1982), pp. 560–569.

[2]See Thomas N. Martin, John R. Schermerhorn, Jr., and Lars L. Larson, "Motivational Consequences of a Supportive Work Environment," *Advances in Motivation and Achievement: Motivation Enhancing Environment,* Vol. 6 (Greenwich, CT: JAI Press, 1989), pp. 179–214.

[3]See Lawrence H. Peters, Edward J. O'Connor, and Joe R. Eulberg, "Situational Constraints: Sources, Consequences, and Future Considerations," in Kendreth M. Rowland and Gerald R. Ferris, eds., *Research in Personnel and Human Resources Management,* Vol. 3 (Greenwich, CT: JAI Press, 1985).

[4]*The New York Times* (April 10, 1990); "Hudson Institute Work Force 2000," *The Wall Street Journal* (May 9, 1989), p. A-6.

[5]See G. N. Powell, *Women and Men in Management* (Beverly Hills, CA: Sage Publications, 1988); T. W. Mangione, "Turnover—Some Psychological and Demographic Correlates," in R. P. Quinn and T. W. Mangione, eds., *The 1969–70 Survey of Working Conditions* (Ann Arbor: University of Michigan Survey Research Center, 1973); R. Marsh and H. Mannari, "Organizational Commitment and Turnover: A Predictive Study," *Administrative Science Quarterly* (March 1977), pp. 57–75; R. J. Flanagan, G. Strauss, and L. Ulman, "Worker Discontent and Work Discontent and Work Place Behavior," *Industrial Relations* (May 1974), pp. 101–23; K. R. Garrison and P. M. Muchinsky, "Attitudinal and Biographical Predictions of Incidental Absenteeism," *Journal of Vocational Behavior* (April 1977), pp. 221–30; G. Johns, "Attitudinal and Nonattitudinal Predictions of Two Forms of Absence from Work," *Organizational Behavior and Human Performance* (December 1978), pp. 431–44; R. T. Keller, "Predicting Absenteeism from Prior Absenteeism, Attitudinal Factors, and Nonattitudinal Factors," *Journal of Applied Psychology* (August 1983), pp. 536–40.

[6]"Word Choice Can Shape Sexual Bias," *Lubbock Avalanche Journal* (December 31, 1989).

[7]Larry L. Cummings and Donald P. Schwab, *Performance in Organizations: Determinants and Appraisal* (Glenview, IL: Scott, Foresman, 1973), p. 8.

[8]Milton Rokeach, *The Nature of Human Values* (New York: Free Press, 1973).

[9]Gordon Allport, Philip E. Vernon, and Gardner Lindzey, *Study of Values* (Boston: Houghton Mifflin, 1931).

[10]Bruce M. Meglino, Elizabeth C. Ravlin, and Cheryl L. Adkins, "Value Congruence and Satisfaction with a Leader: An Examination of the Role of Interaction," unpublished manuscript (1990), University of South Carolina, pp. 8–9.

[11]Adapted from Joseph A. Raelin, "The 60's Kids in the Corporation: More Than 'Daydream Believers'," *Academy of Management Executive,* Vol. 1 (1987), pp. 21–30; Joseph A. Raelin, *Clash of Cultures* (Cambridge, MA: Harvard University Press, 1986).

[12]Ibid.

[13]Meglino, Ravlin, and Adkins, p. 2.

[14]Daniel Yankelovich, *New Rules! Searching for Self-fulfillment in a World Turned Upside Down* (New York: Random House, 1981); Daniel Yankelovich, Hans Zetterberg, Burkhard Strumpel, and Michael Shanks, *Work and Human Values: An International Report on Jobs in the 1980s and 1990s* (Aspen, CO: Aspen Institute for Humanistic Studies, 1983).

[15]See Martin Fishbein and Icek Ajzen, *Belief, Attitude, Intention and Behavior: An Introduction to Theory and Research* (Reading, MA: Addison-Wesley, 1975).

[16]Itzhak Harpaz, "The Importance of Work Goals: An International Perspective," *Journal of International Business Studies,* Vol. 21, No. 1 (1990), pp. 76–93.

[17]Leon Festinger, *A Theory of Cognitive Dissonance* (Palo Alto, CA: Stanford University Press, 1957).

[18]Peter Nulty, "America's Toughest Bosses," *Fortune* (February 27, 1989), pp. 40–52.

[19]Daniel J. Levinson, *The Seasons of a Man's Life* (New York: Alfred A. Knopf, 1978).

[20]Chris Argyris, *Personality and Organization* (New York: Harper & Row, 1957).

[21]J. B. Rotter, "Generalized Expectancies for Internal versus External Control of Reinforcement," *Psychological Monographs,* Vol. 80 (1966), pp. 1–28.

[22]Don Hellriegel, John W. Slocum, Jr., and Richard W. Woodman, *Organizational Behavior,* Fifth Edition (St. Paul: West, 1989), p. 46.

[23]Abstracted from J. Kotkin, "Mr. Iacocca, Meet Mr. Honda," *Inc.* (November 1986), pp. 37–40.

[24]Raymond G. Hunt, Frank J. Krzystofiak, James R. Meindl, and Abdalla M. Yousry, "Cognitive Style and Decision Making," in *Organizational Behavior and Human Decision Processes,* Vol. 44, No. 3 (1989), pp. 436–453.

[25]For additional work on problem-solving styles, see Ferdinand A. Gul, "The Joint and Moderating Role of Personality and Cognitive Style on Decision Making," *The Accounting Review* (April 1984), pp. 264–77; Brian H. Kleiner, "The Interrelationship of Jungian Modes of Mental Functioning with Organizational Factors: Implications for Management Development," *Human Relations* (November 1983), pp. 997–1012; James L. McKenney and Peter G. W. Keen, "How Managers' Minds Work," *Harvard Business Review* (May–June 1974), pp. 79–90.

[26]See Thomas Moore, "Personality Tests Are Back," *Fortune* (March 30, 1987), pp. 74–82.

[27]Niccolo Machiavelli, *The Prince,* George Bull, trans. (Middlesex: Penguin, 1961).

[28]Richard Christie and Florence L. Geis, *Studies in Machiavellianism* (New York: Academic Press, 1970).

[29]Adapted from R. W. Bortner, "A Short Scale: A Potential Measure of Pattern A Behavior," *Journal of Chronic Diseases,* Vol. 22 (1969). Used by permission.

[30]See Meyer Friedman and Ray Roseman, *Type A Behavior and Your Heart* (New York: Alfred A. Knopf, 1974). For another view, see Walter Kiechel III, "Attack of the Obsessive Managers," *Fortune* (February 16, 1987), pp. 127–128.

[31]See Andrew Kakabodse and Gill McWilliam, "Superpowers' Superwomen," *Management Today* (September 1987), pp. 73–74.

[32]Barry Z. Posner, James M. Kouzes, and Warren H. Schmidt, "Shared Values Make a Difference: An Empirical Test of Corporate Culture," *Human Resource Management,* Vol. 24 (Fall 1985), pp. 293–309.

[33]From *Values Clarification: A Handbook of Practical Strategies for Teachers,* by Sidney Simon, Leland Howe, and Howard Kirschenbaum. Copyright 1972 by Hart Publishing Co., Inc. Used with permission.

[34]John M. Champion and John H. James, *Critical Incidents in Management,* 5th Ed. © Richard D. Irwin, Inc., 1985, pp. 218–219. All rights reserved. Used with permission.

## CHAPTER 5

[1]For a good review article that identifies the need for more integration among motivation theories, see Terrence R. Mitchell, "Motivation—New Directions for Theory, Research and Practice," *Academy of Management Review,* Vol. 7 (January 1982), pp. 80–88.

[2]Lyman W. Porter, "Job Attitudes in Management: II. Perceived Importance of Needs as a Function of Job Level," *Journal of Applied Psychology,* Vol. 47 (April 1963), pp. 141–148.

[3]Douglas T. Hall and Khalil E. Nougaim, "An Examination of Maslow's Need Hierarchy in an Organizational Setting," *Organization Behavior and Human Performance,* Vol. 3 (1968), pp. 12–35.

[4]Lyman W. Porter, "Job Attitudes in Management: IV. Perceived Deficiencies in Need Fulfillment as a Function of Size of Company," *Journal of Applied Psychology,* Vol. 47 (December 1963), pp. 386–397.

[5]John M. Ivancevich, "Perceived Need Satisfactions of Domestic Versus Overseas Managers," Vol. 54 (August 1969), pp. 274–278.

[6]Mahmoud A. Wahba and Lawrence G. Bridwell, "Maslow Reconsidered: A Review of Research on the Need Hierarchy Theory," *Academy of Management Proceedings* (1974), pp. 514–520; Edward E. Lawler III and J. Lloyd Suttle, "A Causal Correlational Test of the Need Hierarchy Concept," *Organizational Behavior and Human Performance,* Vol. 7 (1973), pp. 265–287.

[7]See Clayton P. Alderfer, "An Empirical Test of a New Theory of Human Needs," *Organizational Behavior and Human Performance,* Vol. 4 (1969), pp. 142–175; Clayton P. Alderfer, *Existence, Relatedness, and Growth* (New York: Free Press, 1972); Benjamin Schneider and Clayton P. Alderfer, "Three Studies of Need Satisfaction in Organization," *Administrative Science Quarterly,* Vol. 18 (1973), pp. 489–505.

[8]Lane Tracy, "A Dynamic Living Systems Model of Work Motivation," *Systems Research,* Vol. 1 (1984), pp. 191–203; John Rauschenberger, Neal Schmidt, and John E. Hunter, "A Test of the Need Hierarchy Concept by a Markov Model of Change in Need Strength," *Administrative Science Quarterly,* Vol. 25 (1980) pp. 654–670.

[9]Clayton P. Alderfer and R. A. Guzzo, "Life Experiences and Adults" Enduring Strength of Desires in Organizations," *Administrative Science Quarterly,* Vol. 24 (1979), pp. 347–361.

[10]Sources pertinent to this discussion are David C. McClelland, *The Achieving Society* (New York: Van Nostrand, 1961); David C. McClelland, "Business, Drive and National Achievement," *Harvard Business Review,* Vol. 40 (July–August 1962), pp. 99–112; David C. McClelland, "That Urge to Achieve," *Think* (November–December 1966), pp. 19–32; G. H. Litwin and R. A. Stringer, *Motivation and Organizational Climate* (Boston: Division of Research, Harvard Business School, 1966), pp. 18–25.

[11]George Harris, "To Know Why Men Do What They Do: A Conversation with David C. McClelland," *Psychology Today,* Vol. 4 (January 1971), pp. 35–39.

[12]P. Miron and D. C. McClelland, "The Impact of Achievement Motivation Training on Small Businesses," *California Management Review* (Summer 1979), pp. 13–28.

[13]David C. McClelland and David H. Burnham, "Power Is the Great Motivator," *Harvard Business Review,* Vol. 54 (March–April 1976), pp. 100–110; David C. McClelland and Richard E. Boyatzis, "Leadership Motive Pattern and Long-Term Success in Management," *Journal of Applied Psychology,* Vol. 67 (1982), pp. 737–743.

[14]Charles M. Kelly, "The Interrelationship of Ethics and Power in Today's Organizations," *Organizational Dynamics,* Vol. 5 (Summer 1987); Christopher Farrell, "Gutfreund Gives Salmon's Young Lions More Power," *Business Week,* Vol. 32 (October 20, 1986); Jolie Solomon, "Heirs Apparent to Chief Executives Often Trip Over Prospect of Power," *The Wall Street Journal,* Vol. 29 (March 24, 1987).

[15]The complete two-factor theory is well explained by Herzberg and his associates in Frederick Herzberg, Bernard Mausner, and Barbara Bloch Snyderman, *The Motivation to Work,* Second Edition (New York: John Wiley, 1967); and Frederick Herzberg, "One More Time: How Do You Motivate Employees?" *Harvard Business Review,* Vol. 46 (January–February 1968), pp. 53–62.

[16]See Robert J. House and Lawrence A. Wigdor, "Herzberg's Dual-Factor Theory of Job Satisfaction and Motivation: A Review of the Evidence and a Criticism," *Personnel Psychology,* Vol. 20 (Winter 1967), pp. 369–389; and Steven Kerr, Anne Harlan, and Ralph Stogdill, "Preference for Motivator and Hygiene Factors in a Hypothetical Interview Situation," *Personnel Psychology,* Vol. 27 (Winter 1974), pp. 109–124.

[17]See, for example, J. Stacy Adams, "Toward an Understanding of Inequity," *Journal of Abnormal and Social Psychology,* Vol. 67 (1963), pp. 422–436; and J. Stacy Adams, "Inequity in Social Exchange," in L. Berkowitz, ed., *Advances in Experimental Social Psychology,* Vol. 2 (New York: Academic Press, 1965), pp. 267–300.

[18]For an excellent review, see Richard T. Mowday, "Equity Theory Predictions of Behavior in Organizations," in Richard M. Steers and Lyman W. Porter, eds., *Motivation and Work Behavior,* 4th Ed. (New York: McGraw-Hill, 1987), pp. 89–110.

[19]Victor H. Vroom, *Work and Motivation* (New York: John Wiley, 1964).

[20]Gerald R. Salancik and Jeffrey Pfeffer, "A Social Information Processing Approach to Job Atti-

tudes and Task Design," *Administrative Science Quarterly,* Vol. 23 (June 1978), pp. 224–253.

[21]Strictly speaking, Vroom's treatment of instrumentality would allow it to vary from −1 to +1. We use the probability definition here and the 0 to +1 range for pedagogical purposes. This connection remains consistent with the basic notion of instrumentality.

[22]Terence R. Mitchell, "Expectancy Models of Job Satisfaction, Occupational Preference and Effort: A Theoretical, Methodological, and Empirical Appraisal," *Psychological Bulletin,* Vol. 81 (1974), pp. 1053–1077; Mahmoud A. Wahba and Robert J. House, "Expectancy Theory in Work and Motivation: Some Logical and Methodological Issues," *Human Relations,* Vol. 27 (January 1974), pp. 121–147; Terry Connolly, "Some Conceptual and Methodological Issues in Expectancy Models of Work Performance Motivation," *Academy of Management Review,* Vol. 1 (October 1976), pp. 37–47; Terence Mitchell, "Expectancy–Value Models in Organizational Psychology," in N. Feather, ed., *Expectancy, Incentive and Action* (New York: Erlbaum and Associates, 1980).

[23]Lyman W. Porter and Edward E. Lawler III, *Managerial Attitudes and Performance* (Homewood, IL: Richard D. Irwin, 1968).

[24]Mitchell, "Expectancy–Value Models in Organizational Psychology."

[25]Porter and Lawler, op. cit., p. 17.

[26]This integrated model is not based only on the Porter and Lawler model but is consistent with the kind of comprehensive approach suggested by Evans in a recent review. See Martin G. Evans, "Organizational Behavior: The Central Role of Motivation in J. G. Hunt and J. D. Blair, eds., *1986 Yearly Review of Management of the Journal of Management,* Vol. 12 (1986), pp. 203–222.

[27]Adapted from a case assignment prepared by Lee Neely for Professor James G. Hunt, Southern Illinois University at Carbondale. The case appears in John E. Dittrich and Robert A. Zawacki, eds., *People and Organizations: Cases in Management and Organizational Behavior,* pp. 126–128. © Business Publications, 1981. All rights reserved. Used by permission.

## CHAPTER 6

[1]For good overviews, see W. E. Scott, Jr., and P. M. Podsakoff, *Behavioral Principles in the Practice of Management* (New York: John Wiley, 1985); Fred Luthans and Robert Kreitner, *Organizational Behavior Modification and Beyond* (Glenview, IL: Scott, Foresman, 1985).

[2]For some of B. F. Skinner's work, see *Walden Two* (New York: Macmillan, 1948), *Science and Human Behavior* (New York: Macmillan, 1953), and *Contingencies of Reinforcement* (New York: Appleton-Century-Crofts, 1969).

[3]Edward L. Deci, *Intrinsic Motivation* (New York: Plenum Press, 1975), pp. 7–8.

[4]See Robert Kreitner and Fred Luthans, "A Social Learning Approach to Behavioral Management: Radical Behaviorists 'Mellowing Out'," *Organizational Dynamics,* Vol. 13 (Autumn 1984), pp. 47–65.

[5]See, for example, Ann M. Morrison, Randall P. White, and Ellen Van Velsor, *Breaking the Glass Ceiling* (Reading, MA: Addison-Wesley, 1987).

[6]E. L. Thorndike, *Animal Intelligence* (New York: Macmillan, 1911), p. 244.

[7]Based on Fred Luthans and Robert Kreitner, *Organizational Behavior Modification and Beyond* (Glenview, IL: Scott, Foresman, 1985).

[8]Both laws are stated in Keith L. Miller, *Principles of Everyday Behavior Analysis* (Monterey, CA: Brooks/Cole, 1975), p. 122.

[9]"School Tries Attendance Bonuses," *Lubbock Avalanche Journal* (January 8, 1986).

[10]J. Herman, "Effects of Bonuses for Punctuality on the Tardiness of Industrial Workers," *Journal of Applied Behavioral Analysis,* Vol. 6 (1973), pp. 563–570.

[11]"Paying Employees Not to Go to the Doctor," *Business Week* (March 21, 1983), p. 150; "Giving Goodies to the Good," *Time* (November 21, 1985), p. 98; "Incentive Plans Spur Safe Work Habits, Reducing Accidents at Some Plants," *The Wall Street Journal* (January 27, 1987), p. 1.

[12]See Lise M. Saari and Gary P. Latham, "Employee Reactions to Continuous and Variable Ratio Reinforcement Schedules Involving a Monetary Incentive," *Journal of Applied Psychology* (August 1982), pp. 506–508.

[13]Karen M. Evans, "On-the-Job Lotteries: A Low-Cost Incentive that Sparks Higher Productivity," *Compensation and Benefits Review,* Vol. 20, 4 (1988), pp. 68–74.

[14]Adapted in part from W. Clay Hamner, "Using Reinforcement Theory in Organizational Settings," in Henry L. Tosi and W. Clay Hamner, eds., *Organizational Behavior and Management: A Contingency Approach* (Chicago: St. Clair Press, 1977), pp. 388–395.

[15]Adapted from *Organizational Behavior Modification,* by Fred Luthans and Robert Kreitner. © 1975 Scott, Foresman and Company, pp. 125–126. Reprinted by permission.

[16]A. R. Korukonda and James G. Hunt, "Pat on the Back versus Kick in the Pants: An Application of Cognitive Inference to the Study of Leader Reward and Punishment Behaviors," *Group and Organization Studies,* Vol. 14, 3 (1989), pp. 299–324.

[17]Based on an example in Luthans and Kreitner, op. cit. (1975), pp. 127–129.

[18]Developed in part from Hamner, "Using Reinforcement Theory in Organizational Settings."

[19]Edwin A. Locke, "The Myths of Behavior Mod in Organizations," *Academy of Management Review,* Vol. 2 (October 1977), pp. 543–553. For a counterpoint see Jerry L. Gray, "The Myths of the Myths about Behavior Mod in Organizations: A Reply to Locke's Criticisms of Behavior Modification," *Academy of Management Review,* Vol. 4 (January 1979), pp. 121–129.

[20]Robert Kreitner, "Controversy in OBM: History, Misconceptions, and Ethics," in Lee Frederiksen, ed., *Handbook of Organizational Behavior Management* (New York: John Wiley, 1982), pp. 71–91.

[21]W. E. Scott, Jr., and P. M. Podsakoff, *Behavioral Principles in the Practice of Management* (New York: John Wiley, 1985).

[22]Also see W. Clay Hamner, "Reinforcement Theory and Contingency Management in Organizational Settings," in Richard M. Steers and Lyman W. Porters, eds., *Motivation and Work Behavior,* Fourth Edition (New York: McGraw-Hill, 1987), pp. 139–165; Fred Luthans and Robert Kreitner, *Organizational Behavior Modification and Beyond: An Operant and Social Learning Approach* (Glenview, IL: Scott, Foresman, 1985).

[23]Edward E. Lawler, *Pay and Organization Development* (Reading, MA: Addison-Wesley, 1981).

[24]For complete reviews of theory, research, and practice, see Edward E. Lawler III, *Pay and Organizational Effectiveness* (New York: McGraw-Hill, 1971); Edward E. Lawler III, *Pay and Organization Development* (Reading, MA: Addison-Wesley, 1981); Edward E. Lawler III, "The Design of Effective Reward Systems," pp. 255–271, in Jay W. Lorsch (ed.), *Handbook of Organizational Behavior* (Englewood Cliffs, NJ: Prentice-Hall, 1987).

[25]Jude T. Rich, "Reincenting America," *Compensation and Benefits Review,* Vol. 21, 2 (1989), pp. 65–68.

[26]Michael K. Mount, "Coordinating Salary Action and Performance Appraisal," in David B. Balkin and Luis R. Gomez-Mejia, eds., *New Perspectives on Compensation* (Englewood Cliffs, NJ: Prentice Hall, 1987), pp. 187–195.

[27]Jone L. Pearce, "Why Merit Pay Doesn't Work: Implications from Organization Theory," in David B. Balkin and Luis R. Gomez-Mejia, eds., *New Perspectives on Compensation* (Englewood Cliffs, NJ: Prentice-Hall, 1987), pp. 169–178; Jerry M. Newman, "Selecting Incentive Plans to Complement Organizational Strategy," in David R. Balkin and Luis R. Gomez-Mejia, eds., *New Perspectives on Compensation* (Englewood Cliffs, NJ: Prentice-Hall, 1987), pp. 214–224; Edward E. Lawler III, "Pay for Performance: Making It Work," *Compensation and Benefits Review,* Vol 21, 1 (1989), pp. 55–60.

[28]Carla O'Dell and Jerry McAdams, "The Revolution in Employee Rewards," *Compensation and Benefits Review,* Vol. 19 (May–June 1987), pp. 68–73.

[29]O'Dell and McAdams, op. cit., p. 69.

[30]Vida Gulbinas Scarpello and James Ledvinka, *Personnel/Human Resource Management: Environments and Functions* (Boston: PWS Kent, 1988), pp. 416–417; Randall S. Schuler, *Personnel and Human Resource Management,* Third Edition (St. Paul, MN: West, 1987), p. 317.

[31]Thomas Rollins, "Productivity-Based Group Incentive Plans: Powerful, but Use with Caution," *Compensation and Benefits Review,* Vol. 21, 3 (1989), p. 41.

[32]Rollins, op. cit., p. 43.

[33]Theresa M. Welbourne and Luis R. Gomez-Mejia, "Gainsharing Revisited," *Compensation and Benefit Review,* Vol. 20, 4, (1988), pp. 19–28.

[34]O'Dell and McAdams, op. cit. (May–June 1987), pp. 70–71; Rollins, op. cit. (1989), pp. 39–50.

[35]Scarpello and Ledvinka, op. cit. (1988), pp. 449–450.

[36]Developed from Stuart C. Feedman, "Performance-Based Pay: A Convenience Store Case Study," *Personnel Journal,* Vol. 64 (July 1985), pp. 30–34.

## CHAPTER 7

[1]Ramon J. Aldag and Arthur P. Brief, "The Intrinsic–Extrinsic Dichotomy: Toward Conceptual Clarity," *Academy of Management Review,* Vol. 2 (1977), pp. 497–498.

[2]Frederick Herzberg, "One More Time: How Do You Motivate Employees?" *Harvard Business Review,* Vol. 46 (January–February 1968), pp. 53–62.

[3]For a complete description and review of the research, see J. Richard Hackman and Greg R. Oldham, *Work Redesign* (Reading, MA: Addison-Wesley, 1980).

[4]Reported in "You See the Package from Beginning to End," *Business Week* (May 16, 1983), p. 103.

[5]Lisa R. Berlinger, William H. Glick, and Robert C. Rodgers, "Job Enrichment and Performance Improvement," in John P. Campbell, Richard J. Campbell, and associates, *Productivity in Organizations* (San Francisco: Jossey-Bass, 1988), pp. 219–254.

[6]This case is adapted from J. Richard Hackman, Greg Oldham, Robert Janson, and Kenneth Purdy, "A New Strategy for Job Enrichment," *California Management Review,* Vol. 17 (1975), pp. 51–71.

[7]Paul J. Champagne and Curt Tausky, "When Job Enrichment Doesn't Pay," *Personnel,* Vol. 3 (January–February 1978), pp. 30–40.

[8]William W. Winpisinger, "Job Enrichment: A Union View," in Karl O. Magnusen, ed., *Organizational Design, Development and Behavior: A Situational View* (Glenview, IL: Scott, Foresman, 1977), p. 222.

[9]See William A. Pasmore, "Overcoming the Roadblocks to Work-Restructuring Efforts," *Organizational Dynamics,* Vol. 10 (1982), pp. 54–67; Hackman and Oldham, op. cit.

[10]Denis D. Umstot, Terence R. Mitchell, and Cecil H. Bell, Jr., "Goal Setting and Job Enrichment: An Integrated Approach to Job Design," *Academy of Management Review,* Vol. 3 (October 1978), p. 868.

[11]See Edwin A. Locke, Karyll N. Shaw, Lise M. Saari, and Gary P. Latham, "Goal Setting and Task Performance: 1969–1980," *Psychological Bulletin,* Vol. 90 (July–November 1981), pp. 125–152. See also Gary P. Latham and Edwin A. Locke, "Goal Setting—A Motivational Technique That Works," *Organizational Dynamics,* Vol. 8 (Autumn 1979), pp. 68–80; Gary P. Latham and Timothy P. Steele, "The Motivational Effects of Participation versus Goal-Setting on Performance," *Academy of Management Journal,* Vol. 26 (1983), pp. 406–417; Miriam Erez and Frederick H. Kanfer, "The Role of Goal Acceptance in Goal Setting and Task Performance," *Academy of Management Review,* Vol. 8 (1983), pp. 454–463.

[12]Craig C. Pinder, *Work Motivation Theory, Issues, and Applications* (Dallas, TX: Scott, Foresman, 1984), p. 169.

[13]Henry L. Tosi, John R. Rizzo, and Stephen J. Carroll, *Managing Organizational Behavior,* Second Edition (New York: Harper & Row, 1990), p. 323.

[14]For a good review of MBO, see Anthony P. Raia, *Managing by Objectives* (Glenview, IL: Scott, Foresman, 1974); Steven Kerr summarizes the criticisms well in "Overcoming the Dysfunctions of MBO," *Management by Objectives,* Vol. 5, No. 1 (1976).

[15]E. A. Locke and G. P. Latham, *Goal Setting: A Motivational Technique that Works!* (Englewood Cliffs, NJ: Prentice-Hall, 1984), pp. 27–40.

[16]Fred Luthans, *Organizational Behavior,* Fifth Edition (New York: McGraw-Hill, 1989), p. 282.

[17]Pinder, op. cit (1984), pp. 175–176.

[18]J. A. Breaugh, "The 12-Hour Workday: Differing Employee Reactions," *Personnel Psychology,* Vol. 36 (1983), pp. 277–88; S. Ronen and S. B. Primps, "The Compressed Work Week as Organizational Change: Behaviors and Attitudinal Outcomes," *Academy of Management Review,* Vol. 6 (1981), pp. 61–74; Janina C. Latack and Lawrence W. Foster, "Implementation of Compressed Work Schedules: Participation and Job Redesign as Critical Factors for Employee Acceptance," *Personnel Psychology,* Vol. 38 (1985), pp. 75–92.

[19]J. C. Latack and L. W. Foster, "Implementation of Compressed Work Schedules: Participation and Job Redesign as Critical Factors for Employee Acceptance," *Personnel Psychology,* Vol. 38 (1985), pp. 75–92.

[20]Cohen and Gadon, op. cit., pp. 38–46. See also Jon L. Pierce and John W. Newstrom, "Toward a Conceptual Clarification of Employee Responses to Flexible Working Hours: A Work Adjustment Approach," *Journal of Management,* Vol. 6 (1980), pp. 117–134.

[21]*Management World* (July–August 1988), pp. 14–15.

[22]Allan R. Cohen and Herman Gadon, *Alternative Work Schedules: Integrating Individual and Organizational Needs* (Reading, MA: Addison-Wesley, 1978).

[23]M. Creger, "Flexitime Continues to Edge Upwards." *Management World* (July–August 1988), p. 15.

[24]Herbert G. Heneman III, Donald P. Schwab, John A. Fossum and Lee D. Dyer, *Personnel/Human Resource Management,* Fourth Edition (Homewood, Ill.: Irwin, 1989), pp. 399–401.

[25]Randall S. Schuler, *Personnel and Human Resource Management,* Third Edition (St. Paul, MN: West, 1987), p. 464.

[26]*Working Woman* (February 1989), pp. 46, 48, 52; C. Ansberry, "When Employees Work at Home, Management Problems Often Arise," *The Wall Street Journal* (April 20, 1987), p. 21.

[27]Adapted from Norm Alster, "What Flexible Workers Can Do," *Fortune* (February 13, 1989), p. 62.

## CHAPTER 8

[1]Harold J. Leavitt, "Suppose We Took Groups Seriously," in Eugene L. Cass and Frederick G. Zimmer, eds., *Man and Work in Society* (New York: Van Nostrand Reinhold, 1975), pp. 67–77.

[2]See Marvin E. Shaw, *Group Dynamics: The Psychology of Small Group Behavior,* Second Edition, (New York: McGraw-Hill, 1976).

[3]See Bib Latané, Kipling Williams, and Stephen Harkins, "Many Hands Make Light the Work: The Causes and Consequences of Social Loafing," *Journal of Personality and Social Psychology,* Vol. 37 (1978), pp. 822–832; E. Weldon and G. M. Gargano, "Cognitive Effort in Additive Task Groups: The Effects of Shared Responsibility on the Quality of Multiattribute Judgments," *Organizational Behavior and Human Decision Processes,* Vol. 36 (1985), pp. 348–361.

[4]David M. Herold, "The Effectiveness of Work Groups," in Steven Kerr, ed., *Organizational Behavior* (New York, John Wiley, 1979), p. 95.

[5]Edgar H. Schein, *Organizational Psychology,* Second Edition (Englewood Cliffs, N.J.: Prentice Hall, 1970), p. 81.

[6]Developed from Rensis Likert, *New Patterns of Management* (New York: McGraw-Hill, 1961), pp. 166–169.

[7]For further insights see J. Richard Hackman, "The Design of Work Teams," in Jay W. Lorsch, ed., *Handbook of Organizational Behavior* (Englewood Cliffs, NJ: Prentice-Hall, 1987), pp. 343–357.

[8]Linda N. Jewell and H. Joseph Reitz, *Group Effectiveness in Organizations* (Glenview, IL: Scott, Foresman, 1981), pp. 149, 150.

[9]This discussion is developed from Herold, "The Effectiveness of Work Groups," pp. 99–103.

[10]William C. Schutz, *FIRO: A Three-Dimensional Theory of Interpersonal Behavior* (New York: Rinehart & Co., 1958).

[11]William C. Schutz, "The Interpersonal Underworld," *Harvard Business Review,* Vol. 36, No. 4 (July–August, 1958), p. 130.

[12]E. J. Thomas and C. F. Fink, "Effects of Group Size," in Larry L. Cummings and William E. Scott, eds., *Readings in Organizational and Human Performance* (Homewood, IL: Richard D. Irwin, 1969), pp. 394–408.

[13]Shaw, *op. cit.*

[14]George C. Homans, *The Human Group* (New York: Harcourt Brace, 1950).

[15]Burt Scanlan and J. Bernard Keys, *Management and Organizational Behavior, Second Edition (New York: John Wiley, 1983), p. 294.*

[16]William F. Dowling, "Job Redesign on the Assembly Line: Farewell to Blue-Collar Blues," *Organizational Dynamics* (Autumn 1973), pp. 51–67.

[17]See Richard E. Walton, "How to Counter Alienation in the Plant," *Harvard Business Review* (November–December 1972), pp. 70–81; Richard E. Walton, "Work Innovations at Topeka: After Six Years," *Journal of Applied Behavior Science,* Vol. 13 (1977), pp. 422–431; Richard E. Walton, "The Topeka Work System: Optimistic Visions, Pessimistic Hypotheses, and Reality," in Zager and Rosow, eds., *The Innovative Organization,* Chap. 11.

[18]Thomas G. Cummings and Edgar F. Huse, *Organization Development and Change,* Fourth Edition (St. Paul: West, 1990), p. 301.

[19]See Kenichi Ohmae, "Quality Control Circles: They Work and Don't Work," *The Wall Street Journal,* March 29, 1982, p. 16; Robert P. Steel, Anthony J. Mento, Benjamin L. Dilla, Nestor K. Ovalle, and Russell F. Lloyd, "Factors Influencing the Success and Failure of Two Quality Circles Programs," *Journal of Management,* Vol. 11, no. 1 (1985), pp. 99–119; Edward E. Lawler III and Susan A. Mohrman, "Quality Circles: After the Honeymoon," *Organizational Dynamics,* Vol. 15, No. 4 (1987), pp. 42–54.

[20]Example from "Rounding Up Quality at USAA," *AIDE Magazine* (Fall 1983), p. 24.

[21]Example from "Time to Toss Tradition?" *Enterprise* (Fall 1989), pp. 35–39.

[22]Cummings and Huse, op. cit., p. 268.

[23]Exercise adapted by Roy J. Lewicki from *FIRO: A Three Dimensional Theory of Interpersonal Behavior,* by William C. Schultz (New York: Rinehart & Company, 1958).

## CHAPTER 9

[1]For a good discussion of team building, see William D. Dyer, *Team Building,* Second Edition (Reading, MA: Addison-Wesley, 1987).

[2]J. Steven Heinen and Eugene Jacobson, "A Model of Task Group Development in Complex Organization and a Strategy of Implementation," *Academy of Management Review,"* Vol. 1 (Oct. 1976), pp. 98–111.

[3]Developed from a discussion by Edgar H. Schein, *Process Consultation* (Reading, MA: Addison-Wesley, 1969), pp. 32–37; Schein, *Process Consultation: Volume I* (1988), pp. 40–49.

[4]This example is from Roger Harrison, "When Power Conflicts Trigger Team Spirit," *European Business* (Spring 1972), pp. 57–65.

[5]This incident was obtained from Dorothy N. Harlow and Jean J. Hanke, *Behavior in Organizations* (Boston: Little, Brown, 1975), pp. 244–245. The original source cannot be located.

[6]See Daniel C. Feldman, "The Development and Enforcement of Group Norms," *Academy of Management Review,* Vol. 9 (1984), pp. 47–53.

[7]Robert F. Allen and Saul Pilnick, Confronting the Shadow Organization: How to Select and Defeat Negative Norms," *Organizational Dynamics* (Spring 1973), pp. 13–17. See also Alvin Zander, *Making Groups Effective* (San Francisco: Jossey-Bass, 1982), Chap. 4; Daniel C. Feldman, "The Development and Enforcement of Group Norms," *Academy of Management Review,* Vol. 9 (1984), pp. 47–53.

[8]For a good summary of research on group cohesiveness, see Marvin E. Shaw, *Group Dynamics* (New York: McGraw-Hill, 1971), pp. 110–112, p. 192.

[9]Robert F. Bales, "Task Roles and Social Roles in Problem-Solving Groups," in Eleanor E. Maccoby, Theodore M. Newcomb, and E. L. Hartley, eds., *Readings in Social Psychology* (New York: Holt, Rinehart & Winston, 1958).

[10]This discussion is developed from Schein, *Process Consultation:* Volume I, Second Edition (Reading, MA: Addison-Wesley, 1988), pp. 49–53; Rensis Likert, *New Patterns of Management* (New York: McGraw-Hill, 1961), pp. 166–169.

[11]Ibid.

[12]This discussion is developed from Fred E. Fiedler, *A Theory of Leadership Productivity* (New York: McGraw-Hill, 1967); Alex Bavelas, "Communication Patterns in Task-Oriented Groups," *Journal of the Accoustical Society of America,* vol. 22 (1950), pp. 725–730. See also "Research on Communication Networks," as summarized in Shaw, *Group Dynamics,* pp. 137–153.

[13]This discussion is developed from Edgar H. Schein, *Process Consultation: Volume I,* Second Edition (1988), pp. 69–75.

[14]Ibid., p. 73.

[15]Developed from the classic article by Norman R. F. Maier, "Assets and Liabilities in Group Problem Solving," Psychological Review, Vol. 74 (1967), pp. 239–249.

[16]Jerry Harvey, "Managing Agreement in Organizations: The Abilene Paradox," *Organizational Dynamics* (Summer, 1974), pp. 63–80. Used by permission.

[17]Irving L. Janis, "Groupthink," *Psychology Today* (November 1971), pp. 43–46; Irving L. Janis, *Groupthink,* Second Edition (Boston: Houghton Mifflin, 1982). See also J. Longley and D. G. Pruitt, "Groupthink: A Critique of Janis' Theory," in L. Wheeler ed., *Review of Personality and Social Psychology* (Beverly Hills, CA: Sage, 1980); Carrie R. Leana, "A Partial Test of Janis's Groupthink Model: The Effects of Group Cohesiveness and Leader Behavior on Decision Processes," *Journal of Management,* Vol. 11, No. 1 (1985), pp. 5–18.

[18]These techniques are well described in George P. Huber, *Managerial Decision Making* (Glenview, IL: Scott, Foresman, 1980): André L. Delbec, Andrew L. Van de Ven, and David H. Gustafson, *Group Techniques for Program Planning: A Guide to Nominal Groups and Delphi Techniques* (Glenview, IL: Scott, Foresman, 1975); and William M. Fox, "Anonymity and other Keys to Successful Problem-Solving Meetings," *National Productivity Review,* Vol. 8 (Spring 1989), pp. 145–156.

[19]See Gayle W. Hill, "Group versus Individual Performance: Are $N + 1$ Heads Better than One?" *Psychological Bulletin,* Vol. 91 (1982), pp. 517–539.

[20]Schein, *Process Consultation: Volume I* (1988), pp. 106–115.

## CHAPTER 10

[1]See Richard M. Cyert and James G. March, *A Behavioral Theory of the Firm* (Englewood Cliffs, NJ: Prentice Hall, 1963). A good discussion of organizational goals is also found in Charles Perrow, *Organizational Analysis: A Sociological View* (Belmont, CA: Wadsworth, 1970) and in Richard H. Hall, "Organizational Behavior: A Sociological Perspective," in Jay W. Lorsch, ed., *Handbook of Organizational Behavior* (Englewood Cliffs, NJ: Prentice-Hall, 1987), pp. 84–95.

[2]See Richard N. Osborn, James G. Hunt, and Lawrence R. Jauch, *Organization Theory: Integrated Text and Cases* (Melbourne, FL: Krieger, 1985).

[3]H. Talcott Parsons, *Structure and Processes in Modern Societies* (New York: Free Press, 1960).

[4]See, for instance, Thomas J. Peters and Richard Waterman, Jr., *In Search of Excellence: Lessons from America's Best-Run Companies* (New York: Harper & Row, 1982).

[5]See, for instance, I. C. MacMillan and A. Meshulack, "Replacement versus Expansion: Dilemma for Mature U.S. Businesses," *Academy of Management Journal,* Vol. 26 (1983), pp. 708–726.

[6]William H. Starbuck and Paul C. Nystrom, "Designing and Understanding Organizations," in P. C. Nystrom and W. H. Starbuck, eds., *Handbook of Organizational Design: Adapting Organizations to Their Environments* (New York: Oxford University Press, 1981).

[7]See Osborn, Hunt, and Jauch, 1986, op. cit.

[8]See Paul R. Lawrence and Jay W. Lorsch, *Organization and Environment* (Homewood, IL: Irwin, 1969).

[9]For a review, see Osborn, Hunt, and Jauch, 1985, op. cit.

[10]See Paul Carroll, "IBM is Planning Another Staff Redeployment," *The Wall Street Journal* (June 27, 1988), p. 3.

[11]See Osborn, Hunt, and Jauch, 1985, op. cit.

[12]For further discussion, see J. Ivancevich, J. Donnelley, and J. Gibson, *Managing for Performance* (Plano, TX: Business Publications, 1986); Herbert Simon, Making Management Decisions, The Role of Intuition and Emotion," *Academy of Management Executive,* Vol. 1 (1987), pp. 57–64.

[13]William G. Ouchi and M. A. McGuire, "Organization Control: Two Functions," *Administrative Science Quarterly,* Vol. 20 (1977), pp. 559–569.

[14]Arlyn J. Melcher, *Structure and Process of Organizations: A Systems Approach* (Englewood Cliffs, NJ: Prentice Hall, 1976), pp. 219–223, 252.

[15]Also see Kenneth Lebich, "Big Changes and Big Brown," *Fortune* (January 18, 1988), p. 56.

[16]For a discussion, see Stephen P. Robbins, *Organization Theory: Structure, Design and Applications* Third Edition (Englewood Cliffs, NJ: Prentice Hall, 1990), pp. 420–458.

[17]This section is based on Osborn, Hunt, Jauch *Organization Theory* pp. 273–303

[18]For a good discussion of Matrix Structures see Stanley Davis, Paul Lawrence, Harvey Kolodny, and Michael Beer, *Matrix* (Reading Mass: Addison Wesley, 1977).

[19]Exercise adapted from *Mother Jones Magazine* (June 1985). Used with permission.

## CHAPTER 11

[1]R. N. Osborn, J. G. Hunt, and L. Jauch, *Organization Theory: Integrated Text and Cases* (Melbourne, FL: Krieger, 1984), pp. 123–215.

[2]See Henry Mintzberg, *Structure in Fives: Designing Effective Organizations* (Englewood Cliffs, NJ: Prentice Hall, 1983).

[3]For a comprehensive review, see W. Richard Scott, *Organizations: Rational, Natural, and Open Systems,* Second Edition (Englewood Cliffs, NJ: Prentice Hall, 1987).

[4]Max Weber, *The Theory of Social and Economic Organization,* translated by A. M. Henderson and H. T. Parsons (New York: Free Press, 1947).

[5]Tom Burns and G. M. Stalker, *The Management of Innovation* (London: Tavistock, 1961).

[6]Mintzberg, 1983, op. cit.

[7]Mintzberg, 1983, op. cit.

[8]See Osborn et al. 1984, op. cit., for an extended discussion.

[9]See Peter Clark and Ken Starkey, *Organization Transitions and Innovation-Design* (London: Pinter Publications, 1988).

[10]Ibid.

[11]See Peter M. Blau and Richard A. Schoenner, "The Structure of Organizations (New York: Basic Books, 1971).

[12]Joan Woodward, *Industrial Organization: Theory and Practice* (London: Oxford University Press, 1965).

[13]James D. Thompson, *Organization In Action* (New York: McGraw-Hill, 1967).

[14]Woodward, 1965, op. cit.

[15]For reviews, see Osborn et al, 1980, op. cit., and Louis Fry, "Technology-Structure Research: Three Critical Issues," *Academy of Management Journal,* Vol. 25 (1982), pp. 532–552.

[16]Mintzberg, 1983, op. cit.

[17]See R. N. Osborn and C. C. Baughn, "New Patterns in the Formation of U.S./Japanese Cooperative Ventures," *Columbia Journal of World Business,* Vol. 22 (1988), pp. 57–65.

[18]See John Ettlie, "Technology Drives a Marriage," *The Journal of Commerce* (Friday, March 16, 1990), p. 6.

[19]This section is based on R. N. Osborn and J. G. Hunt, "The Environment and Organization Effectiveness," *Administrative Science Quarterly,* Vol. 19 (1974), pp. 231–246, and Osborn et al, 1984, op. cit.

[20]L. R. Jauch and R. N. Osborn, "Toward an Integrated Theory of Strategy," *Academy of Management Review,* Vol. 6 (1981), 491–498; Alfred D. Chandler, *The Visible Hand: The Managerial Revolution in America* (Cambridge, MA: Bellknap, 1977); Karen Bantel and R. N. Osborn, "The Influence of Performance, Environment, and Size on Firm Strategic Clarity," working paper, Department of Management, Wayne State University, 1990.

[21]See M. Porter, *Competitive Strategy* (New York: Free Press, 1980).

[22]Raymond E. Miles and Charles C. Snow, "Fit, Failure and the Hall of Fame," *California Management Review,* Vol. 23 (1984), pp. 10–28.

[23]Adapted from Robert Quinn, *Beyond Rational Management* (New York: Jossey-Bass, 1988). Used with permission.

## CHAPTER 12

[1]E. Schein, "Organizational Culture," *American Psychologist,* Vol. 45 (1990), pp. 109–119.

[2]These examples were reported in an interview with Edgar Schein, "Corporate Culture is the Real Key to Creativity," *Business Month* (May 1989), pp. 73–74.

[3]T. Deal and A. Kennedy, *Corporate Culture* (Reading, MA: Addison-Wesley, 1982).

[4]T. Peters and R. Waterman, *In Search of Excellence* (New York: Harper & Row, 1982).

[5]G. Hofstede and M. H. Bond, "The Confucius Connection: From Cultural Roots to Economic Growth," *Organizational Dynamics,* 16(4), pp. 4–21.

[6]R. A. Cooke and D. M. Rousseau, "Behavioral Norms and Expectations: A Quantitative Approach to the Assessment of Organizational Culture," *Group and Organizational Studies,* Vol. 13 (1988), pp. 245–273.

[7]J. Martin and C. Siehl, "Organization Culture and Counterculture," *Organizational Dynamics,* Vol. 12 (1983), pp. 52–64.

[8]See Anthony F. Buono, James L. Bowditch, and John L. Lewis III, "When Cultures Collide: The Anatomy of a Merger," *Human Relations,* Vol. 38 (1985), pp. 477–500; C. A. Enz, "Value Congruity and Intraorganizational Power: A Supplement to Critical Contingencies Explanation," *Administrative Science Quarterly,* Vol. 32 (1988), pp. 284–304.

[9]Schein, op. cit., 1990.

[10]C. Gertz, *The Interpretation of Culture* (New York: Basic Books, 1973).

[11]J. M. Byer and H. M. Trice, "How an Organization's Rites Reveal Its Culture," *Organizational Dynamics* (Spring 1987), pp. 27–41.

[12]J. Martin, M. S. Feldman, M. J. Hatch, and S. B. Stikin, "The Uniqueness Paradox in Organizational Stories," *Administrative Science Quarterly,* Vol. 28 (1983), pp. 438–453.

[13]H. M. Trice and J. M. Beyer, "Studying Organizational Cultures Through Rites and Ceremonials," *Academy of Management Review,* Vol. 3 (1984), pp. 633–669.

[14]Ibid.

[15]J. S. Ott, *The Organizational Culture Perspective* (Chicago: Irwin Dorsey, 1989), p. 182.

[16]See A. L. Wilkins and N. J. Bristow, "For Successful Organization Culture, Honor Your Past," *Academy of Management Executives,* Vol. 13 (1987), pp. 221–230.

[17]See J. G. Hunt, *Toward a Leadership Paradigm Change* (Newbury Park, CA: Sage, in press); B.

Schneider and J. Rentsch, "Managing Climates and Cultures: A Futures Perspective," to appear in J. Hage, ed., *Futures of Organizations* (Lexington, MA: Lexington Books, in press).

[18]B. Keys and T. R. Miller, "The Japanese Management Theory Jungle," *Academy of Management Review,* Vol. 9 (1984), pp. 342–353; William Ouchi, *Theory Z* (Reading, MA: Addison-Wesley, 1981).

[19]Geret Hofstede, *Culture's Consequences: International Differences in Work-Related Values* (Beverly Hills, CA: Sage, 1980).

[20]Jay B. Barney, "Organizational Culture: Can It Be a Source of Sustained Competitive Advantage," *Academy of Management Review,* Vol. 11 (1986), pp. 656–665.

[21]See Ralph Killman, Mary J. Saxton, and Roy Serpa, "Issues in Understanding and Changing Culture," *California Management Review,* Vol. 28 (1986), pp. 84–96; Ralph Killman, *Beyond the Quick Fix* (San Francisco: Jossey-Bass, 1984); Dennis Keale, "Working at IBM: Intense Loyalty in a Rigid Culture," *The Wall Street Journal* (April 7, 1986), pp. 21–23.

[22]R. N. Osborn and M. Jackson, "Leaders, Riverboat Gamblers or Purposeful Unintended Consequences in the Management of Complex, Dangerous Technologies," *Academy of Management Journal,* Vol. 31 (1988), pp. 924–947.

[23]This discussion is based on the work of Jeffrey Sonnenfeld as reported by Carol Hymowitz, "Which Corporate Culture Fits You?" *The Wall Street Journal* (July 17, 1989), p. B1.

[24]This discussion is based on John B. Cullen, Bart Victor, and Carroll Stephens, "An Ethical Weather Report: Assessing the Organization's Ethical Climate," *Organizational Dynamics* (Winter 1990), pp. 50–63.

[25]Adapted from Victor and Cullen, 1986. Used with permission.

## CHAPTER 13

[1]For an excellent overview, see George P. Huber, *Managerial Decision Making* (Glenview, IL: Scott, Foresman, 1980).

[2]Subsequent discussion is adapted with permission from John R. Schermerhorn, Jr., *Management for Productivity* (New York: John Wiley, 1989), pp. 70–71. Copyright © 1989 John Wiley & Sons. Reprinted by permission of John Wiley & Sons, Inc.

[3]Alan L. Otten, "Ethics on the Job: Companies Alert Employees to Potential Dilemmas," *The Wall Street Journal* (July 14, 1986), p. 17.

[4]Developed in part from ibid. and Schermerhorn, op. cit., pp. 603–610.

[5]Saul W. Gellerman, "Why 'Good' Managers Make Bad Ethical Choices," *Harvard Business Review,* Vol. 64 (July–August 1986), pp. 85–90. See also Barbara Ley Toffler, *Tough Choices: Managers Talk Ethics* (New York: Wiley, 1986).

[6]Developed from Trish Hall, "When Budding MBAs Try to Save Kool-Aid, Original Ideas Are Scarce," *The Wall Street Journal* (November 26, 1986), p. 31.

[7]Henry Mintzberg, "Planning on the Left Side and Managing on the Right," *Harvard Business Review,* Vol. 54 (July–August 1976), pp. 51–63.

[8]Weston H. Agor, *Intuition in Organizations* (Newbury Park, CA: Sage, 1989).

[9]The classic work in this area is found in a series of articles by D. Kahneman and A. Tversky: "Subjective Probability: A Judgement of Representativeness," *Cognitive Psychology,* Vol. 3 (1972), pp. 430–454; "On the Psychology of Prediction," *Psychological Review,* Vol. 80 (1973), pp. 237–251; "Prospect Theory: An Analysis of Decision Under Risk," *Econometrica,* Vol. 47 (1979), pp. 263–291; "Psychology of Preferences," *Scientific American* (1982), pp. 161–173; "Choices, Values, Frames," *American Psychologist,* Vol. 39 (1984), pp. 341–350.

[10]Definition and subsequent discussion based on Max H. Bazerman, *Judgment in Managerial Decision Making,* Second Edition (New York: John Wiley, 1990), pp. 11–39.

[11]Barry M. Staw, "The Escalation of Commitment to a Course of Action," *Academy of Management Review,* Vol. 6 (1981), pp. 577–587; Barry M. Staw and Jerry Ross, "Knowing When to Pull the Plug" *Harvard Business Review,* Vol. 65 (March–April 1987), pp. 68–74. See also Glen Whyte, "Escalating Commitment to a Course of Action: A Reinterpretation," *Academy of Management Review,* Vol. 11 (1986), pp. 311–321.

[12]Bazerman, op. cit., pp. 79–83.

[13]Rubin, J. Z., "Negotiation: An Introduction to Some Issues and Themes," *American Behavioral Scientist,* Vol. 27 (1983), pp. 135–147.

[14]Wallas, G., *The Art of Thought* (New York: Harcourt, 1926). Cited in Bazerman, op. cit.

[15]James A. F. Stoner, *Management,* Second Edi-

tion (Englewood Cliffs, NJ: Prentice Hall, 1982), pp. 167–168.

[16]This discussion is based on James G. March and Herbert A. Simon, *Organizations* (New York: John Wiley, 1958), pp. 137–142.

[17]Ibid. See also Herbert A. Simon. *Administrative Behavior* (New York: Free Press, 1947).

[18]See Victor H. Vroom and Philip W. Yetton, *Leadership and Decision Making* (Pittsburgh: University of Pittsburgh Press, 1973); Victor H. Vroom and Arthur G. Jago, *The New Leadership* (Englewood Cliffs, NJ: Prentice Hall, 1988).

[19]Adapted from ibid., p. 43.

[20]For an excellent overview, see Roger Fisher and William Ury, *Getting to Yes: Negotiating Agreement Without Giving In* (New York: Penguin, 1983). See also James A. Wall, Jr., *Negotiation: Theory and Practice* (Glenview, IL: Scott, Foresman, 1985).

[21]Ibid., pp. 4–7.

[22]Roy J. Lewicki and Joseph A. Litterer, *Negotiation* (Homewood, IL: Irwin, 1985), pp. 316–319.

[23]Ibid., pp. 328–329.

[24]Following discussion based on Fisher and Ury, op. cit., and Lewicki and Litterer, op. cit.

[25]Fisher and Ury, op. cit., pp. 10–14.

[26]This example is developed from Bazerman, op. cit., pp. 106–108.

[27]Developed from Bazerman, op. cit., pp. 127–141.

[28]Fisher and Ury, op. cit., p. 33.

[29]Lewicki and Litterer, op. cit., pp. 177–181.

[30]Exercise developed from Charles Wales and Robert Stages, "The Fishing Trip," under an Exxon Guided Design IMPACT Grant. Used with permission.

## CHAPTER 14

[1]Henry Mintzberg, *The Nature of Managerial Work* (New York: Harper & Row, 1973); See Morgan W. McCall, Jr., Ann M. Morrison, and Robert L. Hannan, *Studies of Managerial Work: Results and Methods,* Technical Report No. 9 (Greensboro, NC: Center for Creative Leadership, 1978); John P. Kotter, *The General Managers* (New York: Free Press, 1982).

[2]William J. Haney, *Communication and Interpersonal Communication: Text and Cases,* Fourth Edition (Homewood, IL: Irwin, 1979).

[3]Thomas J. Peters and Robert H. Waterman, Jr., *In Search of Excellence* (New York: Harper & Row, 1983).

[4]See D. E. Campbell, "Interior Office Design and Visitor Response," *Journal of Applied Psychology*. Vol. 64 (1979), pp. 648–653; P. C. Morrow and J. C. McElroy, "Interior Office Design and Visitor Response: A Constructive Replication," *Journal of Applied Psychology,* Vol. 66 (1981), pp. 646–650.

[5]Richard V. Farace, Peter R. Monge, and Hamish M. Russell, *Communicating and Organizing* (Reading, MA: Addison-Wesley, 1977), pp. 97–98.

[6]The statements are from *Business Week* (July 6, 1981), p. 107.

[7]See Harold J. Leavitt and Romald A. H. Mueller, "Some Effects of Feedback on Communication," *Human Relations,* Vol. 4 (1951), pp. 401–410; Harold J. Leavitt, *Managerial Psychology,* Third Edition (Chicago: University of Chicago Press, 1972).

[8]This research is reviewed by John C. Athanassiades, "The Distortion of Upward Communication in Hierarchical Organizations," *Academy of Management Journal,* Vol. 16 (June 1973), pp. 207–226.

[9]See M. P. Rowe and M. Baker, "Are You Hearing Enough Employee Concerns?" *Harvard Business Review,* Vol. 62 (May–June 1984), pp. 127–135.

[10]This discussion is based on Carl R. Rogers and Richard E. Farson, "Active Listening" (Chicago: Industrial Relations Center of the University of Chicago).

[11]Adapted from John Anderson, "Giving and Receiving Feedback," in Paul R. Lawrence, Louis B. Barnes, and Jay W. Lorsch, eds., *Organizational Behavior and Administration,* Third Edition (Homewood, IL: Irwin, 1976), p. 109. See also John F. Kiloski and Joseph A. Litterer, "Effective Communication in the Performance Appraisal Interview," *Public Personnel Management,* Vol. 9 (Spring 1983), pp. 33–42.

[12]J. Stephen Morris, "How to Make Criticism Sessions Productive," *Wall Street Journal* (October 12, 1981), p. 24.

[13]See Robert L. Kahn, Donald M. Wolfe, Robert F. Quinn, and J. Diedrick Snoek, *Organizational Stress: Studies in Role Conflict and Ambiguity* (New York: John Wiley, 1964); Daniel Katz and Robert L. Kahn, *The Social Psychology of Orga-*

*nizations,* Second Edition (New York: John Wiley, 1978).

[14]Richard E. Walton, *Interpersonal Peacemaking: Confrontations and Third-Party Consultation* (Reading, MA: Addison-Wesley, 1969).

[15]Kenneth W. Thomas and Warren H. Schmidt, "A Survey of Managerial Interests with Respect to Conflict," *Academy of Management Journal,* Vol. 19 (1976), pp. 315–318.

[16]Richard E. Walton and John M. Dutton, "The Management of Interdepartmental Conflict: A Model and Review," *Administrative Science Quarterly,* Vol. 14 (1969), pp. 73–84.

[17]Developed from Don Hellriegel, John W. Slocum, Jr., and Richard W. Woodman, *Organizational Behavior,* 3rd ed. (St. Paul: West, 1983), pp. 471–474.

[18]Developed from Gary Johns, *Organizational Behavior* (Glenview, IL: Scott, Foresman, 1983), pp. 415–417; and Walton and Dutton, op. cit.

[19]These stages are consistent with the conflict models described by Alan C. Filley, *Interpersonal Conflict Resolution* (Glenview, IL: Scott, Foresman, 1975); and Louis R. Pondy, "Organizational Conflict: Concepts and Models," *Administrative Science Quarterly,* Vol. 12 (September 1967), pp. 269–320.

[20]S. P. Robbins, *Organization Theory: Structure Design and Applications* (Englewood Cliffs, NJ: Prentice Hall, 1987).

[21]See Jay Galbraith, *Designing Complex Organizations* (Reading, MA: Addison-Wesley, 1973); Rensis Likert and Jane B. Likert, *New Ways of Managing Conflict* (New York: McGraw-Hill, 1976).

[22]D. Nadler and M. Tushman, *Strategic Organizational Design* (Glenview, IL: Scott, Foresman, 1988).

[23]E. M. Eisenberg and M. G. Witten, "Reconsidering Openness in Organizational Communication," *Academy of Management Review,* Vol. 12 (1987), pp. 418–426.

[24]R. G. Lord and M. C. Kernan, "Scripts as Determinants of Purposeful Behavior in Organizations," *Academy of Management Review,* Vol. 12 (1987), pp. 265–277.

[25]See Filley, op. cit., and L . David Brown, *Managing Conflict at Organizational Interfaces* (Reading, MA: Addison-Wesley, 1983).

[26]Ibid., pp. 27, 29.

[27]Kenneth Thomas, "Conflict and Conflict Management," in M. D. Dunnett, ed., *Handbook of Industrial and Organizational Behavior* (Chicago: Rand McNally, 1976), pp. 889–935.

[28]Kenneth W. Thomas, "Toward Multi-Dimensional Values in Teaching: The Example of Conflict Behaviors," *Academy of Management Review,* Vol. 2 (1977), pp. 484–490.

[29]Developed from an example in Filley, *Interpersonal Conflict Resolution,* p. 24.

[30]Exercise from David Whetten and Kim Cameron, *Developing Management Skills* (Glenview, IL: Scott, Foresman, 1984).

## CHAPTER 15

[1]Rosabeth Moss Kanter, "Power Failure in Management Circuit," *Harvard Business Review* (July–August 1979), pp. 65–75.

[2]John R. P. French and Bertram Raven, "The Bases of Social Power," in Dorwin Cartwright, ed., *Group Dynamics: Research and Theory* (Evanston, IL: Row, Peterson, 1962), pp. 607–623.

[3]See French and Raven, op. cit.

[4]Stanley Milgram, "Behavioral Study of Obedience," in Dennis W. Organ, ed., *The Applied Psychology of Work Behavior* (Dallas: Business Publications, Inc., 1978), pp. 384–398. Also see Stanley Milgram, "Behavioral Study of Obedience," *Journal of Abnormal and Social Psychology,* Vol. 67 (1963), pp. 371–378; Stanley Milgram, "Group Pressure and Action Against a Person," *Journal of Abnormal and Social Psychology,* Vol. 69 (1964), pp. 137–143; "Some Conditions of Obedience and Disobedience to Authority," *Human Relations,* Vol. 1 (1965), pp. 57–76; *Obedience to Authority* (New York: Harper and Row, 1974).

[5]Chester Barnard, *The Functions of the Executive* (Cambridge, MA: Harvard University Press, 1938).

[6]See Steven N. Brenner and Earl A. Mollander, "Is the Ethics of Business Changing," *Harvard Business Review,* Vol. 55 (February 1977), pp. 57–71; Barry Z. Posner and Warren H. Schmidt, "Values and the American Manager: An Update," *California Management Review,* Vol. XXVI (Spring 1984), pp. 202–216.

[7]Barnard, *The Functions of the Executive.*

[8]John P. Kotter, "Power, Success, and Organizational Effectiveness," *Organizational Dynamics,* Vol. 6 (Winter 1978), p. 27.

[9]David A. Whetten and Kim S. Cameron, *Devel-*

*oping Managerial Skills* (Glenview, IL: Scott, Foresman, 1984), pp. 250–259.

[10]Ibid., pp. 260–266.

[11]David Kipinis, Stuart M. Schmidt, Chris Swaffin-Smith, and Ian Wilkinson, "Patterns of Managerial Influence: Shotgun Managers, Tacticians, and Bystanders," *Organizational Dynamics,* Vol. 12 (Winter 1984), pp. 60, 61.

[12]Ibid., pp. 58–67; David Kipinis, Stuart M. Schmidt, and Ian Wilkinson, "Intraorganizational Influence Tactics: Explorations in Getting One's Way," *Journal of Applied Psychology*. Vol. 65 (1980), pp. 440–452.

[13]Warren K. Schilit and Edwin A. Locke, "A Study of Upward Influence in Organizations," *Administrative Science Quarterly,* Vol. 27 (1982), pp. 304–316.

[14]This and the following quote are from Thomas A. Stewart, "New Ways to Exercise Power," *Fortune* (November 6, 1989), pp. 52–64.

[15]For useful and related discussions, see Allan R. Cohen and David L. Bradford, *Influence Without Authority* (New York: John Wiley, 1990) and John P. Kotter, *A Force for Change: How Leadership Differs from Management* (New York: Free Press, 1990).

[16]Although the work on organizational politics is not extensive, useful reviews include a chapter in Robert H. Miles, *Macro Organizational Behavior* (Santa Monica, CA: Goodyear, 1980); Bronston T. Mayes and Robert W. Allen, "Toward a Definition of Organizational Politics," *Academy of Management Review,* Vol. 2 (1977), pp. 672–677; Gerald F. Cavanagh, Denis J. Moberg, and Manuel Velasquez, "The Ethics of Organizational Politics," *Academy of Management Review,* Vol. 6 (July 1981), pp. 363–374; Dan Farrell and James C. Petersen, "Patterns of Political Behavior in Organizations," *Academy of Management Review,* Vol. 7 (July 1982), pp. 403–412; D. L. Madison, R. W. Allen, L. W. Porter, and B. T. Mayes, "Organizational Politics: An Exploration of Managers' Perceptions," *Human Relations,* Vol. 33 (1980), pp. 92–107.

[17]Mayes and Allen, "Toward a Definition of Organizational Politics," p. 675.

[18]Jeffrey Pfeffer, *Power in Organizations* (Marshfield, MA: Pitman, 1981), p. 7.

[19]Madison et al., op. cit.

[20]For a discussion of this perspective, see Pfeffer, 1981, op cit.; M. M. Harmon and R. T. Mayer, *Organization Theory for Public Administration* (Boston: Little Brown, 1986); W. Richard Scott, *Organizations: Rational, Natural and Open Systems* (Englewood Cliffs, NJ: Prentice Hall, 1987).

[21]See Jeffrey Pfeffer, *Organizations and Organization Theory* (Boston: Pitman, 1983); Jeffrey Pfeffer and Gerald R. Salancik, *The External Control of Organizations* (Englewood Cliffs, NJ: Prentice Hall, 1978).

[22]James D. Thompson, *Organizations in Action* (New York: McGraw-Hill, 1967).

[23]R. N. Osborn and D. H. Jackson, "Leaders, Riverboat Gamblers, or Purposeful Unintended Consequences in Management of Complex Technologies," *Academy of Management Journal* Vol. 31 (1988), pp. 924–947; M. Hector, "When Actors Comply: Monitoring Costs and the Production of Social Order," *Acta Sociologica,* Vol. 27 (1984), pp. 161–183; T. Mitchell and W. G. Scott, "Leadership Failures, the Distrusting Public and Prospects for the Administrative State," *Public Administration Review,* Vol. 47 (1987), pp. 445–452.

[24]This discussion is based on Cavanagh, Moberg, and Velasquez, "The Ethics of Organizational Politics," and Manuel Velasquez, Dennis J. Moberg, and Gerald Cavanagh, "Organizational Statesmanship and Dirty Politics: Ethical Guidelines for the Organizational Politician," *Organizational Dynamics,* Vol. 11 (1983), pp. 65–79, both of which offer a fine treatment of the ethics of power and politics.

[25]Adapted from Cavanagh et al., "The Ethics of Organizational Politics," pp. 363–374.

[26]These criteria are developed from ibid.

[27]Saul W. Gellerman, "Why 'Good' Managers Make Bad Ethical Choices," *Harvard Business Review* Vol. 64 (July 1986), pp. 85–97.

[28]See Keith G. Provan, "Power and Politics in Organization," *The Owen Manager* (Spring/Summer 1983), pp. 11–17.

[29]Exercise adapted from R. Christie and F. L. Geis, *Studies in Machiavellianism* (Academic Press, 1970). Used with permission.

## CHAPTER 16

[1]John Kotter, *A Force for Change: How Leadership Differs from Management* (New York: Free Press, 1990).

[2]H. S. Geneen and A. Moscow, *Managing* (Garden City, NY: Doubleday, 1984).

[3]This perspective is based on James C. McElroy,

"Alternative Schemes for Teaching Leadership," *The Organizational Behavior Teaching Review*, Vol. 11 (1986–87), pp. 87–94; James C. McElroy and J. David Hunger, "Leadership Theory as Causal Attributions for Performance," in J. G. Hunt, B. R. Baliga, H. P. Dachler, and C. A. Schriesheim, eds., *Emerging Leadership Vistas* (Lexington, MA: Lexington Books, 1987).

[4]"Wang Founder Apparently Forces His Son to Step Down as President," *The Wall Street Journal* (August 9, 1989), p. A-3.

[5]Ralph M. Stogdill, *Handbook of Leadership* (New York: Free Press, 1974).

[6]Adapted from Richard Brandt, "The Billion-Dollar Whiz Kid," *Business Week* (April 13, 1987), p. 69.

[7]Rensis Likert, *New Patterns of Management* (New York: McGraw-Hill, 1961).

[8]Stogdill, *Handbook of Leadership*, loc. cit., Chap. 11.

[9]Robert R. Blake and Jane S. Mouton, *The New Managerial Grid* (Houston: Gulf, 1978).

[10]See M. F. Peterson, "PM Theory in Japan and China: What's in It for the United States?" *Organizational Dynamics* (Spring 1988), pp. 22–39; J. Misumi and M. F. Peterson, "The Performance–Maintenance Theory of Leadership: Review of a Japanese Research Program," *Administrative Science Quarterly*, Vol. 30 (1985), pp. 198–223; P. B. Smith, J. Misumi, M. Tayeb, M. F. Peterson and M. Bond, "On the Generality of Leadership Style Measures Across Cultures," paper presented at the International Congress of Applied Psychology, Jerusalem, July 1986.

[11]See Henry P. Sims, Jr., "The Leader as a Manager of Reinforcement Contingencies: An Empirical Example and a Model," in J. G. Hunt and L. L. Larson, eds., *Leadership Frontiers* (Kent, OH: Comparative Administration Research Institute, Kent State University, 1977); P. M. Podsakoff, W. D. Toder, R. A. Grover, and V. L. Huber, "Situational and Personality Moderators of Leader Reward and Punishment Behaviors: Fact or Fiction?" *Organizational Behavior and Human Performance*, Vol. 34 (1984), pp. 810–821.

[12]A. R. Korukonda and James G. Hunt, "Pat on the Back versus Kick in the Pants: An Application of Cognitive Inference to the Study of Leader Reward and Punishment Behaviors," *Group and Organization Studies*, Vol. 14, No. 3 (1989), pp. 299–324.

[13]This section is based on R. J. House, "A 1976 Theory of Charismatic Leadership," in J. G. Hunt and L. L. Larson, eds., *Leadership: The Cutting Edge* (Carbondale, IL: Southern Illinois University Press, 1977).

[14]Jay A. Conger and R. N. Kanungo, eds., *Charismatic Leadership: The Elusive Factor in Organizational Effectiveness* (San Francisco: Jossey-Bass, 1988).

[15]Bruce J. Avolio and Bernard M. Bass, "Transformational Leadership, Charisma and Beyond," in J. G. Hunt, B. R. Baliga, H. P. Dachler, and C. A. Schriesheim, eds., *Emerging Leadership Vistas* (Lexington, MA: Lexington Books, 1988).

[16]Kate Ballen, "The No. 1 Leader is Petersen of Ford," *Fortune* (October 24, 1988), pp. 69–70.

[17]Conger and Kanungo, op. cit. (1988), pp. 103–104.

[18]Blake and Mouton, op. cit. (1978).

[19]Bernard M. Bass, "Policy Implications of a New Paradigm of Leadership," in *Military Leadership: Traditions and Future Trends*, United States Naval Academy and the Navy Personnel Research and Development Center Conference, June 10–12, 1987 (Annapolis, MD: Action Printing and Graphics, 1989), pp. 155–164.

[20]This section is based on Fred E. Fiedler and Martin M. Chemers, *The Leader Match Concept*, Second Edition (New York: John Wiley, 1984).

[21]This section is based on Fred E. Fiedler and Joseph E. Garcia, *New Approaches to Effective Leadership* (New York: John Wiley, 1987).

[22]This section is based on Robert J. House and Terence R. Mitchell, "Path–Goal Theory of Leadership," *Journal of Contemporary Business* (Autumn 1977), pp. 81–97.

[23]See the discussion of this approach in Paul Hersey and Kenneth H. Blanchard, *Management of Organizational Behavior* (Englewood Cliffs, NJ: Prentice Hall, 1988).

[24]Hersey and Blanchard, op. cit. (1988).

[25]Robert E. Quinn, Sue R. Faerman, Michael P. Thompson, and Michael R. McGrath, *Becoming a Master Manager* (New York: John Wiley, 1990).

[26]Fiedler and Garcia, op. cit. (1987).

[27]House and Mitchell, op. cit. (Autumn 1977).

[28]For some criticisms, see Claude L. Graeff, "The Situational Leadership Theory: A Critical View,"

*Academy of Management Review,* Vol. 8 (1983), pp. 285–291.

[29]Based on R. E. Quinn, *Beyond Rational Management* (San Francisco: Jossey-Bass, 1988).

[30]F. E. Fiedler, M. M. Chemers, and L. Mahar, *Improving Leadership Effectiveness: The Leader Match Concept* (New York: John Wiley, 1977); Robbins, op. cit. (1989).

[31]Quinn, Faerman, Thompson, and McGrath, op. cit. (1990).

[32]For example, see A. Lowin and J. R. Craig, "The Influence of Level of Performance on Managerial Style: An Experimental Object-Lesson on the Ambiguity of Correlational Data," *Organizational Behavior and Human Performance,* Vol. 3 (1968), pp. 440–458.

[33]Jeffrey Pfeffer, "The Ambiguity of Leadership," *Academy of Management Review,* Vol. 2 (1977), pp. 104–112.

[34]James R. Meindl, "On Leadership: An Alternative to the Conventional Wisdom," in B. M. Staw and L. L. Cummings, eds., *Research in Organizational Behavior,* Vol. 12 (JAI Press, 1990), pp. 159–203.

[35]See Arthur Jago, "Leadership: Perspectives in Theory and Research," *Management Science,* Vol. 28 (1982), pp. 315–336.

[36]James G. Hunt, Kimberly B. Boal, and Ritch L. Sorenson, "Top Management Leadership: Inside the Black Box," *The Leadership Quarterly* (in press, 1990).

[37]The discussion in this section is based on Steven Kerr and John Jermier, "Substitutes for Leadership: Their Meaning and Measurement," *Organizational Behavior and Human Performance,* Vol. 22 (1978), pp. 375–403.

[38]Phillip M. Posakoff, Peter W. Dorfman, Jon P. Howell, and William D. Todor, "Leader Reward and Punishment Behaviors: A Preliminary Test of a Culture-Free Style of Leadership Effectiveness," *Advances in Comparative Management,* Vol. 2 (1989), pp. 95–138; T. K. Peng, "'Substitutes for Leadership in an International Setting," unpublished manuscript, College of Business Administration, Texas Tech University (1990).

[39]Adapted from Jim Wall, *Bosses* (Lexington, MA: Lexington Books, 1986), pp. 129–133, 142–150, 256–260.

[40]Exercise created by W. Warner Burke, Ph.D. Used with permission.

## CHAPTER 17

[1]Developed in part from "Management Discovers the Human Side of Automation," *Business Week* (September 29, 1986), pp. 70–79.

[2]The first example is reported in Anthony Jay, *Management and Machiavelli: An Inquiry into the Politics of Corporate Life* (New York: Holt, Rinehart and Winston, 1967), p. 96.

[3]Developed from James Robins, "Firms Try Newer Approaches to Slash Absenteeism as Carrot and Stick Fail," *The Wall Street Journal,* March 14, 1979.

[4]See, for example, Ralph H. Kilmann, *Beyond the Quick Fix* (San Francisco: Jossey-Bass, 1984); Noel M. Tichy and Mary Anne Devanna, *The Transformational Leader* (New York: John Wiley, 1986).

[5]Robert A. Cooke, "Managing Change in Organizations," in Gerald Zaltman, ed., *Management Principles for Nonprofit Organizations* (New York: American Management Association, 1979). See also David A. Nadler, "The Effective Management of Organizational Change," pp. 358–369 in Jay W. Lorsch, ed., *Handbook of Organizational Behavior* (Englewood Cliffs, NJ: Prentice Hall, 1987).

[6]Kurt Lewin, "Group Decision and Social Change," in G. E. Swanson, T. M. Newcomb, and E. L. Hartley, eds., *Readings in Social Psychology* (New York: Holt, Rinehart and Winston, 1952), pp. 459–473.

[7]Tichy and Devanna, op. cit., p. 44.

[8]Robert Chin and Kenneth D. Benne, "General Strategies for Effecting Changes in Human Systems," in Warren G. Bennis, Kenneth D. Benne, Robert Chin, and Kenneth E. Corey, eds., *The Planning of Change,* Third Edition (New York: Holt, Rinehart and Winston, 1969), pp. 22–45.

[9]The change strategy examples in this part are developed from an exercise reported in J. William Pfeiffer and John E. Jones, *A Handbook of Structured Experiences for Human Relations Training,* Vol. II (La Jolla, CA: University Associates, 1973).

[10]Donald Klein, "Some Notes on the Dynamics of Resistance to Change: The Defender Role," in Bennis et al., eds., *The Planning of Change,* pp. 117–124.

[11]See Everett M. Rogers with F. Floyd Shoemaker, *Communication of Innovations,* Second Edition (New York: Free Press, 1971).

[12]John P. Kotter and Leonard A. Schlesinger, "Choosing Strategies for Change," *Harvard Business Review,* Vol. 57 (March–April 1979), pp. 109–112.

[13]W. Warner Burke, *Organization Development* (Reading, MA: Addison-Wesley, 1987); Wendell L. French and Cecil H. Bell, Jr., *Organization Development,* Fourth Edition (Englewood Cliffs, NJ: Prentice Hall, 1990); Edgar F. Huse and Thomas G. Cummings, *Organization Development and Change,* Fourth Edition (St. Paul: West, 1989).

[14]Huse and Cummings, op. cit., Third Ed, (1985), p. 6. Copyright © 1985, West Publishing Company. All rights reserved.

[15]Warren Bennis, "Using Our Knowledge of Organizational Behavior," pp. 29–49 in Lorsch, op. cit.

[16]Huse and Cummings, op. cit., (1980), pp. 8–9.

[17]A set of ethical guidelines for OD practitioners was published in *Consultation,* Vol. 5 (Fall 1986), pp. 21–218.

[18]See Cummings and Huse, op. cit., Fourth Edition (1989), pp. 32–36, 45.

[19]Excellent overviews are found in ibid; and French and Bell, op. cit.

[20]Richard Beckhard, "The Confrontation Meeting," *Harvard Business Review,* Vol. 45 (March–April 1967), pp. 149–155.

[21]See Dale Zand, "Collateral Organization: A New Change Strategy," *Journal of Applied Behavioral Science,* Vol. 10 (1974), pp. 63–89; Barry A. Stein and Rosabeth Moss Kanter, "Building the Parallel Organization," *Journal of Applied Behavioral Science,* Vol. 16 (1980), pp. 371–386.

[22]J. Richard Hackman and Greg R. Oldham, *Work Redesign* (Reading, MA: Addison-Wesley, 1980).

## CHAPTER 18

[1]Charles Dickens, *A Tale of Two Cities, in the Words of Charles Dickens* (New York: P. F. Collier, 1880), p. 343.

[2]From Arthur P. Brief, Randall S. Schuler, and Mary Van Sell, *Managing Job Stress,* pp. 6–7. Copyright © 1981 by Arthur P. Brief, Randall S. Schuler, and Mary Van Sell. Reprinted by permission of Little Brown and Company.

[3]Brief and Van Sell, op. cit.

[4]Portions of this treatment of stress developed from John R. Schermerhorn, Jr., *Management for Productivity,* Third Edition (New York: John Wiley, 1989), pp. 647–652.

[5]For a classic work see H. Selye, *The Stress of Life,* Rev. ed. (New York: McGraw-Hill, 1976).

[6]Meyer Friedman and Ray Roseman, *Type A Behavior and Your Heart* (New York: Alfred A. Knopf, 1974).

[7]See John D. Adams, "Health, Stress, and the Manager's Life Style," *Group and Organization Studies,* Vol. 6 (September 1981), pp. 291–301.

[8]See John M. Ivancevich and Michael T. Matteson, "Optimizing Human Resources: A Case for Preventive Health and Stress Management," *Organizational Dynamics,* Vol. 9 (Autumn 1980), pp. 6–8; Matteson and Ivancevich, *Controlling Work Stress: Effective Human Resource and Management Strategies* (San Francisco: Jossey-Bass, 1987).

[9]Cary L. Cooper, "Executive Stress Around the World," *University of Wales Review of Business and Economics* (Winter 1987), pp. 3–8.

[10]See Orlando Behling and Arthur L. Darrow, *Managing Work-Related Stress* (Chicago: Science Research Associates, 1984), pp. 14–16.

[11]Friedman and Roseman, *Type A Behavior and Your Heart.*

[12]Adapted from Robert Kreitner, Personal Wellness: It's Just Good Business," *Business Horizons,* Vol. 25 (May–June 1982), pp. 28–35. Copyright 1982 by the Foundation for the School of Business at Indiana University. Reprinted by permission. See also Behling and Darrow, *Managing Work-Related Stress,* pp. 27–31.

[13]Kreitner, "Personal Wellness: It's Just Good Business."

[14]For a research review, see Daniel C. Feldman, "Careers in Organizations: Recent Trends and Future Directions," *Yearly Review of Management,* Vol. 15 (June 1989), pp. 135–156.

[15]Irving Janis and Dan Wheeler, "Thinking Clearly about Career Choices," *Psychology Today* (May 1978), p. 67.

[16]Summarized in part from a discussion by Kae H. Chung and Leon C. Megginson, *Organizational Behavior: Developing Managerial Skills* (New York: Harper & Row, 1981), pp. 539–540, as based on Schein, *Career Dynamics,* pp. 189–199.

[17]Daniel J. Levinson, *The Seasons of a Man's Life* (New York: Alfred A. Knopf, 1978). See also Douglas T. Hall, *Careers in Organizations* (Santa Monica, CA: Goodyear, 1975).

[18]See Lloyd Baird and Kathy Kram, "Career Dynamics: Managing the Superior–Subordinate Relationship," *Organizational Dynamics* (Spring 1983), p. 47; Paul H. Thompson, Robin Zenger Baker, and Norman Smallwood, "Improving Professional Development by Applying the Four-Stage Career Model," *Organizational Dynamics* (Autumn 1986), pp. 49–62.

[19]Thomas P. Ference, James A. F. Stoner, and E. Kirby Warren, "Managing the Career Plateau," *Academy of Management Review*, Vol. 2 (October 1977), pp. 602–612.

[20]For a review, see Uma Sekaran, *Dual-Career Families* (San Francisco: Jossey-Bass, 1986).

[21]For a good summary of the issues, see Felice Schwartz, "Management Women and the New Facts of Life," *Harvard Business Review*, Vol. 68 (January–February 1989), pp. 65–76; Douglas T. Hall, "Promoting Work/Family Balance: An Organization–Change Approach," *Organizational Dynamics*, Vol. X (1990), pp. 5–18.

[22]This study is reported in *Time* (December 4, 1989), p. 86.

[23]Reported in Milo Geyelin, "States Try to Balance Job, Family," *The Wall Street Journal* (May 4, 1990), p. B1.

[24]Based on Ross A. Webber, "13 Career Commandments," *MBA* (May 1975), p. 47; Alan N. Schoonmaker, *Executive Career Strategy* (New York: American Management Association, 1971).

[25]Exercise created by Dorothy M. Hair, 1985. Used with permission.

## SUPPLEMENTARY MODULE A

[1]Paul R. Lawrence, "Historical Development of Organizational Behavior," pp. 1–9 in Jay W. Lorsch, ed., *Handbook of Organizational Behavior* (Englewood Cliffs, NJ: Prentice Hall, 1987).

[2]Frederick W. Taylor, *The Principles of Scientific Management* (New York: W. W. Norton, 1967), p. 9. (The original version of this book was published in New York by Harper, 1911.)

[3]Charles D. Wrege and Amedeo G. Perroni, "Taylor's Pig Tale: A Historical Analysis of Frederick W. Taylor's Pig-Iron Experiments," *Academy of Management Journal*, Vol. 17 (March 1974, pp. 6–27.

[4]Edwin A. Locke, "The Ideas of Frederick W. Taylor: An Evaluation," *The Academy of Management Review*, Vol. 7 (1982), pp. 14–24. See also Edwin A. Locke, "Job Attitudes in Historical Perspective," pp. 5–11 in Daniel A. Wren and John A. Pearce II, eds, *Papers Dedicated to the Development of Modern Management: Celebrating 100 Years of Modern Management* (Academy of Management, 1986).

[5]Ibid., p. 24.

[6]The Hawthorne studies are described in detail in F. J. Roethlisberger and William J. Dickson, *Management and the Worker* (Cambridge, MA: Harvard University Press, 1966); G. Homans, *Fatigue of Workers* (New York: Reinhold, 1941). Both sources were used in preparing the synopsis. See also Ronald G. Greenwood and Charles D. Wrege, "The Hawthorne Studies," pp. 24–35 in Wren and Pearce, op. cit.

[7]For a representative of this school of thought, see Willart E. Parker and Robert W. Kleemeier, *Human Relationships in Supervision: Leadership in Management* (New York: McGraw-Hill, 1951).

[8]Alex Carey, "The Hawthorne Studies: A Radical Criticism," *American Sociological Review*, Vol. 32 (June 1967), pp. 403–416. See also Greenwood and Wrege, op. cit.

[9]For representatives of this school of thought, see Henry C. Metcalfe and L. Urwick, eds., *Dynamic Administration: The Collected Papers of Mary Parker Follet* (New York: Harper & Brothers, 1940); James D. Mooney, *The Principles of Administration*, rev. ed. (New York: Harper & Brothers, 1947); L. Urwick, *The Elements of Administration* (New York: Harper & Brothers, 1943).

[10]The primary source for this discussion of Fayol's work is M. B. Brodie, *Fayol on Administration* (London: Lyon, Grant and Green, 1967).

[11]Available in the English language as Henri Fayol, *General and Industrial Administration* (London: Sir Isaac Pitman & Sons, 1949).

## SUPPLEMENTARY MODULE B

[1]Developed from Eugene Stone, *Research Methods in Organizational Behavior* (Santa Monica, CA: Goodyear, 1978). p. 8.

[2]For a good review of research designs, see Donald T. Campbell and Julian C. Stanley, *Experimental and Quasi-Experimental Designs for Research* (Chicago: Rand-McNally, 1969); Stone, *Research Methods in Organizational Behavior.*

[3]See Stone, *Research Methods in Organizational Behavior,* for a good discussion of threats to internal and external validity.

[4]Ibid.

[5]C. William Emory, *Business Research Methods,* rev. ed. (Homewood, IL: Richard D. Irwin, 1980).

[6]Fred E. Fiedler, Martin M. Chemers, and Linda Mahar, *Improving Leadership Effectiveness: The Leader Match Concept* (New York: John Wiley & Sons, 1976).

[7]Kenneth W. Thomas and Walter G. Tymon, Jr., "Necessary Properties of Relevant Research: Lessons from Recent Criticisms of the Organizational Sciences," *Academy of Management Review,* Vol. 7 (1982), pp. 345–352.

## SUPPLEMENTARY MODULE C

[1]We especially thank Dr. Lawrence Peters, Texas Christian University, for his fine critique of this module in its draft form and the many useful suggestions provided.

[2]Charles J. Fombrun and Robert L. Laud, "Strategic Issues in Performance Appraisal, Theory and Practice," *Personnel,* Vol. 60 (November–December 1983), p. 24.

[3]Ibid., pp. 23–31.

[4]See Gary P. Latham and Kenneth N. Wexley, *Increasing Productivity Through Performance Appraisal* (Reading, MA: Addison-Wesley, 1981), pp. 48–51.

[5]See David L. Devries, Ann M. Morrison, Sandra L. Shullman, and Michael L. Gerlach, *Performance Appraisal on the Line* (Greensboro, NC: Center for Creative Leadership, 1986), Chs. 3, 6.

[6]For discussion of a number of these errors, see ibid, Ch. 3.

[7]For more detail, see Latham and Wexley, *Increasing Productivity Through Performance Appraisal;* Stephen J. Carroll and Craig E. Schneier, *Performance Appraisal and Review Systems* (Glenview, IL: Scott, Foresman, 1982).

[8]For current pro and con discussions of BARS, see R. Jacobs, D. Kafry, and S. Zedeck, "Expectations of Behaviorally Anchored Ratings Scales," *Personnel Psychology,* Vol. 33 (Autumn 1980), pp. 595–640; Frank J. Landy and James L. Farr, "Performance Rating," *Psychological Bulletin,* Vol. 87 (1980), pp. 72–107; Shullman and Gerlach, op. cit., Ch. 3; Devries and Morrison.

[9]For a detailed discussion of MBO, see Steven J. Carroll and Henry L. Tosi, *Management by Objectives: Application and Research* (New York: Macmillan, 1976); Anthony P. Raia, *Managing by Objectives* (Glenview, IL: Scott, Foresman, 1974).

[10]Based on J. J. Bernardin and C. S. Walter, "The Effects of Rater Training and Diary Keeping on Psychometric Error in Ratings," *Journal of Applied Psychology,* Vol. 61 (1977), pp. 64–69; see also R. G. Burnask and T. D. Hollman, "An Empirical Comparison of the Relative Effects of Sorter Response Bias on Three Rating Scale Formats," *Journal of Applied Psychology,* Vol. 59 (1974), pp. 307–312.

[11]Based on W. F. Cascio and H. J. Bernardin, "Implications of Performance Appraisal Litigation for Personnel Decisions," *Personnel Psychology,* Vol. 34 (1981), pp. 211–212. See also Devries, Morrison, Shullman, and Gerlach, op. cit., for a discussion.

[12]Andrew D. Szilagyi, Jr. and Marc J. Wallace, Jr., *Organizational Behavior and Performance,* 3rd ed. (Glenview, IL: Scott, Foresman, 1983), pp. 393–394. Used by permission.

# CREDITS

## VISIONS CREDITS

Chapter 1: *Fortune* (January 29, 1990), p. 46.

Chapter 2: *Newsweek* (October 2, 1989); *Training* (November 1987), pp. 62–66; *Fortune* (March 26, 1990), pp. 36–37.

Chapter 3: Michael Porter, *The Competitive Advantage of Nations* (New York: Free Press, 1990).

Chapter 4: *Working Woman* (January 1990), pp. 74–75.

Chapter 5: *Business Week* (March 26, 1990), pp. 66–74.

Chapter 6: *Fortune* (June 4, 1990), pp. 58–68.

Chapter 7: *Inc.* (May 1990), pp. 124–125; *Business Week* (February 5, 1990), p. 82a.

Chapter 8: *Via Volvo* (Vol. V, 1987); *The New York Times* (June 23, 1987); *Time* (August 28, 1989).

Chapter 9: *Fortune* (May 7, 1990), pp. 52–60.

Chapter 10: *American Way* (August 1, 1987), pp. 23–25; and *Business Week* (June 13, 1988), pp. 100–102.

Chapter 11: *Harvard Business Review* (May–June 1990), p. 110.

Chapter 12: *Harvard Business Review* (May–June 1990), p. 106.

Chapter 13: *Harvard Business Review* (March–April 1990), p. 108.

Chapter 14: *Harvard Business Review* (May–June 1990), p. 108.

Chapter 15: *Fortune* (November 6, 1989), pp. 52–64.

Chapter 16: *Fortune* (July 17, 1989), p. 107.

Chapter 17: *Fortune* (January 15, 1990), pp. 127–131.

Chapter 18: *The Wall Street Journal* (May 21, 1990), p. B1.

## EXAMPLE CREDITS

### CHAPTER 1

Inland Fisher Guide: *The Columbus Dispatch* (March 22, 1990), p. 2C.

British Petroleum: *The Wall Street Journal* (February 13, 1990), pp. 1, A13.

Navistar International Corporation: *The Academy of Management Executives* (Winter 1990), pp. 36–49.

Next, Inc.: *Fortune* (February 26, 1990), pp. 75–79.

Corning, Inc.: *The Wall Street Journal* (February 9, 1990), pp. R6–8.

Shering-Plough Corp.: *The Wall Street Journal* (July 20, 1990), p. B1.

Eastman Kodak: *The Wall Street Journal* (Centennial Edition, 1990).

U.S. West, Inc.: *The Wall Street Journal* (November 22, 1989).

### CHAPTER 2

Sibson & Company: *The Wall Street Journal* (December 8, 1989), p. R23.

Xerox Corporation: *The Wall Street Journal* (November 15, 1989), p. B1.

## CHAPTER 3

The University of Michigan: *Fortune* (November 6, 1989), p. 78.

Motorola: *Business Week* (October 4, 1984), p. 56.

General Electric Company: *The Wall Street Journal* (December 11, 1989), p. B1.

Kotobuki Electronics Industries: *The Wall Street Journal* (October 2, 1989), p. A10.

AT&T Microelectronics: *The Wall Street Journal* (March 26, 1990), p. 1.

Procter & Gamble: *Business Week* (October 30, 1989), p. 40.

Ford Motor Company: *The Wall Street Journal* (December 11, 1989), p. B4.

## CHAPTER 4

Quad/Graphics: *Fortune* (March 22, 1990), p. 134.

General Motors: *The Wall Street Journal* (November 10, 1986), p. 36D.

## CHAPTER 5

Toronto Sun Publishing Corporation: *The Wall Street Journal* (March 9, 1990), pp. B1–2.

## CHAPTER 6

Nordstrom's: *Time* (February 2, 1987), pp. 56–57.

Lincoln Electric: *Success* (October 1989), p. 12.

The Bank Mart: *Inc.* (December 1989), p. 142.

## CHAPTER 7

United Parcel Service: *The Wall Street Journal* (March 22, 1986), pp. 1, 26.

Metroma: Based on an example presented in Edward E. Lawler III, *Motivation in Work Organizations* (Monterey, CA: Brooks/Cole, 1973), pp. 154–155.

Cypress Semiconductor Corporation: *Harvard Business Review* (July–August 1990), pp. 88–89.

Aetna Life & Casualty Company: *The Wall Street Journal* (June 4, 1990, p. R35; June 18, 1990, p. B1).

Northwest Utilities Service Corporation: *The Wall Street Journal* (June 4, 1990), p. R34.

Telecom USA: *The Wall Street Journal* (December 22, 1989), pp. B1–2.

## CHAPTER 8

Aetna Life: *Organizational Dynamics* (Vol. 16, Spring 1988), pp. 4–27.

Corning Glass: *The Wall Street Journal* (February 9, 1990), pp. R6–8.

Volvo: *Time* (August 28, 1989), pp. 90–93.

Federal Express: *The Wall Street Journal* (October 30, 1989) and *Fortune* (May 7, 1990), pp. 52–60.

Saturn: *The Wall Street Journal* (July 9, 1990), pp. A1, A4.

## CHAPTER 9

Union Pacific: *Fortune* (December 18, 1989), p. 134.

NUMMI: *The California Management Review* (Summer 1989), pp. 26–44.

Compaq Computer Corporation: *Harvard Business Review* (July–August 1990), p. 117.

Hallmark Cards, Inc.: *The Wall Street Journal* (February 14, 1990), pp. B1–4.

Union Pacific: *Fortune* (December 18, 1989), p. 134.

Ford: *Fortune* (March 12, 1990), p. 134.

## CHAPTER 10

Owens-Illinois: *Fortune* (November 6, 1989), p. 58.

Heinz: *Fortune* (November 6, 1989), p. 58.

General Motors: *The Columbus Dispatch* (August 2, 1990), p. 2B.

Heinz: *Fortune* (November 6, 1989), p. 58.

## CHAPTER 12

Mary Kay Cosmetics: T. Deal and A. Kennedy, *Corporate Cultures* (Reading, MA: Addison-Wesley, 1982), p. 12.

Hewlett-Packard: *Business Month* (June 1989), p. 58.

Mills College: *The Detroit Free Press* (June 2, 1989), p. 3B.

Apple Computer, Inc.: T. Peters and R. Waterman, *In Search of Excellence* (New York: Harper & Row, 1982), p. 107.

General Motors: *The Detroit Free Press* (November 26, 1986), pp. 1, 26.

General Electric: J. M. Beyer and H. M. Trice, "How an Organization's Rites Reveal Its Culture," *Organizational Dynamics* (Spring 1987), pp. 27–41.

Scandinavian Airlines Services (SAS): *Business Month* (June 1989), p. 58.

Zenith: C. J. Johnson, "HDTV: The Players and

the Perils," unpublished report to Dr. Richard N. Osborn (June 29, 1990).

General Electric: *The Wall Street Journal* (July 31, 1990), p. A10.

Union Pacific: *Fortune* (December 18, 1989), p. 142.

Four Seasons Hotels: *The Wall Street Journal* (April 9, 1990), p. A10.

General Electric: *The Wall Street Journal* (July 17, 1989), p. B1.

Johnson & Johnson: *The Detroit Free Press* (July 3, 1988).

Xerox Corporation: *The New York Times* (October 3, 1990), p. B1.

## CHAPTER 13

Compaq Computer Corporation: *Harvard Business Review* (July–August 1990), p. 119.

## CHAPTER 14

Heinz: *Fortune* (November 6, 1989), p. 62.

Colgate-Palmolive: *Fortune* (November 6, 1989), p. 58.

Progressive: *Fortune* (August 13, 1990), p. 58.

American Express: *Harvard Business Review* (November–December 1989), p. 86.

IBM: *Harvard Business Review* (November–December 1989), p. 86.

## CHAPTER 15

Johnsonville. Thomas A. Stewart, "New Ways to Exercise Power," *Fortune* (November 6, 1989), pp. 62–64.

Torchmark: *The Wall Street Journal* (April 12, 1990), p. B8.

The Ohio State Employment Relations Board: *The Columbus Dispatch* (April 25, 1990), p. 1.

Sara Lee: *Fortune* (November 6, 1989), p. 64.

Pillsbury Company: *The Athens Messenger* (August 1, 1990).

Corning, Inc.: *The Columbus Dispatch* (February 4, 1990), p. 46.

## CHAPTER 16

Disney: *Fortune* (December 4, 1989), p. 116.

## CHAPTER 17

3M Corporation: *Fortune* (January 29, 1990), p. 43.

## CHAPTER 18

U.S. Postal Service: *Time* (December 25, 1989), pp. 3–31.

AT&T: *Fortune* (January 1, 1990), p. 36.

Citicorp: *The Wall Street Journal* (June 12, 1990), p. B1.

Chubb Corporation: *The Wall Street Journal* (June 1, 1990), p. D1.

P.G. &. E.: *The New York Times* (February 27, 1990), p. D1.

Ford: *Time* (December 4, 1989), p. 86.

IBM: *Fortune* (April 23, 1990), pp. 165–181.

Stride Rite: *Executive Female* (July/August 1990), pp. 9, 30.

# NAME INDEX

## U



## V



## W



## Y

# SUBJECT INDEX

## D

## M

## N



## O

## Q



## R

## T



## U



## V